{ CHAPTER OPENERS

{ BRIEF CONTENTS

WileyPLUS

Now with: **ORION**, An Adaptive Experience

WileyPLUS is a research-based, online environment for effective teaching and learning.

WileyPLUS builds students' confidence because it takes the guesswork out of studying by providing students with a clear roadmap:

- **what to do**
- **how to do it**
- **if they did it right**

It offers interactive resources along with a complete digital textbook that help students learn more. With *WileyPLUS*, students take more initiative so you'll have greater impact on their achievement in the classroom and beyond.

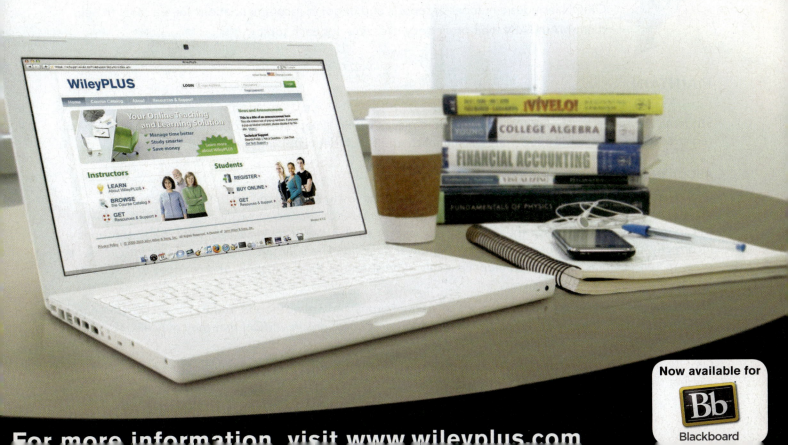

For more information, visit www.wileyplus.com

WileyPLUS with ORION

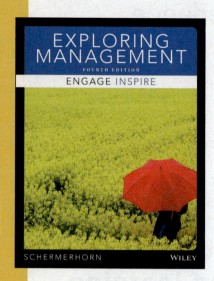

Based on cognitive science, *WileyPLUS* with ORION provides students with a personal, adaptive learning experience so they can build their proficiency on topics and use their study time most effectively.

BEGIN

Unique to ORION, students **BEGIN** by taking a quick diagnostic for any chapter. This will determine each student's baseline proficiency on each topic in the chapter. Students see their individual diagnostic report to help them decide what to do next with the help of ORION's recommendations.

PRACTICE

For each topic, students can either **STUDY**, or **PRACTICE**. Study directs students to the specific topic they choose in *WileyPLUS*, where they can read from the e-textbook or use the variety of relevant resources available there. Students can also practice, using questions and feedback powered by ORION's adaptive learning engine. Based on the results of their diagnostic and ongoing practice, ORION will present students with questions appropriate for their current level of understanding, and will continuously adapt to each student to help build proficiency.

MAINTAIN

ORION includes a number of reports and ongoing recommendations for students to help them **MAINTAIN** their proficiency over time for each topic.

Students can easily access ORION from multiple places within *WileyPLUS*. It does not require any additional registration, and there will not be any additional charge for students using this adaptive learning system.

ABOUT THE ADAPTIVE ENGINE

ORION includes a powerful algorithm that feeds questions to students based on their responses to the diagnostic and to the practice questions. Students who answer questions correctly at one difficulty level will soon be given questions at the next difficulty level. If students start to answer some of those questions incorrectly, the system will present questions of lower difficulty. The adaptive engine also takes into account other factors, such as reported confidence levels, time spent on each question, and changes in response options before submitting answers.

The questions used for the adaptive practice are numerous and are not found in the WileyPLUS assignment area. This ensures that students will not be encountering questions in ORION that they may also encounter in their WileyPLUS assessments.

ORION also offers a number of reporting options available for instructors, so that instructors can easily monitor student usage and performance.

WileyPLUS with ORION helps students learn by learning about them.™

FOURTH EDITION

Exploring Management

John R. Schermerhorn, Jr.

Ohio University

with contributions from

Susan Berston
City College of San Francisco

VICE PRESIDENT & EXECUTIVE PUBLISHER	George Hoffman
EXECUTIVE EDITOR	Lisé Johnson
CONTENT EDITOR	Jennifer Manias
EDITORIAL ASSISTANT	Jacqueline Hughes
DIRECTOR OF MARKETING	Amy Scholz
SENIOR MARKETING MANAGER	Kelly Simmons
MARKETING ASSISTANT	Marissa Carroll
DESIGN DIRECTOR	Harry Nolan
COVER AND INTERIOR DESIGNER	Thomas Nery
SENIOR CONTENT MANAGER	Dorothy Sinclair
SENIOR PRODUCTION EDITOR	Erin Ault
SENIOR PRODUCT DESIGNER	Allison Morris
EDITORIAL OPERATIONS MANAGER	Yana Mermel
MEDIA SPECIALIST	Elena Santa Maria
SENIOR PHOTO EDITOR	Mary Ann Price
PHOTO RESEARCHER	Susan McLaughlin
COVER PHOTO	© FrankMay/dpa/Corbis
EXPLORE YOURSELF PHOTO	© Greg Epperson/iStockphoto
TIPS TO REMEMBER PHOTO	© Helder Almeida/iStockphoto
MANAGER'S LIBRARY PHOTO	© Nikki Bidgood/iStockphoto
STEPS FOR FUTHER LEARNING—BUILD PHOTO	© Cubens 3d/Shutterstock
STEPS FOR FUTHER LEARNING—GET PHOTO	© Stuart Miles/Shutterstock
STEPS FOR FUTHER LEARNING—DO PHOTO	© Sergey Nivens/Shutterstock

This book was typeset in 11/14 Kepler Std Regular at Aptara®, Inc. and printed and bound by Courier/Kendallville. The cover was printed by Courier/Kendallville.

This book is printed on acid free paper. ∞

Founded in 1807, John Wiley & Sons, Inc. has been a valued source of knowledge and understanding for more than 200 years, helping people around the world meet their needs and fulfill their aspirations. Our company is built on a foundation of principles that include responsibility to the communities we serve and where we live and work. In 2008, we launched a Corporate Citizenship Initiative, a global effort to address the environmental, social, economic, and ethical challenges we face in our business. Among the issues we are addressing are carbon impact, paper specifications and procurement, ethical conduct within our business and among our vendors, and community and charitable support. For more information, please visit our website: www.wiley.com/go/citizenship.

ISBN 13 978-1-118-70079-2

Printed in the United States of America.

10 9 8 7 6 5 4 3 2 1

■ *I once again dedicate this book to the person who lovingly helps me explore and appreciate life's wonders: My wife, Ann.*

J.R.S.

■ About the Author

DR. JOHN R. SCHERMERHORN JR. is the Charles G. O'Bleness Emeritus Professor of Management in the College of Business at Ohio University where he teaches undergraduate and MBA courses in management, organizational behavior, and Asian business. He earned a PhD degree in organizational behavior from Northwestern University, after receiving an MBA degree (with distinction) in management and international business from New York University and a BS degree in business administration from the State University of New York at Buffalo.

Dr. Schermerhorn's teaching and writing bridges the gap between the theory and practice of management. He has won awards for teaching excellence at Tulane University, The University of Vermont, and Ohio University, where he was named a *University Professor*, the university's leading campus-wide award for undergraduate teaching. He also received the excellence in leadership award for his service as Chair of the Management Education and Development Division of the Academy of Management.

Dr. Schermerhorn brings a unique global dimension to his scholarship. He holds an honorary doctorate from the University of Pécs in Hungary, awarded for his international scholarly contributions to management research and education. He served as a Visiting Fulbright Professor at the University of Botswana, Visiting Professor of Management at the Chinese University of Hong Kong, on-site Coordinator of the Ohio University MBA and Executive MBA programs in Malaysia, and Kohei Miura Visiting Professor at the Chubu University of Japan. Presently he is Adjunct Professor at the National University of Ireland at Galway, a member of the graduate faculty at Bangkok University in Thailand, and Permanent Lecturer in the PhD program at the University of Pécs in Hungary.

Educators and students alike know Dr. Schermerhorn as author of *Management 12e* (Wiley, 2013) and senior co-author of *Organizational Behavior 12e* (Wiley, 2012). His many books are available in Chinese, Dutch, French, Indonesian, Portuguese, Russian, and Spanish language editions. Dr. Schermerhorn has also published numerous articles in publications such as the *Academy of Management Journal, Academy of Management Review, Academy of Management Executive, Organizational Dynamics, Journal of Management Education,* and the *Journal of Management Development*.

Dr. Schermerhorn is a popular guest speaker. His student and faculty workshop topics include tensions and innovations in business education, high engagement teaching and the millennial generation, global perspectives and student learning, and textbook writing and scholarly manuscript development.

{ DEAR COLLEAGUE:

Welcome to *Exploring Management, Fourth Edition.* I hope you find it a useful and engaging resource for your management course. You'll quickly see that it is a bit different from traditional textbooks, hopefully in a positive way. It has all the content you expect, but ...

- The writing voice is "personal"—students are made part of the conversation and asked to interact with the subject matter while reading.
- The presentation is "chunked"—short content sections that fit how students read are followed by study guides that check their learning and prompt career thinking.
- The content is "live"—pages are full of timely examples, news items, situations, and reflection questions that make management real and launch meaningful discussions.

I like to say that *Exploring Management* is a reflection of how much I have learned from my students about what they value, where they hope to go, and how they like to study and learn. It's also a reflection of my desire to bring the real world into the management class, engage students in interesting discussions of important topics, and offer a variety of assignments and projects that promote critical thinking. And if you are using the flipped classroom or plan to try it, this book is tailored from experience to make "doing the flip" easy, exciting, and highly rewarding for you as well as your students.

I've had a lot of success using *Exploring Management* to bring high student engagement to my classes. Chances are that you will too. Take a moment to review the book's design and built-in pedagogy. Browse some pages to check the writing style, visual presentation, reflection features, and study guides. Does *Exploring Management* offer what you are looking for to build a great management course? Could it help engage your students to the point where they actually read and think about topics before coming to class?

As management educators we bear a lot of responsibility for helping our students learn how to better manage their lives and careers and assist organizations to make real contributions to society. *Exploring Management, Fourth Edition,* is my attempt to make it easier for you to fulfill this responsibility in your own way, with lots of instructional options, and backed by solid text content. Thanks for considering it.

Sincerely,

John Schermerhorn

▪ Preface

||| What makes *Exploring Management* different?

Students tell me over and over again that they learn best when their courses and assignments fit well in the context of their everyday lives, career aspirations, and personal experiences. I have written *Exploring Management Fourth Edition,* to meet and engage the new generation of students in their personal spaces. It uses lots of examples, applications, visual highlights, and learning aids to convey the essentials of management. It also asks students lots of thought-provoking questions as they read. My hope is that this special approach and underlying pedagogy will help management educators find unique and innovative ways to enrich the learning experiences of their students.

▪ *Exploring Management* offers a flexible, topic-specific presentation.

The first thing you'll notice is that *Exploring Management* presents "chunks" of material to be read and digested in short time periods. This is a direct response to my classroom experiences where I, and my students, find typical book chapters cumbersome to handle. Students never read more than several pages in *Exploring Management* before hitting a "Study Guide" that allows them to bring closure to what they have just read. This chunked pedagogy motivates students to read and study assigned material before attending class. And, it helps them perform better on tests and assignments.

Topics in the book are easily assignable and sized just right for a class session. Although presented in the traditional planning, organizing, leading, and controlling framework, chapters can be used in any order based on instructor preferences. Many options are available for courses of different types, lengths, and meeting schedules, including online and distance-learning formats. It all depends on what fits best with course objectives, learning approaches, and instructional preferences.

▪ *Exploring Management* uses an integrated learning design.

Every chapter opens with a catchy subtitle and clear visual presentation that quickly draws students into the topic. The opening **Management Live** vignette links chapter topics with popular culture examples from movies and television. Key learning objectives are listed in **Your Chapter Takeaways** while **What's Inside** highlights five interesting and useful chapter features—Explore Yourself, Role Models, Ethics Check, Facts to Consider, and Manager's Library.

Each chapter section begins with a visual overview that poses a **Takeaway Question** followed by a list of **Answers to Come**. These answers become the subheadings that organize section content. The section ends with a **Study Guide**. This one-page checkpoint asks students to pause, and check learning before moving on to the next section. The Study Guide elements include—

- *Rapid Review*—bullet-list summary of concepts and points
- *Terms to Define*—glossary quiz for vocabulary development
- *Be Sure You Can*—checkpoint of major learning outcomes for mastery
- *Questions for Discussion*—questions to stimulate inquiry and prompt class discussions
- *Career Situation: What Would You Do?*—asks students to apply section topics to a problem-solving situation

▪ *Exploring Management* makes "flipping" the classroom easy.

"Flipped" classrooms shift the focus from instructors lecturing and students listening, to instructors guiding and students engaging. The first step in doing the flip is getting students to read and study assigned materials before class. When they come to class prepared, the instructor has many more options for engagement. The chunked presentation, frequent Study Guides, and integrated learning design of *Exploring Management* help greatly in this regard.

Success in flipping the classroom requires a good short quiz and testing program to assure student learning. *Exploring Management* is nicely integrated with the advanced WileyPLUS online environment (see p. x) to make this easy. And, the flipped classroom also requires the instructor to have a solid inventory of discussion activities, projects, and quick-hitting experiences that turn class time into engaged learning time. *Exploring Management* is packed with interesting features that can be used for flipped classroom activities and discussions, and for individual and team assignments.

- **Role Models**
  Introduces a real person's experience and asks students to answer *What's the Lesson Here?* Examples include Ursula Burns, CEO of Xerox and the first African-American woman to head a *Fortune* 500 firm; Gary Hirshberg, social entrepreneur and co-founder of Stonyfield Farms; and online education innovator Salman Khan, founder of the Khan Academy.

- **Ethics Check**
  Poses an ethical dilemma and asks students to answer *You Decide* questions. Examples include "CEO Gets $96.1 Million Pay Package," "Cyberspace Slackers Love Company Time," "Life and Death at an Outsourcing Factory," and "Social Loafing Is Closer Than You Think."

- **Explore Yourself**
  Reminds students how chapter content relates to important personal skills and characteristics, and asks them to *Get to Know Yourself Better* by taking self-assessments and completing other active learning activities. Examples include "Self-management," "Self-confidence," "Integrity," "Resiliency," and "Cultural Awareness."

- **Facts to Consider**
  Briefly summarizes survey data to stimulate critical inquiry and asks students *What Are Your Thoughts?* Examples include "American Workers Talk about Biggest Fears," "Bosses Overestimate Management Skills," "Office Romance Policies Vary Widely," and "Corruption and Bribes Haunt International Business."

- **Manager's Library**
  Highlights a popular book on the reading lists of managers and asks students to *Reflect and React* to its points and themes. Examples include *Delivering Happiness* by Tony Hsieh, *Lean In* by Sheryl Sandberg, *Fast Future* by David Burstein, and *The New Digital Age* by Eric Schmidt and Jared Cohen.

- **Hot Topics**
  Present timely, even controversial, issues framed for debate and discussion, and ask students to participate in a *Final Faceoff* or give their *Final Take*. Examples include "Time to turn the workplace into a fun place?" "Should Parents Pay for Children's Grades?" "Move Over Old Timer, Time to Make Room for Gen Y," and, "Does Disharmony Help Build a Better Team?"

■ *Exploring Management* uses a conversational and interactive writing style.

The author's voice in *Exploring Management* speaks with students the way you and I do in the classroom—conversationally, interactively, and using lots of questions. Although it may seem unusual to have an author speaking directly to his audience, my goal is to be a real person and to approach readers in the spirit of what Ellen Langer calls *mindful learning*.[1] She describes this as engaging students from a perspective of active inquiry rather than as consumers of facts and prescriptions. I view it as a way of moving textbook writing in the same direction we are moving college teaching—being less didactic and more interactive, trying to involve students in a dialog around meaningful topics, questions, examples, and even dilemmas.

■ *Exploring Management* helps students earn grades and build career skills.

Exploring Management is written and designed to help students prepare for quizzes and tests, and earn the best possible grades. In addition to chunked reading and **Study Guides**, the end-of-chapter **Test Prep** asks students to answer multiple-choice, short response, and integration and application questions as a starting point for testing success. They are next directed to active learning and personal development activities in the end-of-book **Skill-Building Portfolio**. It offers **Self-Assessments**, **Class Exercises**, and **Team Projects** carefully chosen to match chapter content with skills development opportunities. A further selection of **Cases for Critical Thinking** engages students in analysis of timely situations and events involving real people and organizations.

[1]Ellen J. Langer, *The Power of Mindful Learning* (Reading, MA: Perseus, 1994).

■ **WileyPLUS**

A natural fit with the flipped classroom, *WileyPLUS* is an innovative, research-based, online environment for effective teaching and learning. It builds students' confidence by taking the guesswork out of studying and providing students with a clear roadmap for **what to do, how to do it, and if they did it right**. The *WileyPLUS* interactive approach focuses on:

CONFIDENCE: Research shows that students experience a great deal of anxiety over studying. That's why we provide a structured learning environment that helps students focus on **what to do**, along with the support of immediate resources.

MOTIVATION: To increase and sustain motivation throughout the semester, *WileyPLUS* helps students learn **how to do it** at a pace that's right for them. Our integrated resources—available 24/7—function like a personal tutor, directly addressing each student's demonstrated needs with specific problem-solving techniques.

SUCCESS: *WileyPLUS* helps to assure that each study session has a positive outcome by putting students in control. Through instant feedback and study objective reports, students know **if they did it right,** and where to focus next, so they achieve the strongest results.

With *WileyPLUS*, our efficacy research shows that students improve their outcomes by as much as one letter grade. *WileyPLUS* helps students take more initiative, so you'll have greater impact on their achievement in the classroom and beyond.

||| What do students receive with *WileyPLUS* for *Exploring Management*?

- The complete digital textbook, saving students up to 60% off the cost of a printed text.
- Question assistance, including links to relevant sections in the online digital textbook.
- Immediate feedback and proof of progress, 24/7.
- Integrated, multi-media resources including the following resources and many more that provide multiple study paths and encourage more active learning.
  - Animated figures
  - CBS/BBC videos
  - Self-assessment quizzes students can use to test themselves on topics such as emotional intelligence, diversity awareness, and intuitive ability.
  - Management calendar including daily management tips
  - Flash cards
  - Hot topic modules
  - Crossword puzzles
  - Interactive self-assessments

||| What do instructors receive with *WileyPLUS* for *Exploring Management*?

Customizable Course Plan: *WileyPLUS* comes with a precreated Course Plan designed by a subject matter expert uniquely for this course. Simple drag-and-drop tools make it easy to assign the course plan as-is or modify it to reflect your course syllabus.

Precreated Activity Types Include:
- Questions
- Readings and resources
- Presentation
- Print Tests
- Concept Mastery
- Project

Course Materials and Assessment Content:
- Lecture Notes PowerPoint Slides
- Classroom Response System (Clicker) Questions
- Image Gallery
- Instructor's Manual
- Question Assignments: all end-of-chapter problems
- Testbank

- Pre- and Post-Lecture Quizzes
- Web Quizzes
- Video Teaching Notes—includes questions geared toward applying text concepts to current videos.

www.wileyplus.com

■ WileyPLUS inside Blackboard Learn™

Discover the advantage of integrating all your course materials in one place with WileyPLUS and Blackboard.

Digital content in higher education is advancing rapidly—moving from static content to dynamic digital assets that provide for personalized, interactive learning. That's why Blackboard and Wiley have partnered to deliver all the benefits of WileyPLUS within the familiar Blackboard Learn™ experience. Tested by instructors and students, this best-in-class integration is designed to meet varying levels of digital usage.

With direct access to WileyPLUS inside Blackboard Learn™, you can create a unified learning experience for your students. You'll have everything you need for teaching and learning all in one place:

- Single sign-on provides faculty and students with direct access to all WileyPLUS content with the convenience of one login.
- Direct links to WileyPLUS readings and assignments give faculty greater control over how they deliver information and allow students to conveniently access their course work.
- Gradebook synchronization ensures all grades appear in the Blackboard Grade Center, saving instructors time and increasing student accountability.
- Student data privacy compliance means student data is always protected and secure.

It's easy to get Started with WileyPLUS and Blackboard. The free WileyPLUS Building Block is available now on Behind the Blackboard for U.S. and international higher education institutions that license Blackboard Learn 9.1, Service Pack 5 and higher. Download the Building Block today.

■ WileyPLUS with ORION

Helping you learn by learning about you™.

WileyPLUS **with ORION** is an adaptive, personal learning experience that helps students find their way as they make new discoveries about how they learn. Highlighting both strengths and problem areas, *WileyPLUS* **with ORION** is the guide that helps all types of learners navigate through their studies to get optimal results in the most efficient amount of time.

WileyPLUS with ORION provides students with a personal, adaptive learning experience so they can build their proficiency on topics and use their study time most effectively. ORION helps students learn by learning about them.

- Unique to ORION, students **begin** by taking a quick diagnostic for any chapter. This will determine each student's baseline proficiency on each topic in the chapter. Students see their individual diagnostic report to help them decide what to do next with the help of ORION's recommendations.
- For each topic, students can either **Study** or **Practice**. Study directs students to the specific topic they choose in *WileyPLUS*, where they can read from the e-textbook or use the variety of relevant resources available there. Students can also practice, using questions and feedback powered by ORION's adaptive learning engine. Based on the results of their diagnostic and ongoing practice, ORION presents students with questions appropriate for their current level of understanding. The system continuously adapts to each student so that he or she can build proficiency.
- *WileyPLUS* with ORION includes a number of reports and ongoing recommendations for students to help them **maintain** their proficiency over time for each topic.

■ Student and Instructor Resources

⫶ What additional special materials does *Exploring Management* offer to both students and instructors?

My colleagues at John Wiley & Sons have worked hard to design supporting materials that extend the goals of this book.

- **Companion Web Site** The Companion Web site for *Exploring Management* at www.wiley.com/college/schermerhorn contains myriad tools and links to aid both teaching and learning, including nearly all the resources described in this section.

- **Annotated Instructor's Edition** With teaching notes prepared by Susan Berston, City College of San Francisco, the Annotated Instructor's Edition includes a brief *Teaching Note* for each section of the book. These notes are designed to stimulate deeper discussion, energize the class, and improve learning through reinforcement and application.

- **Instructor's Resource Guide** Also prepared by Susan Berston, the Instructor's Resource Guide includes a *Conversion Guide, Chapter Outlines, Chapter Objectives, Lecture Notes, Teaching Notes,* and *Suggested Answers* for all quiz, test, and case questions.

- **Test Bank** The Test Bank prepared by Amit Shah, Frostburg State University, consists of nearly 80 true/false, multiple-choice, and short-answer questions per chapter. It was specifically designed so that the questions vary in degree of difficulty, from straightforward recall to challenging, to offer instructors the most flexibility when designing their exams. The *Computerized Test Bank*, includes a test-generating program that allows instructors to customize their exams.

- **PowerPoint Slides** A set of interactive PowerPoint slides prepared by Shelley Smith includes lecture notes and talking points. An *Image Gallery*, containing jpg files for all of the figures in the text, is also provided for instructor convenience.

- **Personal Response System** PRS or "Clicker" content for each chapter will spark additional discussion and debate in the classroom. For more information on PRS, please contact your local Wiley sales representative.

- **Web Quizzes** This resource, prepared by Amit Shah, Frostburg State University, is available on the student portion of the *Exploring Management* companion Web site. It offers online quizzes with questions varying in level of difficulty, designed to help students evaluate their individual progress through a chapter.

- **Management Weekly Updates** These timely updates keep you and your students updated and informed on the very latest in business news stories. Each week you will find links to five new articles, video clips, business news stories, and so much more with discussion questions to elaborate on the stories in the classroom. http://wileymanagementupdates.com

- **Videos and Video Teaching Guide** This set of short video clips from current news programming provides an excellent starting point for lectures or for general classroom discussion. The *Video Teaching Guide*, prepared by Susan Berston, includes video summaries, approaches for using video in the classroom, and assessment questions for each video clip.

- **Darden Business Cases** Through the Wiley Custom Select Web site, you can choose from thousands of cases from Darden Business Publishing to create a book with any combination of cases, Wiley textbook chapters, and original material. Visit http://www.customselect.wiley.com/collection/dardencases for more information.

■ Acknowledgments

Exploring Management, Fourth Edition, is a "concept" book, which began, grew, and found life and form in its first three editions over many telephone conversations, conference calls, e-mail exchanges, and face-to-face meetings. It has since matured and been refined in content, style, and direction as a fourth edition through the useful feedback provided by many satisfied faculty and student users and reviewers.

There wouldn't be an *Exploring Management* without the support, commitment, creativity, and dedication of the following members of the Wiley team. My thanks go to: Lisé Johnson, *Executive Editor*; George Hoffman, *Vice President and Publisher*; Jennifer Manias, *Content Editor*; Jacqueline Hughes, *Editorial Assistant*; Kelly Simmons, *Marketing Manager*; Erin Bascom, *Senior Production Editor*; Harry Nolan, *Creative Director*; Tom Nery, *Senior Designer*; Mary Ann Price, *Photo Manager*; and, Susan McLaughlin, *Photo Researcher*.

My special thanks go to two colleagues who helped make *Exploring Management 4/e* a true resource for student engagement. Susan Berston of City College of San Francisco edited the portfolio of *Cases for Critical Thinking*, contributed to chapter features, and prepared the instructor's guide and resource package. Robert E. (Lenie) Holbrook of Ohio University contributed *Management Live* features that introduce each chapter and authored the creative supplement *Art Imitates Life*.

Focus Group Participants:

Maria Aria, *Camden County College*
Ellen Benowitz, *Mercer County Community College*
John Brogan, *Monmouth University*
Lawrence J. Danks, *Camden County College*
Matthew DeLuca, *Baruch College*
David Fearon, *Central Connecticut State University*
Stuart Ferguson, *Northwood University*
Eugene Garaventa, *College of Staten Island*
Scott Geiger, *University of South Florida, St. Petersburg*

Larry Grant, *Bucks County Community College*
Fran Green, *Pennsylvania State University, Delaware County*
F. E. Hamilton, *Eckerd College*
Don Jenner, *Borough of Manhattan Community College*
John Podoshen, *Franklin and Marshall College*
Neuman Pollack, *Florida Atlantic University*
David Radosevich, *Montclair State University*
Moira Tolan, *Mount Saint Mary College*

Virtual Focus Group Participants:

George Alexakis, *Nova Southeastern University*
Steven Bradley, *Austin Community College*
Paula Brown, *Northern Illinois University*
Elnora Farmer, *Clayton State University*
Paul Gagnon, *Central Connecticut State University*
Eugene Garaventa, *College of Staten Island*
Larry Garner, *Tarleton State University*
Wayne Grossman, *Hofstra University*
Dee Guillory, *University of South Carolina, Beaufort*
Julie Hays, *University of St. Thomas*
Kathleen Jones, *University of North Dakota*
Marvin Karlins, *University of South Florida*

Al Laich, *University of Northern Virginia*
Vincent Lutheran, *University of North Carolina, Wilmington*
Douglas L. Micklich, *Illinois State University*
David Oliver, *Edison College*
Jennifer Oyler, *University of Central Arkansas*
Kathleen Reddick, *College of Saint Elizabeth*
Terry L. Riddle, *Central Virginia Community College*
Roy L. Simerly, *East Carolina University*
Frank G. Titlow, *St. Petersburg College*
David Turnipseed, *Indiana University—Purdue University, Fort Wayne*
Michael Wakefield, *Colorado State University, Pueblo*
George A. (Bud) Wynn, *University of Tampa*

Reviewers:

M. David Albritton, *Northern Arizona University*
Mitchell Alegre, *Niagara University*
Allen Amason, *University of Georgia*
Mihran Aroian, *University of Texas, Austin*
Karen R. Bangs, *California State Polytechnic University*
Heidi Barclay, *Metropolitan State University*
Reuel Barksdale, *Columbus State Community College*
Patrick Bell, *Elon University*
Michael Bento, *Owens Community College*
William Berardi, *Bristol Community College*
Robert Blanchard, *Salem State University*
Laquita Blockson, *College of Charleston*
Peter Geoffrey Bowen, *University of Denver*
Victoria Boyd, *Claflin University*
Ralph R. Braithwaite, *University of Hartford*
David Bright, *Wright State University-Dayton*
Kenneth G. Brown, *University of Iowa*
Diana Bullen, *Mesa Community College*
Beverly Bugay, *Tyler Junior College*
Robert Cass, *Virginia Wesleyan College*
Savannah Clay, *Central Piedmont Community College*
Paul Coakley, *Community College of Baltimore County*
Suzanne Crampton, *Grand Valley State University*
Kathryn Dansky, *Pennsylvania State University*
Susan Davis, *Claflin University*
Jeanette Davy, *Wright State University*
Matt DeLuca, *Baruch College*
Karen Edwards, *Chemeketa Community College*
Valerie Evans, *Lincoln Memorial University*
Paul Ewell, *Bridgewater College*
Gary J. Falcone, *LaSalle University*
Elnora Farmer, *Clayton State University*
Gail E. Fraser, *Kean University*
Nancy Fredericks, *San Diego State University*
Tamara Friedrich, *Savannah State University*
Larry Garner, *Tarleton State University*
Cindy Geppert, *Palm Beach State College*
Richard J. Gibson, *Embry-Riddle University*
Dee Guillory, *University of South Carolina, Beaufort*
Linda Hefferin, *Elgin Community College*
Aaron Hines, *SUNY New Paltz*
Merrily Hoffman, *San Jacinto College*
Jeff Houghton, *West Virginia University*
Tammy Hunt, *University of North Carolina Wilmington*
Debra Hunter, *Troy University*

Kimberly Hurnes, *Washtenaw Community College*
Gary S. Insch, *West Virginia University*
Barcley Johnson, *Western Michigan University*
Louis Jourdan, *Clayton State University*
Brian Joy, *Henderson Community College*
Edward Kass, *University of San Francisco*
Renee King, *Eastern Illinois University*
Judith Kizzie, *Howard Community College*
Robert Klein, *Philadelphia University*
John Knutsen, *Everett Community College*
Al Laich, *University of Northern Virginia*
Susan Looney, *Delaware Technical & Community College*
Vincent Lutheran, *University of North Carolina, Wilmington*
Jim Maddox, *Friends University*
John Markert, *Wells College*
Marcia Marriott, *Monroe Community College*
Brenda McAleer, *Colby College*
Randy McCamery, *Tarleton State University*
Gerald McFry, *Coosa Valley Technical College*
Diane Minger, *Cedar Valley College*
Michael Monahan, *Frostburg State University*
Dave Nemi, *Niagara County Community College*
Nanci Newstrom, *Eastern Illinois University*
Lam Nguyen, *Palm Beach State College*
Joelle Nisolle, *West Texas A&M University*
Penny Olivi, *York College of Pennsylvania*
Jennifer Oyler, *University of Central Arkansas*
Barry Palatnik, *Burlington County Community College*
Kathy Pederson, *Hennepin Technical College*
Sally Proffitt, *Tarrant County College*
Nancy Ray-Mitchell, *McLennan Community College*
Catherine J. Ruggieri, *St. John's University*
Joseph C. Santora, *Essex County College*
Charles Seifert, *Siena College*
Sidney Siegel, *Drexel University*
Gerald F. Smith, *University of Northern Iowa*
Wendy Smith, *University of Delaware*
Howard Stanger, *Canisius College*
Peter Stone, *Spartanburg Community College*
Henry A. Summers, *Stephen F. Austin State University*
Daryl J. Taylor, *Pasadena City College*
Ann Theis, *Adrian College*
Jody Tolan, *University of Southern California, Marshall School of Business*

David Turnipseed, *Indiana University—Purdue University, Fort Wayne*
Robert Turrill, *University of Southern California*
Vickie Tusa, *Embry-Riddle University*
Aurelio Valente, *Philadelphia University*

Michael Wakefield, *Colorado State University, Pueblo*
Charles D. White, *James Madison University*
Daniel Wubbena, *Western Iowa Tech Community College*
Alan Wright, *Henderson State University*
Ashley Wright, *Spartanburg Community College*

Class Test Participants

Verl Anderson, *Dixie State College*
Corinne Asher, *Henry Ford Community College*
Forrest Aven, *University of Houston Downtown*
Richard Bartlett, *Columbus State Community College*
John Bird, *West Virginia State University*
Dr. Sheri Carder, *Florida Gateway College*
Susie Cox, *McNeese State University*
Robert Eliason, *James Madison University*
Trent Engbers, *Indiana University*
Shelly Gardner, *Augustana College*
Ann Gilley, *Ferris State University*
Janie Gregg, *The University of West Alabama*
Jay Hochstetler, *Anderson University*
Tacy Holliday, *Montgomery College*
David Hollomon, *Victor Valley College*

Cheryl Hughes, *Indiana University*
David Jalajas, *Long Island University*
Angelina Kiser, *University of the Incarnate Word*
Cindy Murphy, *Southeastern Community College*
Chandran Mylvaganam, *Northwood University*
Greg Petranek, *Eastern Connecticut State University*
Tracy Porter, *Cleveland State University*
Renee Rogers, *Forsyth Technical Community College*
Richard Sharman, *Lone Star College–Montgomery*
Catherine Slade, *Augusta State University*
Susan Steiner, *The University of Tampa*
Donald Stout, *Saint Martin's University*
Alec Zama, *Grand View University*
Nancy Zimmerman, *The Community College of Baltimore County*

Student Focus Group Participants, Baruch College:

Faculty Conveners: Alvin L. Booke, Matthew J. De Luca, Sara Grant, Louis Myers, Abe Tawil, James Walsh.

Student Contributors: Farhana Alam, Laureen Attreed, Sarah Bohsali, Susanna Eng, Dino Genzano, Annie Gustave, Andrew Josefiak, Diana Pang, Vidushi Parmar, Dulari Ramkishun, Vicky Roginskaya, Jessica Scheiber, Ruta Skarbauskaite, Darren Smith, Anita Alickaj, Dana Fleischer, Mandie Gellis, Haider Mehmood, and Dina Shlafman

■ Brief Contents

▪Detailed Contents

Cases for Critical Thinking   C-1

FOURTH EDITION

Exploring Management

Annotated Instructor's Edition

Zappos CEO Tony Hsieh is into happiness. His goal is "to set up an environment where the personalities, creativities, and individuality of all different employees come out and shine."

Brad Swonetz/Redux Pictures

Managers and the Management Process

Everyone Becomes a Manager Someday

Management Live

Warner Bros/Photofest

Self-Management and *Slumdog Millionaire*

*T*he *Times* of London called this movie an "exotic, edgy thriller," while the *New York Times* described it as a "gaudy, gorgeous rush of color, sound and motion." What's your take on this rags-to-riches story of an orphan growing up in Mumbai, India, and finding his way to a TV game show offering him the chance to be a "slumdog millionaire"?

When the disgruntled game-show host has the police chief rough up the main character Jamal (Dev Patel) the night before the big show, he asks: "What the hell can a slum boy possibly know?" Facing the chief and the prospect of more mistreatment, Jamal looks him in the eye and says in return: "The answers."

This movie is a study in discipline, confidence, and self-management—the capacity to act with a strong sense of self-awareness. As a career skill, this ability helps us stay confident, build on strengths, overcome weaknesses, and avoid viewing ourselves both more favorably or more negatively than is justified.

You have to admire the way Jamal held up under the police chief's torture. And, he didn't fall prey to the quiz master's repeated attempts to deceive and pressure him into not believing his own best answers. It's a classic case of self-management in action.

Even if you've already seen it, *Slumdog Millionaire* is worth another viewing. Watch for lessons on management and personal career development that you might explore with your friends and classmates.

YOUR CHAPTER 1 TAKEAWAYS

1. Understand what it means to be a manager.

2. Know what managers do and what skills they use.

3. Recognize important career issues in the new workplace.

WHAT'S INSIDE

Explore Yourself
More on **self-management**

Role Models
Ursula Burns leads Xerox with confidence and a strategic eye

Ethics Check
Watch out for bad apples at farmers' markets

Facts to Consider
Employment contradictions in workforce diversity

Manager's Library
Delivering Happiness: A Path to Profits, Passion, and Purpose by Tony Hsieh

Takeaway 1.1
What Does It Mean to Be a Manager?

ANSWERS TO COME

- Organizations have different types and levels of managers.
- Accountability is a cornerstone of managerial performance.
- Effective managers help others achieve high performance and satisfaction.
- Managers must meet multiple and changing expectations.

IN A BOOK CALLED *THE SHIFT: THE FUTURE OF WORK IS ALREADY HERE*, SCHOLAR Lynda Gratton describes the difficult times in which we live and work. "Technology shrinks the world but consumes all of our time," she says, while "globalization means we can work anywhere, but must compete with people from everywhere; there are more of us, and we're living longer; traditional communities are being yanked apart as people cluster in cities; and there is rising energy demand and fewer traditional resources."[1]

What does all this mean in terms of planning for career entry and advancement? At a minimum there are few guarantees of long-term employment, and jobs are increasingly earned and re-earned every day through one's performance accomplishments. Careers are being redefined along the lines of "flexibility," "free agency," "skill portfolios," and "entrepreneurship." The fact is: Career success today requires lots of initiative and self-awareness, as well as continuous learning. The question is: Are you ready?

Organizations have different types and levels of managers.

You find them everywhere, in small and large businesses, voluntary associations, government agencies, schools, hospitals, and wherever people work together for a common cause. Even though the job titles vary from team leader to department head, project leader, president, administrator, and more, the people in these jobs all share a common responsibility—helping others do their best work. We call them **managers**—persons who directly supervise, support, and help activate work efforts to achieve the performance goals of individuals, teams, or even an organization as a whole. In this sense, I think you'll agree with the chapter subtitle: Everyone becomes a manager someday.

Take a good look at **Figure 1.1**. It describes an organization as a series of layers, each of which represents different levels of work and managerial responsibilities.[2]

First-Line Managers and Team Leaders

"I've just never worked on anything that so visibly, so dramatically changes the quality of someone's life. Some days you wake up, and if you think about all the work you have to do it's so overwhelming, you could be paralyzed." These are the words of Justin Fritz as he described his experiences leading a 12-member team to launch a new product at Medtronic, a large medical products company. He is a **first-line manager**—a team leader or supervisor who is formally in charge of a

A **manager** is a person who supports and is responsible for the work of others.

First-line managers are team leaders and supervisors in charge of people who perform nonmanagerial duties.

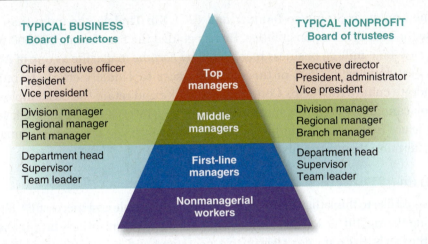

FIGURE 1.1
What Are the Typical Job Titles and Levels of Management in Organizations?
The traditional organization is structured as a pyramid. The top manager, typically a CEO, president, or executive director, reports to a board of directors in a business or to a board of trustees in a nonprofit organization. Middle managers report to top managers, and first-line managers or team leaders report to middle managers.

small work group composed of nonmanagerial workers. About the challenge of managerial work, Fritz says: "You just have to get it done."[3]

A first job in management typically involves serving as a team leader or supervisor. Typical job titles for these first-line managers include department head, team leader, and unit manager. For example, the leader of an auditing team is considered a first-line manager, as is the head of an academic department in a university. Even though most people enter the workforce as technical specialists such as auditor, market researcher, or systems analyst, sooner or later they advance to these positions of initial managerial responsibility. And they serve as essential building blocks for organizational performance.[4]

Middle Managers

Look again at Figure 1.1. This time consider where Justin may be headed in his career. At the next level above team leader we find **middle managers**—persons in charge of relatively large departments or divisions consisting of several smaller work units or teams.

Middle managers usually supervise several first-line managers. Examples include clinic directors in hospitals; deans in universities; and division managers, plant managers, and regional sales managers in businesses. Because of their position "in the middle," these managers must be able to work well with people from all parts of the organization—higher, lower, and side-to-side. As Justin moves up the career ladder to middle management, there will be more pressure and new challenges. But there should also be rewards and satisfaction.

Middle managers oversee the work of large departments or divisions.

Top Managers

Some middle managers advance still higher in the organization, earning job titles such as chief executive officer (CEO), chief operating officer (COO), chief financial officer (CFO), chief information officer (CIO), president, and vice president. These **top managers** are part of a senior management team that is responsible for the performance of an organization as a whole or for one of its larger parts. They must be alert to trends and developments in the external environment, recognize potential problems and opportunities, set strategy, craft the internal culture, build a talent pool, and overall lead the organization to success.[5] The best of them are future-oriented thinkers who make good decisions even in face of uncertainty and tough competition.

Top managers guide the performance of the organization as a whole or of one of its major parts.

The Container Store's co-founder and CEO, Kip Tindell, has more than met these top manager responsibilities. He has guided the firm from a $35,000 start-up to a $700+ million business recognized by *Fortune* magazine as one of America's best employers.[6] Part of this success traces to Tindell's efforts to build a corporate culture that helps Container Store hire and retain the best employees. All job candidates go through extensive screening interviews. Once hired, salespeople are paid twice the industry average and given 263 hours of training per year, far more than the industry average of eight.[7]

Boards of Directors

We would like to think that all top managers are responsible and successful—always making the right decisions and doing things in their organization's best interests. But, the fact is that some don't live up to expectations and even take personal advantage of their positions, perhaps to the point of ethics failures and illegal acts. Who or what keeps CEOs and other senior managers focused and high performing?

If you look back at Figure 1.1, you'll see that even the CEO or president of an organization reports to a higher-level boss. In business corporations, this is a **board of directors**, whose members are elected by stockholders to represent their ownership interests. In nonprofit organizations, such as a hospital or university, top managers report to a *board of trustees*. These board members may be elected by local citizens, appointed by government bodies, or invited to serve by existing members.

In both business and the public sector, the basic responsibilities of a board are the same. Its members are supposed to oversee the affairs of the organization and the performance of its top management. In other words, they are supposed to make sure that the organization is always being run right. This is called **governance**, the oversight of top management by an organization's board of directors or board of trustees.

‖ Accountability is a cornerstone of managerial performance.

Throughout the workplace, not just at the top, the term **accountability** describes the requirement of one person to answer to a higher authority for performance achieved in his or her area of work responsibility. This notion of accountability is an important aspect of managerial performance. In the traditional organizational pyramid, accountability flows upward. Team members are accountable to a team leader, the team leader is accountable to a middle manager, the middle manager is accountable to a top manager, and the top manager is accountable to a board of directors.

Let's not forget that accountability in managerial performance is always accompanied by dependency. At the same time that any manager is being held accountable by a higher level for the performance results of her or his area of supervisory responsibility, the manager is dependent on others to do the required work. In fact, we might say that a large part of the study of management is all about learning how to best manage the dynamics of accountability and dependency as shown in the small figure.

---

*Members of a **board of directors** are elected by stockholders to represent their ownership interests.*

***Governance** is oversight of top management by a board of directors or board of trustees.*

***Accountability** is the requirement to show performance results to a supervisor.*

Work team members

Working Mother Looks for the Best

Great Employers Put Top Value on People

Working Mother magazine's annual listing of the "100 Best Companies for Working Mothers" has become an important management benchmark—both for employers who want to be among the best and for potential employees who want to work only for the best. The magazine is worth a look for topics ranging from kids to health to personal motivation and more.

Self-described as helping women "integrate their professional lives, their family lives and their inner lives," *Working Mother* mainstreams coverage of work–life balance issues and needs for women. One issue reported on moms who "pushed for more family-friendly benefits and got them." The writer described how Kristina Marsh worked to get lactation support for nursing mothers as a formal benefit at Dow Corning, and how Beth Schiavo started a Working Moms Network in Ernst & Young's Atlanta offices and then got it approved as a corporate program nationwide.

A list of best employers for multicultural women includes Allstate, American Express, Deloitte, Ernst & Young, IBM, and General Mills. *Working Mother* says: "All of our winning companies not only require manager training on diversity issues but also rate manager performance partly on diversity results, such as how many multicultural women advance."

Find Inspiration

Pick up a copy of *Working Mother* magazine or browse the online version. It's a chance to learn more about the complexities of work–life balance, including the challenges faced by women blending motherhood with a career. It's also a place to learn which employers are truly great in respecting quality of work life issues.

An **effective manager** successfully helps others achieve high performance and satisfaction in their work.

Quality of work life is the overall quality of human experiences in the workplace.

⦀ Effective managers help others achieve high performance and satisfaction.

This discussion of performance accountability and related challenges may make you wonder: What exactly is an effective manager? Most people, perhaps you, would reply that an effective manager is someone who helps people and organizations perform. That's a fine starting point, but we should go a step further. I define an **effective manager** as someone who successfully helps others achieve both high performance and satisfaction in their work.

The concern for not just work performance but also job satisfaction is a central theme in our society. It calls attention to **quality of work life** (QWL) issues—the overall quality of human experiences in the workplace. Have you experienced a "high QWL" environment? Most people would describe it as a place where they are respected and valued by their employer. They would talk about fair pay, safe work conditions, opportunities to learn and use new skills, room to grow and progress in a career, and protection of individual rights. They would say everyone takes pride in their work and the organization.

Are you willing to work anywhere other than in a high QWL setting? Would you, as a manager, be pleased with anything less than helping others achieve not just high performance but also job satisfaction? Sadly, the real world doesn't always live up to these expectations. Talk to parents, relatives, and friends who go to work every day. You might be surprised. Many people still labor in difficult, sometimes even hostile and unhealthy, conditions—ones we would consider low QWL for sure.[8]

⦀ Managers must meet multiple and changing expectations.

As president and CEO of Cornerstone Research, Cindy Zollinger directly supervises 24 people. But she says: "I don't really manage them in a typical way; they largely run themselves. I help them in dealing with obstacles they face, or in making the most of opportunities they find."[9] As Cindy's comments suggest, we are in a time when the best managers are known more for "helping" and "supporting" than for "directing" and "order giving." The terms "coordinator," "coach," and "team leader" are heard as often as "supervisor" or "boss." The fact is that most organizations need more than managers who simply sit back and tell others what to do.

Take a moment to jot down a few notes on the behaviors and characteristics of the *best* managers you've ever had. My students describe theirs as leading by example, willing to do any job, treating others as equals and with respect, acting approachable, being enthusiastic, expecting outstanding performance, and helping others grow. They talk about managers who often work alongside those they supervise, spending most of their time providing advice and support so that others can perform to the best of their abilities and with satisfaction. How does this listing compare with your experiences?

Figure 1.2 uses the notion of an **upside-down pyramid** to describe a new mindset for managers—a real expression of what it means to act as a coach rather than an order giver. The concept of the upside-down pyramid fits well with Cindy Zollinger's description of her job as a manager, and it should also be consistent with how you described your best manager.

Sitting prominent at the top of the upside-down pyramid are nonmanagerial workers—people who interact directly with customers and clients or produce products and services for them. Managers are shown a level below. Their attention is concentrated on supporting these workers so they can best serve the organization's customers.

In the upside-down pyramid view, there is no doubt that the organization exists to serve its customers. It keeps clear that managers are there to help and support the people whose work makes that possible. As the Container Store's CEO Kip Tindell says: "If employees aren't happy, customers aren't happy and then shareholders won't be happy."[10] Given the success he's had with all three, isn't that a pretty strong endorsement for all managers to try flipping the organizational pyramid upside-down?

The **upside-down pyramid** view of organizations puts customers at the top and being served by nonmanagerial workers, who are supported by team leaders and higher-level managers.

FIGURE 1.2
How Do Mindsets Change When the Organization Is Viewed as an Upside-Down Pyramind?
If we turn the traditional organizational pyramid upside down, we get a valuable look at how managerial work is viewed today. Managers are at the bottom of the upside-down pyramid, and they are expected to support the operating workers above them. Their goal is to help these workers best serve the organization's customers at the top. The appropriate mindset of this supportive manager is more "coaching" and "helping" than "directing" and "order giving."

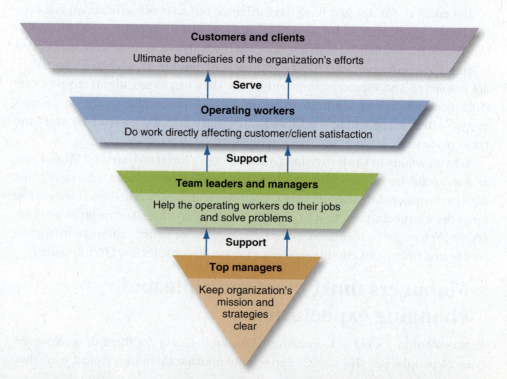

STUDY GUIDE

Takeaway 1.1
What Does It Mean to Be a Manager?

Terms to Define

Accountability

Board of directors

Effective manager

First-line manager

Governance

Manager

Middle managers

Quality of work life

Top managers

Upside-down pyramid

Rapid Review

- Managers support and facilitate the work efforts of other people in organizations.
- Top managers scan the environment and pursue long-term goals; middle managers coordinate activities among large departments or divisions; first-line managers, like team leaders, supervise and support nonmanagerial workers.
- Everyone in an organization is accountable to a higher-level manager for his or her performance accomplishments; at the highest level, top managers are held accountable by boards of directors or boards of trustees.
- Effective managers help others achieve both high performance and high levels of job satisfaction.
- New directions in managerial work emphasize "coaching" and "supporting," rather than "directing" and "order giving."
- In the upside-down pyramid view of organizations, the role of managers is to support nonmanagerial workers who serve the needs of customers at the top.

Questions for Discussion

1. Other than at work, in what situations do you expect to be a manager during your lifetime?
2. Why should a manager be concerned about the quality of work life in an organization?
3. In what ways does the upside-down pyramid view of organizations offer advantages over the traditional view of the top-down pyramid?

Be Sure You Can

- explain how managers contribute to organizations
- describe the activities of managers at different levels
- explain how accountability operates in organizations
- describe an effective manager
- list several ways the work of managers is changing from the past
- explain the role of managers in the upside-down pyramid

Career Situation: What Would You Do?

When people are promoted to become managers they often end up supervising friends and colleagues. Put yourself in this situation. As a new manager of a team full of friends, what can and should you do to quickly earn the respect of others and build a smoothly functioning work team?

Takeaway 1.2
What Do Managers Do, and What Skills Do They Use?

ANSWERS TO COME

- Managerial work is often intense and demanding.
- Managers plan, organize, lead, and control.
- Managers enact informational, interpersonal, and decisional roles.
- Managers pursue action agendas and engage in networking.
- Managers use a variety of technical, human, and conceptual skills.
- Managers can and should learn from experience.

THE MANAGERS WE HAVE BEEN DISCUSSING ARE INDISPENSABLE TO ORGANIZATIONS. Their efforts bring together resources, technology, and human talents to get things done. Some are fairly routine tasks that are repeated day after day. Many others, however, are challenging and novel, often appearing as unexpected problems and opportunities. But regardless of the task at hand, managers are expected to make things happen in ways that best serve the goals of the organization, the needs of its customers, and the interests of its employees or members.

Managerial work is often intense and demanding.

> The manager can never be free to forget the job, and never has the pleasure of knowing, even temporarily, that there is nothing else to do. . . . Managers always carry the nagging suspicion that they might be able to contribute just a little bit more. Hence they assume an unrelenting pace in their work.[11]

Although what managers do may seem straightforward, this quote from scholar and consultant Henry Mintzberg shows that putting it into practice can be much more complicated. In his classic book, *The Nature of Managerial Work*, Mintzberg describes the daily work of corporate chief executives this way. "There was no break in the pace of activity during office hours. The mail . . . telephone calls . . . and meetings . . . accounted for almost every minute from the moment these executives entered their offices in the morning until they departed in the evenings."[12] Today, we might add the constant demands of our smart phones, ever-full e-mail and voice-mail in-boxes, and constant streams of instant messages and social media alerts to Mintzberg's list of executive preoccupations.[13]

Can you imagine a day filled with managerial responsibilities? The managers Mintzberg observed had little free time because unexpected problems and continuing requests for meetings consumed almost all the time that was available. Their workdays were intense, hectic, and fast paced; the pressure for always improving performance was all-encompassing. Any manager, according to Mintzberg, must be ready to work long hours on fragmented and varied tasks at an intense pace, while getting things done through communication and interpersonal relationships.

⦀ Managers plan, organize, lead, and control.

If you are ready to perform as a manager or to get better as one, a good starting point is Figure 1.3. It shows the four functions in the **management process**—planning, organizing, leading, and controlling. The belief is that all managers, regardless of title, level, and organizational setting, are responsible for doing each of them well.[14]

The **management process** is planning, organizing, leading, and controlling the use of resources to accomplish performance goals.

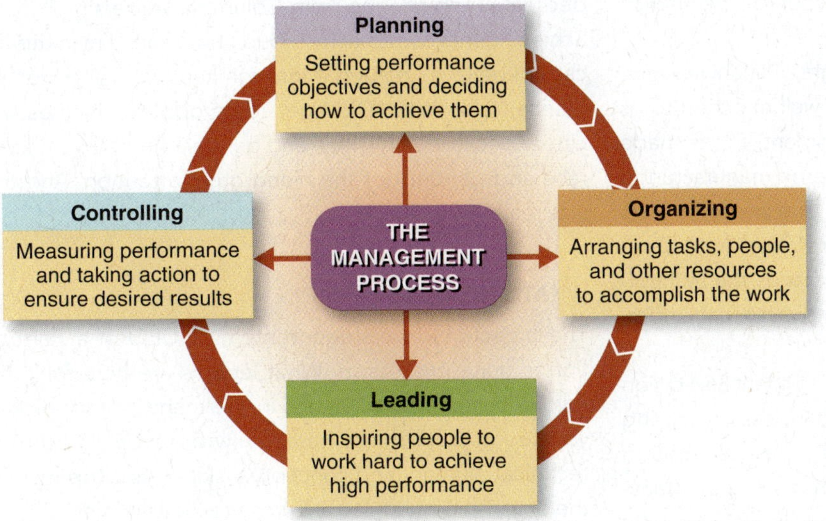

FIGURE 1.3
What Four Functions Make Up the Management Process?
The management process consists of four functions: planning, organizing, leading, and controlling. Planning sets the direction as performance objectives. Organizing arranges people and tasks to do the work. Leading inspires others to work hard. Controlling measures performance to make sure that plans and objectives are accomplished.

Planning
Setting performance objectives and deciding how to achieve them

Controlling
Measuring performance and taking action to ensure desired results

THE MANAGEMENT PROCESS

Organizing
Arranging tasks, people, and other resources to accomplish the work

Leading
Inspiring people to work hard to achieve high performance

Planning

In management, **planning** is the process of setting performance objectives and determining what actions should be taken to accomplish them. When managers plan, they set goals and objectives and select ways to achieve them.

There was a time, for example, when Ernst & Young's top management grew concerned about the firm's retention rates for women.[15] Why? Turnover rates at the time were much higher among women than among men, running some 22% per year and costing the firm about 150% of each person's annual salary to hire and train a replacement. Then Chairman Philip A. Laskawy responded to the situation by setting a planning objective to reduce turnover rates for women.

Planning is the process of setting objectives and determining what should be done to accomplish them.

Organizing

Even the best plans will fail without strong implementation. Success begins with **organizing**, the process of assigning tasks, allocating resources, and coordinating the activities of individuals and groups. When managers organize, they bring people and resources together to put plans into action.

At Ernst & Young, Laskawy organized to meet his planning objective by convening and personally chairing a Diversity Task Force of partners. He also established a new Office of Retention and hired Deborah K. Holmes, now Global Director of Corporate Responsibility, to head it. As retention problems were identified in various parts of the firm, Holmes created special task forces to tackle them and recommend location-specific solutions.

Organizing is the process of assigning tasks, allocating resources, and coordinating work activities.

{ **"I'M IN THIS JOB BECAUSE I BELIEVE I EARNED IT THROUGH HARD WORK AND HIGH PERFORMANCE."**

Role Models

■ Ursula Burns Leads Xerox with Confidence and a Strategic Eye

"Frankness," sharp humor," "willingness to take risks," "deep industry knowledge," "technical prowess." These are all phrases used to describe Ursula Burns, CEO of Xerox Corporation. She started as a mechanical engineering intern and moved up to become the first African American woman to head a *Fortune* 500 firm.

When she took over the firm at the height of financial crisis, her experience and leadership skills were well matched to its many challenges. In her prior role as president, Burns made tough decisions on downsizing, closed Xerox manufacturing operations, and changed the product mix. She also knew how to work well with the firm's board. Director Robert A. McDonald of Procter & Gamble says. "She understands the technology and can communicate it in a way that a director can understand it."

Burns took a significant risk as new CEO and spent $6.4 billion to acquire the computer outsourcing and business processing company Affiliated Computer Services. This acquisition changed the size, scope, and focus of Xerox. ACS is a transportation solutions company providing services like electronic toll collection, management of cities' parking systems, and photo traffic enforcement.

A working mother and spouse, Burns was raised by a single mom in New York City public housing. She earned a master's degree in engineering from Columbia University. Pride in her achievements comes across loud and clear: "I'm in this job because I believe I earned it through hard work and high performance," she said. "Did I get some opportunities early in my career because of my race and gender? Probably . . . I imagine race and gender got the hiring guys' attention. And the rest was really up to me."

WHAT'S THE LESSON HERE?

The trajectory from student intern to CEO of a *Fortune* 500 firm is quite impressive. What lessons are here for others to follow? Which four functions in the management process do you see at work in this case? How does Ursula Burns utilize technical, human, and conceptual skills? As a top manager of the organization, what are Burns's responsibilities?

Leading

Leading is the process of arousing enthusiasm and inspiring efforts to achieve goals.

The management function of **leading** is the process of arousing people's enthusiasm to work hard and inspiring their efforts to fulfill plans and accomplish objectives. When managers lead, they build commitments to plans and influence others to do their best work in implementing them. This is one of the most talked about managerial responsibilities, and it deserves lots of personal thought. Not every manager is a good leader, but every great manager is one for sure.

Deborah Holmes actively pursued her leadership responsibilities at Ernst & Young. She noticed that, in addition to the intense work at the firm, women often faced more stress because their spouses also worked. She became a champion of improved work–life balance and pursued it relentlessly. She started "call-free holidays," where professionals did not check voice mail or e-mail on weekends and holidays. She also started a "travel sanity" program that limited staffers' travel to four days a week so that they could get home for weekends. And she started a Woman's Access Program to provide mentoring and career development.

Controlling

Controlling is the process of measuring performance and taking action to ensure desired results.

Controlling is the process of measuring work performance, comparing results to objectives, and taking corrective action as needed. As you have surely experienced, things don't always go as planned. When managers control, they stay in contact with people as they work, gather and interpret information on performance results, and use this information to make adjustments.

At Ernst & Young, Laskawy and Holmes regularly measured retention rates for women at the firm and compared them to the rate that existed when their new programs were started. By comparing results with plans and objectives, they were able to track changes in work-life balance and retention rates and pinpoint where they needed to make further adjustments in their programs. Over time, turnover rates for women were, and continue to be, reduced at all levels in the firm.[16]

⦀ Managers enact informational, interpersonal, and decisional roles.

When you consider the four management functions, don't be unrealistic. The functions aren't always performed one at a time or step-by-step. Remember the manager's workday as earlier described by Mintzberg—intense, fast-paced, and stressful. The reality is that managers must plan, organize, lead, and control continuously while dealing with the numerous events, situations, and problems of the day.

To describe how managers actually get things done, Mintzberg identified three sets of roles that he believed all good managers enact successfully.[17] These are the interpersonal, informational, and decisional roles shown in the small figure.

INTERPERSONAL ROLES	INFORMATIONAL ROLES	DECISIONAL ROLES
How a manager interacts with other people • Figurehead • Leader • Liaison	How a manager exchanges and processes information • Monitor • Disseminator • Spokesperson	How a manager uses information in decision making • Entrepreneur • Disturbance handler • Resource allocator • Negotiator

A manager's *informational roles* focus on the giving, receiving, and analyzing of information. The *interpersonal roles* reflect interactions with people inside and outside the work unit. The *decisional roles* involve using information to make decisions to solve problems or address opportunities.[18] It is through performing all these roles, so to speak, that managers fulfill their planning, organizing, leading, and controlling responsibilities.

Speaking of roles, each chapter of this book has a Role Models feature that introduces you to successful managers and executives in a variety of settings. Ursula Burns of Xerox was just featured as our first role model, and her story is well worth a look.

⦀ Managers are busy people that pursue action agendas and engage in networking.

Managers must not only master the four management functions and the roles just discussed; they must implement them in intense and complex work settings. And without any doubt, managerial work is busy, demanding, and stressful at all levels of responsibility. The managers Mintzberg studied had little free time to themselves.[19] And in our age of high-tech smart devices, little has changed. A recent study found that just 15% of a typical CEO's day is spent working alone.[20] The workdays of most managers are hectic, and the pressure for improving performance is often intense.[21]

- Long hours
- Intense pace
- Fragmented and varied tasks
- Lots of communication
- Filled with interpersonal relationships

While we are discussing workday realities, consider this description of just one incident from the life of a general manager.[22]

> On the way to a scheduled meeting, a general manager met a staff member who did not report to him. They exchanged "hellos" and in a two-minute conversation the manager: (a) asked two questions and received helpful information; (b) reinforced his relationship with the staff member by sincerely complimenting her on recent work; and (c) enlisted the staff member's help on another project.

Can you see the pattern here? In just 2 short minutes, this general manager accomplished a lot. In fact, he demonstrated excellence with two activities that management consultant and scholar John Kotter considers critical to succeeding with the management process—agenda setting and networking.[23]

Agenda Setting

Agenda setting involves identifying clear action priorities.

Through **agenda setting**, managers identify clear action priorities. These agendas may be incomplete and loosely connected in the beginning. But over time, as the manager utilizes information continually gleaned from many different sources, the agendas become more specific. Kotter believes that the best managers keep their agendas always in mind so they can quickly recognize and take advantage of opportunities to advance them. In the example here, what might have happened if the manager had simply nodded "hello" to the staff member and continued on to his meeting?

Networking

Networking involves building and maintaining positive relationships with other people.

Through **networking**, managers build and maintain positive relationships with other people, ideally those whose help might be useful someday. These networks create the opportunities through which priority agenda items can be fulfilled.

Much of what managers need to get done is beyond their individual capabilities alone. The support and contributions of other people often make the difference between success and failure. Networking is a way of developing all-important **social capital**—the capacity to attract support and help from others. You can think of it as a capacity to get things done with the help of people you know and relate well with.

Social capital is the capacity to attract support and help from others to get things done.

The manager in the prior example needed help from someone who did not report directly to him. Although he wasn't in a position to order the staff person to help him out, this wasn't a problem. Because of the working relationship they maintained through networking, she wanted to help when asked. Most managers maintain extensive networks with peers, members of their work teams, higher-level executives, and people at various points elsewhere in the organization at the very least. Many are expected to network even more broadly, such as with customers, suppliers, and community representatives.

Managers use a variety of technical, human, and conceptual skills.

The discussion of roles, agendas, and networking is but a starting point for inquiry into your personal portfolio of management skills. Another step forward is found in the work of Harvard scholar Robert L. Katz. He classified the essential skills of managers into three categories—technical, human, and conceptual. As shown in **Figure 1.4**, the relative importance of each skill varies by level of managerial responsibility.[24]

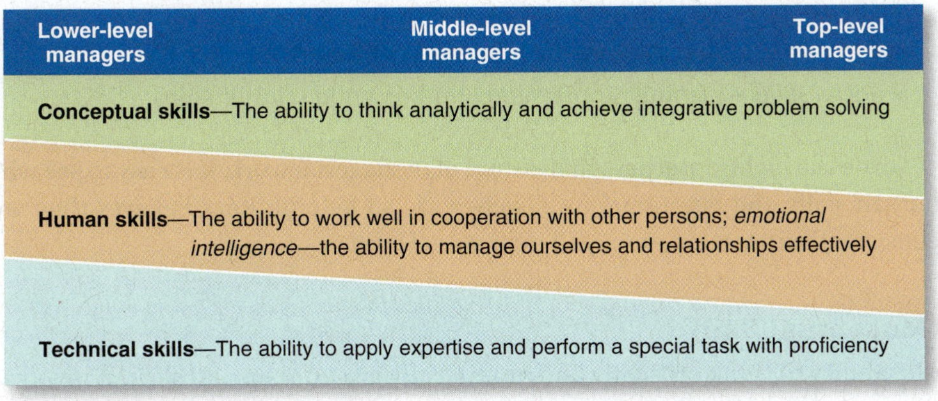

Lower-level managers	Middle-level managers	Top-level managers

Conceptual skills—The ability to think analytically and achieve integrative problem solving

Human skills—The ability to work well in cooperation with other persons; *emotional intelligence*—the ability to manage ourselves and relationships effectively

Technical skills—The ability to apply expertise and perform a special task with proficiency

FIGURE 1.4 What Are Three Essential Managerial Skills, and How Does Their Importance Vary Across Levels?
All managers need essential technical, human, and conceptual skills. At lower levels of management, the technical skills are more important than conceptual skills, but at higher levels of management, the conceptual skills become more important than technical skills. Because managerial work is so heavily interpersonal, human skills are equally important across all management levels.

Technical Skill

A **technical skill** is the ability to use a special proficiency or expertise to perform particular tasks. Accountants, engineers, market researchers, financial planners, and systems analysts, for example, possess obvious technical skills. Other baseline technical skills for any college graduate today include such things as written and oral communication, computer literacy, and math and numeracy.

> A **technical skill** is the ability to use expertise to perform tasks with proficiency.

In Katz's model, technical skills are very important at career entry levels. So how do you get them? Formal education is an initial source for learning these skills, but continued training and job experiences are important in further developing them. Why not take a moment to inventory your technical skills, the ones you have and the ones you still need to learn for your future career? Katz tells us that the technical skills are especially important at job entry and early career points. Surely, you want to be ready the next time a job interviewer asks the bottom-line question: "What can you really do for us?"

Human Skill

The ability to work well with others is **a human skill**, and it is a foundation for managerial success. How can we excel at networking, for example, without an ability and willingness to relate well with other people? How can we develop social capital without it? A manager with good human skills will have a high degree of self-awareness and a capacity to understand or empathize with the feelings of others. You would most likely observe this person working with others in a spirit of trust, enthusiasm, and genuine involvement.

> A **human skill** is the ability to work well in cooperation with other people.

Emotional intelligence is the ability to manage ourselves and our relationships effectively.

A manager with good human skills is also likely to be high in **emotional intelligence (EI)**. Considered an important leadership attribute, EI is defined by scholar and consultant Daniel Goleman as the "ability to manage ourselves and our relationships effectively."[25] He believes that emotional intelligence is built on the following five foundations.

Five Foundations of Emotional Intelligence ≫

1. *Self-awareness*—understanding moods and emotions
2. *Self-regulation*—thinking before acting; controlling disruptive impulses
3. *Motivation*—working hard and persevering
4. *Empathy*—understanding the emotions of others
5. *Social skills*—gaining rapport and building good relationships

Given the highly interpersonal nature of managerial work, it is easy to see why human skills and emotional intelligence are so helpful. Katz believes they are consistently important across all managerial levels.

Conceptual Skill

A **conceptual skill** is the ability to think analytically and solve complex problems.

The ability to think critically and analytically is a **conceptual skill**. It involves the capacity to break down problems into smaller parts, see the relations between the parts, and recognize the implications of any one problem for others.

As Figure 1.4 previously showed, Katz believes conceptual skills gain in relative importance as we move from lower to higher levels of management. This is because the problems faced at higher levels of responsibility are often ambiguous and unstructured, accompanied by many complications and interconnections, and full of longer-term consequences for people and organizations. In respect to personal development, the question to ask is: "Am I developing the strong critical-thinking and problem-solving capabilities I will need for sustained career success?" The Steps for Further Learning selections at the end of each chapter are good ways to test your conceptual skills in a management context.

⦀ Managers can and should learn from experience.

Functions, roles, agendas, networks, skills! How can anyone develop and be consistently good at all these things? How can the capacity to do them all well be developed and maintained for long-term career success?

This book can be a good starting point for career development, a foundation for the future. Take your time, and give some thought to answering the questions that I ask as you read. Consider also how you might apply what you are learning to your current situations—school, work, and personal. And then ask what you can learn from these situations in turn. It is well recognized that successful managers do this all the time. We call it learning from experience.

Lifelong learning is continuous learning from daily experiences.

The challenge for all of us is to be good at **lifelong learning**—the process of continuously learning from our daily experiences and opportunities. Consider the following point by State Farm CEO Edward B. Rust, Jr.[26]

I think the whole concept of lifelong learning is more relevant today than ever before. It's scary to realize that the skill sets we possess today are likely to be inadequate five years from now, just due to the normal pace of change. As more young people come into the workforce, they need a deeper, fundamental understanding of the basic skills—not just to get a job, but to grow with the job as their responsibilities change over their lifetimes.

Does Rust's assessment of lifelong learning sound daunting? Or is it a challenge you are confident in meeting? Do you agree that this is an accurate description of today's career environment? If you do, and I believe you should, you'll also have to admit that learning, learning, and more learning are top priorities in our lives. Why not use Table 1.1, Six "Must-Have" Managerial Skills, as a preliminary checklist for assessing your managerial learning and career readiness? How do you stack up?

Table 1.1 Six "Must-Have" Managerial Skills

Teamwork Able to work effectively as team member and leader; strong on team contributions, leadership, conflict management, negotiation, and consensus building

Self-Management Able to evaluate self, modify behavior, and meet obligations; strong on ethical reasoning, personal flexibility, tolerance for ambiguity, and performance responsibility

Leadership Able to influence and support others to perform complex and ambiguous tasks; strong on diversity awareness, project management, and strategic action

Critical Thinking Able to gather and analyze information for problem solving; strong on information analysis and interpretation, creativity and innovation, judgment, and decision making

Professionalism Able to sustain a positive impression and instill confidence in others; strong on personal presence, initiative, and career management

Communication Able to express self well in communication with others; strong on writing, oral presentation, giving and receiving feedback, and technology utilization

With the prior list as a starting point, the rest of this book should be valuable for your personal development. And in this regard, another question is worth asking. Given all the hard work and challenges that it involves, why would anyone want to be a manager? Beyond the often-higher salaries, there is one very compelling answer—pride! As pointed out by management theorist Henry Mintzberg, being a manager is an important and socially responsible job.[27]

No job is more vital to our society than that of the manager. It is the manager who determines whether our social institutions serve us well or whether they squander our talents and resources. It is time to strip away the folklore about managerial work, and time to study it realistically so that we can begin the difficult task of making significant improvement in its performance.

STUDY GUIDE

Takeaway 1.2

What Do Managers Do, and What Skills Do They Use?

Terms to Define

Agenda setting

Conceptual skill

Controlling

Emotional intelligence

Human skill

Leading

Lifelong learning

Management process

Networking

Organizing

Planning

Social capital

Technical skill

Rapid Review

- The daily work of managers is often intense and stressful, involving long hours and continuous performance pressures.
- In the management process, planning sets the direction, organizing assembles the human and material resources, leading provides the enthusiasm and direction, and controlling ensures results.
- Managers perform interpersonal, informational, and decision-making roles while pursuing high-priority agendas and engaging in successful networking.
- Managers rely on a combination of technical skills (ability to use special expertise), human skills (ability to work well with others), and conceptual skills (ability to analyze and solve complex problems).
- Everyday experience is an important source of continuous lifelong learning for managers.

Questions for Discussion

1. Is Mintzberg's view of the intense and demanding nature of managerial work realistic, and if so, why would you want to do it?
2. If Katz's model of how different levels of management use essential skills is accurate, what are its career implications for you?
3. Why is emotional intelligence an important component of one's human skills?

Be Sure You Can

- describe the intensity and pace of a typical workday for a manager
- give examples of each of the four management functions
- list the three managerial roles identified by Mintzberg
- explain how managers use agendas and networks in their work
- give examples of a manager's technical, human, and conceptual skills
- explain how these skills vary in importance across management levels
- explain the importance of experience as a source of managerial learning

Career Situation: What Would You Do?

It's time now to take a first interview for your "dream" job. The interviewer is sitting across the table from you. She smiles, looks you in the eye, and says: "You have a very nice academic record, and we're impressed with your extracurricular activities. Now tell me exactly, what can you do for us that will add value to our organization right from day one?" How do you respond in a way that clearly shows you are "job ready" with strong technical, human, and conceptual skills?

Takeaway 1.3
What Are Some Important Career Issues in the New Workplace?

ANSWERS TO COME

- Globalization and job migration are changing the world of work.
- Failures of ethics and corporate governance are troublesome.
- Diversity and discrimination are continuing social priorities.
- Intellectual capital and self-management skills are essential for career success.

YOU MIGHT ALREADY HAVE NOTICED THAT THIS TEXT MAY DIFFER FROM OTHERS you've read. I'm going to ask you a lot of questions and expose you to different viewpoints and possibilities. This process of active inquiry begins with the recognition that we live and work in a time of great changes, ones that are not only socially troublesome and personally challenging, but also likely to increase, not decrease, in number, intensity, and complexity in the future.

Are you ready for the challenges ahead? Are you informed about the issues and concerns that complicate our new workplace? Are you willing to admit that this is no time for complacency?

⦀ Globalization and job migration are changing the world of work.

At last count there were some 5.3 million or 3.5% of Americans working in the United States for foreign employers.[28] We buy foreign cars like Toyota, Nissan, and Mercedes-Benz that are assembled in America. We buy appliances from the Chinese firm Haier and Eight O'Clock Coffee from India's Tata Group. Top managers at Starbucks, IBM, Sony, Ford, and other global corporations have little need for the words "overseas" or "international" in everyday business vocabulary. They operate as global businesses that serve customers and suppliers wherever in the world they may be located, and that hire talent from around the world wherever it may be available at the lowest costs. Take Hewlett-Packard.[29] It operates in 170 countries, and most of its 330,000+ employees work outside the United States. Although headquartered in Palo Alto, California, one has to wonder: Is HP truly an American company anymore?

There are many faces of **globalization**, the worldwide interdependence of resource flows, product markets, and business competition that characterize our economy.[30] Government leaders now worry about the competitiveness of nations, just as corporate leaders worry about business competitiveness.[31] Countries and people are not just interconnected through the news, in travel, and lifestyles; they are interconnected in labor markets and employment patterns and in financial and business dealings. At a time when more Americans find that their customer service call is answered in Ghana, their CAT scan read by a radiologist in India, and their tax return prepared by an accountant in the Philippines, the fact that globalization offers both opportunities and challenges is quite clear indeed.

Globalization is the worldwide interdependence of resource flows, product markets, and business competition.

Global sourcing involves contracting for work to be performed in other countries.

Job migration occurs when global outsourcing shifts jobs from one country to another.

Reshoring moves jobs back from foreign to domestic locations.

Ethics set moral standards of what is "good" and "right" behavior in organizations and in our personal lives.

Corporate governance is oversight of a company's management by a board of directors.

Businesses engage the global economy to sell goods and services to customers around the world. They also buy the things they need wherever they can be found at the lowest price. This is **global sourcing**—hiring workers and contracting for supplies in other countries. The firms save money by manufacturing and getting jobs done in countries with lower costs of labor.

One controversial side effect to global sourcing is **job migration**, the shifting of jobs from one country to another. The U.S. economy has been a net loser to job migration. Countries such as China, India, and the Philippines have been net gainers. And such countries aren't just sources of unskilled labor anymore. They are now able to offer highly trained workers—engineers, scientists, accountants, health professionals—for as little as one-fifth the cost of an equivalent U.S. worker.

Politicians and policy makers regularly debate how best to deal with the high costs of job migration, as local workers lose their jobs and their communities lose economic vitality. One side looks for new government policies to stop job migration by protecting the jobs of U.S. workers. The other side calls for patience, believing that the global economy will readjust in the long run and create new jobs for U.S. workers. Recent data suggest, in fact, that this is starting to happen as rising global labor and transportation costs make manufacturing at home more attractive. Ford and General Electric are among the firms that have started a practice called **reshoring**. It moves foreign production and jobs back to the United States.[32] Which side are you on—more regulation to save domestic jobs, or letting markets take care of themselves?

⫼ Failures of ethics and corporate governance are troublesome.

When Bernard Madoff was sentenced to 150 years in jail for crimes committed with a multi-billion dollar fraudulent Ponzi scheme, the message was crystal clear.[33] There is no excuse for senior executives in any organization to act illegally and tolerate management systems that enrich the few while damaging the many.

The harm done by Madoff touched individuals who lost lifelong and retirement savings, charitable foundations that had invested monies with his firm, and the employees of his firm and others that went out of business as a result of the fraud. Society also paid a price when faith in the nation's business system was damaged by the scandal.[34] Worse yet, Madoff isn't alone in letting greed overwhelm morality. All too often we learn about more scandals affecting banks and other financial institutions, as well as businesses and organizations of many other types. How would you recover if an employer bankruptcy or major business fraud affected you?

At the end of the day, we depend on individual people, working at all levels of organizations, to act ethically. **Ethics** is a code of moral principles that sets standards of conduct for what is "good" and "right" as opposed to "bad" or "wrong."

Don't let all the scandals make you cynical about ethical behavior in organizations. Even though ethics failures get most of the publicity, there is still a lot of good happening in the world of work. Look around. You'll find stronger **corporate governance**, described earlier as the active oversight of management decisions, corporate strategy, and financial reporting by a company's

{ **"ONE ORGANIC FARMER CLAIMS THAT "PESTICIDES MAY HAVE DRIFTED ONTO HER FIELD FROM NEIGHBORING FARMS."**

Ethics Check

■ Watch Out for Bad Apples at Farmers' Markets

The U.S. Department of Agriculture reports that the number of farmers' markets across the United States is surging. The customer appeal rests with desires for better food quality, lower prices, and a friendly shopping atmosphere, which may even offer entertainment and family activities. Farmers are also thrilled with the selling format and enjoy connecting with customers, selling the fruits of their labor, and socializing with other farmers. The overall message is often "support your local community," and the satisfaction of doing so is infectious.

But, what does "local" mean? A market's management usually determines just how it is defined in terms of radius miles from grower to marketplace. Some farmers markets are "producer only" markets requiring their vendors to produce and grow all products sold. Others allow resellers who essentially purchase produce from third parties and then bring it to the market to sell.

Unfortunately, there are cases where participating "farmers" make false claims. A Los Angeles investigation reported on surprise visits to farms where the produce was claimed to have been grown. Sellers were required by law to have permits and list fields. But some farms were full of weeds and dry dirt instead of rows of vegetables and fruits. Investigators even videotaped some farmers stopping at large whole-sale warehouses enroute to the farmers' markets. Why? They were stocking up with products clearly not grown on their premises.

Additional unsubstantiated and false claims about pesticides were found. Samples from five sellers in a Los Angeles farmers' market were taken to a state-certified lab and tested. Three out of five samples turned up positive for pesticides. When confronted, one so-called organic seller said that pesticides may have "drifted onto her field from neighboring farms."

YOU DECIDE

When discussing integrity issues in this fast-growing farmers' market industry, one blogger states: "We've been told to know our farmers, but it is management who makes the decisions." So, is it the customer's responsibility to know what they're buying and who they are buying it from? Or, is it the farmers' market management that is supposed to make sure all sellers live up to standards? Is it inevitable that once good things start to happen in the local farmer's market—growth, popularity, business success—that unethical people and practices will creep in to spoil them? What's the management to do? They may even be volunteers.

---

board of directors.[35] You'll also find that many people and organizations exemplify an ethical reawakening, one that places high value on personal integrity and moral leadership.

In a book entitled *The Transparent Leader,* Herb Baum, argues that integrity is a major key to ethics in leadership. When CEO of Dial Corporation, he walked the talk—no reserved parking place, open door, honest communication, careful listening, and hiring good people. Believing that most CEOs are overpaid, he once gave his annual bonus to the firm's lowest-paid workers. Baum tells the story of an ethical role model—a rival CEO, Reuben Mark of Colgate Palmolive. Mark called him one day to say that a newly hired executive had brought with him to Colgate a disk containing Dial's new marketing campaign. Rather than read it he returned the disk to Baum, an act Baum called "the clearest case of leading with honor and transparency I've witnessed in my career."[36]

Why not make ethics a personal priority? Your management course and this book are good opportunities to build confidence in dealing with ethics challenges. Take time to read and consider the situations presented in each chapter's Ethics Check.

{ THE PAY GAP FOR WOMEN IN FINANCIAL SERVICES IS THE LARGEST FOR ANY INDUSTRY.

Facts to **Consider**

■ Employment Contradictions in Workforce Diversity

The nonprofit research group Catalyst claims: "Now more than ever, as companies examine how to best weather an economy in crisis, we need talented business leaders, and many of these leaders, yet untapped, are women." But research studies and news reports show contradictions in workforce diversity.

- Women earn some 60% of college degrees, hold 50.6% of managerial jobs, and hold 15.7% of board seats at *Fortune* 500 companies; women of color hold 3.2% of board seats, and only 4% of firms have two women of color on their boards.
- The median compensation of female CEOs in North American firms is 85% that of males; in the largest firms it is 61%.
- For each $1 earned by male managers, female managers earn 79 cents; female managers in finance earn 58.8 cents for each $1 earned by male managers.

- For each $1 earned by men, African-American women earn 64 cents, and Hispanic women earn 52 cents.
- African Americans are 11.5% of the workforce and hold 8.3% of managerial and professional jobs.
- Asian Americans are 4.7% of the workforce and hold 6.3% of managerial and professional jobs.
- Hispanics are 11.1% of the workforce and hold 5% of managerial jobs.

YOUR THOUGHTS?

Do these data fit with your experience? What are the implications for you and your career aspirations? What other contradictions in workforce diversity have you seen, and how can they be explained?

‖ Diversity and discrimination are continuing social priorities.

> **Workforce diversity** describes differences among workers in gender, race, age, ethnicity, religion, sexual orientation, and able-bodiedness.

The term **workforce diversity** describes the composition of a workforce in terms of differences among people on gender, age, race, ethnicity, religion, sexual orientation, and physical ability.[37] The diversity trends of changing demographics are well recognized. Minorities now constitute more than 43% of the U.S. population, and the proportion is growing. The U.S. Census Bureau predicts that the country will become a true plurality by 2060, meaning that no one racial or ethnic group will be in the majority. Whites will be less than half the population, outnumbered by African Americans, Native Americans, Asians, and Hispanics combined. Hispanics are now the fastest-growing community and by 2060 will represent almost one-third of the population. The U.S. population is also aging. By 2030, more than 20% of the population will be 65 or older. Importantly, the proportion of the population that is working age will decline from 62.7% today to 56.9% by 2060.[38]

Even though our society is diverse, many diversity issues in employment remain as open challenges. How, for example can we explain the diversity facts in the nearby box? And consider this. When researchers sent out résumés with white-sounding first names like Brett, they received 50% more responses from potential employers than when identical résumés were sent with black-sounding first names, like Kareem.[39] How can this result be explained?

U.S. laws strictly prohibit the use of demographic characteristics when employers make decisions on hiring, promotion, and firing. But laws are one thing; actions are another. Do you ever wonder why women and minorities hold few top jobs in large companies? One explanation is a subtle form of discrimination known as the **glass ceiling effect**. It occurs when an invisible barrier, or "ceiling,"

> The **glass ceiling effect** is an invisible barrier limiting career advancement of women and minorities.

prevents members of diverse populations from advancing to high levels of responsibility in organizations.[40]

There is little doubt that women and minorities face special work and career challenges in our society at large.[41] Although progress is being made—for example more corporate board seats going to women—diversity bias still exists in too many of our work settings.[42] This bias begins with **prejudice,** the holding of negative, irrational attitudes regarding people who are different from us. Take as an example lingering prejudice against working mothers. The nonprofit Families and Work Institute reports that in 1977 only 49% of men and 71% of women believed that mothers could be good employees; in 2008 the figures had risen to 67% and 80%, respectively.[43] But, don't you wonder why the figures don't show 100% support of working mothers?

Prejudice becomes active **discrimination** when people in organizations treat minority members unfairly and deny them full membership benefits. Discrimination was evident in the résumés study described earlier. And prejudice also becomes discrimination when a male or female manager refuses to promote a working mother in the belief that "she has too many parenting responsibilities to do a good job at this level." Scholar Judith Rosener suggests that employment discrimination of any form comes at a high cost—not just to the individuals involved, but also to society. The organization's loss for any discriminatory practices, she says, is "undervalued and underutilized human capital."[44]

A female vice president at Avon once described the challenges of truly valuing and managing diversity this way: "Consciously creating an environment where everyone has an equal shot at contributing, participating, and most of all advancing."[45] And many voices point out that today's increasingly diverse and multicultural workforce should be an asset that, if tapped, creates opportunities for performance gains. But consultant R. Roosevelt Thomas cautions that too many employers still address diversity with the goal of "making their numbers."[46]

⦀ Intellectual capital and self-management skills are essential for career success.

No matter how you look at it, the future poses a complex setting for career success. And if current trends continue, it will be more and more of a **free-agent economy.** Like professional athletes, many of us will be changing jobs more often and even working on flexible contracts with a shifting mix of employers over time.[47] British scholar and consultant Charles Handy uses the analogy of the **shamrock organization,** shown here, to describe the implications.[48] Each leaf in the shamrock organization represents a different group of workers.

The first leaf in Handy's shamrock organization is a core group of permanent, full-time employees with critical skills, who follow standard career paths. The second leaf consists of workers hired as freelancers and independent contractors. They provide organizations with specialized skills and talents for specific projects and then change employers when projects are completed. An increasing number of jobs in the new economy fall into this category. Some call this a time of *giganomics*, where even well-trained professionals make their livings moving from one "gig" to the next, instead of

Prejudice is the display of negative, irrational attitudes toward women or minorities.

Discrimination actively denies women and minorities the full benefits of organizational membership.

In a **free-agent economy**, people change jobs more often, and many work on independent contracts with a shifting mix of employers.

A **shamrock organization** operates with a core group of full-time long-term workers supported by others who work on contracts and part time.

Full-time core workers

Independent contractors

Part-time temporaries

The shamrock organization

holding a traditional full-time job.[49] The third leaf is a group of temporary part-timers. Their hours of work increase or decrease as the needs of the business rise or fall. They often work without benefits and are the first to lose their jobs when an employer runs into economic difficulties.

As you might guess, today's college graduates must be prepared to succeed in the second and third leaves of Handy's shamrock organization, not just the first. And to achieve success, Handy advises everyone to maintain a portfolio of skills that is always up-to-date and attractive to potential employers, regardless of where in the shamrock your goals may center.

You might begin by thinking seriously about your **intellectual capital**—what you can offer an employer in terms of brainpower, skills, and capabilities. Ideally, these will be things valued by the employer that also differentiate you a bit from others who might want the same job. A good way to address the issue is to use this **intellectual capital equation:**[50]

> **Intellectual capital** is the collective brainpower or shared knowledge of a workforce.

> The **intellectual capital equation** is: IC = competency × commitment.

$$\text{Intellectual Capital} = \text{Competency} \times \text{Commitment.}$$

Competency represents our talents or job-relevant capabilities, whereas commitment represents our willingness to work hard in applying them to important

---

{ *Delivering Happiness: A Path to Profits, Passion, And Purpose*
by Tony Hsieh

Manager's **Library**

"What are you going to be when you grow up?" Those words echo through the mind starting in childhood and grow louder as adulthood approaches. The moment of truth finally arrives. Or has it? According to Tony Hsieh, author of the book *Delivering Happiness* (2010, Business Plus), "being" something is more of a mind-set than an occupation. He thinks the question is answered by simply asking yourself, "What makes you happy?"

Hsieh thinks rules in business are just like rules about hobbies and friends—do what makes you happy with people you like. Hsieh translated youthful interests and associations into two profitable ventures. He founded two Internet start-ups with college friends—LinkExchange and Zappos.com—selling them for $256 million and $1.2 billion, respectively.

As Zappos' CEO, Hsieh cultivates a culture in which customers and employees are treated as friends. He considers this the Zappos brand and its secret to success. He emphasizes customer service and employee training and says adults work best when they playfully share discoveries together, much like children do. Fun events sponsored during work hours enable social ties to cultivate.

Zappos welcomes customer calls and online chats as opportunities to create friendly bonds. They aren't timed, no script is used, and agents are guided by personal judgment. Zappos' mission is to "Deliver WOW," and loyal customers receive surprise upgrades to overnight shipping.

Employees control career progression by choosing which company-designed courses to take and when to complete them. They receive incremental title and pay boosts rather than infrequent employer-driven reviews. This creates a pipeline of wide-ranging talent. Hsieh believes people must decide when and how to advance based on their happiness at each level.

Finding purpose in work comes with finding happiness; staying connected with others in common purpose beyond self-serving needs feels more like play than work. Hsieh reflects on his childhood worm farm and college pizza business as examples where work and friendship merged meaningfully. He stays busy having fun rather than growing up to be "something."

REFLECT AND REACT

Is Hsieh onto something here? How do you think the rules of work compare or contrast to the rules of play? Do you view play and work as individual pursuits or group undertakings? How are friends and coworkers similar or different? What are your pathways to happiness?

tasks. Obviously, both are essential. One without the other is not enough to meet anyone's career needs or any organization's performance requirements. Max DePree, former CEO of Herman Miller, puts it this way: "We talk about the difference between being successful and being exceptional. Being successful is meeting goals in a good way—being exceptional is reaching your potential."[51]

When it comes to human potential, the workplace is well into the *information age* dominated by **knowledge workers**. These are persons whose minds, not just physical capabilities, are critical assets.[52] And things are not standing still. Futurist Daniel Pink says that we are already moving toward a *conceptual age* in which intellectual capital rests with people who are both "high concept"—creative and good with ideas, and "high touch"—joyful and good with relationships.[53] The future, he believes, will belong to those with "whole-mind" competencies, that combine left-brain analytical thinking with right-brain intuitive thinking.

There is no doubt that the free-agent economy places a premium on your capacity for **self-management**, being able to realistically assess and actively manage your personal development. It means showing emotional intelligence, exercising initiative, accepting responsibility for accomplishments and failures, and continually seeking new learning opportunities and experiences. Take a look at the Explore Yourself feature in each chapter. It is designed to better acquaint you with managerial skills and their implications for your career readiness. The first feature is on self-management, and the question you should be asking when reading it is: How well do I stack up?

The fact is that what happens from this point forward in your career is largely up to you. There is no better time than the present to start taking charge of what can be called your "personal brand"—a unique and timely package of skills and capabilities of real value to a potential employer. Management consultant Tom Peters advises that your brand should be "remarkable, measurable, distinguished, and distinctive" relative to the competition—others who want the same career opportunities that you do.[54]

Have you thought about what employers want? Are you clear and confident about the brand called "You"? Does your personal portfolio include new workplace survival skills?

> **Knowledge workers** use their minds and intellects as critical assets to employers.

> **Self-management** is the ability to understand oneself, exercise initiative, accept responsibility, and learn from experience.

{ SELF-MANAGEMENT HELPS US AVOID VIEWING OURSELVES MORE FAVORABLY THAN IS JUSTIFIED

Explore **Yourself**

■ Self-Management

When it comes to doing well as a student and in a career, a lot rests on how well you know yourself and what you do with this knowledge. Self-management involves acting with a strong sense of self-awareness, something that helps us build on strengths, overcome weaknesses, and avoid viewing ourselves more favorably than is justified. This capacity is an important career skill.

It can be easy to talk about self-management but much harder to master it. Why not use the many self-assessments in this book to get in better touch with this and other important career skills?

> Get to know yourself better by taking the self-assessment on Personal Career Readiness and completing other activities in the *Exploring Management* Skill-Building Portfolio.

STUDY GUIDE

Takeaway 1.3
What Are Some Important Career Issues in the New Workplace?

Terms to Define

Corporate governance

Discrimination

Ethics

Free-agent economy

Glass ceiling effect

Global sourcing

Globalization

Intellectual capital

Intellectual capital equation

Job migration

Knowledge workers

Prejudice

Reshoring

Self-management

Shamrock organization

Workforce diversity

Rapid Review

- Globalization has brought increased use of global outsourcing by businesses and concern for the adverse effects of job migration.
- Society increasingly expects organizations and their members to perform with high ethical standards and in socially responsible ways.
- Organizations operate with diverse workforces, and each member should be respected for her or his talents and capabilities.
- Work in the new economy is increasingly knowledge based, relying on people with valuable intellectual capital to drive high performance.
- Careers in the new economy are becoming more flexible, requiring personal initiative to build and maintain skill portfolios that are always up-to-date and valued by employers.

Questions for Discussion

1. How are current concerns about ethics in business, globalization, and changing careers addressed in your courses and curriculum?
2. Is it possible for members of minority groups to avoid being hurt by prejudice, discrimination, and the glass ceiling effect in their careers?
3. In what ways can the capacity for self-management help you to prosper in a free-agent economy?

Be Sure You Can

- describe how corporate governance influences ethics in organizations
- explain how globalization and job migration are changing the economy
- differentiate prejudice, discrimination, and the glass ceiling effect
- state the intellectual capital equation
- discuss career opportunities in the shamrock organization
- explain the importance of self-management to career success

Career Situation: What Would You Do?

One result of globalization is that many people now work domestically for foreign employers that have set up businesses in their local communities. How about you? Does it make any difference if you receive a job offer from a foreign employer such as Haier—a Chinese firm that makes popular home appliances—or a domestic employer? What are the "pluses and minuses" of working at home for a foreign employer? Could the pluses outweigh the minuses for you?

TestPrep 1

Answers to TestPrep questions can be found at the back of the book.

Multiple-Choice Questions

1. If a sales department supervisor is held accountable by a middle manager for the department's performance, on whom is the department supervisor dependent in making this performance possible?
   (a) Board of directors
   (b) Top management
   (c) Customers or clients
   (d) Department salespersons

2. The management function of _____ is being activated when a bookstore manager measures daily sales in the magazine section and compares them with daily sales targets.
   (a) planning
   (b) agenda setting
   (c) controlling
   (d) delegating

3. The process of building and maintaining good working relationships with others who may someday help a manager implement his or her work agendas is called _____.
   (a) governance
   (b) networking
   (c) emotional intelligence
   (d) entrepreneurship

4. According to Robert Katz, _____ skills are more likely to be emphasized by top managers than by first-line managers.
   (a) human
   (b) conceptual
   (c) informational
   (d) technical

5. An effective manager is someone who helps others to achieve high levels of both _____ and _____.
   (a) pay; satisfaction
   (b) performance; satisfaction
   (c) performance; pay
   (d) pay; quality of work life

6. _____ is the active oversight by boards of directors of top management decisions in such areas as corporate strategy and financial reporting.
   (a) Value chain analysis
   (b) Productivity
   (c) Outsourcing
   (d) Corporate governance

7. When a manager denies promotion to a qualified worker simply because of personally disliking her because she is Hispanic, this is an example of _____.
   (a) discrimination
   (b) accountability
   (c) self-management
   (d) a free-agent economy

8. A company buys cloth in one country, has designs made in another country, has the garments sewn in another country, and sells the finished product in yet other countries. This firm is actively engaging in the practice of _____.
   (a) job migration
   (b) performance effectiveness
   (c) value creation
   (d) global sourcing

9. The intellectual capital equation states: Intellectual Capital = _____ × Commitment.
   (a) Diversity
   (b) Confidence
   (c) Competency
   (d) Communication

10. If the direction in managerial work today is away from command and control, what is it toward?
    (a) Coaching and facilitating
    (b) Telling and selling
    (c) Pushing and pulling
    (d) Carrot and stick

11. The manager's role in the "upside-down pyramid" view of organizations is best described as providing _____ so that operating workers can directly serve _____.
    (a) direction; top management
    (b) leadership; organizational goals
    (c) support; customers
    (d) agendas; networking

12. When a team leader clarifies desired work targets and deadlines for a work team, he or she is fulfilling the management function of _____.
    (a) planning
    (b) delegating
    (c) controlling
    (d) supervising

13. The research of Mintzberg and others concludes that most managers _____.
    (a) work at a leisurely pace.
    (b) have blocks of private time for planning.
    (c) always live with the pressures of performance responsibility.
    (d) have the advantages of short workweeks.

14. Emotional intelligence helps us to manage ourselves and our relationships effectively. Someone that is high in emotional intelligence will have the capacity to _____, an ability to think before acting and to control potentially disruptive emotions and actions.
    (a) set agendas
    (b) show motivation
    (c) self-regulate
    (d) act as a leader

15. Which of the following is a responsibility that is most associated with the work of a CEO, or chief executive officer, of a large company?
    (a) Aligning the company with changes in the external environment
    (b) Reviewing annual pay raises for all employees
    (c) Monitoring short-term performance of lower-level task forces and committees
    (d) Conducting hiring interviews for new college graduates

Short-Response Questions

16. What is the difference between prejudice and workplace discrimination?

17. How is the emergence of a free-agent economy changing career and work opportunities?

18. In what ways will the job of a top manager typically differ from that of a first-line manager?

19. How does planning differ from controlling in the management process?

Integration and Application Question

20. Suppose you have been hired as the new supervisor of an audit team for a national accounting firm. With four years of auditing experience, you feel technically well prepared. However, it is your first formal appointment as a manager. The team has 12 members of diverse demographic and cultural backgrounds and varying work experience. The workload is intense, and there is a lot of performance pressure.

    Questions: To be considered *effective* as a manager, what goals will you set for yourself in the new job? What skills will be important to you, and why, as you seek success as the audit team supervisor?

Steps*for* Further Learning

BUILD MARKETABLE SKILLS
DO A CASE ANALYSIS
GET AND STAY INFORMED

BUILD

MARKETABLE SKILLS.
EARN BIG CAREER
PAYOFFS!

Don't miss these
opportunities in the
**Skill-Building
Portfolio**

■ **SELF-ASSESSMENT 1:**
Personal Career Readiness

*Rate your personal characteristics . . . start making a solid
career development plan.*

■ **CLASS EXERCISE 1:**
My Best Manager

*Compare viewpoints on great
managers . . . think about how
you can become one.*

■ **TEAM PROJECT 1:**
Managing Millennials

*Get inside the millennial generation . . . learn to appreciate
individual differences at work.*

Many
learning
resources are
found at the end
of the book and
online within
WileyPLUS.

Take advantage of **Cases for Critical Thinking**

■ **CHAPTER 1 CASE SNAPSHOT:**
Trader Joe's—Managing less to gain more/
Sidebar on Chobani

Trader Joe's is a model of how a company effectively
performs the management functions of planning, organizing, leading, and controlling. The company stands
for unique quality items like olive oil, Greek olives, brie,
and baguettes at peanut butter and jelly prices. How
did this retail grocer grow to $8.5+ billion in sales and
attract an obsessive and diverse cult following of foodies? Much has to do with its unique corporate culture,
which affects everything from how the company meticulously plans its store locations, to how it manages
its employees and purchasing and branding strategies.
A walk down any aisle shows how management fundamentals helped make Trader Joe's more than just the
"average Joe" of food retailers.

DO
A CASE ANALYSIS.
STRENGTHEN YOUR
CRITICAL THINKING!

Dig into this **Hot Topic**

■ **PRO AND CON DEBATE:** **Time to turn the
workplace into a fun place?**

"Goofing off" time is considered valuable time at the
online retailer Zappos.com. Employees are encouraged
to take breaks and have fun, all while on the payroll.
The company even has a "cultural evangelist"—John
Walkses, whose job it is to make sure the organizational
culture stays both happy and productive. He says: "By
allowing team members to participate in nonwork activities and have fun, the office keeps a positive vibe and
people are much happier. Also, they don't burn out as
they are free to take time away from their duties."

GET
AND STAY INFORMED.
MAKE YOURSELF
VALUABLE!

Zappos isn't alone in its commitment to turning the workplace into a fun place. At
WhatIF, an innovation consultancy, PechaKucha sessions are used to engage employees
in sharing interesting things about themselves and their activities outside work. The technique involves making a presentation of 20 slides that show for only 20 seconds each. The
presenter narrates the slide show as a way of helping coworkers get to know them better.

Those in favor of adding fun time to work are likely to say: "You discover new things
about people . . .," "It helps take the pressure off . . .," and "I look forward to seeing people
I've grown to really like." *Those against the practice are likely to say:* "Come on, grow
up. . . .," "I don't think employers should be spending money on these things . . .," and
"Look, work is work, I don't care what package you put it in."

Final Face-off   As an employer, would you consider building "fun" into your workplace?
Are organizations like Zappos and WhatIf ahead of the curve, with many others likely to follow? Or, is all this talk about fun at work just a fad, perhaps something that applies to just a
few employers and organizations and is not to be copied? How about it—should managers
spend time and money to transform the workplace into a fun place?

Great management isn't new, and it isn't all high tech . . . it is part of our history.

Latitudestock/Getty Images

Management Learning

Great Things Grow from Strong Foundations

Buena Vista / Photofest

Management Live

Learning Style and *Mr. Holland's Opus*

Glenn Holland (Richard Dreyfus) is an aspiring musician who wants to compose. He takes a job as a high school music teacher to gain more time for composition. One day he has an epiphany—he realizes his students do not learn music the way he did.

Gertrude Lang (Alicia Witt) desperately wants to play the clarinet because everyone else in her family excels at something. As much as she practices, she never improves. Mr. Holland helps her understand that music is about heart and feeling and that she needs to trust herself to play effectively. So, she learns to play by imagining a song as a sunset.

Louis Russ (Terrence Howard) must learn to play the bass drum to remain eligible for sports. The way he learns is different; he needs action and a model to follow. Mr. Holland gets Russ to understand timing and rhythm by imitating his beat.

Each of us has a preferred **learning style**, a set of ways through which we like to learn by receiving, processing, and recalling new information. For Gertrude Lang, it was being able to create a mental image that allowed music to flow from her heart to her fingertips. Lou Russ's style involved physically feeling and duplicating the rhythm being tapped by his teacher. As in these examples, we can often learn better when our styles are understood. How about you? Are you in touch with your learning style?

YOUR CHAPTER 2 TAKEAWAYS

1. Understand the lessons of the classical management approaches.

2. Identify the contributions of the behavioral management approaches.

3. Recognize the foundations of modern management thinking.

WHAT'S INSIDE

Explore Yourself
More on **learning styles**

Role Models
Oprah Winfrey Multitasks to make a difference in others' lives

Ethics Check
Cyberslackers find company time great for Internet Surfing

Facts to Consider
Generations differ when rating their bosses

Manager's Library
Outliers: The Story of Success by Malcolm Gladwell

TEACHING NOTE:
Many organizations now operate with just a few levels of management and a dispersed workforce. Ask students to show which classical management ideas do or do not have value in such settings.

Takeaway 2.1
What Are the Lessons of the Classical Management Approaches?

ANSWERS TO COME

- Taylor's scientific management sought efficiency in job performance.
- Weber's bureaucratic organization is supposed to be efficient and fair.
- Fayol's administrative principles describe managerial duties and practices.

HISTORIANS TRACE MANAGEMENT AS FAR BACK AS 5000 B.C., WHEN ANCIENT Sumerians used written records to assist in governmental and commercial activities.[1] Management contributed to the construction of the Egyptian pyramids, the rise of the Roman Empire, and the commercial success of 14th-century Venice. During the Industrial Revolution in the 1700s, great social changes helped to prompt a leap forward in the manufacture of basic staples and consumer goods. Adam Smith's ideas of efficient production through specialized tasks and the division of labor further accelerated industrial development.

By the turn of the 20th century, Henry Ford and others were making mass production a mainstay of the emerging economy.[2] What we now call the classical school was launching a path of rapid and continuing development in the science and practices of management.[3] Prominent representatives of this school and their major contributions to management thinking include Frederick Taylor—scientific management, Max Weber—bureaucracy, and Henri Fayol—administrative principles.

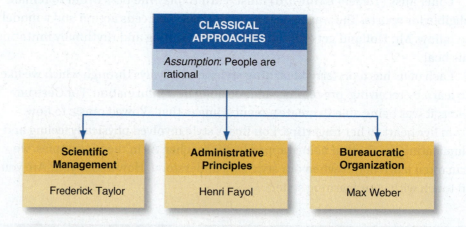

||| Taylor's scientific management sought efficiency in job performance.

In 1911, Frederick W. Taylor stated the following in his book, *The Principles of Scientific Management:* "The principal object of management should be to secure maximum prosperity for the employer, coupled with the maximum prosperity for the employee."[4] Taylor had noticed that many workers did their jobs in their own way—

perhaps haphazard—and without consistent supervision. And it seemed to him that a lack of clear and uniform methods caused workers to lose efficiency and perform below their true capacities. As a result, their organizations also underperformed.

To correct this problem, Taylor identified a system he called **scientific management**. It was based on the notion that jobs should be studied to identify their basic steps and motions as well as determine the most efficient ways of doing them. Once this job "science" was defined, workers could be trained to follow it, and supervisors could be trained to support and encourage workers to perform to the best of their abilities. Taylor's approach to scientific management can be summarized in these four core principles.

1. Develop a "science" for each job—rules of motion, standard work tools, and proper work conditions.
2. Hire workers with the right abilities for the job.
3. Train and motivate workers to do their jobs according to the science.
4. Support workers by planning and assisting their work according to the science.

One of the most enduring legacies of the scientific management approach grew out of Taylor's first principle and involves **motion study**, the science of reducing a job or task to its basic physical motions. Two of Taylor's contemporaries, Frank and Lillian Gilbreth, pioneered the use of motion studies as a management tool.[5] In one famous case, they reduced the number of motions used by bricklayers and tripled their productivity.[6]

Are you clear about the principles of scientific management? Think about what happens when a top coach trains a group of soccer players. If the coach teaches players the techniques of their positions and how the positions fit into the overall team strategy, the team will probably do better in its games, right? In the same way, Taylor hoped to improve the productivity of workers and organizations. With a stopwatch and notebook in hand, he analyzed tasks and motions to describe the most efficient ways to perform them.[7] He then linked these requirements with job training, monetary incentives for performance success, and better direction and assistance from supervisors.

A ready example of how Taylor's ideas are still used is United Parcel Service. Sorters at regional centers are timed according to strict task requirements and are expected to load vans at a set number of packages per hour. GPS technology plots the shortest routes; delivery stops are studied and carefully timed; supervisors

Scientific management emphasizes careful selection and training of workers and supervisory support.

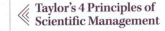 **Taylor's 4 Principles of Scientific Management**

Motion study is the science of reducing a job or task to its basic physical motions.

Tips to **Remember**

■ **Scientific Management Lessons for Today's Managers**

- Make results-based compensation a performance incentive.
- Carefully design jobs with efficient work methods.
- Carefully select workers with the abilities to do these jobs.

- Train workers to perform jobs to the best of their abilities.
- Train supervisors to support workers to best perform their jobs.

generally know within a few minutes how long a driver's pickups and deliveries will take. Industrial engineers also devise precise routines for drivers. The point in classic scientific management fashion is that savings of seconds on individual stops adds up to significant increases in productivity.

‖ Weber's bureaucratic organization is supposed to be efficient and fair.

> The purely bureaucratic type of administrative organization . . . is from a purely technical point of view capable of attaining the highest degree of efficiency. . . . It is superior to any other form in precision, in stability, in the stringency of its discipline, and in its reliability. It thus makes possible a particularly high degree of calculability of results for the heads of the organization and for those acting in relation to it. It is finally superior both in intensive efficiency and in the scope of its operations and is formally capable of application to all kinds of administrative tasks.
>
> Max Weber, *The Theory of Social Economic Organization*

Max Weber was a late-19th-century German intellectual whose insights have made a significant impact on the field of management and the sociology of organizations.[8] Like Taylor, his ideas developed somewhat in reaction to what he considered to be poor performance by the organizations of his day. He was especially concerned that people were in positions of authority not because of their job-related capabilities but because of their social standing or "privileged" status in German society.

Have you seen similar problems? Have you ever been upset that people rise to positions of major responsibility in organizations not because of their competencies, but because of whom they know or how well they play political games? Look around, talk to friends and relatives. Are Weber's concerns at all relevant today?

At the heart of Weber's proposal for correcting performance problems with organizations was a specific approach he called a **bureaucracy**.[9] When staffed and structured along the lines listed in **Table 2.1**, Characteristics of an Ideal Bureaucracy, he believed organizations could be both highly efficient and very fair in treating their

A **bureaucracy** is a rational and efficient form of organization founded on logic, order, and legitimate authority.

Table 2.1 Characteristics of an Ideal Bureaucracy

Clear Division of Labor Jobs are well defined, and workers become highly skilled at performing them.

Clear Hierarchy of Authority Authority and responsibility are well defined, and each position reports to a higher-level one.

Formal Rules and Procedures Written guidelines describe expected behavior and decisions in jobs; written files are kept for the historical record.

Impersonality Rules and procedures are impartially and uniformly applied; no one gets preferential treatment.

Careers Based on Merit Workers are selected and promoted on ability and performance; managers are career employees of the organization.

members and clients. For Weber, an organization of this type—the bureaucracy—was ideal and rational. And in effect, he was recommending that this is how all organizations should be run.

A bureaucracy works well, in theory at least, because of its reliance on logic, order, and legitimate authority. It also works well because people are selected for their jobs because of competency and are only promoted to higher-level ones because of demonstrated performance. But if it is so good, why do we so often hear the terms "bureaucracy" and "bureaucrat" used negatively? That's because bureaucracies don't always live up to Weber's expectations.

Think of the last time you were a client of a traditional bureaucracy, perhaps a government agency or the registrar at your school. Would you agree that they are sometimes slow in handling problems, making changes, and adapting to new customer or client needs? As a customer, have you sometimes encountered employees who seem disconnected, hesitant to make a decision, resistant to change, and even apathetic in relating to you? When was the last time you were frustrated at the service you received and complained about an organization's excessive "red tape"?

These and other disadvantages of bureaucracy are most likely to limit performance and cause problems for organizations that must be flexible and quick in adapting to changing times—a common situation today. And they are irritants for demanding customers, perhaps like you, who want quick service and a quality customer experience.

The bureaucratic model isn't the best choice for all organizations. It works well sometimes, but not all the time. In fact, a major challenge for research on organizational design is to identify when and under what conditions bureaucratic features work well and what the best alternatives are when they don't. Later in the module we'll call this "contingency thinking."

The Classic Bureaucracy

Fair
Impersonal
Career managers
Clear division of labor
Promotion based on merit
Formal hierarchy of authority
Written rules and standard procedures

Don Bayley/iStockphoto

{ **MILLENNIAL GENERATION MORE POSITIVE THAN BABY BOOMERS WHEN RATING BOSSES' PERFORMANCE.**

Facts to **Consider**

■ Generations Differ When Rating Their Bosses

Would it surprise you that Millennials have somewhat different views of their bosses than their Generation X and Baby Boomer coworkers? Check out these data from a Kenexa survey that asked 11,000 respondents to rate their managers' performance.

- Overall performance positive—Boomers 55%, Gen Xers 59%, Millennials 68%
- People management positive—Boomers 50%, Gen Xers 53%, Millennials 62%
- Work management positive—Boomers 52%, Gen Xers 55%, Millennials 63%
- Keeping commitments positive—Boomers 59%, Gen Xers 60%, Millennials 65%

- Outstanding leader—Boomers 39%, Gen Xers 43%, Millennials 51%

YOUR THOUGHTS?

A Kenexa researcher says that Millennials are "more willing to take direction and accept authority," whereas "as we grow older, our ideas become more concrete and less flexible." Does this seem like an accurate conclusion? How can these generational differences in evaluating managers be explained? And, by the way, what do these data suggest if you are managing people from these different generations?

||| Fayol's administrative principles describe managerial duties and practices.

Another branch in the classical approaches to management includes attempts to document and understand the experiences of successful managers. The most prominent writer in this realm is Henri Fayol.

In 1916, after a career in French industry, Henri Fayol published *Administration Industrielle et Générale*.[10] The book outlines his views on the proper management of organizations and the people within them. It identifies five "rules" or "duties" of management in respect to foresight, organization, command, coordination, and control:

> **Fayol's Five Duties of Management** »

- **Foresight**—complete a plan of action for the future.
- **Organization**—provide and mobilize resources to implement plan.
- **Command**—lead, select, and evaluate workers.
- **Coordination**—fit diverse efforts together, ensure information is shared and problems are solved.
- **Control**—make sure things happen according to plan, take necessary corrective action.

Look closely at Fayol's duties. Do you see how they resemble the four functions of management that we talk about today—planning, organizing, leading, and controlling? Importantly, Fayol believed that managers could be taught to put these functions into practice in the best ways. For example, he offered the following "principles" as guides to managerial action. You'll still hear them talked about in the vocabulary of everyday management. Fayol's **scalar chain principle** stated that there should be a clear and unbroken line of communication from the top to the bottom in the organization. His **unity of command principle** stated that each person in an organization should receive orders from only one boss. Would you say that these principles still make sense today?

The **scalar chain principle** states that organizations should operate with clear and unbroken lines of communication top to bottom.

The **unity of command principle** states that a worker should receive orders from only one boss.

© Courtney Keating/ iStockphoto

{ REVOKING PERSONAL INTERNET USE IS NOT VERY REALISTIC. ON THE OTHER HAND, LOST PRODUCTIVITY DUE TO CYBERSLACKING IS A REAL PROBLEM

Ethics **Check**

■ Cyberslackers Find Company Time Great for Internet Surfing

Have you ever passed by a co-worker's desk only to see multiple computer windows open—and not all of them work-related? Did you know that many employers install software to keep track of employee Internet activity? The software identifies browsing time and locations. The target is lost productivity from spending too much time surfing the web for personal use. Working at home doesn't mean workers are safe from prying eyes either. Some software even tracks employee activity remotely.

More and more employers have Internet usage policies—and for the most part, most frown upon excessive Internet use. But how much is too much? Because organizations rely so heavily on the Internet for professional use, employers find themselves in a quandary over what to do. The fact is that using tracking software can create a climate of mistrust in the employer–employee relationship.

Most employers expect that employees may send a few personal e-mails, check stocks, pay bills, or partake in a little online shopping. Revoking personal Internet use is not very realistic. On the other hand, lost productivity due to cyberslacking is a real problem. Systems administrators also worry about personal Internet browsing opening the organization's network to outsiders and creating security risks.

YOU DECIDE

Is "cyberslacking" a real problem in most instances? Or, are today's workers—especially the younger ones, so Internet efficient that personal web browsing doesn't really hurt their work productivity? How do you propose an employer deal with this issue? Suppose you get a job offer from an organization that has a policy against personal use of the Internet and smart phones except during official breaks. What might determine whether you accept the job or not?

STUDY GUIDE

Takeaway 2.1
What Are the Lessons of the Classical Management Approaches?

Terms to Define

Bureaucracy

Motion study

Scalar chain principle

Scientific management

Unity of command principle

Rapid Review

- Taylor's principles of scientific management focused on the need to carefully select, train, support, and reward workers in their jobs.
- Weber considered bureaucracy, with its clear hierarchy, formal rules, well-defined jobs, and competency-based staffing, to be a form of organization that is efficient and fair.
- Fayol suggested that managers learn and fulfill duties we now call the management functions of planning, organizing, leading, and controlling.

Questions for Discussion

1. How did Taylor and Weber differ in the approaches they took to improving the performance of organizations?
2. Should Weber's concept of the bureaucratic organization be scrapped, or does it still have potential value today?
3. What are the risks of accepting the "lessons of experience" offered by successful executives such as Fayol?

Be Sure You Can

- list the principles of Taylor's scientific management
- list key characteristics of bureaucracy
- explain why Weber considered bureaucracy an ideal form of organization
- list possible disadvantages of bureaucracy
- describe how Fayol's "duties" overlap with the four functions of management

Career Situation: What Would You Do?

It's summer job time, and you've found something that just might work—handling customer service inquiries at a local Internet provider. The regular full-time employees are paid by the hour. Summer hires like you fill in when they go on vacation. You will be paid by the call, $0.75 for each customer that you handle. How will this pay plan affect your behavior as a customer service representative? Is this a good way for the Internet provider to pay summer hires? How will things go when you are working side-by-side with full-timers?

TEACHING NOTE:
Ask students to apply the behavioral management approaches to the classroom setting. Discuss their ideas and examples of how an instructor's focus on students as individuals may influence their attitudes and behavior.

Takeaway 2.2
What Are the Contributions of the Behavioral Management Approaches?

ANSWERS TO COME

- Follett viewed organizations as communities of cooperative action.
- The Hawthorne studies focused attention on the human side of organizations.
- Maslow described a hierarchy of human needs with self-actualization at the top.
- McGregor believed managerial assumptions create self-fulfilling prophecies.
- Argyris suggests that workers treated as adults will be more productive.

DURING THE 1920S, EMPHASIS ON THE HUMAN SIDE OF THE WORKPLACE INFLUENCED the emergence of behavioral management approaches. As shown in **Figure 2.1**, this new school of thought included Follett's notion of the organization as a community, the well-known Hawthorne studies, and Maslow's theory of human needs, as well as theories generated from the work of Douglas McGregor and Chris Argyris. The underlying assumptions are that people are social and self-actualizing, and that workers seek satisfying social relationships, respond to group pressures, and search for personal fulfillment. Does that sound like you?

FIGURE 2.1

Who Are the Major Contributors to the Behavioral or Human Resource Approaches to Management Thinking? The human resource approaches shifted management thinking away from physical factors and work structures and toward the human side of organizations. The contributors shown here each focused on people as individuals and how their needs may influence their attitudes and behavior at work.

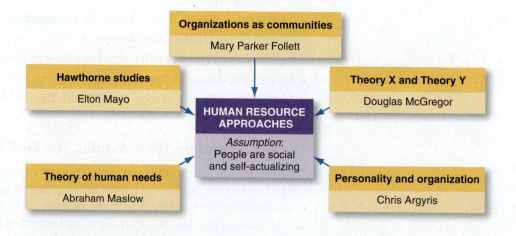

||| Follett viewed organizations as communities of cooperative action.

On her death in 1933, Mary Parker Follett was eulogized as "one of the most important women America has yet produced in the fields of civics and sociology."[11] She has been called a "prophet" of management, and her work is a reminder that good things really do grow from strong foundations.[12]

Even though Follett's ideas were expressed more than 80 years ago, many would consider them very farsighted indeed.[13] Her ideas still offer the wisdom of history. She advocated social responsibility, respect for workers, and better

"Life Is Good" Means Business

Happiness May Be Your Guide to Career Building

Imagine! Yes, you can! Go for it! Life is good. Well, make that: Life is really good! These are thoughts that turn dreams into realities. They're also part and parcel of the $80 million company named Life Is Good. It began with two brothers, Bert and John Jacobs, making T-shirts for street sales and has grown into a 2001 employee company selling a variety of fun apparel and related products in 14 or more countries. *Inc.* magazine calls it a "fine small business that only wants to make me happy."

Bert, Chief Executive Optimist, and Jake, Chief Creative Optimist, built a company devoted to humor and humility. John says: "It's important that we're saying 'Life is good,' not 'Life is great' or 'Life is perfect,' there's a big difference. . . . Don't determine that you're going to be happy when you get the new car or the big promotion or meet that special person. You can decide that you're going to be happy today." And that's the message of the Life Is Good brand.

Bert and Jake have stuck to their values on this journey to business success. They live the brand, enjoying leisure pursuits such as kayaking and ultimate Frisbee; they support philanthropies such as Camp Sunshine for children with serious illnesses and Project Joy for traumatized children; and the company runs seasonal Life Is Good festivals to help raise money for charities.

Life is good.®

Courtesy Life is Good Company

Find Inspiration

Bert and John didn't start with business degrees or experience, but they had good instincts, creativity, and positive views on life. And they learned as they progressed. Each step forward was a chance to capture business and management experience, learn from it, and keep getting better. How about you? Can we say that you're a student of history and use past experiences to improve in the future?

cooperation throughout organizations; she warned against the dangers of too much hierarchy and called for visionary leadership. Many of these themes are still central to management theory, even though we describe them by terms such as "empowerment", "involvement", "flexibility", "self-management", and "transformational leadership".

Follett suggested that making every employee an owner in the business would create feelings of collective responsibility. Today, we address the same issues as "employee ownership," "profit sharing," and "gain-sharing plans." Follet believed that business problems involve a wide variety of factors that must be considered in relationship to one another. Today, we talk about "systems" when describing the same phenomenon. Follett viewed businesses as services, organizations that should always consider making profits vis-á-vis the public good. Today, we pursue the same issues as "managerial ethics" and "corporate social responsibility."

And what can be said about executive success today?[14] I wonder what Follett would say? My guess is that Follett would agree that the successful 21st-century executive must be an inspiring leader who attracts talented people and motivates them in a setting where everyone can do his or her best work. She would argue that every manager, regardless of level, should be an ethical role model—always acting ethically, setting high ethical standards, and infusing ethics throughout the organization. And she would point out that anyone aspiring to managerial success must be an active doer, someone ready to make things happen, focus attention on the right things, and make sure that they really get done.

Women in the Relay Assembly Test Room, ca. 1930. Western Electric Company Hawthorne Studies Collection. Baker Library Historical Collections, Harvard Business School.

The **Hawthorne effect** is the tendency of persons singled out for special attention to perform as expected.

||| The Hawthorne studies focused attention on the human side of organizations.

In 1924, the Western Electric Company commissioned a study of individual productivity at the Hawthorne Works of the firm's Chicago plant.[15] These "Hawthorne studies," with a research team headed by Elton Mayo of Harvard University, sought to determine how economic incentives and physical conditions of the workplace affected the output of workers. But their results were perplexing due to the appearance of unforeseen "psychological factors."

After isolating six relay-assembly workers in a special room, Mayo and his team measured the effect on outputs of various rest pauses as well as lengths of workdays and workweeks. Productivity increased regardless of the changes made. The researchers concluded that, in the new "social setting" of the test room, the workers tried to do what they thought the researchers wanted them to do—a good job. This tendency to try to live up to expectations became known as the **Hawthorne effect**. Have you noticed that people given special attention will tend to perform as expected? Could the Hawthorne effect explain why some students, perhaps you, do better in smaller classes or for instructors who pay more attention to them in class?

The Hawthorne studies continued until the economic conditions of the Depression forced their termination. By then, interest in the human factor had broadened to include employee attitudes, interpersonal relations, and group relations. Results led the researchers to conclude that the same things that satisfied some workers—such as work conditions or wages—led to dissatisfaction for others. They also found that people would restrict their output to avoid the displeasure of the group, even if it meant sacrificing increased pay.

Scholars have criticized the Hawthorne studies for poor research design, weak empirical support for the conclusions drawn, and overgeneralized findings.[16] But they were still turning points in the evolution of management thought. They helped shift attention away from the technical and structural concerns of the classical management approaches and toward social and human concerns as keys to workplace productivity.

Millennials are warming up to part-time employment for full-time pay.

As organizations streamline and adopt new forms, people's work preferences are changing too. It seems that free agency is becoming an "in" thing among millennials. Many are opting to work freelance by personal choice, not just because they don't have alternatives. The term "permalancers" describes new college graduates who string together multiple and shifting part-time contracts to create full-time income. The payoff is employment independence and the personal flexibility that goes along with it. Some call this employment entrepreneurship, because new grads are crafting their own careers.

||| Maslow described a hierarchy of human needs with self-actualization at the top.

The work of psychologist Abraham Maslow in the area of human needs emerged as a key component of the new direction in management thinking.[17] He began with the notion of the human **need**, a physiological or psychological deficiency that a person feels compelled to satisfy. Why, you might ask, is this a significant concept for managers? The answer is because needs create tensions that can influence a person's work attitudes and behaviors.

What needs, for example, are important to you? How do they influence your behavior, the way you study and the way you work? You probably already know that Maslow described the five levels of human needs shown in **Figure 2.2**. They are grouped as lower-order needs—physiological, safety, and social, and higher-order needs—esteem and self-actualization.

A **need** is a physiological or psychological deficiency that a person wants to satisfy.

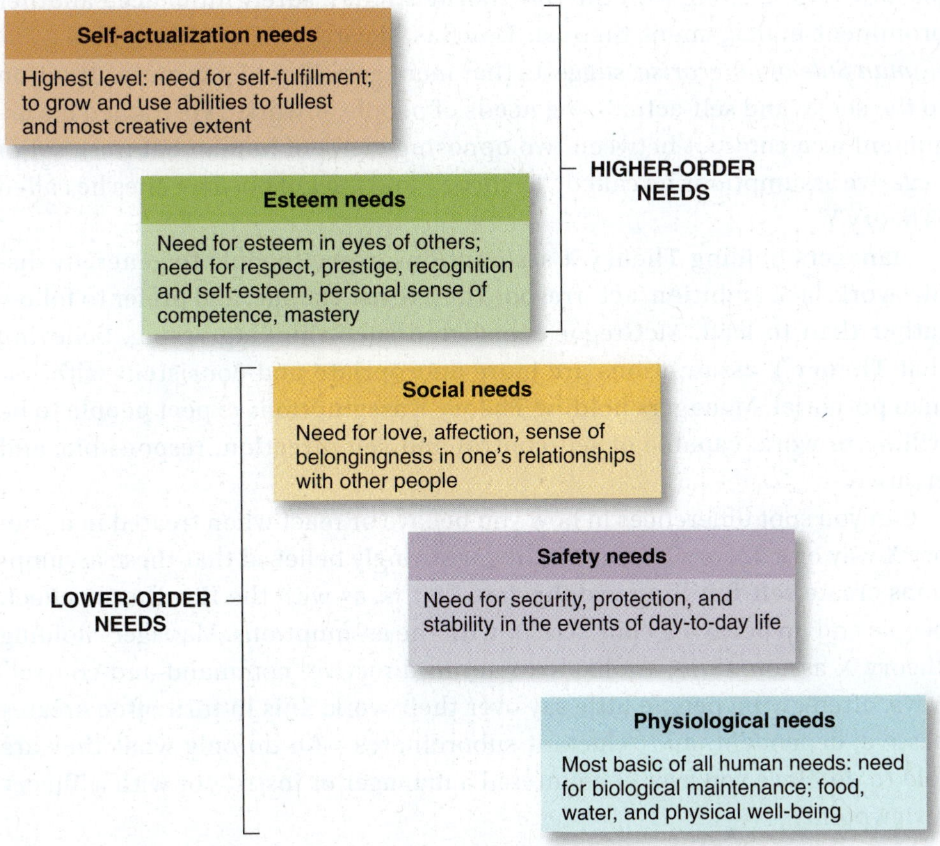

FIGURE 2.2
How Does Maslow's Hierarchy of Human Needs Operate?
In Abraham Maslow's theory, human needs are satisfied in a step-by-step progression. People first satisfy the lower-order needs: physiological, safety, and social. Once these are satisfied, they focus on the higher-order ego and self-actualization needs. A satisfied need no longer motivates behavior, except at the level of self-actualization. At this top level, the need grows stronger the more it is satisfied.

Self-actualization needs
Highest level: need for self-fulfillment; to grow and use abilities to fullest and most creative extent

Esteem needs
Need for esteem in eyes of others; need for respect, prestige, recognition and self-esteem, personal sense of competence, mastery

HIGHER-ORDER NEEDS

Social needs
Need for love, affection, sense of belongingness in one's relationships with other people

Safety needs
Need for security, protection, and stability in the events of day-to-day life

LOWER-ORDER NEEDS

Physiological needs
Most basic of all human needs: need for biological maintenance; food, water, and physical well-being

According to Maslow, people try to satisfy the five needs in sequence, moving step-by-step from the lowest to the highest. He called this the **progression principle**—a need only becomes activated after the next-lower-level need is satisfied. Once a need is activated, it dominates attention and determines behavior until it is satisfied. But then it no longer motivates behavior. Maslow called this the **deficit principle**—people act to satisfy deprived needs for which a satisfaction "deficit" exists. Only at the highest level of self-actualization do

Maslow's **progression principle** is that a need at any level becomes activated only after the next-lower-level need is satisfied.

Maslow's **deficit principle** is that people act to satisfy needs for which a satisfaction deficit exists; a satisfied need doesn't motivate behavior.

the deficit and progression principles cease to operate. The more this need is satisfied, the stronger it grows.

Maslow's theory can help us to better understand people's needs and help find ways to satisfy them through their work. Of course, this is easier said than done. If it were easy, we wouldn't have so many cases of workers going on strike against their employers, complaining about their jobs, or quitting to find better ones. Consider also the case of volunteers working for the local Red Cross, a community hospital, or a youth soccer league. Our society needs volunteers; most nonprofit organizations depend on them. But what needs move people to do volunteer work? How can one keep volunteers involved and committed in the absence of pay?

‖ McGregor believed managerial assumptions create self-fulfilling prophecies.

Maslow's work, along with the Hawthorne studies, surely influenced another prominent management theorist, Douglas McGregor. His classic book, *The Human Side of Enterprise*, suggests that managers should pay more attention to the social and self-actualizing needs of people at work.[18] He framed his argument as a contrast between two opposing views of human nature: a set of negative assumptions he called "Theory X" and a set of positive ones he called "Theory Y."

Managers holding **Theory X** assumptions expect people to generally dislike work, lack ambition, act irresponsibly, resist change, and prefer to follow rather than to lead. McGregor considered such thinking wrong, believing that **Theory Y** assumptions are more appropriate and consistent with human potential. Managers holding Theory Y assumptions expect people to be willing to work, capable of self-control and self-direction, responsible, and creative.

Can you spot differences in how you behave or react when treated in a Theory X way or a Theory Y way? McGregor strongly believed that these assumptions create **self-fulfilling prophecies**. That is, as with the Hawthorne effect, people end up behaving consistently with the assumptions. Managers holding Theory X assumptions are likely to act in directive "command-and-control" ways, often giving people little say over their work. This in turn often creates passive, dependent, and reluctant subordinates who do only what they are told to do. Have you ever encountered a manager or instructor with a Theory X viewpoint?

Managers with Theory Y assumptions behave quite differently. They are more "participative," likely giving others more control over their work. This creates opportunities to satisfy higher-order esteem and self-actualization needs. In response, the workers are more likely to act with initiative, responsibility, and high performance. The self-fulfilling prophecy occurs again, but this time it is a positive one. You should find Theory Y thinking reflected in a lot of the ideas and developments discussed in this book, such as valuing diversity, employee involvement, job enrichment, empowerment, and self-managing teams.[19]

Theory X assumes people dislike work, lack ambition, are irresponsible, and prefer to be led.

Theory Y assumes people are willing to work, accept responsibility, are self-directed, and are creative.

A **self-fulfilling prophecy** occurs when a person acts in ways that confirm another's expectations.

Explore **Yourself**

■ Learning Style

Each of us has a preferred **learning style**, a set of ways through which we like to learn by receiving, processing, and recalling new information. Hopefully, you take advantage of this book to gain insights into your style and where and how it works best.

Given that learning is any change of behavior that results from experience, one of our most significant challenges is to always embrace experiences—at school, at work, and in every-day living—and try our best to learn from them. The same can be said about unlocking the wisdom of history. This chapter is a reminder about management history and how the achievements of the past can still provide insights that can help us deal with the present.

> Get to know yourself better by taking the self-assessment on **Managerial Assumptions** and completing other activities in the *Exploring Management* **Skill-Building Portfolio**.

||| Argyris suggests that workers treated as adults will be more productive.

Ideas set forth by the well-regarded scholar and consultant Chris Argyris also reflect the positive views of human nature advanced by Maslow and McGregor. In his book *Personality and Organization*, Argyris contrasted the management practices found in traditional and hierarchical organizations with the needs and capabilities of mature adults.[20]

Argyris clearly believes that when problems such as employee absenteeism, turnover, apathy, alienation, and low morale plague organizations, they may be caused by a mismatch between management practices and the adult nature of their workforces. His basic point is that no one wants to be treated like a child, but that's just the way many organizations treat their workers. The result, he suggests, is a group of stifled and unhappy workers who perform below their potential.

Does Argyris seem to have a good point? For example, scientific management assumes that people will work more efficiently on better-defined tasks. Argyris would likely disagree, believing that simplified jobs limit opportunities for self-actualization in one's work. In a Weberian bureaucracy, typical of many of our government agencies, people work in a clear hierarchy of authority, with higher levels directing and controlling the work of lower levels.[21] This is supposed to be an efficient way of doing things. Argyris would worry that workers lose initiative and end up being less productive. Also, Fayol's administrative principles assume that efficiency will increase when supervisors plan and direct a person's work. Argyris might suggest that this sets up conditions for psychological failure; psychological success is more likely when people define their own goals.

STUDY GUIDE

Takeaway 2.2
What Are the Contributions of the Behavioral Management Approaches?

Terms to Define

Deficit principle

Hawthorne effect

Need

Progression principle

Self-fulfilling prophecies

Theory X

Theory Y

Rapid Review

- Follett's ideas on groups, human cooperation, and organizations that served social purposes foreshadowed current management themes.
- The Hawthorne studies suggested that social and psychological forces influence work behavior and that good human relations may lead to improved work performance.
- Maslow's hierarchy of human needs suggests the importance of self-actualization and the potential for people to satisfy important needs through their work.
- McGregor criticized negative Theory X assumptions about human nature and advocated positive Theory Y assumptions that view people as independent, responsible, and capable of self-direction in their work.
- Argyris pointed out that people in the workplace are mature adults who may react negatively when management practices treat them as if they were immature.

Questions for Discussion

1. How did insights from the Hawthorne studies redirect thinking from the classical management approaches and toward something quite different?
2. If Maslow's hierarchy of needs theory is correct, how can a manager use it to become more effective?
3. Where and how do McGregor's notions of Theory X and Theory Y overlap with Argyris's ideas regarding adult personalities?

Be Sure You Can

- explain why Follett's ideas were quite modern in concept
- summarize findings of the Hawthorne studies
- explain and illustrate the Hawthorne effect
- explain Maslow's deficit and progression principles
- distinguish between McGregor's Theory X and Theory Y assumptions
- explain the self-fulfilling prophecies created by Theory X and Theory Y
- explain Argyris's concern that traditional organizational practices are inconsistent with mature adult personalities

Career Situation: What Would You Do?

As a manager in a small local firm, you've been told that because of an uncertain economy workers can't be given any pay raises this year. You have some really hardworking and high-performing people on your team, and you were counting on giving them solid raises. What can you do? Can insights from Maslow's hierarchy of needs help you solve this dilemma? Is it possible to find ways other than pay to reward team members for high performance and keep them motivated?

Takeaway 2.3
What Are the Foundations of Modern Management Thinking?

ANSWERS TO COME

■ Managers use quantitative analysis and tools to solve complex problems.

■ Organizations are open systems that interact with their environments.

■ Contingency thinking holds that there is no one best way to manage.

■ Quality management focuses attention on continuous improvement.

■ Evidence-based management seeks hard facts about what really works.

THE NEXT STEP IN THE TIMELINE OF MANAGEMENT HISTORY SETS THE STAGE FOR a stream of new developments that are continuing to this day. Loosely called the modern management approaches, they share the assumption that people and organizations are complex, growing and changing over time in response to new problems and opportunities in their environments. The many building blocks of modern management include the use of quantitative tools and techniques, recognition of the inherent complexity of organizations as systems, contingency thinking that rejects the search for universal management principles, attention to quality management, and the desire to ground management practice in solid scientific evidence.

⦀ Managers use quantitative analysis and tools to solve complex problems.

About the same time that some scholars were developing human resource approaches to management, others were investigating how quantitative techniques could improve managerial decision making. The foundation of these analytical decision sciences approaches is the assumption that mathematical techniques can be used for better problem solving. At Google, for example, a math formula has been developed to aid in retaining talent. It pools information from performance reviews and surveys, promotions, and pay histories to identify employees who might feel underutilized and be open to offers from other firms. Human resource management plans are then developed to try to retain them.[22]

In our world of vast computing power and the easy collection and storage of data, there is renewed emphasis on how to use available data to make better management decisions. This is an area of management practice known as **analytics**, the use of large data bases, often referred to as "big data," to solve problems and make informed decisions using systematic analysis.[23] And in respect to analytics, scholars are very interested in learning how managers can use mathematical tools to conduct quantitative and statistical analyses.

The terms **management science** and **operations research** are often used interchangeably to describe the use of mathematical techniques to solve management problems. A typical quantitative approach proceeds as follows. A problem is encountered, it is systematically analyzed, appropriate mathematical models

Analytics is the systematic use and analysis of data to solve problems and make informed decisions.

Management science and **operations research** apply mathematical techniques to solve management problems.

and computations are applied, and an optimum solution is identified. Consider these examples.

Problem: A real estate developer wants to control costs and finish building a new apartment complex on time. Quantitative approach: Network models break large tasks into smaller components and visually diagram them in step-by-step sequences that track completion of different activities on the required timetables.

Problem: An oil exploration company is worried about future petroleum reserves in various parts of the world. Quantitative approach: Mathematical forecasting helps make future projections for reserve sizes and depletion rates that are useful in the planning process.

Problem: A big box retailer is trying to deal with pressures on profit margins by minimizing costs of inventories while never being "out of stock" for customers. Quantitative approach: Inventory analysis helps control inventories by mathematically determining how much to automatically order and when.

Problem: A grocery store is getting complaints from customers that waiting times are too long for checkouts during certain times of the day. Quantitative approach: Queuing theory helps allocate service personnel and workstations based on alternative workload demands and in a way that minimizes both customer waiting times and costs of service workers.

Problem: A manufacturer wants to maximize profits for producing three different products on three different machines, each of which can be used for different periods of times and at different costs. Quantitative approach: Linear programming is used to calculate how best to allocate production among different machines.

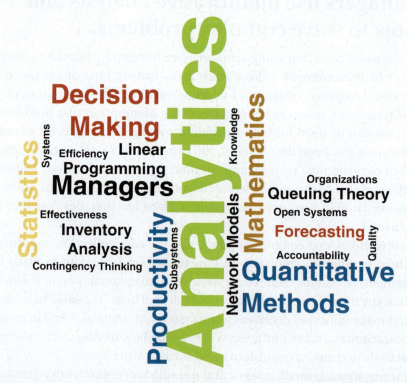

An important counterpart to these management science approaches is **operations management**, which focuses on how organizations produce goods and services efficiently and effectively. The emphasis is on the study and improvement of operations, the transformation process through which goods and services are actually created. The essentials of operations management include such things as business process analysis, workflow designs, facilities layouts and locations, work scheduling and project management, production planning, inventory management, and quality control.

Organizations are open systems that interact with their environments.

The concept of system is a key ingredient of modern management thinking. **Figure 2.3** shows that organizations are **open systems** that interact with their environments to obtain resources—people, technology, information, money, and supplies—that are transformed through work activities into goods and services for their customers and clients. All organizations, from IBM to the U.S. Postal Service to your college or university and the local bookstore, can be described this way.

An **open system** transforms resource inputs from the environment into product outputs.

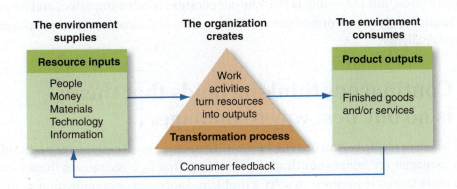

FIGURE 2.3

How Do Organizations as Open Systems Interact with Their External Environments? As open systems, organizations continually interact with their external environments to obtain resource inputs, transform those inputs through work activities into goods and services, and deliver finished products to their customers. Feedback from customers indicates how well they are doing.

The open-systems concept helps explain why there is so much emphasis today on organizations being customer driven. This means they try hard to focus their resources, energies, and goals on continually satisfying the needs of their customers and clients. Look again at Figure 2.3, and you should recognize the logic. Can you see how customers hold the keys to the long-term prosperity and survival of a business, such as an auto manufacturer? Their willingness to buy products or use services provides the revenues needed to obtain resources and keep the cycle in motion. And as soon as the customers balk or start to complain, someone should be listening. This feedback is a warning that the organization needs to change and do things better in the future.

Any organization also operates as a complex network of **subsystems**, or smaller components, whose activities individually and collectively support the work of the larger system.[24] **Figure 2.4** shows the importance of cooperation among organizational subsystems.[25] In the figure, for example, the operations and service management systems serve as a central point. They provide the integration among other subsystems, such as purchasing, accounting, sales, and information, all of which are essential to the work, and the success, of the

A **subsystem** is a smaller component of a larger system.

FIGURE 2.4

How Do Organizations Operate as Complex Networks of Subsystems?
Externally, organizations interact with suppliers and customers in their environments. Internally, many different subsystems must interact and work well together so that high-quality inputs are transformed into products satisfying customers' needs. Common subsystems of a business include purchasing, information technology, operations management, marketing and sales, distribution, human resources, and accounting and finance.

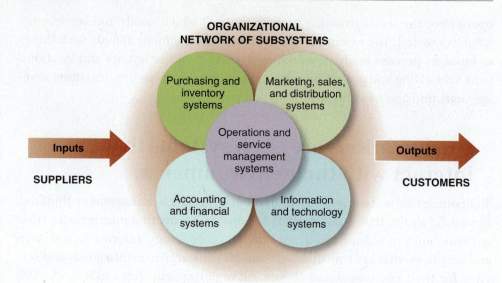

ORGANIZATIONAL NETWORK OF SUBSYSTEMS

- Purchasing and inventory systems
- Marketing, sales, and distribution systems
- Operations and service management systems
- Accounting and financial systems
- Information and technology systems

Inputs → **SUPPLIERS**

Outputs → **CUSTOMERS**

Contingency thinking tries to match management practices with situational demands.

organization. But the reality is that the cooperation is often imperfect and could be improved. Just how organizations achieve this, of course, is a major management challenge.

‖ Contingency thinking holds that there is no one best way to manage.

Rather than trying to find the one best way to manage in all circumstances, modern management adopts **contingency thinking**. That is, it recognizes there is often more than one pathway to solve a problem—personal or organizational. This means that instead of looking for universal or "cookie-cutter" advice, managers should be trying to identify practices that best fit with the unique demands of different situations.

Consider again the concept of bureaucracy. Weber offered it as an ideal form of organization. But from a contingency perspective, the strict bureaucratic form is only one possible way of organizing things. What turns out to be the best structure in any given situation will depend on many factors, including environmental uncertainty, available technology, staff competencies, and more. Contingency thinking recognizes that the structure that works well for one organization may not work well for another in different circumstances. Also, what works well at one point in time may not work as well in the future if circumstances have changed.[26]

You should find a lot of contingency thinking in this book. Its implications extend to all the management functions—from planning and controlling for diverse environmental conditions, to organizing for diverse workforces and multiple tasks, to leading in different performance situations. And this is a good reflection of everyday realities. Don't you use a lot of contingency thinking when solving problems and otherwise going about your personal affairs?

AFP/Newscom

Role Models

■ Oprah Winfrey multitasks to make a difference in other' lives

Oprah Winfrey, America's first female African-American billionaire, has been called the world's most powerful woman. "Making other people happy is what brings me happiness. This principle of giving has brought me enormous good fortune, long before I knew this is how the universe works."

One Christmas at around the age of 12 and living on welfare with a single mother in Milwaukee, WI, Oprah was told by her mother that Santa would not be visiting their home. When three nuns showed up at Winfrey's home with a doll for her, she says, "I remember feeling that I mattered enough to these nuns—and what it meant that they had remembered me. I wasn't forgotten."

It is through her fame that Oprah has been able to satisfy the importance she places on "the principle of giving." The beneficiaries of Oprah's benevolence are causes related to education, women, and children. Through her generosity, Oprah Winfrey, cable network owner, talk show host, philanthropist, writer, actress, and media mogul, has profoundly touched many lives. "What material success does is provide you with the ability to concentrate on other things that really matter," she is quoted as saying.

Oprah's Angel Network, featured oftentimes on *The Oprah Winfrey Show*, is a charity that provided $80 million of support to projects and grants to nonprofits worldwide. Oprah used her show as a platform to inspire her viewers to make a difference in the lives of others—particularly underserved women and children. Oprah personally donated $10 million for Hurricane Katrina relief. Close to 400 students in grades 8 to 12 attend Oprah Winfrey Leadership Academy for girls in Johannesburg, South Africa. At a cost of $40 million and in collaboration with Nelson Mandela, Oprah built the school, which includes state-of-the-art facilities and classrooms. Her advice is: "Think about what you have to give, not in terms of dollars because I believe that your life is about service. It's about what you came to give the world, to your children, to your family."

WHAT'S THE LESSON HERE?

Can you see contingency thinking in Oprah's approach to life and work? What impact has her disadvantaged youth had on her quest to be a benefactor for others? How can her motivation to succeed be explained? What specific needs would you say Oprah has satisfied through her work and philanthropy?

||| Quality management focuses attention on continuous improvement.

The work of W. Edwards Deming is a cornerstone of the quality movement in management.[27] His story began in 1951, when he was invited to Japan to explain quality control techniques that had been developed in the United States. "When Deming spoke," we might say, "the Japanese listened." The principles he taught the Japanese were straightforward, and they worked: Tally defects, analyze and trace them to the source, make corrections, and keep a record of what happens afterward. Deming's approach to quality emphasizes constant innovation, use of statistical methods, and commitment to training in the fundamentals of quality assurance.[28]

One outgrowth of Deming's work was the emergence of **total quality management**, or TQM. This process makes quality principles part of the organization's strategic objectives, applying them to all aspects of operations and striving to meet customers' needs by doing things right the first time. Most TQM approaches begin with an insistence that the total quality commitment applies to everyone

Total quality management is managing with an organizationwide commitment to continuous improvement, product quality, and customer needs.

WHAT IS YOUR PATH TO SUCCESS?

Studies of individual greatness lead many observers to the adage "great leaders are born, not made." But according to author Malcolm Gladwell in the book *Outliers* (2008, Little, Brown and Company), extraordinary people—or outliers—are made, not born. Ingredients like practice, social savvy, and positive attitude are needed along with opportunity to nurture these skills.

Gladwell insists that high IQ cannot predict success and instead a minimum threshold is necessary. Your environment provides more critical elements, and he cites the "10,000 hour rule" that defines the amount of work logged by eventual masters of various disciplines. Gladwell contends that you must practice to become great, not simply once you become great. He contends achievement-oriented individuals possess a can-do attitude and persist through difficulty when others give up. He recommends you choose complex and meaningful interests that promote self-direction. By exerting

and reflecting on your progress, you can train yourself to become a master.

Gladwell argues that success is not an innate ability but something that most can achieve given the right chance. He laments that we select individuals with exceptional ability over those with threshold ability. Those born bright often fail to make themselves successful, whereas those born with modest intellect could flourish given the opportunity to make themselves great.

REFLECT AND REACT

Are you destined for greatness? How much time do you spend on your favorite activity? Are you entitled to good things in life, and how do you assert yourself? When you do poorly on something, do you give up or try until you do well? Is someone with a high GPA more likely to succeed than someone who leads a student organization and works 20 hours a week?

---

in an organization, from resource acquisition and supply chain management, through production and into the distribution of finished goods and services, and ultimately to customer relationship management.

The search for and commitment to quality is now tied to the emphasis modern management gives to the notion of **continuous improvement**—always looking for new ways to improve on current performance.[29] The goal is that one can never be satisfied; something always can and should be improved on.

Continuous improvement involves always searching for new ways to improve work quality and performance.

‖ Evidence-based management seeks hard facts about what really works.

Looking back on the historical foundations of management, one thing that stands out is criticism by today's scholars of the scientific rigor of some historical cornerstones, among them Taylor's scientific management approach and the Hawthorne studies. The worry is that we may be too quick in accepting as factual the results of studies that are based on weak or even shoddy empirical evidence. And if the studies are flawed, perhaps more care needs to be exercised when trying to apply their insights to improve management practices. This problem isn't limited to the distant past.[30]

A book by Jim Collins, *Good to Great*, achieved great acclaim and best-seller status for its depiction of highly successful organizations.[31] But Collins's methods and findings have since been criticized by researchers.[32] After problems appeared at many firms previously considered by him to be "great," he wrote a follow-up book called *How the Mighty Fall*.[33] The point here is not to discredit what keen observers of management practice like Collins and others report. But it is meant to make you cautious and a bit skeptical when it comes to separating fads from facts and conjecture from informed insight.

Scholars Jeffrey Pfeffer and Robert Sutton make the case for **evidence-based management**, or EBM. This is the process of making management decisions on "hard facts"—that is, about what really works—rather than on "dangerous half-truths"—things that sound good but lack empirical substantiation.[34]

Using data from a sample of some 1,000 firms, for example, Pfeffer and a colleague found that firms using a mix of well-selected human resource management practices had more sales and higher profits per employee than those that didn't.[35] Those practices included employment security, selective hiring, self-managed teams, high wages based on performance merit, training and skill development, minimal status differences, and shared information. Examples of other EBM findings include that challenging goals accepted by an employee are likely to result in high performance, and that unstructured employment interviews are unlikely to result in the best person being hired to fill a vacant position.[36]

Scholars pursue a variety of solid empirical studies using proven scientific methods in many areas of management research. Some carve out new and innovative territories, whereas others build on and extend knowledge that has come down through the history of management thought. By staying abreast of such developments and findings, managers can have more confidence that they are acting on a foundation of evidence rather than speculation or hearsay.

> **Evidence-based management** involves making decisions based on hard facts about what really works.

- A research question or problem is identified.
- Hypotheses, or possible explanations, are stated.
- A research design is created to systematically test the hypotheses.
- Data gathered in the research are analyzed and interpreted.
- Hypotheses are accepted or rejected based on the evidence.

≪ **Basic Scientific Methods**

Is Crowdsourcing Grades a Step too Far?

As colleges and universities face pressures to increase productivity in academic programs, online course offerings are proliferating. One development is crowdsourcing of grades previously done by the instructor. An assignment—say an essay—is graded by averaging scores assigned by peers in an online "crowd" of students presumably reading another student's work. It's an attractive option because instructors can handle more students. But critics like Professor Adam Falk of Williams College ask if the educational outcome is the "equivalent of a highly trained professor providing thoughtful evaluation and detailed response."

© Chris Schmidt/iStockphoto

STUDY GUIDE

Takeaway 2.3
What Are the Foundations of Modern Management Thinking?

Terms to Define

Analytics

Contingency thinking

Continuous improvement

Evidence-based management

Management science

Open system

Operations management

Operations research

Subsystem

Total quality management

Rapid Review

- Advanced quantitative techniques in decision sciences and operations management help managers solve complex problems.
- The systems view depicts organizations as complex networks of subsystems that must interact and cooperate with one another if the organization as a whole is to accomplish its goals.
- Contingency thinking avoids "one best way" arguments, recognizing instead that managers need to understand situational differences and respond appropriately to them.
- Quality management focuses on making continuous improvements in processes and systems.
- Evidence-based management uses findings from rigorous scientific research to identify management practices for high performance.

Questions for Discussion

1. Can you use the concepts of open system and subsystem to describe the operations of an organization in your community?
2. In addition to the choice of organization structures, in what other areas of management decision making do you think contingency thinking plays a role?
3. Does evidence-based management allow for managers to learn from their own experiences as well as the experiences of others?

Be Sure You Can

- discuss the importance of quantitative analysis in management decision making
- use the terms *open system* and *subsystem* to describe how an organization operates
- explain how contingency thinking might influence a manager's choices of organization structures
- describe the role of continuous improvement in total quality management
- give examples of workplace situations that can benefit from evidence-based management

Career Situation: What Would You Do?

You've just come up with a great idea for improving productivity and morale in a shop that silk-screens T-shirts for college bookstores. Your idea is to allow 40+ employees to work four 10-hour days if they want instead of the normal five-day/40-hour week. With the added time off, you reason, they'll he happier and more productive while working. But your boss isn't so sure. "Show me some evidence," she says. Can you design a research study that can be done in the shop to show whether or not your proposal is a good one?

TestPrep 2

Answers to TestPrep questions can be found at the back of the book.

Multiple-Choice Questions

1. A management consultant who advises managers to carefully study jobs, train workers to do them with efficient motions, and tie pay to job performance is using ideas from _____.
   - (a) scientific management
   - (b) contingency thinking
   - (c) Henri Fayol
   - (d) Theory Y

2. The Hawthorne studies were important in management history because they raised awareness about the influence of _____ on productivity.
   - (a) organization structures
   - (b) human factors
   - (c) physical work conditions
   - (d) pay and rewards

3. If Douglas McGregor heard an instructor complaining that her students were lazy and irresponsible, he would say these assumptions _____.
   - (a) violated scientific management ideas
   - (b) focused too much on needs
   - (c) would create a negative self-fulfilling prophecy
   - (d) showed contingency thinking

4. If your local bank or credit union is a complex system, then the loan-processing department of the bank would be considered a _____.
   - (a) subsystem
   - (b) closed system
   - (c) learning organization
   - (d) bureaucracy

5. When a manager puts Danté in a customer relations job because he has strong social needs and gives Sherrill lots of daily praise because she has strong ego needs, he is displaying _____.
   - (a) systems thinking
   - (b) Theory X
   - (c) contingency thinking
   - (d) administrative principles

6. Which of the following is one of the characteristics of Weber's ideal bureaucracy?
   - (a) Few rules and procedures
   - (b) Impersonality
   - (c) Promotion by privilege not by merit
   - (d) Ambiguous hierarchy of authority

7. Which principle states that a person should only receive orders from one boss in an organization?
   - (a) Scalar
   - (b) Contingency
   - (c) Hawthorne
   - (d) Unity of command

8. One of the conclusions from the Hawthorne studies was that _____.
   - (a) motion studies could improve performance
   - (b) groups can sometimes restrict the productivity of their members
   - (c) people respond well to monetary incentives
   - (d) supervisors should avoid close relations with their subordinates

9. If an organization was performing poorly, what would Henri Fayol most likely advise as a way to improve things?
   - (a) teach managers to better plan, organize, lead, and control
   - (b) give workers better technology
   - (c) promote only the best workers to management
   - (d) find ways to improve total quality management

10. When a worker is a responsible parent, makes car payments, and is active in local organizations, how might Argyris explain her poor work performance?
    - (a) She isn't treated as an adult at work.
    - (b) Managers are using Theory Y assumptions.
    - (c) Organizational subsystems are inefficient.
    - (d) She doesn't have the right work skills.

11. _____ management assumes people are complex, with widely varying needs.

(a) Classical

(b) Neoclassical

(c) Behavioral

(d) Modern

12. The big interest today in _____ refers to the management practice of using mathematics and computing power to examine "big data" for insights on business.

(a) continuous improvement

(b) Theory X

(c) analytics

(d) total quality management

13. The highest level in Maslow's hierarchy is _____.

(a) safety

(b) esteem

(c) self-actualization

(d) physiological

14. If an organization is considered an open system, work activities that turn resources into outputs are part of the _____ process.

(a) input

(b) transformation

(c) output

(d) feedback

15. When managers make decisions based on solid facts and information, this is known as _____.

(a) continuous improvement

(b) evidence-based management

(c) Theory Y

(d) The scalar chain

Short-Response Questions

16. Give an example of how principles of scientific management can apply in organizations today.

17. How do the deficit and progression principles operate in Maslow's hierarchy?

18. Compare the Hawthorne effect with McGregor's notion of self-fulfilling prophecies.

19. Explain by example several ways a manager might use contingency thinking in the management process.

Integration and Application Question

20. Enrique Temoltzin is the new manager of a college bookstore. He wants to do a good job and decides to operate the store on Weber's concept of bureaucracy.

Question: Is bureaucracy the best approach here? What are its potential advantages and disadvantages? How could Enrique use contingency thinking in this situation?

CHAPTER 2

Steps *for* Further Learning

BUILD

MARKETABLE SKILLS.
EARN BIG CAREER
PAYOFFS!

Don't miss these
opportunities in the
**Skill-Building
Portfolio**

■ **SELF-ASSESSMENT 2:**
Managerial Assumptions

*Assumptions influence
behavior... discover your
Theory X and Theory Y
tendencies.*

■ **CLASS EXERCISE 2:**
**Evidence-Based
Management Quiz**

*It's easy to bet on hearsay...
what the evidence says might
surprise you.*

■ **TEAM PROJECT 2:**
**Management in Popular
Culture**

*Management is all around
us... take time to learn from
everyday experiences.*

> Many learning resources are found at the end of the book and online within WileyPLUS.

Take advantage of **Cases for Critical Thinking**

■ **CHAPTER 2 CASE SNAPSHOT:**
Zara International—Fast Fashion's Style Maker/
Sidebar on Uniqlo

In this world of "hot today, gauche tomorrow," no company does fast fashion better than Zara. Shoppers in 79 countries, and counting, are fans of Zara's knack for bringing the latest styles from sketchbook to clothing rack at lightning speed and reasonable prices. Low prices and a rapid response to fashion trends give Zara a top ranking among global clothing vendors. The chain specializes in quick turnarounds—from sketchbook to clothing rack—of the latest designer trends at prices tailored to the young. Louis Vuitton's fashion director Daniel Piette described Zara as "possibly the most innovative and devastating retailer in the world." But now that Zara has shown the world how to do fast fashion so well, won't others find it easy to copy their success story?

DO
A CASE ANALYSIS.
STRENGTHEN YOUR
CRITICAL THINKING!

Dig into this **Hot Topic**

■ **GOOD IDEA OR NOT?** **Raising Expectations
and Getting Better Feedback**

Dinner Date Question: Does a glass of wine taste better if you have never heard of the vintage or if you have previously read a positive review of it? As you might guess, it will likely be the wine you taste after reading the positive review. The reason traces to issues of perception and expectations. We often end up perceiving things—the glass of wine, a test drive of a new BMW, or a new teammate, as we expect them to be.

So, does this mean that before your next big presentation to the class or to an executive team you should prepare the audience by telling them ahead of time—"You're really going to like this one"? *Those intrigued by the practice* might say it's just another spin on the Hawthorne Effect. You're just proactively shaping the expectations of others so that their feedback goes in your favor. *Those skeptical of the practice* might argue that caution is in order. Raising expectations can be overplayed. When they get set too high there's more chance for disappointment to set in.

Dan Ariely, professor of psychology and behavioral economics, advises that we have to be careful in communicating expectations. If we overhype something while hoping for positive feedback, we may end up getting a negative review. His rule of thumb is that it's okay to send out high expectations if you don't over exaggerate too much. A stretch of about 20% is a comfortable target for moving the perceiver's feedback in a positive direction.

Final Take   This notion of communicating high expectations to get positive feedback is an interesting one to test in everyday experience. Why not try it? See how well you can manage expectations of friends and teammates. Should this be cultivated as an essential management and workplace skill, and one that can also serve us well in many personal situations?

GET
AND STAY INFORMED.
MAKE YOURSELF
VALUABLE!

"How do you excuse betraying thousands?" said Bernard Madoff when sentenced to 150 years in jail for a multibillion dollar financial fraud.

Ethics and Social Responsibility

3

Character Doesn't Stay Home When We Go to Work

Individual Character and *Avatar*

I t was an instant classic combining a great story with interesting characters and super visual effects. But James Cameron's *Avatar* was also a window into a world where cultures clashed over resources and individuals had to confront their ethics.

The Na'vi inhabit a land rich with valuable Unobtainium, the object of greedy Parker Selfridge's quest. He makes a deal with paraplegic Jake Sully to infiltrate the Na'vi land of Pandora in return for corrective surgery. The goal is to get the Unobtanium, even though the Na'vi culture and way of life may be destroyed. Jake ends up valuing the Na'vi and their way of life. He helps them prevail and fight off the ethnocentric business attackers from an outside world.

The film is a cross-cultural journey that also opens a window to sustainable development. But the next time you watch the movie, pay special attention to Jake's personal journey with ethical dilemmas. It's a reminder that **individual character** isn't just something we think about on occasion. Along with its foundation of personal integrity, individual character deserves our constant attention.

Twentieth Century-Fox Film Corporation / Photofest

YOUR CHAPTER 3 TAKEAWAYS

1. Understand how ethics and ethical behavior play out in the workplace.

2. Know how to maintain high standards of ethical conduct.

3. Identify when organizations are and are not acting in socially responsible ways.

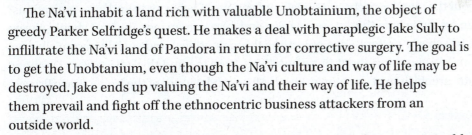

WHAT'S INSIDE

Explore Yourself
More on **individual character**

Role Models
Gary Hirshberg goes for triple bottom line at Stonyfield Farm

Ethics Check
Signing on to a Green Supply Chain

Facts to Consider
Manager behavior key to an ethical workplace

Manager's Library
Conscious Capitalism: Liberating the Heroic Spirit of Business by John Mackey and Raj Sisodia

Takeaway 3.1

How Do Ethics and Ethical Behavior Play Out in the Workplace?

ANSWERS TO COME

- Ethical behavior is values driven.
- What is considered ethical varies among moral reasoning approaches.
- What is considered ethical can vary across cultures.
- Ethical dilemmas arise as tests of personal ethics and values.
- People tend to rationalize unethical behaviors.

DOES LEARNING ABOUT BAD BUSINESS BEHAVIOR SHOCK AND DISMAY YOU? "MADOFF gets 150 years in prison." "Worldcom CEO sentenced to 25 years in prison." "Massey Mine Boss Sentenced; Feds Toughen Mine Safety Rule." Such headlines and their underlying scandals are all too frequent in the news. And the stories underlying them aren't ones of incompetence; they tell tales of personal failures and greed.[1] With bleak reports like these, it's understandable that some people, perhaps a lot of them, are left feeling cynical, pessimistic, and even helpless regarding the state of executive leadership in our society.[2]

So what can be done? For starters, would you say that it is time to get serious about the moral aspects and social implications of behavior in and by organizations? Can we agree here that in your career, and for any manager, the goal should always be to achieve performance objectives through ethical and socially responsible actions? As you think about these questions, keep in mind this advice from Desmond Tutu, archbishop of Capetown, South Africa, and winner of the Nobel Peace Prize.[3]

Schalk van Zuydam/AP

You are powerful people. You can make this world a better place where business decisions and methods take account of right and wrong as well as profitability. . . . You must take a stand on important issues: the environment and ecology, affirmative action, sexual harassment, racism and sexism, the arms race, poverty, the obligations of the affluent West to its less-well-off sisters and brothers elsewhere.

It is tempting to say that any behavior that is legal can also be considered ethical. But this is too easy; the "letter of the law" does not always translate into what others would consider to be ethical actions.[4] U.S. laws once allowed slavery, permitted only men to vote, and allowed young children to work full-time jobs. Today we consider such actions unethical.

Ethics is defined as the code of moral principles that sets standards of good or bad, or right or wrong, in our conduct.[5] Personal ethics are guides for behavior, helping people make moral choices among alternative courses of action. Most typically, we use the term **ethical behavior** to describe what we accept as "good" and "right" as opposed to "bad" or "wrong."

Ethics sets standards of good or bad, or right or wrong, in our conduct.

Ethical behavior is "right" or "good" in the context of a governing moral code.

‖ Ethical behavior is values driven.

It's one thing to look back and make ethical judgments; it is a bit harder to make them in real time. Is it truly ethical for an employee to take longer than necessary to do a job . . . to make personal telephone calls on company time . . . to call in sick and go on vacation instead? Although not strictly illegal, many people would consider any one or more of these acts to be unethical. How about you? How often and in what ways have you committed or observed acts that could be considered unethical in your school or workplace?[6]

Many ethical problems arise at work when people are asked to do something that violates their personal beliefs. For some, if the act is legal, they proceed with confidence and consider their behavior ethical. For others, the ethical test goes beyond legality and extends to personal **values**—underlying beliefs and judgments regarding what is right or desirable and that influence individual attitudes and behaviors.

The psychologist Milton Rokeach distinguishes between "terminal" and "instrumental" values.[7] **Terminal values** focus on desired ends, such as the goal of lifelong learning. Examples of terminal values considered important by managers include self-respect, family security, freedom, inner harmony, and happiness. **Instrumental values** focus on the means for accomplishing these ends, such as the role of intellectual curiosity in lifelong learning. Instrumental values held important by managers include honesty, ambition, courage, imagination, and self-discipline.

Although terminal and instrumental values tend to be quite enduring for any one individual, they can vary considerably from one person to the next. A contrast of such values might help to explain why different people respond quite differently to the same situation. Although two people might share the terminal value of career success, they might disagree on how to balance the instrumental values of honesty and ambition in accomplishing it.

> **Values** are broad beliefs about what is appropriate behavior.

> **Terminal values** are preferences about desired end states.

> **Instrumental values** are preferences regarding the means to desired ends.

Masterfile

{ THE MOST COMMON UNETHICAL ACTS BY MANAGERS INCLUDE VERBAL, SEXUAL, AND RACIAL HARASSMENT.

Facts to **Consider**

■ Behavior of Managers Is Key to an Ethical Workplace

Managers make a big difference in ethical behavior at work, according to a survey conducted for Deloitte & Touche USA. Some findings include

- Forty-two percent of workers say the behavior of their managers is a major influence on an ethical workplace.
- The most common unethical acts by managers and supervisors include verbal, sexual, and racial harassment; misuse of company property; and giving preferential treatment.
- Ninety-one percent of workers are more likely to behave ethically when they have work–life balance; but, 30% say they suffer from poor work–life balance.
- Top reasons for unethical behavior are lack of personal integrity (80%) and lack of job satisfaction (60%).

- Most workers consider it unacceptable to steal from an employer, cheat on expense reports, take credit for another's accomplishments, and lie on time sheets.
- Most workers consider it acceptable to ask a work colleague for a personal favor, take sick days when not ill, and use company technology for personal affairs.

YOUR THOUGHTS?

Are there any surprises in these data? Is this emphasis on manager and direct supervisor behavior justified as the key to an ethical workplace? Would you make any changes to what the workers in this survey report as acceptable and unacceptable work behaviors?

Talk with some of your friends or classmates about their terminal values (what you and they want to achieve) and instrumental values (how you and they are willing to do it). Don't be surprised to find values differences, and don't be surprised to find that these differences create conflicts. Some of them may rest on significant differences in what behaviors are and are not considered ethical.

Consider this situation. About 10% of an MBA class at Duke University was once caught cheating on a take-home final exam.[8] The "cheaters" averaged 29 years of age and six years of work experience; they were also big on music downloads, file sharing, open-source software, text messaging, and electronic collaboration. Some say what happened is a good example of "postmodern learning," where students are taught to collaborate, work in teams, and utilize the latest communication technologies. For others, there is no doubt—it was an individual exam, and those students cheated.

⫿ What is considered ethical varies among moral reasoning approaches.

Figure 3.1 shows four different philosophical views of ethical behavior, with each representing an alternative approach to moral reasoning.[9] They are the utilitarian, individualism, justice, and moral rights views.

FIGURE 3.1

How Do Alternative Moral Reasoning Approaches View Ethical Behavior?
People often differ in the approaches they take toward moral reasoning, and they may use different approaches at different times and situations. Four ways to reason through the ethics of a course of action are utilitarianism, individualism, moral rights, and justice. Each approach can justify an action as ethical, but the reasoning will differ from that of the other views.

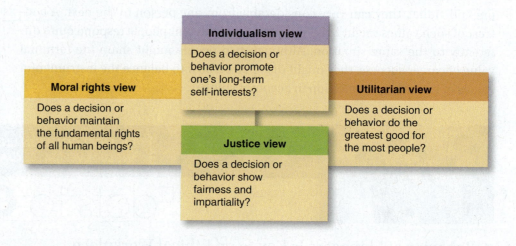

In the **utilitarian view**, ethical behavior delivers the greatest good to the most people.

Utilitarian View

The **utilitarian view** considers ethical behavior to be that which delivers the greatest good to the greatest number of people. Founded in the work of 19th-century philosopher John Stuart Mill, this results-oriented view tries to assess the moral implications of our actions in terms of their consequences. Business executives, for example, might use profits, efficiency, and other performance criteria to judge what decision is best for the most people.

An example of the utilitarian view toward ethical behavior is the manager who decides to cut 30% of a plant's workforce to keep the plant profitable and save the remaining jobs, rather than lose them all to business failure. This decision seems defensible from a utilitarian perspective, but we also have to be careful. Utilitarian thinking relies on the assessment of future outcomes that are often difficult to predict and that are tough to measure accurately. What is the economic value of a human life when deciding how rigid safety regulations need to be on an off-shore drilling rig, for example? Is it even appropriate to try to put an economic value on the potential loss of human life?

Individualism View

Whereas in the utilitarian view ethical behavior delivers the greatest good to the most people, the **individualism view** focuses on the long-term advancement of self-interests. The notion is that people become self-regulating as they strive for individual advantage over time; ethics are maintained in the process. Suppose, for example, that you consider cheating on your next test. You also realize this quest for short-term gain might lead to a long-term loss if you are caught and expelled. This reasoning shows an individualism view toward ethical behavior and should cause you to quickly reject the original inclination to cheat on the exam.

> In the **individualism view**, ethical behavior advances long-term self-interests.

Not everyone, as you might expect, agrees that decisions based on the individualism view will result in honesty and integrity. One complaint is that individualism in business practice too often results in a *pecuniary ethic*. This has been described by one executive as a tendency to "push the law to its outer limits" and "run roughshod over other individuals to achieve one's objectives."[10] The individualism view also presumes that individuals are self-regulating. But we know that not everyone has the same capacity or desire to control their behaviors. Even if only a few individuals take unethical advantage of the freedom allowed under this perspective, such instances can disrupt the degree of trust that exists within a business community and make it difficult to predict how others will act.

Justice View

The **justice view** of moral reasoning considers a behavior to be ethical when people are treated impartially and fairly, according to legal rules and standards. It judges the ethical aspects of any decision on the basis of how equitable it is for everyone affected.[11] Today, researchers often speak about four types of workplace justice—procedural, distributive, interactional, and commutative.

> In the **justice view**, ethical behavior treats people impartially and fairly.

Procedural justice involves the fair administration of policies and rules. For example, does a sexual harassment charge levied against a senior executive receive the same full hearing as one made against a first-level supervisor? **Distributive justice** involves the allocation of outcomes without respect to individual characteristics, such as those based on ethnicity, race, gender, or age. For example, does a woman with the same qualifications and experience as a man receive the same consideration for hiring or promotion?

> **Procedural justice** focuses on the fair application of policies and rules.

> **Distributive justice** focuses on treating people the same regardless of personal characteristics.

Interactional justice focuses on treating everyone with dignity and respect. For example, does a bank loan officer take the time to fully explain to an applicant why he or she was turned down for a loan?[12] **Commutative justice** focuses on the fairness of exchanges or transactions. An exchange is deemed to be fair if all parties enter into it freely, have access to relevant and available information, and obtain some type of benefit from the transaction.[13]

> **Interactional justice** is the degree to which others are treated with dignity and respect.

> **Commutative justice** focuses on the fairness of exchanges or transactions.

You should notice that the justice view of ethical reasoning places an emphasis on fairness and equity. But which type of justice is paramount? Is it more important to ensure that everyone is treated exactly the same way—creating procedural justice, or to ensure that those from different backgrounds are adequately represented in terms of the final outcome—creating distributive justice?

Moral Rights View

In the **moral rights view**, ethical behavior respects and protects fundamental rights.

Finally, a **moral rights view** considers behavior to be ethical when it respects and protects the fundamental rights of people. Based on the teachings of John Locke and Thomas Jefferson, this view believes all people have rights to life, liberty, and fair treatment under the law. In organizations, this translates into protecting the rights of employees to privacy, due process, free speech, free consent, health and safety, and freedom of conscience.

The moral rights view of ethical reasoning protects individual rights, but it doesn't guarantee that the outcomes will be beneficial to the broader society. What happens, for example, when someone's right to free speech conveys messages hurtful to others?

Compounding this problem is the fact that various nations have different laws and cultural expectations. As we grapple with the complexities of global society, human rights are often debated. Even though the United Nations stands by the Universal Declaration of Human Rights passed by the General Assembly in 1948, business executives, representatives of activist groups, and leaders of governments still argue and disagree over rights issues in various circumstances.[14] And without doubt, one of the areas where human rights can be most controversial is the arena of international business.

Excerpts from the Universal Declaration of Human Rights, United Nations

- **Article 1**—All human beings are born free and equal in dignity and right.
- **Article 18**—Everyone has the right to freedom of thought, conscience, and religion.
- **Article 19**—Everyone has the right to freedom of opinion and expression.
- **Article 23**—Everyone has the right to work, to free choice of employment, to just and favorable conditions of work.
- **Article 26**—Everyone has the right to education.

‖ What is considered ethical can vary across cultures.

Andrew Holbrooke / Corbis

Situation: A 12-year-old boy is working in a garment factory in Bangladesh. He is the sole income earner for his family. He often works 12-hour days and was once burned quite badly by a hot iron. One day he is told he can't work. His employer was given an ultimatum by the firm's major American customer—"no child workers if you want to keep our contracts." The boy says: "I don't understand. I could do my job very well. My family needs the money."

"Should this child be allowed to work?" This question is but one example among the many ethics challenges faced in international business. Robert Haas, former Levi CEO, once said that an ethical problem "becomes even more difficult when you overlay the complexities of different cultures and values systems that exist throughout the world."[15] It would probably be hard to find a corporate leader or businessperson engaged in international business who would disagree. Put yourself in their positions. How would you deal with an issue such as child labor in a factory owned by one of your major suppliers?

Those who believe that behavior in foreign settings should be guided by the classic rule of "when in Rome, do as the Romans do" reflect an ethical position of cultural relativism.[16] This is the belief that there is no one right way to behave and that ethical behavior is always determined by its cultural context. An American international business executive guided by rules of cultural relativism, for example, would argue that the use of child labor is okay in another country as long as it is consistent with local laws and customs.

Figure 3.2 contrasts cultural relativism with the alternative of **moral absolutism**. This is a universalist ethical position suggesting that if a behavior or practice is not okay in one's home environment, it is not acceptable practice anywhere else. In other words, ethical standards are absolute and should apply universally across cultures and national boundaries. The American executive in the former example would not do business in a setting where child labor was used because it is unacceptable at home. Critics of the universal approach claim it is a form of **ethical imperialism**, or the attempt to externally impose one's ethical standards on others.

> **Cultural relativism** suggests there is no one right way to behave; cultural context determines ethical behavior.

> **Moral absolutism** suggests ethical standards apply universally across all cultures.

> **Ethical imperialism** is an attempt to impose one's ethical standards on other cultures.

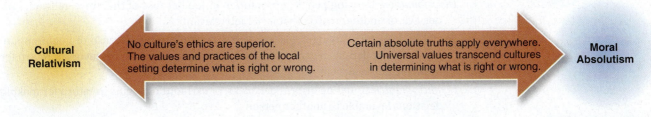

Cultural Relativism — No culture's ethics are superior. The values and practices of the local setting determine what is right or wrong. — Certain absolute truths apply everywhere. Universal values transcend cultures in determining what is right or wrong. — **Moral Absolutism**

When in Rome, do as the Romans do.

Don't do anything you wouldn't do at home.

FIGURE 3.2 **How Do Cultural Relativism and Moral Absolutism Influence International Business Ethics?** The international business world is one of the most challenging settings in respect to ethical decision making. This figure identifies two diametrically opposed extremes. Cultural relativism justifies a decision if it conforms to local values, laws, and practices. Moral absolutism justifies a decision only if it conforms to the ways of the home country. (*Source*: Developed from Thomas Donaldson, "Values in Tension: Ethics Away from Home," *Harvard Business Review*, vol. 74 (September/October 1996), pp. 48–62.)

Business ethicist Thomas Donaldson finds fault with both cultural relativism and moral absolutism. He argues instead that fundamental human rights and ethical standards can be preserved while values and traditions of a local culture are respected.[17] The core values or "hypernorms" that must travel across cultural and national boundaries focus on human dignity, basic rights, and good citizenship. But once these core values have been met, Donaldson believes that international business behaviors can be tailored to local cultures. In the case of child labor, the American executive might ensure that any children employed in a factory under contract to his or her business work in safe conditions and are provided regular schooling during scheduled work hours.[18]

||| Ethical dilemmas arise as tests of personal ethics and values.

It's all well and good to discuss cases about ethical behavior in theory and in the safety of the college classroom. The tough personal test, however, occurs when we encounter a real-life situation that challenges our ethical beliefs and standards. Sooner or later, we all will. Often ambiguous and unexpected, these ethical challenges are inevitable. Think ahead to your next job search. Suppose you have accepted a job offer only to get a better one from another employer two

An **ethical dilemma** is a situation that, although offering potential benefit or gain, is also unethical.

weeks later. Should you come up with an excuse to back out of the first job so that you can accept the second one instead?

An **ethical dilemma** is a situation requiring a decision about a course of action that, although offering potential benefits, may be considered unethical. As a further complication, there may be no clear consensus on what is "right" and "wrong." In these circumstances, one's personal values are often the best indicators that something isn't right. An engineering manager speaking from experience sums it up this way: "I define an unethical situation as one in which I have to do something I don't feel good about."[19]

Take a look at Table 3.1—Common Examples of Unethical Behavior at Work.[20] Have you been exposed to anything like this? Are you ready to deal with these situations and any ethical dilemmas that they may create?

Table 3.1 Common Examples of Unethical Behavior at Work

Discrimination: Denying people a promotion or job because of their race, religion, gender, age, or another reason that is not job relevant

Sexual harassment: Making a co-worker feel uncomfortable because of inappropriate comments or actions regarding sexuality or by requesting sexual favors in return for favorable job treatment

Conflicts of interest: Taking bribes, kickbacks, or extraordinary gifts in return for making decisions favorable to another person

Customer privacy: Giving someone privileged information regarding the activities of a customer

Organizational resources: Using a business e-mail account to communicate personal opinions or to make requests from community organizations

Managers responding to a *Harvard Business Review* survey reported that many of their ethical dilemmas arise out of conflicts with superiors, customers, and subordinates.[21] The most frequent issues involve dishonesty in advertising and in communications with top management, clients, and government agencies. Other ethics problems involve dealing with special gifts, entertainment expenses, and kickbacks.

Isn't it interesting that managers single out their bosses as frequent causes of ethical dilemmas? They complain about bosses who engage in various forms of harassment, misuse organizational resources, and give preferential treatment to certain persons.[22] They report feeling pressured at times to support incorrect viewpoints, sign false documents, overlook the boss's wrongdoings, and do business with the boss's friends. A surprising two-thirds of chief financial officers in a *Newsweek* survey, for example, said that they had been asked by their bosses to falsify financial records. Of them, 45% said they refused the directive, whereas 12% said they complied.[23]

Often found at the top of lists of bad boss behaviors is holding people accountable for unrealistically high performance goals.[24] When individuals feel extreme performance pressures, they sometimes act incorrectly and engage in questionable practices in attempting to meet these expectations. As scholar Archie Carroll says: ". . . otherwise decent people start cutting corners on accuracy or quality, or start covering up incidents, lying or deceiving customers."[25] The management lesson is to be realistic and supportive in what you request of others. As Carroll says: "Good management means that one has to be sensitive to how pressure to perform might be perceived by those who want to please the boss."[26]

⦀ People have tendencies to rationalize unethical behaviors.

What happens after someone commits an unethical act? Most of us generally view ourselves as "good" people. When we do something that is or might be "wrong," it leaves us doubtful, uncomfortable, and anxious. A common response is to rationalize the questionable behavior to make it seem acceptable in our minds. Although rationalizations might give us a false sense of justification, they come at a high cost.[27]

A rationalizer might say: It's not really illegal. This implies that the behavior is acceptable, especially in ambiguous situations. When dealing with shady or borderline situations, you may not be able to precisely determine right from wrong. In such cases, it is important to stop and reconsider things. When in doubt about the ethics of a decision, the best advice is: Don't do it.

A rationalizer might also say: It's in everyone's best interests. This response suggests that just because someone might benefit from the behavior, it is okay. To overcome this "ends justify the means" rationalization, we need to look beyond short-run results and carefully assess longer-term implications.

Sometimes a rationalizer uses a third excuse: No one will ever know about it. This implies that something we do is wrong only if it is discovered. Lack of accountability, unrealistic pressures to perform, and a boss who prefers "not to know" can all reinforce this tendency. But especially in today's world of great transparency, such thinking is risky and hard to accept.

Finally, a rationalizer might try to justify a questionable action on the belief that the organization will stand behind them. This is misperceived loyalty. The individual believes that the organization's best interests stand above all others, that top managers will protect the individual from harm. But if caught doing something wrong, would you want to count on the organization going to bat for you? And when you read about people who have done wrong and then tried to excuse it by saying, "I only did what I was ordered to do," how sympathetic are you?

{ WE HAVE TO KNOW OURSELVES AND OUR PERSONAL VALUES WELL ENOUGH TO MAKE PRINCIPLED DECISIONS.

Explore Yourself

■ Individual Character

Character is something that people tend to think more about during presidential election years or when famous people, such as professional athletes or politicians, commit unethical acts. But, the fact is that **individual character** can't be given only an occasional concern.

Along with its foundation of personal integrity, individual character deserves constant attention. Indeed, it is often tested by ethics and social responsibility situations in organizations today. Ethical dilemmas can arise unexpectedly. To deal with them, we have to know ourselves and our personal values well enough to make principled decisions, ones that we can be proud of and that others will respect. After all, it's the character of people making key decisions that determines whether our organizations act in socially responsible or irresponsible ways.

Get to know yourself better by taking the self-assessment on **Terminal Values** and completing other activities in the *Exploring Management* **Skill-Building Portfolio.**

Takeaway 3.1

How Do Ethics and Ethical Behavior Play Out in the Workplace?

Terms to Define

Commutative justice

Cultural relativism

Distributive justice

Ethical behavior

Ethical dilemmas

Ethical imperialism

Ethics

Individualism view

Instrumental values

Interactional justice

Justice view

Moral absolutism

Moral rights view

Procedural justice

Terminal values

Utilitarian view

Values

Rapid Review

- Ethical behavior is that which is accepted as "good" or "right" as opposed to "bad" or "wrong."
- The utilitarian, individualism, moral rights, and justice views offer different approaches to moral reasoning; each takes a different perspective of when and how a behavior becomes ethical.
- Cultural relativism argues that no culture is ethically superior to any other; moral absolutism believes there are clear rights and wrongs that apply universally, no matter where in the world one might be.
- An ethical dilemma occurs when one must decide whether to pursue a course of action that, although offering the potential for personal or organizational gain, may be unethical.
- Ethical dilemmas faced by managers often involve conflicts with superiors, customers, and subordinates over requests that involve some form of dishonesty.
- Common rationalizations for unethical behavior include believing the behavior is not illegal, is in everyone's best interests, will never be noticed, or will be supported by the organization.

Questions for Discussion

1. For a manager, is any one of the moral reasoning approaches better than the others?
2. Will a belief in cultural relativism create inevitable ethics problems for international business executives?
3. Are ethical dilemmas always problems, or can they be opportunities?

Be Sure You Can

- differentiate between legal behavior and ethical behavior
- differentiate between terminal and instrumental values, and give examples of each
- list and explain four approaches to moral reasoning
- illustrate distributive, procedural, interactive, and commutative justice in organizations
- explain the positions of cultural relativism and moral absolutism in international business ethics
- illustrate the types of ethical dilemmas common in the workplace
- explain how bad management can cause ethical dilemmas
- list four common rationalizations for unethical behavior

Career Situation: What Would You Do?

Today's classroom could be a mirror image of tomorrow's work place. You have just seen one of your classmates snap a cell phone photo of the essay question on an exam. The instructor has missed this, and you're not sure if anyone else observed what just happened. You know that the instructor is giving the exam to another section of the course starting next class period. Do you let this pass, perhaps telling yourself that it isn't all that important? If you can't let it pass, what action would you take?

Takeaway 3.2
How Can We Maintain High Standards of Ethical Conduct?

ANSWERS TO COME

■ Personal character and moral development influence ethical conduct.

■ Managers as positive role models can inspire ethical conduct.

■ Training in ethical decision making can improve ethical conduct.

■ Protection of whistleblowers can encourage ethical conduct.

■ Formal codes of ethics set standards for ethical conduct.

AS QUICK AS WE ARE TO RECOGNIZE THE BAD NEWS AND PROBLEMS ABOUT ETHICAL behavior in organizations, we shouldn't forget that there is a lot of good news, too. There are many organizations out there whose leaders and members set high ethical standards for themselves and others and engage in a variety of methods to encourage consistent ethical behaviors. John Mackey, for example, built Whole Foods with a commitment to "whole food, whole people, and whole planet."[28]

Look around. You'll see many people and organizations operating in ethical and socially responsible ways. Some are quite well known—companies like Patagonia, Stonyfield Farm, and Whole Foods Market are examples. Others are less visible, but still performing every day with high ethical standards. Surely there are examples right in your local community of how "profits with principles" can be achieved. As you think about organizations that do these good things, don't forget that the underlying reasons rest with the people who run them—individuals like you and me.

⦀ Personal character and moral development influence ethical decision making.

There are many possible influences on our personal ethics and how we apply them at work. One set traces to who we are as a person, what might be called our "character," as described in the Explore Yourself feature that ended the last section. Our character is reflected in how we behave and what we stand for. It is a product of family influences, religious beliefs, personal standards, personal values, and even past experiences.

As the chapter subtitle says: Character shouldn't stay home when we go to work. But we also know that it isn't always easy to stand up for what we believe. This problem grows when we are exposed to extreme pressures, when we get contradictory or just plain bad advice, and when our career is at stake. "Do this or lose your job!" is a terribly intimidating message. So it may be no surprise that 56% of U.S. workers in one survey reported feeling pressured to act unethically in their jobs.[29] Sadly, the same survey also revealed that 48% of respondents had themselves committed questionable acts within the past year.

Problems become more manageable when we have solid **ethical frameworks,** or well-thought-out personal rules and strategies for ethical decision making. They can help us to act consistently and confidently. Ethical anchors that give high priority to such virtues as honesty, fairness, integrity, and self-respect can help us make correct decisions even under the most difficult conditions.

Ethical frameworks are well-thought-out personal rules and strategies for ethical decision making.

The many personal influences on ethical decision making come together in the three levels of moral development described by Lawrence Kohlberg and shown in **Figure 3.3**.[30] Kohlberg believes that we move step-by-step through the levels and their stages as we grow in maturity and education. Not everyone, in fact perhaps only a few of us, reaches the postconventional level.

FIGURE 3.3

What Are the Stages in Kohlberg's Three Levels of Moral Development?
At the preconventional level of moral development, the individual focuses on self-interests, avoiding harm and making deals for gain. At the conventional level, attention becomes more social centered, and the individual tries to be consistent and meet obligations to peers. At the postconventional level of moral development, principle-centered behavior results in the individual living up to societal expectations and personal principles.

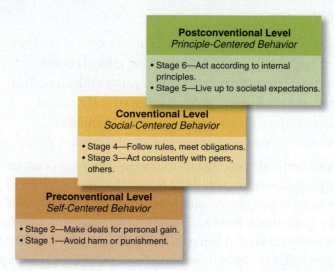

Postconventional Level
Principle-Centered Behavior
- Stage 6—Act according to internal principles.
- Stage 5—Live up to societal expectations.

Conventional Level
Social-Centered Behavior
- Stage 4—Follow rules, meet obligations.
- Stage 3—Act consistently with peers, others.

Preconventional Level
Self-Centered Behavior
- Stage 2—Make deals for personal gain.
- Stage 1—Avoid harm or punishment.

In Kohlberg's *preconventional stage* of moral development, the individual is self-centered. Moral thinking is largely limited to issues of punishment, obedience, and personal interest. Decisions made in the preconventional stage are likely to be directed toward personal gain and based on obedience to rules.

In the *conventional stage*, by contrast, attention broadens to include more social concerns. Decisions made in this stage are likely to be based on following social norms, meeting the expectations of others, and living up to agreed-upon obligations.

In the *postconventional stage* of moral development, also referred to as the principled stage, the individual is strongly driven by core principles and personal beliefs. A strong ethics framework is evident, and the individual is willing to break with norms and conventions, even laws, to act consistent with personal principles. An example is the student who passes on an opportunity to cheat on a take-home examination because he or she believes it is wrong, even though the consequence will be a lower grade. Another example is someone who refuses to use pirated computer software, preferring to purchase it and show respect for intellectual property rights.

When Students Share Assignments, Is It Cheating . . . Or Collaborating?

When a Harvard professor finished reading take-home final examinations from 100+ students in a government class, the conclusion was: Too many answers said close to the same things. When the faculty member reported the incident to the university administration, Harvard had a "cheating" scandal on its hands. Or did it? From the perspective of some students, "collaborating" is a better choice of words. That's the view of a generation that grew up using the Internet and all sorts of collaborative media, and for whom online courses or class activities are a way of life. So, was it cheating or are the professors out of date? Do test-taking rules need better clarification? Are students taking advantage of new situations and technologies?

Managers as positive role models can inspire ethical conduct.

While still a college student, Gabrielle Melchionda started Mad Gab's Inc., an all-natural skin-care business in Portland, Maine. After her sales had risen to over $300,000, an exporter offered to sell $2 million of her products abroad. She turned it down. Why? The exporter also sold weapons, something that contradicted her sense of ethical behavior. Melchionda's personal values guide all her business decisions, from offering an employee profit-sharing plan to hiring disabled adults to using only packaging designs that minimize waste.[31]

The way business owners and top managers approach ethics can make a big difference in what happens in their organizations. They have a lot of power to shape an organization's policies and set its moral tone. Some of this power works through the attention given to policies that set high ethics standards—and to their enforcement. Another and significantly large part of this power works through the personal examples those at the top set as role models. To have a positive impact on ethical conduct throughout an organization, they, like Gabrielle Melchionda, must walk the talk.

Of course, it's not just the owners and top managers who have the power to shape ethical behavior and the responsibility to use that power well. Managers at all levels have more power than they realize to influence the ethical behavior of others. Again, part of this power is walking the talk, setting the example, and acting as an ethical role model. Another part is just practicing good management day by day, keeping goals and performance expectations realistic and achievable, for example. A *Fortune* survey reported that 34% of its respondents felt a company president can help to create an ethical climate by setting reasonable goals "so that subordinates are not pressured into unethical actions."[32]

As you think about managers as ethics role models, consider these ideas from management scholar Archie Carroll. He makes the distinction between amoral, immoral, and moral managers as shown here.[33]

The **immoral manager**, in Carroll's view, chooses to behave unethically. He or she does something purely for personal gain and intentionally disregards the ethics of the action or situation. The **amoral manager** also disregards the ethics of an act or decision, but does so unintentionally. This manager simply fails to consider the ethical consequences of his or her actions.

In contrast to both prior types, the **moral manager** considers ethical behavior as a personal goal. He or she always makes decisions and acts in full consideration of ethical issues. We can say that this manager has a strong ethical framework and moral individual character. In Kohlberg's terms, this manager operates at the postconventional or principled stage of moral development.[34]

An **immoral manager** chooses to behave unethically.

An **amoral manager** fails to consider the ethics of her or his behavior.

A **moral manager** makes ethical behavior a personal goal.

Although it may seem surprising, Carroll suggests that most of us act amorally as managers and in work roles. Although well intentioned, we remain mostly uninformed or undisciplined in considering the ethical aspects of our behavior. Should we just accept this as some natural human tendency? Or is Carroll's observation better considered a call to action—a challenge to seek the moral high ground at work and in our personal lives?

Training in ethical decision making can improve ethical conduct.

Ethics training seeks to help people understand the ethical aspects of decision making and to incorporate high ethical standards into their daily behavior.

It would be nice if people had access through their employers to **ethics training** that helps them understand and best deal with ethical aspects of decision making. Although not all will have this opportunity, more and more are getting it, including college students. Most business schools, for example, now offer required and elective courses on ethics or integrate ethics into courses on other subjects.[35]

One of the biggest differences between facing an ethical dilemma in a training seminar or as part of class discussions is pressure. Many times we must, or believe we must, move fast. Tips to Remember offers a reminder that it often helps to pause and double-check important decisions before taking action in uncomfortable circumstances. It presents a seven-step checklist that is used in some corporate training workshops.

Spotlight questions highlight the risks from public disclosure of one's actions.

Would you agree that the most powerful of the steps in the decision checklist is Step 6? This is what some call the test of the **spotlight questions**. You might think of it as highlighting the risk of public disclosure for your actions. Asking and answering the spotlight questions about how you would feel if family, friends, and role models learn of your actions is a powerful way to test whether a decision is consistent with your ethical standards.[36] By the way, never underestimate the risk of Internet exposure. Hardly a day goes by that we don't hear of someone, even public officials, who are publicly embarrassed to the point of career damage by something they said or photos they posted on the Web.

{ **"HOW WOULD I FEEL IF MY FAMILY FOUND OUT ABOUT MY DECISION?"**

Tips to **Remember**

■ **Checklist for Dealing with Ethical Dilemmas**

Step 1. Recognize the ethical dilemma.
Step 2. Get the facts.
Step 3. Identify your options.
Step 4. Test each option: Is it legal? Is it right? Is it beneficial?
Step 5. Decide which option to follow.
Step 6. Ask spotlight questions to double-check your decision.
Step 7. Take action.

- *"How would I feel if my family found out about my decision?"*
- *"How would I feel if my decision is reported in the local newspaper or posted on the Internet?"*
- *"What would the person I know who has the strongest character and best ethical judgment say about my decision?"*

Protection of whistleblowers can encourage ethical conduct.

Agnes Connolly pressed her employer to report two toxic chemical accidents.

Dave Jones reported that his company was using unqualified suppliers in constructing a nuclear power plant.

Margaret Newsham revealed that her firm allowed workers to do personal business while on government contracts.

Herman Cohen charged that the ASPCA in New York was mistreating animals.

Barry Adams complained that his hospital followed unsafe practices.

Who are these people? They are **whistleblowers**, persons who expose organizational misdeeds to preserve ethical standards and protect against wasteful, harmful, or illegal acts.[37] They were also all fired from their jobs.

Have you ever encountered a student cheating on an exam or homework assignment? If so, did you blow the whistle by informing the instructor? A survey by the Ethics Resource Center reports that some 44% of U.S. workers fail to report the wrongdoings they observe at work. The top reasons for not reporting are "the belief that no corrective action would be taken, and the fear that reports would not be kept confidential."[38]

Whistleblowers take significant career risks when they expose wrongdoing in organizations. Although there are federal and state laws that offer whistleblowers some defense against "retaliatory discharge," the protection is still inadequate overall. Laws vary from state to state, and the federal laws mainly protect government workers. Furthermore, even with legal protection, there are other reasons why potential whistleblowers might hesitate to act.

Another reason we don't hear about more whistleblowing is that the very nature of organizations as power structures creates potential barriers that

Whistleblowers expose misconduct of organizations and their members.

Performance not up to par? Maybe there's not enough women on board.

The consulting firm McKinsey & Company reports that women are hired to fill more than 50% of professional jobs in America's large corporations. But then they start leaking from the career pipeline. They hold 3% of CEO positions, 14% of C-suite jobs, and 28% of director positions on corporate boards. The low percentage of women serving at the top of corporate hierarchy doesn't match well with data showing their presence has a positive performance impact. A Millward Brown Optimor study found that top global companies with women on their boards showed 66% brand growth over a 5-year period, whereas those with no female board members had 6% brand growth. An Ernst & Young study concludes: "having more women at the top improves financial performance." A Catalyst report also points out that gender diversity on corporate boards is linked to more philanthropic giving and more environment-linked social responsibility.

© Trista Weibel/iStockphoto

discourage the practice. A strict chain of command can make it hard to bypass the boss if he or she is the one doing something wrong. Strong work group identities can discourage whistleblowing and encourage loyalty and self-censorship. And, working under conditions of ambiguous priorities can sometimes make it hard to distinguish right from wrong.[39]

||| Formal codes of ethics set standards for ethical conduct.

At Gap Inc., global manufacturing is governed by a formal Code of Vendor Conduct.[40] You'll find statements like these in the code.

- **Discrimination**—"Factories shall employ workers on the basis of their ability to do the job, not on the basis of their personal characteristics or beliefs."
- **Forced labor**—"Factories shall not use any prison, indentured or forced labor."
- **Working conditions**—"Factories must treat all workers with respect and dignity and provide them with a safe and healthy environment."
- **Freedom of association**—"Factories must not interfere with workers who wish to lawfully and peacefully associate, organize or bargain collectively."

A **code of ethics** is a formal statement of values and ethical standards.

Many, if not most, organizations now operate with a **code of ethics** that formally states the values and ethical principles members are expected to display. Some employers even require new hires to sign and agree to their ethics code as a condition of employment. Don't be surprised if you are asked to do this someday. Ethics codes may be specific on how to behave in situations susceptible to ethical dilemmas—such as how sales representatives and purchasing agents should handle giving and receiving gifts. They might also specify consequences for unethical acts like taking bribes and kickbacks.

Ethics codes are common in the complicated world of international business. Global firms like the Gap rely on them where situations such as use of child labor and unfair or unsafe work conditions by contractors are possible and perplexing.[41] Now that corporate executives realize customers and society hold them accountable for the actions of their foreign suppliers, they are much stricter in using ethics codes and policing their international operations.[42]

But don't forget that you have to be careful in expecting too much of ethics codes. They set forth nice standards, but they can't guarantee good conduct.[43] That, we might say, depends once again on employing people with the right moral character and putting them in a work environment where they are led by strong and positive ethics role models.

STUDY GUIDE

Takeaway 3.2
How Can We Maintain High Standards of Ethical Conduct?

Terms to Define

Amoral manager

Code of ethics

Ethical frameworks

Ethics training

Immoral manager

Moral manager

Spotlight questions

Whistleblowers

Rapid Review

- Ethical behavior is influenced by an individual's character and represented by core values and beliefs.
- Kohlberg describes three levels of moral development—preconventional, conventional, and postconventional—with each of us moving step-by-step through the levels as we grow ethically over time.
- Ethics training can help people better understand how to make decisions when dealing with ethical dilemmas at work.
- Whistleblowers who expose the unethical acts of others have incomplete protection from the law and can face organizational penalties.
- All managers are responsible for acting as ethical role models for others.
- Immoral managers choose to behave unethically; amoral managers fail to consider ethics; moral managers make ethics a personal goal.
- Formal codes of conduct spell out the basic ethical expectations of employers regarding the behavior of employees and other contractors.

Questions for Discussion

1. Is it right for organizations to require ethics training of employees?
2. Should whistleblowers have complete protection under the law?
3. Should all managers be evaluated on how well they serve as ethical role models?

Be Sure You Can

- explain how ethical behavior is influenced by personal factors
- list and explain Kohlberg's three levels of moral development
- explain the term "whistleblower"
- list three organizational barriers to whistleblowing
- compare and contrast ethics training, ethics role models, and codes of conduct for their influence on ethics in the workplace
- state the spotlight questions for double-checking the ethics of a decision
- describe differences between the inclinations of amoral, immoral, and moral managers when facing difficult decisions

Career Situation: What Would You Do?

One of your first assignments as a summer intern for a corporate employer is to design an ethics training program for the firm's new hires. Your boss says that the program should familiarize newcomers with the corporate code of ethics. But, it should go beyond this to provide them with a foundation for handling ethical dilemmas in a confident and moral way. What will your lesson plan for the training program look like?

TEACHING NOTE:
Ask students to quickly go online and find an example of how a company evaluates itself in its social responsibility report. After discussion, turn to the question: what aspects of social responsibility can and should be measured?

Takeaway 3.3
What Should We Know About the Social Responsibilities of Organizations?

ANSWERS TO COME

- Social responsibility is an organization's obligation to best serve society.
- Scholars argue cases for and against corporate social responsibility.
- Shared value integrates corporate social responsibility into business strategy.
- Social businesses and social entrepreneurs are driven by social responsibility.
- Social responsibility audits measure the social performance of organizations.
- Sustainability is an important social responsibility goal.

Stakeholders are people and institutions most directly affected by an organization's performance.

THE ORGANIZATIONS, GROUPS, AND PERSONS WITH WHOM AN ORGANIZATION interacts and conducts business are known as its **stakeholders** because they have a direct "stake" or interest in its performance. They are affected in one way or another by what the organization does and how it performs. As **Figure 3.4** shows, the stakeholders include customers, suppliers, competitors, regulators, investors/owners, and employees, as well as future generations.

Importantly, an organization's stakeholders can have different interests. Customers typically want value prices and quality products; owners want profits as returns on their investments; suppliers want long-term business relationships; communities want good corporate citizenship and support for public services; employees want good wages, benefits, security, and satisfaction in their work.

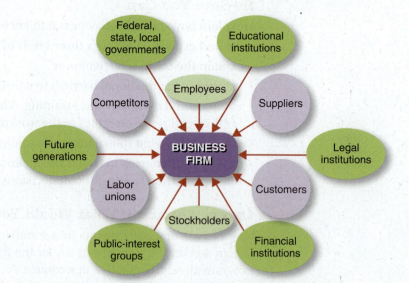

FIGURE 3.4 Who Are the Stakeholders of Organizations?
Stakeholders are the individuals, groups, and other organizations that have a direct interest in how well an organization performs. A basic list of stakeholders for any organization would begin with the employees and contractors who work for the organization, customers and clients who consume the goods and services, suppliers of needed resources, owners who invest capital, regulators in the form of government agencies, and special-interest groups such as community members and activists.

⫼ Social responsibility is an organization's obligation to best serve society.

The way organizations behave in relationship with their many stakeholders is a good indicator of their underlying ethical characters. When we talk about the "good" and the "bad" in business and societal relationships, **corporate social responsibility** is at issue. Often called CSR, it is defined as an obligation of the organization to act in ways that serve both its own interests and the interests of its stakeholders, representing society at large.

Even though corporate "irresponsibility" seems to get most of the media's attention, we can't forget that a lot of responsible behavior is taking place as well. Increasingly this has become part of what is called the **triple bottom line**—how well an organization performs when measured not only on financial criteria but also on social and environmental ones. Some call this triple bottom line the **3 Ps of organizational performance**—profit, people, and planet.[44] The triple bottom line in business decision making is checked by asking these questions: Profit—Is the decision economically sound? People—Is the decision socially responsible? Planet—Is the decision environmentally sound?

Showing CSR and concerns for the triple bottom line is most likely the way you'd like your future employers to behave. "Students nowadays want to work for companies that help enhance the quality of life in their surrounding community," says an observer.[45] In one survey, 70% of students report that "a company's reputation and ethics" was "very important" when deciding whether or not to accept a job offer; in another survey, 79% of 13- to 25-year-olds say they "want to work for a company that cares about how it affects or contributes to society."[46]

Corporate social responsibility is the obligation of an organization to serve its own interests and those of its stakeholders.

The **triple bottom line** of organizational performance includes financial, social, and environmental criteria.

The **3 Ps of organizational performance** are profit, people, and planet.

Jodi Hilton/The New York Times /Redux Pictures

{ "OFFER A PURE AND HEALTHY PRODUCT THAT TASTES GOOD AND EARN A PROFIT WITHOUT HARMING THE ENVIRONMENT."

Role Models

■ Gary Hirshberg Goes for Triple Bottom Line at Stonyfield Farm

President, CEO, and co-founder of Stonyfield Farm, Gary Hirshberg, makes a career out of organic yogurt. He's also a firm believer that "business is the most powerful force in the world." Considered a social entrepreneur, Hirshberg has always been at the forefront of movements for environmental and social transformation. He studied climate change at Hampshire College, built energy-producing windmills, and worked at a nonprofit research center.

At Stonyfield Farm he's helping craft a clear mission: "Offer a pure and healthy product that tastes good and earn a profit without harming the environment." Indeed, Hirshberg says "we factor the planet into all of our decisions."

Stonyfield Farm focuses on the triple bottom line of being economically, socially, and environmentally responsible—

what some call profit, people, and planet. "It's a simple strategy but a powerful one," says Hirshberg proudly. "Going green is not just the right thing to do, but a great way to build a successful business." His results speak for themselves. Stonyfield Farm is now the number-one maker of organic yogurt in the world.

WHAT'S THE LESSON HERE?

Granted, Stonyfield Farm has succeeded with Hirshberg's social business model and a commitment to the three Ps of profit, people, and planet. But can something like this be done only when starting a firm from scratch? Can an existing firm be turned in this direction? What does it take to lead organizations with a commitment to ethics and social responsibility?

‖ Scholars argue cases for and against corporate social responsibility.

It may seem that corporate social responsibility, or CSR, is one of those concepts and goals that most everyone agrees on. There are, however, two contrasting views that stimulate debate in academic and public-policy circles. The classical view takes a stand against making corporate social responsibility a business priority, whereas the socioeconomic view advocates for it.[47]

The **classical view of CSR** holds that management's only responsibility in running a business is to maximize profits and shareholder value. It puts the focus on the single bottom line of financial performance. In other words: "The business of business is business." This narrow stakeholder perspective is represented in the views of the late Milton Friedman, a respected economist and Nobel Laureate. He says: "Few trends could so thoroughly undermine the very foundations of our free society as the acceptance by corporate officials of social responsibility other than to make as much money for their stockholders as possible."[48]

The arguments against corporate social responsibility include fears that its pursuit will reduce business profits, raise business costs, dilute business purpose, and give business too much social power. Yet events such as the huge BP oil spill in the Gulf of Mexico seem to argue otherwise. The public was outraged about the oil spill. Demands were quickly made for stronger government oversight and control over corporate practices such as deepwater oil drilling that might put our natural world at risk.

The **socioeconomic view of CSR** holds that management of any organization should be concerned for the broader social welfare, not just corporate profits. This broad stakeholder perspective puts the focus on the expanded triple bottom line of not just financial performance, such as shareholder returns, but also social and environmental performance. It is supported by Paul Samuelson, another distinguished economist and also a Nobel laureate.

Those in favor of corporate social responsibility argue that it will add long-run profits for businesses, improve their public images, and help them avoid government regulation. They believe that because businesses often have vast resources with the potential for great social impact, business executives have ethical obligations to ensure that their firms act in socially responsible ways. And, researchers are finding it hard to argue that social responsibility will hurt the financial bottom line.[49] A worst-case scenario seems to be no adverse impact. The best-case scenario is a **virtuous circle**, where corporate social responsibility leads to improved financial performance that leads to more socially responsible actions in the future.[50]

‖ Shared value integrates corporate social responsibility into business strategy.

What's your position on these alternative views of corporate social responsibility? More and more today you will find people arguing that businesses have an obligation to "give back" to society. This means doing more than offering useful products and services and providing jobs. It means that businesses should balance the pursuit of profit with genuine contributions to the public good.

The **classical view of CSR** is that business should focus on the pursuit of profits.

The **socioeconomic view of CSR** is that businesses should focus on contributions to society, not just making profits.

A **virtuous circle** exists when corporate social responsibility leads to improved financial performance that leads to more social responsibility.

"Business Education Must Reframe The 'Winner Takes All' Mentality"

Business School Students Challenged to Serve the Greater Good

She didn't fit the stereotype—visiting Afghanistan, Pakistan, Ethiopia, Zambia, and more. But when Carolyn Y. Woo was dean of the Mendoza College of Business at the University of Notre Dame, she was a dean with a purpose. She says "a true business education must ultimately engage and enlighten students," causing them to "feel a sense of urgency that the collective good of society depends on them."

Anton Oparin / Shutterstock

Dr. Woo, now president and CEO of Catholic Relief Services, believes that "Business is a necessary good, not a tolerated evil" . . . "corporate social responsibility is no longer exogenous to business" . . . "business education must reframe the 'winner takes all' mentality." She points to the U.N. Global compact as an exemplar of values that should guide business behavior. The compact focuses attention on human rights (protect rights and avoid abuses), labor (uphold free association and eliminate slave labor, child labor, and discrimination), environment (act responsibly and use environmentally friendly technologies), and corruption (work against it in all forms).

Find Inspiration

Dr. Woo says that business can be a force for the better or worse in society. Can you describe recent examples or situations from your experiences that would fit in the "best" and "worst" categories? What does she mean by saying business students should abandon the "winner takes all" mentality? Is it possible for an undergraduate business education to shift student mindsets in this direction?

This thinking is consistent with the notion of **shared value** advocated by Michael Porter and Mark Kramer.[51] They say: "The purpose of a corporation must be redefined as creating shared value, not just profit per se."[52] Their point is that executives can and should make business decisions with full understanding that economic gains and social progress are fundamentally interconnected. In other words, businesses can make profits while striving to do good and overcome social ills such as pollution, poverty, illiteracy, and disease.

One of the problems with the pro and con CSR debate is that it pits the interests of shareholders and owners against other stakeholders in win-lose fashion. Instead, the notion of shared value takes a win-win perspective. Another problem is that even when CSR is made a priority it becomes more of an add-on initiative than a strategically integrated one. Activities like local philanthropy and environment projects may end up serving mainly reputational and branding goals for the firm. Instead, the notion of shared value integrates social contribution into corporate strategy.

Shared value approaches business decisions with understanding that economic gains and social progress are interconnected.

Business decisions in the shared value model are made so that economic value is created by pursuing social value. Business advantage is found by aligning practices and strategies with social contributions. Think of it in terms of examples.[53]

- Len Sauers, Procter & Gamble's vice president of global sustainability, says that reducing waste is a top priority and that doing so "almost always results in cost savings."
- Nestlé pushes local sourcing and supports rural businesses near its factories. This reduces distribution costs and ensures supplies of high-quality products.
- IBM found a new market when it realized cities could benefit from more integrated computer systems and analytics. It started a "Smarter Cities" business to help cities use IBM technologies to solve problems with traffic flows, public health, schools, housing, and crime.

Manager's **Library**

CAN BUSINESS LEADERS COMMIT TO STAKEHOLDER SERVICE?

In the aftermath of the global financial crisis, business and capitalism have come in for lots of criticism. Does that mean they are fundamentally bad for society? Not at all! state John Mackey and Raj Sisodia in their book *Conscious Capitalism: Liberating the Heroic Spirit of Business* (Harvard Business Review Press, 2013). In fact, they argue just the opposite: business and capitalism are fundamentally good. But, they also add that it's the job of business leaders to make sure things turn out that way.

Mackey and Sisodia's book was called "chicken soup for the Davos soul" by *The Wall Street Journal*—a reference to the annual global economic forum in Davos, Switzerland, where economic ideas are presented and debated. The concept behind the acclaim is "conscious capitalism," described by the authors as capitalism pursued by leaders who understand that business can create lots of value for society, act ethically, and help people and communities gain prosperity.

The key to conscious capitalism is for the business leader to understand that the needs of all stakeholders must be considered and that the purpose of the business has to go beyond just making profit for the owners. As Mackey, CEO founder of

Whole Foods Market, and Sisodia, Bentley College marketing professor, say: "When any profession becomes primarily about making money, it starts to lose its true identity and its interests start to diverge from what is good for society."

When businesses do the right things, Mackey and Sisodia believe capitalism becomes "heroic" by achieving societal impact that does good for people, planet, and environment. But to get there, business leaders must achieve their own states of consciousness and be "primarily motivated by service to the purposes of the business and its stakeholders, and not by the pursuit of power and personal enrichment."

REFLECT AND REACT

Does this concept of conscious capitalism sound a lot like "shared value"? Is this a book that you might like to read to learn more about how businesses can do good for society, or even to help you pick a good employer someday? If you look into Mackey's approach to Whole Foods Market—things like capping executive pay at 19 times that of the average worker— does he seem to live up to the standards set in this book? And how about your academic program, is it designed to help students become conscious business leaders of the future?

⦀ Social business and social entrepreneurs are driven by social responsibility.

Muhammad Yunus won a Nobel prize for his pioneering work in Bangladesh creating the Grameen Bank.[54] At one level it was a business innovation—bringing microcredit lending into the forefront. But at another level it is a **social business** in that the underlying business model directly addresses a social problem—using microcredit lending to help fight poverty. And in the expanding domain of social business, Yunus's ideas and examples have set benchmarks.

Social businesses are profit driven. But, instead of the profits being returned to investors or owners, they are used to pay off initial start-up costs and then reinvested to expand the social business to serve more clients and customers. These businesses are developed by **social entrepreneurs**, people who take business risk with the goal of finding novel ways to solve pressing social problems at home and abroad.[55] Social entrepreneurs are like business entrepreneurs with one big difference: They are driven by a social mission, not financial gain.[56] They pursue original thinking and innovations to help solve social problems and make lives better for people who are disadvantaged.

You'll be hearing and reading a lot more about social businesses and social entrepreneurs. They are already being called the new "fourth sector" of our

A **social business** is one in which the underlying business model directly addresses a social problem.

Social entrepreneurs take business risks to find novel ways to solve pressing social problems.

economy—joining private for-profit businesses, public government organizations, and nonprofits.[57] As the late management guru Peter Drucker once said: "Every single social and global issue of our day is a business opportunity in disguise."[58]

Housing and job training for the homeless . . . Bringing technology to poor families . . . Improving literacy among disadvantaged youth . . . Bringing expanded healthcare to impoverished communities . . . and more. What wonderful possibilities. Could social business and social entrepreneurship be part of your future some day?

Social Entrepreneur Finds Unique Way to Fight Hunger at Home

Step up to the counter at Denise Cerreta's restaurant—the One World Café—in Salt Lake City, and you will be asked a question: "How much would you like to pay?" This is her novel approach to combating hunger. The menu shows a suggested price, but people can pay more . . . or less . . . or they can do volunteer work for the price of the meal. When Cerreta started the practice, she was in debt, and her restaurant was struggling. Now she's out of debt and has started the One World Everybody Eats Foundation. It is devoted to opening similar eateries around the country—at least 30 so far. Cerreta says: "What these restaurants are doing is building a sense of community. Once you have that, you're not going to let your neighbor suffer. And from that point, all sorts of good things happen."

Douglas C. Pizac / AP

‖ Social responsibility audits measure the social performance of organizations.

If we are to get serious about social responsibility, we need to get rigorous about measuring corporate social performance and holding business leaders accountable for the results. A **social responsibility audit** can be used at regular intervals to report on and systematically assess an organization's performance in various areas of corporate social responsibility.

The social performance of business firms varies along a continuum that ranges from compliance—acting to avoid adverse consequences, to conviction—acting to create positive impact.[59] As shown in the figure, an audit of corporate social performance might cover the organization's performance on four criteria for evaluating socially responsible practices: economic, legal, ethical, and discretionary.[60]

An organization is meeting its economic responsibility when it earns a profit through the provision of goods and services desired by customers. Although it might seem unusual to focus on financial performance as a component of CSR, a firm's economic performance provides the foundation on which all the other types of responsibility rest. If a firm is not financially viable, it will not be able to take care of its owners or employees or engage in any of the other aspects of CSR. Legal responsibility is fulfilled when an organization operates within the law and according to the requirements of various external regulations. An organization meets its ethical responsibility when its

A **social responsibility audit** measures and reports on an organization's performance in various areas of corporate social responsibility.

Zone of Compliance		Zone of Conviction	
Economic Responsibility: *Be Profitable*	Legal Responsibility: *Obey the Law*	Ethical Responsibility: *Do What Is Right*	Discretionary Responsibility: *Contribute to Community*

{ AFTER INVESTING IN CRADLE-TO-GRAVE MANUFACTURING, THE FIRM EXPERIENCED "SO MUCH INNOVATION THAT WE SAW A SWIFT PAY OUT."

Ethics Check

■ Signing on to a Green Supply Chain

It's called "cradle-to-grave manufacturing," and you might wonder why more companies aren't involved. The basic principle is that you must start with nonhazardous materials and then build products that are disassembled at the end of their lives to become biodegradable waste or new products.

The approach was adopted by Stef Kranendijk, CEO of Desso, a carpet manufacturer, when he set new sustainability goals for the firm. He saw it as a potential stimulus to innovation and a way to differentiate his company from the competition. In his words: "We launched it as a design and quality initiative that would boost our innovation capability with positive effects on the environment and public health."

The pathways to cradle-to-grave manufacturing aren't easy. Shareholders and owners have to agree on the goals and benefits; suppliers have to join in the quest for sustainable materials; designs have to be created to meet the end-of-product-life goals.

But Kranendijk found that Desso's employees were highly supportive and reported increased satisfaction. He also said the firm experienced "so much innovation that we saw a swift pay out."

YOU DECIDE

Desso's commitment to cradle-to-grave manufacturing requires lots of investment, both monetary and otherwise, from the manufacturer and its supply chain members. But is it ethical for a business to turn its back on such possibilities? Should we as consumers push for these types of sustainability initiatives? Or, is it unethical to try to force businesses to pursue green goals before the market as a whole does it for us? And while you are thinking about the issues, is it ethical to claim social responsibility for pursuing environmentally friendly practices only to avoid government regulation or adverse publicity? In other words, does it make a difference if a firm does "good things" for selfish reasons?

---

actions voluntarily conform not only to legal expectations but also to the broader values and moral expectations of society.

The highest level of social performance comes through the satisfaction of discretionary responsibility. At this level, the organization moves beyond basic economic, legal, and ethical expectations to provide leadership in advancing the well-being of individuals, communities, and society as a whole. An example is found at the Bellisio Foods plant in Jackson, Ohio, where manager Ryan Wright has found a number of ways to "green up" manufacturing. A large treatment plant digests food waste and uses bio-organisms to create methane for fuel to run the factory's boilers. The process cuts CO_2 output by saving on costs of natural gas and transporting waste to a landfill. Although the price of the system was $4.65 million, Wright says: "It's a great project; we're proud of it; it's the right thing to do."[61]

||| Sustainability is an important social responsibility goal.

Think about the issues of our day—things like resource scarcity, climate change, carbon footprints, and alternative energy. Think about popular terms and slogans—ones like renew, recycle, conserve, and preserve. They all reflect the importance of **sustainability** as a goal, one that addresses the rights of present and future generations as stakeholders of the world's natural resources.

"With a global population at 6.5 billion," Gavin Neath, vice president for Unilever, says, "we are already consuming resources at a rate far in excess of nature's capacity to replenish them. Water is becoming scarce and global warming and climate change are accelerating."[62] Little wonder that 93% of CEOs in a recent survey admit

Sustainability is a goal that addresses the rights of present and future generations as costakeholders of present-day natural resources.

that the future success of their firms depends in part on how well they meet sustainability challenges.[63] And as United Nations General Secretary Ban Ki-moon says, "It means thinking differently about how and where we invest, thinking differently about creating markets of the future, and creating opportunities for growth."[64]

Sustainable Business and Sustainable Development

The prior points and ideas introduce the notion of **sustainable business**, where firms operate in ways that both meet the needs of customers and protect or advance the well-being of our natural environment.[65] A sustainable business operates in harmony with nature rather than by exploiting nature. Its actions produce minimum negative impact on the environment and help preserve it for future generations. The hallmarks of sustainable business practices include less waste, less toxic materials, more resource efficiency, more energy efficiency, and more renewable energy.

> **Sustainable business** is where firms operate in ways that both meet the needs of customers and protect or advance the well-being of our natural environment.

If sustainability is a business goal, just what is **sustainable development**? The World Business Council for Sustainable Development, whose membership includes the CEOs of global corporations, defines it as "forms of progress that meet the needs of the present without compromising the ability of future generations to meet their needs."[66]

> **Sustainable development** is making use of natural resources to meet today's needs while also preserving and protecting the environment for use by future generations.

A useful term in sustainable development is **environmental capital** or **natural capital.** It refers to the available storehouse of natural resources that exist in the atmosphere, land, water, and minerals that we use to sustain life and produce goods and services for society.[67] The importance of environmental capital is reflected in **ISO 14001**, a global quality standard that requires certified organizations to set environmental objectives and targets; account for the environmental impact of their activities, products, or services; and continuously improve environmental performance.[68]

> **Environmental capital** or **natural capital** is the storehouse of natural resources—atmosphere, land, water, and minerals—that we use to sustain life and produce goods and services for society.

The conversation about sustainable development stands at the interface between how people live and how organizations operate, and the capacity of the natural environment to support them. We want prosperity, convenience, comfort, and luxury in our everyday lives. But we are also more aware that attention must be given to the "costs" of these aspirations and how those costs can be borne in a way that doesn't impair the future. At PepsiCo, for example, CEO Indra Nooyi has said that her firm's "real profit" should be assessed as: Revenue less Cost of Goods Sold less Costs to Society. "All corporations operate with a license from society," says Nooyi. "It's critically important that we take that responsibility very, very seriously; we have to make sure that what corporations do doesn't add costs to society."[69]

> **ISO 14001** is a global quality standard that certifies organizations that set environmental objectives and targets, account for the environmental impact of their activities, and continuously improve environmental performance.

Human Sustainability

The notion of sustainability and the pursuit of sustainable development goals can be made much broader than a focus on the natural environment alone. Scholar Jeffrey Pfeffer offers a strong case in favor of giving management attention not only to issues of ecological and environmental sustainability—traditional green management themes—but also to social and human sustainability. He says: "Just as there is concern for protecting natural resources, there could be a similar level of concern for protecting human resources. . . . Being a socially responsible business ought to encompass the effect of management practices on employee physical and psychological well-being."[70] You might think of Pfeffer's point this way: While valuing the "planet," don't forget that "people" are also part of the 3 Ps of organizational performance.

STUDY GUIDE

Takeaway 3.3
What Should We Know About the Social Responsibilities of Organizations?

Terms to Define

Classical view of CSR

Corporate social responsibility

Environmental capital or natural capital

ISO 14001

Shared value

Social business

Social entrepreneurs

Social responsibility audit

Socioeconomic view of CSR

Stakeholders

Sustainability

Sustainable business

Sustainable development

Three Ps of organizational performance

Triple bottom line

Virtuous circle

Rapid Review

- Corporate social responsibility is an obligation of the organization to act in ways that serve both its own interests and the interests of its stakeholders.
- In assessing organizational performance today, the concept of the triple bottom line evaluates how well organizations are doing on economic, social, and environmental performance criteria.
- Criteria for evaluating corporate social performance include how well it meets economic, legal, ethical, and discretionary responsibilities.
- The argument against corporate social responsibility says that businesses should focus on making profits; the argument for corporate social responsibility says that businesses should use their resources to serve broader social concerns.
- The concept of sustainable development refers to making use of environmental resources to support societal needs today while also preserving and protecting the environment for use by future generations.
- Social businesses and social entrepreneurs pursue business models that help to directly address important social problems.

Questions for Discussion

1. Choose an organization in your community. What questions would you ask to complete an audit of its social responsibility practices?
2. Is the logic of the virtuous circle a convincing argument in favor of corporate social responsibility?
3. Should government play a stronger role in making sure organizations commit to sustainable development?

Be Sure You Can

- explain the concept of social responsibility
- summarize arguments for and against corporate social responsibility
- illustrate how the virtuous circle of corporate social responsibility might work
- explain the notion of social business

Career Situation: What Would You Do?

It's debate time, and you've been given the task of defending corporate social responsibility. Make a list of all possible arguments for making CSR an important goal for any organization. For each item on the list, find a good current example that confirms its importance based on real events. In what order of priority will you present your arguments in the debate? And, what arguments "against" CSR will you be prepared to defend against?

TestPrep 3

Answers to TestPrep questions can be found at the back of the book.

Multiple-Choice Questions

1. A business owner makes a decision to reduce a plant's workforce by 10% to cut costs and be able to save jobs for the other 90% of employees. This decision could be justified as ethical by using the _____ approach to moral reasoning.
   - (a) utilitarian
   - (b) individualism
   - (c) justice
   - (d) moral rights

2. If a manager fails to enforce a late-to-work policy for all workers—that is, by allowing some favored employees to arrive late without penalties—this would be considered a violation of _____.
   - (a) human rights
   - (b) personal values
   - (c) distributive justice
   - (d) cultural relativism

3. According to research on ethics in the workplace, _____ is/are often a major and frequent source of pressures that create ethical dilemmas for people in their jobs.
   - (a) Declining morals in society
   - (b) Long work hours
   - (c) Low pay
   - (d) Requests or demands from bosses

4. Someone who exposes the ethical misdeeds of others in an organization is usually called a/an _____.
   - (a) whistleblower
   - (b) ethics advocate
   - (c) ombudsman
   - (d) stakeholder

5. Two employees are talking about ethics in their workplaces. Jay says that ethics training and codes of ethical conduct are worthless; Maura says they are the only ways to ensure ethical behavior by all employees. Who is right, and why?
   - (a) Jay—no one really cares about ethics at work.
   - (b) Maura—only the organization can influence ethical behavior.
   - (c) Neither Jay nor Maura—training and codes can encourage but never guarantee ethical behavior.
   - (d) Neither Jay nor Maura—only the threat of legal punishment will make people act ethically.

6. Which ethical position has been criticized as a source of "ethical imperialism"?
   - (a) Individualism
   - (b) Absolutism
   - (c) Utilitarianism
   - (d) Relativism

7. If a manager takes a lot of time explaining to a subordinate why he did not get a promotion and sincerely listens to his concerns, this is an example of an attempt to act ethically according to _____ justice.
   - (a) utilitarian
   - (b) commutative
   - (c) interactional
   - (d) universal

8. At what Kohlberg calls the _____ level of moral development, an individual can be expected to act consistent with peers, meet obligations, and follow rules of social conduct.
   - (a) postconventional
   - (b) conventional
   - (c) preconventional
   - (d) nonconventional

9. In respect to the link between bad management and ethical behavior, research shows that _____.
   - (a) managers who set unrealistic goals can cause unethical behavior
   - (b) most whistleblowers just want more pay
   - (c) only top managers really serve as ethics role models
   - (d) a good code of ethics makes up for any management deficiencies

10. A person's desires for a comfortable life and family security represent _____ values, whereas his or her desires to be honest and hard working represent _____ values.
   - (a) terminal; instrumental
   - (b) instrumental; terminal
   - (c) universal; individual
   - (d) individual; universal

11. A proponent of the classical view of corporate social responsibility would most likely agree with which of these statements?

   (a) Social responsibility improves the public image of business.
   (b) The primary responsibility of business is to maximize profits.
   (c) By acting responsibly, businesses avoid government regulation.
   (d) Businesses should do good while they are doing business.

12. The triple bottom line of organizational performance would include measures of financial, social, and _____ performance.

   (a) philanthropic   (b) environmental
   (c) legal   (d) economic

13. An amoral manager _____.

   (a) always acts in consideration of ethical issues
   (b) chooses to behave unethically
   (c) makes ethics a personal goal
   (d) acts unethically but does so unintentionally

14. In a social responsibility audit of a business firm, positive behaviors meeting which of the following criteria would measure the highest level of commitment to socially responsible practices?

   (a) Legal—obeying the law
   (b) Economic—earning a profit
   (c) Discretionary—contributing to community
   (d) Ethical—doing what is right

15. What organizational stakeholder would most likely get top priority attention if a corporate board is having a serious discussion regarding how the firm could fulfill its obligations in respect to sustainable development?

   (a) Owners or investors
   (b) Customers
   (c) Suppliers
   (d) Future generations

Short-Response Questions

16. How does distributive justice differ from procedural justice?

17. What are the three spotlight questions that people can use for double-checking the ethics of a decision?

18. If someone commits an unethical act, how can he or she rationalize it to make it seem right?

19. What is the virtuous circle of corporate social responsibility?

Integration and Application Questions

20. A small outdoor clothing company in the United States has just received an attractive proposal from a business in Tanzania to manufacture the work gloves that it sells. Accepting the offer from the Tanzanian firm would allow for substantial cost savings compared to the current supplier. However, the American firm's manager has recently read reports that some businesses in Tanzania are forcing people to work in unsafe conditions in order to keep their costs down. The manager is now seeking your help in clarifying the ethical aspects of this opportunity.

Question: How would you describe to this manager his or her alternatives in terms of cultural relativism and moral absolutism? What would you identify as the major issues and concerns in terms of the cultural relativism position versus the absolutist position? Finally, what action would you recommend in this situation, and why?

Steps*for* FurtherLearning

BUILD MARKETABLE SKILLS
DO A CASE ANALYSIS
GET AND STAY INFORMED

BUILD
MARKETABLE SKILLS.
EARN BIG CAREER
PAYOFFS!

Don't miss these
opportunities in the
**Skill-Building
Portfolio**

■ **SELF-ASSESSMENT 3:**
Terminal Values

*Values count and values
differ … what do you hold as
important?*

■ **CLASS EXERCISE 3:**
**Confronting Ethical
Dilemmas**

*No one can predict when a
dilemma will hit … now is a
good time to test your ethics.*

■ **TEAM PROJECT 3:**
**Organizational Commitment
to Sustainability**

*Sustainability is easy to talk
about … it can be hard to
measure how well organizations
really do.*

> **Many
> learning
> resources are
> found at the end
> of the book and
> online within
> WileyPLUS.**

Take advantage of **Cases for Critical Thinking**

■ **CHAPTER 3 CASE SNAPSHOT:**
*Patagonia: Leading a Green Revolution /
Sidebar on Philanthrocapitalism*

Patagonia has managed to stay both green and profitable even when the economy is down, consumers are tight for cash, and "doing the profitable thing" is not necessarily doing the right thing. How has Patagonia achieved its success without compromising its ideals? A look to the firm's founder, Yvon Chouinard, provides lots of insight. Patagonia succeeds by staying true to his vision. Chouinard is committed to having a successful outdoor clothing company that is steadfastly committed to environmental sustainability. And he's been consistently on target. "They've become the Rolls-Royce of their product category," says one industry analyst. "When people were stepping back, and the industry became copycat, Chouinard didn't sell out, lower prices, and dilute the brand. Sometimes, the less you do, the more provocative and true of a leader you are."

DO
A CASE ANALYSIS.
STRENGTHEN YOUR
CRITICAL THINKING!

Dig into this **Hot Topic**

■ **GOOD RESULT OR NOT?** **Sustainability ranks
low among chief executive challenges**

A global poll of 729 business leaders by the Conference Board asked them to rank the top ten challenges facing them in the year ahead. The results showed the top four concerns in order were 1—human capital, 2—operational excellence, 3—innovation, and 4—customer relationships. The bottom three challenges in order of importance were 8—corporate brand and reputation, 9—sustainability, and 10—trust in business. Are these results reassuring in terms of sustainability values and practices by global business leaders or troubling?

GET
AND STAY INFORMED.
MAKE YOURSELF
VALUABLE!

Those finding these results reassuring are likely to say: "This shows confidence that sustainability issues are under control" … "We don't need to think that sustainability is a crisis concern anymore" … "It's good that trust and reputation are considered solid and not problematical for these business leaders." *Those finding these results troubling are likely to say:* "It's clear that sustainability isn't a front-runner goal in the executive suite" … "The executives don't seem to view business reputation and sustainability as pathways to profits" … "The lack of attention to trust in the eyes of stakeholders shows arrogance and a disconcerting disconnect with society."

Final Take How do you read these data and their implications for how global businesses behave? Is it time to recognize that sustainability is firmly attached to executive priorities and basically secure as a corporate value? Or, are we seeing here that much of the sustainability talk is just that—"talk," and that the issues of sustainability, reputation, and trust are still not getting the attention they deserve?

Estamos bien en el refugio–los 33. For 69 days shift leader Luis Urzúa kept the men trapped in the Chilean mine organized and hopeful. On the 70th day, he was the last man safely out.

Managers as Decision Makers

4

There Is No Substitute for a Good Decision

Dreamworks/Photofest

Self-Confidence and *Red Eye*

Things get hectic in *Red Eye* when the Lux Atlantic Hotel manager Lisa Reisert (Rachel McAdams) is away attending her grandmother's funeral. Her assistant, Cynthia (Jayma Mays), proves unable to handle a series of problems that arise. So, she calls Reisert who is en route to the airport for a return flight to Miami. Reisert calmly talks Cynthia through the handling of a deleted reservation for frequent guests, identifies another issue as a nonproblem, and gives details for handling a high-security guest who is arriving 12 hours early.

Clearly, Reisert is confident in her abilities and can deal with multiple issues even under pressure. This confidence comes into play later in the movie when she develops a strategy to defeat a terrorist who wants to use her to threaten the high-security guest.

How is it that some managers always seem to make the right moves while others cave in at the slightest sign of trouble? One key difference may be **self-confidence**. Really good managers believe in their decisions and the information foundations for them.

The many topics in this chapter can improve your decision-making skills. A better understanding of your personal style in gathering and processing information can also help build your self-confidence as a decision maker.

YOUR CHAPTER 4 TAKEAWAYS

1. Recognize how managers use information to solve problems.

2. Identify five steps in the decision-making process.

3. Understand current issues in managerial decision making.

WHAT'S INSIDE

Explore Yourself
More on **self-confidence**

Role Models
Indra Nooyi leads Pepsico through uncertainty and risk

Ethics Check
Left to die on Mt. Everest

Facts to Consider
American workers talk about their biggest fears

Manager's Library
The Shallows: What the Internet is Doing to Our Brains by Nicholas Carr

Takeaway 4.1
How Do Managers Use Information to Solve Problems?

ANSWERS TO COME

- Managers use technological, informational, and analytical competencies to solve problems.
- Managers deal with problems posing threats and offering opportunities.
- Managers can be problem avoiders, problem solvers, or problem seekers.
- Managers make programmed and nonprogrammed decisions when solving problems.
- Managers can use both systematic and intuitive thinking.
- Managers use different cognitive styles to process information for decision making.
- Managers make decisions under conditions of certainty, risk, and uncertainty.

WHEN THE SAN JOSÉ COPPER AND GOLD MINE COLLAPSED IN CHILE; 32 MINERS, along with their shift leader, Luis Urzúa, were trapped inside.[1] "The most difficult moment was when the air cleared and we saw the rock," said Urzúa, "I had thought maybe it was going to be a day or two days, but not when I saw the rock . . ." In fact, the miners were trapped 2,300 feet below the surface for 69 days. Their plight caught the attention of the entire world. After the rescue shaft was completed, Urzúa was the last man out. "The job was hard," he said, "they were days of great pain and sorrow." But the decisions Urzúa made as shift leader—organizing the miners into work shifts, keeping them busy, studying mine diagrams, making escape plans, raising morale—all contributed to the successful rescue. After embracing Urzúa when he arrived at the surface, Chile's President Sebastian Pinera said, "He was a shift boss who made us proud."

Most managers will never have to face such an extreme crisis, but decision making and problem solving are parts of every manager's job. Not all decisions are going to be easy ones; some will have to be made under tough conditions, and not all decisions will turn out right. But as with the case of Urzúa, the goal is to do the best you can under the circumstances.

⦀ Managers use technological, informational, and analytical competencies to solve problems.

All those case studies, experiential exercises, class discussions, and even essay exam questions are intended to engage students in the complexities of managerial decision making, the potential problems and pitfalls, and even the pressures of crisis situations. From the classroom forward, however, it's all up to you. Only you can determine whether you step ahead and make the best of very difficult problems or collapse under pressure.

Problem solving is the process of identifying a discrepancy between an actual and a desired state of affairs and then taking action to resolve it. The context for managerial problem solving is depicted in **Figure 4.1**. It shows why managers fit the definition of **knowledge workers**, persons whose value to organizations rests with their intellectual, not physical, capabilities.[2]

Problem solving involves identifying and taking action to resolve problems.

Knowledge workers add value to organizations through their intellectual capabilities.

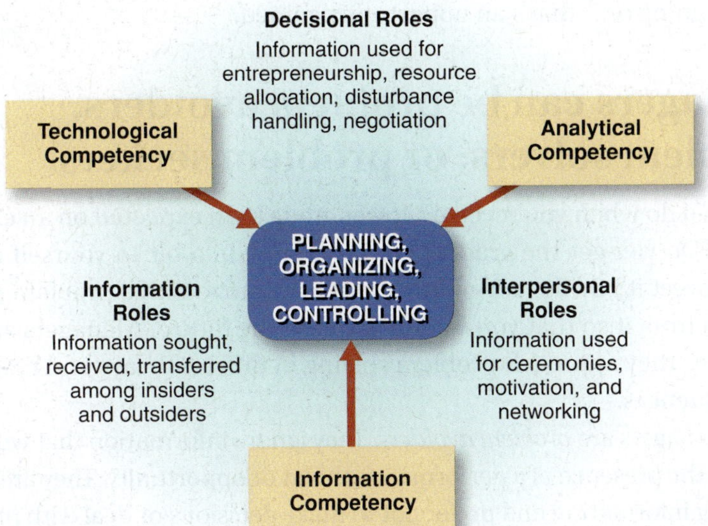

FIGURE 4.1

In What Ways Do Managers Serve as Information Nerve Centers in Organizations? Managers sit at the center of complex networks of information flows; they serve as information-processing hubs or nerve centers. Each of the management functions—planning, organizing, leading, and controlling—requires the gathering, use, and transfer of information in these networks. Managers must have the information competencies needed to perform well in these roles.

All managers continually solve problems as they gather, give, receive, and process information from many sources. In fact, your career and personal success increasingly requires three "must-have" competencies. **Technological competency** is the ability to understand new technologies and use them to their best advantage. In many ways this involves moving skills we already use in everyday personal affairs—social media, Internet, smart devices—into work-related applications. **Information competency** is the ability to locate, retrieve, organize, and display information of potential value to decision making and problem solving. This means, for example, not just getting information from hearsay or off the Internet; it means locating credible and valuable information. **Analytical competency** is the ability to evaluate and analyze information to make actual decisions and solve real problems.[3] This involves being able to digest and sort through information, even very large amounts of data, and then use it well to make good decisions that solve real problems How about it—are you ready?

Technological competency is the ability to understand new technologies and to use them to their best advantage.

Information competency is the ability to gather and use information to solve problems.

Analytical competency is the ability to evaluate and analyze information to make actual decisions and solve real problems.

‖ Managers deal with problems posing threats and offering opportunities.

The most obvious problem-solving situation for managers, or anyone for that matter, is a **performance threat**. This occurs as an actual or potential performance deficiency. Something is wrong or is likely to be wrong in the near future. Hurricane Katrina is an example worth remembering. There were lots of warnings about this storm, but many underestimated or were either ambivalent or overconfident in preparing for it. Too many people weren't ready when Katrina slammed into New Orleans, and a high price was paid for their errors.

A **performance threat** is a situation where something is wrong or likely to be wrong.

Let's not forget, however, that problem solving often involves, or should involve, chances to deal with a **performance opportunity**. This is a situation that offers the possibility of a better future if the right steps are taken now. Suppose a regional manager notices that sales at one retail store are unusually high. Does she just say, "Great," and go on about her business? That's an opportunity missed. A really sharp manager says: "Wait a minute, there may be something happening here that I could learn from and possibly transfer to other stores. I had better find out what's going on." That's an opportunity gained.

Managers can be problem avoiders, problem solvers, or problem seekers.

What do you do when you receive a lower grade than expected on an exam or assignment? Do you get the grade, perhaps complain a bit to yourself or friends, and then forget it? Or do you get the grade, recognize that a problem exists, and try to learn from it so that you can do better in the future? Managers are just like you and me. They approach problem solving in different ways and realize different consequences.

Some managers are *problem avoiders*. They ignore information that would otherwise signal the presence of a performance threat or opportunity. They are not active in gathering information and prefer not to make decisions or deal with problems.

Other managers are *problem solvers*. They make decisions and try to solve problems, but only when required. They are reactive, gathering information and responding to problems when they occur, but not before. These managers may deal reasonably well with performance threats, but they are likely to miss many performance opportunities.

Still other managers, the really better ones, are *problem seekers*. They are always looking for problems to solve or opportunities to explore. True problem seekers are proactive as information gatherers, and they are forward thinking. They anticipate threats and opportunities, and they are eager to take action to gain the advantage in dealing with them.

Managers make programmed and nonprogrammed decisions when solving problems.

So far in this discussion, we have used the word "decision" rather casually. From this point forward, though, let's agree that a **decision** is a choice among possible alternative courses of action. Let's also agree that decisions can be made in different ways, with some ways working better than others in various circumstances.

Some management problems are routine and repetitive. They can be addressed through **programmed decisions** that apply preplanned solutions based on the lessons of past experience. Such decisions work best for structured problems that are familiar, straightforward, and clear with respect to information needs. In human resource management, for example, decisions always have to be made on things such as vacations and holiday work schedules. Forward-looking managers can use past experience and plan ahead to make these decisions in programmed, not spontaneous, ways.

Many management problems arise as new or unusual situations full of ambiguities and information deficiencies. These unstructured problems require **nonprogrammed decisions** that must craft novel solutions to meet the unique demands of a situation. In the recent financial crisis, for example, all eyes were on President Obama's choice of Treasury Secretary Timothy Geithner. His task was to solve the problems with billions in bad loans made by the nation's banks and restore stability to the financial markets. But it was uncharted territory; no prepackaged solutions were readily available. Geithner and his team did what they believed was best. But in difficult and dynamic circumstances, the nonprogrammed decisions they made were hotly debated, and only time would tell if they were the right ones.

A **nonprogrammed decision** applies a specific solution that has been crafted to address a unique problem.

Managers can use both systematic and intuitive thinking.

Managers differ in their use of "systematic" and "intuitive" thinking. In **systematic thinking** a person approaches problems in a rational, step-by-step, and analytical fashion. You might recognize this when someone you are working with tries to break a complex problem into smaller components that can be addressed one by one. We might expect systematic managers to make a plan before taking action and to search for information and proceed with problem solving in a fact-based and step-by-step fashion.

Systematic thinking approaches problems in a rational and analytical fashion.

A systematic thinker approaches problems in a step-by-step and linear fashion

An intuitive thinker approaches problems in flexible and spontaneous fashion

Someone using **intuitive thinking** is more flexible and spontaneous than the systematic thinker, and they may be quite creative.[4] You might observe this pattern in someone who always seems to come up with an imaginative response to a problem, often based on a quick and broad evaluation of the situation. Intuitive managers tend to deal with many aspects of a problem at once, jump quickly from one issue to another, and act on either hunches based on experience or on spontaneous ideas.

Intuitive thinking approaches problems in a flexible and spontaneous fashion.

Amazon.com's Jeff Bezos says that when it's not possible for the firm's top managers to make systematic fact-based decisions, "you have to rely on experienced executives who've honed their instincts" and are able to make good judgments.[5] In other words, there's a place for both systematic and intuitive decision making in management.

Managers use different cognitive styles to process information for decision making.

When US Airways Flight 1549 took off from LaGuardia airport on January 15, 2009, all was normal. It was normal, that is, until the plane hit a flock of birds, and both engines failed. Flight 1549 was going to crash. Pilot Chesley Sullenberger quickly realized he couldn't get to an airport and decided to land in the Hudson River—a highly risky move. But he had both a clear head and a clear sense of what he had been trained to do. The landing was successful, and no lives were lost.

Called a "hero" for his efforts, Sullenberger described his thinking this way. "I needed to touch down with the wings exactly level. I needed to touch down with the nose slightly up. I needed to touch down at ... a descent rate that was survivable. And I needed to touch down just above our minimum

flying speed but not below it. And I needed to make all these things happen simultaneously." [6]

This example raises the issue of **cognitive styles**, or the way individuals deal with information while making decisions. If you take the self-assessment "Intuitive Ability" at the end of the book, you can examine your cognitive style in problem solving. This involves a contrast of tendencies toward information gathering (sensation vs. intuition) and information evaluation (feeling vs. thinking). Pilot Sullenberger would most likely score high in both sensation and thinking, and that is probably an ideal type for his job. But as shown in the figure, this is only one of four master **cognitive styles**. [7]

Cognitive style is the way an individual deals with information while making decisions.

	Sensing	Intuition
Thinking	Sensation Thinkers "STs"—like facts, goals	Intuitive Thinkers "ITs"—idealistic, theoretical
Feeling	Sensation Feelers "SFs"—like facts, feelings	Intuitive Feelers "IFs"—thoughtful, flexible

Information Evaluation

Information Processing

- *Sensation thinker*—STs tend to emphasize the impersonal rather than the personal and take a realistic approach to problem solving. They like hard "facts," clear goals, certainty, and situations of high control.

- *Intuitive thinkers*—ITs are comfortable with abstraction and unstructured situations. They tend to be idealistic, prone toward intellectual and theoretical positions; they are logical and impersonal but also avoid details.

- *Intuitive feelers*—IFs prefer broad and global issues. They are insightful and tend to avoid details, being comfortable with intangibles; they value flexibility and human relationships.

- *Sensation feelers*—SFs tend to emphasize both analysis and human relations. They tend to be realistic and prefer facts; they are open communicators and sensitive to feelings and values.

The descriptions above show how people with different cognitive styles may approach problems and make decisions in ways quite different from one another. This is why it's so important to understand our cognitive styles and those of others. In the social context of the workplace, lots of decisions are made by people working together in small groups and teams. The more diverse the cognitive styles, the more difficulty we might expect as they try to make decisions.

||| Managers make decisions under conditions of certainty, risk, and uncertainty.

It's not just personal styles that differ in problem solving; the environment counts, too. **Figure 4.2** shows three different conditions or problem environments in which managers make decisions—certainty, risk, and uncertainty.

As you might expect, the levels of risk and uncertainty in problem environments tend to increase the higher one moves in management ranks. You might think about this each time you hear about Coca-Cola or Pepsi launching a new flavor or product or advertising campaign. Are the top executives making these decisions *certain* that the results will be successful? Or are they taking *risks* in market situations that are *uncertain* as to whether the new flavor or product or ad will be positively received by customers?

A **certain environment** offers complete information on possible action alternatives and their consequences.

It would be nice if we could all make decisions and solve problems in the relative predictability of a **certain environment**. This is an ideal decision situation where factual information exists for the possible alternative courses of action and their consequences. All a decision maker needs to do is study the alternatives and choose the best solution. It isn't easy to find examples of decision situations with such

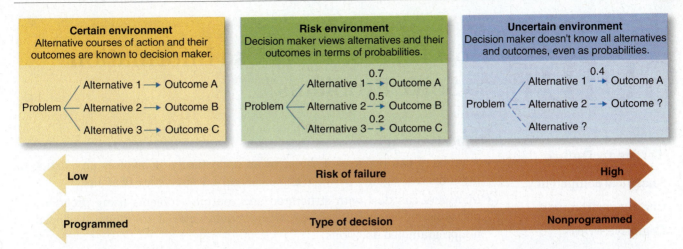

FIGURE 4.2 What Are the Differences Between Certain, Risk, and Uncertain Decision-Making Environments?
Managers rarely face a problem where they can know all the facts, identify all alternatives and their consequences, and chart a clear course of action. Such *certainty* is more often than not replaced by problem environments involving risk and uncertainty. *Risk* is where alternatives are known but their consequences can be described in terms of probabilities. *Uncertainty* is where all alternatives are not known, and their consequences are highly speculative.

certain conditions. One possibility is a decision to take out a "fixed-rate" loan—say for college studies or a new car. At least you can make the decision knowing future interest costs and repayment timetables. But this situation changes significantly, doesn't it, if the lender is offering you a "variable-rate" loan? In this case the interest rate you have to pay will vary in the future according to what happens with market interest rates. How willing are you to take a loan while not knowing if interest rates will go down (to your gain) or up (to your loss) in the future?

Whereas absolute certainty is the best scenario for decision makers, the reality is that in our personal lives and in management, we more often face **risk environments** where information and facts are incomplete. An example is the offer of a variable-rate loan as just discussed. In risk conditions, alternative courses of action and their consequences can be analyzed only as *probabilities* (e.g., 4 chances out of 10). One way of dealing with risk is by gathering as much information as possible, perhaps in different ways. In the case of a new product, such as Coke Zero or even a college textbook like this, it is unlikely that marketing executives would make go-ahead decisions without lots of data gathering and analysis. Often this involves getting reports from multiple focus groups that test the new product in its sample stages.

When facts are few and information is so poor that managers have a hard time even assigning probabilities to things, an **uncertain environment** exists. This is the most difficult decision condition.[8] It's also more common than you might think. And, the border line between risk and uncertainty isn't always clear. When the Japanese built a nuclear power plant at Fukushima—on the seacoast and in an earthquake zone, were decision makers just taking a calculated risk, or were they acting in the face of absolute uncertainty?

Decisions made in uncertain conditions depend greatly on intuition, judgment, informed guessing, and hunches—all of which leave considerable room for error. When things are uncertain, group discussion and decisions are often useful. The more information, perspectives, and creativity that can be brought to bear on the situation, the better. This increases chances for a good decision, or at least a better one than the individual alone might make.

A **risk environment** lacks complete information but offers probabilities of the likely outcomes for possible action alternatives.

An **uncertain environment** lacks so much information that it is difficult to assign probabilities to the likely outcomes of alternatives.

STUDY GUIDE

Takeaway 4.1
How Do Managers Use Information to Solve Problems?

Rapid Review

- A problem can occur as a threat or an opportunity; it involves an existing or potential discrepancy between an actual and a desired state of affairs.
- Managers can deal with structured and routine problems using programmed decisions; novel and unique problems require special solutions developed by nonprogrammed decisions.
- Managers deal with problems in different ways, with some being problem avoiders, others being reactive problem solvers, and still others being proactive problem seekers.
- Managers using systematic thinking approach problems in a rational step-by-step fashion; managers using intuitive thinking approach them in a more flexible and spontaneous way.
- Managers display different cognitive styles when dealing with information for decision making—sensation thinkers, intuitive thinkers, intuitive feelers, and sensation feelers.
- The problems that managers face occur in environments of certainty, risk, or uncertainty.

Questions for Discussion

1. Can a manager be justified for acting as a problem avoider in certain situations?
2. Would an organization be better off with mostly systematic or mostly intuitive thinkers?
3. Is it possible to develop programmed decisions for use in conditions of risk and uncertainty?

Be Sure You Can

- explain the importance of information competency for successful problem solving
- differentiate programmed and nonprogrammed decisions
- describe different ways managers approach and deal with problems
- discuss the differences between systematic and intuitive thinking
- identify differences between the four cognitive styles used in decision making
- explain the challenges of decision making under conditions of certainty, risk, and uncertainty environments

Career Situation: What Would You Do?

Even though some problems in organizations seem to "pop up" unexpectedly, many of them can be anticipated. Examples are an employee who calls in sick at the last minute, a customer who is unhappy with a product or service and wants a refund, and even a boss who asks you to do something that isn't job relevant. How might you anticipate handling such situations as a decision maker?

Takeaway 4.2
What Are Five Steps in the Decision-Making Process?

ANSWERS TO COME

- Step 1 is to identify and define the problem.
- Step 2 is to generate and evaluate alternative courses of action.
- Step 3 is to decide on a preferred course of action.
- Step 4 is to implement the decision.
- Step 5 is to evaluate results.
- Ethical reasoning is important at all steps in decision making.

THE **DECISION-MAKING PROCESS** INVOLVES A STRAIGHTFORWARD SERIES OF STEPS shown in Figure 4.3—Identify and define the problem, generate and evaluate alternative solutions, decide on a preferred course of action, implement the decision, and then evaluate results. An ethics double-check should be done at each step along the way.[9]

The **decision-making process** begins with identification of a problem and ends with evaluation of implemented solutions.

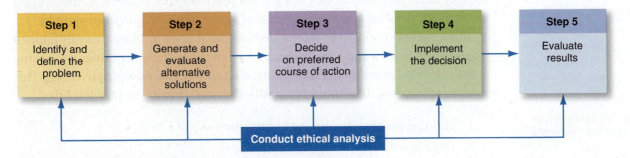

FIGURE 4.3 **What Are Five Steps in the Decision-Making Process?**
Decision making can be viewed as a series of steps—(1) find and define the problem, (2) generate and evaluate solutions, (3) choose a preferred alternative, (4) implement the decision, and (5) evaluate the results. It is important to conduct ethical analysis at all steps in the decision-making process—from initial problem identification all the way to the evaluation of results. When the ethics of a decision are questioned, it's time to stop and rethink the entire process. This helps the decision maker to be confident that all underlying moral problems have been identified and dealt with in the best possible ways.

Let's look at this process with a timely example. When General Motors announced it was closing nine plants in North America and cutting 30,000 jobs, it was a blow to workers, their families, and their communities.[10] The following case isn't quite as sensational, but it's equally real. It helps show how the decision-making steps apply in real situations.

The Ajax Case

On December 31, the Ajax Company decided to close down its Murphysboro plant. Market conditions and a recessionary economy were forcing layoffs, and the company hadn't been able to find a buyer for the plant. Of the 172 employees, some had been with the company as long as 18 years, others as little as 6 months. Ajax needed to terminate all of them. Under company policy, they would be given severance pay equal to one week's pay per year of service.

This opening to the Ajax case reflects how competition, changing times, and the forces of globalization can take their toll on organizations, the people that work for them, and the communities in which they operate. How would you feel—as one of the affected employees, as the mayor of this small town, or as an Ajax executive having to make tough decisions in this situation?

‖ Step 1 is to identify and define the problem.

The first step in decision making is to identify and define the problem. This is a stage of information gathering, information processing, and deliberation. It is also where goals are clarified to specify exactly what a decision should accomplish. The more specific the goals, the easier it is to evaluate results after implementing the decision.

Three mistakes are common in this critical first step in decision making. First, we may define the problem too broadly or too narrowly. To take a classic example, instead of stating the problem as "Build a better mousetrap," we define it as "Get rid of the mice." Ideally, problems are defined in ways that give them the best possible range of problem-solving options.

Second, we may focus on symptoms instead of causes. Symptoms only indicate that problems may exist; they aren't the problems themselves. Of course, managers need to be good at spotting problem symptoms (e.g., a drop in performance). But instead of just treating symptoms (such as simply encouraging higher performance), managers need to seek out and address their root causes (e.g., discovering the workers' need for training in the use of a complex new computer system).

Third, we may choose the wrong problem to deal with. This can easily happen when we are rushed and time is short, or when there are many things happening at once. Instead of just doing something, it's important to do the right things. This means setting priorities and dealing with the most important problems first.

Common Mistakes When Identifying Problems ≫

1. Defining problem too broadly or too narrowly
2. Dealing with symptoms, not real causes
3. Focusing on wrong problem to begin with

Back to the Ajax Case

Closing the plant will result in a loss of jobs for a substantial number of people from the small community of Murphysboro. The unemployment created will negatively affect these individuals, their families, and the community as a whole. The loss of the Ajax tax base will further hurt the community. Ajax management, therefore, defines the problem as how to minimize the adverse impact of the plant closing on the employees, their families, and the community.

‖ Step 2 is to generate and evaluate alternative courses of action.

After the problem is defined, the next step in decision making is to gather the needed facts and information. Managers must be clear here on exactly what they know and what they need to know. Extensive information gathering should identify alternative courses of action as well as their anticipated consequences. Key stakeholders in the problem should be identified, and the effects of each possible course of action on them should be considered. In the case of GM's plant closings and layoffs, for example, a union negotiator said: "While GM's continuing decline in market share isn't the fault of workers or our communities, it is these groups that will suffer."

Most managers use some form of **cost-benefit analysis** to evaluate alternatives. This compares what an alternative will cost with its expected benefits. At a minimum, benefits should exceed costs. In addition, an alternative should be timely, acceptable to as many stakeholders as possible, and ethically sound. And most often, the better the pool of alternatives and the better the analysis, the more likely it is that a good decision will result.

Back to the Ajax Case

Ajax will definitely close the plant; keeping it open is no longer an option. These alternatives are considered—close the plant on schedule and be done with it; delay the plant closing and try again to sell it to another firm; offer to sell the plant to the employees and/or local interests; close the plant and offer employees transfers to other Ajax plant locations; close the plant, offer transfers, and help the employees find new jobs in and around Murphysboro.

‖ Step 3 is to decide on a preferred course of action.

Management theory recognizes two quite different ways that alternatives get explored and decisions get made: the classical and behavioral models shown in **Figure 4.4**. The **classical decision model** views the manager as acting rationally and in a fully informed manner. The problem is clearly defined, all possible action alternatives are known, and their consequences are clear. As a result, he or she makes an **optimizing decision** that gives the absolute best solution to the problem.

CLASSICAL MODEL		BEHAVIORAL MODEL
• Structured problem • Clearly defined • Certain environment • Complete information • All alternatives and consequences known	Rationality Acts in perfect world Manager as decision maker Bounded rationality Acts with cognitive limitations	• Unstructured problem • Not clearly defined • Uncertain environment • Incomplete information • Not all alternatives and consequences known
OPTIMIZING DECISION Choose absolute best among alternatives		**SATISFICING DECISION** Choose first "satisfactory" alternative

Although the classical model sounds ideal, most of the time it's too good to be true. Because there are limits to our information-processing capabilities, something called *cognitive limitations*, it is hard to be fully informed and make perfectly rational decisions in all situations. Recognizing this, the premise of the **behavioral decision model** is that people act only in terms of their perceptions, which are frequently imperfect. Armed with only partial knowledge about the available action alternatives and their consequences, decision makers are likely to choose the first alternative that appears satisfactory to them. Herbert Simon, who won a Nobel Prize for his work, calls this the tendency to make **satisficing decisions**.[11] What do you think? Does this seem accurate in describing how we make a lot of decisions?

Back to the Ajax Case

Ajax executives decide to close the plant, offer employees transfers to company plants in another state, and offer to help displaced employees find new jobs in and around Murphysboro.

Cost-benefit analysis involves comparing the costs and benefits of each potential course of action.

The **classical decision model** describes decision making with complete information.

An **optimizing decision** chooses the alternative providing the absolute best solution to a problem.

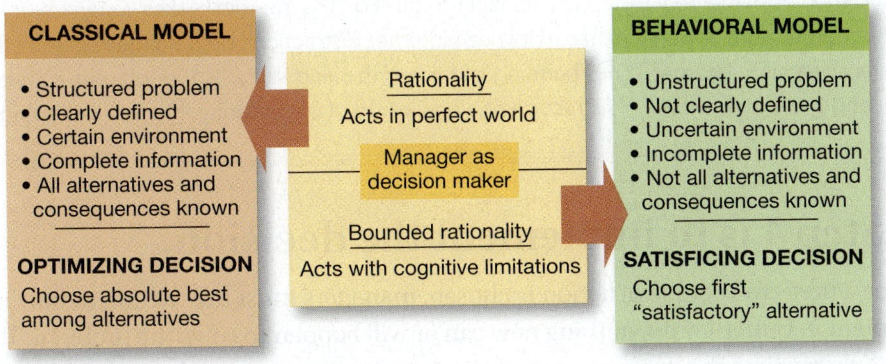

FIGURE 4.4
How Does the Classical Model of Managerial Decision Making Differ from the Behavioral Model?
The classical model views decision makers as having complete information and making optimum decisions that are the absolute best choices to resolve problems. The behavioral model views decision makers as having limited information-processing capabilities. They act with incomplete information and make satisficing decisions, choosing the first satisfactory alternative that comes to their attention.

The **behavioral decision model** describes decision making with limited information and bounded rationality.

A **satisficing decision** chooses the first satisfactory alternative that presents itself.

Manager's **Library**

YOUR BRAIN ON THE INTERNET—MORE ENLIGHTENED, OR LIGHTENED?

The World Wide Web has forever altered human culture. One profound impact is on the human brain, which evolves along with the tools that we use to communicate. Although the Internet has enlightened us in various ways, it may also be lightening our thinking by replacing deep thought and reflection with shallow-minded pursuits.

In the book *The Shallows: What the Internet is Doing to Our Brains* (2010, W. W. Norton & Company), Nicholas Carr discusses how human minds have changed along with communication technologies ranging from the spoken word to the written tablet, and the printing press to the Internet. Research shows that brains are "rewired" when using the Web as the "hypermedia" of links and audio-visual stimuli overwhelm its cognitive capacity. Brains cope with information overload by changing their neural networks of operation. "Linear" thought—deep thinking and slow reflection using long-term memory, is replaced by "nonlinear" thought—temporary thinking and rapid scanning using short-term memory.

Carr cites research showing book readers outperform "hypertext" readers in comprehension, memory, and learning. Internet brains are distracted by abundant stimuli and grow their short-term memory circuits by converting and replacing long-term memory circuits. Permanent memory requires time and calm for ideas to pass into the unconscious mind, so he describes the Internet as a "technology of forgetfulness" and a "Web of distraction." Carr warns that critical mental skills are lost and advises caution in Internet use. He thinks users should be purpose driven, focus on fewer tasks simultaneously, and spend time away from the Web to read, ponder, and discuss ideas verbally.

It's not all bad news, though. Carr concedes that new skills are developed by Net use—"power browsing" through titles, content pages, and abstracts to quickly obtain ideas and "hunting and gathering" more efficiently for additional and varied facts. He speculates Web use may someday advance brains to multitask effectively. But, he still worries those tasks may be less complex as humans' brains evolve to accommodate the shallow thinking demands of the Internet.

REFLECT AND REACT

Do you think time spent on the Internet makes you more or less smart? How can Internet distractions be managed? Is the Internet harming our linear thinking skills? Is the Internet a Web of distraction or a new world of opportunity that is still evolving?

⫶ Step 4 is to implement the decision.

Once a preferred course of action is chosen, managers must take action to fully implement it. Until they do, nothing new can or will happen to solve the problem. This not only requires the determination and creativity to arrive at a decision, but it also requires the ability and personal willingness to act. Most likely it also requires the support of many other people. And more often than you might realize, it is lack of support that sabotages the implementation of many perfectly good decisions.

Managers fall prey to the **lack-of-participation error** when they don't include in the decision-making process those persons whose support is necessary for implementation. When managers use participation wisely, by contrast, they get the right people involved from the beginning. This not only brings their inputs and insights to bear on the problem, but it also helps build commitments to take actions supporting the decision and make sure it all works as intended.

Lack-of-participation error is failure to include the right people in the decision-making process.

Back to the Ajax Case

Ajax management ran an ad in the local and regional newspapers for several days. It announced to potential employers an "Ajax skill bank" composed of "qualified, dedicated, and well-motivated employees with a variety of skills and experiences." The ad urged interested employers to contact Ajax for further information.

NATALIA KOLESNIKOVA/
AFP/Getty Images

{ "WHATEVER ANYBODY SAYS OR DOES, ASSUME POSITIVE INTENT. YOU WILL BE AMAZED AT HOW YOUR WHOLE APPROACH TO A PERSON OR PROBLEM BECOMES VERY DIFFERENT."

Role Models

■ Indra Nooyi Leads Pepsico Through Uncertainty and Risk

Indra Nooyi, Pepsico's Chairman and CEO, says the best advice she ever got came from her father. He said: "Whatever anybody says or does, assume positive intent. You will be amazed at how your whole approach to a person or problem becomes very different. . . . You are trying to understand and listen because at your basic core you are saying, 'Maybe they are saying something to me that I am not hearing.'"

Nooyi believes she must earn her job as Pepsi CEO each day—knowing that it can, at any time, be taken away. Running a global enterprise facing obesity as a top health issue, Nooyi faces tough decisions to keep PepsiCo—maker of Pepsi, Mountain Dew, Lay's potato chips, Doritos, Cheetos, and hundreds of other foods and drinks— "transforming while performing."

Conditions of uncertainty and risk are commonplace for Nooyi. But Nooyi's early experience as a strategy consultant with Boston Consulting Group (BCG) taught her the power of "inductive thinking." "It taught me how to think of the problem in micro terms, "she says," but also to zoom out and put the problem in the context of its broader environment and then zoom back in to solve the problem." In other words, she not only focuses on the big picture, but also on the details.

When she decided that PepsiCo needed a research and development operation to get ahead of the looming obesity and health threat, this meant taking sugar, salt, and fat out of products. To implement, she hired Mehmood Khan, previously a pharmaceutical research director and chief of the Diabetes, Endocrine, and Nutritional Trials unit of the Mayo Clinic to build an R&D (Research and Development) program. Khan asked: "It will take five years before we'll see any results. Do you have the patience for that?" Her response: "It's not whether I have the patience. I don't have a choice."

WHAT'S THE LESSON HERE?

Indra Nooyi makes many strategic and consequential decisions every day. One trend that could make or break PepsiCo is the worldwide rise of lifestyle diseases like diabetes and coronary artery disease. How can Nooyi blend profits with social responsibility at a company that encourages people to consume snacks and soft drinks? If you were Pepsico's head, what criteria would you use when making decisions to move the firm into the future?

⫴ Step 5 is to evaluate results.

A decision isn't much good if it doesn't achieve the desired outcomes or causes undesired side effects. This is why the decision-making process is not complete until results are evaluated. Doing so is a form of control, gathering data so that performance results can be measured against initial goals. If things aren't going well it means reassessing and perhaps redoing earlier steps in the decision-making process. If things are better than expected, it means trying to learn why, so these lessons can be used in the future.

Back to the Ajax Case

How effective was Ajax's decision? Well, we don't know for sure. After Ajax ran the skill-bank advertisement for 15 days, the plant's industrial relations manager said: "I've been very pleased with the results." However, we really need a lot more information for a true evaluation. How many employees got new jobs locally? How many transferred to other Ajax plants? How did the local economy perform in the following months? Probably you can add evaluation questions of your own to this list.

Ethical reasoning is important at all steps in decision making.

If you look back to Figure 4.3, you'll see that each step in the decision-making process is linked with ethical reasoning.[12] Attention to ethical analysis helps identify any underlying moral problems. You can think of this as an ongoing "ethics double-check." It is accomplished by asking and answering two sets of questions.

The first set of ethics questions is based on four criteria described in the work of ethicist Gerald Cavanagh and his associates.[13]

1. *Utility*—Does the decision satisfy all constituents or stakeholders?
2. *Rights*—Does the decision respect the rights and duties of everyone?
3. *Justice*—Is the decision consistent with the canons of justice?
4. *Caring*—Is the decision consistent with my responsibilities to care?

The second set of ethics questions opens a decision to public disclosure and the prospect of shame.[14] These so-called **spotlight questions**, discussed also in the last chapter, are especially powerful when the decision maker comes from a morally scrupulous family or social structure.

1. "How would I feel if my family found out about this decision?"
2. "How would I feel if this decision was published in the local newspaper or posted on the Internet?"
3. "What would the person I know who has the strongest character and best ethical judgment say about my decision?"

Spotlight questions highlight the risks of public disclosure of one's actions.

STR/AFP / Getty Images

{ "HUMAN LIFE IS FAR MORE IMPORTANT THAN JUST GETTING TO THE TOP OF A MOUNTAIN."

Ethics Check

■ Left to Die on Mt. Everest

Some 40 climbers are winding their ways to the top of Mt. Everest. About 1,000 feet below the summit sits a British mountain climber in trouble, collapsed in a shallow snow cave. Most of those on the way up just look while continuing their climbs. Sherpas from one passing team pause to give him oxygen before moving on. Within hours, David Sharp, 34, is dead of oxygen deficiency on the mountain.

A climber who passed by says: "At 28,000 feet it's hard to stay alive yourself . . . he was in very poor condition . . . , it was a very hard decision . . . he wasn't a member of our team."

Someone who made the summit in the past says: "If you're going to go to Everest . . . I think you have to accept responsibility that you may end up doing something that's not ethically nice . . . you have to realize that you're in a different world."

After hearing about this case, the late Sir Edmund Hillary, who reached the top in 1953, said: "Human life is far more important than just getting to the top of a mountain."

YOU DECIDE

Who's right and who's wrong here? And, by the way, in our personal affairs, daily lives, and careers, we are all, in our own ways, climbing Mt. Everest. What are the ethics of our climbs? How often do we notice others in trouble, struggling along the way? And, like the mountain climbers heading to the summit of Everest, how often do we pass them by to continue our own journeys? Can you identify examples—from business, school, career, sports, and so on—that pose similar ethical dilemmas?

STUDY GUIDE

Takeaway 4.2
What Are Five Steps in the Decision-Making Process?

Terms to Define

Behavioral decision model

Classical decision model

Cost-benefit analysis

Decision-making process

Lack-of-participation error

Optimizing decision

Satisficing decision

Spotlight questions

Rapid Review

- The steps in the decision-making process are (1) identify and define the problem, (2) generate and evaluate alternatives, (3) decide on the preferred course of action, (4) implement the decision, (5) evaluate the results, and conduct ethics double-check in all steps.
- A cost-benefit analysis compares the expected costs of a decision alternative with its expected results.
- In the classical model, an optimizing decision chooses the absolute best solution from a known set of alternatives.
- In the behavioral model, cognitive limitations lead to satisficing decisions that choose the first satisfactory alternative to come to attention.
- The ethics of a decision can be checked on the criteria of utility, rights, justice, and caring, as well as by asking the spotlight questions.

Questions for Discussion

1. Do the steps in the decision-making process have to be followed in order?
2. Do you see any problems or pitfalls for managers using the behavioral decision model?
3. Is use of the spotlight questions sufficient to ensure an ethical decision?

Be Sure You Can

- list the steps in the decision-making process
- apply these steps to a sample decision-making situation
- explain cost-benefit analysis
- compare and contrast the classical and behavioral decision models
- illustrate optimizing and satisficing in your personal decision-making experiences
- list and explain the criteria for evaluating the ethics of a decision
- list three questions for double-checking the ethics of a decision

Career Situation: What Would You Do?

You are under a lot of pressure as a team leader because of social loafing and poor performance by one of your team members. You have come up with a reason to remove her from the team. But, you feel very uneasy. After doing the ethics analysis, the decision you are about to make fails all three of the recommended spotlight questions. What do you do now?

Takeaway 4.3
What Are Some Current Issues in Managerial Decision Making?

ANSWERS TO COME

- Creativity can be unlocked and encouraged for better decision making.
- Group decision making has both advantages and disadvantages.
- Judgmental heuristics and other biases and traps may cause decision-making errors.
- Managers must be prepared for crisis decision making.

ONCE YOU ACCEPT THE FACT THAT EACH OF US IS LIKELY TO MAKE IMPERFECT decisions at least some of the time, it makes sense to probe even further into the how's and why's of decision making in organizations. One popular issue is creativity and how to unlock its power in decision making. Some common concerns relate to the handling of group versus individual decisions, judgmental heuristics and decision biases, and decision making under crisis conditions.

‖ Creativity can be unlocked and encouraged for better decision making.

Situation—Elevator riders in a new high-rise building are complaining about long waiting times. *Building engineer's advice*—upgrade the entire system at substantial cost. Why? He assumed that any solutions to a slow elevator problem had to be mechanical ones. *Creativity consultant's advice*—place floor-to-ceiling mirrors by the elevators. Why? People, he suspected, would not notice waiting times because they were distracted by their and others' reflections. *Outcome*—the creativity consultant was right.[15]

We can define **creativity** as the generation of a novel idea or unique approach to solving performance problems or exploiting performance opportunities.[16] The potential for creativity is one of our greatest personal assets, even though this capability may be too often unrecognized by us and by others.

One reason we often underestimate our creativity skills is too much focus on what researchers call **Big-C creativity**—when extraordinary things are done by exceptional people.[17] Think Big-C creativity when you use or see someone using an iPhone or iPad—Steve Jobs's creativity, or browse Facebook—Mark Zuckerburg's creativity. Even though not always aware of it, most of us also show a lot of **Little-C creativity**—when average people come up with unique ways to deal with daily events and situations. Think Little-C creativity, for example, the next time you solve relationship problems at home, build something for the kids, or even find ways to pack too many things into too small a suitcase. But are we similarly creative when it would really help in solving workplace problems?

Just imagine what can be accomplished with all the creative potential—Big-C and Little-C—that exists in an organization. How do you turn that potential into creative decisions? One source of insight is the three-component model of personal creativity drivers—task expertise, task motivation, and creativity skills.[18]

Creativity is the generation of a novel idea or unique approach that solves a problem or crafts an opportunity.

Big-C creativity occurs when extraordinary things are done by exceptional people.

Little-C creativity occurs when average people come up with unique ways to deal with daily events and situations.

{ **MANAGERS ARE DECISION MAKERS . . .
THEY ARE ALSO DECISION IMPLEMENTERS.**

Explore **Yourself**

■ Self-confidence

Managers are decision makers. And if they are to make consistently good decisions, they must be skilled at gathering and processing information. Managers are also implementers. Once decisions are made, managers are expected to rally people and resources to put them into action. This is how problems get solved and opportunities get explored in organizations.

In order for all this to happen, managers must have the **self-confidence** to turn decisions into action accomplishments; they must believe in their decisions and the information foundations for them. A good understanding of the many topics in this chapter can improve your decision-making skills. A better understanding of your personal style in gathering and processing information can also go a long way toward building your self-confidence as a decision maker.

> Get to know yourself better by taking the self-assessment on **Cognitive Style** and completing other activities in the *Exploring Management* **Skill-Building Portfolio**.

From a management standpoint, the model shown here is helpful because it points us in the direction of actions that can be taken to build creativity drivers into the work setting and encourage creativity in decision making.

Creative decisions are more likely to occur when the person or team has a lot of task expertise. Creativity often extends in new directions something we are already good at or know something about. Creative decisions are more likely when people are highly task motivated. They occur in part because people work exceptionally hard to resolve a problem and end up accomplishing something new and different. Creative decisions are also more likely when the people involved have strong creativity skill sets. The popular spin on this contrasts "right-brain" thinking—imagination, intuition, spontaneity, and emotion—and "left-brain" thinking—logic, order, method, and analysis.

Just what are we talking about here? Is creativity something that is built into some of us and not built into others? Or, is creativity something that one can work to develop along with other personal skills and competencies? Most researchers tend to agree that most of us can develop creativity skill sets like the following.[19]

- Work with high energy
- Hold one's ground in the face of criticism
- Be resourceful even in difficult situations
- Think "outside the box"—divergent thinking
- Use "lateral thinking"—looking at diverse ways to solve problems
- Transfer learning from one setting to others
- Able to "step back," be objective, and question assumptions

Personal Creativity Drivers

≪ **Characteristics of
Creative People**

Table 4.1 Potential Advantages and Disadvantages of Group Decision Making.[20]

Why group decisions are often good

More information—More information, expertise, and viewpoints are available to help solve problems.

More alternatives—More alternatives are generated and considered during decision making.

Increased understanding—There is increased understanding and a greater acceptance of the decision by group members.

Greater commitment—There is an increased commitment of group members to work hard and support the decision.

Why group decisions can be bad

Conformity with social pressures—Some members feel intimidated by others and give in to social pressures to conform.

Domination by a few members—A minority dominates; some members get railroaded by a small coalition of others.

Time delays—More time is required to make decisions when many people try to work together.

Group decision making has both advantages and disadvantages.

Whether to make decisions alone or with the help of others shouldn't be an either/or choice. Effective managers and team leaders typically switch back and forth between individual and group decision making, trying to use the best methods for the problems at hand.

In respect to advantages, group decisions can be good because they bring greater amounts of information, knowledge, and expertise to bear on a problem. They often expand the number and even the creativity of action alternatives examined. And as noted earlier in our discussion of lack-of-participation error, participation helps group members gain a better understanding of any decisions reached. This increases the likelihood that they will both accept decisions made and work hard to help implement them.

In respect to disadvantages, we all know that it is sometimes difficult and time consuming for people to make group decisions. The more people involved, the longer it can take to reach a group decision, and the more likely that problems will arise. There may be social pressure to conform that leads to premature consensus and agreement in group situations. Some individuals may feel intimidated or compelled to go along with the apparent wishes of others who have authority or who act aggressive and uncompromising. Minority domination might cause some members to feel forced or railroaded into a decision advocated by one vocal individual or a small coalition. And, lots of decisions get made quickly or at the last minute just because a group is running out of meeting time.

Judgmental heuristics and other biases and traps may cause decision-making errors.

Why do well-intentioned people sometimes make bad decisions? The reason often traces to simplifying strategies we use when making decisions with limited information, time, and even energy. These strategies, known as heuristics, can cause decision-making errors.[21]

The **availability heuristic** occurs when people use information "readily available" from memory as a basis for assessing a current event or situation. You may decide, for example, not to buy running shoes from a company if your last pair didn't last long. The potential bias is that the readily available information may be wrong or irrelevant. Even though your present running shoes are worn out, you may have purchased the wrong model for your needs or used them in the wrong conditions.

The **representativeness heuristic** occurs when people assess the likelihood of something happening based on its similarity to a stereotyped set of past occurrences. An example is deciding to hire someone for a job vacancy simply because he or she graduated from the same school attended by your last and most successful new hire. Using the representative stereotype may mask the truly important factors relevant to the decision—the real abilities and career expectations of the new job candidate; the school attended may be beside the point.

The **anchoring and adjustment heuristic** involves making decisions based on adjustments to a previously existing value or starting point. For example, a manager may set a new salary level for a current employee by simply raising the prior year's salary by a percentage increment. The problem is that this increment is anchored in the existing salary level, one that may be much lower than the employee's true market value. Rather than being pleased with the raise, the employee may be unhappy and start looking elsewhere for another, higher-paying job.

In addition to heuristic biases, **framing error** is another potential decision trap. Framing occurs when managers evaluate and resolve a problem in the context in which they perceive it—either positive or negative. You might consider

The **availability heuristic** uses readily available information to assess a current situation.

The **representativeness heuristic** assesses the likelihood of an occurrence using a stereotyped set of similar events.

The **anchoring and adjustment heuristic** adjusts a previously existing value or starting point to make a decision.

Framing error is solving a problem in the context perceived.

MSPhotographic / Shutterstock

{ WORKERS MAY BE FEELING MORE JOB SECURITY, BUT SIZE OF PAYCHECK IS STILL AN ISSUE FOR MANY.

Facts to **Consider**

■ American Workers Talk About Their Biggest Fears

The job market is getting better, and fewer Americans are losing their jobs. But a Harris interactive survey still uncovered worker fears and concerns.

- *Low wages*—11% of workers listed "flat paychecks" as a stressor. Among women the figure was 14% and for men 8%. Low wages bothered 11% of college-educated workers versus 14% for those with high school educations.

- *Wrong career*—11% of women felt stressed by having to work in jobs that weren't their career choices, whereas 5% of men said the same.

- *Unreasonable workload*—A sense of being overworked to an unreasonable extent bothers 9% of survey respondents.

- *Other factors*—Also identified as stressors in daily work life were irritating coworkers and commuting issues.

YOUR THOUGHTS?

When you look at these data, do you sense that all of these concerns are beyond a worker's control? Or, could better decisions—past and present—result in better feelings about one's work? Do some people perceive they are trapped in bad jobs while working to support themselves and their families, but really have more options than they are willing to admit or go after? When does a past decision become a trap that makes it hard for someone to move on to better things?

this as the "glass is half empty versus the glass is half full" dilemma. Suppose marketing data show that a new product has a 40% market share. What does this really mean? A negative frame says there's a problem because the product is missing 60% of the market. "What are we doing wrong?" is the likely follow-up question. But if the marketing team used a positive frame and considered the 40% share as a success story, the conversation might well be: "How can we do even better?" By the way, we are constantly exposed to framing in the world of politics; the word used to describe it is "spin."

Another of our tendencies is to try to find ways to justify a decision after making it. In the case of unethical acts, for example, we try to rationalize with statements like: "No one will ever find out" or "The boss will protect me." Such thinking causes a decision-making trap known as **confirmation error**. This means that we notice, accept, and even seek out only information that confirms or is consistent with a decision we have just made. Other and perhaps critical information is downplayed or denied. This is a form of selective perception. The error is that we neglect other points of view or disconfirming information that might lead us to a different decision.

Yet another decision-making trap is **escalating commitment**. This is a tendency to increase effort and perhaps apply more resources to pursue a course of action that signals indicate is not working.[22] It is an inability or unwillingness to call it quits even when the facts suggest this is the best decision under the circumstances. Ego and the desire to avoid being associated with a mistake can play a big role in escalation.

How about it? Are you disciplined enough to minimize the risk of escalating commitments to previously chosen, but erroneous, courses of action? Fortunately, researchers have provided some good ideas on how to avoid the escalation trap.[23] They include

> **Confirmation error** is when we attend only to information that confirms a decision already made.

> **Escalating commitment** is the continuation of a course of action even though it is not working.

> **Tips for Avoiding the Escalation Trap** »

- Set advance limits on your involvement in and commitment to a particular course of action; stick with these limits.
- Make your own decisions; don't follow the lead of others because they are also prone to escalation.
- Carefully determine just why you are continuing a course of action; if there are insufficient reasons to continue, don't.
- Remind yourself of the costs of a course of action; consider saving these costs as a reason to discontinue.

⦀ Managers must be prepared for crisis decision making.

> A **crisis** is an unexpected problem that can lead to disaster if not resolved quickly and appropriately.

Think back to the example of shift leader Luis Urzúa and the Chilean mine disaster that opened this chapter. One of the most challenging of all decision situations is the **crisis**. This is an unexpected problem that can lead to disaster if not resolved quickly and appropriately. Although not all crises are as sensational and life-threatening as the mine disaster, they still require special handling and they still generate lots of mistakes. Indeed, the ability to deal successfully with crises could well be the ultimate test of any manager's decision-making capabilities.

Nestlé faced an unexpected social media problem when Greenpeace posted a YouTube video claiming the firm's Kit Kat brand was using palm oil produced by unsustainable forestry in Indonesia.[24] Executives at Nestlé quickly had the video removed based on copyright violation. But, this resulted in more social media protests, and the video was reposted elsewhere.

Realizing that the social media world was out of the firm's control, Nestlé changed its approach. Operations manager José Lopez formed a crisis management team. It quickly decided to stop sourcing from the Indonesian supplier and held meetings with Greenpeace to share and review the firm's supply chains. The Forest Trust nonprofit was hired to audit its suppliers, and Nestlé joined the Roundtable for Sustainable Palm Oil.

By engaging rather than trying to censure its critics, Lopez's team managed the immediate crisis and lowered future risks by cleaning up Nestlé's supply chain. It also strengthened the company's commitment to sustainability leadership as a corporate goal—a "win-win" for all stakeholders.

Not everyone does as well in crisis situations. In fact, managers sometimes react to crises by doing exactly the wrong things. Instead of opening up and reaching out they end up isolating themselves and trying to solve the problem alone or in a small, closed group.[25] This denies them access to crucial information at the very time that they need it the most. It not only sets them up for poor decisions, but it may create even more problems. This is why many organizations are developing formal crisis management programs. They train managers in crisis decision making (see Tips to Remember), assign people ahead of time to crisis management teams, and develop crisis management plans to deal with various contingencies.

Fire and police departments, the Red Cross, and community groups plan ahead and train to best handle civil and natural disasters; airline crews train for flight emergencies. So too can managers and work teams plan ahead and train to best deal with organizational crises.[26] This only makes sense, doesn't it?

{ **THE ABILITY TO HANDLE CRISES COULD BE THE ULTIMATE TEST OF YOUR DECISION-MAKING CAPABILITIES.**

Tips to **Remember**

■ Six Rules for Crisis Management

1. *Figure out what is going on*—Dig in to thoroughly understand what's happening and the conditions under which the crisis must be resolved.

2. *Remember that speed matters*—Attack the crisis as quickly as possible, trying to catch it when it is small and before it gets overwhelmingly large.

3. *Remember that slow counts, too*—Know when to back off and wait for a better opportunity to make progress with the crisis.

4. *Respect the danger of the unfamiliar*—Understand the danger of entering all-new territory where you and others have never been before.

5. *Value the skeptic*—Don't look for and get too comfortable with early agreement; appreciate skeptics and let them help you see things differently in sorting out what to do.

6. *Be ready to "fight fire with fire"*—When things are going wrong and no one seems to care, you may have to fuel the crisis to get their attention.

STUDY GUIDE

Takeaway 4.3
What Are Some Current Issues in Managerial Decision Making?

Rapid Review

- Creativity in decision making can be enhanced by the personal creativity drivers of individual creativity skills, task expertise, and motivation.
- Group decisions offer the potential advantages of more information, greater understanding, and expanded commitments; a major disadvantage is that they are often time consuming.
- Judgmental heuristics such as availability, anchoring and adjustment, and representativeness can bias decisions by oversimplifying the situation.
- Framing errors influence decisions by placing them in either a negative or a positive situational context; confirmation error focuses attention only on information that supports a decision.
- Escalating commitment occurs when one sticks with a course of action even though evidence indicates that it is not working.
- A crisis problem occurs unexpectedly and can lead to disaster if managers fail to handle it quickly and properly.

Questions for Discussion

1. How can you avoid being hurt by the anchoring and adjustment heuristic in your annual pay raises?
2. What are some real-world examples of how escalating commitment is affecting decision making in business, government, or people's personal affairs?
3. Is it really possible to turn a crisis into an opportunity, and, if so, how?

Be Sure You Can

- identify personal factors that can be developed or used to drive greater creativity in decision making
- list potential advantages and disadvantages of group decision making
- explain the availability, representativeness, and anchoring and adjustment heuristics
- illustrate framing error and continuation error in decision making
- explain and give an example of escalating commitment
- describe what managers can do to prepare for crisis decisions

Career Situation: What Would You Do?

You have finally caught the attention of senior management. Top executives asked you to chair a task force to develop ideas that can breathe new life into an existing product line. First, you need to select the members of the task force. What criteria will you use to choose members who are most likely to bring high levels of creativity to this team?

TestPrep 4

Answers to TestPrep questions can be found at the back of the book.

Multiple-Choice Questions

1. A manager who is reactive and works hard to address problems after they occur is described as a _____.
   (a) problem seeker
   (b) problem solver
   (c) rational thinker
   (d) strategic opportunist

2. A problem is a discrepancy between a/an _____ situation and a desired situation.
   (a) unexpected
   (b) risk
   (c) actual
   (d) uncertain

3. If a manager approaches problems in a rational and analytical way, trying to solve them in step-by-step fashion, he or she is well described as a/an _____.
   (a) systematic thinker
   (b) intuitive thinker
   (c) problem seeker
   (d) behavioral decision maker

4. The first step in the decision-making process is to _____.
   (a) generate a list of alternatives
   (b) assess the costs and benefits of each alternative
   (c) identify and define the problem
   (d) perform the ethics double-check

5. When the members of a special task force are asked to develop a proposal for hitting very aggressive targets for the international sales of a new product, this problem most likely requires a _____ decision.
   (a) routine
   (b) programmed
   (c) crisis
   (d) nonprogrammed

6. Costs, benefits, timeliness, and _____ are among the recommended criteria for evaluating alternative courses of action in the decision-making process.
   (a) ethical soundness
   (b) past history
   (c) availability
   (d) simplicity

7. The _____ decision model views managers as making optimizing decisions, whereas the _____ decision model views them as making satisficing decisions.
   (a) behavioral; judgmental heuristics
   (b) classical; behavioral
   (c) judgmental heuristics; ethical
   (d) crisis; routine

8. One reason why certainty is the most favorable environment for problem solving is because the problems can be addressed by using _____ decisions.
   (a) satisficing
   (b) optimizing
   (c) programmed
   (d) intuitive

9. A common mistake made by managers facing crisis situations is _____.
   (a) trying to get too much information before responding
   (b) relying too much on group decision making
   (c) isolating themselves to make crisis decisions alone
   (d) forgetting to use their crisis management plan

10. In which decision environment does a manager deal with probabilities regarding possible courses of action and their consequences?

    (a) Risk

    (b) Certainty

    (c) Uncertainty

    (d) Optimal

11. A manager who decides against hiring a new employee that just graduated from Downstate University because the last person hired from there turned out to be a low performer is falling prey to _____ error.

    (a) availability

    (b) adjustment

    (c) anchoring

    (d) representativeness

12. Which decision-making error is most associated with the old adage: "If you don't succeed, try and try again"?

    (a) Satisficing

    (b) Escalating commitment

    (c) Confirmation

    (d) Too late to fail

13. You go to your boss and ask for a pay raise. She says: "Well, let's take a look first at what you are making now." The risk you face in this situation is that your boss's decision will be biased because of _____.

    (a) a framing error

    (b) escalating commitment

    (c) anchoring and adjustment

    (d) strategic opportunism

14. Personal creativity drivers include creativity skills, task expertise, and _____.

    (a) strategic opportunism

    (b) management support

    (c) organizational culture

    (d) task motivation

15. The last step in the decision-making process is to _____.

    (a) choose a preferred alternative

    (b) evaluate results

    (c) find and define the problem

    (d) generate alternatives

Short-Response Questions

16. How does an optimizing decision differ from a satisficing decision?

17. What is the difference between a risk environment and an uncertain environment in decision making?

18. How can you tell from people's behavior if they tend to be systematic or intuitive in problem solving?

19. What is escalating commitment, and how can it be avoided?

Integration and Application Question

20. With the goals of both expanding your resumé and gaining valuable experience, you have joined a new mentoring program between your university and a local high school. One of the first activities is for you and your teammates to offer "learning modules" to a class of sophomores. You have volunteered to give a presentation and engage them in some learning activities on the topic: "Individual versus group decision making: Is one better than the other?"

    Question: What will you say and do, and why?

Steps *for* Further Learning

BUILD MARKETABLE SKILLS
DO A CASE ANALYSIS
GET AND STAY INFORMED

BUILD

MARKETABLE SKILLS. EARN BIG CAREER PAYOFFS!

Don't miss these opportunities in the **Skill-Building Portfolio**

■ **SELF-ASSESSMENT 4:**
Intuitive Ability

Check your capacity for intuition . . . turn it into a decision-making skill.

■ **CLASS EXERCISE 4:**
Lost at Sea

Sometimes group decisions are best . . . how do you make a good group decision?

■ **TEAM PROJECT 4:**
Crisis Management Scenario

Crisis handling is always a hot topic . . . turn the experiences of others into learning for yourself.

Many learning resources are found at the end of the book and online within WileyPLUS.

Take advantage of **Cases for Critical Thinking**

■ **CHAPTER 4 CASE SNAPSHOT:**
Amazon.com—Keeping the Fire Hot /
Sidebar on Netflix

Amazon.com is not only the e-commerce company to beat, it also keeps changing as it grows. No one is ever sure what will come next under the guidance of founder and CEO Jeff Bezos. Seeming not to worry about current earnings per share, Bezos keeps investing to make his company stronger and harder to catch. Its millions of square feet of distribution fulfillment space keep growing domestically and around the globe. The firm's products and services are continuously upgraded and expanded. Just go to the website and check multiple versions of the Kindle Fire e-book reader, Prime Instant Video TV and movie content streamed on demand, and a variety of cloud computer services. A *New York Times* article says that "within a few years, Amazon's creative destruction of both traditional book publishing and retailing may be footnotes to the company's larger and more secretive goal: giving anyone on the planet access to an almost unimaginable amount of computing power through its cloud services." What drives Bezos's decisions, and will his investments pay off in the years to come?

DO

A CASE ANALYSIS. STRENGTHEN YOUR CRITICAL THINKING!

Dig into this **Hot Topic**

■ **GOOD IDEA OR NOT?** Yahoo! bans telecommuting—good or bad decision?

Situation All eyes were on Marissa Mayer when she left a successful stint at Google to become Yahoo!'s CEO. But not everyone liked what they heard when she told employees there would be no more working from home. "Bye-bye telecommuting" was the message. Mayer's stated goal was to bring face-to-face collaboration back to the Yahoo! culture and increase innovation in the process.

GET

AND STAY INFORMED. MAKE YOURSELF VALUABLE!

Critics of Mayer's decision claim it flies in the face of evidence that says not only do most employees want the option of telecommuting—as high as 80+ percent in some reports, but they're both hard working and more satisfied when they can spend time working from home. "Telecommuting . . . has allowed me to have a career as well as be a mother," said a posting by "digital mom" on Babble.com, an online Web site for parents.

Those who support Mayer's decision point to other employers—including Bank of America, Google, and Twitter—that are either cutting back on or discouraging work-at-home choices. When asked, "How many people telecommute at Google?" the firm's chief financial officer replied: "As few as possible."

Final Take What is your position on telecommuting? Does experience tell you that it works or doesn't? Is it something that you are looking for in an employer? Does Mayer's decision show courage in the face of a popular but not necessarily performance-friendly practice? Or, was it a premature rush to blame work-at-home practices for what she perceived as Yahoo!'s failures of collaboration and innovation?

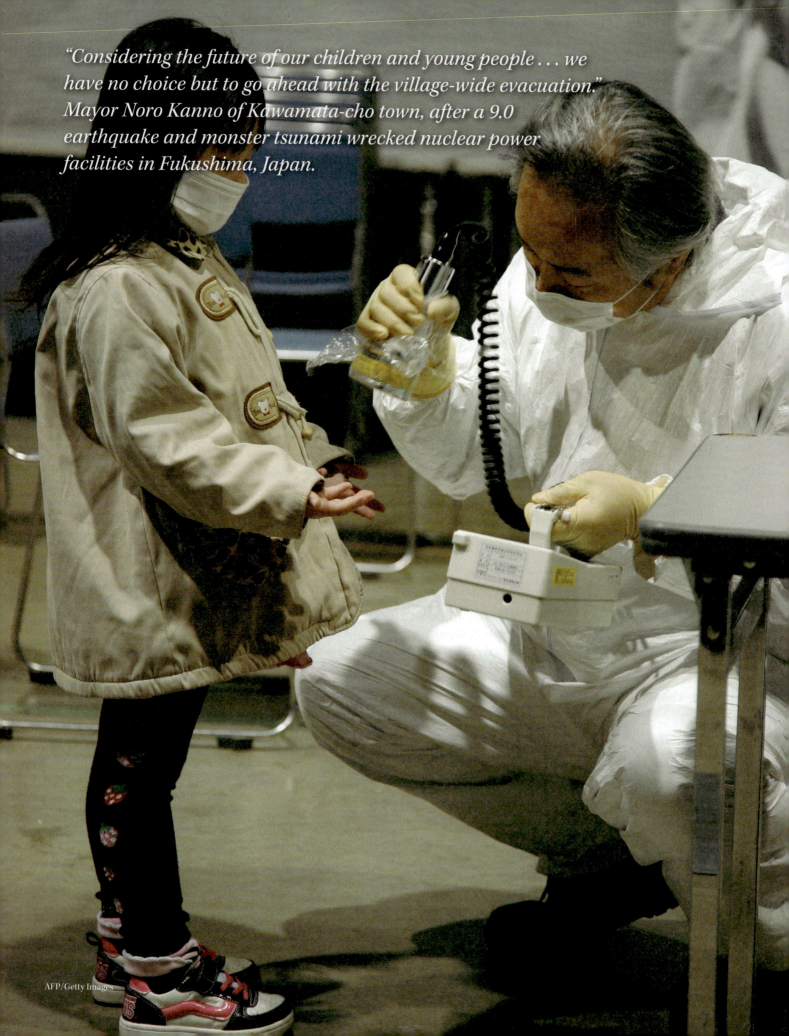

"Considering the future of our children and young people ... we have no choice but to go ahead with the village-wide evacuation." Mayor Noro Kanno of Kawamata-cho town, after a 9.0 earthquake and monster tsunami wrecked nuclear power facilities in Fukushima, Japan.

Plans and Planning Techniques

Get There Faster with Objectives

Fox 2000 Pictures/Photofest

5

Management Live

Time Management and 27 *Dresses*

In 27 *Dresses*, Jane Nichols (Katherine Heigl) works as a personal assistant for George (Edward Burns), the owner of Urban Everest. Jane has a penchant for detail and also lives a second life as "professional" bridesmaid and unofficial wedding planner.

The movie opens with Jane standing in for a bride as final alterations are made on the dress, then scurrying off to attend two weddings occurring almost simultaneously. We learn that Jane is a fastidious planner who keeps a "file of facts" and a tight schedule.

Managing time involves more than writing to-do lists. Jane is an excellent example. Unlike some who are good at writing things down but then never get the really important work done, Jane follows through. We might say she has a flair for wrapping things up with style.

What about you? You probably juggle multiple responsibilities, such as school, a job, relationships, and extracurricular activities. **Time management** is an essential planning skill in the fast-paced and complicated world of business and for new graduates entering the workforce. Are you able to do it like Jane, consistently getting the right things done in the right ways? Look for insights in this chapter to help improve your planning skills.

YOUR CHAPTER 5 TAKEAWAYS

1. Understand how and why managers use the planning process.
2. Identify the types of plans used by managers.
3. Describe useful planning tools and techniques.

WHAT'S INSIDE

Explore Yourself
More on **time management**

Role Models
Don Thompson keeps the focus for career success

Ethics Check
E-waste graveyards offer easy way out

Facts to Consider
Policies on office romances vary widely

Manager's Library
Analytics at Work: Smarter Decisions, Better Results by Thomas Davenport, Jeanne Harris, and Robert Morison

Takeaway 5.1
How and Why Do Managers Use the Planning Process?

ANSWERS TO COME

- Planning is one of the four functions of management.
- Planning is the process of setting objectives and identifying how to achieve them.
- Planning improves focus and action orientation.
- Planning improves coordination and control.
- Planning improves time management.

IT CAN BE EASY TO GET SO ENGROSSED IN THE PRESENT THAT WE FORGET ABOUT the future. Yet a mad rush to the future can sometimes go off track without solid reference points in the past. The trick is to blend past experiences and lessons with future aspirations and goals and to be willing to adjust as new circumstances arise. The management function of **planning** helps us do just that. It is a process of setting goals and objectives and determining how to best accomplish them. Said a bit differently, planning involves looking ahead, identifying exactly what you want to accomplish, and deciding how best to go about it.

Planning is the process of setting performance objectives and determining how to accomplish them.

⦀ Planning is one of the four functions of management.

Among the four management functions shown in **Figure 5.1**, planning comes first. When done well, it sets the stage for the others: organizing—allocating and arranging resources to accomplish tasks; leading—guiding the efforts of human resources to ensure high levels of task accomplishment; and controlling—monitoring task accomplishments and taking necessary corrective action.

In today's demanding organizational and career environments, effective planning is essential to staying one step ahead of the competition. An Eaton Corporation annual report, for example, once stated: "Planning at Eaton means taking the hard decisions before events force them upon you, and anticipating the future needs of the market before the demand asserts itself."[1]

You really should take these words to heart. But instead of a company, think about your personal situation. What hard decisions do you need to make? Where are the job markets going? Where do you want to be in your career and personal life in the next 5 or 10 years?

FIGURE 5.1 Why Does Planning Play a Central Role in the Management Process?
Planning is the first of the four management functions. It is the process of setting objectives—deciding where you want to go—and then identifying how to accomplish them—determining how to get there. When planning is done well, it provides a strong foundation for success with the other management functions.

‖ Planning is the process of setting objectives and identifying how to achieve them.

From experience alone, you are probably familiar with planning and all that it involves. But it also helps to understand Table 5.1—Steps in the Planning Process and its action implications.

Table 5.1 Steps in the Planning Process

Step 1. Define your objectives Know where you want to go; be specific enough to know you have arrived when you get there and how far off you are along the way.

Step 2. Determine where you stand vis-à-vis objectives Know where you presently stand in reaching the objectives; identify strengths that work in your favor and weaknesses that can hold you back.

Step 3. Develop premises regarding future conditions Generate alternative scenarios for what may happen; identify for each scenario things that may help or hinder progress toward your objectives.

Step 4. Make a plan Choose the action alternative most likely to accomplish your objectives; describe what must be done to implement this course of action.

Step 5. Implement the plan and evaluate results Take action; measure progress toward objectives as implementation proceeds; take corrective actions and revise the plan as needed.

Step 1 in planning is to define your **objectives** and to identify the specific results or desired goals you hope to achieve. This step is important enough to stop and reflect a moment. Whether you call them goals or objectives, they are targets. They point us toward the future and provide a frame of reference for evaluating progress. With them, as the module subtitle suggests, you should get where you want to go and get there faster.

Step 2 in planning is to compare where you are at present with the objectives. This establishes a baseline for performance; the present becomes a standard against which future progress can be gauged. Step 3 is to formulate premises about future conditions. It is where one looks ahead, trying to figure out what may happen. Step 4 is to make an actual **plan**. This is a list of actions that must be taken to accomplish the objectives. Step 5 is to implement the plan and evaluate results. This is where action takes place and measurement happens. Results are compared with objectives, and if needed, plans are modified to improve things in the future.

Have you thought about how well you plan and how you might do it better? Managers should be asking the same question. They rarely get to plan while working alone in quiet rooms free from distractions. Because of the fast pace and complications of the typical workday, managerial planning is ongoing. It takes place even as one deals with a constant flow of problems in a sometimes hectic and demanding work setting.[2] Yet it's all worth it: Planning offers many benefits to people and organizations.[3]

- **Action oriented**—keeping a results-driven sense of direction
- **Priority oriented**—making sure the most important things get first attention
- **Advantage oriented**—ensuring that all resources are used to best advantage
- **Change oriented**—anticipating problems and opportunities so they can be best dealt with

Objectives are specific results that one wishes to achieve.

A **plan** is a statement of intended means for accomplishing objectives.

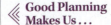 **Good Planning Makes Us . . .**

{ *Analytics at Work: Smarter Decisions, Better Results*
by Thomas Davenport, Jeanne Harris, and Robert Morison

Manager's **Library**

FACE THE FACTS, THOSE GUT FEELINGS COULD BE MISLEADING YOU

In the book *Analytics at Work: Smarter Decisions, Better Results* (2010, Harvard Business Press), authors Thomas Davenport, Jeanne Harris, and Robert Morison argue that organizations can improve their strategies by making better use of available information to guide decisions. A key point is that organizations have access to vast amounts of data but often fail to leverage it for competitive gain. Analytical approaches to decision making can yield smarter choices with improved results. Data sources include, among others, transactional records within enterprise systems and databases, clickstream data from Web activity, checkout scanner data, and information from customer loyalty programs.

The authors suggest that all aspects of organizations are ripe for analytic improvement. Customer relationships can be enhanced by segmenting types, understanding preferences, predicting desires, and identifying loyal or departing patrons. Supply chains can be streamlined by optimizing inventory levels, delivery routes, and production schedules. Human resources can be improved by hiring those likely to stay and predicting those prone to depart.

Analytics are great tools, and we need to get better at using them. The authors say organizations are more intelligent when managers use facts, and not feelings, to guide decisions.

REFLECT AND REACT

Choose a business and describe the analytics it might use to plan improvements in a process such as customer relationship management. For example, how might it determine which products are most popular, most profitable, or trending toward less popular? How might it optimize inventory levels or hire better workers? And by the way, do you also agree that better analytics can help improve personal planning?

The **complacency trap** is being lulled into inaction by current successes or failures.

||| Planning improves focus and action orientation.

Planning can help sharpen focus and increase flexibility, both of which improve performance. An organization with focus knows what it does best and what it needs to do. Individuals with focus know where they want to go in a career or situation, and they keep that focus even when difficulties arise. An organization with flexibility is willing and able to change and adapt to shifting circumstances. An individual with flexibility adjusts career plans to fit new and developing opportunities.

Planning helps us avoid the **complacency trap** of being lulled into inaction by successes or failures of the moment. Instead of being caught in the present, planning keeps us looking toward the future. Management consultant Stephen R. Covey described this as an action orientation with a clear set of priorities.[4] He said the most successful executives "zero in on what they do that adds value to an organization." They know what is important, and they work first on the things that really count. They don't waste time by working on too many things at once.

Would a friend or relative describe you as focused on priorities, or as always jumping from one thing to another? Could you achieve more by getting your priorities straight and working hard on things that really count?

Planning improves coordination and control.

Organizations consist of many people and subsystems doing many different things at the same time. But even as they pursue the various tasks, their accomplishments must add together meaningfully if the organization is to succeed. Good planning facilitates coordination by linking people and subsystems in a **hierarchy of objectives**. This is a means–ends chain in which lower-level objectives (the means) lead to the accomplishment of higher-level objectives (the ends). An example is the total quality management program shown in **Figure 5.2**.

In a **hierarchy of objectives**, lower-level objectives help to accomplish higher-level ones.

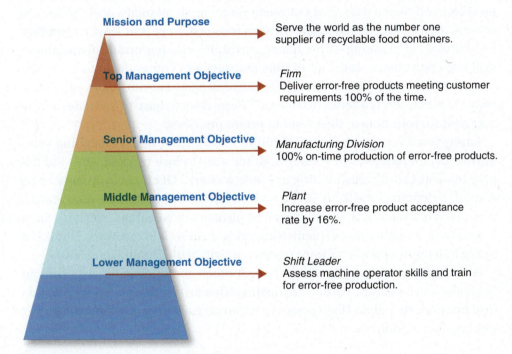

Mission and Purpose
Serve the world as the number one supplier of recyclable food containers.

Top Management Objective
Firm
Deliver error-free products meeting customer requirements 100% of the time.

Senior Management Objective
Manufacturing Division
100% on-time production of error-free products.

Middle Management Objective
Plant
Increase error-free product acceptance rate by 16%.

Lower Management Objective
Shift Leader
Assess machine operator skills and train for error-free production.

FIGURE 5.2
How Might a Hierarchy of Objectives Guide a Quality Management Program in a Manufacturing Firm?
A hierarchy of objectives identifies a means–ends chain through which lower-level objectives become the pathways for accomplishing higher-level ones. In the case of total quality management, the top-level objective (delivering error-free products that meet customer needs 100% of the time) moves step-by-step down the hierarchy until the point where a shift supervisor supports TQM with the objective of making sure that machine operators are trained well enough to do error-free work.

Good planning also sets the stage for controlling in the management process. It's hard to exercise control if you haven't set objectives. Without control, plans may fail because of a lack of follow-through. With both, it's a lot easier to see when things aren't going well and make the necessary adjustments. Two years after launching a costly information technology upgrade, for example, the CEO of McDonald's realized that the system couldn't deliver on its promises. He stopped the project, took a loss of $170 million, and refocused the firm's resources on projects with more direct impact on customers.[5]

Planning improves time management.

When Daniel Vasella was CEO of Novartis AG and its 98,000 employees spread across 140 countries, he was calendar bound—"locked in by meetings, travel and other constraints." To stay on track, he would list priorities of things to do. As CEO of ING US Wealth Management, Kathleen Murphy was also calendar bound, with conferences and travel booked a year ahead. She scheduled meetings at half-hour intervals, worked 12-hour days, and spent 60% of her time traveling.

She also made good use of her time on planes, where, she says, "no one can reach me by phone and I can get reading and thinking done."[6]

How to Better Manage Your Time »

- Set priorities for what really needs to get done.
- Work on the most important things first.
- Leave details for later, or delegate them to others.
- Say "No!" to requests that divert attention from your priorities.
- Take charge of your schedule; don't let others control what you do and when.
- Stick with your choices; not everything deserves immediate attention.

These are common executive stories—tight schedules, little time alone, lots of meetings and phone calls, and not much room for spontaneity. And the keys to success in these classic management scenarios rest, in part at least, on another benefit of good planning—time management. It is an important management skill and competency, and a lot of time management comes down to discipline and priorities. Lewis Platt, former chairman of Hewlett-Packard, once said: "Basically, the whole day is a series of choices."[7] These choices have to be made in ways that allocate your time to the most important priorities.

Surely you have experienced difficulties in balancing time-consuming commitments and requests. Indeed, it is all too easy to lose track of time and fall prey to what consultants identify as "time wasters." Of course, you have to be careful in defining "waste." It isn't a waste of time to occasionally relax, take a breather from work, and find humor and pleasure in social interactions. Such breaks help us gather and replenish energies to do well in our work. But it is a waste to let other people or nonessential activities dominate your time.[8]

Although to-do lists can help, they aren't much good unless the lists contain the high-priority things. We need to distinguish between things that we must do (top priority), should do (high priority), might do (low priority), and really don't need to do (no priority).

{ **TO-DO LISTS ARE OFTEN PUT TOGETHER WITH BEST INTENTIONS BUT FAIL TO DELIVER RESULTS AT THE END OF THE DAY.**

Explore **Yourself**

■ Time Management

One of the most consistently top rated "must-have" skills for new graduates entering fast-paced and complicated careers in business and management is **time management**. Many, perhaps most, of us keep to-do lists. But it's the rare person who is consistently successful in living up to one.

Time management is a form of planning, and planning can easily suffer the same fate as the to-do lists—put together with the best of intentions, but with little or nothing to show in terms of results at the end of the day. There are a lot of good ideas in this chapter on how to plan, both in man-

agement and in our personal lives. Now is a good time to get in touch with your time management skills and to start improving your capabilities to excel with planning as a basic management function.

Get to know yourself better by taking the **Time Management Profile** self-assessment and completing other activities in the *Exploring Management* **Skill-Building Portfolio**.

STUDY GUIDE

Takeaway 5.1
How and Why Do Managers Use the Planning Process?

Terms to Define

Complacency trap

Hierarchy of objectives

Objectives

Plan

Planning

Rapid Review

- Planning is the process of setting performance objectives and determining how to accomplish them.
- A plan is a set of intended actions for accomplishing important objectives.
- The steps in the planning process are (1) define your objectives, (2) determine where you stand vis-à-vis objectives, (3) develop premises regarding future conditions, (4) make a plan to best accomplish objectives, (5) implement the plan, and evaluate results.
- The benefits of planning include better focus and action orientation, better coordination and control, and better time management.
- Planning improves time management by setting priorities and avoiding time wasters.

Questions for Discussion

1. Should all employees plan, or just managers?
2. Which step in the planning process do you think is the hardest to accomplish?
3. How could better planning help in your personal career development?

Be Sure You Can

- explain the importance of planning as the first of four management functions
- list the steps in the formal planning process
- explain the important link between planning and controlling as management functions
- illustrate the benefits of planning for a business or an organization familiar to you
- illustrate the benefits of planning for your personal career development
- list at least three things you can do now to improve your time management

Career Situation: What Would You Do?

Someone you really care about wants you to take a step forward in time management. She asks you to make a list of all the things you plan to do tomorrow and identify which ones are (A) *most important*—top priority, (B) *important*—not top priority, and (C) *least important*—low priority. Next, she says to double-check your Bs—asking if any should be As or Cs, and your As—to see if any should be Bs or Cs? So do it, and see how things turn out. Can an exercise like this help you take charge of your time and get the really important things done first?

TEACHING NOTE:
Have students read and discuss Facts to Consider on p. 123—"Policies on Office Romances vary Widely." Ask where they stand on the issue. What's their take on the individual and employer points of view? How would they recommend employers deal with romance in the work environment?

Takeaway 5.2
What Types of Plans Do Managers Use?

ANSWERS TO COME

- Managers use short-range and long-range plans.
- Managers use strategic and operational plans.
- Organizational policies and procedures are plans.
- Budgets are plans that commit resources to activities.

MANAGERS FACE DIFFERENT PLANNING CHALLENGES IN THE FLOW AND PACE OF activities in organizations. In some cases, the planning environment is stable and predictable. In others, it is more dynamic and uncertain. To meet these different needs, managers rely on a variety of plans.

||| Managers use short-range and long-range plans.

We live and work in a fast-paced world where planning horizons are becoming compressed. We now talk about planning in Internet time, where businesses are continually changing and updating plans. Even most top managers would likely agree that *long*-range planning is becoming shorter and shorter. A reasonable rule of thumb in this context is that **short-range plans** cover a year or less, whereas **long-range plans** look ahead three or more years into the future.[9]

Quite frankly, the advent of Internet time and shorter planning horizons might be an advantage for many of us. Management researcher Elliot Jaques found that very few people have the capacity to think long term.[10] As shown in the figure, he believes that most of us work comfortably with only three-month time spans; some can think about a year into the future; only about one person in several million can handle a 20-year time frame.

Do Jaques's conclusions match your experience? And if we accept his findings, what are their implications for managers and career development? Although a team leader's planning challenges may rest mainly in the weekly or monthly range, a chief executive needs to have a vision extending at least some years into the future. Career progress to higher management levels still requires the conceptual skills to work well with longer-range time frames.[11]

Short-range plans usually cover a year or less.

Long-range plans usually cover three years or more.

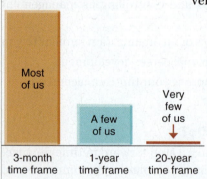

||| Managers use strategic and operational plans.

When planning for the organization as a whole or a major component, the focus is on **strategic plans**. These longer-term plans set broad and comprehensive directions for an organization. Well crafted strategic plans create a framework for allocating resources for best long-term performance impact. They take a **vision** that clarifies the purpose of the organization and what it hopes to be in the future and set out the ways to turn that vision into reality.

A **strategic plan** identifies long-term directions for the organization.

A **vision** clarifies the purpose of the organization and expresses what it hopes to be in the future.

Apple Plans for "Made in USA" to Become Part of Its New Mac Strategy

There was a time early in Apple's life when all Mac computers were made at U.S. factories. Then the strategy shifted to outsourcing with foreign suppliers and assembly plants. But problems with worker safety and employments conditions in some of its contractors' plants created uncomfortable publicity. Political pressures to bring jobs home added more fuel to the outsourcing fires. Now Apple CEO Tim Cook—considered the genius behind the firm's global supply chains, is planning to invest $100 million to shift at least some of that foreign production of Macs back to American soil. It won't be easy, and the plan is not a guaranteed success say analysts. Labor costs, worker skills, and even Federal Trade Commission rules on importing parts and qualifying for "Made in USA" labeling all add risk to the move.

Paul Sakuma/AP

When a sports team enters a game, it typically does so with a "strategy." Most often this strategy is set by the head coach in conjunction with assistants. The goal is clear—win the game. But as the game unfolds, a variety of situations arise that require adjustments and responses to solve problems or exploit opportunities. They call for "tactics" that deal with the situation at hand while advancing the overall strategy for winning against the competition. These tactics are often decided on by assistant coaches, perhaps in consultation with the head coach.

The same logic holds true for organizations. **Operational plans**, also called **tactical plans,** are developed to implement strategic plans. They are shorter-term and step-by-step means for putting the strategies into action. In the sports context, you might think of tactical plans as involving the use of "special teams" plans or as "special plays" designed to meet a particular threat or opportunity. In business, tactical plans often take the form of **functional plans** that indicate how different parts of the enterprise will contribute to the overall strategy. Such functional plans might include the following:

> An **operational plan** or **tactical plan** sets out ways to implement a strategic plan.

- *Financial plans* deal with money required to support various operations.
- *Facilities plans* deal with facilities development and work layouts.
- *Marketing plans* deal with the requirements of selling and distributing goods or services.
- *Human resource plans* deal with the recruitment, selection, and placement of people into various jobs.
- *Production plans* deal with the methods and technology needed by people in their work.

> A **functional plan** identifies how different parts of an enterprise will contribute to accomplishing strategic plans.

⦀ Organizational policies and procedures are plans.

In addition to strategic and operational plans, organizations also need plans that provide members with day-to-day guidance on such things as attendance, hiring practices, ethical behavior, privacy, trade secrets, and more. This is often provided in the form of organizational policies and procedures.

Yves Logghe/AP

{ **"HE HAS THE ABILITY TO LISTEN, BLEND IN, ANALYZE, AND COMMUNICATE. PEOPLE FEEL AT EASE WITH HIM."**

Role **Models**

■ Don Thompson Keeps the Focus for Career Success

Some call Don Thompson, President and CEO of McDonald's, the "accidental executive." He's not only one of the youngest top managers in the *Fortune* 500, but he also may have followed the most unusual career path. After graduating from Purdue University with a degree in electrical engineering, Thompson went to work for Northrop Grumman, a leading global security company. One day he received a call from a head-hunter. Thompson thought the job being offered was at McDonnell Douglas Company, a firm in which engineering is central. After finding out it was at McDonald's, he almost turned the opportunity down. But, after some encouragement he took the interview.

The first step in Thompson's career path at McDonald's was purchasing kitchen equipment. Later, and after he failed to win an annual McDonald's President's Award, the firm's diversity officer recommended that he speak with Raymond Mines, at the time the firm's highest-ranking African-American executive. When Thompson confided that he "wanted to have an impact on decisions," Mines told him to move out of engineering and into the operations side of the business. The advice was right on, and Thompson listened well. His work not only excelled, but he also got the attention needed to advance to ever-higher

responsibilities that spanned restaurant operations, franchisee relations, strategic management, and eventually being appointed the company's first African-American CEO.

Thompson works from a corner office that has no door, and the building is configured with an open floor plan—all that fits well with Thompson's style and personality. His former mentor Raymond Mines says: "He has the ability to listen, blend in, analyze, and communicate. People feel at ease with him. A lot of corporate executives have little time for those below them. Don makes everyone a part of the process." As for Thompson, he says, "I want to make sure others achieve their goals, just as I have."

WHAT'S THE LESSON HERE?

As a leader—Thompson is described as "a real people guy and a teddy bear of a man who often greets people with a hug." How much of Thompson's success traces to strong motivation, good planning, and clear goals? Is the resiliency he showed when things didn't always go according to plan a strength that many others might lack? Are there lessons here that could help others have successful careers?

A **policy** is a standing plan that communicates broad guidelines for decisions and action.

A **procedure** or rule precisely describes actions to take in specific situations.

A **policy** communicates broad guidelines for making decisions and taking action in specific circumstances. Common human resource policies address such matters as employee hiring, termination, performance appraisals, pay increases, promotions, discipline, and civility. Consider the issue of sexual harassment. How should individual behavior be guided? A sample sexual harassment policy states: "Sexual harassment is specifically prohibited by this organization. Any employee found to have violated the policy against sexual harassment will be subject to immediate and appropriate disciplinary action including but not limited to possible suspension or termination."

Procedures, or *rules*, describe exactly what actions to take in specific situations. They are often found in employee handbooks or manuals as SOPs (standard operating procedures). Whereas a policy sets broad guidelines, procedures define specific actions to be taken. A sexual harassment policy, for example, should be backed up with procedures that spell out how to file a sexual harassment complaint, as well as the steps through which any complaint will be handled.[12] When Judith Nitsch started her engineering consulting business, for example, she defined a sexual harassment policy, established clear procedures for its enforcement, and designated both a male and a female employee for others to talk with about sexual harassment concerns.[13]

Allison Michael Orenstein/
Getty Images

{ EIGHTY PERCENT OF EMPLOYERS PROHIBIT RELATIONSHIPS BETWEEN SUPERVISORS AND THEIR SUBORDINATES.

Facts to **Consider**

■ Policies on Office Romances Vary Widely

A former CEO of Boeing was asked to resign by the firm's board after his relationship with a female executive became public. But, employer policies on office relationships vary.

- 80% prohibit relationships between supervisors and subordinates.
- 24% prohibit relationships among persons in the same department.
- 13% prohibit relationships among persons who have the same supervisor.
- 5% have no restrictions on office romances.

- New trend—"love contracts," where employees pledge that their romantic relationships in the office won't interfere with their work.

YOUR THOUGHTS?

Do you know anyone who has been involved in an office relationship? What are your thoughts? Is this an area that employers should be regulating, or should office romance be left to the best judgments of those involved?

⫿ Budgets are plans that commit resources to activities.

A **budget** is a plan that commits resources to activities, programs, or projects. It is a powerful tool that allocates scarce resources among multiple and often competing uses. Managers typically negotiate with their bosses to obtain budgets that support the needs of their work units or teams. They are also expected to achieve performance objectives while keeping within their budgets.

Managers deal with and use various types of budgets. *Financial budgets* project cash flows and expenditures. *Operating budgets* plot anticipated sales or revenues against expenses. *Nonmonetary* budgets allocate resources such as labor, equipment, and space. A *fixed budget* allocates a fixed amount of resources for a specific purpose, such as $50,000 for equipment purchases in a given year. A *flexible budget* allows resources to vary in proportion with various levels of activity, such as monies to hire temporary workers when workloads exceed certain levels.

All budgets play important roles in organizations by linking planned activities with the resources needed to accomplish them. But budgets can also get out of control. Sometimes, perhaps much too often, they creep higher and higher without getting enough critical scrutiny. If in doubt, just tune in to the latest debates over local and national government budgets. One of the most common problems is that resource allocations are rolled over from one time period to the next without any real performance review. A **zero-based budget** deals with this problem by approaching each budget period as if it were brand new. No guarantee exists for renewing any past funding. Instead, all proposals compete with a fresh start for available resources. This helps eliminate waste by making sure scarce resources are not spent on unproductive, outdated, or low-priority activities.

A **budget** is a plan that commits resources to projects or activities.

A **zero-based budget** allocates resources as if each budget was brand new.

STUDY GUIDE

What Types of Plans Do Managers Use?

Terms to Define

Budget

Functional plan

Long-range plan

Operational (tactical) plan

Policy

Procedure

Short-range plan

Strategic plan

Vision

Zero-based budget

Rapid Review

- Short-range plans tend to cover a year or less, whereas long-range plans extend out to three years or more.
- Strategic plans set critical long-range directions; operational plans are designed to support and help implement strategic plans.
- Policies, such as a sexual harassment policy, are plans that set guidelines for the behavior of organizational members.
- Procedures are plans that describe actions to take in specific situations, such as how to report a sexual harassment complaint.
- Budgets are plans that allocate resources to activities or projects.
- A zero-based budget allocates resources as if each new budget period is brand new; no "rollover" resource allocations are allowed without new justifications.

Questions for Discussion

1. Is there any need for long-range plans in today's fast-moving environment?
2. What types of policies do you believe are essential for any organization?
3. Are there any possible disadvantages to zero-based budgeting?

Be Sure You Can

- differentiate short-range and long-range plans
- differentiate strategic and operational plans
- explain how strategic and operational plans complement one another
- differentiate policies and procedures, and give examples of each
- explain the benefits of a zero-based budget

Career Situation: What Would You Do?

One of the persons under your supervision has contacted you about a "possible" sexual harassment complaint against a co-worker. But, she says that the organization's procedures are not clear. You also decide they're not clear and take the matter to your boss. He tells you to draft a set of procedures that can be taken to top management for approval. What procedures will you recommend so that future sexual harassment complaints can be dealt with in a fair manner?

Takeaway 5.3
What Are Some Useful Planning Tools and Techniques?

ANSWERS TO COME

■ Forecasting tries to predict the future

■ Contingency planning creates backup plans for when things go wrong

■ Scenario planning crafts plans for alternative future conditions

■ Benchmarking identifies best practices used by others

■ Participatory planning improves implementation capacities

■ Goal setting helps align plans and activities throughout an organization

TEACHING NOTE: MOOCs, massive open online courses, are an emerging force in higher education. Ask students to brainstorm 2-3 alternative future scenarios for them at your college or university. Ask about their planning implications for the institution's current leadership.

THE BENEFITS OF PLANNING ARE BEST REALIZED WHEN PLANS ARE BUILT FROM strong foundations. Useful planning tools and techniques include forecasting, contingency planning, scenarios, benchmarking, participatory planning, and use of goal setting.

⫴ Forecasting tries to predict the future.

Crystal balls are notoriously cloudy when it comes to foreseeing the future. Who would have predicted just a few years ago that the time-tested auto brand Volvo would be bought by China's Geely, or that Jaguar and Land Rover would be bought by India's Tata group? Who would have predicted that two of America's giants—General Motors and Chrysler—would go in and out of bankruptcy while China was emerging as the largest car market in the world?

What about future conditions in the world at large? When asked recently to identify "where the danger lurks" ahead, 48% of top global executives chose climate change, 17% water shortages, 14% Middle East conflicts, 14% nuclear proliferation, and 6% pandemics.[14] But, are they focused on the right things and staying on top of the right trends? At least one corporate CEO, GE's Jeffery Immelt, is frank about his failure to plan well for the recent economic and financial crisis before it actually hit. "I should have done more to anticipate the radical changes that occurred" he says. He's since been restructuring GE around a model he believes is more consistent with new economic realities.[15]

Forecasting is the process of predicting what will happen in the future. Periodicals such as *Business Week, Fortune*, and *The Economist* regularly report forecasts of industry conditions, interest rates, unemployment trends, and national economies, among other issues.[16] Some rely on qualitative forecasting, which uses expert opinions to predict the future. Others involve quantitative forecasting, which uses mathematical models and statistical analysis of historical data and surveys.

Most plans involve forecasts of some sort. But, any forecast should be used with caution. Forecasts are planning aids, not planning substitutes. It is said that a music agent once told Elvis Presley: "You ought to go back to driving a truck because you ain't going nowhere." That's the problem with forecasts. They always rely on human judgment, and that judgment can be wrong.

Forecasting attempts to predict the future.

||| Contingency planning creates backup plans for when things go wrong.

Of course things often go wrong. It is highly unlikely that any plan will ever be perfect. But picture this scene. A golfer is striding down the golf course with an iron in each hand. The one in her right hand is "the plan"; the one in her left is the "backup plan." Which club she uses will depend on how the ball lies on the fairway. One of any professional golfer's greatest strengths is being able to adjust to the situation by putting the right club to work in the circumstances at hand.

Planning in our work and personal affairs is often like that of the golfer. By definition, planning involves thinking ahead. But the more uncertain the environment, the more likely one's original assumptions, forecasts, and intentions may prove inadequate or wrong. And when they do, the best managers and organizations have alternative plans ready to go.

Contingency planning identifies alternative courses of action that can be implemented to meet the needs of changing circumstances. A really good contingency plan will contain "trigger points" for activating preselected alternatives. This is really an indispensable planning tool. But, it's surprising how many organizations lack good contingency plans to deal with unexpected events.

Poor contingency planning was very much in the news when debates raged over how BP managed the disastrous Deepwater Horizon oil spill in the Gulf of Mexico. Everyone from the public at large to U.S. lawmakers to oil industry experts criticized BP not only for failing to contain the spill quickly, but also for failing to anticipate and have contingency plans in place to handle such a crisis.

A BP spokesperson initially said—"You have here an unprecedented event . . . the unthinkable has become thinkable and the whole industry will be asking questions of itself."

An oil industry expert responded—"There should be a technology that is preexisting and ready to deploy at the drop of a hat . . . it shouldn't have to be designed and fabricated now, from scratch."

Former BP CEO Tony Hayward finally admitted—"There are some capabilities that we could have available to deploy instantly, rather than creating as we go."[17]

The lesson in the BP example is hard-earned but very clear. Contingency planning can't prevent crises from occurring. But when things do go wrong, there's nothing better to have in place than good contingency plans.

||| Scenario planning crafts plans for alternative future conditions.

A long-term version of contingency planning, called **scenario planning**, identifies several alternative future scenarios. Managers then make plans to deal with each, so they will be better prepared for whatever occurs.[18] In this sense, scenario planning forces them to really think far ahead.

This approach was developed years ago at Royal Dutch/Shell, when top managers asked themselves a perplexing question: "What would Shell do after its oil supplies ran out?" Although recognizing that scenario planning can never be inclusive of all future possibilities, a Shell executive once said that it helps "condition the organization to think" and better prepare for "future shocks."[19]

Contingency planning
identifies alternative courses of action to take when things go wrong.

CHRISTOPHE SIMON/AFP/Getty Images

Scenario planning identifies alternative future scenarios and makes plans to deal with each.

Shell uses scenario planning to tackle such issues as climate change, sustainable development, fossil-fuel alternatives, human rights, and biodiversity. Most typically it involves descriptions of "worst cases" and "best cases." In respect to oil supplies, for example, a worst-case scenario might be that global conflict and devastating effects on the natural environment occur as nations jockey with one another to secure increasingly scarce supplies of oil and other natural resources. A best-case scenario might be that governments work together to find pathways that take care of everyone's resource needs while supporting the sustainability of global resources.

⦀ Benchmarking identifies best practices used by others.

All too often managers become too comfortable with the ways things are going. They fall into the complacency trap discussed earlier and let habits and overconfidence trick them into believing the past is a good indicator of the future. Planning helps us deal with such tendencies by challenging the status quo and reminding us not to always accept things as they are. One way to do this is through **benchmarking**, a planning technique that makes use of external comparisons to better evaluate current performance.[20]

Benchmarking uses external comparisons to gain insights for planning.

budgetstockphoto/iStockphoto

{ OUR UNWANTED ELECTRICAL PRODUCTS OFTEN END UP IN OFFSHORE E-WASTE GRAVEYARDS.

Ethics **Check**

■ E-Waste Graveyards Offer Easy Way Out

"Give me a plan," says the boss. "We need to get rid of our electronic waste."

This isn't an uncommon problem. Have you ever considered where your old cell phone or computer monitor ends up when discarded in favor of a new one? Rapid changes in technology, effective advertising, and planned or built-in product obsolescence—designing a product with a limited useful life so that it becomes obsolete—have fueled what may be called an "e-waste monster."

Lots of e-waste ends up in less-developed countries in Asia and Africa. The waste arrives by sea container or barge and goes into huge dumps. Local laborers, perhaps including children, disassemble the waste products under unsafe conditions and using methods like open-air incineration and acid baths. Their goal is to salvage valuable metals like platinum, silver, and gold and base metals like copper, iron, and aluminum.

Exporting to e-waste graveyards overseas may be less expensive than dealing with the waste at home, but what are the adverse environmental and health effects? What is the harm to people and planet? It isn't a stretch to say that the workers often inhale toxic fumes; nearby streams can be polluted with runoff waste; and even the streets and living areas of the workers become cluttered with electronic debris. Monitors or TVs with cathode-ray tubes contain up to four pounds of toxic lead. If improperly disposed, it can cause harm to health and environment. Hazardous substances such as lead, cadmium, mercury, and chromium are part of many electronics. When released, they can pollute groundwater and cause neurological damage in children.

It can be expensive to properly dispose of electronic waste. Regulatory controls or laws on its export tend to be light. Going offshore with e-waste may be cheap and easy. But, is it the correct thing to do?

YOU DECIDE

As countries become profitable hosts for e-waste, their governments may look the other way when it comes to environmental and human costs. Some even argue that e-waste business helps with a country's development. Whose responsibility is it to deal with the adverse consequences of e-waste disposal? Is it just a local matter? Do the originating country and consumer have obligations as well? If a manager gives the directive to "ship the waste overseas" is this acceptable business practice?

Managers use benchmarking to discover what other people and organizations are doing well and plan how to incorporate these ideas into their own operations. They search for **best practices** inside and outside the organization and among competitors and noncompetitors alike. These are things that others are doing and that help them to achieve superior performance. As a planning tool, benchmarking is basically a way of learning from the successes of others. There's little doubt that sports stars benchmark one another; scientists and scholars do it; executives and managers do it. Could you be doing it, too?

Many top firms make good use of best practices benchmarks. Xerox, for example, has benchmarked L. L. Bean's warehousing and distribution methods, Ford's plant layouts, and American Express's billing and collections. In building its "world car," the Fiesta, Ford benchmarked BMW's 3 series. James D. Farley, Ford's global marketing head says: "The ubiquity of the 3 series engenders trust in every part of the world, and its design always has a strong point of view. . . ."[21] And in the fast-moving apparel industry, the Spanish retailer Zara has become a benchmark for both worried competitors and others outside the industry.[22] Zara is praised for excellence in affordable "fast-fashion." The firm's design and manufacturing systems allow it to get new fashions from design to stores in 2 weeks, whereas competitors may take months. Zara produces only in small batches that sell out and create impressions of scarcity. Shoppers at Zara know they have to buy now because an item will not be replaced, whereas at competitors, shoppers often wait for sales and inventory clearance bargains.

Best practices are methods that lead to superior performance.

Participatory planning includes the persons who will be affected by plans and/or who will be asked to implement them.

‖ Participatory planning improves implementation capacities.

When it comes to implementation, participation can be a very important word in planning. **Participatory planning**, as shown in **Figure 5.3**, includes in all steps of the process those people whose ideas and inputs can benefit the plans and whose support is needed for implementation. It has all the advantages of group decision making discussed in Chapter 4.

Participatory planning can increase the creativity and information available, it can increase understanding and acceptance of plans, and it can build stronger commitments to a plan's success. When 7-Eleven executives planned for new upscale products and services, such as selling fancy meals-to-go, they learned this lesson the hard way. Although their ideas sounded good at the top, franchise owners and managers disagreed. Their resistance taught the executives the value of taking time to involve lower levels in planning new directions for the stores.[23]

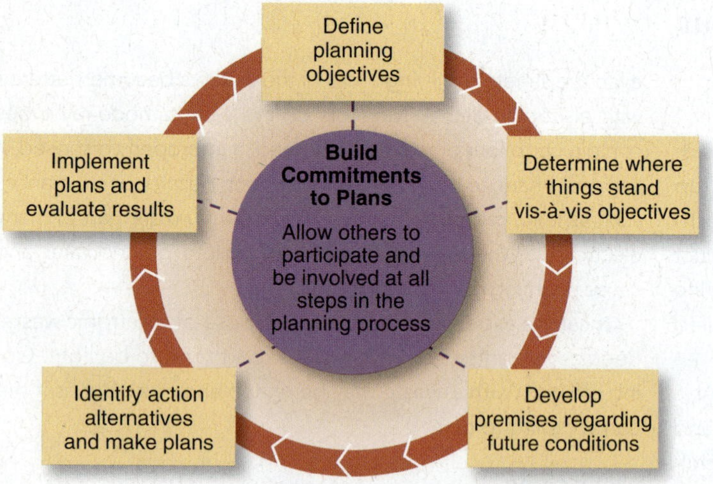

FIGURE 5.3 **How Do Participation and Involvement Help Build Commitments to Plans?**
Any plan needs the efforts and support of many people to make it work. It is easier and more likely to get this commitment when the people responsible for implementation have had the opportunity to participate in developing the plans in the first place. When managers use participatory planning and allow others to become involved in the planning process, it leads to better plans, a deeper understanding of the plans, and a strengthened commitment to fully implementing the plans.

‖ Goal setting helps align plans and activities throughout an organization.

In the dynamic and highly competitive technology industry, CEO T. J. Rodgers of Cypress Semiconductor Corp. supports a planning system where employees work with clear and quantified work goals that they help set. He believes the system helps people find problems before they interfere with performance. Says Rodgers: "Managers monitor the goals, look for problems, and expect people who fall behind to ask for help before they lose control of or damage a major project.[24]

Although Rodgers makes us aware of the importance of goal setting in management, he may make it look too easy. Just how goals are set can make a big difference in whether they work well or poorly to point people in the right directions and make sure plans are well implemented. If they are to have the desired effects, goals and objectives have to be good ones; they should push us to achieve substantial, not trivial, things. Jack Welch, former CEO of GE, believed in **stretch goals**—performance targets that we have to work extra hard and really stretch to reach.[25] Would you agree that stretch goals can add real strength to the planning process, for organizations and for individuals?

The following guidelines are starting points in moving from "no goals" and even just everyday run-of-the-mill "average goals" to having really "great goals"—ones that result in plans being successfully implemented. Great goals are

> **Stretch goals** are performance targets that we have to work extra hard and stretch to reach.

1. *Specific*—clearly target key results and outcomes to be accomplished.
2. *Timely*—linked to specific timetables and "due dates."
3. *Measurable*—described so results can be measured without ambiguity.
4. *Challenging*—include a stretch factor that moves toward real gains.
5. *Attainable*—although challenging, realistic and possible to achieve.

> « **5 Criteria for Great Goals**

Even when individual goals are well set as part of a plan, managers must still make sure that the goals and plan for one person or work unit help accomplish the goals of the organization as a whole. It's always important to align goals from one level to the next so that the right things happen at the right times throughout an organization. Goals set anywhere in the organization should ideally help advance its overall mission or purpose. Strategic goals set by top management should cascade down the organization to become goals and objectives for lower levels. Ideally, goals link together across levels in a consistent "means–end" fashion as suggested earlier in Figure 5.2. When a hierarchy of goals and objectives is well defined through good planning, this helps improve coordination among the multiple tasks, components, and levels of work in organizations.

STUDY GUIDE

Takeaway 5.3
What Are Some Useful Planning Tools and Techniques?

Terms to Define

Benchmarking

Best practices

Contingency planning

Forecasting

Participatory planning

Scenario planning

Stretch goals

Rapid Review

- Forecasting, which attempts to predict what might happen in the future, is a planning aid but not a planning substitute.
- Contingency planning identifies alternative courses of action to implement if and when circumstances change and an existing plan fails.
- Scenario planning analyzes the implications of alternative versions of the future.
- Benchmarking utilizes external comparisons to identify best practices that could become planning targets.
- Participation and involvement open the planning process to valuable inputs from people whose efforts are essential to the effective implementation of plans.

Questions for Discussion

1. If forecasting is going to be imperfect, why bother with it?
2. Shouldn't all planning provide for contingency plans?
3. Are stretch goals a good fit for today's generation of college students when they enter the workplace?

Be Sure You Can

- differentiate among forecasting, contingency planning, scenario planning, and benchmarking
- explain the importance of contingency planning
- describe the benefits of participatory planning as a special case of group decision making

Career Situation: What Would You Do?

As CEO you've decided to hire a consulting firm to help write a strategic plan for your organization. The plan is important, but you are worried about getting "buy-in" from all members, not just those at the top. What guidelines will you give the consultants so that they come up with a solid strategic plan that has strong commitments to its implementation by all members of your organization?

TestPrep 5

Answers to TestPrep questions can be found at the back of the book.

Multiple-Choice Questions

1. Planning is best described as the process of _____ and _____.
   (a) developing premises about the future; evaluating them
   (b) measuring results; taking corrective action
   (c) measuring past performance; targeting future performance
   (d) setting objectives; deciding how to accomplish them

2. The benefits of planning often include _____.
   (a) improved focus
   (b) less need for controlling
   (c) more accurate forecasts
   (d) guaranteed success

3. The first step in the planning process is to _____.
   (a) decide how to get where you want to go
   (b) define your objectives
   (c) identify possible future conditions or scenarios
   (d) act quickly to take advantage of opportunities

4. As a first step to help implement her firm's strategic plans, the CEO of a business firm would want marketing, manufacturing, and finance executives to develop clear and appropriate _____.
   (a) procedures
   (b) operational plans
   (c) zero-based budgets
   (d) forecasts

5. _____ planning identifies alternative courses of action that can be quickly taken if problems occur with the original plan.
   (a) Benchmark
   (b) Participatory
   (c) Staff
   (d) Contingency

6. Having a clear sexual harassment policy won't help an organization much unless it is accompanied by clear _____ that let all members know for sure how it will be implemented.
   (a) contingencies
   (b) benchmarks
   (c) procedures
   (d) budgets

7. When a manager is asked to justify a new budget proposal on the basis of projected activities rather than as an incremental adjustment to the prior year's budget, this is an example of _____.
   (a) zero-based budgeting
   (b) strategic planning
   (c) operational planning
   (d) contingency planning

8. One of the expected benefits of participatory planning is _____.
   (a) faster planning
   (b) less need for forecasting
   (c) greater attention to contingencies
   (d) more commitment to implementation

9. When managers use benchmarking in the planning process, they usually try to _____.
   (a) set up flexible budgets
   (b) identify best practices used by others
   (c) find the most accurate forecasts that are available
   (d) use expert staff planners to set objectives

10. In a hierarchy of objectives, plans at lower levels are supposed to act as _____ for accomplishing higher-level plans.
    (a) means
    (b) ends
    (c) scenarios
    (d) benchmarks

11. If a team leader wants to tap the advantages of participatory planning, what type of decision-making method should he or she use?

(a) Authority

(b) Quantitative

(c) Group

(d) Zero-based

12. From a time management perspective, which manager is likely to be in best control of his or her time? One who _____.

(a) tries to never say "no" to requests from others

(b) works on the most important things first

(c) immediately responds to instant messages

(d) always has "an open office door"

13. A marketing plan in a business firm would most likely deal with _____.

(a) production methods and technologies

(b) money and capital investments

(c) facilities and workforce recruiting

(d) sales and product distribution

14. The best planning goals or objectives would have which of the following characteristics?

(a) Easy enough so that no one fails to reach them

(b) Realistic and possible to achieve, while still challenging

(c) Open ended, with no clear end point identified

(d) No set timetable or due dates

15. The planning process isn't complete until _____.

(a) future conditions have been identified

(b) stretch goals have been set

(c) plans are implemented and results evaluated

(d) budgets commit resources to plans

Short-Response Questions

16. List the five steps in the planning process, and give examples of each.

17. How does planning facilitate controlling?

18. What is the difference between contingency planning and scenario planning?

19. Why is participation good for the planning process?

Integration and Application Question

20. My friends Curt and Rich own a local bookstore. They are very interested in making plans for improving the store and better dealing with competition from the other bookstores that serve college students in our town. I once heard Curt saying to Rich: "We should be benchmarking what some of the successful coffee shops, restaurants, and novelty stores are doing." Rich replied: "I don't see why; we should only be interested in bookstores. Why don't we study the local competition and even look at what the best bookstores are doing in the big cities?"

Questions: Who is right, Curt or Rich? If you were hired as a planning consultant to them, what would you suggest as the best way to utilize benchmarking as a planning technique to improve their bookstore? And, how would you use the planning process to help Curt and Rich come to a point of agreement on the best way forward for their bookstore?

Steps*for* FurtherLearning

BUILD MARKETABLE SKILLS
DO A CASE ANALYSIS
GET AND STAY INFORMED

BUILD

MARKETABLE SKILLS. EARN BIG CAREER PAYOFFS!

Don't miss these opportunities in the Skill-Building Portfolio

■ **SELF-ASSESSMENT 5:**
Time Management Profile
Time does count, but who really counts time? . . . check your time management skills.

■ **CLASS EXERCISE 5:**
The Future Workplace
Good jobs are hard to find . . . look ahead and prepare for tomorrow's opportunities.

■ **TEAM PROJECT 5:**
Personal Career Planning
Your career planning should have started yesterday . . . it's not too late to build a plan for success.

Many learning resources are found at the end of the book and online within WileyPLUS.

Take advantage of **Cases for Critical Thinking**

■ **CHAPTER 5 CASE SNAPSHOT:**
Nordstrom—"High Touch" with "High Tech"/
Sidebar on Global Supply Chains

A trip to the local department store isn't always a turn on. But a trip to Nordstrom's . . . well that's usually a trip worth taking. How has Nordstrom managed to stay fashionable and profitable in an economy of recession-weary consumers? How does it keep up with, or ahead of, changing fashion trends and intense competition among retailers? The fourth generation of family members running this business has brought time-honored retail practices into a new era. But in many ways, it's just the basics with an added dash of technology that makes the difference. Nordstrom provides a quality customer experience via personalized service, a compelling merchandise offering, a pleasant shopping environment and tight inventory management. Acute attention to detail and well-laid plans have allowed the company to navigate difficult times better than many rivals.

DO

A CASE ANALYSIS. STRENGTHEN YOUR CRITICAL THINKING!

Dig into this **Hot Topic**

■ **PRO AND CON DEBATE** Keep your career plan tight and focused, or loosen up?

Executive 1. "Career planning is more art than science. . . . Nonetheless, some form of plan can greatly enhance the evaluation of various opportunities and enable you to make better career decisions. A career plan allows you to identify how to use your basic strengths to maximum advantage, set major career objectives, and establish immediate milestones to measure personal development and advancement."

GET

AND STAY INFORMED. MAKE YOURSELF VALUABLE!

Executive 2. "A career . . . is a series of accidental changes of job and shifts of scenery on which you look back later, weaving through the story retroactively some thread of logic that was not visible at the time. If you try to carefully to plan your life, the danger is that you will succeed—succeed in narrowing your options and closing off avenues of adventure that cannot now be imagined."

Those in favor of tight career planning are likely to say: "You need a plan to give yourself a sense of direction." . . . "Having a career objective is highly motivating." . . . . "Without a plan you'll wander and not accomplish much of anything." *Those against tight career planning are likely to say:* "How can you know today what the future might offer?" . . . "If you are too tightly focused you won't spot unique opportunities." . . . "We grow and change over time, our career plans should too."

Final Faceoff. Both executives are talking from experience and personal success. Is executive 1's advice right for most people—careers should be carefully planned and then implemented step-by-step to achieve a long-term goal? Or is executive 2's advice right for most people—careers are best built with flexibility and spontaneity to take advantage of opportunities that pop up along the way? How do these perspectives fit with what we know about job markets and career directions today? Which position do you favor? Or, would you rather blend a bit of both to carve a pathway to career success?

"Over the past two weeks we have been receiving a lot of feed-back about Apple's repair and warranty policy in China. . . . We express our sincere apologies for any concerns or misunder-standings this gave consumers."

Controls and Control Systems

What Gets Measured Happens

Resiliency and *Forest Gump*

Growing up in the Deep South, Forrest Gump (Tom Hanks) is no stranger to adversity. Despite being bullied about his learning disability, he develops as a runner and turns this into an opportunity to play football at the University of Alabama. Gump is wounded while saving soldiers, including his dying friend Bubba, during the Vietnam War. He receives the Medal of Honor from President Kennedy.

Instead of retiring after the war on a military pension for his wounds, Gump seizes another opportunity. He learns how to play Ping-Pong during his recovery and gets to take part in a sports exchange to improve diplomatic relations with China. He returns to the United States and makes good on a promise to start the Bubba Gump Shrimp Company—named for his wartime friend.

Gump's positive outlook—often stated using the phrase "Life is like a box of chocolates"—and actions demonstrate **resiliency**. This is the ability to call on inner strength and keep moving forward even when things are tough.

How well do you respond to adversity? Watch *Forrest Gump*. It's a feel-good story with plenty of emotion. Ask yourself whether you would be able to bounce back as often as Gump does. As you review this chapter, think about ways you can develop internal control mechanisms and make yourself more resilient.

Paramount Pictures/Photofest

YOUR CHAPTER 6 TAKEAWAYS

1. Understand how and why managers use the control process.

2. Identify types of controls used by managers.

3. Describe useful control tools and techniques.

WHAT'S INSIDE

Explore Yourself
More on **resiliency**

Role Models
Bill Gates calls for better measurement to fix global problems

Ethics Check
Global privacy and censorship worries

Facts to Consider
Distractions can be goal killers

Manager's Library
Lean In: Women, Work and the will to Lead by Sheryl Sandberg

TEACHING NOTE:
Turn the discussion personal by asking students to read and discuss the Facts to Consider feature on "distractions." Get them to describe common distractions they face. Next have them show how the steps in the control process might be used to better deal with distractions in their daily lives.

Takeaway 6.1
How and Why Do Managers Use the Control Process?

ANSWERS TO COME

- Controlling is one of the four functions of management.
- Step 1—Control begins with objectives and standards.
- Step 2—Control measures actual performance.
- Step 3—Control compares results with objectives and standards.
- Step 4—Control takes corrective action as needed.

"KEEPING IN TOUCH" . . . "STAYING INFORMED" . . . "BEING IN CONTROL." THESE ARE important responsibilities for every manager. Yet "control" is a word like "power." If you aren't careful when and how the word is used, it leaves a negative connotation. But control plays a positive and necessary role in the management process. To have things "under control" is good; for things to be "out of control" is generally bad.[1]

So, you might ask: What happened at these well-known companies?[2]

Toyota—Recalled more than 6 million vehicles to fix throttle problems. Afterwards, Toyota North America's president and COO Jim Lentz said: "I am truly sorry for the concern our recalls have caused, and want you to know we're doing everything we can—as fast as we can—to make things right. . . . We'll continue to do everything we can to meet—and exceed—your expectations and justify your continued trust in Toyota."

Apple—Faced government criticism and customer push back in China over questions about warranty policies and repair charges. With China representing some 15% of Apple revenues, CEO Tim Cook was quick to issue a public apology. "We are aware that a lack of communications . . . led to the perception that Apple is arrogant and doesn't care to attach enough importance to customer feedback," he said. "We express our sincere apologies for any concerns or misunderstanding this gave consumers."

Lululemon—Recalled 17% of its black yoga pants after customers discovered that they were see-through when worn. Full refunds were offered and the cost to the firm was damaged reputation plus some $60 million in lost revenues. Addressing the issue of transparent yoga tights, Lululemon's CEO Christine Day, since replaced, seemed to look for excuses when she said: "The only way to test for the problem is to put the pants on and bend over."

⫼ Controlling is one of the four functions of management.

Controlling is the process of measuring performance and taking action to ensure desired results.

Managers understand **controlling** as a process of measuring performance and taking action to ensure desired results. Its purpose is straightforward—to make sure that plans are achieved and that actual performance meets or surpasses objectives. Like any aspect of decision making, the foundation of control is information. Henry Schacht, former CEO of Cummins Engine Company, once discussed control in terms of what he called "friendly facts." "Facts that reinforce what you are doing . . . are nice," he said, "because they help in terms of psychic reward. Facts that raise alarms are equally friendly, because they give you clues about how to respond, how to change, where to spend the resources."[3]

Just how does control fit in with the other management functions? Planning sets the directions. Organizing arranges people and resources for work. Leading inspires people toward their best efforts. And as shown in **Figure 6.1**, controlling sees to it that the right things happen, in the right way, and at the right time. If things go wrong, control helps get things back on track.

Effective control offers the great opportunity of learning from experience. Consider, for example, the program of **after-action review** pioneered by the U.S. Army and now utilized in many other organization settings. It is a structured review of lessons learned and results accomplished through a completed project, task force assignment, or special operation. Participants answer questions like: "What was the intent?" "What actually happened?" "What did we learn?"[4] The after-action review encourages everyone involved to take responsibility for his or her performance efforts and accomplishments.

Even though improving performance through learning is one of the great opportunities offered by the control process, the potential benefits are realized only when learning is translated into corrective actions. For example, after IBM executives learned that male attitudes were major barriers to the success of female managers they made male senior executives report annually on the progress of women managers in their divisions. This action substantially increased the percentage of women in IBM's senior management ranks.[5]

‖ Step 1—Control begins with objectives and standards.

The control process consists of the four steps shown in **Figure 6.2**. The process begins with setting performance objectives and standards for measuring them. It can't start any other way. This is the planning part: setting the performance objectives against which results can eventually be compared. Measurement standards are important, too. It isn't always easy to set them, but they are essential.

We often hear about earnings per share, sales growth, and market shares as standards for measuring business performance. Others include quantity and quality of production, costs incurred, service or delivery time, and error rates. But how about other types of organizations, such as a symphony orchestra? When the Cleveland Orchestra wrestled with

FIGURE 6.1 Why Is Controlling So Important in the Management Process?
Controlling is one of the four management functions. It is the process of measuring performance—finding out how well you are doing, and taking action to ensure desired results—making sure results meet expectations. When controlling is done well, it sets a strong foundation for performance. As the old adage says: What gets measured happens.

After-action review is a structured review of lessons learned and results accomplished through a completed project, task force assignment, or special operation.

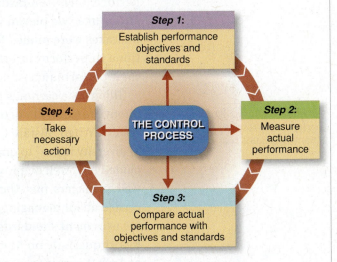

FIGURE 6.2 What Are the Four Steps in the Control Process?
The control process is straightforward: (1) set performance objectives and standards, (2) measure actual performance, (3) compare actual performance with objectives and standards, (4) take corrective action as needed. Although essential to management, these steps apply equally well to personal careers. Without career objectives, how do you know where you really want to go? How can you allocate time and other resources to take best advantage of opportunities? Without measurement, how can you assess how well you are doing and make adjustments to do better in the future?

Facts to **Consider**

■ Distractions can be Goal Killers

Most of us work with good intentions. But when distractions hit, focus gets lost, plans fall by the wayside, and progress suffers. Whether it's chatting with co-workers, following social media, or tackling electronic in-boxes, interruptions are more plentiful than we might admit.

- Office workers get distracted as often as once every 3 minutes and it takes an average of 23 minutes to refocus after a major interruption.
- Handling up to 100 electronic messages can kill up to one-half a workday.
- Facilitators of disruptions include open-plan office spaces, use of multiple electronic devices, and constant checking of social media and messaging windows.

Lacy Roberson, eBay's director of learning and organization development, calls the situation "an epidemic" and says it's hard for people to get their work done with all the interruptions and stress they cause. The fight against disruptions causes some workers to start extra early or stay late to get their jobs done. Employers are starting to fight back and try to protect "real work" time.

"No devices" is a rule at some eBay meetings. Intel is experimenting with allowing workers blocks of "think time" where they don't answer messages or attend meetings. Abbot Laboratories is retraining workers to use the telephone rather than e-mail for many internal office communications.

YOUR THOUGHTS

How prone are you to letting distractions consume your time? Does this problem apply to your personal affairs and relationships, not just work? It's interesting that some employers are trying to step in and set policies that might minimize the negative impact of distractions, particularly electronic ones. Where's the self-control? Aren't there things we can all do to protect our time and keep our work and goals on track?

---

performance standards, the members weren't willing to rely on vague generalities like "we played well," "the audience seemed happy," and "not too many mistakes were made." Rather, they decided to track standing ovations, invitations to perform in other countries, and how often other orchestras copied their performance styles.[6]

Things like earnings per share for a business and standing ovations for a symphony are examples of **output standards**. They measure actual outcomes or work results. When Allstate Corporation launched a new diversity initiative, it created a "diversity index" to quantify performance on diversity issues. The standards included how well employees met the goals of bias-free customer service and how well managers met the firm's diversity expectations.[7] When GE became concerned about managing ethics in its 320,000-member global workforce, it created measurement standards to track compliance. Each business unit was required to report quarterly on how many of its members attended ethics training sessions and what percentage signed the firm's "Spirit and Letter" ethics guide.[8]

The control process also uses **input standards** to measure work efforts. These are helpful in situations where outputs are difficult or expensive to measure. Examples of input standards for a college professor might be having an orderly course syllabus, showing up at all class sessions, and returning exams and assignments in a timely fashion. Of course, as this example might suggest, measuring inputs doesn't mean that outputs, such as high-quality teaching and learning, are necessarily achieved. Other examples of input standards in the workplace include conformance with rules and procedures, efficiency in the use of resources, and work attendance or punctuality.

An **output standard** measures performance results in terms of quantity, quality, cost, or time.

An **input standard** measures work efforts that go into a performance task.

{ YOU CAN ACHIEVE INCREDIBLE PROGRESS IF YOU SET A CLEAR GOAL AND FIND A MEASURE THAT WILL DRIVE PROGRESS TOWARD THAT GOAL.

Role Models

Bill Gates Calls for Better Measurement to Fix Global Problems

"Measure them!" advises Bill Gates. The world's problems will remain unsolved unless we do it and do it well. He says: "I have been struck by how important measurement is to improving the human condition. You can achieve incredible progress if you set a clear goal and find a measure that will drive progress toward that goal." Gates believes that failures to fix social problems like polio and poor education are often due to missing or poor measurement combined with an unwillingness to listen to data and make changes based on it. "We can do better," he says. "We have the tools at hand."

The United Nations and its commitment to The Millennium Development Goals earn Gates's praise. This compact commits 189 nations to make measured improvements by 2015 in the health, education, and income of their populations. Its value, according to Gates, comes from consensus to focus on clear and important priorities and to follow through with concrete measurement of progress made or lost. One Millennium Development Goal is to lower child mortality by 2015 to two-thirds of its rate in 1990. Through investments in community health workers and measurement of their impact, Ethiopia has already achieved a 60% decline.

Gates describes the challenge this way. "In the U.S. we should be measuring the value added by colleges. . . . In agriculture, creating a global productivity target would help countries focus on a key but neglected area: the efficiency and output of hundreds of millions of small farmers who live in poverty. . . In poor countries we still need better ways to measure the effectiveness of the many government workers providing health services . . . I'd love to have a way to measure how exposure to risks like disease, infection, malnutrition and problem pregnancies impact children's potential."

In making his case for "extraordinary measures," Bill Gates is offering society a pathway to progress through big goals and big accomplishments. His message is basic management, a lesson on control learned from success in building Microsoft into a global corporation. Progress begins with the right goals and plans. Progress is achieved when results are measured and adjustments are made so that things can keep getting better in the future.

WHAT'S THE LESSON HERE?

It may be tempting to dismiss Gates's call to action as the musings of a rich man. It's a lot smarter to listen and learn. How can this call for better measurement and more willingness to listen to data apply to organizations that you work for or are familiar with? Can this advice help advance your life and career goals? Do you have an aversion to measurement? If so, how can you turn measurement into a friend rather than an enemy?

⦀ Step 2—Control measures actual performance.

The second step in the control process is to measure actual performance. Accurate and timely measurement is essential to spot differences between what is really taking place and what was originally planned. Unless we are willing to measure, very little control is possible. But a willingness to measure has its rewards: What gets measured tends to happen.

The "what gets measured happens" lesson can go a long way in nurturing a career. Linda Sanford, senior vice president for enterprise transformation at IBM, grew up on a family farm, where she developed an appreciation for measuring results. "At the end of the day, you saw what you did, knew how many rows of strawberries you picked." This experience carried over into her work at IBM. She earned an early career reputation for walking around the factory just to see "at the end of the day how many machines were going out of the back dock."[9]

Step 3—Control compares results with objectives and standards.

The third step in the control process is to compare actual results with objectives and standards. You might remember its implications by this **control equation**:

$$\text{Need for Action} = \text{Desired Performance} - \text{Actual Performance}$$

The control equation is a valuable tool made possible by goals that identify desired performance, and measurements that define actual performance. When actual is less than desired, a performance threat or deficiency exists. When actual is more than desired, a performance opportunity exists.

Some organizations use *engineering comparisons* to identify desired performance. An example is UPS. The firm carefully measures the routes and routines of its drivers to establish the times expected for each delivery. When a delivery manifest is scanned as completed, the driver's time is registered in an electronic performance log closely monitored by supervisors. Some make use of *historical comparisons*. These use past experience as a basis for evaluating current performance. And, *relative comparisons* are also common. They benchmark performance against that being achieved by other people, work units, or organizations.

Step 4—Control takes corrective action as needed.

The final step in the control process occurs when action is taken to address gaps between desired and actual performance. You might hear the term **management by exception** used in this regard. It is the practice of giving attention to high-priority situations that show the greatest need for action.

Management by exception basically adds discipline to our use of the control equation by focusing attention not just on needs for action but also on the highest-priority needs for action. In this way it can save valuable time, energy, and other resources that might be spent addressing things of little or no importance while those of great importance get missed or delayed.

Management by exception focuses attention on differences between actual and desired performance.

{ **WE NEED THE COURAGE TO ADMIT WHEN THINGS ARE GOING WRONG.**

Explore **Yourself**

■ Resiliency

The control process is one of the ways through which managers help organizations best use their resources and systems to achieve productivity. In many ways our daily lives are similar quests for productivity, and the control process counts there, too. But how well we do depends a lot on our capacity for **resiliency**—the ability to call on inner strength and keep moving forward even when things are tough. We need the courage and confidence to admit when things are going wrong, to change ways that aren't working well, and to hold on and keep things moving forward, even in the face of adversity.

> Get to know yourself better by taking the self-assessment on **Internal/External Control** and completing other activities in the *Exploring Management* **Skill-Building Portfolio**.

Takeaway 6.1
How and Why Do Managers Use the Control Process?

Terms to Define

After-action review

Controlling

Input standards

Management by exception

Output standards

Rapid Review

- Controlling is the process of measuring performance and taking corrective action as needed.
- The control process begins when performance objectives and standards are set; both input standards for work efforts and output standards for work results can be used.
- The second step in control is to measure actual performance in the control process.
- The third step compares results with objectives and standards to determine the need for corrective action.
- The final step in the control process involves taking action to resolve problems and improve things in the future.
- The control equation states: Need for action = Desired performance − Actual performance.
- Management by exception focuses attention on the greatest need for action.

Questions for Discussion

1. What performance standards should guide a hospital emergency room or fire department?
2. Can one control performance equally well with input standards and output standards?
3. What are the possible downsides to management by exception?

Be Sure You Can

- explain the role of controlling in the management process
- list the steps in the control process
- explain how planning and controlling should work together in management
- differentiate output standards and input standards
- state the control equation
- explain management by exception

Career Situation: What Would You Do?

A work colleague comes to you and confides that she feels "adrift in her career" and "just can't get enthused about what she's doing anymore." Your take is that this might be a problem of self-management and personal control. How will you explain to her that using the steps in the management control process might help in better understanding and correcting her situation?

Takeaway 6.2
What Types of Controls Are Used by Managers?

ANSWERS TO COME

- Managers use feedforward, concurrent, and feedback controls.
- Managers use both internal and external controls.
- Managing by objectives is a way to integrate planning and controlling.

||| **Managers use feedforward, concurrent, and feedback controls.**

You should recall discussions in earlier modules of how organizations operate as open systems that interact with their environments in an input-throughput-output cycle. **Figure 6.3** now shows how three types of managerial controls—feedforward, concurrent, and feedback—apply to each phase.[10]

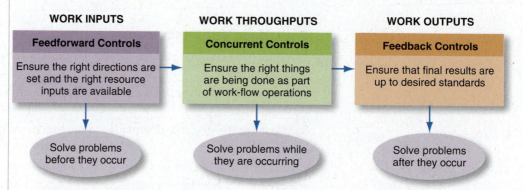

FIGURE 6.3 What Are the Differences Between Feedforward, Concurrent, and Feedback Controls?
Organizations are input-throughput-output systems, and each point in the cycle offers its own opportunities for control over performance. Feedforward controls try to solve problems before they occur, by making sure the production systems have high-quality inputs. Concurrent controls try to solve problems as they occur, by monitoring and correcting problems during the work process. Feedback controls try to correct problems after they have occurred and inform the system so that similar mistakes can be avoided in the future.

Feedforward control ensures clear directions and needed resources before the work begins.

Feedforward controls, also called *preliminary controls*, take place before work begins. Their goal is to prevent problems before they occur. This is a forward-thinking and proactive approach to control, one that we should all try to follow whenever we can. At McDonald's, for example, preliminary control of food ingredients plays an important role in the firm's quality program. Suppliers of its hamburger buns produce them to exact specifications, covering everything from texture to uniformity of color. Even in overseas markets, the firm works hard to develop local suppliers of dependable quality.[11]

Finding Quality at Whole Foods Markets

Employees control the tone for high performance.

Whole Foods Market is a sweetheart of the supermarket industry. And the Austin, Texas, company's management philosophies leave no room for complacency. It competes in a $560 billion industry with profit margins described by one business writer as "slimmer than angel-hair pasta." The high-end retail grocer has survived a squeamish economy and cutbacks in discretionary consumer spending. You may wonder how. A good place to start is its culture of "open books, open doors, and open people."

Included in *Fortune* magazine's annual list of the "100 Best Companies to Work For" every year since the list began, Whole Foods is a benchmark for continuous improvement. The company's employees embrace its mission to promote a healthy lifestyle. It only sells products that meet its internal quality control standards for being "natural," which the store defines as "minimally processed foods that are free of artificial preservatives, colors, flavors, sweeteners and hydrogenated fats." It maintains an online "Unacceptable Food Ingredients" list.

Co-CEO Walter Robb emphasizes that "employees are everything." One of the company's core values is team member happiness and excellence. Robb says . . . that is something we believe in our hearts and something that guides our actions every day as a company. . . If we're taking care of one another, the customers are going to feel that." The company's culture is one of inclusiveness so that employees feel that not only are they being taken care of, they have responsibilities to take care of one another.

Concurrent controls focus on what happens during the work process; they take place while people are doing their jobs. The goal is to solve problems as they occur. Sometimes called *steering controls*, they make sure that things are always going according to plan. The ever-present shift leaders at McDonald's restaurants are a good example of how this happens through direct supervision. They constantly observe what is taking place, even while helping out with the work. They are trained to correct things on the spot. The question continually asked is: "What can we do to improve things right now?"

Feedback controls, or *post-action controls*, take place after a job or project is completed. Think about your experiences as a student. Most course evaluation systems ask, "Was this a good learning experience?" only when the class is almost over. Think also about your experiences as a restaurant customer. Very often we're asked, "Was everything alright?" when it's time to pay the bill. And think of the electronic devices you buy. Probably the last question a cell phone maker asks before your device is shipped from the factory floor is, "Does it work?" Although the prior questions are good ones most often asked in good faith, feedback controls focus on the quality of finished products. Although this type of control may prevent you from receiving a defective cell phone, it may not help you much while taking a poorly organized college course or after eating a bad meal.

Find Inspiration

Whole Foods Market caps the salaries of top executives at 19 times the average worker pay every year. "It helps us keep faith with one another," says Robb, who emphasizes the importance of "all living by the same rules." He also criticizes traditional CEO salaries that can run to 400 times that of average worker pay. Although some companies struggle to find ways to improve performance, Whole Foods Market trusts its employees to deliver. Control for whole foods comes from inside the culture. Shouldn't this be the case in all organizations?

Concurrent control focuses on what happens during the work process.

Feedback control takes place after completing an action.

WOMEN SHOULD TAKE BACK CAREER CONTROL

First-time author Sheryl Sandberg got lots of attention with her book *Lean In: Women, Work and the Will to Lead* (2013, Knopf). Formerly with Google, and now Chief Operating Officer of Facebook, Sandberg describes her "aha moment" with research using a business school case study, "Heidi vs. Howard." The case about a real Silicon Valley CEO, entrepreneur, and venture capitalist was given to two groups of students. One received a version with the real CEO named—Heidi Roizen; the other received the identical case with one change—the CEO was Howard Roizen.

When students were asked if they preferred to work for Heidi or Howard, most agreed that both were equally competent. But, they preferred to work for Howard because of Heidi's aggressive, assertive, "out for herself" demeanor and political prowess. Of course, Howard displayed the same behaviors. Sandberg's takeaway was that gender bias stereotypes are deeply ingrained in our culture, and likeability and success do not always correlate for women.

Sandberg says women have to take charge of their careers and stop making bad decisions. She believes they do too much "leaning back" (e.g., taking a back or corner seat at a meeting table) and "leaning out" (e.g., not accepting new responsibilities because motherhood is planned sometime in the future). Instead, Sandberg's advises women to "lean in" and "don't leave before you leave." Think of this as women taking control of their own destinies.

Sandberg admits that stereotypes, corporate cultures, and traditional structures can hold women back. And she calls for better policies on things like maternity and paternity leave. She also warns about "benevolent sexism," where men act sympathetic but still treat women differently. But, her book is really about empowering women to take control and make better career decisions. Sandberg wants women to believe in their dreams and in themselves . . . and to achieve their full potential.

REFLECT AND REACT

Is Sandberg on to something here, or is she being too critical? Have you witnessed or experienced the "leaning back" or "leaning out" types of behaviors Sandberg discusses? Are women largely to blame for their lack of presence in the executive suite? Can this call for women to take charge of their careers by "leaning in" really lead to positive change? Is it broadly applicable? Or, is Sandberg talking from the largely unrealistic position of a super successful and wealthy woman, someone who "has it all," so to speak?

‖ Managers use both internal and external controls.

We all exercise self-control in our daily lives; we do so in respect to managing our money, our relationships, our work-life balance, and more.[12] Managers can take advantage of this human capacity by unlocking and setting up conditions that support **internal control**, or **self-control**, in the workplace. According to Douglas McGregor's Theory Y perspective, discussed in Chapter 2, people are ready and willing to exercise self-control in their work.[13] This potential is increased when capable people have a clear sense of organizational mission, know their goals, and have the resources necessary to do their jobs well.

In addition to encouraging and allowing internal control, managers also set up and use various forms of **external control** to structure situations so that things happen as planned.[14] The alternatives include bureaucratic or administrative control, clan control, and market control.

Internal control, or **self-control**, occurs as people exercise self-discipline in fulfilling job expectations.

External control occurs through direct supervision or administrative systems.

The logic of **bureaucratic control** is that authority, policies, procedures, job descriptions, budgets, and day-to-day supervision help make sure that people behave in ways consistent with organizational interests. As discussed in the previous chapter on planning, for example, organizations typically have policies and procedures regarding sexual harassment. They are designed to make sure people behave toward one another respectfully and without sexual pressures or improprieties.

Whereas bureaucratic control emphasizes hierarchy and authority, **clan control** influences behavior through social norms and peer expectations. This is the power of collective identity; persons who share values and identify strongly with each other tend to behave in ways that are consistent with one another's expectations. Just look around the typical college classroom and campus. You'll see clan control reflected in dress, language, and behavior as students tend to act consistent with the expectations of those peers and groups they identify with. The same holds true in organizations where close-knit employees display common behavior patterns.

Market control is essentially the influence of market competition on the behavior of organizations and their members. Business firms adjust products, pricing, promotions, and other practices in response to customer feedback and competitor moves. An example is the growing emphasis on "green" products and practices. When a firm such as Wal-Mart starts to get good publicity from its expressed commitment to eventually power all its stores with renewable energy, the effect is felt by its competitors.[15] They have to adjust practices to avoid giving up this public relations advantage to Wal-Mart. In this sense, the time-worn phrase "Keeping up with the competition" is really another way of expressing the dynamics of market controls in action.

> **Bureaucratic control** influences behavior through authority, policies, procedures, job descriptions, budgets, and day-to-day supervision.

> **Clan control** influences behavior through social norms and peer expectations.

> **Market control** is essentially the influence of market competition on the behavior of organizations and their members.

‖ Managing by objectives is a way to integrate planning and controlling.

A useful technique for integrating planning and controlling is **managing by objectives**. Often called MBO, it is a structured process of regular communication in which a supervisor or team leader and a subordinate or team member jointly set performance objectives and review accomplished results.[16] As **Figure 6.4**

> **Managing by objectives** is a process of joint objective setting between a superior and a subordinate.

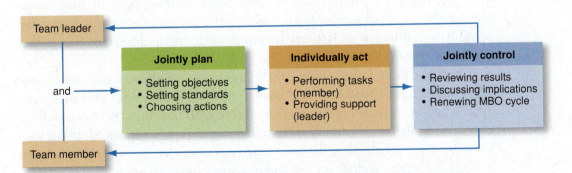

FIGURE 6.4 How Does Managing by Objectives Help to Integrate Planning and Controlling?
Managing by objectives is a structured process of communication between a supervisor and a subordinate, or team leader and team members. Planning is accomplished when both parties communicate to identify the subordinate's performance objectives. This is a form of participatory planning, and the goal is agreement. Informed by the objectives, the supervisor provides support for the subordinate as work progresses. Controlling is accomplished when the two parties meet at scheduled times to jointly discuss progress and results and make new plans setting future performance objectives.

Tips to **Remember**

■ How to Write a Good Performance Objective

- *Clarify the target*—be specific; clearly describe the key result to be accomplished.
- *Make it measurable*—state how the key result will be measured and documented.
- *Define the timetable*—identify a date by which the key result will be accomplished.

- *Avoid the impossible*—be realistic; don't promise what cannot be accomplished.
- *Add challenge*—be optimistic; build in "stretch" to make the accomplishment significant.
- *Don't overcomplicate*—stick to the essentials; write to fit a Post-it note reminder.

Improvement objectives document intentions to improve performance in a specific way.

Personal development objectives document intentions to accomplish personal growth, such as expanded job knowledge or skills.

shows, the process creates an agreement between the two parties regarding performance objectives for a given time period, plans for accomplishing them, standards for measuring them, and procedures for reviewing them.

In the previous chapter on planning, we talked about "great goals." You can think of them in the present context as objectives that have real meaning in terms of significant performance consequences. When a team leader and team member are working together in a managing by objectives approach, for example, it is helpful to consider two types of objectives that can have an element of "greatness" to them. **Improvement objectives** document intentions for improving performance in a specific way. An example is "to reduce quality rejects by 10%." **Personal development objectives** focus on expanding job knowledge or skills. An example is "to learn the latest version of a computer spreadsheet package."

Whether we are talking about improvement or personal objectives, it's important to remember that the best objectives are specified as clearly as possible. Ideally, this involves agreement on a *measurable end product*, for example, "to reduce housekeeping supply costs by 5% by the end of the fiscal year." But this can be hard to do in some cases. Instead, performance objectives can be stated as *verifiable work activities*. For example, a team leader can commit to holding weekly team meetings as a means for achieving better communications.

You might already be wondering if managing by objectives can become too complicated a process.[17] The answer is "yes." Critics note that problems arise when objectives are linked too closely with pay, focused too much on easy accomplishments, involve excessive paperwork, and end up being dictated by supervisors. But, it's also true that there are many advantages to making objectives a clear part of the ongoing conversation between managers and those reporting to them.[18] This keeps workers focused on the most important tasks and priorities and keeps supervisors focused on the best ways to help them meet agreed-upon objectives. Because the process requires lots of communication, furthermore, it helps build good interpersonal relationships. And by increasing participation in goal setting, it encourages self-management.[19]

STUDY GUIDE

Takeaway 6.2
What Types of Controls Are Used by Managers?

Terms to Define

Bureaucratic control

Clan control

Concurrent control

External control

Feedback control

Feedforward control

Improvement objectives

Internal control (self-control)

Managing by objectives

Market control

Personal development objectives

Rapid Review

- Feedforward controls try to make sure things are set up right before work begins; concurrent controls make sure that things are being done correctly; feedback controls assess results after an action is completed.
- Internal control is self-control that occurs as people take personal responsibility for their work.
- External control is accomplished by use of bureaucratic, clan, and market control systems.
- Management by objectives is a process through which team leaders work with team members to "jointly" set performance objectives and "jointly" review performance results.

Questions for Discussion

1. How does bureaucratic control differ from clan control?
2. What is Douglas McGregor's main point regarding internal control?
3. Can MBO work when there are problems in the relationship between a team leader and a team member?

Be Sure You Can

- illustrate the use of feedforward, concurrent, and feedback controls
- explain the nature of internal control or self-control
- differentiate among bureaucratic, clan, and market controls
- list the steps in the MBO process as it might operate between a team leader and a team member

Career Situation: What Would You Do?

You have a highly talented work team whose past performance has been outstanding. Recently, though, team members are starting to act like the workday is mainly a social occasion. Getting the work done seems less important than having a good time and performance is on the decline. How can you use external controls in a positive way to restore team performance to high levels?

Takeaway 6.3
What Are Some Useful Control Tools and Techniques?

ANSWERS TO COME

- Quality control is a foundation of modern management.
- Gantt charts and CPM/PERT improve project management and control.
- Inventory controls help save costs.
- Breakeven analysis shows where revenues will equal costs.
- Financial ratios measure key areas of financial performance.
- Balanced scorecards help top managers exercise strategic control.

MOST ORGANIZATIONS USE A VARIETY OF COMPREHENSIVE AND SYSTEM-WIDE controls. You should be familiar with quality control, purchasing and inventory controls, and breakeven analysis, as well as the use of key financial controls and balanced scorecards.

⫴ Quality control is a foundation of modern management.

If managing for high performance is a theme of the day, *quality control* is one of its most important watchwords. As pointed out in Chapter 2, the term **total quality management (TQM)** is quite common in modern management. It is used to describe operations that make quality an everyday performance objective and strive to always do things right the first time.[20] A foundation of TQM is the quest for **continuous improvement**, meaning that one is always looking for new ways to improve on current performance.[21] The notion is that you can never be satisfied, that something always can and should be improved on.[22]

The basic cornerstone of quality control in any organization is measurement. If you want quality, you have to tally defects, analyze and trace them to the sources, make corrections, and keep records of what happens afterwards.[23] A quality tool often used in manufacturing, for example, is the **control chart** shown here.

Total quality management (TQM) commits to quality objectives, continuous improvement, and doing things right the first time.

Continuous improvement involves always searching for new ways to improve work quality and performance.

Control charts are graphical ways of displaying trends so that exceptions to quality standards can be identified.

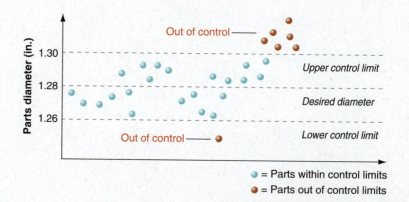

Control charts are graphical ways of displaying trends so that exceptions to quality standards can be identified for special attention. In the prior figure, for example, an upper control limit and a lower control limit specify the allowable tolerances for measurements of a machine part. As long as the manufacturing process produces parts that fall within these limits, things are "in control." However, as soon as parts start to fall outside the limits, it is clear that something is going wrong that is affecting quality. The process can then be investigated, even shut down, to identify the source of the errors and correct them.

The use of statistics adds power to sampling as a basis for decision making and quality management. Many manufacturers now use a **Six Sigma** program, meaning that statistically the firm's quality performance will tolerate no more than 3.4 defects per million units of goods produced or services completed. This translates to a perfection rate of 99.9997%. As tough as it sounds, Six Sigma is a common quality standard for many, if not most, major competitors in our demanding global marketplace.

> **Six Sigma** is a quality standard of 3.4 defects or less per million products or service deliveries.

⦀ Gantt charts and CPM/PERT improve project management and control.

It might be something personal such as planning an anniversary party for one's parents, preparing for a renovation to your home, or watching the completion of a new student activities building on a campus. What these examples and others like them share in common is that they are relatively complicated tasks. Multiple components must be completed in a certain sequence, within budget, and by a specified date. In management we call them **projects**.

> **Projects** are one-time activities with many component tasks that must be completed in proper order and according to budget.

Project management is responsibility for the overall planning, supervision, and control of projects. Basically, a project manager's job is to ensure that a project is well planned and then completed according to plan—on time, within budget, and consistent with objectives. In practice, this is often assisted by two control techniques known as Gantt charts and CPM/PERT.

> **Project management** makes sure that activities required to complete a project are planned well and accomplished on time.

A **Gantt chart** like the one shown here graphically displays the scheduling of tasks that go into completing a project. As developed in the early 20th century by Henry Gantt, an industrial engineer, this tool has become a mainstay of project management. One of the biggest problems with projects, for example, is that delays in early activities create problems for later ones. The Gantt chart's visual overview shows what needs to be done when, and allows for progress checks at different time intervals. It helps with activity sequencing to make sure that things get accomplished in time for later work to build on them.

> A **Gantt chart** graphically displays the scheduling of tasks required to complete a project.

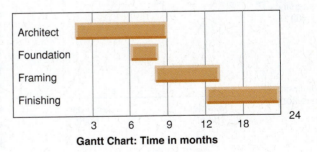

Gantt Chart: Time in months

A more advanced use of the Gantt chart is found in something called **CPM/PERT**—a combination of the critical path method and the program evaluation and review technique. Project planning based on CPM/PERT uses network charts that break a project into a series of small subactivities with clear beginning and end points. These points become "nodes" in the charts, and the arrows between nodes show in what order things must be done. The full

> **CPM/PERT** is a combination of the critical path method and the program evaluation and review technique.

diagram shows all the interrelationships that must be coordinated for the entire project to be successfully completed.

Use of CPM/PERT techniques helps project managers track activities to make sure they happen in the right sequence and on time. If you look at the CPM/PERT network shown here, you should notice that the time required for each activity can be easily computed and tracked. The pathway from start to conclusion that involves the longest completion times is called the **critical path**. It represents the quickest time in which the entire project can be finished, assuming everything goes according to schedule and plans. In the example, the critical path is 38 days.

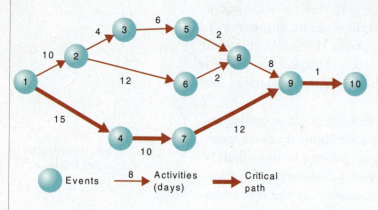

The **critical path** is the pathway from project start to conclusion that involves the longest completion times.

Inventory controls help save costs.

Cost control ranks right up there with quality control as an important performance concern. And a very good place to start is with inventory. The goal of **inventory control** is to make sure that any inventory is only big enough to meet one's immediate performance needs.

Inventory control ensures that inventory is only big enough to meet immediate needs.

The **economic order quantity** method places new orders when inventory levels fall to predetermined points.

The **economic order quantity** form of inventory control, shown in the figure, automatically orders a fixed number of items every time an inventory level falls to a predetermined point. The order sizes are mathematically calculated to minimize costs of inventory. A good example is your local supermarket. It routinely makes hundreds of daily orders on an economic order quantity basis.

Another and very popular approach to inventory control is **just-in-time scheduling (JIT)**. First made popular by the Japanese, these systems reduce costs and improve workflow by scheduling materials to arrive at a workstation or facility just in time for use. Because JIT nearly eliminates the carrying costs of inventories, it is an important business productivity tool. But, the recent tsunami and nuclear disaster in Japan also showed some of the risks of JIT. Many global companies, among them Boeing and Dell, faced product delays when just-in-time shipments were disrupted as Japanese firms in their supply chains were closed or their operations scaled back due to the disaster.[24]

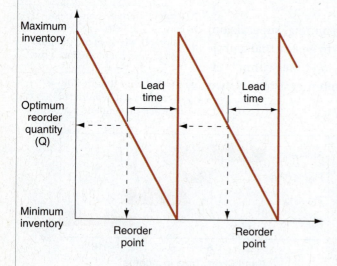

Just-in-time scheduling (JIT) routes materials to workstations just in time for use.

Breakeven analysis shows where revenues will equal costs.

When business executives are deliberating new products or projects, a frequent control question is: "What is the **breakeven point**?" **Figure 6.5** shows that breakeven occurs at the point where revenues just equal costs. You can also think of it

The **breakeven point** occurs where revenues just equal costs.

as the point where losses end and profit begins. A breakeven point is computed using this formula.

$$\text{Breakeven Point} = \text{Fixed Costs} \div (\text{Price} - \text{Variable Costs})$$

Managers rely on **breakeven analysis** to perform what-if calculations under different projected cost and revenue conditions. Suppose, for example, the proposed target price for a new product is $8 per unit, fixed costs are $10,000, and variable costs are $4 per unit. What sales volume is required to break even? (*Answer:* Breakeven at 2,500 units.) What happens if you are good at cost control and can keep variable costs to $3 per unit? (*Answer:* Breakeven at 2,000 units.) Now, suppose you can only produce 1,000 units in the beginning and at the original costs. At what price must you sell them to break even? (*Answer:* $14.) Business executives perform these types of cost control analyses every day.

> **Breakeven analysis** performs what-if calculations under different revenue and cost conditions.

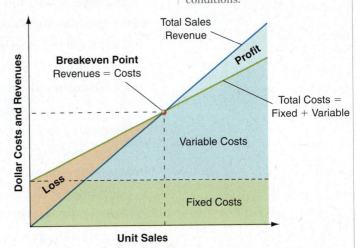

‖ Financial ratios measure key areas of financial performance.

The pressure is always on for organizations to use their financial resources well to achieve high performance. And, the analysis of an organization's financial performance is an important aspect of managerial control.

The foundation for analysis using financial controls rests with a firm's balance sheet and income statement. The **balance sheet** shows assets and liabilities at a point in time. It will be displayed in an Assets = Liabilities format. The **income statement** shows profits or losses at a point in time. It will be displayed in a Sales − Epenses = Net Income format. You can remember both from an accounting course or as summarized below.

Information from balance sheets and income statements is used to create a variety of financial performance measures. At a minimum, managers should be able to understand the performance and control implications of several important financial ratios.

FIGURE 6.5 **How Do Managers Use Breakeven Analysis to Make Informed What-If Decisions?**
A common question asked by managers when considering a new product or service investment is: "What is the breakeven point?" A breakeven point is computed using this formula: Breakeven Point × Fixed Costs ÷ (Price − Variable Costs). As shown in this figure, breakeven occurs at the point where revenues just equal costs. You can also think of it as the point where losses end and profit begins. This approach helps managers perform what-if calculations under different projected cost and revenue conditions.

> A **balance sheet** shows assets and liabilities at one point in time.

> An **income statement** shows profits or losses at one point in time.

Balance Sheet

Assets	Liabilities
Current Assets	**Current Liabilities**
• Cash	• Accounts payable
• Receivables	• Accrued expenses
• Inventories	• Taxes payable
Fixed Assets	**Long-term Liabilities**
• Land	• Mortgages
• Buildings	• Bonds
Less Depreciation	**Owner's Equity**
	• Outstanding stock
	• Retained earnings
Total Assets	**= Total Liabilities**

Income Statement

Gross Sales
    less Returns
Net Sales
    less Expenses and Cost of Goods Sold
Operating Profits
    plus Other Income
Gross Income
    less Interest Expense
Income Before Taxes
    less Taxes
Net Income

**Insights of Key
Financial Ratios** ≫

Liquidity—measures ability to meet short-term obligations.

- *Current Ratio* = Current Assets ÷ Current Liabilities
- *Quick Ratio* = (Current Assets − Inventory) ÷ Current Liabilities

↑ Higher is better: You want more assets and fewer liabilities.

Leverage—measures use of debt.

- *Debt Ratio* = Total Debts ÷ Total Assets

↓ Lower is better: You want fewer debts and more assets.

Asset Management—measures asset and inventory efficiency.

- *Asset Turnover* = Sales ÷ Total Assets
- *Inventory Turnover* = Sales ÷ Average Inventory

↑ Higher is better: You want more sales and fewer assets or lower inventory.

Profitability—measures profit generation.

- *Net Margin* = Net Income ÷ Sales
- *Return on Assets* (ROA) = Net Income ÷ Total Assets
- *Return on Equity* (ROE) = Net Income ÷ Owner's Equity

↑ Higher is better: You want as much net income or profit as possible for sales, assets, and equity.

These and other financial ratios can be used for historical comparisons within the firm and for external benchmarking relative to industry performance. They can also be used to set company-level financial targets or goals to be shared with employees and tracked to indicate success or failure. At Civco Medical Instruments, for example, financial results are distributed monthly to all employees. They always know exactly how well the firm is doing. This helps them focus on what they can do differently and better to help improve the firm's bottom line.[25]

⫴ Balanced scorecards help top managers exercise strategic control.

If "what gets measured happens," then managers should take advantage of "scorecards" to record and track performance results. When an instructor takes class attendance and assigns grades based on it, students tend to come to class. When an employer tracks the number of customers each employee serves per day, employees tend to serve more customers. Do the same principles hold for organizations?

A **balanced scorecard** measures performance on financial, customer service, internal process, and innovation and learning goals.

Strategic management consultants Robert S. Kaplan and David P. Norton think so. They advocate using what is called the **balanced scorecard** in respect to management control.[26] It gives top managers, as they say, "a fast but comprehensive view of the business." The basic principle is that to do well and to win, you have to keep score. And like sports teams, organizations perform better when all members know the score.

Developing a balanced scorecard for any organization begins with a clarification of the organization's mission and vision—what it wants to be and how it wants to be perceived by its key stakeholders. Next, the following questions are asked and answered to develop balanced scorecard goals and performance measures.

- *Financial Performance*—"How well do our actions directly contribute to improved financial performance?" To improve financially, how should we appear to our shareholders? Sample goals: survive, succeed, and prosper. Sample measures: cash flow, sales growth and operating income, increased market share, and return on equity.

- *Customer Satisfaction*—"How well do we serve our customers and clients?" To achieve our vision, how should we appear to our customers? Sample goals: new products, responsive supply. Sample measures: percentage sales from new products, percentage on-time deliveries.

- *Internal Process Improvement*—"How well do our activities and processes directly increase value provided to our customers and clients?" To satisfy our customers and shareholders, at what internal business processes should we excel? Sample goals: manufacturing productivity, design excellence, new product introduction. Sample measures: cycle times, engineering efficiency, new product time.

- *Innovation and Learning*—"How well are we learning, changing, and improving things over time?" To achieve our vision, how will we sustain our ability to change and improve? Sample goals: technology leadership, time to market. Sample measures: time to develop new technologies, new product introduction time versus competition.

When balanced scorecard measures are taken, recorded, shared, and critically reviewed, Kaplan and Norton expect organizations to perform better. Their point is one we've made before: What gets measured happens. Think about the possibilities here. Couldn't the balanced scorecard approach work in an elementary school, a hospital, a community library, a mayor's office, a fast-food restaurant? And if balanced scorecards make sense, why is it that more organizations don't use them?

Masterfile

{ WHO WINS AND LOSES WHEN GLOBAL INTERNET FIRMS AND LOCAL GOVERNMENTS BATTLE FOR CONTROL?

Ethics **Check**

■ Global Privacy and Censorship Worries

London—Amnesty International claimed that Yahoo!, Microsoft, and Google violated human rights in China by complying with government requests for censorship. Amnesty said that "corporate values and policies" are compromised in the quest for profits. A spokesperson for Yahoo!'s China business, Alibaba.com, said: "By creating opportunities for entrepreneurs and connecting China's exporters to buyers around the world, Alibaba.com and Yahoo! China are having an overwhelmingly positive impact on the lives of average people in China."

Beijing—Skype is told by the Chinese government that its software must filter words that the Chinese leadership considers offensive from text messages. If the company doesn't, it can't do business in the country. After refusing at first, company executives finally agreed. Phrases such as "Falun Gong" and "Dalai Lama" no longer appear in text messages delivered through Skype's Chinese joint venture partner, Tom Online.

YOU DECIDE

Skype co-founder Niklas Zennstrom says: "I may like or not like the laws and regulations to operate businesses in the UK or Germany or the U.S., but if I do business there I choose to comply." What do you think? Do company executives have any choice but to comply with the requests of governments? Are there times when profits should be sacrificed for principles? When should business executives stand up and challenge laws and regulations used to deny customers the privacy they expect?

STUDY GUIDE

Takeaway 6.3
What Are Some Useful Control Tools and Techniques?

Terms to Define

Balance sheet

Balanced scorecard

Breakeven analysis

Breakeven point

Continuous improvement

Control chart

Critical path

CPM/PERT

Economic order quantity

Gantt chart

Income statement

Inventory control

Just-in-time scheduling (JIT)

Project

Project management

Six Sigma

Total quality management (TQM)

Rapid Review

- Total quality management tries to meet customers' needs and do things right on time, the first time, and all the time.
- Organizations use control charts and statistical techniques such as the Six Sigma system to measure the quality of work samples for quality control purposes.
- Economic order quantities and just-in-time deliveries are common approaches to inventory cost control.
- The breakeven equation is: Breakeven Point = Fixed Costs ÷ (Price − Variable Costs).
- Breakeven analysis identifies the points where revenues will equal costs under different pricing and cost conditions.
- Financial control of business performance is facilitated by use of financial ratios, such as those dealing with liquidity, leverage, assets, and profitability.
- The balanced scorecard measures overall organizational performance in respect to four areas: financial, customers, internal processes, innovation.

Questions for Discussion

1. Can a firm such as Wal-Mart ever go too far in controlling its inventory costs?
2. Is the concept of total quality management out of date?
3. Does the "balanced scorecard" as described in this chapter measure the right things?

Be Sure You Can

- explain the role of continuous improvement in TQM
- explain how Gantt charts and CPM/PERT help organizations with project management
- explain two common approaches to inventory cost control
- state the equation to calculate a breakeven point and its use in explaining breakeven analysis
- state the common financial ratios used in organizational control
- identify the balanced scorecard components and control questions

Career Situation: What Would You Do?

You've had three years of solid work experience after earning your undergraduate degree. A lot of your friends are talking about going to graduate school and they're pushing you to take time out to earn an MBA degree. There are potential costs and benefits if you go for the MBA. How can breakeven analysis help you make the decision to: (1) go or not go, (2) go full time or part time, and (3) even where to go?

TestPrep 6

Answers to TestPrep questions can be found at the back of the book.

Multiple-Choice Questions

1. After objectives and standards are set, what step comes next in the control process?

   (a) Measure results.

   (b) Take corrective action.

   (c) Compare results with objectives.

   (d) Modify standards to fit circumstances.

2. When a soccer coach tells her players at the end of a losing game, "You did well in staying with our game plan," she is using a/an _____ as a measure of performance.

   (a) input standard

   (b) output standard

   (c) historical comparison

   (d) relative comparison

3. When an automobile manufacturer is careful to purchase only the highest-quality components for use in production, this is an example of an attempt to ensure high performance through _____ control.

   (a) concurrent

   (b) statistical

   (c) inventory

   (d) feedforward

4. Management by exception means _____.

   (a) managing only when necessary

   (b) focusing attention where the need for action is greatest

   (c) the same thing as concurrent control

   (d) the same thing as just-in-time delivery

5. A total quality management program is most likely to be associated with _____.

   (a) EOQ

   (b) continuous improvement

   (c) return on equity

   (d) breakeven analysis

6. The _____ chart graphically displays the scheduling of tasks required to complete the project.

   (a) exception

   (b) Taylor

   (c) Gantt

   (d) after-action

7. When MBO is done right, who does the review of a team member's performance accomplishments?

   (a) The team member

   (b) The team leader

   (c) Both the team member and team leader

   (d) The team leader, the team member, and a lawyer

8. A good performance objective is written in such a way that it _____.

   (a) has a flexible timetable

   (b) is general and not too specific

   (c) is impossible to accomplish

   (d) can be easily measured

9. A team leader is not living up to the concept of MBO if he or she _____.

   (a) sets performance objectives for individual team members

   (b) stays in touch and tries to support team members in their work

   (c) jointly reviews performance results with each team member

   (d) keeps a written record of performance objectives for team members

10. If an organization's top management establishes a target of increasing new hires of minority and female candidates by 15% in the next six months, this is an example of a/an _____ standard for control purposes.

    (a) input

    (b) output

    (c) clan

    (d) market

11. When a supervisor works alongside an employee and corrects him or her immediately when a mistake is made, this is an example of _____ control.
    (a) feedforward
    (b) external
    (c) concurrent
    (d) preliminary

12. When one team member advises another team member that "your behavior is crossing the line in terms of our expectations for workplace civility," she is exercising a form of _____ control over the other person's inappropriate behaviors.
    (a) clan
    (b) market
    (c) internal
    (d) preliminary

13. In CPM/PERT, "CPM" stands for _____.
    (a) critical path method
    (b) control planning management
    (c) control plan map
    (d) current planning matrix

14. In a CPM/PERT analysis, the focus is on _____ and the event _____ that link them together with the finished project.
    (a) costs; budgets
    (b) activities; sequences
    (c) timetables; budgets
    (d) goals; costs

15. Among the financial ratios often used for control purposes, Current Assets/Current Liabilities is known as the _____.
    (a) debt ratio
    (b) net margin
    (c) current ratio
    (d) inventory turnover ratio

Short-Response Questions

16. What type of control is being exercised in the U.S. Army's after-action review?

17. How could clan control be used in a TQM program?

18. How can a just-in-time system reduce inventory costs?

19. What four questions could be used to set up a balanced scorecard for a small business?

Integration and Application Question

20. Put yourself in the position of a management consultant who specializes in MBO. The local Small Business Enterprise Association has asked you to be the speaker for its luncheon next week. The president of the association says that the group would like to learn more about the topic: "How to Use Management by Objectives for Better Planning and Control."

    Questions: Your speech will last 15 to 20 minutes. What is the outline for your speech? How will you explain the potential benefits of MBO to this group of small business owners?

Stepsfor Further Learning

BUILD MARKETABLE SKILLS

DO A CASE ANALYSIS

GET AND STAY INFORMED

BUILD

MARKETABLE SKILLS. EARN BIG CAREER PAYOFFS!

Don't miss these opportunities in the **Skill-Building Portfolio**

■ **SELF-ASSESSMENT 6:** Internal / External Control

Is what happens up to you, or not? . . . Learn about your control tendencies.

■ **CLASS EXERCISE 6:** Stakeholder Maps

Organizations can have lives of their own . . . gain insight into stakeholder perspectives.

■ **TEAM PROJECT 6:** After Meeting Project Review

It's rare that things go perfectly right . . . a good review process can make things go better the next time.

Many learning resources are found at the end of the book and online within WileyPLUS.

Take advantage of **Cases for Critical Thinking**

■ **CHAPTER 6 CASE SNAPSHOT:**

Chipotle—Control Keeps Everything Fresh/ *Sidebar on Mint.com*

If controlling is the process of measuring performance and taking action to ensure desired results, your next meal from Chipotle's should be a good one. Since its humble beginnings in Denver, Colorado, Chipotle has implemented the control process with fervor, catapulting the company to where it is today. Nothing is left to chance, and everything counts. Input standards make sure that meal ingredients are up to the firm's high expectations. After all, putting good ingredients in makes it more likely that good burritos will come out. Output standards measure performance results in terms of quantity, quality, cost, or time. For Chipotle this means reviewing sales to cost ratios, same-store sales figures

DO

A CASE ANALYSIS. STRENGTHEN YOUR CRITICAL THINKING!

speed check-out times during peak lunch hour, and tracking its stock performance. All those burritos come from a high performance culture that thrives on control.

Dig into this **Hot Topic**

■ **PRO AND CON DEBATE** Should parents pay for children's grades?

Managing is a lot like parenting, and allocating rewards isn't easy in either situation. How often have you heard someone say: "We pay for 'A's'?" Perhaps you've said it yourself, or plan to. But is this the correct thing to do? Can paying for grades improve parental control over children's study habits?

Those in favor of paying for grades are likely to say: "It gets the kid's attention." . . . "It motivates them to study more." . . . "It gets them ready for work where pay and performance go together." *Those against the practice are likely to say:* "Once they get paid for As, they'll be studying for financial gain not real learning." . . . "It hurts those who work hard but still can't get the high grades." . . . "If there's more than one child in the family, it's unfair if they don't all get rewards."

GET

AND STAY INFORMED. MAKE YOURSELF VALUABLE!

Final Faceoff As a parent will you pay for grades or not? How can you justify your position? Hit the books and go to the Web, find out what scholars have to say. Perhaps you'll change your mind. There are a number of issues here that any manager, leader, or parent needs to understand—pay for performance, extrinsic versus intrinsic rewards, equity in rewards, valuing effort versus valuing achievement. By the way, what can parenting teach us about managing people at work?

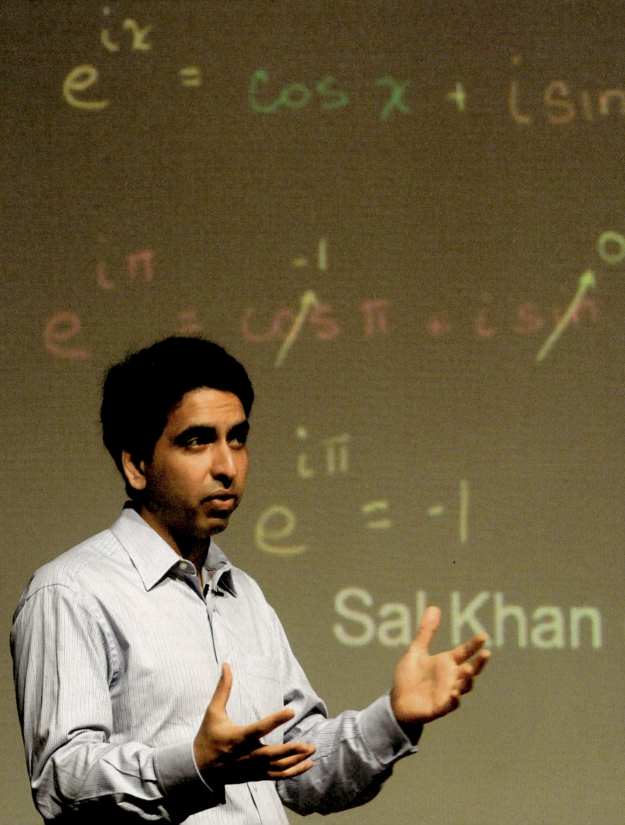

"There is a fundamental disconnect between the providers of education and the consumers of education . . . this whole online debate or what's happening now is actually starting to clarify things. At Khan Academy we're 100% focused on the learning side . . ."

Salman Khan, founder of the Khan Academy

Strategy and Strategic Management

7

Insight and Hard Work Deliver Results

Walt Disney Pictures / Photofest

Critical Thinking and *Tron: Legacy*

Acting on a mysterious pager message sent to a family confidant, Sam Flynn (Garrett Hedlund) finds himself in a virtual world known as The Grid. Sam is captured and designated as a game player, with his only instruction being to "survive."

Welcome to the sci-fi movie *Tron: Legacy*. Sam knows nothing about this new virtual world. He is left to anticipate what will happen and use his instincts to stay alive. By keen observation he quickly learns how to use his disc and a light cycle to defeat other players. Sam is eventually reunited with his father, Kevin Flynn (Jeff Bridges), and uses his intuition to save Quorra (Olivia Wilde).

Pretty heady stuff that you only see in the movies, right? Not so. The complexity and uncertainty of our fast-changing world forces all of us to deal with daily challenges in similar ways. The core issue is strategic management—of ourselves and our organizations—and the baseline requirement is strength in **critical thinking** skills. They give us the capability to dig in to situations, understand their intricacies, gather and interpret relevant information, and think everything through to the point where decisions made today position us well for the future.

Case studies and other problem-based methods of learning can help develop your critical thinking skills. Just remember, though, that case studies are often neat and tidy while the real world can be much more complex and unstructured. The more practice you get now with critical thinking, the better prepared you will be when you encounter uncertainties.

YOUR CHAPTER 7 TAKEAWAYS

1. Identify the types of strategies used by organizations.

2. Understand how managers formulate and implement strategies.

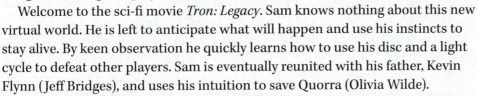

WHAT'S INSIDE

Explore Yourself
More on **critical thinking**

Role Models
Wendy Kopp tackles the culture of low achievement

Ethics Check
Life and death at an outsourcing factory

Facts to Consider
Disposable workers are indispensible to business profits

Manager's Library
Rebooting Work: Transform How You Work in the Age of Entrepreneurship by Maynard Webb

TEACHING NOTE: Choose an organization—local or other, and have students describe what they consider to be its strategy. Ask them to suggest examples of organizations following different strategies. Use this to launch a discussion of "sustainable" competitive advantage—organizational and personal.

Takeaway 7.1

What Types of Strategies Are Used by Organizations?

ANSWERS TO COME

- Strategy is a comprehensive plan for achieving competitive advantage.
- Organizations use corporate, business, and functional strategies.
- Growth strategies focus on expansion.
- Restructuring and divestiture strategies focus on consolidation.
- Global strategies focus on international business initiatives.
- Cooperation strategies focus on alliances and partnerships.
- E-business strategies focus on using the Internet for business success.

DON'T TAKE THE OPENING PHOTO OF SAL KHAN TOO LIGHTLY. HIS INNOVATIVE ONLINE Khan academy has the goal of "changing education for the better by providing a free world-class education for anyone anywhere." Its success helped spur the development of MOOCs—massive open online courses—as "disrupters" of the traditional university model of face-to-face delivery of pay-per-credit courses.[1] Some MOOCs are free, they're being launched in increasing numbers from top universities, and new start-ups like Coursera and Udacity are marketing them on a global scale.

Fast Company magazine once said: "If you want to make a difference as a leader, you've got to make time for strategy."[2] And, higher education today ranks high among industries facing strategic challenges. But leaders in any industry should remember past lessons. There was a time when Henry Ford could say: "The customer can have any color he wants as long as it's black." Those days are gone for the automakers, and they're gone for universities, public institutions, and businesses as well. A senior IBM executive described this shift in strategic landscape as the "difference between a bus which follows a set route, and a taxi which goes where customers tell it to go."[3]

There will be lots of strategy and strategic management ideas and insights in this chapter. As you read, remember that everything applies equally well to your career. What's your personal strategy? Are you acting like the bus following the set route, the taxi following opportunities, or some combination of both?

‖‖ Strategy is a comprehensive plan for achieving competitive advantage.

A **strategy** is a comprehensive action plan that identifies long-term direction for an organization and guides resource utilization to accomplish its goals. Strategy focuses leadership attention on the competitive environment. It represents a "best guess" about what to do to be successful in the face of rivalry and changing conditions.

A good strategy provides leaders with a plan for allocating and using resources with consistent **strategic intent**. Think of this as having all organizational energies directed toward a unifying and compelling target or mission, one that is highly aspirational.[4] At for-profit Coca-Cola, for example, strategic intent is described as "To put a Coke within 'arm's reach' of every consumer in the world."

A **strategy** is a comprehensive plan guiding resource allocation to achieve long-term organization goals.

Strategic intent focuses organizational energies on achieving a compelling goal.

The mission of the not-for-profit Khan Academy, discussed earlier, is to provide "a free world-class education for anyone anywhere."

Ultimately, a good strategy helps an organization achieve **competitive advantage.** This means that it is able to outperform rivals. The very best strategies provide **sustainable competitive advantage.** This doesn't mean that the competitive advantage lasts forever, but it does mean that for a period of time their success is hard for competitors to imitate.

> A **competitive advantage** is an ability to outperform rivals.

> A **sustainable competitive advantage** is achieved in ways that are difficult to imitate.

When you think about the "sustainability" of competitive advantage, think about Apple and its iPad. It was first to market with an innovative product linking design, technology, and customer appeal. And, it was all backed by a super efficient supply chain. As one industry analyst said, "Apple moved the goal posts before most of their competitors even took the field."[5] But Apple's industry dominance eventually came into question as competitors caught on and developed similar competencies. Android tablets from Samsung and Google, Kindle Fires from Amazon, and even more iPad alternatives moved the game out of Apple's favor. While lots of people waited for its next big success story, some wondered if Apple's best days of competitive advantage had already passed.

⦀ Organizations use corporate, business, and functional strategies.

You can identify strategies at three levels in most organizations. At the top level, **corporate strategy** provides direction and guides resource allocation for the organization as a whole. The *strategic question* at the corporate strategy level is: In what industries and markets should we compete? In large, complex organizations, such as PepsiCo, IBM, and General Electric, decisions on corporate strategy identify how the firm intends to compete across multiple industries, businesses, and markets.

> A **corporate strategy** sets long-term direction for the total enterprise.

Business strategy focuses on the strategic intent for a single business unit or product line. The *strategic question* at the business strategy level is: How are we going to compete for customers within this industry and in this market? Typical business strategy decisions include choices about product and service mix, facilities locations, new technologies, and the like. For smaller, single-business enterprises, business strategy is the corporate strategy.

> A **business strategy** identifies how a division or strategic business unit will compete in its product or service domain.

Functional strategy guides activities to implement higher-level business and corporate strategies. This level of strategy unfolds within a specific functional area such as marketing, manufacturing, finance, and human resources. The *strategic question* for functional strategies is: How can we best utilize resources within the function to support implementation of the business strategy? Answers to this question involve a wide variety of practices and initiatives to improve things such as operating efficiency, product quality, customer service, or innovativeness.

> A **functional strategy** guides activities within one specific area of operations.

⦀ Growth strategies focus on expansion.

You often read and hear about organizations trying to get bigger. They are pursuing **growth strategies** to increase the size and scope of current operations. Many executives view growth as necessary for long-run profitability. But you should probably question this assumption and probe deeper right from the start. Is growth always the best path? And if the strategic choice is to grow, how should it be accomplished?

> A **growth strategy** involves expansion of the organization's current operations.

{ AS A COLLEGE STUDENT, WENDY KOPP'S VISION WAS TO "ELIMINATE EDUCATIONAL INEQUITIES. . . . THAT VISION STILL DRIVES TEACH FOR AMERICA'S STRATEGY"

Role Models

■ Wendy Kopp Tackles the Culture of Low Achievement

Wendy Kopp, Chief Executive Officer and founder of Teach for America, proposed the creation of her nonprofit in an undergraduate thesis at Princeton University. Two short decades later, her strategic leadership had inspired 38,000+ teacher participants and reached more than 3 million children nationwide.

Kopp's vision as a college student was to "eliminate educational inequities," regardless of a child's family income. That vision still guides Teach for America's strategy.

Kopp's ability to engage in continuous change and performance enhancement is part of her organization's success story. "Change is Possible," states the organization's Web site, "We can provide an excellent education for kids in low-income communities . . . they can achieve at the highest levels."

Part of Kopp's strategy was to identify target "priority regions" like Detroit and Memphis. Well over half of the regions in need have requested math and science teachers. The demand for subject areas like early childhood education,

special education, and, Spanish/bilingual education remains strong.

Teach for America's goal is to help children growing up in poverty beat what Kopp calls "the culture of low achievement." Her strategy is to enlist high-achieving recent college graduates and professionals to make a difference by two-year teaching stints in low-income urban and rural communities. Now, isn't that a teachable moment?

WHAT'S THE LESSON HERE?

How much of Teach for America's success is due to Kopp's clear and compelling vision for social change? What lessons on the link between vision and strategy does this example offer organizations of any type? Is it easier to inspire people to implement strategy in a nonprofit with a social mission than in a business that is profit driven? How can the leader of a business gain high levels of employee commitment to the strategy?

Growth through concentration means expansion within an existing business area.

Growth through diversification means expansion by entering related or new business areas.

Growth through vertical integration occurs by acquiring suppliers or distributors.

A strategy of growth through **concentration** seeks expansion within an existing business area, one in which the firm has experience and presumably expertise. You don't see McDonald's trying to grow by buying bookstores or gasoline stations; it keeps opening more restaurants at home and abroad. You don't see Wal-Mart trying to grow by buying a high-end department store chain or a cellphone company; it keeps opening more Wal-Mart stores. These are classic growth by concentration strategies.

Growth can also take place through **diversification,** where expansion occurs by entering new business areas. As you might expect, diversification involves risk because the firm may be moving outside existing areas of competency. One way to moderate the risk is to pursue *related diversification*, expanding into similar or complementary new business areas. PepsiCo did this when it purchased Tropicana. Although Tropicana's fruit juices were new to Pepsi, the business is related to its expertise in the beverages industry.

Some firms pursue *unrelated diversification* by seeking growth in entirely new business areas. Did you know, for example, that Exxon once owned Izod? Does that make sense? Can you see the risk here and understand why growth through unrelated diversification might cause problems? Research, in fact, is quite clear that business performance may decline for firms that get into too much unrelated diversification.[6]

Diversification can also take the form of **vertical integration**. This is where a business acquires its suppliers (*backward vertical integration*) or its distributors (*forward vertical integration*). Backward vertical integration has been a historical pattern in the automobile industry as firms purchased parts suppliers, although recent trends are to reverse this. It's now evident at Apple Computer. The firm has bought chip manufacturers to give it more privacy and sophistication in developing microprocessors for products like the iPad. In beverages, both Coca-Cola and PepsiCo have pursued forward vertical integration by purchasing some of their major bottlers.

‖ Restructuring and divestiture strategies focus on consolidation.

When organizations run into performance difficulties, perhaps because of too much growth and diversification, these problems have to be solved. A **retrenchment strategy** seeks to correct weaknesses by making radical changes to current ways of operating.

The most extreme form of retrenchment is **liquidation,** where a business closes down and sells its assets to pay creditors. A less extreme and more common form of retrenchment is **restructuring.** This involves making major changes to cut costs, gain short-term efficiencies, and buy time to try new strategies to improve future success.

When a firm is in desperate financial condition and unable to pay its bills, a situation faced by Chrysler and General Motors during the financial crisis, restructuring by **Chapter 11 bankruptcy** is an option under U.S. law. This protects the firm from creditors while management reorganizes things in an attempt to restore solvency. The goal is to emerge from bankruptcy as a stronger and profitable business, something achieved by both GM and Chrysler.

Downsizing is a restructuring approach that often makes the news. It cuts the size of operations and reduces the workforce.[7] When you learn of organizations downsizing by across-the-board cuts, however, you might be a bit skeptical. Research shows that downsizing is most successful when cutbacks are done selectively and focused on key performance objectives.[8]

Finally, restructuring by **divestiture** involves selling parts of the organization to refocus on core competencies, cut costs, and improve operating efficiency. This type of retrenchment often occurs when organizations have become

A **retrenchment strategy** changes operations to correct weaknesses.

Liquidation occurs when a business closes and sells its assets to pay creditors.

Restructuring reduces the scale or mix of operations.

Chapter 11 bankruptcy protects an insolvent firm from creditors during a period of reorganization to restore profitability.

Downsizing decreases the size of operations.

Divestiture involves selling off parts of the organization to refocus attention on core business areas.

{ **MANAGERS RARELY HAVE THE LUXURY OF FULL INFORMATION BOXED UP FOR ANALYSIS IN A NICE NEAT CASE FORMAT.**

Explore **Yourself**

■ Critical Thinking

Strategic management requires managers to deal with a complex array of forces and uncertainties. All must be analyzed to craft a strategy that moves an organization forward with success.

Critical thinking is a "must-have" for success in strategic management. It is what enables you to perceive problems, hone in on their more essential aspects, gather and interpret useful information, and make good decisions in complex conditions.

The same critical thinking that is part of a case study in your course is what helps managers create winning strategies. But with all the uncertainties that exist today, managers rarely have

the luxury of full information boxed up for analysis in a nice neat case format. Critical thinking in the real world must be multidimensional and embrace both the systematic and intuitive aspects of decision making.

> Get to know yourself better by taking the self-assessment on **Handling Facts and Inferences** and completing other activities in the *Exploring Management* **Skill-Building Portfolio.**

overdiversified. eBay once spent $3.1 billion to buy the Internet telephone service Skype. After the expected synergies between Skype and eBay's online auction business never developed, Skype was sold to private investors.[9] They, in turn, sold it to Microsoft, which is still trying to integrate Skype into its business model.

⫴ Global strategies focus on international business initiatives.

International business offers a variety of growth opportunities. Many large U.S. firms—including McDonald's, IBM, and Colgate-Palmolive—now get the majority of their revenues internationally. But, many challenges also come with the growth opportunities of international business. And, firms strategically engage them in different ways.[10]

Firms pursuing a **globalization strategy** tend to view the world as one large market. They try to advertise and sell standard products for use everywhere. For example, Gillette sells and advertises its latest razors around the world; you get the same product in Italy or South Africa as in America.

Firms pursuing a *multidomestic strategy* customize products and advertising to fit local cultures and needs. Bristol Myers, Procter & Gamble, and Unilever all vary their products to match consumer preferences in different countries and cultures.[11]

A third approach is the *transnational strategy*, where firms seek a balance between efficiencies in global operations and responsiveness to local markets. A transnational firm tries to operate without a strong national identity, hoping instead to blend with the global economy. Firms using a **transnational strategy** try to fully utilize business resources and tap customer markets worldwide. Ford, for example, draws on design, manufacturing, and distribution expertise all over the world to build car platforms. These are then modified within regions to build cars that meet local tastes.

> A **globalization strategy** adopts standardized products and advertising for use worldwide.

> A **transnational firm** tries to operate globally without having a strong national identity.

YM YIK/EPA/Landov

{ THE WORK IS MEANINGLESS, NO CONVERSATION IS ALLOWED ON THE PRODUCTION LINES, AND BATHROOM BREAKS ARE LIMITED.

Ethics Check

■ Life and Death at an Outsourcing Factory

Foxconn, the trade name for Hon Hai Precision Industry, is a major outsourcing firm. Its plants in China make products for Apple, Dell, and Hewlett-Packard, among others. One large complex employs over 300,000 people.

The firm has been the target of complaints over worker safety, overtime, and underage hiring practices. A clash between workers and security forces focused on rules perceived as too strict for China's newest generation of workers. At a factory in Shenzen, China, safety netting was draped around dormitories after a rash of employee suicides.

Foxconn employees have complained that the work is meaningless, no conversation is allowed on the production lines, and bathroom breaks are limited. One says: "I do the same thing every day. I have no future."

A Foxconn supervisor points out that the firm provides counseling services and that most workers are young and this is the first time they have been away from their homes. "Without their families," says the supervisor, "they're left without direction. We try to provide them with direction and help." Recent changes at the company include more focus on working conditions, higher wages, less overtime, and even more automation of simple jobs.

YOU DECIDE

What ethical responsibilities do global firms have when outsourcing in foreign plants? Whose responsibility is it to make sure workers are well treated? Should price-conscious consumers support bad practices by buying products from firms whose outsourcing partners treat workers poorly?

Cooperation strategies focus on alliances and partnerships.

The trend today is toward more cooperation among organizations, often in **strategic alliances,** where two or more organizations join together in partnership to pursue an area of mutual interest. A common form involves *outsourcing alliances*, contracting to purchase specialized services from another organization. Many organizations today, for example, are outsourcing their IT function to firms such as Infosys and IBM. The belief is that these services are better provided by a firm with special expertise in this area.

Cooperation in the supply chain also takes the form of *supplier alliances*, which guarantee a smooth and timely flow of quality supplies among alliance partners. We also see cooperation in *distribution alliances* where firms join together to accomplish product or services sales and distribution.

Some cooperation strategies even involve strategic alliances with competitors. Known as **co-opetition,** it has been called a "revolution mindset" that business competitors can be co-operating partners.[12] United and Lufthansa are international competitors, but they cooperate in the Star Alliance network that allows customers to book each other's flights and share frequent flyer programs. Likewise, luxury car competitors Daimler and BMW are cooperating to co-develop new motors and components for hybrid cars.[13]

> In a **strategic alliance**, organizations join together in partnership to pursue an area of mutual interest.

> **Co-opetition** is the strategy of working with rivals on projects of mutual benefit.

E-business strategies focus on using the Internet for business success.

A common question asked of business executives is: "What is your **e-business strategy?**" This refers to the strategic use of the Internet to gain competitive advantage. **Table 7.1**—Web-Based Business Models—lists some examples.[14]

B2B business strategies are business-to-business. They use the Web to vertically link organizations with members of their supply chains. For example, Dell Computer sets up special Web site services that allow major corporate customers to manage their accounts online. Wal-mart links its suppliers to the firm's information systems so they can electronically manage inventories for their own

> An **e-business strategy** strategically uses the Internet to gain competitive advantage.

> A **B2B business strategy** uses IT and Web portals to link organizations vertically in supply chains.

Table 7.1   Web-Based Business Models

Advertising model: Provide free information or services and then generate revenues from paid advertising to viewers (e.g., Yahoo!, Google)

Brokerage model: Bring buyers and sellers together for online business transactions and take a percentage from the sales (e.g., eBay, Priceline)

Community model: Provide a meeting point sold by subscription or supported by advertising (e.g., eHarmony, Facebook)

Freemium model: Offer a free service and encourage users to buy extras (e.g., Skype, Zynga)

Infomediary model: Provide a free service while collecting information on users and selling it to other businesses (e.g., Epinions, Yelp)

Merchant model: Sell products direct to customers through the Web—e-tailing (e.g., Amazon, Apple iTunes Store)

Referral model: Provide free listings and get referral fees from online merchants after directing customers to them (e.g., Shopzilla, PriceGrabber)

Subscription model: Sell access to high-value content through a subscription Web site (e.g., Netflix, Wall Street Journal Interactive)

B2C business strategy uses IT and Web portals to link businesses with customers.

products. B2C business strategies are business-to-customer. They use the Web to link businesses with customers. Whenever you buy a music download from Apple's iTunes Store, order a book from Amazon.com, or shop Patagonia.com for the latest outdoor gear, you are the "C" in a B2C strategy.

A **social media strategy** uses social media to better engage with an organization's customers, clients, and external audiences in general.

There's a lot of buzz today about **social media strategy.** Think of this as an organization using social media such as Facebook or Twitter to better engage with customers, clients, and external audiences. How often do you hear or read "Find us on Facebook"? That's what Procter & Gamble says. Its Facebook page on Pampers sells the product, hosts a discussion forum for users, and encourages viewers to enter free Pampers sweepstakes.

A **crowdsourcing** strategy uses the Internet to engage customers and potential customers in providing opinions and suggestions on products and their designs.

Crowdsourcing is a special type of social media strategy. It uses the Internet to engage customers and potential customers to make suggestions and express opinions on products and their designs. An example is Threadless.com. The firm's website allows online visitors to submit designs for T-shirts. The designs are voted on by other viewers—the "crowd"—and top-rated ones get selected for production and sale to customers.[15]

{ *Rebooting Work: Transform How You Work in the Age of Entrepreneurship*
by Maynard Webb

Manager's **Library**

TIME TO GET YOUR CAREER STRATEGY UP TO DATE

Strategy and strategic management isn't just for organizations, it also applies to personal affairs and goals. Career strategy is right up there in importance. Things are changing so fast today that the career strategies that helped past generations to succeed might not work as well for present ones. Here's some ideas from a book that might just be worth reading.

Rebooting Work: Transform How You Work in the Age of Entrepreneurship (2013, John Wiley & Sons), by Maynard Webb, is a practical guide to navigating the new era of what many call the "entrepreneurial workplace." Webb, former chief operating officer of eBay, is a Silicon Valley angel investor, philanthropist, entrepreneur, and company builder. One of the career strategies he discusses is mentoring. Surely you've heard about the value of finding a good mentor. But have you thought about how the mentoring strategy plays out in today's hyper-competitive, hyper-quick workplace?

This book describes a decline of age-old face-to-face mentoring relationships between senior managers and their juniors. Reasons include technology replacing in-person communication and the shorter and more temporary tenure of employment contracts. Flatter organizations that operate with fewer middle managers offer less mentoring opportunities.

Even though Webb claims that "the mentor-protégé model has gone the way of the mainframe computer," mentoring is still high on his list of career priorities. Given today's entrepreneurial workplace, he sees it as a strategy more and more driven by the power of self-management. It's important, he says, to take control of your own destiny and abandon the dated notion that an employer will take care of your professional development.

Webb's message is that mentors are out there, but we have to find and access them on our own. Good developmental job opportunities exist, but we have to seek out the new roles and responsibilities for ourselves. Webb recommends we "seek mentors and aspire to be a mentor" and "focus on being voted on the team each day." With proper self management it's possible to stay inspired, empowered, and successful in the entrepreneurial workplace.

REFLECT AND REACT

Does this notion of the entrepreneurial workplace seem to describe the career settings ahead for you? How about the mentoring strategy? If you don't have a mentor and your employer isn't being helpful, how can you get yourself one? Can mentoring work as well online as face-to-face?

STUDY GUIDE

Takeaway 7.1
What Types of Strategies Are Used by Organizations?

Terms to Define

B2B business strategy

B2C business strategy

Business strategy

Chapter 11 bankruptcy

Competitive advantage

Concentration

Co-opetition

Corporate strategy

Crowdsourcing

Diversification

Divestiture

Downsizing

E-business strategy

Functional strategy

Globalization strategy

Growth strategy

Liquidation

Restructuring

Retrenchment strategy

Social media strategy

Strategic alliance

Strategic intent

Strategy

Sustainable competitive advantage

Transnational firm

Vertical integration

Rapid Review

- A strategy is a comprehensive plan that sets long-term direction for an organization and guides resource allocations to achieve competitive advantage, operating in ways that outperform the competition.
- Corporate strategy sets the direction for an entire organization; business strategy sets the direction for a large business unit or product division; functional strategy sets the direction within business functions.
- Growth strategies seek to expand existing business areas through concentration or add new ones by related or unrelated diversification.
- Retrenchment strategies try to streamline or consolidate organizations for better performance through restructuring and divestiture.
- Global strategies pursue international business opportunities.
- Cooperative strategies make business use of alliances and partnerships.
- E-business strategies use the Internet to pursue competitive advantage.

Questions for Discussion

1. With things changing so fast today, is it really possible for a business to achieve "sustainable" competitive advantage?
2. Why is growth such a popular business strategy?
3. Is it good news or bad news for investors when a business announces that it is restructuring?

Be Sure You Can

- differentiate strategy, strategic intent, and competitive advantage
- differentiate corporate, business, and functional levels of strategy
- list and explain major types of growth and diversification strategies
- list and explain restructuring and divestiture strategies
- explain alternative global strategies
- differentiate B2B and B2C as e-business strategies

Career Situation: What Would You Do?

A neighborhood business association has members from the local coffee bistro, bookstore, drugstore, hardware store, and bicycle shop. The owners of these businesses are interested in how they might "cooperate" for better success. Be a business consultant to the association. What would you propose as possible strategic alliances and cooperation strategies so that these businesses can work together for mutual gain?

Takeaway 7.2
How Do Managers Formulate and Implement Strategies?

ANSWERS TO COME

- The strategic management process formulates and implements strategies.
- Strategy formulation begins with the organization's mission and objectives.
- SWOT analysis examines strengths, weaknesses, opportunities, and threats.
- Porter's five forces model identifies industry attractiveness.
- Porter's competitive strategies model identifies business or product strategies.
- Portfolio planning examines strategies across multiple businesses or products.
- Strategic leadership ensures strategy implementation and control.

THE LATE AND GREAT MANAGEMENT GURU PETER DRUCKER ONCE SAID: "THE future will not just happen if one wishes hard enough. It requires decision—now. It imposes risk—now. It requires action—now. It demands allocation of resources, and above all, of human resources—now. It requires work—now."[16] Drucker's point fits squarely with the chapter subtitle: Insight and hard work deliver results. It's now time to talk more about the hard work of strategic management.

⫿ The strategic management process formulates and implements strategies.

Strategic management is the process of formulating and implementing strategies.

Strategy formulation is the process of creating strategies.

Figure 7.1 shows **strategic management** as the process of formulating and implementing strategies to accomplish long-term goals and sustain competitive advantage. **Strategy formulation** is the process of crafting strategy. It reviews current mission, objectives, and strategies, assesses the organization and

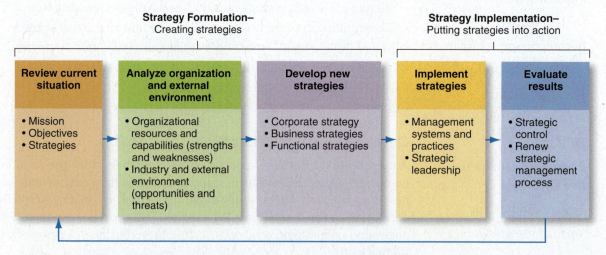

Strategy Formulation– Creating strategies   Strategy Implementation– Putting strategies into action

Review current situation	Analyze organization and external environment	Develop new strategies	Implement strategies	Evaluate results
• Mission • Objectives • Strategies	• Organizational resources and capabilities (strengths and weaknesses) • Industry and external environment (opportunities and threats)	• Corporate strategy • Business strategies • Functional strategies	• Management systems and practices • Strategic leadership	• Strategic control • Renew strategic management process

FIGURE 7.1 What Are the Steps in the Strategic Management Process?
The strategic management process involves responsibilities for both formulating and implementing organizational strategies. The process begins with review of existing mission, objectives, and strategies to set a baseline for further action. Next, organizational strengths and weaknesses as well as environmental opportunities and threats are analyzed. Strategies are then crafted at corporate, business, and functional levels. Finally, the strategies are put into action. This requires strategic leadership and control to ensure that all organizational resources and systems fully support strategy implementation.

environment, and develops new strategies to deliver future competitive advantage. **Strategy implementation** is the process of putting strategies into action. It leads and activates the entire organization to put strategies to work.

Can you see that both activities are necessary, that success is only possible when strategies are both well formulated and well implemented? Competitive advantage in business or in a career doesn't just happen. It is created when great strategies are implemented to full advantage.

⫴ Strategy formulation begins with the organization's mission and objectives.

Strategy formulation begins with review of the organization's mission, current strategies, and objectives.[17] You should know that the **mission** describes the purpose of an organization, its reason for existence in society.[18] The best organizations have clear missions that communicate a sense of direction and motivate members to work hard in their behalf.[19] They also link these missions with well-chosen **operating objectives** that serve as short-term guides to performance.[20] A sampling of typical business operating objectives includes profitability, cost efficiency, market share, product quality, innovation, and social responsibility.

When mission and objectives are clear, a strategic planning baseline is established. The next step in strategy formulation is to understand how well the organization is currently positioned to achieve competitive advantage.

⫴ SWOT analysis examines strengths, weaknesses, opportunities, and threats.

A **SWOT analysis** involves a detailed examination of organizational strengths and weaknesses as well as environmental opportunities and threats. As **Figure 7.2** shows, the results of this examination can be portrayed in a straightforward and very useful planning matrix.

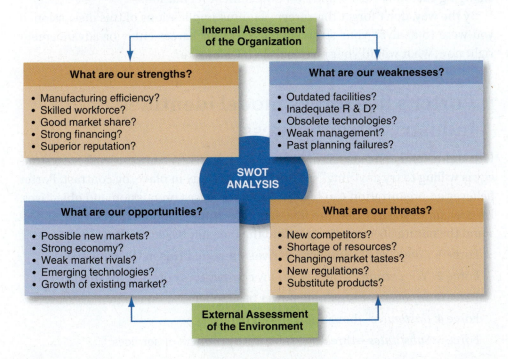

> **Strategy implementation** is the process of putting strategies into action.

> The **mission** is the organization's reason for existence in society.

> **Operating objectives** are specific results that organizations try to accomplish.

> A **SWOT analysis** examines organizational strengths and weaknesses, as well as environmental opportunities and threats.

FIGURE 7.2
What Does a SWOT Analysis Try to Discover?
The SWOT analysis is a way of identifying organizational strengths and weaknesses as well as environmental opportunities and threats. It forces strategists to discover key facts and conditions with potential consequences for strategic performance. It also organizes this information in a structured manner that is useful for making strategy decisions. Managers using a SWOT analysis should be looking for organizational strengths that can be leveraged as core competencies to make future gains, as well as environmental opportunities that can be exploited.

Tips to **Remember**

■ Key Operating Objectives of Organizations

When it is time to measure performance and assess how well an organization is doing, operating objectives like the following are often under scrutiny.

- *Profits*—operating with revenues greater than costs
- *Cost efficiency*—operating with low costs; finding ways to lower costs
- *Market share*—having a solid and sustainable pool of customers
- *Product quality*—producing goods and services that satisfy customers

- *Talented workforce*—attracting and retaining high-quality employees
- *Innovation*—using new ideas to improve operations and products
- *Social responsibility*—earning the respect of multiple stakeholders
- *Sustainability*—developing sustainable processes, products, and supply chains

---

> A **core competency** is a special strength that gives an organization a competitive advantage.

When looking at the organization's *strengths*, one goal is to identify **core competencies.** These are special strengths that the organization has or does exceptionally well in comparison with its competitors. When an organization's core competencies are unique and costly for others to imitate—say, for example, Amazon's "1-Click" order technology and efficient logistics, they become potential sources of competitive advantage.[21] Organizational *weaknesses* are the flip side of the picture. They must also be understood to gain a realistic sense of the organization's capabilities.

The same analytical discipline holds when examining conditions in the environment. It's not only the *opportunities* that count—such as new markets, a strong economy, weak competitors, and emerging technologies. The *threats* count too—perhaps the emergence of new competitors, resource scarcities, changing customer tastes, and new government regulations.

By the way, don't forget the career planning implications of this discussion. If you were to analyze your strategic readiness for career entry or advancement right now, what would your personal SWOT look like?

⦀ Porter's five forces model identifies industry attractiveness.

Harvard scholar and consultant Michael Porter says, "A company without a strategy is willing to try anything."[22] With a good strategy in place, by contrast, Porter believes an organization can best focus its resources on mission and objectives. He goes on to suggest that the first step in crafting a good strategy is to understand the nature of competition within the industry based on these "five forces."

Force 1: *Competitors*—intensity of rivalry among firms in the industry

Force 2: *New entrants*—threats of new competitors entering the market

Force 3: *Suppliers*—bargaining power of suppliers

Force 4: *Customers*—bargaining power of buyers

Force 5: *Substitutes*—threats of substitute products or services[23]

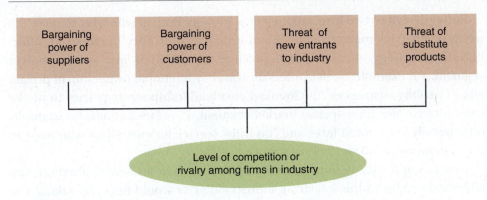

FIGURE 7.3
What Is Porter's Five Forces Model of Industry Attractiveness?
Strategic management is very challenging in an *unattractive industry* that has intense competitive rivalries, substantial threats in the form of possible new entrants and substitute products, and powerful suppliers and buyers who dominate any bargaining with the firm. Strategy management is less of a problem in an *attractive industry* that has little existing competition, few threats from new entrants or substitutes, and low bargaining power among suppliers and buyers.

Porter's five forces model of industry attractiveness is shown in **Figure 7.3**. An unattractive industry will have intense competitive rivalries, substantial threats in the form of possible new entrants and substitute products, and powerful suppliers and buyers who dominate any bargaining with the firm. As you might expect, this is a very challenging environment for strategy formulation.

A very attractive industry will have little existing competition, few threats from new entrants or substitutes, and low bargaining power among suppliers and buyers. These are much more favorable conditions for strategy formulation.

⫴ Porter's competitive strategies model identifies business or product strategies.

Once industry forces are understood, attention shifts to how a business or its products can be strategically positioned relative to competitors. Porter believes that competitive strategies can be built around differentiation, cost leadership, and focus.

A **differentiation strategy** seeks competitive advantage through uniqueness. This means developing goods and services that are clearly different from the competition. The strategic objective is to attract customers who stay loyal to the firm's products and lose interest in those of its competitors.

Success with a differentiation strategy depends on customer perceptions of product quality and uniqueness. This requires organizational strengths in marketing, research and development, and creativity. An example is Polo Ralph Lauren, retailer of upscale classic fashions and accessories. In Ralph Lauren's words, "Polo redefined how American style and quality is perceived. Polo has always been about selling quality products by creating worlds and inviting our customers to be part of our dream."[24] If you've seen any Polo ads in magazines or on television, you'll know that the company aggressively markets this perception.

A **cost leadership strategy** seeks competitive advantage by operating with lower costs than competitors. This allows organizations to make profits while selling products or services at low prices their competitors can't profitably match. The objective is to continuously improve operating efficiencies in purchasing, production, distribution, and other organizational systems.

Success with the cost leadership strategy requires tight cost and managerial controls, as well as products or services that are easy to create and distribute. This is what might be called the "Wal-Mart" strategy—do everything you can to keep costs so low that you can offer customers lower prices than competitors and still make a reasonable profit.

A **differentiation strategy** offers products that are unique and different from those of the competition.

A **cost leadership strategy** seeks to operate with lower costs than competitors.

A **focused differentiation strategy** offers a unique product to a special market segment.

A **focused cost leadership strategy** seeks the lowest costs of operations within a special market segment.

Porter describes two forms of the focus strategy, both of which try to serve the needs of a narrow market segment better than anyone else. The **focused differentiation strategy** offers a unique product to customers in a special market segment. For example, NetJets offers air travel by fractional ownership of private jets to wealthy customers. The **focused cost leadership strategy** tries to be the low-cost provider for a special market segment. Low-fare airlines, for example, offer heavily discounted fares and "no frills" service for customers who want to travel point-to-point for the lowest prices.

Can you apply these four competitive strategies to an actual situation, say, alternative sodas in the soft-drink industry? Porter would begin by asking and answering two questions for each soda: What is the market scope—broad or narrow? What is the potential source of competitive advantage—low price or product uniqueness? **Figure 7.4** shows how answers to these questions might strategically position some soft drinks with which you might be familiar.

FIGURE 7.4
What Are the Strategic Options in Porter's Competitive Strategies Model? Porter's competitive strategies model asks two basic questions to identify alternative business and product strategies. First, what is the market scope—broad or narrow? Second, what is the expected source of competitive advantage—lower price or product uniqueness? The four possible combinations of answers result in differentiation, cost leadership, focused differentiation, and focused cost leadership strategies. The figure uses examples from the soft-drink industry to show how these strategies can be used for different products.

The makers of Coke and Pepsi follow a differentiation strategy. They spend millions on advertising to convince consumers that their products are of high quality and uniquely desirable. Bubba Cola, a Save-A-Lot Brand, and Go2 Cola, a Safeway Brand, sell as cheaper alternatives. To make a profit at the lower selling price, these stores must follow a cost leadership strategy.

What about a can of A & W Root Beer or a can of Mountain Dew? In Porter's model, they represent a strategy of focused differentiation—products with unique tastes for customers wanting quality brands. This is quite different from the strategy behind Giant store's Quist or Stop & Shop's Sun Pop. These are classic cases of focused cost leadership—a product with a unique taste for customers who want a low price.

Porter's Competitive Strategies »

- *Differentiation*—make products that are unique and different.
- *Cost leadership*—produce at lower cost and sell at lower price.
- *Focused differentiation*—use differentiation and target needs of a special market.
- *Focused cost leadership*—use cost leadership and target needs of a special market.

⫶ Portfolio planning examines strategies across multiple businesses or products.

As you might expect, strategic management gets quite complicated for companies that operate multiple businesses selling many different products and services. A good example is the global conglomerate General Electric. The firm owns a portfolio of diverse businesses ranging from jet engines, to financial services, to medical systems, to power systems, and even more. The CEO of GE faces a difficult strategic question all the time: How should the firm's resources be allocated across this mix, or portfolio, of businesses? This portfolio-planning question is better made systematically than haphazardly.[25]

The Boston Consulting Group recommends a portfolio planning approach summarized in **Figure 7.5** and known as the **BCG Matrix**. This strategic framework asks managers to analyze business and product strategies based on market growth rate and market share.[26]

Stars in the BCG Matrix have high market shares in high-growth markets. They produce large profits through substantial penetration of expanding markets. The preferred strategy for stars is growth. The BCG Matrix recommends making further resource investments in them. Stars are not only high performers in the present, they also offer future potential to do the same or even better.

Cash cows have high market shares in low-growth markets. They produce large profits and a strong cash flow, but with little upside potential. Because the markets offer little growth opportunity, the preferred strategy for cash cows is stability or modest growth. Like real dairy cows, the BCG Matrix advises firms to "milk" these businesses to generate cash for investing in other more promising areas.

Question marks have low market shares in high-growth markets. Although they may not generate much profit at the moment, the upside potential is there because of the growing markets. Question marks make for difficult strategic decision making. The BCG Matrix recommends targeting only the most promising question marks for growth, while retrenching those that are less promising.

Dogs have low market shares in low-growth markets. They produce little if any profit, and they have low potential for future improvement. The preferred strategy for dogs is straightforward: retrenchment by divestiture.

The **BCG Matrix** analyzes business opportunities according to market growth rate and market share.

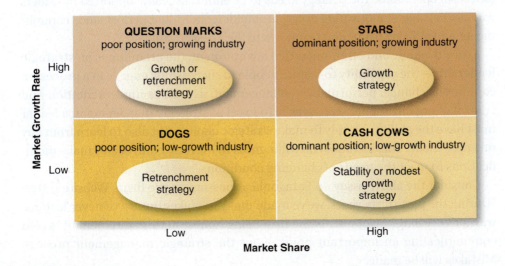

FIGURE 7.5

Why Is the BCG Matrix Useful in Strategic Planning? The BCG Matrix is useful in situations where managers must make strategic decisions that allocate scarce organizational resources among multiple and competing uses. This is a typical situation for organizations that have a range of businesses or products. The BCG Matrix sorts businesses or products into four strategic types (dogs, stars, question marks, and cash cows), based on market shares held and market growth rates. Specific master strategies are recommended for each strategic type.

Climbing High with Patagonia, Inc.

Passion and Values Make for Strategic Success

Headquartered in Ventura, California, Patagonia sells top-quality and high-priced outdoor clothing and gear. That may seem like nothing special perhaps, but the company is noteworthy. It is known for a commitment to sustainability and respect for the natural environment. Some go so far as to call the firm "fanatical about environmental concerns."

Even though Patagonia's commitment to green products is a source of market advantage, there is uniqueness evident on many fronts at this company. And, it all drives competitive advantage. The firm's earnings are consistently above the industry average. Its workforce is loyal and inspired. Its products are always on top of the quality chain.

Most analysts would call Patagonia a strategic success story anchored to its clear mission: "Build the best product, cause no unnecessary harm, use business to inspire and implement solutions to the environmental crisis." There's no doubt founder Yvon Chouinard has a personal commitment to sustainability and expects the firm to live up to its responsibilities as a steward of the natural environment. He says: "Most people want to do good things but don't. At Patagonia it's an essential part of your life." He backed this statement by filing papers for Patagonia to become California's first "benefit corporation." This means that its policies will always "crate a material positive impact on society and the environment."

Find Inspiration

Yvon Chouinard believes a compelling mission plus great talent is a recipe for self-control. "I have an M.B.A. theory of management," he says, "Management by Absence. I take off for weeks at a time and never call in. We hire the best people we can and then leave them to do their jobs." Can inspiring leadership be this easy?

Strategic leadership inspires people to implement organizational strategies.

▌▌▌ Strategic leadership ensures strategy implementation and control.

The rest of *Exploring Management* is really all about strategy implementation. In order to successfully put strategies into action, the entire organization and all its resources and systems must be mobilized in support of them. This, in effect, involves the complete management process—from planning and controlling through organizing and leading. No matter how well or elegantly planned, a strategy requires supporting structures, a good allocation of tasks and workflow designs, and the right people to staff all aspects of operations. The strategy needs to be enthusiastically supported by leaders who are capable of motivating everyone, building individual performance commitments, and utilizing teams and teamwork to their best advantage.

In our dynamic and often-uncertain environment, the premium is on **strategic leadership**—the capability to inspire people to successfully engage in a process of continuous change, performance enhancement, as well as implementation and control of organizational strategies.[27] To excel at strategic management, a leader must have the ability not only to make strategic choices but also to learn from any mistakes made. This includes the willingness to exercise control and make modifications to meet the needs of changing conditions.

Consider the above essay on Patagonia. A posting on the firm's Website states: "During the past thirty years, we've made many mistakes but we've never lost our way for very long."[28] Not only is the firm being honest in this statement, it is also communicating an important point about the strategic management process: Mistakes will be made.

Kai Nedden/laif/Redux Pictures

Stuart Rayner/iStockphoto

Facts to **Consider**

■ Disposable Workers Are Becoming Indispensible to Business Profits

We're now in the era of the disposable worker says Northwestern University economist Robert Gordon. And the facts certainly support his claim. Businesses seem enamoured with the idea of hiring less full-timers and more part-time or temporary workers that can be added and let go according to demand. Professor Susan J. Lambert of the University of Chicago blames some of the switch to disposable workers on labor union decline. Others simply point out the cost advantages to employers who only have to pay for workers as needed.

- A McKinsey survey of 2,000 employers found 58% planning to hire more workers on a part-time, temporary, and contract basis.
- The U.S. Bureau of Labor Statistics reports that 1 million full-time jobs have been cut and 500,000 part-time ones added by retail and wholesale employers in the last six years.

- Almost 3 of every 10 retail/wholesale jobs are filled part-time. Among part-timers, 30.6% want full-time work.
- Compensation for part-timers in retail/wholesale averaged $10.92 per hour ($8.90 wages and $2.02 benefits) versus $17.18 for full-timers ($12.25 wages and $4.93 benefits).
- A survey of retailers in New York City found half of jobs filled by part-timers. Only 1 in 10 of them had set work schedules.

YOUR THOUGHTS?

Is this switch to employing more disposable workers a good long-term strategy for businesses and other organizations? What are the possible downsides to the employer and the remaining full-time employees? How might this trend affect you? Is this something that you have already factored into your career plan?

No matter how thorough or well intended the analysis, the chance exists that one's strategic choices might be wrong. One of the lessons business firms learned from the recent economic crisis is that a strategic leader has to maintain **strategic control**. This means that the CEO and other top managers must always be in touch with the strategy, know whether it is generating performance success or failure, and recognize when the strategy needs to be tweaked or changed.[29]

Michael Porter, whose five forces and competitive strategy models for strategic management were discussed earlier, emphasizes the role of CEO as chief strategist. He describes the task in the following ways.[30]

- *A strategic leader has to be the guardian of trade-offs.* It is the leader's job to make sure that the organization's resources are allocated in ways consistent with the strategy. This requires the discipline to sort through many competing ideas and alternatives to stay on course and not get sidetracked.

- *A strategic leader needs to create a sense of urgency.* The leader must not allow the organization and its members to grow slow and complacent. Even when doing well, the leader keeps the focus on getting better and being alert to conditions that require adjustments to the strategy.

- *A strategic leader must make sure that everyone understands the strategy.* Unless strategies are understood, the daily tasks and contributions of people lose context and purpose. Everyone might work very hard, but unless efforts are aligned with strategy, the impact is dispersed and fails to advance common goals.

- *A strategic leader must be a teacher.* It is the leader's job to teach the strategy and make it a "cause," says Porter. In order for strategy to work, it must become an ever-present commitment throughout the organization. This means that a strategic leader must be a great communicator. Everyone must understand the strategy and how it makes the organization different from others.

Strategic control makes sure strategies are well implemented and that poor strategies are scrapped or changed.

《 **Strategic Leadership Responsibilities**

STUDY GUIDE

Takeaway 7.2
How Do Managers Formulate and Implement Strategies?

Terms to Define

BCG Matrix

Core competencies

Cost leadership strategy

Differentiation strategy

Focused cost leadership strategy

Focused differentiation strategy

Mission

Operating objectives

Strategic control

Strategic leadership

Strategic management

Strategy formulation

Strategy implementation

SWOT analysis

Rapid Review

- Strategic management is the process of formulating and implementing strategies to achieve a sustainable competitive environment.
- A SWOT analysis sets a foundation for strategy formulation by systematically assessing organizational strengths and weaknesses as well as environmental opportunities and threats.
- Porter's five forces model analyzes industry attractiveness in terms of competitors, threat of new entrants, substitute products, and the bargaining powers of suppliers and buyers.
- Porter's competitive strategies describes business and product strategies based on differentiation (distinguishing one's products from the competition), cost leadership (minimizing costs relative to the competition), and focus (concentrating on a special market segment).
- The BCG Matrix is a portfolio-planning approach that describes strategies for businesses classified as stars, cash cows, question marks, or dogs.
- Strategic leadership is the responsibility for activating people, organizational resources, and management systems to continually pursue and fully accomplish strategy implementation.

Questions for Discussion

1. Can an organization have a good strategy but a poor sense of mission?
2. Would a monopoly receive a perfect score for industry attractiveness in Porter's five forces model?
3. Does the BCG Matrix oversimplify a complex strategic management problem?

Be Sure You Can

- describe the strategic management process
- explain Porter's five forces model
- explain Porter's competitive strategies model
- describe the purpose and use of the BCG Matrix
- explain the responsibilities of strategic leadership

Career Situation: What Would You Do?

For some years now, you've owned a small specialty bookshop in a college town. You sell some textbooks but mainly cater to a broader customer base. Your store always stocks the latest fiction, nonfiction, and children's books. Recent numbers show a steep decline in sales, including of books that would normally be considered best sellers. You suspect this is because of the growing popularity of e-books and e-readers such as the Amazon Kindle and Barnes & Noble Nook. Some of your friends say it's time to close up because your market is dying. Is it hopeless, or is there a business strategy that might yet save the store?

TestPrep 7

Answers to TestPrep questions can be found at the back of the book.

Multiple-Choice Questions

1. Which is the best question to ask to start the strategic management process?

    (a) "What is our mission?"

    (b) "How well are we currently doing?"

    (c) "How can we get where we want to be?"

    (d) "Why aren't we doing better?"

2. The ability of a business firm to consistently outperform its rivals is called _____.

    (a) vertical integration

    (b) competitive advantage

    (c) strategic intent

    (d) core competency

3. General Electric is a complex conglomerate that owns many firms operating in very different industries. The strategies pursued for each individual firm within GE umbrella would best be called _____level strategies.

    (a) corporate

    (b) business

    (c) functional

    (d) transnational

4. An organization that is downsizing by cutting staff to reduce costs can be described as pursuing a _____strategy.

    (a) liquidation

    (b) divestiture

    (c) retrenchment

    (d) stability

5. When you buy music downloads online, the firm selling them to you is engaging in which type of e-business strategy?

    (a) B2C

    (b) B2B

    (c) infomediary

    (d) crowdsourcing

6. The alliances that link firms in supply chain management relationships are examples of how businesses can use _____strategies.

    (a) B2C

    (b) growth

    (c) cooperation

    (d) concentration

7. Among the global strategies that international businesses might pursue, the _____strategy most directly tries to customize products to fit local needs and cultures in different countries.

    (a) concentration

    (b) globalization

    (c) transnational

    (d) multidomestic

8. If Google's top management were to announce that the firm was going to buy Federal Express, this would be a strategy of growth by _____.

    (a) diversification

    (b) concentration

    (c) horizontal integration

    (d) vertical integration

9. _____are special strengths that an organization has or does exceptionally well and that help it outperform competitors.

    (a) Core competencies

    (b) Strategies

    (c) Alliances

    (d) Operating objectives

10. A _____in the BCG Matrix would have a high market share in a low-growth market.

    (a) dog

    (b) cash cow

    (c) question mark

    (d) star

11. In Porter's five forces model, which of the following conditions is most favorable from the standpoint of industry attractiveness?

(a) Many competitive rivals

(b) Many substitute products

(c) Low bargaining power of suppliers

(d) Few barriers to entry

12. The two questions Porter asks to identify the correct competitive strategy for a business or product line are: 1—What is the market scope? 2—What is the _____?

(a) market share

(b) source of competitive advantage

(c) core competency

(d) industry attractiveness

13. When Coke and Pepsi spend millions on ads trying to convince customers that their products are unique, they are pursuing what Porter calls a _____ strategy.

(a) transnational

(b) concentration

(c) diversification

(d) differentiation

14. A firm that wants to compete with rivals by selling a very-low-priced product in a broad market would need to successfully implement a _____ strategy.

(a) retrenchment

(b) differentiation

(c) cost leadership

(d) diversification

15. In addition to focusing on strategy implementation and strategic control, the responsibility for strategic leadership of an organization involves success with _____.

(a) motivating a disposable workforce

(b) the process of continuous change

(c) Chapter 11 bankruptcy

(d) growth by liquidation

Short-Response Questions

16. What is the difference between corporate strategy and functional strategy?

17. Why is a cost leadership strategy so important when one wants to sell products at lower prices than competitors?

18. What strategy should be pursued for a "question mark" in the BCG Matrix, and why?

19. What is strategic leadership?

Integration and Application Question

20. Kim Harris owns and operates a small retail store that sells the outdoor clothing of an American manufacturer to a predominantly college-student market. A large national-chain department store has come to town and started selling similar but lower-priced clothing manufactured in China, Thailand, and Bangladesh. Kim is losing business to this store. She has asked your instructor to have a student team analyze the situation and propose some strategic alternatives to best deal with this threat. You are on the team.

Questions: How can a SWOT analysis be helpful in addressing Kim's strategic management problem? How could Porter's competitive strategies model be helpful as well?

Steps *for* Further Learning

BUILD MARKETABLE SKILLS
DO A CASE ANALYSIS
GET AND STAY INFORMED

BUILD

MARKETABLE SKILLS.
EARN BIG CAREER PAYOFFS!

Don't miss these opportunities in the **Skill-Building Portfolio**

■ **SELF-ASSESSMENT 7:**
Handling Facts and Inferences

Not all situations are clear-cut . . . get better at separating facts from inferences.

■ **CLASS EXERCISE 7:**
Strategic Scenarios

It's risky to make decisions on past experience . . . practice getting a sense of the future.

■ **TEAM PROJECT 7:**
Contrasting Strategies

There's often more than one way to a goal . . . but some strategies are still better than others

Many learning resources are found at the end of the book and online within WileyPLUS.

Take advantage of **Cases for Critical Thinking**

■ **CHAPTER 7 CASE SNAPSHOT:**
Dunkin' Donuts—Growth Feeds a Sweet Tooth /
Sidebar on Jamba Juice

Long before Starbucks was even a glimmer in anyone's entrepreneurial mind Dunkin' Donuts was as a well-known chain of coffee shops in the Northeast. It began in Boston in 1950, grew nicely, and today has positioned itself as a global player. This java giant is broadly expanding both its food and coffee menus to ride the wave of fresh trends appealing to a new generation of more health-conscious customers. Dunkin's long reputation for quality gives it an advantage in earning the trust of customers. But it's a highly competitive industry, and change has to constantly be on the menu. With Starbucks rethinking its positioning strategy and McDonald's offering a great-tasting coffee at a reasonable price, Dunkin' Donuts is hoping that careful strategic planning will keep its customers "Runnin on Dunkin."

DO

A CASE ANALYSIS.
STRENGTHEN YOUR CRITICAL THINKING!

Dig into this **Hot Topic**

■ **PRO AND CON DEBATE** How about a "double Irish" with a "Dutch sandwich"?

No, it's not a drink and a sandwich we're talking about. It's a global business strategy used to reduce corporate income taxes paid in America. Ireland offers corporations that put offices and plants there a 12.5% corporate tax rate. That compares with the standard 40% rate due at home. If you set up two Irish companies and arrange to funnel foreign earnings through them—the double Irish move—you pay the lesser tax bill. If those same earnings are then routed out and back to Ireland through the Netherlands and Bermuda, the tax bill goes down further—the Dutch sandwich. Who does it? Apple, Google, and Microsoft are among the players.

GET

AND STAY INFORMED.
MAKE YOURSELF VALUABLE!

Those in favor of the practice are likely to say: "It's perfectly legal." . . . "It boosts corporate earnings." . . . "You'd be a fool not to take advantage of the situation." *Those against the practice are likely to say:* "Wait a minute, I pay my full taxes why shouldn't they?". . . "Something isn't right here, isn't this just a blatant tax avoidance scheme?" . . . "We all lose when global corporations don't pay their taxes here at home."

Final Face-off Global business is a complicated world, and tax laws vary widely from one country to the next. International business executives have to be sophisticated and informed when it comes to managing financial transactions across borders. Are you among those who applaud executives who find and execute strategies like the double Irish with a Dutch sandwich? Or, are you among those who want to put a stop to such practices?

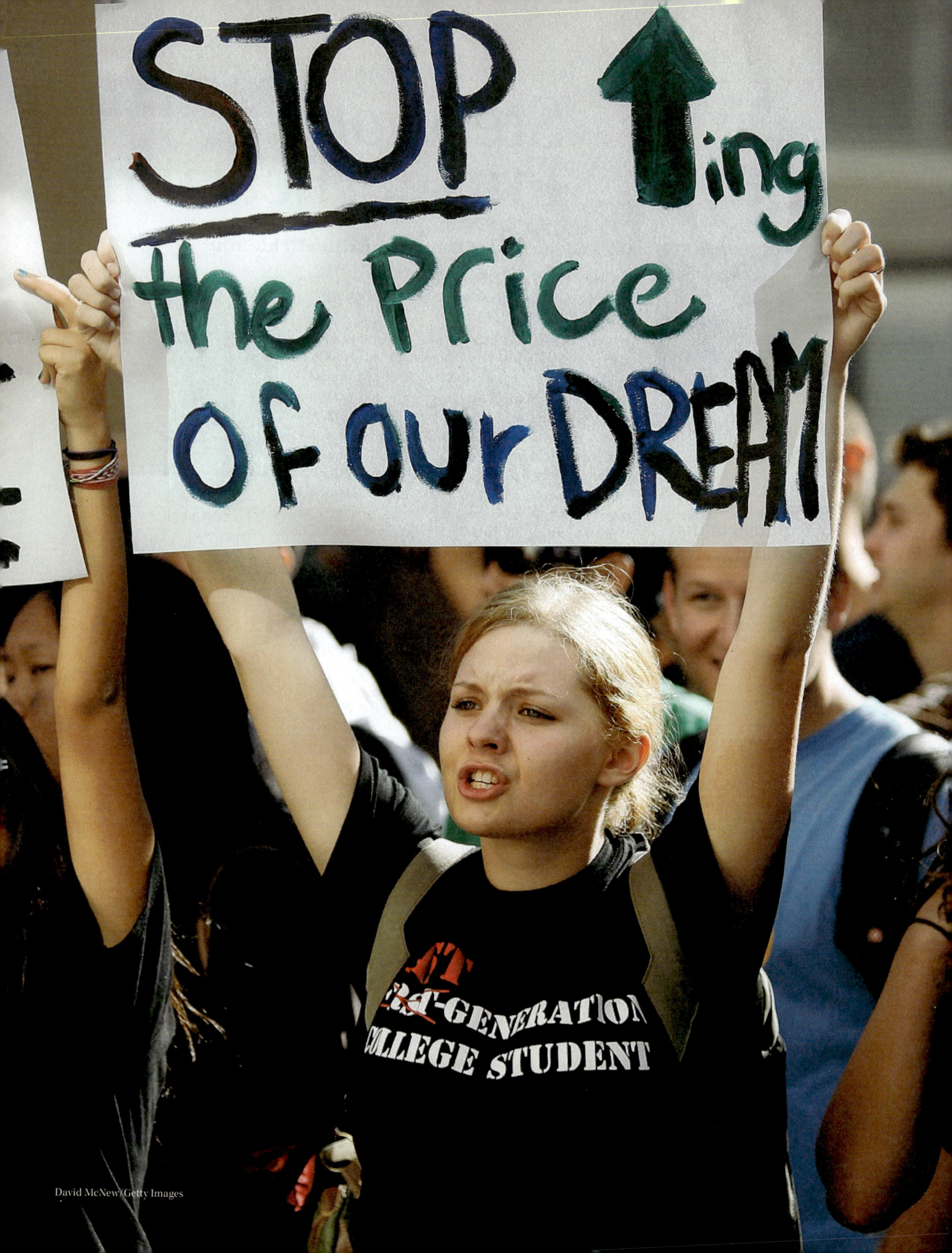

David McNew/Getty Images

Organization Structure and Design

It's All About Working Together

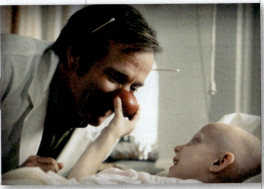

Blue Wolf/Photofest

8

Management Live

Empowerment and *Patch Adams*

The movie *Patch Adams* is based on the true-life story of Hunter "Patch" Adams. In the movie, Adams (Robin Williams) becomes increasingly disillusioned with medical bureaucracy. After a heart-wrenching incident at the hospital where he volunteers, Adams is inspired to create a new kind of hospital—one free from the usual constraints. The idea involves unconventional methods of treatment. Doctors and patients work side by side; patients take responsibility for their own care. Adams believed medical treatment would be more effective when patients had control.

This is how **empowerment** works in any setting. It frees people to make decisions about how they do things. It respects and unlocks their full potential. Although there are many types of organization structures, they aren't always empowering and they don't always match well with situational demands. But in the best organizations, everything is aligned to support high performance.

As you read about organizational structures and new work arrangements, try to imagine the advantages and disadvantages of each. One thing is certain—organizations are only as good as the people who work within them. Too many managers and team leaders fail at empowerment, and end up wondering why their organizations underperform. The last time you had a problem with a product or service, how was the situation resolved? Did the person you dealt with have the freedom to best resolve your problem?

YOUR CHAPTER 8 TAKEAWAYS

1. Understand organizing as a managerial responsibility.

2. Identify common types of organizational structures.

3. Recognize current trends in organizational design.

WHAT'S INSIDE

Explore Yourself
More on **empowerment**

Role Models
Alan Mulally hits the mark by restructuring Ford

Ethics Check
Flattened into exhaustion

Facts to Consider
Bosses may be overestimating their managing skills

Manager's Library
The Truth About Middle Managers: Heroes, Villains, and the Reinvention of Middle Management by Paul Osterman

Takeaway 8.1
What Is Organizing as a Managerial Responsibility?

ANSWERS TO COME

- Organizing is one of the management functions.
- Organization charts describe the formal structures of organizations.
- Organizations also operate with informal structures.
- Informal structures have good points and bad points.

FIGURE 8.1 What Is the Importance of Organizing in the Management Process?
Organizing is one of the four management functions. It is the process of arranging people and resources to create structures so that they work well together in accomplishing goals. Key organizing decisions made by managers include those that divide up the work to be done, staff jobs with talented people, position resources for best utilization, and coordinate activities.

Organizing arranges people and resources to work toward a common goal.

LIKE MOST THINGS, IT IS MUCH EASIER TO TALK ABOUT high-performing organizations than to actually create them. In true contingency fashion, there is no one best way to do things; no one organizational form meets the needs of all circumstances. And what works well at one moment in time can quickly become outdated, even dysfunctional, in another. This is why you often read and hear about organizations making changes and reorganizing in an attempt to improve their performance.

The fact that nothing is constant in most organizations, at least not for long, is a major reason why management scholar Henry Mintzberg pointed out that people often have problems.[1] Whenever job assignments and reporting relationships change, whenever the organization grows or shrinks, whenever old ways of doing things are reconfigured, people naturally struggle to understand the new ways of working. And perhaps even more important, they will worry about the implications for their jobs and careers.

Organizing is one of the management functions.

Most of us like to be organized—at home, at work, when playing games. We tend to get uncomfortable and anxious when things are disorganized. It shouldn't surprise you, therefore, that people in organizations need answers to such questions as: "Where do I fit in?" "How does my work relate to that of others?" and "Who runs things?"[2] People need these answers when they first join an organization, when they take new jobs, and whenever things are substantially changed. If they don't get good answers to this questions, the risk is that they will become disengaged. And with disengagement comes more absenteeism, turnover, dissatisfaction, and lower performance.[3]

This is where and why **organizing** plays a key role as one of the four functions of management shown in **Figure 8.1**. Think of it as the process of arranging people and resources so that they can work together to accomplish goals. Once goals are set in the planning phase, organizing puts people and resources in place to carry them out.[4] When it is done right organizing clarifies jobs and working relationships. It identifies who is to do what and who is in charge of whom. And it sets the stage so that different people and different parts of the organization are coordinated and work well with one another. All this, of course, can be accomplished in different ways. The manager's challenge is to choose the best organizational form to fit the people, the strategy, and other situational demands.

‖ Organization charts describe the formal structures of organizations.

When managers organize things, they arrange people and jobs into meaningful working relationships. They clarify who is to do what, who is in charge of whom, and how different people and work units are supposed to cooperate. This creates what we call the **organization structure**, a formal arrangement that links the various parts of an organization.

You probably know the concept of structure best in terms of an **organization chart**. This is a diagram of positions and reporting relationships within an organization.[5] A typical organization chart identifies major job titles and shows the hierarchy of authority and communication that links them. It describes the organization's **division of labor**—people and groups performing different jobs, ideally ones for which they are well skilled.

Check out Table 8.1—What You Can Learn from an Organization Chart. And indeed you can learn quite a bit from an organization chart, but only in respect to the **formal structure**. This is the "official" structure, or the way things are supposed to operate. It aligns positions, people, and responsibilities in the best ways. But as things change over time, managers find themselves tinkering with the formal structure to get the alignment right. And sometimes, the current structure doesn't make sense. When Carol Bartz asked to see Yahoo's organization chart before taking over as CEO, for example, she said: "It was like a Dilbert cartoon. It was very odd." Her response was: "You need management here."[6]

One organization structure issue making recent news is appointing the same person to be both chairman of the board and CEO. What happens to corporate governance when the CEO essentially reports to himself or herself? How does this structure provide for critical oversight of top management? Many firms are now changing their organization charts to strengthen governance by separating the job of board chairman from that of CEO.[7]

Organization structure is a system of tasks, reporting relationships, and communication linkages.

An **organization chart** describes the arrangement of work positions within an organization.

The **division of labor** means that people and groups perform different jobs.

Formal structure is the official structure of the organization.

Table 8.1 **What You Can Learn from an Organization Chart**

Division of work—Positions and job titles show individual work responsibilities.

Supervisory relationships—Lines between positions show who reports to whom in the chain of command.

Communication channels—Lines between positions show routes for formal communication flows.

Major subunits—How jobs are grouped together identify work units, teams, or divisions.

Levels of management—The number of management layers are shown top to bottom.

Lots to Learn at Build-A-Bear

Reuters/Chip East/Landov

Organizing Is Like Creating a Work of Art

Maxine Clark started Build-A-Bear Workshop Inc. with a simple concept: Pick out a bear or bunny or turtle that you like, add stuffing, and then personalize your own pet with clothing, shoes, and accessories. Each pet is unique—soccer player, teacher, doctor . . . you name it—and tailored to the user's tastes and interests.

Build-A-Bear stores are arranged in a streamlined production process. Guest Bear Builders move along the Bear Pathway from the Choose Me workstation on to Stuff Me and finally to Name Me as their personal creation takes shape. Sounds a lot like organizations, doesn't it? Until you get to the "making it personal" part. That's where organizations often struggle—how to bring together hundreds, thousands, even hundreds of thousands of people in arrangements that make sense and allow personal talents to shine through.

Find Inspiration

Clark crafted Build-A-Bear from its beginnings in St. Louis to a 400-store operation. But the company Clark needs today isn't the same one that was successful a few years back. It's time to "build a new bear," so to speak. When you think about it, isn't this the situation most organization structures face at different points in time?

The **informal structure** or **shadow organization** is the network of unofficial relationships among an organization's members.

Informal Structures and the Shadow Organization

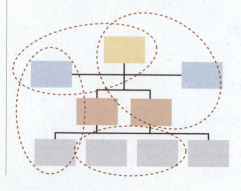

Organizations also operate with informal structures.

Picture this scene: A worker in his office cubicle overhears a conversation taking place in the next cubicle. Words such as "project being terminated" and "job cuts will be necessary" are used. At lunch he shares this with friends; word quickly spreads that their employer is going to announce layoffs. What's happening in this scenario falls outside the formal structure of the organization; it takes place in the "shadows."

An important fact of organizational life is that behind every formal structure also lies an **informal structure**. You might think of this as a **shadow organization** made up of unofficial relationships between organizational members. Like any shadow, the shape of the informal structure will be blurry and change with time. You may have to work hard to understand its full complexities.

If you could draw the informal structure for your organization—and this would be an interesting exercise—you would find relationships cutting across levels and moving from side to side. Some would be work related, reflecting how people have found the best ways to get their jobs done. Many others would be personal, reflecting who meets for coffee, stops in for office chats, meets together in exercise groups, and spends time together as friends, not just co-workers.[8]

It used to be that most informal structures were based on face-to-face relationships. Now, information technology is the driving force behind many of them. Social media links people together within organizations as well as outside of them. As organizations try to tap social media to create things like knowledge sharing networks and crowdsourcing support for problem solving, the relationships they empower make boundaries between "informal" and "formal" increasingly hard to define.

A tool known as **social network analysis** is one way of identifying the informal structures and their embedded social relationships that are active in an organization. It asks people to identify others whom they turn to for help most often, whom they communicate with regularly, and who energizes and de-energizes them.[9] The results of a social network analysis are often described as a map with lines running from person to person according to frequency of communication and type of relationship maintained. The map shows who is linked with whom and how a lot of work really gets done in organizations, in contrast to the formal arrangements shown on the organization chart. This information can be used to redesign the formal structure for better performance and identify who the key people are for possible leadership and mentoring roles.[10]

> **Social network analysis** identifies the informal structures and their embedded social relationships that are active in an organization.

‖ Informal structures have good points and bad points.

One of the first things you probably learned in college was that knowing secretaries and departmental assistants is a very good way to get into classes that are "closed" or find out about new courses that will be offered. Think about all the different ways you use informal structures to get things done. Most people in most organizations do the same.

Let's start with the good points of informal structures and both face-to-face and media-enriched social networks. As just pointed out, they can be very helpful in getting work accomplished. Indeed, they may be essential in many ways to organizational success. They fill gaps missing in the formal structure and help compensate for its inadequacies.

The relationships available in the informal structure are often important in helping people learn their jobs and solve problems while doing them. This occurs as people assist each other, not because the structure requires it, but because they know and trust one another. It can be really nice, as you already know from personal experience, to be able to tap into the wisdom of friends or even an anonymous social media crowd when needing advice on a particular

---

Creative People Add Zest to Organizational Networks

Would you like to work with a box of used kitty litter under your conference table? A group of executives had mixed reactions after finding out that was the case—many laughed; two left the room. The culprit was Amanda Zolten. She did the stunt as part of a pitch for her agency Grey New York to do ads for the firm's kitty litter products. Zolten says she was trying to achieve a "memorable experience." Her boss, Tor Myhren, said, "there was enough chaos in the room we didn't know if it was a good or bad thing." But this burst of creativity earned Zolten an Heroic Failure Award, set up by Myhren to stimulate risk taking and avoid risk aversion at the fast-growing ad agency.

Yuri Arcurs/Alamy

problem. Informal relationships also provide a lot of social and emotional support. They give people access to friendships, support groups, conversations, and advice that can help make the normal workday pleasant and a bad workday less troublesome.

Informal structures can be especially helpful during times of change, when out-of-date formal structures just don't deal well with new or unusual situations. Because it takes time to change or modify formal structures, the informal structure helps fill the void. For these reasons and possibly more, it can be argued that informal structures are essential for any organization to succeed.

Now let's consider the potential bad points of informal structures. Because they exist outside the formal system, things that happen in informal structures may work against the best interests of the organization as a whole. These shadow structures can be susceptible to rumor, carry inaccurate information, breed resistance to change, and even distract members from their work. And if you happen to end up as an "outsider" rather than an "insider in the informal networks," you may feel less a part of things. Some American managers in Japanese firms, for example, have complained about being excluded from what they call the "shadow cabinet"—an informal group of Japanese executives who hold the real power and sometimes act to the exclusion of others.[11]

Crisis or difficult situations can sometimes bring out the downsides of informal structures. For example, after the economy suffered a round of massive layoffs, the Society for Human Resource Management reported a 23% increase in workplace eavesdropping and a 54% increase in "gossip and rumors about downsizings and layoffs." Cafeterias were hotspots for gossip, and one HR director says she even noticed people trying to hang out in hallways and sit as close as possible to executives in cafeterias in attempts to overhear conversations. A manager who admitted eavesdropping on employee conversations called this "alert listening."[12]

Gallup Says that Organizations with More Engaged Employees Perform Better

Mangostock / Shutterstock

The Gallup organization pays close attention to employee engagement. It uses an "engagement ratio" as an indicator of organizational health. Its research finds that in the best organizations actively engaged employees outnumber the disengaged ones by a ratio of 9.57 to 1. In average organizations the ratio falls to 1.83 to 1. The benefits derived from an actively engaged workforce extend to profitability, safety records, intentions to leave, and customer orientation. In support of its belief that employee engagement drives success, Gallup points out that in high-performing organizations "engagement is more than a human resources initiative—it is a strategic foundation for the way they do business."

Takeaway 8.1
What Is Organizing as a Managerial Responsibility?

Terms to Define

Division of labor

Formal structure

Informal structure

Organization chart

Organization structure

Organizing

Shadow organization

Social network analysis

Rapid Review

- Organizing is the process of arranging people and resources to work toward a common goal.
- Structure is the system of tasks, reporting relationships, and communication that links people and positions within an organization.
- Organization charts describe the formal structure and how an organization should ideally work.
- The informal structure of an organization consists of the unofficial relationships that develop among its members.
- Informal structures create helpful relationships for social support and task assistance, but they can be susceptible to rumors.

Questions for Discussion

1. Why is organizing such an important management function?
2. If organization charts are imperfect, why bother with them?
3. Could an organization consistently perform well without the help of its informal structure?

Be Sure You Can

- explain what you can learn from an organization chart
- differentiate formal and informal structures
- discuss potential good and bad points about informal structures

Career Situation: What Would You Do?

As the new manager of a branch bank location, you will be supervising 22 employees, most of whom have worked together for a number of years. How will you identify the informal structure of the branch? How will you try to use this structure to help establish yourself as an effective manager in the new situation?

TEACHING NOTE: Try something different. Start class with a quick hitter version of Team Project 8—"Network U." Have students complete it as a short team exercise and debate the strong and weak points of a network structure from their perspectives.

Takeaway 8.2

What Are the Most Common Types of Organization Structures?

ANSWERS TO COME

- Functional structures group together people using similar skills.
- Divisional structures group together people by products, customers, or locations.
- Matrix structures combine the functional and divisional structures.
- Team structures use many permanent and temporary teams.
- Network structures extensively use strategic alliances and outsourcing.

Departmentalization is the process of grouping together people and jobs into work units.

A TRADITIONAL PRINCIPLE OF ORGANIZING IS THAT HIGH PERFORMANCE DEPENDS on having a good division of labor whose parts are well coordinated. The process of arranging people by tasks and work groups is called **departmentalization**.[13] The most basic forms are the functional, divisional, matrix, team, and network structures. As you read about each, don't forget that organizations rarely use only one type of structure. Most often they will use a mixture, with different parts and levels having different structures because of their unique needs.

⦀ Functional structures group together people using similar skills.

A **functional structure** groups together people with similar skills who perform similar tasks.

Take a look at **Figure 8.2**. What organizing logic do you see? These are **functional structures** where people having similar skills and performing similar tasks are grouped together into formal work units. The assumption is that if the functions are well chosen and each acts properly, the organization should operate successfully. In business, for example, typical functions include marketing, finance, accounting, production, management information systems, and human resources. But functional structures are not limited to businesses. The figure also shows how other organizations such as banks and hospitals may use them.

Functional structures work well for small organizations that produce only one or a few products or services. They also tend to work best for organizations, or parts of organizations, that have relatively stable environments where the problems are predictable and demands for change are limited. And they offer benefits to individuals. Within a given function—say, marketing—people share technical expertise, interests, and responsibilities. They can also advance in responsibilities and pursue career paths within the function.

Although functional structures have a clear logic, there are some potential downsides as well. When an organization is divided into functions it can be hard to pinpoint responsibilities for things such as cost containment, product or service quality, and innovation.

Potential Advantages of Functional Structures

- Economies of scale make efficient use of human resources.
- Functional experts are good at solving technical problems.
- Training within functions promotes skill development.
- Career paths are available within each function.

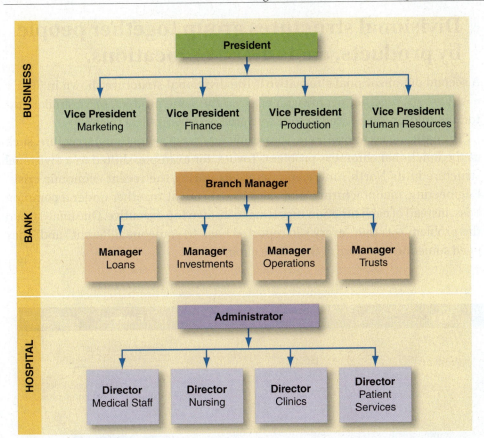

FIGURE 8.2
What Does a Typical Functional Organization Structure Look Like?
Functional structures are common in organizations of all types and sizes. In a typical business you might have vice presidents or senior managers heading the traditional functions of accounting, human resources, finance, manufacturing, marketing, and sales. In a bank, they may head such functions as loans, investments, and trusts. In a hospital, managers or administrators are usually in charge of functions such as nursing, clinics, and patient services.

And with everyone focused on meeting functional goals, the sense of working for the good of the organization as a whole may get lost. People may also find that they get trapped in functional career niches that are hard to break out of to gain career-broadening experiences in other areas.

Another concern is something that you might hear called the **functional chimneys** or **functional silos problem**. Shown in the small figure, this problem occurs as a lack of communication, coordination, and problem solving across functions. Instead of cooperating with one another, members of functional units sometimes end up either competing or selfishly focusing on functional goals rather than broader organizational objectives. CEO Carol Bartz described a functional silo problem she discovered at Yahoo this way: "The home page people didn't want to drive traffic to the finance page because they wanted to keep them on the home page."[14] Such problems of poor cooperation and even just plain lack of helpfulness across functions can be very persistent. It often takes alert and strong managers such as Bartz to get things resolved.

Mars Inc. is the world's largest candy company, and like most firms of its size, it also suffers from the functional chimneys problem. When Paul Michaels took over as CEO, he says, "The top team was siloed and replete with unspoken agendas. Members did not see the benefit of working together as a team; they were only concerned about success in their own region." Michaels's solution was to break the habits of functional thinking by realigning people and mindsets around teams and teamwork.[15]

The **functional chimneys or functional silos problem** is a lack of communication and coordination across functions.

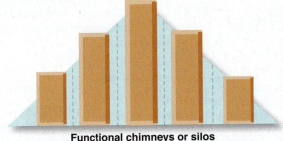

Functional chimneys or silos
· Too little communication across functions
· Too many problems referred upward for solution

Divisional structures group together people by products, customers, or locations.

A **divisional structure** groups together people working on the same product, in the same area, or with similar customers.

A second organizational alternative is the **divisional structure** shown in Figure 8.3. It groups together people who work on the same product, serve similar customers, and/or are located in the same area or geographical region.[16]

The basic idea is to overcome the disadvantages of a functional structure, such as the functional chimneys problem. Toyota, for example, shifted to a divisional structure in its North American operations during the recent economic crisis. Engineering, manufacturing, and sales were brought together under a common boss, instead of each function reporting to its own top executive. One analyst said the problem was that "every silo reported back to someone different" and "they need someone in charge of the whole choir."[17]

Type	Focus	Example
Product	Good or service produced	General Manager → Grocery products / Drugs and toiletries
Geographical	Location of activity	President → Asian division / European division
Customer	Customer or client serviced	Agency Administrator → Problem youth / Senior citizens
Process	Activities part of same process	Catalog Sales Manager → Product purchasing / Order fulfillment

FIGURE 8.3 **What Are Some Ways Organizations Use Divisional Structures?**
In products structures, divisions are based on the product or service provided, such as consumer products and industrial products. In geographic structures, divisions are based on geography or territories, such as an Asia–Pacific division and a North American division. In customer structures, divisions are based on customers or clients served, such as graduate students and undergraduate students in a university.

A **product structure** groups together people and jobs working on a single product or service.

Product structures group together jobs and activities devoted to a single product or service. They identify a common point of managerial responsibility for costs, profits, problems, and successes in a defined market area. An expected benefit is that the product division will be able to respond quickly and effectively to changing market demands and customer tastes. When Fiat took over Chrysler after it emerged from bankruptcy, CEO Sergio Marchionne said he wanted a new structure to "speed decision making and improve communication flow." He reorganized into product divisions for the firm's three brands—Chrysler, Jeep, and Dodge. Each was given its own chief executive and assigned responsibility for its own profits and losses.[18] The "new" General Motors took the same approach and reorganized around four product divisions—Buick, Cadillac, Chevrolet, and GMC.[19]

Geographical structures, or *area structures*, group together jobs and activities in the same location or geographical region. Companies use geographical divisions when they need to focus attention on the unique product tastes or operating requirements of particular regions. As UPS operations expanded worldwide, for example, the company announced a change from a product to a geographical organizational structure. The company created two geographical divisions—the Americas and Europe/Asia—with each area responsible for its own logistics, sales, and other business functions.

> A **geographical structure** brings together people and jobs performed in the same location.

Customer structures group together jobs and activities that serve the same customers or clients. The major appeal of customer divisions is the ability to best serve the special needs of the different customer groups. This is a common structure for complex businesses in the consumer products industries. 3M Corporation, for example, structures itself to focus on such diverse markets as consumer and office, specialty materials, industrial, health care, electronics and communications, transportation, graphics, and safety. Customer structures are also useful in service companies and social agencies. Banks, for example, use them to give separate attention to consumer and commercial customers for loans; government agencies use them to focus on different client populations.

> A **customer structure** groups together people and jobs that serve the same customers or clients.

Divisional structures are supposed to avoid some of the major problems of functional structures, including functional chimneys. But, as with any structural alternative, they also have potential disadvantages. They can be costly when economies of scale are lost through the duplication of resources and efforts across divisions. They can also create unhealthy rivalries where divisions end up competing with one another for scarce resources, prestige, or special top management attention.

‖ Matrix structures combine the functional and divisional structures.

The **matrix structure**, often called the *matrix organization*, combines the functional and divisional structures to try to gain the advantages of each. This is accomplished by setting up permanent teams that operate across functions to support specific products, projects, or programs.[20] Workers in a typical matrix structure, like **Figure 8.4**, belong to at least two formal groups at the same time—a functional group and a product, program, or project team. They also report to two bosses—one within the function and the other within the team.

> A **matrix structure** combines functional and divisional approaches to emphasize project or program teams.

The use of permanent **cross-functional teams** in matrix structures creates several potential advantages. These are teams whose members come together from different functional departments to work on a common task. Everyone, regardless of his or her departmental affiliation, is required to work closely with others and focus on team goals—no functional chimneys thinking is allowed. Expertise and information is shared to solve problems at the team level and make sure that things are accomplished in the best ways possible.

> A **cross-functional team** brings together members from different functional departments.

Potential Advantages of Divisional Structures

- Expertise is focused on special products, customers, or regions.
- Better coordination exists across functions within divisions.
- There is better accountability for product or service delivery.
- It is easier to grow or shrink in size as conditions change.

FIGURE 8.4

How Does a Matrix Structure Combine Functional and Divisional Structures?
A matrix structure is designed to combine the best of the functional and divisional forms. In a typical matrix, the normal functions create a traditional vertical structure, with heads of marketing and manufacturing, and so on. Then a new horizontal structure is added to create cross-functional integration. This is done using teams that are staffed by members from the functions.

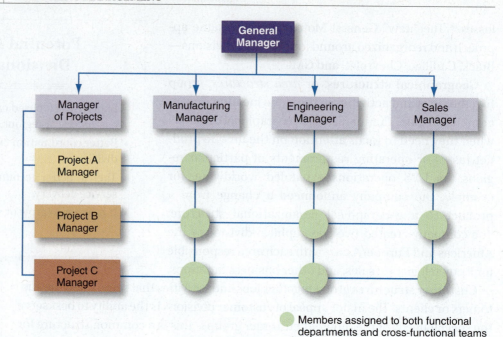

Members assigned to both functional departments and cross-functional teams

Potential Advantages of Matrix Structures

- Performance accountability rests with program, product, or project managers.
- Better communication exists across functions.
- Teams solve problems at their levels.
- Top managers spend more time on strategy.

A **team structure** uses permanent and temporary cross-functional teams to improve lateral relations.

Still, matrix structures aren't perfect; they can't overcome all the disadvantages of their functional and divisional parents. The two-boss system of the matrix can lead to power struggles if functional supervisors and team leaders make confusing or conflicting demands on team members. Matrix structures can be costly because they require a whole new set of managers to lead the cross-functional teams.[21] And as you might guess, team meetings in the matrix can be time consuming.

The matrix structure has gained a strong foothold in the workplace. Applications are found in such diverse settings as manufacturing (e.g., aerospace, electronics, pharmaceuticals), service industries (e.g., banking, brokerage, retailing), professional fields (e.g., accounting, advertising, law), and the nonprofit sector (e.g., government agencies, hospitals, universities).

‖ Team structures use many permanent and temporary teams.

Many organizations adopt **team structures** that extensively use permanent and temporary teams to solve problems, complete special projects, and accomplish day-to-day tasks.[22] As **Figure 8.5** shows, these teams are often formed across functions and staffed with members whose talents match team tasks.[23] The goals are to reduce the functional chimneys problem, tap the full benefits of group decision making, and gain as much creativity in problem solving as possible. At Polaroid Corporation, a research team developed a new medical imaging system in three years, when most had predicted it would take six. As one Polaroid executive noted, "Our researchers are not any smarter, but by working together they get the value of each other's intelligence almost instantaneously."[24]

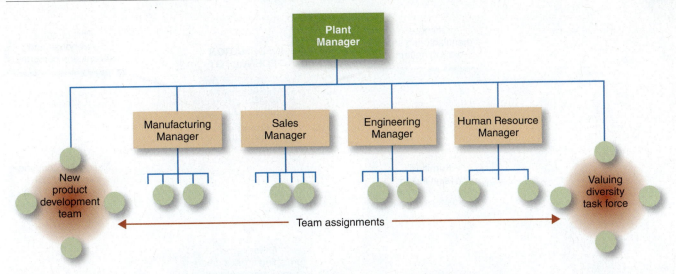

FIGURE 8.5 How Do Team Structures Capture the Benefits of Cross-Functional Teams?
Team structures make extensive use of teams to improve organizations through better communication and problem solving across functions. Some teams are temporary, such as a project team that convenes to create a new product and then disbands when finished. Other teams are more permanent. They bring together members from different functions to work together on standing issues and common problems, such as quality control, diversity management, labor–management relations, or health care benefits.

Sometimes things don't always work as hoped in team structures because the complexities of teams and teamwork create problems. As with the matrix, team members sometimes have to deal with conflicting loyalties between their team and functional assignments. Teamwork always takes time. And as in any team situation, the quality of results often depends on how well the team is managed and how well team members gel as a group. This is why you'll most likely find that organizations with team structures invest heavily in team building and team training.

Potential Advantages of Team Structures

- Team assignments improve communication, cooperation, and decision making.
- Team members get to know each other as persons, not just job titles.
- Team memberships boost morale and increase enthusiasm and task involvement.

⫴ Network structures extensively use strategic alliances and outsourcing.

Another development in organizational structures uses strategic alliances and outsourcing to dramatically reduce the need for full-time staff. Shown in **Figure 8.6**, a **network structure** links a central core of full-time employees with "networks" of relationships to outside contractors and partners that supply essential services. Because the central core is relatively small and the surrounding networks can be expanded or shrunk as needed, the potential advantages are lower costs, more speed, and greater flexibility in dealing with changing environments.[25]

The example in Figure 8.6 shows a network structure for a company that sells lawn and deck furniture over the Internet and by mail order. The firm employs only a few full-time "core" employees. Other business requirements are met through a network of alliances and outsourcing relationships. A consultant creates product designs, and suppliers produce them at low-cost sites around

A **network structure** uses IT to link with networks of outside suppliers and service contractors.

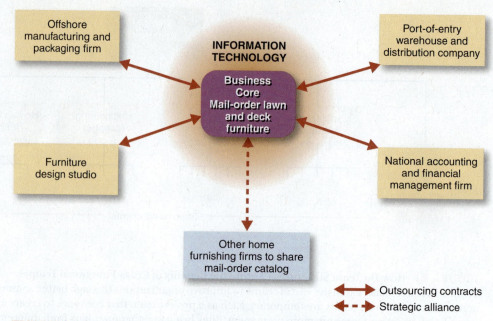

FIGURE 8.6 How Do Network Structures Take Advantage of Strategic Alliances and Outsourcing?

Organizations using network structures replace some full-time positions and functions with services provided by alliance partners and outsourcing contractors. In these structures, "core" employees perform essential operations at the center of a "network" that links them with a shifting mix of outside partners and contractors. The example in this figure shows that a small group of people can run a mail-order business in this manner. A lot of network activities are made easy and cost efficient by using the latest information technologies.

the world. A supply chain management firm gets products shipped to and distributed from an outsourced warehouse. A quarterly catalog is mailed as part of a strategic alliance with two other firms that sell different home furnishings. Accounting services are outsourced. Even the company Web site that supports customer and network relationships is maintained by an outside contractor.

This may sound a bit radical, but it isn't. It is an increasingly common arrangement that raises lots of entrepreneurial opportunities. Could the growing popularity of network organization concepts make it easier for you to start your own business someday?

If network structures are highly streamlined, efficient, and adaptable, don't you wonder why even more organizations aren't adopting them? Part of the answer may lie in inertia, simply being caught up in old ways and finding it very hard to change. Another reason is the management complication of having to deal with a vast and sometimes shifting network of contracts and alliances.

When one part of the network breaks down or fails to deliver, the entire system may suffer the consequences. The recent Japanese tsunami and nuclear disaster is a good case in point. Many global firms suffered when their Japanese contractors and partners had to shut down or scale back operations. Too much reliance on outsourcing might also have hidden costs. Not too long ago, for example, Delta Air announced that it was shutting down its call-center operations in India

Potential Advantages of Network Structures

- Lower costs due to fewer full-time employees.
- Better access to expertise through specialized alliance partners and contractors.
- Easy to grow or shrink with market conditions.

because so many customers complained about communication difficulties with service providers.[26]

As information technology continues to evolve, a variation of the network structure is appearing. Called the **virtual organization**, it uses information technologies to operate a constantly shifting network of alliances.[27] The goal is to use virtual networks to eliminate boundaries that traditionally separate a firm from its suppliers and customers and its internal departments and divisions from one another. The intense use of IT allows virtual relationships to be called into action on demand. When the work is done, they are disbanded or left idle until next needed.

If you really think about it, each of us is probably already a part of virtual organizations. Do you see similarities, for example, with the Facebook, Twitter, or LinkedIn communities? Isn't the virtual organization concept similar to how we manage our online relationships—signing on, signing off, getting things done as needed with different people and groups, and all taking place instantaneously, temporarily, and without the need for face-to-face contacts?

> A **virtual organization** uses information technologies to operate as a shifting network of alliances.

{ *The Truth About Middle Managers: Heroes, Villains, and the Reinvention of Middle Management*
by Paul Osterman

Manager's **Library**

Modern organizations still rely largely on hierarchical efficiencies. A few top executives determine hourly work for many below them, whereas managers in between align those decisions and actions. Expectations of middle managers shift as organizations adapt to swings in the economy and they are revealed as heroes, or cast as villains.

Now middle managers have undergone a makeover as organizations restructure. They've reinvented their roles to match new organizational demands.

In the book *The Truth About Middle Managers* (2008, Harvard Business School Publishing Corporation), Paul Osterman describes the changing landscape for managers nestled between levels of top management and hourly workers. Restructuring trends—fewer levels of management between top management and hourly workers and fewer employees overall—require middle managers to assume broader duties and work longer hours. They have less autonomy because top managers are closer in the hierarchy and less control as information technology allows monitoring and feedback, anytime, anywhere.

Osterman finds middle managers have increased job insecurity due to restructuring. Job tenure, or length of time spent with one employer, is decreasing, and they are more likely to job hop. Stress has increased due to new realities, and they are less loyal to employers. They see top management as greedy, self-serving, and distant and are frustrated by executive hires outside the organization. Many lose ambition because flat hierarchies mean fewer paths to the top.

Despite the challenges, Osterman believes middle managers are highly committed to their work. They enjoy their jobs as craft and thrive on skill execution. Restructuring has pushed high-level duties on many, and they welcome new strategic roles. They make key decisions involving resource allocations and negotiations with varied interests. They spend more time in informal interaction and unplanned activities and experience more variety and complexity in assignments.

REFLECT AND REACT

Organizations now have fewer management levels and employees, so how would you describe middle management jobs and skills? Middle managers view work not only as a means to an end—money or promotion, but an end in itself—craftwork and fulfillment. Why is this? And by the way, what is the future likely to hold for middle managers as more organizations take on team, network, and virtual characteristics?

STUDY GUIDE

Takeaway 8.2
What Are the Most Common Types of Organization Structures?

Terms to Define

Cross-functional teams

Customer structure

Departmentalization

Divisional structure

Functional chimneys, or functional silos, problem

Functional structure

Geographic structure

Matrix structure

Network structure

Product structure

Team structure

Virtual organization

Rapid Review

- Functional structures group people using similar skills to perform similar activities.
- Divisional structures group people who work on a similar product, work in the same geographical region, or serve the same customers.
- A matrix structure uses permanent cross-functional teams to try to gain the advantages of both the functional and divisional approaches.
- Team structures make extensive use of permanent and temporary teams, often cross-functional ones, to improve communication, cooperation, and problem solving.
- Network structures maintain a staff of core full-time employees and use contract services and strategic alliances to accomplish many business needs.

Questions for Discussion

1. Why use functional structures if they are prone to functional chimneys problems?
2. Could a matrix structure improve performance for an organization familiar to you?
3. How can the disadvantages of group decision making hurt team structures?

Be Sure You Can

- compare the functional, divisional, and matrix structures
- draw charts to show how each structure might be used in a business
- list advantages and disadvantages of each structure
- explain the functional chimneys problem
- describe how cross-functional and project teams operate in team structures
- illustrate how an organization familiar to you might operate as a network structure
- list advantages and disadvantages of the network approach to organizing

Career Situation: What Would You Do?

The typical university business school is organized on a functional basis, with departments such as accounting, finance, information systems, management, and marketing all reporting to a dean. Practice your consulting skills. How would you redesign things to increase communication and collaboration across departments, as well as improve curriculum integration across all areas of study?

Takeaway 8.3
What Are the Trends in Organizational Design?

ANSWERS TO COME

- Organizations are becoming flatter, with fewer levels of management
- Organizations are increasing decentralization
- Organizations are increasing delegation and empowerment
- Organizations are becoming more horizontal and adaptive
- Organizations are using more alternative work schedules

JUST AS ORGANIZATIONS VARY IN SIZE AND TYPE, SO, TOO, DO THE VARIETY OF problems and opportunities they face.[28] This is why they use different ways of organizing—from the functional, divisional, and matrix structures to the team and network approaches reviewed in the previous modules. Now it's time to probe further. There is still more to the story of how managers try to align their organizations with the unique situations they face.

This process of alignment is called **organizational design**. It deals with the choices managers make to configure their organizations to best meet the problems and opportunities posed by their environments.[29] And because every organization faces unique challenges, there is no "one fits all" best design. Organizational design is a problem-solving activity where managers strive to get the best configuration to meet situational demands.

> **Organizational design** is the process of configuring organizations to meet environmental challenges.

▌▌ Organizations are becoming flatter, with fewer levels of management.

When organizations grow in size, they tend to get taller by adding more and more levels of management. This raises costs. It also increases the distance between top management and lower levels, making it harder for the levels to communicate with one another. Even with the benefits of new technologies, this increases the risks of slow and poorly informed decisions.

Taller organizations are generally viewed as less efficient, less flexible, and less customer sensitive.[30] You shouldn't be surprised that the trend is toward flatter structures. But, one of the issues behind the chapter opening photo is that many universities seem to be doing just the opposite—adding administrative positions and non-academic units. One Purdue professor says "I have no idea what these people do," while another at the University of Arkansas says "Administrative bloat is clearly contributing to the overall cost of higher education.[31]

One of the things affected when organizations do get flatter is **span of control**—the number of persons directly reporting to a manager. When span of control is narrow, as shown in the small figure, a manager supervises only a few people. Taller organizations have many levels of management and narrow spans of control. A manager with a wide span of control supervises many people. Flatter organizations with fewer levels of management have wider spans of control.

> **Span of control** is the number of persons directly reporting to a manager.

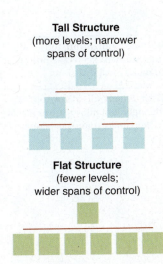

Tall Structure
(more levels; narrower spans of control)

Flat Structure
(fewer levels; wider spans of control)

Tom Gril/Getty Images

{ MY BOSS DOESN'T GET IT. I NEVER HEAR HER ASK: "HENRY, ARE YOU WORKING TOO MUCH?"

Ethics **Check**

■ Flattened into Exhaustion

Dear Stress Doctor:

My boss has come up with this great idea of cutting some supervisor positions, assigning more workers to those of us who remain, and calling us "coaches" instead of supervisors. She says this is all part of a new management approach to operate with a flatter structure and more empowerment.

For me this means a lot more work coordinating the activities of 17 operators instead of the 6 that I previously supervised. I can't get everything cleaned up on my desk most days, and I end up taking a lot of paperwork home.

As my organization "restructures" and cuts back staff, it puts a greater burden on those of us that remain. We get exhausted, and our families get short-changed and even angry. I even feel guilty now taking time to watch my daughter play soccer on Saturday mornings. Sure, there's some decent pay involved, but that doesn't make up for the heavy price I'm paying in terms of lost family times.

But you know what? My boss doesn't get it. I never hear her ask: "Henry, are you working too much; don't you think it's time to get back on a reasonable schedule?" No! What I often hear instead is "Look at Andy; he handles our new management model really well, and he's a real go-getter. I don't think he's been out of here one night this week before 8 p.m." What am I to do, just keep it up until everything falls apart one day? Is a flatter structure with fewer managers always best? Am I missing something in regard to this "new management"?

Sincerely,
Overworked in Cincinnati

YOU DECIDE

Is it ethical to restructure, cut management levels, and expect the remaining managers to do more work? Or is it simply the case that managers used to the "old" ways of doing things need extra training and care while learning "new" management approaches? And what about this person's boss—is she on track with her management skills? Aren't managers supposed to help people understand their jobs, set priorities, and fulfill them, while still maintaining a reasonable work-life balance?

‖ Organizations are increasing decentralization.

> With **centralization**, top management keeps the power to make most decisions.

> With **decentralization**, top management allows lower levels to help make many decisions.

While we are talking about levels of management, the next question becomes: Should top management make the decisions and the lower levels just carry them out? The answer is "No," at least not for all decisions. When top management keeps the power to make most decisions, the setup is called **centralization**. When top management allows lower levels to make decisions on matters where they are best prepared or informed, the setup is called **decentralization**.

If you had to choose right now, wouldn't you go for decentralization? Well, you wouldn't be wrong given the trends.[32] But you wouldn't be exactly right either. Do you really want lower levels making major decisions and changing things whenever they see fit?

The reality is that there is no need for a trade-off; an organization can have both. One of the unique opportunities of today's high-tech world is that top management can decentralize and still maintain centralized control. Computer technology and information systems allow top managers to easily stay informed

{ **"THE SPEED WITH WHICH MULALLY HAS TRANSFORMED FORD INTO A MORE NIMBLE AND HEALTHY OPERATION HAS BEEN ONE OF THE MORE IMPRESSIVE JOBS I'VE SEEN."**

Role Models

Alan Mulally Hits the Mark by Restructuring Ford

Why is it that a CEO brought in from outside the industry fared the best when the Big Three automakers were in crisis mode during the economic downturn? That's a question that Ford Motor Company's chairman, William Clay Ford Jr., has been happy to answer. And the person he's talking about is Alan Mulally, a former Boeing executive Ford hired to retool the firm and put it back on a competitive track.

Many wondered at the time if an "airplane guy" could run an auto company. It isn't easy to come in from outside an industry and successfully lead a huge firm. But Mulally's management experience and insights have proved well up to the task. One consultant says: "The speed with which Mulally has transformed Ford into a more nimble and healthy operation has been one of the more impressive jobs I've seen."

In addition to making changes to modernize plants and streamline operations, Mulally quickly tackled the bureaucratic problems common to many extremely large organizations—particularly those dealing with functional chimneys and a lack of open communication. William Ford says that the "old" Ford had a culture that "loved to meet" and in which managers got together to discuss the message they wanted to communicate to the top executives. Mulally changed all that. One of his senior managers says: "I've never had such consistency of purpose before."

Mulally focused on transparency and data-based decision making. He pushed for greater cooperation between Ford's divisions. And he pursued a more centralized approach to global operations, building vehicles to sell in many markets. When some of the senior executives balked and tried to go directly to Ford with their complaints, Mulally refused: "I didn't permit it," he says, thus reinforcing his authority to run the firm his way.

Ford's a dividend-paying stock once again, and Mulally has gained lots of respect for his executive prowess. Most recently his international experience at Boeing has helped him lead Ford's major push to expand in China. The next big question for the company is: "Who's going to replace Mulally?" He's due for retirement soon.

WHAT'S THE LESSON HERE?

It takes a lot of confidence to come in from outside an industry and lead an organization with vision and a clear strategy. Mulally seems to be doing a good job of blending a strong central authority with decentralized action. He's got support from the board and has built his own top management team. How will you act when taking over a new position someday?

---

about day-to-day performance results throughout an organization. This makes it easier for them to operate in more decentralized ways.[33]

‖ Organizations are increasing delegation and empowerment.

Decentralization brings with it another trend that is good for organizations and their members: increased delegation and empowerment. **Delegation** is the process of entrusting work to others by giving them the right to make decisions and take action.

You can think of delegation as the foundation for decentralization. Its three steps are:

(1) *Assign responsibility*—explain tasks and expectations to others.

(2) *Grant authority*—allow others to act as needed to complete tasks.

(3) *Create accountability*—require others to report back on the completed tasks.

Delegation is the process of entrusting work to others.

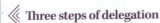 **Three steps of delegation**

Explore **Yourself**

■ Empowerment

Structures help bring order to organizational complexity. They put people together in ways that, on paper at least, make good sense in terms of getting tasks accomplished. But although there are many structural alternatives as described in this chapter, they all struggle for success at times.

Things can change so fast that you might think of today's organization structures as solutions to yesterday's problems. This puts a great burden on people to fill in the gaps and deal spontaneously with things that the formal structures don't or can't cover at any point in time.

Empowerment is a way of unlocking talent and motivation so that people can act in ways that make a performance differ-

ence. It gives them freedom to make decisions about how they work. But, many managers fail when it comes to empowerment. And when they do, their organizations often underperform.

Are you willing, and able, to embrace empowerment as you work with others?

> Get to know yourself better by taking the self-assessment on **Empowering Others** and completing other activities in the *Exploring Management* **Skill-Building Portfolio.**

Empowerment gives people freedom to do their jobs as they think best.

Every manager really needs to know how and when to delegate. Even if you are already good at it, there are probably ways to get even better. On those days when you complain, "I just can't get everything done," the real problem may be that you are trying to do everything yourself. Delegation involves deciding what work to do yourself and what you should allow others to accomplish. It sounds easy, but there is skill in doing delegation right.[34]

A classical management principle states that authority should equal responsibility when a supervisor delegates work to a subordinate. In other words, managers shouldn't delegate without giving the subordinate sufficient authority to perform. Can you think of a time when you were asked to get something done but didn't have the authority to do it? This was probably frustrating, and it may have even caused you to lose respect for the manager.

Some managers mistakenly go even one step further; they fail to delegate at all. Whether because they are unwilling or unable to trust others or are too inflexible in how they want things done, the failure to delegate is more common than you might think. And it creates problems. A failure to delegate not only makes it hard for people to do their jobs, but it also overloads the manager with work that really should be done by others.

Let's remember that the trend is toward more, not less, delegation. And let's not forget that when delegation is done well it leads to **empowerment**. This is the process of giving people the freedom to contribute ideas, make decisions, show initiative, and do their jobs in the best possible ways. Empowerment unlocks the full power of talent, experience, and intellect that people bring to their jobs. It is the engine that powers decentralization. And when it becomes part of the organizational culture, it helps everyone act faster and be more flexible when dealing with today's dynamic environments.

⫴ Organizations are becoming more horizontal and adaptive.

You should remember the concept of **bureaucracy** from earlier discussion in this book. Its distinguishing features are clear-cut division of labor, strict hierarchy of authority, formal rules and procedures, and promotion based on competency. According to Max Weber, bureaucracies should be orderly, fair, and highly efficient.[35] Yet chances are that your image of a bureaucracy is an organization bogged down with "red tape," which acts cumbersome and impersonal and is sometimes overcome to the point of inadequacy by rules and procedures.

Where, you might ask, are the decentralization, delegation, and empowerment that we have just been talking about? Well, researchers have looked into the question and arrived at some interesting answers. When Tom Burns and George Stalker investigated 20 manufacturing firms in England, they found that two quite different organizational forms could be successful.[36] The key was the "fit" between the form and challenges in the external environment.

A more bureaucratic form of organization, which Burns and Stalker called the **mechanistic design**, thrived in stable environments. It was good at doing routine things in predictable situations. But in rapidly changing and uncertain situations, a much less bureaucratic form, called the **organic design**, performed best. It was adaptable and better suited to handle change and less-predictable situations.

Figure 8.7 portrays these two approaches as opposite extremes on a continuum of organizational design alternatives. You can see that organizations with mechanistic designs typically operate as "tight" structures of the traditional vertical and bureaucratic form.[37] They are good for production efficiency. A ready example is your local fast-food restaurant. But what about a company like the software giant Microsoft?

What's your take on Microsoft? The company is a popular target for critics. *Business Week* once claimed it suffers from "bureaucratic red tape" and endless meetings that bog employees down and limit their abilities to be creative and on top of market demands.[38] The *Wall Street Journal* suggested it should be broken into smaller pieces to free the firm from the "bureaucracy that's stifling entrepreneurial spirits."[39] The

> A **bureaucracy** emphasizes formal authority, rules, order, fairness, and efficiency.

> **Mechanistic designs** are bureaucratic, using a centralized and vertical structure.

> **Organic designs** are adaptive, using a decentralized and horizontal structure.

FIGURE 8.7

What Are the Major Differences Between Mechanistic and Organic Organizations Designs? Some indicators of a more organic design are decentralization, few rules and procedures, wider spans of control, sharing of tasks, use of teams and task forces, and informal or personal approaches to coordination. This organic design is most associated with success in dynamic and changing environments. The more mechanistic design has mainly bureaucratic features and is more likely to have difficulty in change environments but to be successful in more stable ones.

MECHANISTIC DESIGNS Bureaucratic organizations		ORGANIC DESIGNS Adaptive organizations
Predictability	Goal	Adaptability
Centralized	Authority	Decentralized
Many	Rules and procedures	Few
Narrow	Spans of control	Wide
Specialized	Tasks	Shared
Few	Teams and task forces	Many
Formal and impersonal	Coordination	Informal and personal

{ IT DOESN'T MATTER WHAT INDUSTRY YOU'RE IN. PEOPLE
HAVE BLIND SPOTS ABOUT WHERE THEY ARE WEAK."

Facts to **Consider**

■ Bosses May be Overestimating Their Managing Skills

A survey by Development Dimensions International, Inc., finds that managers may be overestimating their managing skills. "It doesn't matter what industry you're in. People have blind spots about where they are weak," says DDI vice president Scott Erker. Check these results from a sample of 1,100 first-year managers:

- 72% never question their ability to lead others.
- 58% claim planning and organizing skills as strengths.
- 53% say they are strong in decision making.
- 50% say they are strong in communication.

- 32% claim proficiency in delegating.
- Skills rated as needing most development were delegating, gaining commitment, and coaching.

YOUR THOUGHTS?

Would you, like managers in this survey, probably overestimate your strengths in management skills? What might explain such tendencies toward overconfidence? And among the skills needing work, why would delegating be the one about which even very confident managers still feel some inadequacy?

---

idea is that the new and smaller components would be faster and more innovative in our changing world of technology. In other words, over time and with increasing size, Microsoft may have become too mechanistic for its own good.

The organic organizational design is more horizontal and less vertical than its mechanistic counterpart. It emphasizes empowerment and teamwork and gets a lot of work done through informal structures and interpersonal networks.[40] The result is an organization that is adaptive and flexible and whose employees are allowed to be more spontaneous in dealing with changing markets and environments.[41] This design is good for creativity and innovation. Doesn't it sound like just the type of organization most likely to succeed in the technology industry today?[42]

||| Organizations are using more alternative work schedules.

There's yet another organizing trend that's quite likely to become very important to you someday, if it isn't already—the use of alternative work schedules. The fact is that just because it was normal to work 40 hours each week in the past doesn't make this the only or best way to schedule work time.[43] Here are some possibilities.

A **compressed workweek** allows a worker to complete a full-time job in less than the standard five days of 8-hour shifts.[44] The most common form is the "4–40," that is, accomplishing 40 hours of work in four 10-hour days. It's well used at USAA, a diversified financial services company that ranks among the 100 best companies to work for in America. A large part of the firm's San Antonio workforce is on a four-day schedule, with some working Monday through Thursday and others working Tuesday through Friday.[45]Although compressed workweeks can cause scheduling problems, possible customer complaints, and even union objections, the benefits are there as well. USAA reports improved morale, lower overtime costs, less absenteeism, and decreased use of sick leave.

The term **flexible working hours**, also called *flextime*, describes any work schedule that gives employees some choice in daily work hours. A typical

A **compressed workweek** allows a worker to complete a full-time job in less than five days.

Flexible working hours give employees some choice in daily work hours.

flextime schedule offers choices of starting and ending times, while still putting in a full workday. Some may start earlier and leave earlier, while others do the opposite. The flexibility provides opportunities to attend to personal affairs such as parenting, elder care, medical appointments, and home emergencies. All top 100 companies in *Working Mother* magazine's list of best employers for working moms offer flexible scheduling. They find it reduces stress and unwanted job turnover.[46]

More and more people now do some form of **telecommuting**.[47] They spend at least a portion of scheduled work hours at home or outside the office linked with co-workers, customers, and bosses by a variety of information technologies.[48] From the employer side it makes for savings in office space and real estate. It's a good recruiting tool—reports indicate that up to 80% of employees desire it. Evidence also suggests most telecommuters are hard working and satisfied.[49] Positives on the employee side include freedom to be your own boss and having more free time.

> **Telecommuting** involves using IT to work at home or outside the office.

Even though the evidence largely supports telecommuting or work-at-home practices, there are potential downsides. Some telecommuters say they end up working too much and actually have less time to themselves and for family.[50] And, some employers worry about adverse impact on teamwork and collaboration. Yahoo! CEO Marissa Mayer took a lot of criticism when she decided to ban working from home. Right or wrong, she believed that doing so would help revitalize face-to-face collaboration and increase innovation at the firm.[51] Time will tell if she did the right thing.[52]

A recent development in telecommuting is the **co-working center**, essentially a place where telecommuters go to share an office environment outside the home. A marketing telecommuter says: "We have two kids, so the ability to work from home—it just got worse and worse. I found myself saying, 'If daddy could just have two hours. . . .'" Now he has started his own co-working center to cater to his needs and those of others. One of those using his center says: "What you're paying for is not the desk, it's access to networking creativity and community."[53]

> A **co-working center** is a place where telecommuters share office space outside the home.

Yet another flexible scheduling option is **job sharing**, where two or more persons split one full-time job. This often involves each person working one-half day, but it can also be done via weekly or monthly sharing arrangements. Both the employees and the organizations benefit when talented people who cannot work full days or weeks are kept in or brought back into the workforce.

> **Job sharing** splits one job between two people.

Flexibility in Work Scheduling Helps Employers Beat the "Mommy Drain"

It's well known that attracting and retaining talented workers has to be one of the top priorities for any organization. But what happens with new Moms? How do you get them onboard when you want to hire them? How do you keep them onboard when you already have them? The "Mommy drain"—loss of mothers from the workforce—is real. And we're also starting to talk about a "Daddy drain." Flexibility is a way of dealing with them. Jobs that allow flexible hours, work-at-home time, and job sharing are essential. Extended pay and time off for maternity and parental leaves, as well as in-house career networks that support working parents are helpful too.

Mango Productions/Corbis Corp

STUDY GUIDE

What Are the Trends in Organizational Design?

Terms to Define

Bureaucracy

Centralization

Compressed workweek

Co-working center

Decentralization

Delegation

Empowerment

Flexible working hours

Job sharing

Mechanistic design

Organic design

Organizational design

Span of control

Telecommuting

Rapid Review

- Organizations are becoming flatter—having fewer management levels, combining decentralization with centralization, and using more delegation and empowerment.
- Mechanistic organizational designs are vertical and bureaucratic; they perform best in stable environments with mostly routine and predictable tasks.
- Organic organizational designs are horizontal and adaptive; they perform best in change environments requiring adaptation and flexibility.
- Organizations are using alternative work schedules such as the compressed workweek, flexible working hours, and job sharing.

Questions for Discussion

1. Is "empowerment" just a buzzword, or is it something that can really make a difference in organizations today?
2. Knowing your personality, will you fit in better with an organization that has a mechanistic or an organic design?
3. How can alternative work schedules work to the benefit of both organizations and their members?

Be Sure You Can

- illustrate the link between tall or flat organizations and spans of control
- explain how decentralization and centralization can work together
- list the three steps in delegation
- differentiate mechanistic and organic organizational designs
- differentiate compressed workweek, flexible working hours, and job sharing
- list advantages and disadvantages of telecommuting

Career Situation: What Would You Do?

As the owner of a small computer repair and services business you would like to allow employees more flexibility in their work schedules. But, you also need consistency of coverage to handle drop-in customers as well as at-home service calls. There are also times when customers need "emergency" help outside normal 8 a.m. to 5 p.m. office hours. A meeting with the employees is scheduled for next week. How can you work with them to develop a staffing plan that includes flexible work options that meet their needs as well as yours?

TestPrep 8

Answers to TestPrep questions can be found at the back of the book.

Multiple-Choice Questions

1. The main purpose of organizing as a management function is to _____.
   (a) make sure that results match plans
   (b) arrange people and resources to accomplish work
   (c) create enthusiasm for the needed work
   (d) link strategies with operational plans

2. An organization chart is most useful for _____.
   (a) mapping informal structures
   (b) eliminating functional chimneys
   (c) showing designated supervisory relationships
   (d) describing the shadow organization

3. Rumors and resistance to change are potential disadvantages often associated with _____.
   (a) virtual organizations
   (b) informal structures
   (c) functional chimneys
   (d) cross-functional teams

4. When an organization chart shows that vice presidents of marketing, finance, manufacturing, and purchasing all report to the president, top management is using a _____ structure.
   (a) functional
   (b) matrix
   (c) network
   (d) product

5. The "two-boss" system of reporting relationships is both a potential source of problems and one of the key aspects of _____ structures.
   (a) functional
   (b) matrix
   (c) network
   (d) product

6. A manufacturing business with a functional structure has recently acquired two other businesses with very different product lines. The president of the combined company might consider using a _____ structure to allow a better focus on the unique needs of each product area.
   (a) virtual
   (b) team
   (c) divisional
   (d) network

7. An organization using a _____ structure should expect that more problems will be solved at lower levels and that top managers will have more time free to engage in strategic thinking.
   (a) virtual
   (b) matrix
   (c) functional
   (d) product

8. The functional chimneys problem occurs when people in different functions _____.
   (a) fail to communicate with one another
   (b) try to help each other work with customers
   (c) spend too much time coordinating decisions
   (d) focus on products rather than functions

9. An organization that employs just a few "core" or essential full-time employees and outsources a lot of the remaining work shows signs of using a _____ structure.
   (a) functional
   (b) divisional
   (c) network
   (d) team

10. A "tall" organization will likely have _____ spans of control than a "flat" organization with the same number of members.

    (a) wider

    (b) narrower

    (c) more ambiguous

    (d) less centralized

11. If a student in one of your course groups volunteers to gather information for a case analysis and the other members tell him to go ahead and choose the information sources he believes are most important, the group is giving this student _____ to fulfill the agreed-upon task.

    (a) responsibility

    (b) accountability

    (c) authority

    (d) values

12. The bureaucratic organization described by Max Weber is similar to the _____ organization described by Burns and Stalker.

    (a) adaptive

    (b) mechanistic

    (c) organic

    (d) horizontal

13. Which organization design would likely be a good fit for a dynamic and changing external environment?

    (a) Vertical

    (b) Centralized

    (c) Organic

    (d) Mechanistic

14. Workers following a compressed workweek schedule often work 40 hours in _____ days.

    (a) 3 ½

    (b) 4

    (c) 5

    (d) a flexible schedule of

15. Which alternative work schedule is identified by *Working Mother* magazine as being used by all companies on its list of "100 Best Employers for Working Moms"?

    (a) Telecommuting

    (b) Job sharing

    (c) Flexible hours

    (d) Part-time

Short-Response Questions

16. Why should an organization chart be trusted "only so far"?

17. In what ways can informal structures be good for organizations?

18. How does a matrix structure combine functional and divisional forms?

19. Why is an organic design likely to be quicker and more flexible in adapting to changes than a mechanistic design?

Integration and Application Question

20. Imagine you are a consultant to your university or college president. The assignment is: Make this organization more efficient without sacrificing its educational goals. Although the president doesn't realize it, you are a specialist in network structures. You are going to suggest building a network organization, and your ideas are going to be radical and provocative.

    Questions: What would be the core of the network—is it the faculty members, who teach the various courses, or is it the administration, which provides the infrastructure that students and faculty use in the learning experience? What might be outsourced—grounds and facilities maintenance, food services, security, recreation programs, even registration? What types of alliances might prove beneficial—student recruiting, faculty, even facilities?

Steps *for* Further Learning

BUILD MARKETABLE SKILLS
DO A CASE ANALYSIS
GET AND STAY INFORMED

BUILD

MARKETABLE SKILLS. EARN BIG CAREER PAYOFFS!

Don't miss these opportunities in the **Skill-Building Portfolio**

■ **SELF-ASSESSMENT 8:**
Empowering Others

It can be hard to let go . . . check your willingness to loosen the strings.

■ **CLASS EXERCISE 8:**
Organizational Metaphors

Organizations as brains? . . . metaphors can be a key to greater understanding.

■ **TEAM PROJECT 8:**
Network "U"

Times are changing at the nation's universities . . . is it reasonable that students could help design better ones?

Many learning resources are found at the end of the book and online within WileyPLUS.

Take advantage of **Cases for Critical Thinking**

■ **CHAPTER 8 CASE SNAPSHOT:**
Law Firms Try the Case for New Structures/
Sidebar on Goodbye Office

The traditional organization structure of a large or mid-sized law firm has remained unchanged for years. It was a clear, tight, and even intimidating pyramid with all-powerful partners sitting at the top. In good economic times a new attorney's goal was clear—climb the ladder, become a partner, and enjoy the rewards. Joining the ranks of partner brought higher earnings, prestige, and clout. But as times have changed and the economy corrected, many law firms have had to adjust also. Potential clients now have alternatives to pay-by-the-hour brick and mortar firms. Online law offerings have gained legitimacy. Quality services at more predictable and sometimes flat-rate prices are proliferating. Law firms face a new future. Can changing structures help them deal with it?

DO

A CASE ANALYSIS.
STRENGTHEN YOUR CRITICAL THINKING!

Dig into this **Hot Topic**

■ **GOOD IDEA OR NOT: Crowdsourcing Evaluations as a Way to Flatten Organizational Structures**

It used to be that one of a manager's most important tasks was conducting annual performance reviews. Technology now offers a way to make reviews more timely while also flattening structures and reducing administrative costs. "Bye bye manager!" some are saying as more performance reviews move online and crowdsourcing becomes the feedback mechanism of choice.

GET

AND STAY INFORMED.
MAKE YOURSELF VALUABLE!

Management scholars and consultants have long suggested the value of 360° reviews that include feedback from peers and others working with or for the person being assessed. New technology makes it easy to do all this, and more, online and in real time—think anyone, anytime, any project.

Online reviews are in at the San Francisco-based social media outfit Hearsay Social, Inc. The firm runs on teamwork and involves constantly shifting projects. And there aren't many managers. All 90 employees are part of a crowdsourced feedback system that allows them to comment on one another's work. The feedback is anonymous. Chief Technology officer Steve Garrity says: "We are decentralizing as much decision making as we can, so we also need to decentralize reviews."

Final Take? More of us are going to be on the giving and receiving ends of online reviews and crowdsourced performance feedback in the future. But San Francisco State management professor John Sullivan worries that people may end up evaluating others whose jobs they don't know enough about. Online peer reviews are easy and cost effective, but are they good replacements for the formal sit-down with a team leader or manager? When does technology flatten a structure too far?

"...we're very clear not everyone fits in this quirky company. We put potential hires through seven to eight interviews. Sometimes people look at us like we're crazy and run away. When employees don't understand the team atmosphere, we let them go..."

Kip Tindell, CEO of Container Store

Organizational Cultures, Innovation, and Change

Adaptability and Values Set the Tone

9

Management Live

Tolerance for Ambiguity and *The Terminal*

Dreamworks/Photofest

In *The Terminal*, Viktor Navorski (Tom Hanks) travels from his native Krakozhia to New York City to get an autograph for his father from jazz musician Benny Golson. While he is in transit, Krakozhian soldiers overthrow their government, and the United States no longer recognizes passports from Krakozhia. Navorski is refused entry, but he can't go home because Krakozhian airspace is closed.

Confined to the international transit lounge, Navorski at first doesn't know where to sleep, how to find food, or how to maintain personal hygiene. But he figures out how to do all of this. In addition, he earns money, first by rounding up unreturned baggage carts and then by getting an airport construction job. All this is evidence of his **tolerance for ambiguity**, an ability to deal with uncertainty even when events are beyond personal control.

The Terminal is loosely based on the true story of Mehran Nasseri, a dispossessed Iranian who spent 18 years living in Charles de Gaulle Airport. It is an almost unimaginable situation. But then again all of us live and work in changing, often uncertain, times. Do you find that you are able to deal effectively with circumstances that are unpredictable? How do you respond when something unexpected comes your way?

YOUR CHAPTER 9 TAKEAWAYS

1. Understand the nature of organizational culture.

2. Recognize how organizations support and achieve innovation.

3. Describe how managers lead the process of organizational change.

WHAT'S INSIDE

Explore Yourself
More on **tolerance for ambiguity**

Role Models
Tom Szaky puts eco-capitalism to work at Terra Cycle

Ethics Check
Facebook follies versus corporate culture

Facts to Consider
Organization cultures face up to work-life trends

Manager's Library
Change by Design: How Design Thinking Transforms Organizations and Inspires Innovation
by Tim Brown

TEACHING NOTE: Start discussion with the notion of "person-culture fit." Ask students to explain what it means in general and to them specifically. Make a list of culture characteristics they consider important in finding a good fit between themselves and first jobs after graduation.

Takeaway 9.1
What Is the Nature of Organizational Culture?

ANSWERS TO COME

- Organizational culture is the personality of the organization.
- Organizational culture shapes behavior and influences performance.
- Not all organizational cultures are alike.
- The observable culture is what you see and hear as an employee or customer.
- The core culture is found in the underlying values of the organization.
- Value-based management supports a strong organizational culture.

YOU PROBABLY HEAR THE WORD "CULTURE" A LOT THESE DAYS. IN TODAY'S GLOBAL economy, how can we fail to appreciate the cultural differences between people or nations? However, there's another type of culture that can be just as important: the cultures of organizations. Just as nations, ethnic groups, and families have cultures, organizations do too. These cultures help distinguish organizations from one another and give members a sense of collective identity. As noted by the Container Store example in the opening photo, the "fit" between the individual and an organization's culture is very important. A good fit should be good for both parties. And, how to find the right fit is a real career issue for you to consider.

⫴ Organizational culture is the personality of the organization.

Organizational culture is a system of shared beliefs and values guiding behavior.

Think of the stores that you shop in, the restaurants that you patronize, the place where you work. What is the "atmosphere" like, and does it draw you in or hurry you out? Do you notice how major retailers like Anthropologie, J. Crew, and Williams-Sonoma have Web sites and store climates that seem to fit their brands and customer identities?[1] Such aspects of the internal environments of organizations are important in management. They help display the **organizational culture** as a system of shared beliefs and values that develops within an organization and guides the behavior of its members.[2]

Whenever someone speaks of "the way we do things here," he or she is talking about the organization's culture. You can think of this as the personality of the organization, the atmosphere within which people work. Sometimes called the *corporate culture*, it can have a strong impact on an organization's performance and the quality of work experiences of its members.

Have you heard of or even purchased something from Zappos.com? Its CEO, Tony Hsieh, has built a fun, creative, and customer-centered organizational culture. Amazon CEO Jeff Bezos liked Zappos so much he bought the company. The Girl Scouts are among organizations that send executives to study Zappos and bring back ideas for improving their own cultures. Hsieh says that "the original idea was to add a little fun," and things moved to the point where everyone shared in the idea that "we can do it better." Now the notion of an unhappy Zappos customer is almost unthinkable: "They may only call once in their life," says Hsieh, "but that is our chance to wow them."[3]

Healthy Living Sets the Tone At Clif Bar

Have you had your Clif Bar today? Lots of people have, thanks to a long bike ride during which Gary Erickson decided he just couldn't eat another of the available energy bars. He went back to experiment in his mother's kitchen and produced the first Clif Bar two years later.

Despite its growth from a one-man operation to one employing 270+ people, Clif's still runs with a commitment to what it calls the "5 aspirations"—"sustaining our planet . . . community . . . people . . . business . . . brands."

Picture the "Clifies" working this way.

- Every employee an owner.
- Paid sabbatical leaves of 6 to 8 weeks after seven years.
- Flexible schedule to get every other Friday free.
- Pay for 2.5 hours of workout time each week.
- Bring your pet to work and wear casual clothes.
- Get $6,500 toward a hybrid or biodiesel automobile.

MCT/Getty Images

⫴ Organizational culture shapes behavior and influences performance.

"If we get the culture right," Zappos's Tony Hsieh says, "most of the other stuff, like brand and the customer service, will just happen."[4] And he's mostly right. Although culture isn't the only determinant of what happens in organizations, it does influence what they accomplish. Organizational culture helps to set values, shape attitudes, reinforce beliefs, direct behavior, and establish performance expectations and the motivation to fulfill them.[5] In these ways an organization's culture helps set its moral character and performance tone. In organizations like Zappos and Clif Bars, this culture will be both strong and positive.

In **strong culture** organizations, the culture is clear, well defined, performance driven, and widely shared by members. The culture fits the nature of the business and the talents of the employees. It discourages dysfunctional behaviors and encourages helpful ones while keeping a clear performance vision front and center for all to rally around.[6]

Strong and positive cultures don't happen by chance. They are created by leaders who set the tone, and they are reinforced through **socialization**.[7] This is the process of helping new members learn the culture and values of the organization, as well as the behaviors and attitudes that are shared among its members.[8] Each new Disney employee, for example, attends a program called "traditions." It educates them on the company mission, history, language, lore, traditions, and expectations. This commitment to socialization and a strong culture began with the founder, Walt Disney. He once said: "You can dream, create, design and build the most wonderful place in the world, but it requires people to make the dream a reality."[9]

Strong cultures are clear, well defined, and widely shared among organization members.

Socialization is the process through which new members learn the culture of an organization.

⫴ Not all organization cultures are alike.

It takes a keen eye to be able to identify and understand an organization's culture. But such understanding can be a real asset to employees and job hunters alike.

Alternative Organizational Cultures

Team Culture	Hierarchial Culture
• Authority shared, distributed	• Authority runs the system
• Teams and teamwork rule	• Traditions, roles clear
• Collaboration, trust valued	• Rules, hierarchy valued
• Emphasis on mutual support	• Emphasis on predictability
Entrepreneurial Culture	**Rational Culture**
• Authority goes with ideas	• Authority serves the goals
• Flexibility and creativity rule	• Efficiency, productivity rule
• Change and growth valued	• Planning, process valued
• Emphasis on entrepreneurship	• Emphasis on modest change

Who wants to end up in a situation with a bad person–culture fit? Management scholars offer ideas for reading organizational cultures by asking questions about such things as innovation and risk taking, teamwork, people orientation, and emphasis on outcomes.[10]

One of the popular descriptions of organizational cultures is shown in the small figure. Based on a model called the competing values framework, it identifies four different culture types.[11] *Hierarchical cultures* emphasize authority, tradition, and clear roles. *Rational cultures* emphasize process, efficiency, and slow change. *Entrepreneurial cultures* emphasize change, growth, creativity, and competition. *Team cultures* emphasize teamwork, collaboration, and trust. How do these options sound to you? According to a study by LeadershipIQ, employees are likely to give entrepreneurial cultures the highest marks for engagement and motivation, and as good places to work.[12]

Figure 9.1 shows how you as an employee or customer can understand an organization's culture. The outermost level is the "observable" culture, and the inner level is the "core" culture.[13] You might think of this distinction in the sense of an iceberg. What lies below the surface and is harder to see is the core culture. What stands out above the surface and is visible to the eye is the observable culture.

FIGURE 9.1

What Are the Main Components of Organizational Culture?

With a bit of effort, one can easily identify the organizational culture. The most visible part is the observable culture. It is shown in the stories, rituals, heroes, and symbols that are part of the everyday life of the organization. The deeper, below-the-surface part is the core culture. It consists of the values that influence the beliefs, attitudes, and work practices among organizational members.

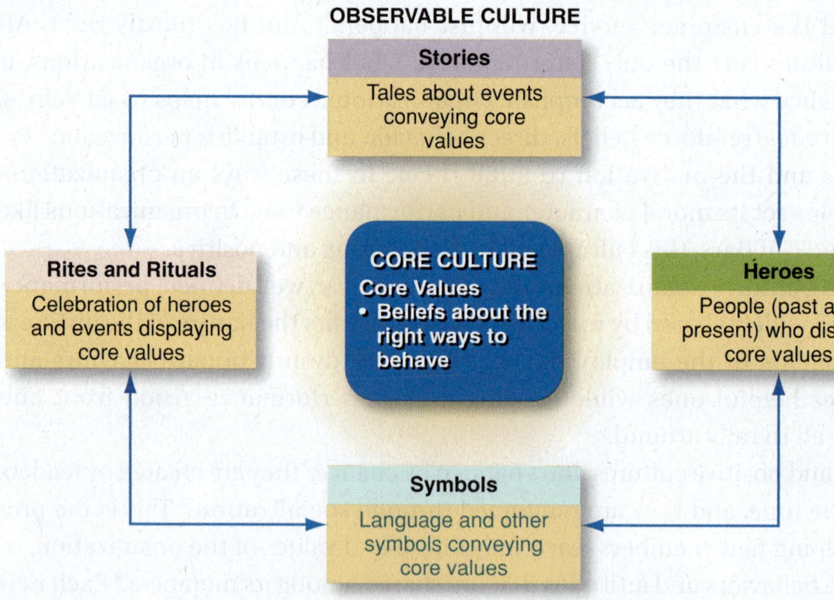

OBSERVABLE CULTURE

Stories
Tales about events conveying core values

Rites and Rituals
Celebration of heroes and events displaying core values

CORE CULTURE
Core Values
• Beliefs about the right ways to behave

Heroes
People (past and present) who display core values

Symbols
Language and other symbols conveying core values

The **observable culture** is what you see and hear when walking around an organization.

‖ The observable culture is what you see and hear as an employee or customer.

The **observable culture** is what you see in people's behaviors and hear in their conversations. It is reflected in how people dress at work, arrange their offices, speak to and behave toward one another, and talk about and treat their customers. You'll notice it not only as an employee but also as a customer or client. Test this out the next time you go into a store, restaurant, or service establishment.

{ BOTH BABY BOOMERS AND GEN YS RATE FLEXIBLE WORK AS IMPORTANT.

Facts to **Consider**

■ Organization cultures face up to work-life trends

If you have any doubts at all regarding the importance of work-life issues and their implications for organizational cultures and management practices, consider these facts:

- 78% of American couples are dual-wage earners.
- 63% believe they don't have enough time for their spouses or partners.
- 74% believe they don't have enough time for their children.
- 35% are spending time caring for elderly relatives.
- Both Baby Boomers (87%) and Gen Ys (89%) rate flexible work as important.

- Both Baby Boomers (63%) and Gen Ys (69%) want opportunities to work remotely at least part of the time.

YOUR THOUGHTS?

What organizational culture issues are raised by these facts? What should employers do to best respond to the situation described here? And when it comes to you, are you prepared to succeed in a work setting that doesn't respect these facts? Or, are you preparing right now to always find and be attractive to employers that do?

How do people look, act, and behave? How do they treat one another? How do they treat customers? What's in their conversations? Are they enjoying themselves? When you answer these questions, you are starting to describe the observable culture of the organization.

The observable culture is also found in the stories, heroes, rituals, and symbols that are part of daily organizational life. In the university, it includes the pageantry of graduation and honors ceremonies; in sports teams, it's the pregame rally, sidelines pep talk, and all the "thumping and bumping" that takes place after a good play. In workplaces it can be spontaneous celebrations of a work accomplishment or personal milestone such as a co-worker's birthday or wedding. And in organizations like Apple, Hewlett-Packard, Zappos, Google, and Amazon, it's in the stories told about the founders and the firm's history.

The presence or absence of these observable things, and the ways they are practiced, can say a lot about an organization's culture. They represent, communicate, and carry the culture over time, keeping it visible and clear in all members' eyes. New members learn the organization's culture through them, and all members keep the culture alive by sharing and joining in them.

‖ The core culture is found in the underlying values of the organization.

A second and deeper level of organizational culture is called the **core culture**. It consists of the **core values**, or underlying assumptions and beliefs, that shape and guide people's behaviors. Values in some of the best companies, for example, often emphasize performance excellence, innovation, social responsibility, integrity, worker involvement, customer service, and teamwork.[14]

Values statements are typically found on Web sites, in mission statements, and in executive speeches. Here are some examples. Merck—"highest level of scientific excellence." Whole Foods—"Creating ongoing win-win partnerships with our suppliers." Under Armour—"Innovation, Inspiration, Reliability and Integrity."

The **core culture** is found in the underlying values of the organization.

Core values are beliefs and values shared by organization members.

Tips to **Remember**

■ **SCORES—How to Read an Organization's Culture**

S—How tight or loose is the *structure*?
C—Are decisions *change* oriented or driven by the status quo?
O—What *outcomes* or results are most highly valued?
R—What is the climate for *risk taking*, innovation?
E—How widespread is *empowerment*, worker involvement?
S—What is the competitive *style*, internal and external?

Tesla—"the best electric car and electric power trains in the world." Honest Tea—"We strive to live up to our name in the way we conduct our business."[15]

When trying to read or understand an organization's core culture, don't be fooled by values statements alone. It's easy to write a set of values, post them on the Web, and talk about them. It's a lot harder to live up to them. If an organization's stated values are to have any positive effects, everyone in the organization from top to bottom must know the values and live up to them in day-to-day actions. It's in this sense that managers have a special responsibility to "walk the values talk" and make the expressed values real. After all, how might you react if you found out senior executives in your organization talked up values such as honesty and ethical behavior, but were also known to spend company funds on lavish private parties and vacations?

||| **Value-based management supports a strong organizational culture.**

When managers practice the core values, model them for others, and communicate and reinforce them in all that they do, this is called **value-based management**. It is managing with a commitment to actively help develop, communicate, and represent shared values within an organization.

An incident at Tom's of Maine provides an example of value-based management.[16] After making a big investment in a new deodorant, founder Tom Chappell learned that customers were very dissatisfied with it. He quickly decided to reimburse customers and pull the product from the market, even though it would cost the company more than $400,000. Tom had founded the company on values of fairness and honesty in all matters. Rather than trying to save costs, he did what he believed was the right thing.

Tom Chappell's decision in this case lives up to the company's values and sets a positive example for others in the firm to follow in future situations. It was value-based management in action. And, it also showed his strengths as a **symbolic leader**, someone who uses language well to communicate core values and whose actions illustrate the desired organizational culture.[17] They talk the "language" of the organization and are ever-present role models for others to emulate and follow.

Value-based management actively develops, communicates, and enacts shared values.

A **symbolic leader** uses language and symbols and actions to establish and maintain a desired organizational culture.

Joe Raedle/Getty Images

CJG-Technology/Alamy

{ BE CAREFUL, OR YOUR FACEBOOK STATUS MAY CHANGE TO "JUST GOT FIRED!"

Ethics **Check**

■ Facebook Follies versus Corporate Culture

Facebook is fun, but don't post before checking your organization's culture. If you put the wrong things on your Facebook page—photo, snide comment, or complaints about your boss—your status might change to "Just got fired!"

Bed-surfing banker— After a Swiss bank employee called in sick with the excuse that she "needed to lie in the dark," company officials observed her surfing Facebook. She was fired, and the bank's statement said it "had lost trust in the employee."

Angry mascot—The Pittsburgh Pirates fired their mascot after he posted criticisms of team management on his Facebook page. A Twitter campaign by supporters helped him get hired back.

Short-changed server—A server at a North Carolina pizza parlor used Facebook to call her customers "cheap" for not giving good tips. After finding out about the posting, her bosses fired her for breaking company policy.

YOU DECIDE

Where do you draw the line? Isn't a person's Facebook page separate from one's work? Shouldn't people be able to speak freely about their jobs, co-workers, and even bosses when outside the workplace? Or is there an ethical boundary that travels from work into one's public communications that needs to be respected? What are the ethics here—on the employee's and the employer's side?

You'll often notice that symbolic leaders tell key stories over and over again, and encourage others to tell them as well. They may refer to the "founding story" about the entrepreneur whose personal values set a key tone for the enterprise. And, they remind everyone about organizational heroes, past and present, whose behaviors exemplify core values. Symbolic leaders make use of language metaphors—positive examples from another context—to make key points in powerful ways. Newly hired workers at Disney, for example, are told to think of themselves not as employees but as key "members of the cast" that work "on stage." After all, they learn, Disney isn't just any business; it is an "entertainment" business.

The notion of **workplace spirituality** is sometimes linked with value-based management and symbolic leadership. Although the first tendency might be to associate the term "spirituality" with religion, it is used in management to describe practices that try to enrich people's lives by bringing meaning to their work and helping them engage one another with a sense of shared community.[18]

A culture of workplace spirituality will have strong ethical foundations, recognize the value of individuals and respect their diversity, and focus efforts on meaningful jobs that offer real value to society. In other words, anyone working in a culture of workplace spirituality should derive pleasure from knowing that what is being accomplished is personally meaningful, created through community, and valued by others. You might think of an organization built around a culture of workplace spirituality as living up to core values such as the following.

- Meaningful purpose
- Trust and Respect
- Honesty and openness
- Personal growth and development
- Worker-friendly practices
- Ethics and social responsibility

Workplace spirituality involves practices that create meaning and shared community among organizational members.

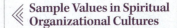 **Sample Values in Spiritual Organizational Cultures**

STUDY GUIDE

Takeaway 9.1
What Is the Nature of Organizational Culture?

Terms to Define

Core culture

Core values

Observable culture

Organizational culture

Socialization

Strong cultures

Symbolic leader

Value-based management

Workplace spirituality

Rapid Review

- Organizational culture is a climate of shared values and beliefs that guides the behavior of members; it creates the character and personality of the organization and sets its performance tone.
- The observable culture is found in the everyday rites, rituals, stories, heroes, and symbols of the organization.
- The core culture consists of the core values and fundamental beliefs on which the organization is based.
- Value-based management communicates, models, and reinforces core values throughout the organization.
- Symbolic leadership uses words, symbols, and actions to communicate the organizational culture.

Questions for Discussion

1. Can an organization achieve success with a good organizational design but a weak organizational culture?
2. When you are in your local bank or any other retail establishment as a customer, what do you see and hear around you that identifies its observable culture?
3. What core values would you choose if you were creating a new organization and wanted to establish a strong performance-oriented culture?

Be Sure You Can

- explain organizational culture as the personality of an organization
- describe how strong cultures influence organizations
- define and explain the process of socialization
- distinguish between the observable and the core cultures
- explain value-based management
- explain symbolic leadership

Career Situation: What Would You Do?

You have two really nice job offers and will soon have to choose between them. They are both in the same industry, but you wonder which employer would be the "best fit" for you. Make a list of the key aspects of the cultures of these organizations that you would investigate to help make your job choice. Why are these aspects of organizational culture important to you?

Takeaway 9.2
How Do Organizations Support and Achieve Innovation?

ANSWERS TO COME

- Organizations pursue process, product, and business model innovations.
- Green innovations pursue and support the goals of sustainability.
- Social innovations seek solutions to important societal problems.
- Commercializing innovation turns new ideas into salable products.
- Disruptive innovation uses new technologies to displace existing practices.
- Innovative organizations share many common characteristics.

THE iPAD, KINDLE, POST-IT NOTES, SUPER-SOAKER WATER GUN, ATMS, ROBOTS ON assembly lines, streaming movie rentals, overnight package deliveries, and more. Name your favorites! What we are discussing here are examples of **innovation**, the process of developing new ideas and putting them into practice.[19] The late management consultant Peter Drucker called innovation "an effort to create purposeful, focused change in an enterprise's economic or social potential."[20] Said a bit differently, it is the act of turning new ideas into usable applications.

Innovation is the process of taking a new idea and putting it into practice.

⦀ Organizations pursue process, product, and business model innovations.

Innovation in and by organizations is often discussed in three forms. **Process innovations** result in better ways of doing things. **Product innovations** result in the creation of new or improved goods and services. **Business model innovations** result in new ways of making money for the firm.[21] Consider these examples.[22]

- *Process innovation*—Southwest Airlines streamlines operations to fit its low-cost business strategy; IKEA sells furniture and fixtures in assemble-yourself kits; Amazon.com's "one-click" makes online shopping easy; Nike lets customers design their own sneakers.
- *Product innovation*—Geico put insurance underwriting online; Apple introduced the iPod, iPhone, and iPad, and made the "app" a must-have for smart phones and tablets; Amazon brought us the Kindle e-book reader; Facebook and Twitter made social media a part of everyday life.
- *Business model innovation*—Netflix turned movie rental into a subscription business; eBay profits by connecting users of its online marketplace; Google thrives on advertising revenues driven by ever-expanding Web technologies; Zynga made paying for "extras" profitable with free online games; Salesforce.com sold cloud-based software not as a product but as a service.

Process innovations result in better ways of doing things.

Product innovations result in new or improved goods or services.

Business model innovations result in ways for firms to make money.

⦀ Green innovations pursue and support the goals of sustainability.

Today we can add **green innovation,** or **sustainable innovation,** to the list of innovation types. Such innovations support sustainability by reducing the carbon

Green innovation or **sustainable innovation** reduces the carbon footprint of an organization or its products.

Jose F. Moreno/AP

Role Models

■ Tom Szaky Puts Eco-capitalism to Work at TerraCycle

Decisions . . . hunches . . . achievements? It's all about being tuned in to the environment. That's a message that seems well learned by Tom Szaky. He's ridden the roller coaster of all roller coasters, taking ideas for "sustainability," "green," and "recycling" from dorm room banter to the shelves of Wal-mart. If you read Tom Szaky's book *Revolution in a Bottle*, you enter the world of "upcycling"—the art, if you will, of turning waste that isn't recyclable into reusable packaging.

Szaky is what many call an "eco-capitalist," someone who brings environmentalism into the world of business and consumers. While a freshman at Princeton University, he ordered a million red worms with the goal of learning how to use them to recycle campus garbage. In conversations with classmate Jon Beyer, the original idea of eco-friendly waste management became one of creating and selling liquid fertilizer made from worm excrement. But they couldn't afford the expensive plastic bottles for packaging. More conversations, this time with entrepreneur Robin Tator, led to a new firm called TerraCycle with a mission to "find a meaningful use for waste materials."

Szaky's original liquid fertilizer became TerraCycle Plant Food. Now the firm *upcycles* a variety of waste products like cookie wrappers, drink containers, and discarded juice packs into usable products ranging from tote bags to containers of various sorts to pencil cases. And, yes, lots of them are found on Wal-mart's shelves. Szaky says: "Unlike most companies, which spend years in product development and testing, TerraCycle moves through these stages very quickly. First we identify a waste stream, then we figure out what we can make from that material. This is our strength—creatively solving the "what the hell do we make from it" issue. If a retailer bites, we are in full production in a matter of weeks."

WHAT'S THE LESSON HERE?

Tom Szaky made many decisions as he moved into the entrepreneurial world of eco-capitalism. It could have ended when the experiment with red worms and campus recycling proved more difficult than expected. But Szaky and his friends didn't stop there; learning from the experience, they persevered and made changes—more than once. We all talk about the planet, sustainability, and social values. But how often do we turn decisions into positive actions? Is there a bit of Tom Szaky in you?

---

footprint of an organization or its products. They are found in areas like energy use, water use, packaging, waste management, and transportation practices, as well as in product development. The possibilities abound. Replacing air travel with videoconferencing not only reduces travel costs for the organization, it also reduces carbon emissions otherwise put out by air travel. Getting energy from biogas or solar energy may cut electricity costs for a business, but it also reduces air pollution. Recycling used garments and reweaving the fibers into new clothing can save on both energy costs and carbon emissions. [23]

⫼ Social innovations seek solutions to important societal problems.

Although the tendency is to view innovation in a purely economic or business context, it's important to remember that it applies equally well to the world's social problems—poverty, famine, literacy, diseases, and the general conditions for social development. **Social innovation** can be described as innovation driven by a social conscience. It stems from creativity in **social entrepreneurship** that pursues innovative ways to solve pressing social problems. [24] And, the whole concept is very relevant today. Management consultant Peter Drucker once said: "Every single social and global issue of our day is a business opportunity in disguise." [25]

Social innovation is business innovation driven by a social conscience.

Social entrepreneurship pursues innovative ways to solve pressing social problems.

According to Dipak C. Jain, dean of INSEAD, business schools "should be producing leaders of real substance who put their knowledge to work in ways that make the world a better place."[26]

Commercializing innovation turns new ideas into salable products.

Whatever the goal—new product, improved process, unique business model, better sustainability, or social problem solving, the innovation process begins with *invention*—the act of discovery—and ends with *application*—the act of use.[27] In business it is the process of **commercializing innovation**—that turns new ideas—the inventions—into actual products, services, or processes—the applications—that generate profits through more sales or lower costs.[28] 3M Corporation, for example, owes its success to the imagination of employees such as Art Fry. He's the person whose creativity turned an adhesive that "wasn't sticky enough" into the blockbuster product known worldwide today as Post-it Notes®.

It's tempting to believe that commercializing an innovation such as the Post-it Note is easy. You might even consider it a "no-brainer." But it isn't necessarily so. Art Fry and his colleagues had to actively "sell" the Post-it idea to 3M's marketing group and senior management before getting the financial support they needed to turn their invention into a salable product. **Figure 9.2** shows how new product ideas such as Post-it might move through the typical steps of commercializing innovation.

Commercializing innovation is the process of turning new ideas into salable products.

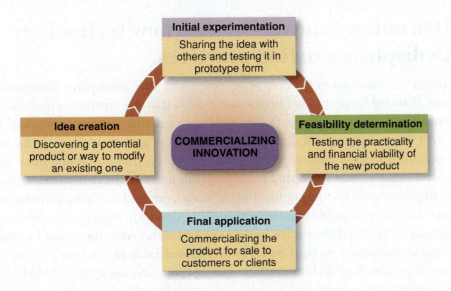

Initial experimentation
Sharing the idea with others and testing it in prototype form

Idea creation
Discovering a potential product or way to modify an existing one

COMMERCIALIZING INNOVATION

Feasibility determination
Testing the practicality and financial viability of the new product

Final application
Commercializing the product for sale to customers or clients

FIGURE 9.2

How Do Organizations Commercialize Innovation? In business it is the process of commercializing innovation that turns new ideas into actual products, services, or processes that can increase profits through greater sales or reduced costs. This requires management encouragement and support for idea creation (invention and the act of discovery), experimentation and feasibility determination, and final application (actually putting the tested idea into use).

One of the newer developments in commercializing innovation is called **reverse innovation**. Sometimes called *trickle-up innovation*, the concept got its start in the world of global business.[29] Firms have shifted away from only viewing innovation as something done "at home" and then transferred to "foreign or emerging markets." Instead, reverse innovation takes products and services developed in emerging markets, often subject to pricing constraints, and finds ways to use them elsewhere. In fact, management scholar C. K. Prahalad goes so far as to call emerging market settings "laboratories for radical innovation."[30] GE is a major believer. The firm has found expanded markets for handheld and portable electrocardiogram and ultrasound machines that sell for a fraction of the price of larger units. The smaller units were developed in India and China and

Reverse innovation recognizes the potential for valuable innovations to be launched from lower organizational levels and diverse locations, including emerging markets.

Social Entrepreneur Empowers Small Farmers to Fight Rural Poverty

Khalik Senosi/AP

Chronic hunger is the leading cause of death among African children. So, what can be done? Sympathy wasn't enough for Andrew Youn. He's a social entrepreneur whose efforts have made a world of difference for many African families. Using $7,000 of his own money he set up an innovative program called the One Acre Fund. It provides small loans to poor families in Burundi, Kenya, and Rwanda, enabling them to work their land with high-quality seed, fertilizer, equipment, and training. The goal is to help farmers "grow their way out of poverty" by finding ways to increase crop yields and avoid the devastating effects of Kenya's three-month "hunger season." Farmer repayments to the fund have reached $10 million annually. The One Acre Fund won the SC Johnson Award for Socially Responsible Entrepreneurship and has expanded into Rwanda. Says Youn: "The mothers are absolutely inspiring. The things they do out of necessity are heroic."

then moved through reverse innovation into the United States. Their mobility and lower prices have made them popular with emergency units.

||| Disruptive innovation uses new technology to displace existing practices.

> **Disruptive innovation** creates products or services that become so widely used that they largely replace prior practices and competitors.

At times the innovation process is so successful that **disruptive innovation** occurs. Harvard Scholar Clay Christensen defines it as the creation of an innovative product or service that starts out small scale and then moves "up market" to where it is so widely used it displaces prior practices and competitors.[31] Historical examples include cellular phones that disrupted traditional landlines and discount retailers that disrupted traditional full-line department stores. Online e-retailers are now disrupting fixed-place stores, and online video gaming and movie streaming businesses are disrupting "buy and own" business models.

As you think about disruptive innovation and technology, the world of Apple Computer and Steve Jobs can't be far away. His leadership at Apple is a model for harnessing technology and innovating—continuously and disruptively.[32] His knack was turning raw technology into consumer-friendly and captivating innovative products. How about the iPad? Wouldn't you agree that we could also use the term "disruptive" to describe its impact on the personal computer market? And then there's Amazon's Jeff Bezos, called "the ultimate disrupter" by *Fortune* magazine.[33] He put electronic books on a Kindle and put the Kindle in our purses and on our nightstands. Wasn't this disruptive innovation in the book publishing industry?

||| Innovative organizations share many common characteristics.

Do you view Microsoft as a firm whose strategy and culture drive an innovation powerhouse? Or do you see what *PC World* once described as "a stodgy old corporation churning out boring software"?[34] There are quite a few critics who believe Microsoft meets the latter description, not the former. Truly innovative organizations—from large corporations like 3M and Amazon to small start-ups—tend to share features such as the following.[35]

HIGHLY INNOVATIVE ORGANIZATIONS				
Strategy includes innovation	Culture values innovation	Structures support innovation	Staffing builds talent for innovation	Leadership drives innovation

In highly innovative organizations the *corporate strategy and culture embrace innovation*. The strategies of the organization include and highlight innovation; the culture of the organization, as reflected in visions and values, emphasizes an innovation spirit. If you go to the Web site for the design firm IDEO, you'll find this description: "Our values are part mad scientist (curious, experimental), bear-tamer (gutsy, agile), *reiki* master (hands-on, empathetic), and midnight tax accountant (optimistic, savvy). These qualities are reflected in the smallest details to the biggest endeavors, composing the medium in which great ideas are born and flourish."[36] There's little doubt that core values at IDEO encourage innovation and allow new ideas to continually flourish.

In highly innovative organizations, *organization structures support innovation*. Bureaucracy is the enemy of innovation. Innovative organizations take advantage of organic designs and team structures that empower people and eliminate cumbersome bureaucratic ways. *BusinessWeek* says: "Instead of assembly line, think swarming beehive. Teams of people from different disciplines gather to focus on a problem. They brainstorm, tinker and toy with different approaches."[37] The term **skunkworks** is often used to describe special units set free from the normal structure and given separate locations, special resources, and their own managers, all with the purpose of achieving innovation.

In highly innovative organizations, *staffing builds talent for innovation*. Step one in meeting this goal is to make creativity an important criterion when hiring and moving people into positions of responsibility. Step two is allowing their creative talents to fully operate by inspiring and empowering them by the practices just discussed—strategy, culture, and structure, as well as the right leadership.

In highly innovative organizations, *leadership drives innovation*. Sometimes this support is policy driven. Google, for example, gives engineers freedom to spend 20% of their time on projects of their own choosing. Other times this support is style driven—a direct reflection of the leader. When asked to identify the "most important source of a culture of innovation," for example, 69% of respondents in one survey chose the CEO of their organizations.[38] The best top managers not only encourage new ideas, but they also tolerate criticism and differences of opinion. They know that success doesn't always come in a straight line and admit that mistakes are often part of the innovation process. When talking about the firm's innovative electronic reader, the Kindle, Amazon's CEO Jeff Bezos said: "Our willingness to be misunderstood, our long-term orientation and our willingness to repeatedly fail are the three parts of our culture that make doing this kind of thing possible."[39]

Skunkworks are special creative units set free from the normal structure for the purpose of innovation.

STUDY GUIDE

Takeaway 9.2
How Do Organizations Support and Achieve Innovation?

Terms to Define

Business model innovation

Commercializing innovation

Disruptive innovation

Green innovation

Innovation

Process innovations

Product innovations

Reverse innovation

Skunkworks

Social innovation

Social entrepreneurship

Sustainable innovation

Rapid Review

- Innovation is a process that turns creative ideas into products or processes that benefit organizations and their customers.
- Organizations pursue process, product, and business model innovations.
- Organizations pursue green innovations that support sustainability.
- Organizations pursue social business innovations to tackle important societal problems.
- The process of commercializing innovation turns new ideas into useful applications.
- Highly innovative organizations tend to have supportive cultures, strategies, structures, staffing, and top management.

Questions for Discussion

1. Are there any potential downsides to making organizational commitments to green innovation?
2. What are the biggest trouble points in a large organization that might prevent a great idea from becoming a commercialized innovation?
3. What difference does a leader make in terms of how innovative an organization becomes?

Be Sure You Can

- discuss differences among process, product, and business model innovations
- explain green innovation and social business innovation
- list five steps in the process of commercializing innovation
- list and explain four characteristics of innovative organizations

Career Situation: What Would You Do?

Take a look around your present organization, be it a school or workplace. What three ideas can you come up with right away for possible innovations? How would your ideas, if implemented, benefit both the organization and society at large? What are the potential obstacles to getting your ideas implemented? What steps could you take as an "innovation champion" to turn your ideas into real practices?

Takeaway 9.3

How Do Managers Lead the Processes of Organizational Change?

ANSWERS TO COME

- Organizations pursue both transformational and incremental changes.
- Three phases of planned change are unfreezing, changing, and refreezing.
- The change process is dynamic and improvising is often essential.
- Managers use force-coercion, rational persuasion, and shared power change strategies.
- Change leaders identify and deal positively with resistance to change.

What if the existing structure or culture of an organization is flawed, doesn't drive high performance, and in general causes problems? Just "change things," you might say. The fact is that we use the word "change" so much that the tendency may be to think changing things is easy, almost a matter of routine. But that's not always the case.[40] Former British Airways CEO Sir Rod Eddington once said, for example, that "altering an airline's culture is like trying to perform an engine change in flight."[41]

Just look at the business news. You'll always find firms that are struggling, and it's not always because they don't have the right ideas—it's because they aren't adapting well to new circumstances. In other words, they have difficulty creating organizational change. There are times when managers at all levels in organizations have to succeed as **change leaders** and take initiative to change the existing pattern of behavior of another person or social system.[42]

Change leaders are supposed to make things happen even when inertia has made systems and people reluctant to embrace new ways of doing things. They are supposed to be alert to cultures, situations, and people needing change; open to good ideas and opportunities; and ready and able to support the implementation of new ideas in actual practice. But, the reality described in the small figure shows a big difference between true change leaders and status quo managers. All too often people in organizations have major tendencies toward the status quo—accepting things as they are and not wanting to change. And it's the status quo that creates lots of difficulties when managers and leaders push organizations to innovate and adapt to changing times.

A **change leader** tries to change the behavior of another person or social system.

Change leaders	Status quo managers
• Confident of ability • Willing to take risks • Seize opportunity • Expect surprise • Make things happen	• Threatened by change • Bothered by uncertainty • Prefer predictability • Support the status quo • Wait for things to happen

▌ Organizations pursue both transformational and incremental changes.

Changes led from top levels are likely to be large-scale, frame breaking, and strategic. They are repositioning changes focused on big issues that affect the organization as a whole. We call this **transformational change**. It is supposed to result in a major and comprehensive redirection of the organization—new vision, new strategy, new culture, new structure, and even new people.[43]

Transformational change results in a major and comprehensive redirection of the organization.

As you might expect, transformational change is intense, highly stressful, and very complex to achieve. Lots of large-scale change efforts actually fail, and the main reason for failure is bad implementation. [44] One of the most common implementation mistakes is management failure to build commitments so that everyone accepts and works hard to accomplish change goals. [45] Popular advice to would-be leaders of large-scale changes includes the following guidlines. [46]

How to Lead Transformational Change »

- Establish a sense of urgency for change.
- Form a powerful coalition to lead the change.
- Create and communicate a change vision.
- Empower others to move change forward.
- Celebrate short-term wins, and recognize those who help.
- Build on success; align people and systems with new ways.
- Stay with it; keep the message consistent; champion the vision.

Let's not forget that there is another more modest and frame-bending side to organizational change. It deals with ongoing adjustments in structures, systems, technologies, products, and staffing to improve performance. This is **incremental change** that tweaks and nudges people, systems, and practices to better align them with emerging problems and opportunities. The intent isn't to break and remake the system, but to move it forward through continuous improvements.

Incremental change bends and adjusts existing ways to improve performance.

Leadership of incremental change focuses on building on existing ways of doing things with the goal of doing them better in the future. Common incremental changes in organizations involve new products, new processes, new technologies, new work systems, and new human resource approches.

Organizational Change Pyramid

Few strategic, large-scale changes to reposition organization

Major changes to improve performance through new structures, systems, technologies, products, and people

Frequent, smaller-scale changes to fine-tune performance, enable short-term gains, and provide continuous improvements in operations

One shouldn't get the idea, by the way, that incremental change is inferior to transformational change. Both are important in the organizational change pyramid shown here. [47] You are likely to find that organizations are most successful over time when they are able to successfully put transformational and incremental change together. Think of it this way. Incremental changes keep things tuned up—like the engine on a car—in between transformations—when the old car is replaced with a new one.

⦀ Three phases of planned change are unfreezing, changing, and refreezing.

Managers seeking to lead change in organizations can benefit from a simple but helpful model developed by the psychologist Kurt Lewin. He describes how change situations can be analyzed and addressed in three phases: *unfreezing*—preparing a system for change; *changing*—making actual changes in the system; and *refreezing*—stabilizing the system after change. [48]

Unfreezing is the stage in which managers help others to develop, experience, and feel a real need for change. The goal here is to get people to view change as a way of solving a problem or taking advantage of an opportunity. Some might call this the "burning bridge" phase, arguing that to get people to jump off a bridge, you might just have to set it on fire. Managers can simulate the burning bridge by

Unfreezing is the phase during which a situation is prepared for change.

engaging people with facts and information that communicate the need for change—environmental pressures, declining performance, and examples of alternative approaches. And as you have probably experienced, conflict can help people to break old habits and recognize new ways of thinking about or doing things.

The **changing** phase is where actual change takes place. Ideally these changes are planned in ways that give them the best opportunities for success, having maximum appeal and posing minimum difficulties for those being asked to make them. Although this phase should follow unfreezing in Lewin's model, he believes it is often started too early. When change takes place before people and systems are ready for it, the likelihood of resistance and change failure is much greater. In this sense Lewin might liken the change process to building a house: You need to put a good foundation in place before you begin the framing.

As shown in **Figure 9.3**, the final stage in the planned change process is **refreezing**. Here, the focus is on stabilizing the change to make it as long lasting as needed. Linking change with rewards, positive reinforcement, and resource support all help with refreezing. Of course, in today's dynamic environments there may not be a lot of time for refreezing before things are ready to change again. You may well find that refreezing in Lewin's sense probably gives way quite often to another phase of evaluating and reassessing. In other words, we begin preparing for or undertaking more change even while trying to take full advantage of the present one.

> **Changing** is the phase where a planned change actually takes place.

> **Refreezing** is the phase at which change is stabilized.

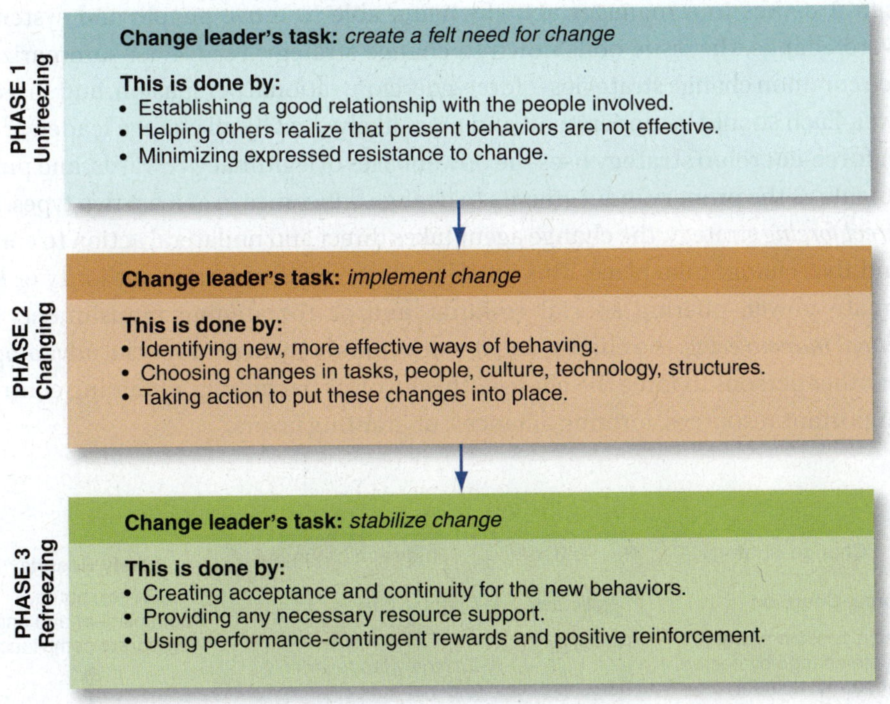

PHASE 1 Unfreezing

Change leader's task: *create a felt need for change*

This is done by:
- Establishing a good relationship with the people involved.
- Helping others realize that present behaviors are not effective.
- Minimizing expressed resistance to change.

PHASE 2 Changing

Change leader's task: *implement change*

This is done by:
- Identifying new, more effective ways of behaving.
- Choosing changes in tasks, people, culture, technology, structures.
- Taking action to put these changes into place.

PHASE 3 Refreezing

Change leader's task: *stabilize change*

This is done by:
- Creating acceptance and continuity for the new behaviors.
- Providing any necessary resource support.
- Using performance-contingent rewards and positive reinforcement.

FIGURE 9.3 What Are the Change Leader Responsibilities in Lewin's Three Phases of Planned Change?
Kurt Lewin identified three phases of the planned change process. The first is unfreezing, the phase where people open up and become receptive to the possibility of change. The second is changing, where the actual change happens and the new ways of doing things are put into place. Third is refreezing, the phase where changes are stabilized to become part of ongoing routines. Lewin believed that change agents often neglect unfreezing and move too quickly into the changing phase, thus setting the stage for change failures. They may also neglect refreezing, with the result that any achieved change has only temporary effects.

The change process is dynamic and improvising is often essential.

Although Lewin's three-phase model depicts change as a linear, step-by-step process, with clear beginning and end points, the reality is that change is dynamic and uncertain. Change leaders often deal with the change phases simultaneously and even incompletely. It's not uncommon for new change to begin before refreezing ever takes place with an old one. The sheer complexity of organizations also creates a need for **improvisational change** where adjustments are continually made as changes are being implemented[49]

Consider the case of bringing new technology into an organization or work unit. A technology that is attractive in concept may appear complicated to the new users. The full extent of its benefits or inadequacies may not become known until it is tried. To succeed in such situations a change leader should be continually gathering feedback on how the change is going and then improvising to revise and customize the new technology to best meet users' needs.

Managers use force-coercion, rational persuasion, and shared power change strategies.

When it comes to a manager actually being able to move people and systems toward change, the issue boils down to change strategy. **Figure 9.4** summarizes three common change strategies—force-coercion, rational persuasion, and shared power. Each should be understood and most likely used by all change leaders.[50]

A **force-coercion strategy** uses the power bases of legitimacy, rewards, and punishments as the primary inducements to change.[51] It comes in at least two types. In a *direct forcing* strategy, the change agent takes direct and unilateral action to command that change take place. This involves the exercise of formal authority or legitimate power, offering special rewards, and/or threatening punishment. In *political maneuvering*, the change agent works indirectly to gain special advantage over other persons to force the change. This involves bargaining, obtaining control of important resources, forming alliances, or granting favors.

Improvisational change makes continual adjustments as changes are being implemented.

A **force-coercion strategy** pursues change through formal authority and/or the use of rewards or punishments.

FIGURE 9.4

What Happens When a Change Leader Uses Different Types of Change Strategies? Force-coercion strategies use authority, offers of rewards, and threats of punishment to push change forward. The likely results are, at best, temporary compliance. Rational persuasion strategies use information, facts, and logic to present a persuasive case in support of change. The likely outcomes are compliance with reasonable commitment. Shared power strategies engage others and allow them to participate in the change process, from initial planning through implementation. The high involvement tends to build more internalization and greater commitments to change.

Change Strategy	Power Bases	Managerial Behavior	Likely Results
Force–Coercion Using position power to create change by decree and formal authority	Legitimacy Rewards Punishments	*Direct forcing* and unilateral action *Political maneuvering* and indirect action	Faster, but low commitment and only temporary compliance
Rational Persuasion Creating change through rational persuasion and empirical argument	Expertise	*Informational efforts* using credible knowledge, demonstrated facts, and logical argument	
Shared Power Developing support for change through personal values and commitments	Reference	*Participative efforts* to share power and involve others in planning and implementing change	Slower, but high commitment and longer term internalization

One thing to remember is that most people will probably respond to force-coercion with temporary compliance. They'll act in a limited way and only out of fear of punishment or hope for a reward. But the new behavior continues only so long as the possibilities for rewards and punishments exist. This is why force-coercion may be most useful as an unfreezing strategy. It can help to break people from old habits and try new ones that eventually prove valuable enough to be self-sustaining. An example is General Electric's Work-Out program, discussed earlier.[52] Jack Welch started Work-Out to create a forum for active employee empowerment. But he made participation mandatory from the start; he used his authority to force employees to participate. And he was confident in doing so because he believed that, once started, the program would prove valuable enough to survive and prosper on its own. It did.

An alternative to force-coercion is the **rational persuasion strategy**, attempting to bring about change through persuasion backed by special knowledge, information, facts, and rational argument. The likely outcome of rational persuasion is compliance with reasonable commitment. This is actually the strategy that you learn and practice so much in school when writing reports and making formal presentations on group projects. You'll do a lot of rational persuasion in the real world as well. But as you probably realize, success with the strategy

> A **rational persuasion strategy** pursues change through empirical data and rational argument.

{ *Change by Design: How Design Thinking Transforms Organizations and Inspires Innovation*
by Tim Brown

Manager's **Library**

BE CREATIVE AND IMPROVE BY NOT THINKING STRAIGHT

Some people like strong coffee and a quiet space to dream up new ideas, whereas other people prefer crowded social settings and hands-on activities to get their creative juices flowing. Either approach helps because creative thinking is nonroutine. Maybe the key to innovation is just avoid an ordinary mindset and try not to think straight!

In the book *Change by Design: How Design Thinking Transforms Organizations and Inspires Innovation* (2009, HarperCollins), author Tim Brown discusses methods that people and organizations can use to change their regular approach and advance innovation. He says "design thinking" implies that people of all functions are innovators, not just artists, engineers, and marketers. Those near "externalities"—technology, consumers, and market forces outside the organization—are best placed and motivated to innovate.

Brown thinks human-centered ideas, not technology-centered ones, capture sustainable gains. New ideas should consider and alter human experiences—those of customers, employees, or business partners—and avoid use of existing resources to improve functionality for incremental but predictable gains. Services are particularly ripe, and he urges construction of ideas with emotional benefits, saying a shift to an "experience economy" means consumers are actively seeking emotive experiences in products and services and avoiding basic feature improvements.

The anecdotes in this book come from Brown's career as a design consultant. He advocates building prototypes early in the design phase—ones that are rough and cheap. The goal is not to have working models, but to generate tangible results from abstract thought and realize their strengths and weaknesses. Prototyping "slows down the process to speed it up." In a sense, not thinking straight yields innovation because the road to success is less cluttered. Perhaps creative thought requires less effort than most people think?

REFLECT AND REACT

Describe products or services that provide you with an emotional experience rather than a functional utility. How can these feelings be evoked in other products or services? Describe circumstances where members of your organization interact with externalities—customers, technologies, or broader society. How can their observations yield innovations? And by the way, do you agree slowing down to speed up enables creative thinking?

depends on having very good facts and information—the rational part, and then being able to communicate them well—the persuasion part.

The rational persuasion strategy works best when the change agent has credibility as an expert. This credibility can come from possessing special information or having a reputation as an expert. It can also be gained from bringing in external consultants or experts, showing case examples or benchmarks, and conducting demonstration projects. Ford, for example, has sent managers to Disney World to learn about customer loyalty, hoping to stimulate them to lead customer service initiatives of their own. A Ford vice president says, "Disney's track record is one of the best in the country as far as dealing with customers."[53] In this sense the power of rational persuasion is straightforward: If it works for Disney, why can't it work for Ford?

A **shared power strategy** engages people in a collaborative process of identifying values, assumptions, and goals from which support for change will naturally emerge. Although slow, the process is likely to yield high commitment. Sometimes called a *normative re-educative strategy*, this approach relies on empowerment and participation. The change leader engages others as a team to develop the consensus needed to support change. This requires being comfortable and confident in allowing others to influence decisions that affect the planned change and its implementation. And because it entails a high level of involvement, this strategy is often quite time consuming. But shared power can deliver major benefits in terms of longer-lasting and internalized change.

The great strength of the shared power strategy lies with unlocking the creativity and experience of people within the system. Still, many managers hesitate to use it for fear of losing control or of having to compromise on important organizational goals. Harvard scholar Teresa M. Amabile points out, however, that managers and change leaders can share power regarding choice of means and processes, even if they can't debate the goals. "People will be more creative," she says, "if you give them freedom to decide how to climb particular mountains. You needn't let them choose which mountains to climb."[54]

A **shared power strategy** pursues change by participation in assessing change needs, values, and goals.

{ YOUR TOLERANCE FOR AMBIGUITY IS A GOOD INDICATOR OF HOW YOU DEAL WITH CHANGE.

Explore **Yourself**

■ Tolerance for Ambiguity

The next time you are driving somewhere and following a familiar route only to find a "detour" sign ahead, test your **tolerance for ambiguity**. Is the detour no big deal and you go forward without any further thought? Or is it a bit of a deal, perhaps causing anxiety or anger and demonstrating your tendencies to resist change in your normal routines?

Your tolerance for ambiguity is a good predictor of how you like to work and deal with change. Some organizations are structured and directive, whereas others are the opposite. Some of us embrace change, whereas others resist it. But remember, people today are being asked to be ever more creative and innovative in their work; organizations are, too.

Change, we often hear said, is now a given. And in so many ways it is. At work we are expected to support change initiatives launched from the top; we are also expected to be change leaders in our own teams and work units. This is a good time to check your readiness to meet the challenges of change in organizations and in personal affairs.

Get to know yourself better by taking the self-assessment on **Tolerance for Ambiguity** and completing other activities in the *Exploring Management* **Skill-Building Portfolio**.

Change leaders identify and deal positively with resistance to change.

You may have heard the adage that "change can be your best friend." At this point, however, we should probably add: "but only if you deal with resistance in the right ways."

When people resist change, they are most often defending something important to them and that now appears threatened. It is tempting to view such resistance as something that must be overcome or defeated. But this mindset can easily cause problems. Perhaps a better way is to view resistance as feedback, as a source of information about how people view the change and its impact on them. A change leader can learn a lot by listening to resistance and then using it to develop ideas for improving the change and the change process.[55]

The list in **Table 9.1**—Why People May Resist Change—probably contains some familiar items. Surely you've seen some or all of these types of change resistance in your own experience. And honestly now, haven't you also been a resister at times? When you were, how did the change leader or manager respond? How do you think they should have responded?

Table 9.1 Why People May Resist Change

Fear of the unknown—not understanding what is happening or what comes next
Disrupted habits—feeling upset to see the end of the old ways of doing things
Loss of confidence—feeling incapable of performing well under the new ways of doing things
Loss of control—feeling that things are being done "to" you rather than "by" or "with" you
Poor timing—feeling overwhelmed by the situation or feeling that things are moving too fast
Work overload—not having the physical or psychic energy to commit to the change
Loss of face—feeling inadequate or humiliated because it appears that the old ways weren't good ways
Lack of purpose—not seeing a reason for the change and/or not understanding its benefits

Researchers have found that once resistance appears in organizations, managers try to deal with it in various ways, and some of their choices are better than others.[56] *Education and communication* use discussions, presentations, and demonstrations to educate people about a change before it happens. *Participation and involvement* allows others to contribute ideas and help design and implement the change. *Facilitation and support* provide encouragement and training, channels for communicating problems and complaints, and ways of helping to overcome performance pressures. *Negotiation and agreement* offer incentives to those who are actively resisting or ready to resist, trying to make trade-offs in exchange for cooperation.

Although very different, each of the prior strategies for dealing with resistance to change has a role to play in organizations. Two other approaches, also found in management practice, are considerably more risky and prone to negative side effects. Change leaders who use *manipulation and cooptation* try to covertly influence resisters by providing information selectively and structuring events in favor of the desired change. Those using *explicit and implicit coercion* try to force resisters to accept change by threatening them with a variety of undesirable consequences if they don't go along as asked. Would you agree that most people don't like to be on the receiving end of these strategies?

STUDY GUIDE

Takeaway 9.3
How Do Managers Lead the Processes of Organizational Change?

Terms to Define

Change leader

Changing

Force-coercion strategy

Incremental change

Improvisational change

Rational persuasion strategy

Refreezing

Shared power strategy

Transformational change

Unfreezing

Rapid Review

- Transformational change makes radical changes in organizational directions; incremental change makes continuing adjustments to existing ways and practices.
- Change leaders are change agents who take responsibility for helping to change the behavior of people and organizational systems.
- Lewin's three phases of planned change are unfreezing (preparing a system for change), changing (making a change), and refreezing (stabilizing the system with a new change in place).
- Successful change agents understand the force-coercion, rational persuasion, and shared power change strategies, and the likely outcomes of each.
- People resist change for a variety of reasons, including fear of the unknown and force of habit; this resistance can be a source of feedback that can help improve the change process.
- Change agents deal with resistance to change in a variety of ways, including education, participation, facilitation, negotiation, manipulation, and coercion.

Questions for Discussion

1. When is it better to pursue incremental rather than transformational change?
2. Can the refreezing phase of planned change ever be completed in today's dynamic environment?
3. Should managers avoid the force-coercion change strategy altogether?

Be Sure You Can

- differentiate transformational and incremental change
- discuss a change leader's responsibilities for each phase of Lewin's change process
- explain the force-coercion, rational persuasion, and shared power change strategies
- list reasons why people resist change
- identify strategies for dealing with resistance to change

Career Situation: What Would You Do?

Times are tough at your organization, and, as the director of human resources, you have a problem. The company's senior executives have decided that 10% of the payroll has to be cut immediately. Instead of laying off people, you would like to have everyone cut back their work hours by 10%. This would cut the payroll but let everyone keep their jobs. You've heard this idea isn't popular with all the workers. Some are already grumbling that it's a "bad idea" and the company is just looking for excuses "to cut wages." How can you best handle this situation as a change leader?

TestPrep 9

Answers to TestPrep questions can be found at the back of the book.

Multiple-Choice Questions

1. Stories told about an organization's past accomplishments and heroes such as company founders are all part of what is called the _____ culture.
   (a) observable
   (b) underground
   (c) functional
   (d) core

2. Planned and spontaneous ceremonies and celebrations of work achievements illustrate how the use of _____ helps build strong corporate cultures.
   (a) rewards
   (b) structures
   (c) rites and rituals
   (d) core values

3. An organization with a strong culture is most likely to have a _____.
   (a) tight, bureaucratic structure
   (b) loose, flexible design
   (c) small staff size
   (d) clearly communicated mission

4. Honesty, social responsibility, and customer service are examples of _____ that can become foundations for an organization's core culture.
   (a) rites and rituals
   (b) values
   (c) subsystems
   (d) ideas

5. Product innovations create new goods or services for customers, whereas _____ innovations create new ways of doing things in the organization.
   (a) content
   (b) process
   (c) quality
   (d) task

6. The Kindle e-reader by Amazon and the iPad by Apple are examples of _____ innovations.
   (a) business model
   (b) social
   (c) product
   (d) process

7. Movie downloads by subscription (Netflix) and advertising revenues from Internet searches (Google) are examples of _____ innovations.
   (a) business model
   (b) social
   (c) product
   (d) process

8. Green innovation is most associated with the concept of _____.
   (a) observable culture
   (b) core culture
   (c) sustainability
   (d) skunkworks

9. The innovation process isn't really successful in an organization until a new idea is _____.
   (a) tested as a prototype
   (b) proven to be financially feasible
   (c) put into practice
   (d) discovered or invented

10. The basic purpose of a starting a skunkworks is to _____.
    (a) add more bureaucratic structure to the innovation process
    (b) provide special space for people to work together and achieve innovation
    (c) make sure that any innovation occurs according to preset plans
    (d) give people free time in their jobs to be personally creative

11. _____ change results in a major change of direction for an organization, whereas _____ change makes small adjustments to current ways of doing things.
    (a) Frame breaking; radical
    (b) Frame bending; incremental
    (c) Transformational; frame breaking
    (d) Transformational; incremental

12. A manager using a force-coercion strategy is most likely relying on the power of _____ to bring about planned change.
    (a) expertise
    (b) reference
    (c) legitimacy
    (d) information

13. The most participative of the planned change strategies is _____.
    (a) negotiation and agreement
    (b) rational persuasion
    (c) shared power
    (d) education and communication

14. The responses most likely to be associated with use of a force-coercion change strategy are best described as _____.
    (a) internalized commitment
    (b) temporary compliance
    (c) passive cooptation
    (d) active resistance

15. When a change leader tries to deal with resistance by trying to covertly influence others, offering only selective information and/or structuring events in favor of the desired change, this is an example of _____.
    (a) rational persuasion
    (b) manipulation and cooptation
    (c) negotiation
    (d) facilitation

Short-Response Questions

16. What core values might be found in high-performance organizational cultures?

17. What is the difference between process, product, and business model innovation?

18. How do a manager's responsibilities for change leadership vary among Lewin's three phases of planned change?

19. What are the possible differences in outcomes for managers using force-coercion and shared power change strategies?

Integration and Application Question

20. One of the common experiences of new college graduates in their first jobs is that they often "spot things that need to be changed." They are full of new ideas, and they are ready and quick to challenge existing ways of doing things. They are enthusiastic and well intentioned. But more often than most probably expect, their new bosses turn out to be skeptical, not too interested, or even irritated; co-workers who have been in place for some time may feel and act the same.

    Questions: What is the new employee to do? One option is to just forget it and take an "I'll just do my job" approach. Let's reject that. So then, how can you be an effective change leader in your next new job? How can you use change strategies and deal with resistance from your boss and co-workers in a manner that builds your reputation as someone with good ideas for positive change?

Steps*for* FurtherLearning

BUILD MARKETABLE SKILLS
DO A CASE ANALYSIS
GET AND STAY INFORMED

BUILD
MARKETABLE SKILLS.
EARN BIG CAREER
PAYOFFS!

Don't miss these opportunities in the **Skill-Building Portfolio**

■ **SELF-ASSESSMENT 9:**
Tolerance for Ambiguity
Measure your reactions to ambiguity . . . make it a friend not a foe.

■ **CLASS EXERCISE 9:**
Force-Field Analysis
Change situations are complex . . . mapping the forces can clarify the pathways.

■ **TEAM PROJECT 9:**
Organizational Culture Walk
Organizational cultures are all around us . . . we can learn a lot as informed observers.

Many learning resources are found at the end of the book and online within WileyPLUS.

Take advantage of **Cases for Critical Thinking**

■ **CHAPTER 9 CASE SNAPSHOT:**
LinkedIn—Networking for Career Opportunities/
Sidebar on Gamers Welcome

With a lot of uncertainty and insecurity about the future, both the employed and the unemployed can benefit from time spent in active networking. This need is met by LinkedIn, an online networking and job site. It has created a solution not only for recruiters in search of candidates, but also for job candidates in full search mode or anyone wanting to make good career connections. LinkedIn offers access to faster recruiting and faster networking. If you are looking for a job or have a job and are interested in a better one, the message is: Why not create a profile on LinkedIn and "get connected"? Innovation has driven the company's success. It was the first ever social network to go public. But, does it have what it takes to stay ahead of constant challenges?

DO
A CASE ANALYSIS.
STRENGTHEN YOUR
CRITICAL THINKING!

Dig into this **Hot Topic**

■ **GOOD IDEA OR NOT?** "Move over old timer, time to make room for GenY."

Employers find a lot to like in the skills Generation Y members—the Millennials—bring to the workplace. No problem with technology—they're natives always on the cusp of things. No problem with collaboration—they've grown up with teamwork and social media. No problem either with motivation—they're task-oriented and career focused.

GET
AND STAY INFORMED.
MAKE YOURSELF
VALUABLE!

But, Gen Ys also need special handling. They can be spoiled and self-centered. They're quick to complain when their bosses don't communicate enough, when their skills aren't fully tapped, and when work rules and bureaucracy get too restrictive. They're also impatient for new assignments, promotions and flexible work arrangements. And when they don't get them, they're quick to move on. Loyalty to a single employer career isn't part of their DNA.

Situation Some employers are going to great lengths to keep their Gen Ys happy, even to the point where "older" employers feel a bit put upon. The online book service Chegg cut middle management positions to make room for younger employees to advance. CEO Dan Rosensweig says: "If they don't feel like they're making a contribution to a company overall quickly, they don't stay." Software firm Aprimo guarantees Gen Ys promotion and a raise in a year if they perform up to expectations. When some of the older workers balked at this special treatment, President Bob Boehnlein says: "I had to strong-arm a little bit."

Final Take Do Gen Ys deserve special treatment? If and when they get it, is it fair that it comes at the expense of their more senior co-workers? Just how do you blend the needs and interests of a new generation of workers with others who have been around awhile—perhaps quite awhile? Who gains and who loses when the new generation pushes employers to rethink the nature of the traditional employment contract?

A Pew Research study reports that 50% of working fathers and 56% of working mothers have "very" or "somewhat difficult times balancing work and family . . . 50% of working fathers and 23% of working mothers feel they "spend too little time with kids."

Human Resource Management

10

Nurturing Turns Potential into Performance

Paramount Pictures/Photofest

Professionalism and *Iron Man 2*

Tony Stark (Robert Downey Jr.) is the rich, playboy owner of Stark Industries, a military weapons company started by his father. Tony was a child prodigy in technology, and when his father dies, the company becomes his. The problem is that Tony doesn't know how to run a business. So, he turns it over to his faithful assistant Pepper Potts (Gwyneth Paltrow). Potts is the consummate professional, always willing to do whatever it takes to keep her boss on schedule and to keep the company running effectively. When Potts becomes CEO and Tony comes to the office acting in typical arrogant and self-centered fashion, she dismisses him.

Professionalism involves more than expertise. It means behaving with internalized commitments to special standards. Those standards may be determined by personal values, academic degrees, professional affiliations, and most certainly, company culture and practices. Managers need to be thoroughly professional in all areas of work responsibility, including how they interact with and make decisions affecting human resources.

Just where do you stand on professionalism? Take advantage of opportunities to test your professional commitment. They're all around. Chances are your school has a student branch of the Society for Human Resource Management or some other professional organization. Consider getting involved for contributions and skills development.

YOUR CHAPTER 10 TAKEAWAYS

1. Understand the purpose and legal context of human resource management.
2. Identify essential human resource management practices.
3. Recognize current issues in human resource management.

WHAT'S INSIDE

Explore Yourself
More on **professionalism**

Role Models
Family values lead CEO Dave Goldberg to Survey Monkey

Ethics Check
CEO gets $96.1 million pay package

Facts to Consider
Human resource executives worry about performance measurement

Manager's Library
Fast Future: How the Millennial Generation is Shaping Our World by David Burstein

TEACHING NOTE: Write the job title Chief Talent Officer on the board or screen. Ask students what the holder of this position would do on a day-to-day basis. Where should this position fit on an organization chart and why? Finish discussion by having them brainstorm a possible career path for someone who would like to hold this title someday.

Takeaway 10.1
What Are the Purpose and Legal Context of Human Resource Management?

ANSWERS TO COME

- Human resource management attracts, develops, and maintains a talented workforce.
- Strategic human resource management aligns human capital with organizational strategies.
- Government legislation protects against employment discrimination.
- Laws can't guarantee that employment discrimination will never happen.

The key to managing people in ways that lead to profit, productivity, innovation, and real organizational learning ultimately lies in how you think about your organization and its people. . . . When you look at your people, do you see costs to be reduced? . . . Or, when you look at your people do you see intelligent, motivated, trustworthy individuals—the most critical and valuable strategic assets your organization can have?

THESE COMMENTS ARE FROM JEFFREY PFEFFER'S BOOK, *THE HUMAN EQUATION: Building Profits by Putting People First.*[1] What is your experience? Do you find employers treating people as costs or as assets? And what difference does this seem to make? Pfeffer and his colleague, John F. Veiga, believe it makes a performance difference, a potentially big one. They conclude: "There is a substantial and rapidly expanding body of evidence . . . that speaks to the strong connection between how firms manage their people and the economic results achieved."[2]

The core argument just advanced is that organizations will perform better when they treat their members better.[3] And when it comes to talent and how people are treated at work, we enter the territory of human resource management.

‖ Human resource management attracts, develops, and maintains a talented workforce.

A marketing manager at IDEO, the Palo Alto–based design firm, once said: "If you hire the right people . . . if you've got the right fit . . . then everything will take care of itself."[4] It really isn't quite that simple, but getting the right people on board is certainly a great starting point for success. The process of **human resource management (HRM)** is supposed to do just that—attract, develop, and maintain a talented and energetic workforce. Its purpose is to ensure that an organization is always staffed with the best people so that all jobs get done in the best possible ways. You might think of the goal of HRM this way—to build organizational performance capacity through people.

The three major responsibilities of human resource management are typically described as follows.

1. *Attracting a quality workforce*—focus on employee recruitment and selection
2. *Developing a quality workforce*—focus on employee orientation, training and development, and performance management
3. *Maintaining a quality workforce*—focus career development, work-life balance, compensation and benefits, retention and turnover, and labor-management relations

> **Human resource management (HRM)** is the process of attracting, developing, and maintaining a high-quality workforce.

Human Resource Management → Attracting talented employees → Developing talented employees → Keeping talented employees

⫼ Strategic human resource management aligns human capital with organizational strategies.

High-performing organizations thrive on strong foundations of **human capital**, the economic value of people's abilities, knowledge, experience, ideas, energies, and commitments. When Sheryl Sandberg left her senior management post with Google to become Facebook's chief operating officer, she made human capital her top priority. She strengthened the firm's human resource management systems with updated approaches for employee performance reviews, innovative recruiting methods, and new management training.[5] These initiatives are consistent with the concept of **strategic human resource management**—mobilizing human capital through the HRM process to best implement organizational strategies.[6]

> **Human capital** is the economic value of people with job-relevant abilities, knowledge, ideas, energies, and commitments.

> **Strategic human resource management** mobilizes human capital to implement organizational strategies.

There are many career opportunities in human resource management. HRM departments are must-haves in most organizations. The job title of Chief Talent Officer is appearing in many senior executive suites. And, HRM specialists of many types are increasingly important in an employment environment complicated by legal issues, talent shortages, economic turmoil, new corporate strategies, changing social values, and more. Such complexity has led to the growth of HRM firms that provide expert services in recruiting, compensation, training, outplacement, HR data mining, and the like. The Society for Human Resource Management, or SHRM, is a professional organization dedicated to keeping its membership up to date in all aspects of HRM from fundamental practices to current events and issues.

The Office Sensationalized Dysfunction in Human Resource Management

© AF archive/Alamy

Want a laugh? Watch some old episodes of *The Office*. Want to learn what you shouldn't do as a manager? Watch some more. Although many of the politically incorrect situations may make you cringe, the show's diverse and outrageous characters also challenge us to think about how we could improve our workplaces. Almost every episode focuses attention on critical issues in human resource management. If you're willing to look behind the laughs, good answers to basic questions can be found. What behavior violates employment law? Should employees attend diversity training sessions? How can we do a better job of handling rivalries between colleagues? When does trying to be funny cross the line into being unprofessional?

Job discrimination occurs when someone is denied a job or job assignment for non-job-relevant reasons.

Equal employment opportunity (EEO) is the right to employment and advancement without regard to race, sex, religion, color, or national origin.

⦀ Government legislation protects against employment discrimination.

"Why didn't I get invited for a job interview? Is it because my first name is Omar?" "Why didn't I get that promotion? Is it because I'm so visibly pregnant?" If valuing people is at the heart of human resource management, **job discrimination** is the enemy. It occurs when an organization denies someone employment or a job assignment or an advancement opportunity for reasons that are not performance relevant.[7]

An important cornerstone of U.S. laws designed to protect workers from job discrimination is Title VII of the Civil Rights Act of 1964, amended by the Equal Employment Opportunity Act of 1972 and the Civil Rights Act (EEOA) of 1991. These acts provide for **equal employment opportunity (EEO)**, giving everyone the right to employment without regard to sex, race, color, national origin, or religion. It is illegal under Title VII to use any of these as criteria when making decisions about hiring, promoting, compensating, terminating, or otherwise changing someone's terms of employment.

Case to Consider: Wal-Mart v. Dukes When the U. S. Supreme Court ruled 5–4 in favor of Wal-Mart it set off a flurry of controversy.[8] The case was a class-action lawsuit filed on behalf of some 1.5 million women who claimed Wal-Mart violated Title VII of the Civil Rights Act by favoring men in pay and promotions. The ruling did not say that individual women had not been discriminated against; it said the "class" action did

Jacquelyn Martin/AP

not show a policy of company-wide discriminatory practices. A company press release stated: "Walmart has had strong policies against discrimination for many years . . . the plaintiffs' claims were worlds away from showing a companywide discriminatory pay and promotion policy." Writing for the minority, Justice Ruth Bader Ginsburg said: "Managers, like all humankind, may be prey to biases of which they are unaware. The risk of discrimination is heightened when those managers are predominantly of one sex, and are steeped in a corporate culture that perpetuates gender stereotypes."

Although the legal debates are still there, the intent of Title VII and equal employment opportunity is clear: To ensure everyone the right to gain and keep employment based only on their ability and job performance. The Equal Employment Opportunity Commission (EEOC) enforces the legislation through its federal power to file civil lawsuits against organizations that do not provide timely resolution of any discrimination charges lodged against them. These laws generally apply to all public and private organizations that employ 15 or more people.

Title VII also requires organizations to show **affirmative action** in their efforts to ensure equal employment opportunity for members of *protected groups*, those historically underrepresented in the workforce. Employers are expected to analyze existing workforce demographics, compare them with those in the relevant labor markets, and set goals for correcting any underrepresentation that might exist. These goals are supported by *affirmative action plans* that are designed to ensure that an organization's workforce represents women and minorities in proportion to their labor market availability.[9]

You are likely to hear discussion over the pros and cons of affirmative action. Critics tend to focus on the use of group membership, female or minority status, as a criterion in employment decisions.[10] The issues raised include claims of *reverse discrimination* toward members of majority populations. White males, for example, may claim that preferential treatment given to minorities in a particular situation interferes with their individual rights.

As a general rule, the legal protections of EEO do not restrict an employer's right to establish **bona fide occupational qualifications**. These are criteria for employment that an organization can clearly justify as relating to a person's capacity to perform a job. However, EEO bars the use of employment qualifications based on race and color under any circumstances; those based on sex, religion, and age are very difficult to support.[11]

Table 10.1 is a reminder that legal protection against employment discrimination is quite extensive. But we must still be realistic. Laws help, but this doesn't mean you will never be affected by employment discrimination.[12]

> **Affirmative action** is an effort to give preference in employment to women and minority group members.

> **Bona fide occupational qualifications** are employment criteria justified by capacity to perform a job.

Table 10.1 A Sample of U.S. Laws Against Employment Discrimination

- *Pay*—The Equal Pay Act of 1963 requires equal pay for women and men doing equal work. It describes equal work in terms of skills, responsibilities, and working conditions.
- *Age*—The Age Discrimination in Employment Act of 1967 as amended in 1978 and 1986 protects workers against mandatory retirement ages. Age discrimination occurs when a qualified individual is adversely affected by a job action that replaces him or her with a younger worker.
- *Pregnancy*—The Pregnancy Discrimination Act of 1978 protects female workers from discrimination because of pregnancy. A pregnant employee is protected against termination or adverse job action because of the pregnancy and is entitled to reasonable time off work.
- *Disabilities*—The Americans with Disabilities Act of 1990 as amended in 2008 prevents discrimination against people with disabilities. The law requires employment decisions be based on a person's abilities and what he or she can do.
- *Family matters*—The Family and Medical Leave Act of 1993 protects workers who take unpaid leaves for family matters from losing their jobs or employment status. Workers are allowed up to 12 weeks of leave for childbirth, adoption, personal illness, or illness of a family member.

Laws can't guarantee that employment discrimination will never happen.

Not too long ago, a woman wrote to the *Wall Street Journal* with this question: "I was interviewing for a sales job and the manager asked me what child care arrangements

I had made. . . . Was his question legal?" The answer, according to an employment attorney, is that the manager's question is "a perfect example of what not to ask a job applicant" and "could be considered direct evidence of gender bias against women based on negative stereotypes."[13]

Employee privacy is the right to privacy on and off the job.

One of the emerging areas of controversy in employment discrimination involves social media use and **employee privacy**—the rights of employees to privacy on and off the job.[14] Technology allows most employers to monitor telephone calls, e-mails, social media usage, and Internet searches to track your activities while on the job. The best advice on privacy at work is to assume you have none and act accordingly. But what about an employee's right to privacy *outside* work? While vacationing in Europe, a Florida teacher posted to her "private setting" Facebook pages photos that showed her drinking alcoholic beverages. After it came to the attention of school administrators, she was asked to resign. She did, but later filed a lawsuit stating her resignation was forced.[15] The number of such social media lawsuits is growing, and their resolutions may help clear up just what is and is not against the law in the nonwork zone of employee privacy.

Mark Wilson/Getty Images

Pay discrimination is against the law. So when Lilly Ledbetter was about to retire from Goodyear and realized that male co-workers were being paid more, she sued. She initially lost the case because the Supreme Court said she had waited too long to file the claim. But she was smiling when the Lilly Ledbetter Fair Pay Act became the very first bill signed by President Barack Obama. It expanded workers' rights to sue employers on equal pay issues. Obama said he signed it in honor not only of Lilly but also of his own grandmother, "who worked in a bank all her life, and even after she hit that glass ceiling, kept getting up again." When he signed the Lilly Ledbetter Fair Pay Act, President Obama said, "Making our economy work means making sure it works for everybody."[16]

Pay discrimination occurs when men and women are paid differently for doing equal work.

Pregnancy discrimination penalizes a woman in a job or as a job applicant for being pregnant.

How about **pregnancy discrimination**? It's also against the law, but pregnancy bias complaints filed with the U.S. Equal Employment Opportunity Commission are still common. A spokesperson for the National Partnership of Women & Families said that problems of pregnancy discrimination are "escalating" and require "national attention."[17] Recent scholary research paints a bleak picture as well. One study had actors playing roles of visibly pregnant and nonpregnant applicants for jobs as corporate attorneys and college professors. Results showed that interviewers were more negative toward the "pregnant" females, even making comments such as "she'll try to get out of doing work" and "she would be too moody."[18]

Age discrimination penalizes an employee in a job or as a job applicant for being over the age of 40.

Age discrimination, too, is against the law. But the EEOC is reporting an increased number of age bias complaints. Federal age discrimination laws protect employees aged 40 and up, and the proportion of workers in this age group is increasing with the "graying" of the American workforce. The possibility of age discrimination exists whenever an older worker is laid off or loses his or her job. But as one attorney points out: "There's always the fine line between what discrimination is and what is a legitimate business decision." About 20% of age discrimination suits result in some financial settlement in favor of the person filing the claim; however, this doesn't always include getting the job back. And, older workers often face tough job searches. Data indicate that unemployment for workers over 50 lasts 27 more weeks than for younger ones.[19]

STUDY GUIDE

Takeaway 10.1
What Are the Purpose and Legal Context of Human Resource Management?

Terms to Define

Affirmative action

Age discrimination

Bona fide occupational qualifications

Employee privacy

Equal employment opportunity (EEO)

Human capital

Human resource management (HRM)

Job discrimination

Pay discrimination

Pregnancy discrimination

Strategic human resource management

Rapid Review

- The human resource management process involves attracting, developing, and maintaining a quality workforce.
- Job discrimination occurs when someone is denied an employment opportunity for reasons that are not job relevant.
- Equal employment opportunity legislation guarantees people the right to employment and advancement without discrimination.
- Current legal issues in the work environment deal with workplace privacy, pay, pregnancy, and age, among other matters.

Questions for Discussion

1. How might the forces of globalization affect human resource management in the future?
2. Are current laws protecting American workers against discrimination in employment sufficient, or do we need additional ones?
3. What employee-rights issues and concerns would you add to those discussed here?

Be Sure You Can

- explain the purpose of human resource management
- differentiate job discrimination, equal employment opportunity, and affirmative action
- identify major U.S. laws protecting against employment discrimination
- explain the issues of workplace privacy that today's college graduates should be prepared to face

Career Situation: What Would You Do?

If you were appointed to a student committee asked to investigate gender equity in sports on your campus, what would you propose the committee look at? Based on your understanding of campus affairs, what changes would you suggest in athletic funding and administration to improve gender equity?

Takeaway 10.2
What Are the Essential Human Resource Management Practices?

ANSWERS TO COME

- The employee value proposition aligns people and organizations.
- Recruitment attracts qualified job applicants.
- Selection makes decisions to hire qualified job applicants.
- Socialization and orientation integrate new hires into an organization.
- Training continually develops employee skills and capabilities.
- Performance management reviews and rewards accomplishments.
- Retention and career development provide career paths.

THE FOCUS OF HUMAN RESOURCE MANAGEMENT IS ON TALENT, SEEKING TO ATTRACT and retain the right people so that an organization always has the best possible workforce. To do this, one must first know exactly what type of people and skill sets are needed. This requires a clear understanding of the jobs to be done and the talents people need to do them well. It also requires having the right systems in place—recruitment, selection, training, and performance management—so that jobs are always filled with enthusiastic and high-performing workers.

The employee value proposition aligns people and organizations.

The employee value **proposition**, or EVP, is the exchange of value between what the individual and the employer offer in the employment relationship.

The best place to start any discussion of human resource management is with the concept of an **employee value proposition,** or EVP. Think of it as an exchange of value, what the organization offers the employee in return for his or her work contributions.[20] The value offered by the individual includes things like effort, loyalty, commitment, creativity, and skills. The value offered by the employer includes things like pay, benefits, meaningful work, flexible schedules, and personal development opportunities.

Getting everything to come together with balance is the key issue for an employee value proposition. Each party needs to believe that the exchange of values is fair and that it is getting what it needs from the other. Any perceived imbalance among the components shown in the nearby figure is likely to cause problems. From the individual's side, a perceived lack of inducements from the employer may cause dissatisfaction, loss of motivation, and poor performance. From the employer's side, a perceived lack of contributions from the individual may cause a loss of confidence in and commitment to the employee as well as reduced rewards for work delivered.

Person-job fit is the match of individual skills, interests, and personal characteristics with the job.

Person-organization fit is the match of individual values, attitudes, and behavior with the organizational culture.

The foundation for a healthy and positive employee value proposition is "fit." **Person-job fit** is the extent to which an individual's skills, interests, and personal characteristics match well with the requirements of the job. **Person-organization fit** is the extent to which and individual's values, interests, and behavior are consistent with the culture of the organization. The importance of a good fit to

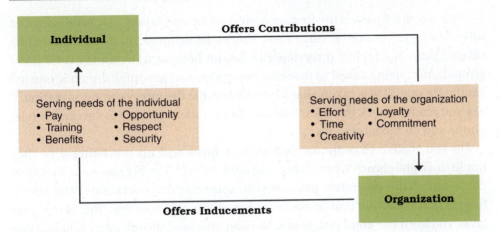

Serving needs of the individual
• Pay • Opportunity
• Training • Respect
• Benefits • Security

Serving needs of the organization
• Effort • Loyalty
• Time • Commitment
• Creativity

the employee value proposition is highlighted to the extreme at Zappos.com. Believe it or not, if a new employee is unhappy with the firm after going through initial training, Zappos pays them to quit. At last check the "bye-bye bounty" was $4,000, and some 2 to 3% of new hires were taking it each year.[21]

‖ Recruitment attracts qualified job applicants.

Employers engage in **recruitment** to attract a qualified pool of applicants to the organization. The word "qualified" is especially important here. Recruiting should bring employment opportunities to the attention of people whose skills, abilities, and interests meet job requirements. The process involves advertising the job, collecting a pool of applicants, and screening them to identify those who are most promising in terms of potential employability.

Recruiters now rely heavily on the Web to disseminate job openings and search for qualified applicants. Job boards like Monster.com and CareerBuilder.com are well-established destinations, but social media sites are becoming go-to-for-sure options. The founder of TheMuse.com, a career resource website, calls Twitter "the new elevator pitch."[22] Among young professionals, LinkedIn is still the top site for job seekers and employers alike. It's especially useful for "opportunistic" recruiting where potential—not necessarily active—candidates can keep credentials visible to employers who may be browsing résumés looking for their skill sets. Adobe, for example, fills as many as half of new hires through LinkedIn.

> **Recruitment** is a set of activities designed to attract a qualified pool of job applicants.

Words to the Wise: Online Job Seekers Need the Right Presentation Strategy

When you use the Web to disseminate your résumé, fill your online profile with key words that clearly display your skills as matches for employer interests. Most positings are read by computers, not people. Employers use special software to scan online profiles for key words that indicate real job skills and experiences that fit their needs. And, clean up your Web presence. Some one-third of executives in a CareerBuilder.com survey said information on social network sites caused them to not hire a job applicant.[23]

Jin Lee/Bloomberg/Getty Images

After a résumé passes the first screening, many employers now conduct a first interview by telephone or video chat. This make-or-break moment shouldn't be taken lightly. The typical interview can last an hour or more and cover a lot of ground. After being asked to describe her major past accomplishments, one job candidate said, "I was taken aback by how specific the interviewer was getting."[24] Are you ready? Check out Tips to Remember for ideas on how to succeed in telephone and online interviews.[25]

Do you realize that almost 50% of new hires end up not being sure they made the right choice when accepting a job offer?[26] The big reason is that they come out of the interview process with unrealistic expectations. The lesson here is that it's important to press for a **realistic job preview**. This is one that gives you both the good points and the bad points of the job and organization, and fully answers all your questions . . . before you make the decision to join or not.[27]

It's easy to be misled by an interviewer that adopts a traditional "tell-and-sell" approach, perhaps trying to hide or gloss over the potential negatives of the job, location, or employer. It's far better to get a realistic and full picture of the situation before, not after, you decide to accept an offer. Instead of "selling" only positive features, a realistic job preview tries to be open and balanced in describing favorable and unfavorable aspects of the job and organization.

How can you tell if you are getting a realistic job preview? The interviewer might use phrases such as "Of course, there are some downsides . . ." "Things don't always go the way we hope . . ." "Something that you will want to be prepared for is . . ." "We have found that some new hires had difficulty with . . ." If you don't hear these phrases, ask the tough questions yourself. The answers you get will help establish realistic job expectations and better prepare you for the inevitable ups and downs of a new job. Recruiters benefit too when new hires have higher levels of early job satisfaction and less inclination to quit prematurely.

Realistic job previews provide job candidates with all pertinent information about a job and organization.

{ YOUR IMPRESSION WILL BE MADE QUICKLY . . . DRESSING RIGHT INCREASES CONFIDENCE . . . FIND OUT HOW TO FOLLOW UP.

Tips to **Remember**

■ Steps to Success in Telephone and Online Interviews

- *Prepare ahead of time*—Study the organization; carefully list your strengths and capabilities; have materials ready for note taking.
- *Interview in private*—Make sure you are in a quiet room, with privacy and without the possibility of interruptions; turn smart phone and computer alerts off so that you are not interrupted.
- *Dress as a professional*—Don't be casual, even though at home; dressing right increases confidence and sets a tone for your side of the conversation.
- *Practice your interview "voice" and "screen presence"*— Your impression will be made quickly; how you sound and

look counts; speak slowly, look at the camera, and enunciate clearly; it helps to smile when you talk because it will change the tone of your voice.

- *Have reference materials handy*—Your résumé and other supporting documents should be within easy reach.
- *Have a list of questions ready*—Don't be caught unprepared; intersperse your best questions during the interview.
- *Ask what happens next*—Find out how to follow up by telephone or e-mail; ask what other information you can provide; ask about the time frame for a decision.
- *Follow up*—Don't forget to send a thank-you email to reiterate your interest in the job.

Selection makes decisions to hire qualified job applicants.

Once a good set of job candidates is identified, the employer's next step is to decide whom to hire. **Selection** involves choosing to hire applicants who offer the greatest performance potential. This is really an exercise in prediction—trying to anticipate whether the candidate will perform well once on the job. The typical sequence involves in-depth interviewing, some form of testing, perhaps a real-time assessment of how well the candidate works on actual or simulated job tasks, and background checks that may include Web searches and reviews of personal postings on social media sites.

It's quite common for job candidates to be asked to take employment tests. Some test job-specific knowledge and skills; others focus more on intelligence, aptitudes, personality, and even ethics. Regardless of the intent, any employment test should be both reliable and valid. **Reliability** means that the test provides a consistent measurement, returning the same results time after time. **Validity** means that the test score is a good predictor of future job performance, with a high score associated with high job performance and vice versa.

One of the popular developments in employment testing is the use of **assessment centers**. They allow recruiters to evaluate a person's job potential by observing his or her performance in experiential activities designed to simulate daily work. A related approach is **work sampling**, which asks candidates to work on actual job tasks while observers grade their performance. Google uses a form of this called "Code Jams." These are essentially contests that the firm runs to find the most brilliant software coders. Winners get financial prizes and job offers. Code Jams are held worldwide, and a company spokesperson says: "Wherever the best talent is, Google wants them."[28]

Socialization and orientation integrate new employees into the organization.

Once hired, a new member of any organization has to "learn the ropes" and become familiar with "the way things are done." **Socialization** is the process of influencing the expectations, behavior, and attitudes of a new hire in a desirable way. It begins with the human resource management practice of **orientation**— a set of activities designed to familiarize new employees with their jobs, co-workers, and key values, policies, and other aspects of the organization as a whole.

For years, Disney has been considered a master at socialization. During orientation at its Disney World Resort in Buena Vista, Florida, new employees learn the corporate culture. They also learn that the company places a premium on personality and expects all employees—from entertainers to ticket sellers to groundskeepers—"to make the customer happy." A Disney HRM specialist says: "We want people who are enthusiastic, who have pride in their work, who can take charge of a situation without supervision."[29]

Selection is choosing whom to hire from a pool of qualified job applicants.

Reliability means that a selection device gives consistent results over repeated measures.

Validity means that scores on a selection device have demonstrated links with future job performance.

An **assessment center** examines how job candidates handle simulated work situations.

Work sampling evaluates applicants as they perform actual work tasks.

Socialization systematically influences the expectations, behavior, and attitudes of new employees.

Orientation familiarizes new employees with jobs, co-workers, and organizational policies and services.

||| Training continually develops employee skills and capabilities.

At this point, you should probably be keeping a list of things to look for in your next employer. Here's a big one: a willingness to invest in training so that you are continuously learning and updating your job skills. Training is so important at Procter & Gamble that managers are rated on how well they train and develop those reporting to them. And, those that develop reputations as great trainers usually get the promotions.[30]

We all need training. But it's especially critical today because new knowledge and technologies quickly make so many of our existing skills obsolete. A great employer won't let this happen. Instead of trying to avoid training to save costs, it willingly spends on training as an investment in human resources.[31] This is a classic case of valuing employees as assets. In fact, you should probably ask questions about training opportunities in any job interview. And if the interviewer struggles for answers or evades the questions, you're getting a pretty good indication that the organization isn't likely to pass the "great employer" test.

One training approach you might inquire about is **coaching**. This is where an experienced person provides performance advice to someone else. Ideally, a new employee is assigned a coach who can model desired work behaviors and otherwise help him or her to learn and make progress. Sometimes, the best coach is the manager. At other times, it may be a co-worker.

You should also be interested in **mentoring**. This is where a new or early-career employee is assigned as a protégé to someone senior in his or her area of expertise, perhaps a high-level manager. Good mentoring programs can be a great boost to a newcomer's career. Mentors are supposed to take an interest in the junior person, provide guidance and advice on skills and career progress, and otherwise inform him or her about how one gets ahead careerwise in the organization.

Some employers are using **reverse mentoring** where younger employees mentor seniors. A good example is technology-savvy Gen Ys tutoring their seniors on how to use social media in their jobs. Reverse mentoring programs are not only informative for senior managers, but they also provide younger employees with an important sense of buy-in and contribution. One human resource management consultant says: "It's exactly the kind of thing that's needed today because Gen Y-rs really want to be involved."[32]

Coaching occurs as an experienced person offers performance advice to a less-experienced person.

Mentoring assigns early-career employees as protégés to more senior ones.

In **reverse mentoring**, younger and newly hired employees mentor senior executives, often on latest developments with digital technologies.

Does Success Come from Hard Work, Luck, or a Bit of Both?

John Turner/Stone/Getty Images

A survey of LinkedIn members in 15 countries reports that 84% believe that luck influences their careers—both to the good and bad. They also say that luck is something we create for ourselves and that good luck tends to come to those who have a strong work ethic. Things believed to drive good luck include communication skills, networking, being flexible, and acting on opportunities when they arise.

Performance management reviews and rewards accomplishments.

Once a person is hired and on the job, one of the important functions of HRM is performance management. This involves using various techniques of **performance review** or **performance appraisal** to formally assess and give feedback on someone's work accomplishments.[33] The purposes of a performance review are twofold. First, it measures and documents performance for the record. Second, it initiates a process of development that can improve performance in the future.[34] For an appraisal method to serve these two purposes with credibility, it must satisfy the same reliability and validity criteria as do employment tests.[35]

The **graphic rating scale** is one of the most basic performance review methods. Think of it as a checklist or scorecard for rating an employee on criteria such as work quality, attendance, and punctuality. Although simple and quick, graphic rating scales have questionable reliability and validity. They should probably be used only along with additional appraisal tools.

The **behaviorally anchored rating scale (BARS)** is a more advanced approach to performance review. It describes actual behaviors that exemplify various levels of performance achievement in a job. The example in **Figure 10.1** shows a BARS for a customer service representative. Note that "Extremely poor" performance is described with the behavioral anchor "treats a customer rudely and with disrespect." Because the BARS relates performance assessments to specific descriptions of work behavior, it is more reliable and valid than the graphic rating scale. The behavioral anchors can also be used for training in job skills and objectives.

Performance review or appraisal is the process of formally evaluating performance and providing feedback to a jobholder.

A **graphic rating scale** uses a checklist of traits or characteristics to evaluate performance.

A **behaviorally anchored rating scale (BARS)** uses specific descriptions of actual behaviors to rate various levels of performance.

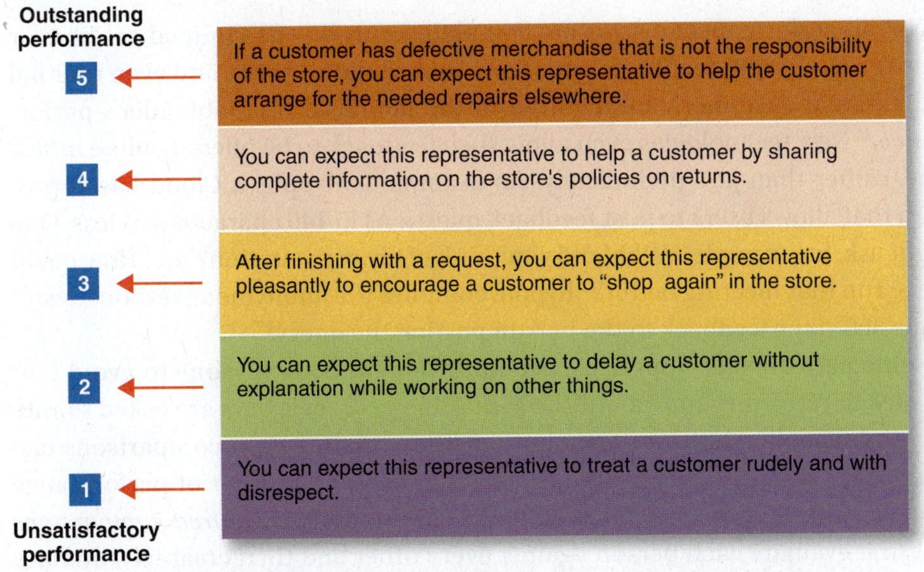

FIGURE 10.1 What Does a Behaviorally Anchored Rating Scale Look Like?
A *behaviorally anchored rating scale (BARS)* uses actual descriptions of positive and negative job behaviors to anchor rating points. In this example of how a customer service representative handles a merchandise return, various alternative behaviors are clearly identified. Consistent and documented rude or disrespectful behavior toward customers by a salesperson would earn a rating of "extremely poor." This specificity makes the BARS more reliable and valid.

{ **ONLY 3% OF HRM EXECUTIVES GIVE "A" GRADES TO THEIR FIRMS' PERFORMANCE MEASUREMENT SYSTEMS.**

Facts to **Consider**

■ Human Resource Executives Worry About Performance Measurement

A survey of human resource executives published in the *Wall Street Journal* reveals they aren't pleased with the way managers in their organizations do performance reviews. Some are so concerned that they suggest dropping reviews altogether. Among survey findings:

- 30% of the HR executives believed that employees trust their employer's performance measurement system.
- 40% rated their performance review systems as B, and only 3% rated them as A.
- Many were concerned that managers aren't willing to face employees and give constructive feedback.

- Many also complained that employees don't have a clear enough understanding of what rates as good and bad performance.

YOUR THOUGHTS?

Performance measurement is often a hot topic these days as things like "merit pay" and "performance accountability" are discussed in many job settings. Based on your experience, what should be done about it? Is it really possible to have a performance measurement system that is respected by all? Can a performance review be accomplished in ways good for employers and workers alike?

The **critical-incident technique** keeps a log of someone's effective and ineffective job behaviors.

360° feedback includes superiors, subordinates, peers, and even customers in the appraisal process.

A **multiperson comparison** compares one person's performance with that of others.

The **critical-incident technique** keeps an actual log of a person's effective and ineffective job behaviors. Using the case of the customer service representative again, a critical-incident log might include this *positive example*: "Took extraordinary care of a customer who had purchased a defective item from a company store in another city." Or, it might include this *negative example*: "Acted rudely in dismissing the complaint of a customer who felt that we mistakenly advertised a sale item."

Not all performance reviews are completed only by one's immediate boss or team leader. In **360° feedback**, superiors, subordinates, peers, and even internal and external customers are involved in the appraisal of a jobholder's performance.[36] New technologies even allow such feedback to be offered online in real time, rather than just periodically. An example is Rypple, a Cloud-based program that allows users to post feedback questions in 140 characters or less. One might ask, for example, "What did you think of my presentation?" or "How could I have run that meeting better?" Rypple compiles the anonymous responses and sends 360°-type feedback to the person posting the query.[37]

Some performance appraisals use **multiperson comparisons** to avoid tendencies to rate everyone "about the same." Instead, reviewers are asked to rate and rank people relative to one another. These multiperson comparisons can be done by *rank-ordering* people from top to bottom in order of performance achievement, with no ties allowed. They can be done by *paired comparisons* that first evaluate each person against every other and then create a summary ranking based on the number of superior scores. Or, they can be done by a *forced distribution* that places each person into a frequency distribution with fixed performance classifications—such as top 10%, next 40%, next 40%, and bottom 10%.

‖ Retention and career development provide career paths.

It seems a no-brainer that employers are foolish after a successful recruitment campaign to neglect efforts to retain the best employees for as long as possible. Yet many fail the test. Sometimes it's a problem with compensation and benefits. But often it's an issue of **career development**—the process of managing how a person grows and progresses from one point in a career to the next.

After initial entry, career paths can take off in many directions. Lots of choices will have to be made about promotions, transfers, training, mentors, higher degrees, even alternative employment and eventual retirement. Ideally, the employer and the individual work closely together in making these choices. Procter & Gamble's global human resources officer, Moheet Nagrath, says his company builds career tracks to match individual goals with company needs. If someone wants to become a top manager someday, the company will plot career moves through jobs in various brands as well as domestic and international assignments. "If you train people to work in different countries and businesses," he says, "you develop a deep bench."[38]

With more people now changing jobs frequently and working as independent contractors and freelancers, career development is becoming more and more a personal responsibility. This means that we each have to be diligent in **career planning**, the process of systematically matching career goals and individual capabilities with opportunities for their fulfillment. It involves regularly asking and answering such questions as "Who am I?" "What can I do?" "Where do I want to go?" and "How do I get there?"

> **Career development** is the process of managing how a person grows and progresses in a career.

> **Career planning** is the process of matching career goals and individual capabilities with opportunities for their fulfillment.

{ **MANAGERS SHOULD BE THOROUGHLY PROFESSIONAL IN ALL ASPECTS OF HUMAN RESOURCE MANAGEMENT.**

Explore **Yourself**

■ Professionalism

Chances are that your school has a student branch of the Society for Human Resource Management. It's a great example of how **professionalism** plays a role in management. When students work together on SHRM projects, they are not just learning HRM techniques and practices. They are also learning to behave with internalized commitments to external standards.

All managers should show professionalism in their own areas of expertise and work responsibility. And, of course, they should be thoroughly professional in all aspects of human resource management discussed in this chapter—from recruiting and selecting new hires, to training and developing them, to appraising performance, to handling issues like compensation and work-life balance.

> Get to know yourself better by taking the self-assessment on **Performance Appraisal Assumptions** and completing the other activities in the *Exploring Management* **Skill-Building Portfolio.**

Manager's **Library**

THE MOST GLOBALLY MINDED AND CONNECTED OF ALL?

Members of the Millennial generation, known as Generation Y, have grown up in the midst of explosive technological growth, as well as global change and turmoil. And, they hold attitudes about work and life that can be quite different from those of their parents. The fascination with Millennials has many, including those who manage them, trying to understand just who these ambitious young people are and what matters most to them.

Millennials draw their fair share of criticism, living with labels like "spoiled," "entitled," and "impatient." Yet, they are having quite an impact on business, technology, politics, and beyond. They are also at the forefront of causes and issues ranging from climate crisis to education and poverty to immigration to marriage equality.

In his book, *Fast Future: How the Millennial Generation is Shaping Our World* (2013, Beacon Press), David Burstein—a Millennial thought leader and author—portrays his cohort through well-crafted eyes. With the desire to accurately describe his generation, Burstein conducted extensive research and interviewed a broad range of Millennial peers. His book paints a picture of a diverse, tech-savvy, and empowered generation of young people whose story needed to be told, as he says, "in our own words."

The book's title, *Fast Future*, focuses attention on the environment in which Millennials have come of age—global awareness, constant connectedness, and many available media platforms in which to share their lives and personal stories. Burstein believes Millennials not only understand the new "operating system" that governs the world in which they live, but they are also continuing to script it in new variations.

Despite facing one of the country's worst recessions in history at the start of their careers, they seem quite able to seamlessly navigate the challenges faced. Why? Burstein claims it's because they know the rules and have the right tools. In his words, Millennials like himself are "masters of and can operate in this fast-changing future world . . . there are more things we can do than things we cannot."

REFLECT AND REACT

Does Burstein's view of the Millennial generation seem accurate? What else could you add to his story line? Why are Millennials often judged and labeled a bit harshly by older generations? Some, perhaps many, Millennials reject the need to have a traditional career. They seem more interested in creating, adapting, and moving in and out of different career options. Does this apply to you?

Some suggest that we should view a career as something to be rationally planned and pursued in a careful step-by-step fashion. Others argue for flexibility, allowing a career to unfold along different pathways as we respond to unexpected opportunities. But think about it. A well-managed career will probably include elements of each. A carefully thought-out career plan helps point you in a clear direction; an eye for opportunity helps fill in the details as you proceed along the way. Are you ready?

STUDY GUIDE

Takeaway 10.2
What Are the Essential Human Resource Management Practices?

Terms to Define

Assessment center

Behaviorally anchored rating scale (BARS)

Career development

Career planning

Coaching

Critical-incident technique

Employee value proposition (EVP)

Graphic rating scale

Mentoring

Multiperson comparison

Orientation

Performance appraisal

Performance review

Person-job fit

Person-organization fit

Realistic job preview

Recruitment

Reliability

Reverse mentoring

Selection

Socialization

360° feedback

Validity

Work sampling

Rapid Review

- Recruitment is the process of attracting qualified job candidates to fill vacant positions; realistic job previews try to provide candidates with accurate information on the job and organization.
- Assessment centers and work sampling that mimic real job situations are increasingly common selection techniques.
- Orientation is the process of formally introducing new employees to their jobs and socializing them to the culture and performance expectations.
- Training keeps workers' skills up to date and job relevant; important training approaches include coaching and mentoring.
- Performance appraisal methods include graphic rating scales, behaviorally anchored rating scales, the critical-incidents technique, 360° feedback, and multi-person comparisons.
- Employee retention programs try to keep skilled workers in jobs and on career paths satisfying to them and beneficial to the employer.

Questions for Discussion

1. Is it realistic to expect that you can get a realistic job preview during the interview process?
2. If a new employer doesn't formally assign someone to be your coach or mentor, what should you do?
3. What are some of the possible downsides to receiving 360° feedback?

Be Sure You Can

- list steps in the recruitment process
- explain realistic job previews
- illustrate reliability and validity in employment testing
- illustrate how an assessment center might work
- explain the importance of socialization and orientation
- describe coaching and mentoring as training approaches
- discuss strengths and weaknesses of alternative performance appraisal methods

Career Situation: What Would You Do?

After taking a new job as head of retail merchandising at a department store, you are disappointed to find that the salesclerks are evaluated on a graphic rating scale. It uses a simple list of traits to gauge their performance. You want to propose an alternative and better approach that will make performance reviews really valuable. Your boss says: "Give me a plan." Exactly what will you suggest in your proposal, and how will you present it to the salesclerks as well as the boss?

Takeaway 10.3

What Are Current Issues in Human Resource Management?

ANSWERS TO COME

- Today's lifestyles increase demands for flexibility and work-life balance.
- Organizations use more independent contractors and part-time workers.
- Compensation plans influence employee recruitment and retention.
- Fringe benefits are an important part of employee compensation packages.
- Labor relations and collective bargaining are closely governed by law.

"HIRING GOOD PEOPLE IS TOUGH," STARTS AN ARTICLE IN THE *HARVARD BUSINESS REVIEW*. The sentence finishes with "keeping them can be even tougher."[39] The point is that it isn't enough to hire and train workers to meet an organization's immediate needs. They must also be successfully nurtured, supported, and retained. When the Society for Human Resource Management surveyed employers, it learned that popular tools for maintaining a quality workforce included flexible work schedules and personal time off, as well as competitive salaries and good benefits—especially health insurance.[40]

▌▌▌ Today's lifestyles increase demands for flexibility and work-life balance.

E-mail from working dad to team members—"Folks, can I propose a slight change? I decided to work from home this morning so I could take my toddler to day care and help my wife with our newborn . . . May I suggest a conference call? Dial-in information below."[41]

Fast-paced and complicated lifestyles raise concerns about **work-life balance**. You have or will soon encounter it as the balance—or lack of balance—between the demands of careers and personal and family needs.[42] Not surprisingly, the "family-friendliness" of an employer is now frequently used as a screening criterion by job candidates. It is also used in "best employer" rankings by magazines such as *Business Week*, *Working Mother*, and *Fortune*.

Work-life balance improves when we have flexibility in scheduling work hours, work locations, and even such things as vacations and personal time off. This helps manage both personal needs and work responsibilities. The results can be good for both the individual—greater job satisfaction, and the employer—less intention to leave.[43] About four out of five employees say they would like the work-at-home or telecommuting option and consider it a "significant job perk."[44] But, employers also worry that too much flexibility disrupts schedules and causes a loss of important face-to-face work time.[45] Marisa Mayer, Yahoo!'s CEO, was willing to face criticism when she decided to disallow telecommuting. Her reasoning was that working from home detracted from Yahoo!'s collaborative culture and ability to innovate.[46]

Employers have many options for increasing job flexibility and work-life balance. Some directly help workers handle family matters by providing such

Work-life balance involves balancing career demands with personal and family needs.

things as on-site day care and elder care. Some have moved into innovative programs that include work sabbaticals—Schwab offers four weeks after five years' employment; unlimited vacation days—Netflix lets workers take as many vacation days as they want; purchased vacation time—Xerox allows workers to buy vacation days using payroll deductions; and on-call doctors—Microsoft sends doctors to employees' homes to keep them out of emergency rooms.[47] The accounting firm KPMG goes so far as to keep a "wellness scorecard" on employees to see if they are missing vacations or working too hard. If so, they are contacted by supervisors to discuss work patterns and ways to slow down.[48]

⫼ Organizations are using more independent contractors and part-time workers.

Don't be surprised if you are asked some day to work only "as needed," as a "freelancer," or as an **independent contractor**. This means you are expected to work for an agreed-upon period or for an agreed-upon task, and without becoming part of the permanent workforce. You may be paid well, but there's no job security.

Another trend, and the source of most new jobs being created in the U.S. economy, is the growing use of temporary and part-time workers. We call them **contingency workers** because they supplement the full-time workforce by

> **Independent contractors** are hired on temporary contracts and are not part of the organization's permanent workforce.

> **Contingency workers** work as needed and part-time, often on a longer-term basis.

Julie Jacobson/AP

{ AFTER THE FIFTH TIME OF LENGTHY DELAYS AT LOS ANGELES INTERNATIONAL AIRPORT, GOLDBERG HAD AN "AHA MOMENT."

Role Models

■ Family Values Lead CEO Dave Goldberg to Survey Monkey

If you've ever created or taken an online survey using Survey Monkey, you know how good it feels to say goodbye to paper questionnaires and the accompanying task of tallying and making sense of results. All of the *Fortune* 100 companies agree—they're users too. Dave Goldberg, CEO of Survey Monkey, has grown the Web survey solutions and analytics provider to over 12 million registered users worldwide. He and his wife, Sheryl Sandberg, Chief Operating Officer of Facebook, are a well-known power couple with two young children.

Already a successful entrepreneur and venture capitalist, Goldberg had family in mind when he decided to join Survey Monkey, founded by Ryan Finley. In an article entitled "Hard Choices," he tells *Business Week* that when his wife joined Facebook and knowing her job would require some travel, he decided to pass up a number of other opportunities and go with Survey Monkey. He wanted at least one parent to be at home with the children every night.

For a while Goldberg commuted from Los Angeles to Silicon Valley. But after the fifth time of lengthy delays at Los Angeles International Airport, he had an "aha moment." More was needed to balance his work-life equation. Goldberg moved

Survey Monkey from Portland, Oregon to Silicon Valley, giving him greater flexibility and more time with family.

Matching career demands with personal and family needs is what work-life balance is all about—and specifically what Goldberg and wife Sheryl Sandberg work hard to accomplish. For her part, Sandberg set off quite a stir in the tech world when she admitted to an interviewer that she leaves work daily at 5:30 p.m. to be home for dinner with her family. "I did that when I was at Google, I did that here, and I would say it's not until the last year, two years that I'm brave enough to talk about it publicly," she says.

WHAT'S THE LESSON HERE?

Employers have become increasingly aware that "balance" is important to today's employees. Goldberg and Sandberg have found ways to balance things as senior executives. But, what can a regular worker and dual-career couple do? Is asking for flexibility and respect for family life something to hide or be ashamed of in today's competitive work environment? What will your priorities be when it comes to the work-life balancing act?

working as-needed and part-time, often on a long-term basis. Their increasing presence in the workforce leads some to say a "permanent temp economy" is the new reality for job hunters.[49] And, employers tend to like it because contingency workers are easy to hire and fire to control costs and respond to cyclical demand.[50]

BusinessWeek sums the employer's advantage in hiring part-timers this way: "easy to lay off, no severance; no company funded retirement plan; pay own health insurance; get zero sick days and no vacation."[51] Things can be a lot less rosy for the part-timers. They may be paid less than full-timers, experience stress due to their temporary job status, and lack access to benefits such as health insurance, pension plans, and paid vacations. Gerry Grabowski of Pittsburgh knows the downside and the upside firsthand. But with initiative he turned a temporary job in real estate into a full-time one. Says Grabowski: "A lot of people say it's a raw deal, and I guess it can be. But if I were an entrepreneur, I would never do a straight hire. I would use a contractor or temp first."[52]

||| Compensation plans influence employee recruitment and retention.

Pay! It may be that no other work issue receives as much attention. And, the trend in compensation today is largely toward "pay-for-performance."[53] Pay increases for those on a **merit pay** system are based on some assessment of actual performance. A high merit raise sends a positive signal to high performers, whereas a low one sends a negative signal to poor performers. The notion is that this encourages both to work hard in the future.

Although the pay-for-performance logic makes sense, merit systems are not problem free. In many ways they are only as good as the methods used to measure

Merit pay awards pay increases in proportion to performance contributions.

Jacopo Raule/Getty Images

{ **$96.1 MILLION FOR ONE YEARS WORK! . . . CEOs EARN 354 TIMES MORE THAN THE AVERAGE WORKER**

Ethics Check

■ CEO Gets $96.1 Million Pay Package

That's $96.1 million for one year's work by the way! The person behind the paycheck is Oracle CEO Larry Ellison. Is something wrong here? Or, is this a motivator to make your career plan a real success story?

Richard Trumka, president of the AFL-CIO, thinks CEO pay is way out of whack. His organization is the largest federation of trade unions in the United States, 56 unions in all, and it's a voice for workers. Trumpka says: "They struggle every day to make ends meet, their wages are stagnant, their companies are trying to take away their health care and pensions, and they're angry." Little wonder that he and his organization are critical of big executive paychecks.

The AFL-CIO reports that while CEOs of the largest firms took in an average of $12.3 million in 2012, the average worker in their firms earned just $34,645. In simple math, the

CEOs outearned the workers by 354 times. That's a bit less than the 525 times reported in 2000, but a lot more than the 42 times in 1980. By comparison, Trumpka's pay as president of AFL-CIO was 8.7 times the average worker's pay, a total of $302,000.

YOU DECIDE

Can you justify the super pay earned by CEOs like Larry Ellison? Is it right that CEO pay is so much higher in proportion to that earned by workers in general? Trumka has asked for regulations to enforce a Wall Street reform rule that requires companies listed on stock exchanges to reveal CEO versus worker pay comparisons. Do you support his position? Should caps be put in place on CEO pay? Or, is CEO pay better left to market forces and kept outside regulatory oversight?

performance. And this is a problem. A survey reported by the *Wall Street Journal* found that only 23% of employees believed they understood their companies' systems.[54] Typical questions are: Who assesses performance? Suppose the employee doesn't agree with the assessment? Is the system fair and equitable to everyone involved? Is there enough money available to make the merit increases meaningful for those who receive them?

When Brian Bader attended an orientation for his new tech-support job at Apple, he and others were told not to discuss their pay with co-workers. With curiosity aroused, he learned from break time chats that most everyone was getting between $10 and 12 an hour. His $12 pay compared well. But just three months later he quit . . . after getting a pay raise. Even though his performance was rated twice that of the lowest performer, the raise was just 20% higher. "It irked me," he said, "why am I not seeing double the pay?"[55]

While some employers struggle with merit pay plans, others use them well. If you are one of the high-performing employees that Applebee's managers want to retain, you might be on the receiving end of "Applebucks"— small cash awards that are given to reward performance and raise loyalty to the firm.[56] This is an example of **bonus pay**—one-time or lump-sum payments to employees based on the accomplishment of specific performance targets or some other extraordinary contribution, such as an idea for a work improvement. Perhaps you will someday receive a letter like one sent to two top executives by Amazon.com's chairman Jeff Bezos. "In recognition and appreciation of your contributions," his letter read, "Amazon.com will pay you a special bonus in the amount of $1,000,000."[57]

> **Bonus pay** plans provide one-time payments based on performance accomplishments.

In contrast to giving outright bonuses, **profit sharing** distributes to employees a proportion of net profits earned by the organization in a performance period. **Gain sharing** extends the profit-sharing concept by allowing groups of employees to share in any savings or "gains" realized when their efforts result in measurable cost reductions or productivity increases.[58]

> **Profit sharing** distributes to employees a proportion of net profits earned by the organization.

Yet another merit pay approach is to grant employees **stock options** linked to their performance.[59] Stock options give them the right to buy shares of stock at a future date at a fixed price. Employees holding options gain financially when the stock price rises above the original option price; they lose when it moves lower. Some companies "restrict" the stock options so that they come due only after designated periods of employment. This practice is meant to tie high performers to the employer and is often called the *golden handcuff*.

> **Gain sharing** allows employees to share in cost savings or productivity gains realized by their efforts.

> **Stock options** give the right to purchase shares at a fixed price in the future.

⫴ Fringe benefits are an important part of employee compensation packages.

Benefits! They rank right up there with pay as a way of helping to attract and retain workers. How many times does a graduating college student hear, "Be sure to get a job with benefits!"?[60]

An employee's **fringe benefits** include nonmonetary forms of compensation such as health insurance and retirement plans. And, they can be a hot button in conversations about work today. Benefits, especially medical insurance and retirement, can add as much as 20% or more to a typical worker's earnings, but the cost to employers can increase faster than the cost of wages and salaries.

> **Fringe benefits** are nonmonetary forms of compensation such as health insurance and retirement plans.

Zumba at work? More Employers and Employees Dance to the Tune of Wellness Benefits.

NBC NewsWire/Getty Images

Want to take a work break? Try employer-sponsored Zumba. True enough. More and more employers are focusing their benefits contributions on things that can help the bottom line, and employee wellness is one of them. That's why employees at Dallas/Forth Worth International Airport get their Zumba class as a perk. Other benefits include "lunch and learn" seminars on healthy eating and handling chronic diseases. As just one measure of success, the airport notes that the number of sick days fell by 47% in a year. Employer surveys also show increasing use of work-at-home policies, lactation rooms, legal counseling, and paid or subsidized off-site fitness.

Family-friendly benefits help employees achieve better work-life balance.

Flexible benefits programs allow choice to personalize benefits within a set dollar allowance.

Employee assistance programs help employees cope with personal stresses and problems.

A **labor union** is an organization that deals with employers on the workers' collective behalf.

Fringe benefits costs are a major worry for employers. Many are attempting to gain control over health care expenses by shifting more of the insurance costs to the employee and by restricting options in choosing health care providers. Many are offering wellness programs and encouraging healthy lifestyles as a way of decreasing health insurance claims. As pointed out earlier, many are also hiring part-timers to minimize benefit costs or avoid them altogether.

A variety of **family-friendly benefits** are designed to help employees with work-life balance. These include child care, elder care, flexible schedules, and parental leave among others. Also popular are **flexible benefits** that give employees budgets to choose a set of benefits that best meet their needs. There are also **employee assistance programs** that help with troublesome personal problems, such as dealing with stress, counseling on alcohol and substance abuse, domestic violence and sexual abuse, and family and marital difficulties.

Labor relations and collective bargaining are closely governed by law.

Labor unions are organizations to which workers belong and that deal with employers on the workers' behalf. They act as a collective "voice" for their members, one that wouldn't be available to them as individuals. Historically, this voice of the unions has played an important role in American society. And even though unions are often associated with wage and benefit concerns, workers also join unions because of things like poor relationships with supervisors, favoritism or lack of respect by supervisors, little or no influence with employers, and failure of employers to provide a mechanism for grievance and dispute resolution.[61]

The average percentage of workers in the United States who belong to unions has been on the decline. Figures show that 11.3% of workers overall now belong to unions versus 14.9% in 1996. The percentage of public-sector workers who belong to unions—teachers, police, firefighters, and local government employees—now stands at 35.6% of workers versus 6% in the private sector.[62] What do you think? Does the decline in private-sector union membership mean that workers have pretty much decided they don't need union representation anymore? Just what explains the downword trend? And, why is union membership increasing in the public sector?

Unions negotiate legal contracts affecting many aspects of the employment relationship for their members. These **labor contracts** typically specify the rights and obligations of employees and management with respect to wages, work hours, work rules, seniority, hiring, grievances, and other conditions of work.

The front line in labor-management relationship is **collective bargaining**, the process that brings management and union representatives together in negotiating, administering, and interpreting labor contracts. During a collective bargaining session, these parties exchange a variety of demands, proposals, and counterproposals. Several rounds of bargaining may take place before a contract is reached or a dispute resolved. Sometimes the process breaks down, and one or both parties walk away. The impasse can be short or lengthy, in some cases leading to labor actions that can last months and even years before agreements are reached.

One of the areas where unions and employers can find themselves on different sides of the bargaining issue relates to so-called **two-tier wage systems**. These are systems that pay new hires less than more senior workers already doing the same jobs. Agreeing to a two-tier system in collective bargaining isn't likely to be the preference of union negotiators. At a Goodyear factory in Alabama where a two-tiered system is in place, one of the high-seniority workers says: "If I was doing the same job, working just as hard and earning what they make, I'd be resentful."[63] But, the management side offers a counter argument. Getting a two-tier agreement in the labor contract can help keep the firm profitable and retain jobs in America that would otherwise be lost to foreign outsourcing. Such agreements are now in place at all the big U.S. automakers.[64]

When labor-management relations take on the adversarial character shown in **Figure 10.2**, the conflict can be prolonged and costly for both sides. That's not good for anyone, and there is quite a bit of pressure these days for more cooperative union-management relationships. Wouldn't it be nice if unions and management would work together in partnership, trying to address the concerns of both parties in ways that best meet the great challenges and competitive pressures of a global economy?

A **labor contract** is a formal agreement between a union and an employer about the terms of work for union members.

Collective bargaining is the process of negotiating, administering, and interpreting a labor contract.

Two-tier wage systems pay new hires less than workers already doing the same jobs with more seniority.

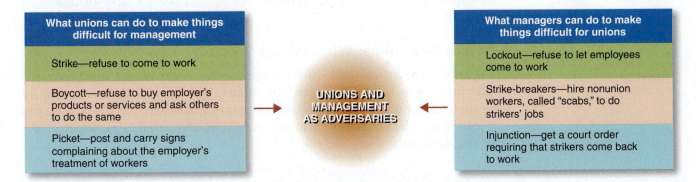

FIGURE 10.2 What Happens When Labor–Management Relations Become Adversarial?
When union and management representatives meet in collective bargaining, it would be nice if things were always cooperative. Unfortunately, they sometimes turn adversarial, and each side has weapons at its disposal to make things hard for the other. Unions can resort to strikes, boycotts, and picketing. Management can use lockouts, strike-breakers, and court injunctions to force strikers back to work. Although each side can find justifications in defense of using such tactics, they can also come with high price tags in terms of lost worker earnings and company profits.

STUDY GUIDE

Takeaway 10.3
What Are Current Issues in Human Resource Management?

Rapid Review

- Complex job demands and family responsibilities have made work-life balance programs increasingly important in human resource management.
- Compensation and benefits packages must be attractive so that an organization stays competitive in labor markets.
- Labor unions are organizations to which workers belong and that deal with employers on the employees' behalf.
- Collective bargaining is the process of negotiating, administering, and interpreting a labor contract.
- Labor relations and collective bargaining are closely governed by law and can be cooperative or adversarial in nature.

Questions for Discussion

1. Are we giving too much attention these days to issues of work-life balance?
2. Can a good argument be made that merit pay just doesn't work?
3. Given economic trends, is it likely that unions will gain in future popularity?

Be Sure You Can

- define work-life balance and discuss its significance for the human resource management process
- explain why compensation and benefits are important in human resource management
- differentiate bonuses and profit sharing as forms of performance-based pay
- define the terms "labor union," "labor contract," and "collective bargaining"
- compare the adversarial and cooperative approaches to labor-management relations

Career Situations: What Would You Do?

You have become aware of a drive to organize the faculty of your institution and have them represented by a union. The student leaders on campus are holding a forum to gather opinions on the pros and cons of a unionized faculty. Because you represent a student organization in your college, you are asked to participate in the forum. What will you say, and why?

Answers to TestPrep questions can be found at the back of the book.

Multiple-Choice Questions

1. Human resource management is the process of _____, developing, and maintaining a high-quality workforce.

   (a) attracting

   (b) compensating

   (c) appraising

   (d) selecting

2. A _____ is a criterion that organizations can legally justify for use in screening job candidates.

   (a) job description

   (b) bona fide occupational qualification

   (c) realistic job preview

   (d) BARS

3. _____ programs are designed to ensure equal employment opportunities for groups historically underrepresented in the workforce.

   (a) Realistic recruiting

   (b) Mentoring

   (c) Affirmative action

   (d) Coaching

4. Which of the following questions can an interviewer legally ask a job candidate during a telephone interview?

   (a) Are you pregnant or planning to soon start a family?

   (b) What skills do you have that would help you do this job really well?

   (c) Will you be able to work at least ten years before hitting the retirement age?

   (d) Do you get financial support from a spouse or companion who is also a wage earner?

5. An employment test that yields different results over time when taken by the same person lacks _____.

   (a) validity   (b) reliability

   (c) realism   (d) behavioral anchors

6. Which phrase is most consistent with a recruiter offering a job candidate a realistic job preview?

   (a) "There are just no downsides to this job."

   (b) "No organization is as good as this one."

   (c) "I can't think of any negatives."

   (d) "Here's something you might not like about the job."

7. Socialization of newcomers occurs during the _____ step of the staffing process.

   (a) orientation

   (b) recruiting

   (c) selection

   (d) advertising

8. The assessment center approach to employee selection uses on _____ to evaluate a candidate's job skills.

   (a) intelligence tests

   (b) simulations and experiential exercises

   (c) 360° feedback

   (d) formal one-on-one interviews

9. The selection technique known as _____ asks a job candidate to actually perform on the job for a period of time while being observed by a recruiter.

   (a) mentoring

   (b) work sampling

   (c) job coaching

   (d) critical incident testing

10. The _____ purpose of performance review is being addressed when a manager describes training options that might help an employee improve future performance.

(a) development

(b) evaluation

(c) judgmental

(d) legal

11. When a team leader must rate 10% of team members as "superior," 80% as "good," and 10% as "unacceptable," this is an example of the _____ approach to performance appraisal.

(a) graphic

(b) critical-incident

(c) behaviorally anchored rating scale

(d) forced distribution

12. What is one of the reasons why employers are hiring more part-time or contingency workers?

(a) It's hard to get people to work full-time anymore.

(b) Part-timers are known to work much harder than full-timers.

(c) Full-time employees don't have up-to-date job skills.

(d) It's easy to hire part-timers when you need them and let them go when you don't.

13. Whereas bonus plans pay employees for special accomplishments, gain-sharing plans reward them for _____.

(a) helping to recruit new workers

(b) regular attendance

(c) positive work attitudes

(d) cost reductions that have been achieved

14. An employee with family problems that are starting to interfere with work would be pleased to learn that his employer had a(n) _____ plan.

(a) employee assistance

(b) flexible benefits

(c) comparable worth

(d) stock options

15. When representatives of management and a labor union meet and negotiate the terms of a new labor contract, this process is known as _____.

(a) boycotting

(b) collective bargaining

(c) 360° feedback

(d) profit sharing

Short-Response Questions

16. Why is orientation important in the HRM process?

17. How does mentoring work as an on-the-job training approach?

18. When is an employment test or a performance appraisal method reliable?

19. How do the graphic rating scale and the BARS differ as performance appraisal methods?

Integration and Application Question

20. Sy Smith is not doing well in his job. The problems began to appear shortly after Sy's job changed from a manual to a computer-based operation. He has tried hard but is just not doing well in learning how to use the computer to meet performance expectations. He is 45 years old and has been with the company for 18 years. Sy has been a great worker in the past and is both popular and influential among his peers. Along with his performance problems, you have also noticed that Sy is starting to sometimes "badmouth" the firm.

Questions: As Sy's manager, what options would you consider in terms of dealing with the issue of his retention in the job and in the company? What could you do by way of career development for Sy, and why?

Steps*for* Further Learning

BUILD MARKETABLE SKILLS
DO A CASE ANALYSIS
GET AND STAY INFORMED

BUILD

MARKETABLE SKILLS. EARN BIG CAREER PAYOFFS!

Don't miss these opportunities in the **Skill-Building Portfolio**

■ **SELF-ASSESSMENT 10:**
Performance Review Assumptions
Test your judgment when assessing others . . . make the best of performance management.

■ **CLASS EXERCISE 10:**
Upward Appraisal
Sometimes feedback has to flow up . . . with practice, you can get better at it.

■ **TEAM PROJECT 10:**
The Future of Labor Unions
Union membership is on the decline . . . does this mean all is well in the workplace?

> **Many learning resources are found at the end of the book and online within WileyPLUS.**

Take advantage of **Cases for Critical Thinking**

■ **CHAPTER 10 CASE SNAPSHOT:**
Silicon Valley's "Chief Executive Mom" /
Sidebar on New Workplace Perks

Before becoming CEO of Yahoo!, Marissa Mayer was best known for her senior role at Google, where she spent 13 years. She was Google's 20th employee and the company's first female engineer. Her move to Yahoo! had a compensation package valued at over $100 million over five years. The company had struggled through a series of CEOs, and she came in with high expectations. But, she wasn't only challenged to turn around the one-time Internet sweetheart; . . . she also became a new mom. Considered by industry observers as a last-chance savior for Yahoo! Mayer's early moves as CEO were closely watched. And, her status as a new mother created some fairly interesting buzz as well.

DO

A CASE ANALYSIS. STRENGTHEN YOUR CRITICAL THINKING!

Dig into this **Hot Topic**

■ **GOOD IDEA OR NOT? Teammates may know you best. Should they pay you as well?**

Tradition is that managers or team leaders make final pay raise decisions. But times may be changing in our crowdsourcing world.

Picture this. Fifteen members of a work team log into to an online exchange run by their employer. Their task is to distribute a pool of 1200 stock options as annual bonuses to their teammates. The only rule is that they can't give any to themselves. Each person's final

GET

AND STAY INFORMED. MAKE YOURSELF VALUABLE!

bonus options are the sum of what other team members give them. When the exchange closes each individual gets notified of their bonus awards and the distribution of bonuses awarded in the team—no names attached.

The example is real. It's from a San Francisco start-up called Coffee & Power. The pay practice was initiated by entrepreneur and co-founder Philip Rosedale. The idea is that because teammates know one another best, they also know who deserves to be recognized at bonus time.

Those in favor of the practice might say that by giving the bonus decisions to the team, it empowers members who get to invest in and reward one another for performance and contributions. One Coffee & Power employee says the approach "lets me reward people that management may not always recognize." *Those against the practice might say* it's a bit like having students give each other grades on a team project. There's too much room for results to be manipulated according to friendships and perceived "need." Too often, performance falls by the wayside as an award criterion.

Final Faceoff You've surely done peer evaluations in teams and perhaps even assigned grades to team members. What's your take on the Coffee & Power approach to bonuses? Does this use of technology really dig down to the level of truly rewarding individual contributions to team performance? Or, is it a practice that might open up more problems than it's worth?

"*I have a dream,*" *said Martin Luther King, Jr., and his voice has traveled from the steps of the Lincoln Memorial in Washington, D.C., on August 28, 1963, across generations. Like other visionary leaders, he communicated shared dreams and inspired others to pursue lofty goals.*

Leadership

A Leader Lives in Each of Us

Management Live

Integrity and *Love Happens*

Universal Pictures/Photofest

Burke Ryan (Aaron Eckhardt) is a successful self-help guru. He travels around the country promoting his book and hosting workshops to help people overcome tragedies and move on in their lives. The only problem is that Ryan has not dealt effectively with his own tragedy—the death of his wife in a car accident.

While hosting a week-long seminar in Seattle, his former home, he meets eclectic florist Eloise Chandler (Jennifer Anniston). He also comes face-to-face with his father-in-law (Martin Sheen) for the first time since the tragedy. These forces help Ryan realize he can no longer live the lie. On the last day of the workshop, he makes a painful public admission that the accident was his fault and he has never forgiven himself. The audience erupts in a standing ovation as Ryan receives a tearful embrace of forgiveness from his father-in-law.

This movie helps remind us about the importance of integrity—being honest, credible, and consistent while living up to personal values. And it moves us to think more about leadership. Real leaders have lots of integrity. It helps them as they try to help others achieve their full potential. Real leaders are also humble, willing to serve others more than be in the spotlight.

How often do you think about integrity when it comes to leadership? When news media cover leaders, do their reports indicate integrity or its absence? What does this say about the status of leadership integrity in our society?

YOUR CHAPTER 11 TAKEAWAYS

1. Understand the foundations for effective leadership.

2. Identify insights of the contingency leadership theories.

3. Discuss current issues and directions in leadership development.

WHAT'S INSIDE

Explore Yourself
More on **integrity**

Role Models
Lorraine Monroe's leadership turns vision into inspiration

Ethics Check
When the boss asks too much

Facts to Consider
Workers report shortcomings of leaders and top managers

Manager's Library
Power: Why Some People Have It and Others Don't by Jeffrey Pfeffer

Takeaway 11.1
What Are the Foundations for Effective Leadership?

ANSWERS TO COME

- Leadership is one of the four functions of management.
- Leaders use position power to achieve influence.
- Leaders use personal power to achieve influence.
- Leaders bring vision to leadership situations.
- Leaders display different traits in the quest for leadership effectiveness.
- Leaders display different styles in the quest for leadership effectiveness.

Leadership is the process of inspiring others to work hard to accomplish important tasks.

A GLANCE AT THE SHELVES IN YOUR LOCAL BOOKSTORE WILL QUICKLY CONFIRM that **leadership**, the process of inspiring others to work hard to accomplish important tasks, is one of the most popular management topics.[1] Consultant and author Tom Peters says that the leader is "rarely—possibly never—the best performer."[2] They don't have to be; leaders thrive through and by the successes of others. But not all managers live up to these expectations. Warren Bennis, a respected scholar and consultant, claims that too many U.S. corporations are "over-managed and under-led." Grace Hopper, the first female admiral in the U.S. Navy, advised that "you manage things; you lead people."[3] The bottom line is that leaders become great by bringing out the best in people.

FIGURE 11.1 Why Is Leading So Important in the Management Process?
Leading is one of the four management functions. It is the process of inspiring others to work hard to accomplish important tasks. Managers who are effective leaders act in ways that create high levels of enthusiasm among people to use their talents fully to accomplish tasks and pursue important plans and goals.

Leadership is one of the four functions of management.

Leadership is one of the four functions that make up the management process shown in **Figure 11.1**. *Planning* sets the direction and objectives; *organizing* brings together the resources to turn plans into action; *leading* builds the commitment and enthusiasm that allow people to apply their talents to help accomplish plans; and *controlling* makes sure things turn out right.

Of course, managers sometimes face daunting challenges in their quest to succeed as leaders. The time frames for getting things accomplished are becoming shorter. Second chances are sometimes few and far between. The problems to be resolved through leadership are often complex, ambiguous, and multidimensional. And, leaders are expected to stay focused on long-term goals even while dealing with problems and pressures in the short term.[4]

Anyone aspiring to career success in leadership must rise to these challenges and more. They must become good at using all the interpersonal skills discussed in this part of *Exploring Management, 4/e*—power and influence, communication, motivation, teamwork, conflict, and negotiation. Where do you stand on leadership skills and capabilities? If, as the chapter subtitle states, "A leader lives in each of us," what leader resides in you?

||| Leaders use position power to achieve influence.

Are you surprised that our discussion of leadership starts with power? Harvard professor Rosabeth Moss Kanter once called it "America's last great dirty word."[5] She worries that too many managers are uncomfortable with the concept and don't realize it is indispensable to leadership.

Power is the ability to get someone else to do something you want done, the ability to make things happen the way you want them to. Isn't that a large part of management, being able to influence other people? So, where and how do managers get power?

> **Power** is the ability to get someone else to do something you want done.

Most often we talk about two sources of managerial power that you might remember by this equation[6]:

$$\text{Managerial Power} = \text{Position Power} + \text{Personal Power.}$$

First is the power of the position, being "the manager." This power includes rewards, coercion, and legitimacy. Second is the power of the person, who you are and what your presence means in a situation. This power includes expertise and reference. Of course, some of us do far better than others at mobilizing and using the different types of power.[7]

Power of the POSITION: *Based on things managers can offer to others*	
Rewards:	"If you do what I ask, I'll give you a reward."
Coercion:	"If you don't do what I ask, I'll punish you."
Legitimacy:	"Because I am the boss, you *must* do as I ask."

If you look at the small figure, you'll see that **reward power** is the capability to offer something of value as a means of achieving influence. To use reward power, a manager says, in effect: "If you do what I ask, I'll give you a reward." Common rewards are things like pay raises, bonuses, promotions, special assignments, and compliments. As you might expect, reward power can work well as long as people want the reward and the manager or leader makes it continuously available. But take the value of the reward or the reward itself away, and that power is quickly lost.

> **Reward power** achieves influence by offering something of value.

Coercive power is the capability to punish or withhold positive outcomes as a way of influencing others. To mobilize coercive power, a manager is really saying: "If you don't do what I want, I'll punish you." Managers have access to lots of possible punishments, including reprimands, pay penalties, bad job assignments, and even termination. But how do you feel when on the receiving end of such threats? If you're like me, you'll most likely resent both the threat and the person making it. You might act as requested or at least go through the motions, but you're unlikely to continue doing so once the threat no longer exists.

> **Coercive power** achieves influence by punishment.

Legitimate power is the capacity to influence through formal authority. It is the right of the manager, or person in charge, to exercise control over persons in subordinate positions. To use legitimate power, a manager is basically saying: "I am the boss; therefore, you are supposed to do as I ask." When an instructor assigns homework, exams, and group projects, don't you most often do what is requested? Why? You do it because the requests seem legitimate to the course. But if the instructor moves outside course boundaries, perhaps asking you to attend a sports event, the legitimacy is lost, and your compliance is less likely.

> **Legitimate power** achieves influence by formal authority.

Manager's **Library**

DO YOURSELF SOME GOOD AND SCHEDULE A POWER TRIP—YOUR CAREER DEPENDS ON IT!

People who believe good work in life gets noticed and leads to just rewards should take pause. Research shows the most critical factor for success is having power—authority and control over work environments, resources, and decisions.

In the book *Power: Why Some People Have It and Others Don't* (2010, HarperCollins), author Jeffrey Pfeffer says research shows a person's organizational power correlates positively with career success, job performance, salary, and even one's life span. He urges people to use political savvy to rise within hierarchies to control more resources and decisions and build power, status, and influence.

Pfeffer says research links political savvy to career success. Effective leaders who are critical of others are seen as intelligent, whereas less-effective leaders who are nice to others are viewed as weak.

Many people face obstacles and fail to gain power. They believe the world is just—rewards for good deeds and punishments for bad ones—and fail to learn from situations, both good and bad, and from people, even those they dislike. They fear failure, so they avoid trying to preserve their self-image.

Pfeffer believes that attaining power requires will and skill, so personal qualities of ambition, energy, and focus are needed. Ambition keeps attention on achieving influence over others, especially those higher up. Energy fuels hard work and effort; it is contagious and signals commitment to others. Focus limits activities and skills to areas that will lead to more power, status, and influence.

REFLECT AND REACT

Think about the formal or informal hierarchies that you belong to. How are members selected and dismissed, and how are members' tasks assigned? How are resources selected and used? How are decisions made and by whom? Are those in power perceived positively, negatively, intelligent, or weak? Do you agree that some people fail to gain power because they fear failure and avoid trying?

‖ Leaders use personal power to achieve influence.

After all is said and done, we need to admit that position power alone isn't going to be sufficient for any manager. In fact, how much personal power you can mobilize through expertise and reference may well make the difference someday between success and failure in a leadership situation—and even in a career.

Expert power achieves influence by special knowledge.

As shown in the small figure, **expert power** is the ability to influence the behavior of others because of special knowledge and skills. When a manager uses expert power, the implied message is: "You should do what I want because of my special expertise or information."

A leader's expertise may come from technical understanding or access to information relevant to the issue at hand. It can be acquired through formal education and evidenced by degrees and credentials. It is also acquired on the job, through experience, and by gaining a reputation as someone who is a high performer and really understands the work. Building expertise in these ways, in fact, may be one of your biggest early career challenges.

There's still more to personal power. Think of all the television commercials that show high-visibility athletes and personalities advertising consumer products.

Power of the PERSON:
Based on how managers are viewed by others

Expertise—as a source of special knowledge and information

Reference—as a person with whom others like to identify

{ THE JOB OF A GOOD LEADER IS TO UPLIFT HER PEOPLE . . .
AS INDIVIDUALS OF INFINITE WORTH IN THEIR OWN RIGHT.

Role Models

■ Lorraine Monroe's Leadership Turns Vision into Inspiration

Dr. Lorraine Monroe's career in the New York City Schools began as a teacher. She went on to serve as assistant principal, principal, and vice chancellor for curriculum and instruction. But her career really took off when she founded the Frederick Douglass Academy, a public school in Harlem, where she grew up. Under her leadership as principal, the school became highly respected for educational excellence. The academy's namesake was an escaped slave who later became a prominent abolitionist and civil rights leader.

Monroe sees leadership as vision driven and follower centered. She believes leaders must always start at the "heart of the matter" and that "the job of a good leader is to articulate a vision that others are inspired to follow." She believes in making sure all workers know that they are valued and that their advice is welcome. She also believes that workers and managers should always try to help and support one another. "I have never undertaken any project," she says, "without first imagining on paper what it would ultimately look like . . . all the doers who would be responsible for carrying out my imaginings have to be informed and let in on the dream."

As a consultant on public leadership, Monroe states: "We can reform society only if every place we live—every school, workplace, church, and family—becomes a site of reform." Her many leadership ideas are summarized in what is called the "Monroe Doctrine." It begins with this advice: "The job of the leader is to uplift her people—not just as members of and contributors to the organization, but as individuals of infinite worth in their own right."

WHAT'S THE LESSON HERE?

Is visionary leadership something that works only at the very top of organizations? Should the leader of a work team also have a vision? Follower-centered leadership is high on Lorraine Monroe's list of priorities. And she's made a fine career by putting its principles to work. What is there in the Monroe Doctrine that can help you succeed as a leader? Do you have what it takes to truly value people who look up to you for leadership?

What's really going on here? The intent is to attract customers to the products through identification with the athletes and personalities. The same holds true in leadership. **Referent power** is the ability to influence the behavior of others because they admire and want to identify positively with you. When a manager uses referent power, the implied message is: "You should do what I want in order to maintain a positive self-defined relationship with me."

If referent power is so valuable, do you know how to get it? It comes in large part from good interpersonal relationships, ones that create admiration and respect for us in the eyes of others. My wife sums this up very simply by saying: "It's a lot easier to get people to do what you want when they like you than when they dislike you." Doesn't this make sense? This is good advice for how to approach your job and the people with whom you work every day.

> **Referent power** achieves influence by personal identification.

⫿ Leaders bring vision to leadership situations.

"Great leaders," it is said, "get extraordinary things done in organizations by inspiring and motivating others toward a common purpose."[8] In other words, they use their power exceptionally well. And frequently today, successful leadership is associated with **vision**—a future that one hopes to create or achieve in order to improve on the present state of affairs. According to the late John Wooden, a standout men's basketball coach at UCLA for 27 years: "Effective leadership means having a lot of people working toward a common goal. And

> A **vision** is a clear sense of the future.

Visionary leadership brings to the situation a clear sense of the future and an understanding of how to get there.

when you have that with no one caring who gets the credit, you're going to accomplish a lot."[9]

The term **visionary leadership** describes a leader who brings to the situation a clear and compelling sense of the future, as well as an understanding of the actions needed to get there successfully.[10] But simply having the vision of a desirable future is not enough. Truly great leaders are extraordinarily good at turning their visions into accomplishments. This means being good at communicating the vision and getting people motivated and inspired to pursue the vision in their daily work. You can think of it this way. Visionary leadership brings meaning to people's work; it makes what they do seem worthy and valuable.

⫴ Leaders display different traits in the quest for leadership effectiveness.

For centuries, people have recognized that some persons use power well and perform successfully as leaders, whereas others do not. You've certainly seen this yourself. How can such differences in leadership effectiveness be explained?

An early direction in leadership research tried to answer this question by identifying traits and personal characteristics shared by well-regarded leaders.[11] Not surprisingly, results showed that physical characteristics such as height, weight, and physique make no difference. But a study of over 3,400 managers found that followers rather consistently admired leaders who were honest, competent, forward-looking, inspiring, and credible.[12] Another comprehensive review is summarized in Table 11.1—Traits Often Shared by Effective Leaders.[13] You might use this list as a quick check of your leadership potential.

Table 11.1 Traits Often Shared by Effective Leaders

Drive—Successful leaders have high energy, display initiative, and are tenacious.

Self-confidence—Successful leaders trust themselves and have confidence in their abilities.

Creativity—Successful leaders are creative and original in their thinking.

Cognitive ability—Successful leaders have the intelligence to integrate and interpret information.

Business knowledge—Successful leaders know their industry and its technical foundations.

Motivation—Successful leaders enjoy influencing others to achieve shared goals.

Flexibility—Successful leaders adapt to fit the needs of followers and the demands of situations.

Honesty and integrity—Successful leaders are trustworthy; they are honest, predictable, and dependable.

⫴ Leaders display different styles in the quest for leadership effectiveness.

In addition to leadership traits, researchers have also studied how successful and unsuccessful leaders behave when working with followers. Most of this research focused on two sets of behaviors: task-oriented behaviors and people-oriented behaviors. A leader high in concern for task plans and defines work goals, assigns task responsibilities, sets clear work standards, urges task completion, and monitors performance results. A leader high in concern for people acts warm and supportive

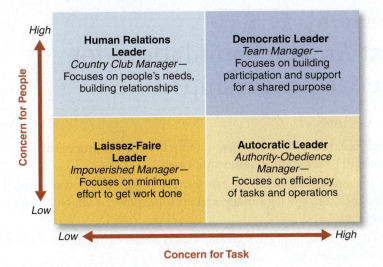

FIGURE 11.2 What Are the Classic Leadership Styles?
It is common to describe leaders in terms of how their day-to-day styles show concern for people and concern for task. In this figure the leader low in concern for both people and task is described as "laissez-faire" and is very ineffective. The leader high in concern for task but low in concern for people is "autocratic" and focused on performance. The leader high in concern for people and low in concern for task has a "human relations" style that focuses mainly on people and relationships. The "democratic" leader is high in concern for both people and task. This person is often highly successful as a true team manager who is able to engage people to accomplish common goals.

toward followers, maintains good relations with them, respects their feelings, shows sensitivity to their needs, and displays trust in them.

Leaders who show different combinations of task and people behaviors are often described as having unique leadership styles, such as you have probably observed in your own experiences. A popular summary of classic **leadership styles** used by managers is shown in **Figure 11.2**.[14]

Someone who emphasizes task over people is often described as an **autocratic leader**. This manager focuses on authority and obedience, delegates little, keeps information to himself or herself, and tends to act in a unilateral command-and-control fashion. Have you ever worked for someone fitting this description? How would you score his or her leadership effectiveness?

A leader who emphasizes people over task is often referred to as a **human relations leader**. This leader is interpersonally engaging, cares about others, is sensitive to feelings and emotions, and tends to act in ways that emphasize harmony and good working relationships.

Interestingly, researchers at first believed that the human relations style was the most effective for a leader. However, after pressing further, the conclusion emerged that the most effective leaders were strong in concerns for both people and task.[15] Sometimes called a **democratic leader,** a manager with this style shares decisions with followers, encourages participation, and supports the teamwork needed for high levels of task accomplishment.

One result of this research on leader behaviors was the emergence of training programs designed to help people become better leaders by learning how to be good at both task-oriented and people-oriented behaviors. How about you? Where do you fit on this leadership diagram? What leadership training would be best for you? Hopefully you're not starting out as an "impoverished" manager with a **laissez-faire leader,** low on both task and people concerns.

Leadership style is the recurring pattern of behaviors exhibited by a leader.

An **autocratic leader** acts in unilateral command-and-control fashion.

A **human relations leader** emphasizes people over tasks.

A **democratic leader** encourages participation with an emphasis on task and people.

A **laissez-faire** leader is disengaged, showing low task and people concerns.

STUDY GUIDE

Takeaway 11.1
What Are the Foundations for Effective Leadership?

Terms to Define

Autocratic leader

Coercive power

Democratic leader

Expert power

Human relations leader

Laissez-faire leader

Leadership

Leadership style

Legitimate power

Power

Referent power

Reward power

Vision

Visionary leadership

Rapid Review

- Leadership, as one of the management functions, is the process of inspiring others to work hard to accomplish important tasks.
- Leaders use power from two primary sources: position power—which includes rewards, coercion, and legitimacy, and personal power—which includes expertise and reference.
- The ability to communicate a vision or clear sense of the future is considered essential to effective leadership.
- Personal characteristics associated with leadership success include honesty, competency, drive, integrity, and self-confidence.
- Research on leader behaviors focused attention on concerns for task and concerns for people, with the leader high on both and using a democratic style considered most effective.

Questions for Discussion

1. When, if ever, is a leader justified in using coercive power?
2. How can a young college graduate gain personal power when moving into a new job as team leader?
3. Why might a leader with a human relations style have difficulty getting things done in an organization?

Be Sure You Can

- illustrate how managers use position and personal power
- define vision and give an example of visionary leadership
- list five traits of successful leaders
- describe alternative leadership styles based on concern for task and concern for people

Career Situation: What Would You Do?

Some might say it was bad luck. Others will say it's life and you'd better get used to it. You've just gotten a new boss, and within the first week it was clear that she is as autocratic as can be. The previous boss led in a very democratic way, and so does the next-higher-level manager with whom you have a good working relationship. So, do you just sit tight and live with it? Or, are there things you and your co-workers can do to remedy this situation without causing harm to anyone, including the new boss?

Takeaway 11.2

What Can We Learn from the Contingency Leadership Theories?

ANSWERS TO COME

■ Fiedler's contingency model matches leadership styles with situational differences.

■ The Hersey-Blanchard situational leadership model matches leadership styles with the maturity of followers.

■ House's path-goal theory matches leadership styles with task and follower characteristics.

■ Leader–member exchange theory describes how leaders treat in-group and out-group followers.

■ The Vroom-Jago model describes a leader's choice of alternative decision-making methods.

EVEN AS YOU CONSIDER YOUR LEADERSHIP STYLE AND TENDENCIES, YOU SHOULD know that researchers eventually concluded that no one style always works best. Not even the democratic, or "high-high," leader is successful all the time. This finding led scholars to explore a **contingency leadership perspective**, one that recognizes that what is successful as a leadership style varies according to the nature of the situation and people involved.

The **contingency leadership perspective** suggests that what is successful as a leadership style varies according to the situation and the people involved.

‖ Fiedler's contingency model matches leadership styles with situational differences.

One of the first contingency models of leadership was put forth by Fred Fiedler. He proposed that leadership success depends on achieving a proper match between your leadership style and situational demands.[16] He also believed that each of us has a predominant leadership style that is strongly rooted in our personalities. This is important because it suggests that a person's leadership style, yours or mine, is going to be enduring and hard to change.

Fiedler uses an instrument called the *least-preferred co-worker scale (LPC)* to classify our leadership styles as either task motivated or relationship motivated. The LPC scale is available in the end of book *Skill-Building Portfolio*. Why not complete it now and see how Fiedler would describe your style?

Leadership situations are analyzed in Fiedler's model according to three contingency variables—leader–member relations, task structure, and position power. These variables can exist in eight different combinations, with each representing a different leadership challenge. The most favorable situation provides high control for the leader. It has good leader–member relations, high task structure, and strong position power. The least favorable situation puts the leader in a low control setting. Leader–member relations are poor, task structure is low, and position power is weak.

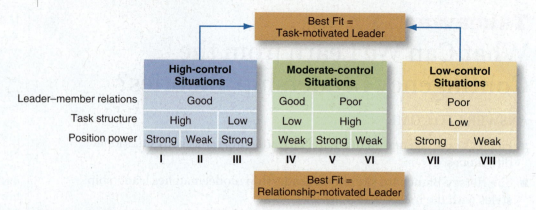

FIGURE 11.3 **What Are the Best Matches of Leadership Style and Situation According to Fiedler's Contingency Model?**
Fiedler believes that leadership success requires the right style–situation match. He classifies leadership styles as either task motivated or relationship motivated and views them as strongly rooted in our individual personalities. He describes situations according to the leader's position power, quality of leader–member relations, and amount of task structure. In situations that are most favorable and unfavorable for leaders, his research shows the task-motivated style as the best fit. In more intermediate situations, the relationship-motivated style provides the best fit.

Fiedler's research revealed an interesting pattern when he studied the effectiveness of different styles in different leadership situations. As shown in Figure 11.3, a task-motivated leader is most successful in either very favorable (high-control) or very unfavorable (low-control) situations. In contrast, a relationship-motivated leader is more successful in situations of moderate control.

Don't let the apparent complexity of the figure fool you. Fiedler's logic is quite straightforward and, if on track, has some interesting career implications. It suggests that you must know yourself well enough to recognize your predominant leadership style. You should seek out or create leadership situations for which this style is a good match. And, you should avoid situations for which your style is a bad match.

Let's do some quick examples. First, assume that you are the leader of a team of bank tellers. The tellers seem highly supportive of you, and their job is clearly defined. You have the authority to evaluate their performance and to make pay and promotion recommendations. This is a high-control situation consisting of good leader–member relations, high task structure, and high position power. By checking Figure 11.3, you can see that a task-motivated leader is recommended.

Now suppose you are chairperson of a committee asked to improve labor–management relations in a manufacturing plant. Although the goal is clear, no one knows exactly how to accomplish it—task structure is low. Further, not everyone believes that a committee is even the right way to approach the situation— poor leader–member relations are likely. Finally, committee members are free to quit any time they want—you have little position power. Figure 11.3 shows that in this low-control situation, a task-motivated leader should be most effective.

Finally, assume that you are the new head of a fashion section in a large department store. Because you won the job over one of the popular salesclerks you now supervise, leader–member relations are poor. Task structure is high because the clerk's job is well defined. Your position power is low because clerks work under a seniority system, with a fixed wage schedule. Figure 11.3 shows that this moderate-control situation requires a relationship-motivated leader.

⫴ The Hersey-Blanchard situational leadership model matches leadership styles with the maturity of followers.

In contrast to Fiedler's notion that leadership style is hard to change, the Hersey-Blanchard situational leadership model suggests that successful leaders do adjust their styles. They do so contingently and based on the maturity of followers, as indicated by their readiness to perform in a given situation.[17] "Readiness," in this sense, is based on how able and willing or confident followers are to perform required tasks. As shown in Figure 11.4, the possible combinations of task and relationship behaviors result in four leadership styles.

- *Delegating*—allowing the group to take responsibility for task decisions; a low-task, low-relationship style
- *Participating*—emphasizing shared ideas and participative decisions on task directions; a low-task, high-relationship style
- *Selling*—explaining task directions in a supportive and persuasive way; a high-task, high-relationship style
- *Telling*—giving specific task directions and closely supervising work; a high-task, low-relationship style

The delegating style works best in high-readiness situations with able and willing or confident followers. The telling style works best at the other extreme of low readiness, where followers are unable and unwilling or insecure. The participating style is recommended for low-to-moderate readiness (followers are able but unwilling or insecure); the selling style works best for moderate-to-high readiness (followers are unable but willing or confident).

Hersey and Blanchard further believe that leadership styles should be adjusted as followers change over time. The model also implies that if the correct styles are used in lower-readiness situations, followers will "mature" and grow in ability, willingness, and confidence. This allows the leader to become less directive as followers mature. Although this situational leadership model is intuitively appealing, limited research has been accomplished on it to date.[18]

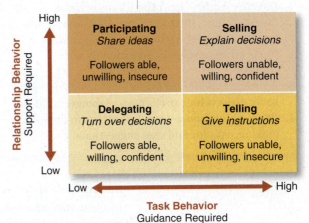

FIGURE 11.4   What Are the Leadership Implications of the Hersey-Blanchard Situational Leadership Model? The Hersey-Blanchard situational leadership model suggests that successful leaders adjust their styles based on the maturity of followers or how willing and able they are to perform in a given situation. The four style–follower matches are delegating style for able and willing followers, participating style for able but unwilling followers, selling style for unable but willing followers, and telling style for unable and unwilling followers.

⫴ House's path-goal theory matches leadership styles with task and follower characteristics.

Another contingency leadership approach is the path-goal theory advanced by Robert House.[19] This theory suggests that leaders are effective when they help followers move along paths through which they can achieve both work goals and personal goals. The best leaders create positive path-goal linkages, raising motivation by removing barriers and rewarding progress.

Like Fiedler's approach, House's path-goal theory seeks the right fit between leadership and situation. But unlike Fiedler, House believes that a leader can move back and forth among the four leadership styles: directive, supportive, achievement-oriented, and participative.

Four Leadership Styles in House's Path-Goal Theory

1. *Directive leader*—lets others know what is expected; gives directions, maintains standards
2. *Supportive leader*—makes work more pleasant; treats others as equals, acts friendly, shows concern
3. *Achievement-oriented leader*—sets challenging goals; expects high performance, shows confidence
4. *Participative leader*—involves others in decision making; asks for and uses suggestions

Substitutes for leadership are factors in the work setting that direct work efforts without the involvement of a leader.

When choosing among the different styles, House suggests that the leader's job is to "add value" to a situation. This means acting in ways that contribute things that are missing and not doing things that can otherwise take care of themselves. If you are the leader of a team whose members are expert and competent at their tasks, for example, why would you need to be directive? Members have the know-how to provide their own direction. More likely, the value you can add to this situation would be found in a participative leadership style that helps unlock the expertise of team members and apply it fully to the tasks at hand.

Path-goal theory provides a variety of research-based guidance of this sort to help leaders contingently match their styles with situational characteristics.[20] When job assignments are unclear, *directive leadership* helps to clarify task objectives and expected rewards. When worker self-confidence is low, *supportive leadership* can increase confidence by emphasizing individual abilities and offering needed assistance. When task challenge is insufficient in a job, *achievement-oriented leadership* helps to set goals and raise performance aspirations. When performance incentives are poor, *participative leadership* might clarify individual needs and identify appropriate rewards.

This contingency thinking has contributed to the recognition of what are called **substitutes for leadership**.[21] These are aspects of the work setting and the people involved that can reduce the need for a leader's personal involvement. In effect, they make leadership from the "outside" unnecessary because leadership is already provided from within the situation.

Possible substitutes for leadership include subordinate characteristics such as ability, experience, and independence; task characteristics such as how routine it is and the availability of feedback; and organizational characteristics such as clarity of plans and formalization of rules and procedures. When these substitutes are present, managers are advised to avoid duplicating them. Instead, they should concentrate on doing other and more important things.

||| Leader–member exchange theory describes how leaders treat in-group and out-group followers.

One of the things you may have noticed in your work and study groups is the tendency of leaders to develop "special" relationships with some team members. This notion is central to leader–member exchange theory, or LMX theory, as it is often called.[22] The theory is highlighted in the nearby figure and recognizes that in most, or at least many, leadership situations, not everyone is treated the same. People fall into "in-groups" and "out-groups," and the group you are in can have quite a significant influence on your experience with the leader.

The premise underlying leader–member exchange theory is that as a leader and follower interact over time, their exchanges end up defining the follower's role.[23] Those in a leader's in-group are often considered the best performers. They enjoy special and trusted high-exchange relationships with the leader that can translate into special assignments, privileges, and access to information. Those in the out-group are often excluded from these benefits due to low-exchange relationships with the leader.

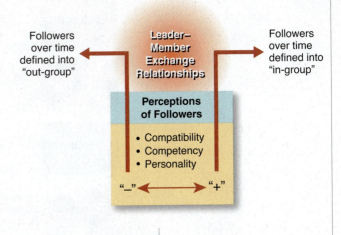

For the follower in a high-LMX relationship, being part of the leader's inner circle or in-group can be a real positive. It's often motivating and satisfying to be on the inside of things in terms of getting rewards and favorable treatments. Being in the out-group because of a low-LMX relationship, however, can be a real negative, bringing fewer rewards and less-favorable treatment. As to the leader, it is nice to be able to call on and depend on the loyal support of those in the in-group. But the leader may also be missing out on opportunities that might come from working more closely with out-group members.

Research on leader–member exchange theory places most value on its usefulness in describing leader–follower interactions. The notions of high-LMX and low-LMX relationships seem to make sense and correspond to working realities experienced by many people. Look around, and you're likely to see examples of this in classroom situations between instructors and certain students, and in work situations between bosses and certain subordinates. In such settings, research finds that members of in-groups get more positive performance evaluations, report higher levels of satisfaction, and are less prone to turnover than are members of out-groups.[24]

⦀ The Vroom-Jago model describes a leader's choice of alternative decision-making methods.

Yet another contingency leadership theory focuses on how managers lead through their use of decision-making methods. The Vroom-Jago leader-participation model views a manager as having three decision options, and in true contingency fashion, no one option is always superior to the others.[25]

1. **Authority decision**—The manager makes an individual decision about how to solve the problem and then communicates the decision to the group.

2. **Consultative decision**—The manager makes the decision after sharing the problem with and getting suggestions from individual group members or the group as a whole.

3. **Group decision**—The manager convenes the group, shares the problem, and then either facilitates a group decision or delegates the decision to the group.

Leadership success results when the manager's choice of decision-making method best matches the nature of the problem to be solved.[26] The rules for making the choice involve three criteria: (1) *decision quality*—based on who has the information needed for problem solving; (2) *decision acceptance*—based on the importance of follower acceptance of the decision to its eventual

An **authority decision** is made by the leader and then communicated to the group.

A **consultative decision** is made by a leader after receiving information, advice, or opinions from group members.

A **group decision** is made by group members themselves.

FIGURE 11.5 What Are the Leadership Implications of the Vroom-Jago Leader-Participation Model?
The leader-participation model suggests that leaders are effective when they use the appropriate decision method to solve a problem situation. Three criteria govern the choice among possible authority, consultative, and team or group decisions: (1) *decision quality*—based on who has the information needed for problem solving; (2) *decision acceptance*—based on the importance of follower acceptance of the decision to its eventual implementation; and (3) *decision time*—based on the time available to make and implement the decision.

implementation; and (3) *decision time*—based on the time available to make and implement the decision. These rules are shown in **Figure 11.5**.

In true contingency fashion each of the decision methods is appropriate in certain situations, and each has advantages and disadvantages.[27] Authority decisions work best when leaders have the expertise needed to solve the problem, they are confident and capable of acting alone, others are likely to accept and implement the decision they make, and little time is available for discussion. By contrast, consultative and group decisions are recommended when:

> **When consultative and group decisions work best**

- The leader lacks sufficient expertise and information to solve this problem alone.
- The problem is unclear, and help is needed to clarify the situation.
- Acceptance of the decision and commitment by others are necessary for implementation.
- Adequate time is available to allow for true participation.

Using consultative and group decisions offers important leadership benefits.[28] Participation helps improve decision quality by bringing more information to bear on the problem. It helps improve decision acceptance as others gain understanding and become committed to the process. It also contributes to leadership development by allowing others to gain experience in the problem-solving process. However, a potential cost of participation is lost efficiency. Participation often adds to the time required for decision making, and leaders don't always have extra time available. When problems must be resolved immediately, the authority decision may be the only option.[29]

STUDY GUIDE

Takeaway 11.2

What Can We Learn from the Contingency Leadership Theories?

Terms to Define

Authority decision

Consultative decision

Contingency leadership perspective

Group decision

Substitutes for leadership

Rapid Review

- Fiedler's contingency model describes how situational differences in task structure, position power, and leader–member relations may influence the success of task-motivated and relationship-motivated leaders.
- The Hersey-Blanchard situational model recommends using task-oriented and people-oriented behaviors, depending on the "maturity" levels of followers.
- House's path-goal theory describes how leaders add value to situations by using supportive, directive, achievement-oriented, and/or participative styles as needed.
- Leader–member exchange theory recognizes that leaders respond differently to followers in their in-groups and out-groups.
- The Vroom-Jago leader-participation theory advises leaders to choose decision-making methods—authority, consultative, group—that best fit the problems to be solved.

Questions for Discussion

1. What are the potential career development lessons of Fiedler's contingency leadership model?
2. What are the implications of follower maturity for leaders trying to follow the Hersey-Blanchard situational leadership model?
3. Is it wrong for a team leader to allow the formation of in-groups and out-groups in his or her relationships with team members?

Be Sure You Can

- explain Fiedler's contingency model for matching leadership style and situation
- identify the three variables used to assess situational favorableness in Fiedler's model
- identify the four leadership styles in the Hersey-Blanchard situational leadership model
- explain the importance of follower "maturity" in the Hersey-Blanchard model
- describe the best use of directive, supportive, achievement-oriented, and participative leadership styles in House's path-goal theory
- explain how leader–member exchange theory deals with in-groups and out-groups among a leader's followers

Career Situation: What Would You Do?

You've just been hired as a visual effects artist by a top movie studio. Members of the team you are joining have already been working together for about two months. There's obviously an in-group when it comes to team leader and team member relationships. This job is important to you and the movie is going to be great résumé material. But, you're worried about the leadership dynamics and your role as a newcomer to the team. What can you do to quickly become a valued team member?

TEACHING NOTE: Prepare for a good debate. Ask students the following questions. a) In your experience—family, school, work, sports, leisure—do women lead differently than men? b) If or when they do, exactly how does their leadership differ from that shown by men? c) How do any differences influence the attitudes and performance of other people? d) What are the leadership development implications of this discussion?

Takeaway 11.3
What Are Current Issues and Directions in Leadership Development?

ANSWERS TO COME

- Transformational leadership inspires enthusiasm and great performance
- Emotionally intelligent leadership handles emotions and relationships well
- Interactive leadership emphasizes communication, listening, and participation
- Moral leadership builds trust from a foundation of personal integrity
- Servant leadership is follower centered and empowering

YOU SHOULD NOW BE THINKING SERIOUSLY ABOUT YOUR LEADERSHIP QUALITIES, tendencies, styles, and effectiveness. You should also be thinking about your personal development as a leader. And, in fact, if you look at what people say about leaders in their workplaces, you should be admitting that most of us have considerable room to grow in this regard.[30]

Transformational leadership inspires enthusiasm and great performance.

A **charismatic leader** develops special leader–follower relationships and inspires followers in extraordinary ways.

It is popular to talk about "superleaders," persons whose visions and strong personalities have an extraordinary impact on others.[31] Martin Luther King, in his famous "I have a dream" speech delivered in August 1963 on the Washington Mall, serves as a good example. Some call people like King **charismatic leaders** because of their ability to inspire others in exceptional ways. We used to think charisma was limited to only a few lucky persons. Today, it is considered one of several personal qualities—including honesty, credibility, and competence, that we should be able to develop with foresight and practice.

Transactional leadership directs the efforts of others through tasks, rewards, and structures.

Leadership scholars James MacGregor Burns and Bernard Bass have pursued this theme. They begin by describing the traditional leadership approaches we have discussed so far as **transactional leadership.**[32] You might picture the transactional leader engaging followers in a somewhat mechanical fashion, "transacting" with them by using power, employing behaviors and styles that seem to be the best choices at the moment for getting things done.

What is missing in the transactional approach, say Burns and Bass, is attention to things typically linked with superleaders—enthusiasm and inspiration, for example. These are among the charismatic qualities that they associate with something called **transformational leadership.**[33]

Transformational leadership is inspirational and arouses extraordinary effort and performance.

Transformational leaders use their personalities to inspire followers and get them so highly excited about their jobs and organizational goals that they strive for truly extraordinary performance accomplishments. Indeed, the easiest way to spot a truly transformational leader is through his or her followers. They are likely to be enthusiastic about the leader and loyal and devoted to his or her ideas and to work exceptionally hard together to support them.

The goal of achieving excellence in transformational leadership is a stiff personal development challenge. It is not enough to possess leadership traits, know the leadership behaviors, and understand leadership contingencies. One must also be prepared to lead in an inspirational way and with a compelling personality. Transformational leaders raise the confidence, aspirations, and performance of followers through these special qualities.[34]

《 **Qualities of Transformational Leaders**

- *Vision*—has ideas and a clear sense of direction; communicates them to others; develops excitement about accomplishing shared "dreams"
- *Charisma*—uses the power of personal reference and emotion to arouse others' enthusiasm, faith, loyalty, pride, and trust in themselves
- *Symbolism*—identifies "heroes," and holds spontaneous and planned ceremonies to celebrate excellence and high achievement
- *Empowerment*—helps others grow and develop by removing performance obstacles, sharing responsibilities, and delegating truly challenging work
- *Intellectual stimulation*—gains the involvement of others by creating awareness of problems and stirring their imaginations
- *Integrity*—is honest and credible; acts consistently and out of personal conviction; follows through on commitments

⫿ Emotionally intelligent leadership handles emotions and relationships well.

The role of personality in transformational leadership raises another area of inquiry in leadership development—**emotional intelligence**. Popularized by the work of Daniel Goleman, emotional intelligence, or EI for short, is an ability to understand emotions in yourself and others and use this understanding to handle one's social relationships effectively.[35] "Great leaders move us," say Goleman and his colleagues. "Great leadership works through emotions."[36]

Emotional intelligence (EI) is the ability to manage our emotions in leadership and social relationships.

Emotional intelligence is an important influence on leadership success, especially in more senior management positions. In Goleman's words: "The higher the rank of the person considered to be a star performer, the more emotional intelligence capabilities showed up as the reason for his or her effectiveness."[37] This is a pretty strong endorsement for making EI one of your leadership assets.[38] In fact, you'll increasingly hear the term **EQ**, or **emotional intelligence quotient**, used in this regard as more employers start to actually measure it as a part of their recruitment screening.

Emotional intelligence quotient (EQ) is a measure of a person's ability to manage emotions in leadership and social relationships.

Consider the four primary emotional intelligence competencies shown in the small figure. *Self-awareness* is the ability to understand our own moods and emotions and to understand their impact on our work and on others. *Social awareness* is the ability to empathize, to understand the emotions of others, and to use this understanding to better deal with them. *Self-management,* or self-regulation, is the ability to think before acting and to be in control of otherwise disruptive impulses. *Relationship management* is the ability to establish rapport with others in ways that build good relationships and influence their emotions in positive ways.

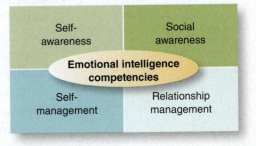

Kraft Foods Feeds Its Sweet Tooth

REUTERS/John Gress/Landov

kraft
Mak___ y deli_

Leaders Provide the Roadmaps

When Kraft Foods was bidding to buy Cadbury, Irene Rosenfeld was often in the news. She was leading a dramatic attempt to capture the British candymaker against its wishes. It was all part of Rosenfeld's desire to transform Kraft—a firm she described as "not living up to our potential." Her leadership roadmap focused on making Kraft a global powerhouse. This included completing the Cadbury acquisition against all odds. And she succeeded.

Rosenfeld is described as a risk taker who makes "bold" moves—the latest being to split Kraft into two companies. She leads by pushing decision authority down the hierarchy, letting managers control their budgets and operations. She focuses on top management teamwork to bring perspectives in from all parts of the company. And, she urges top managers to focus resources on what they do best in their customer markets.

Throughout her life, from school to work, Rosenfeld says, "I just never gave much thought to the fact I couldn't do it." Her advice to leaders is to "get the right people on the bus," "give them a roadmap," and "communicate frequently, consistently and honestly."

Find Inspiration

This example of Irene Rosenfeld is designed to get you thinking about your leadership qualities and looking at the leadership models that abound in your experiences. Just who is the leader in you? What can you do to keep that leader growing and confident in the days and years ahead?

The **gender similarities hypothesis** holds that males and females have similar psychological makeups.

⫼ Interactive leadership emphasizes communication, listening, and participation.

When Sara Levinson was president of NFL Properties Inc., she once asked the all-male members of her management team: "Is my leadership style different from a man's?"[39] Would you be surprised to learn that they answered "Yes," telling her that just by asking the question she was providing evidence of the difference? They described her as a leader who emphasized communication, always gathering ideas and opinions from others. And when Levinson probed further by asking, "Is this a distinctly 'female' trait?" they again said "yes," it was.

Are there gender differences in leadership? Before you jump in with your own answer, consider three things. First, research largely supports the **gender similarities hypothesis** that males and females are very similar to one another in terms of psychological properties.[40] Second, research leaves no doubt that both women and men can be effective leaders.[41] Third, research shows that men and women are sometimes perceived as using different leadership styles, perhaps arriving at success from different angles.[42]

Some studies report that male leaders are viewed as directive and assertive, using position power to get things done in traditional command-and-control ways.[43] Other studies report female leaders are viewed as more participative than men. They are also rated by peers, subordinates, and supervisors as strong on motivating others, emotional intelligence, persuading, fostering communication, listening to others, mentoring, and supporting high-quality work.[44] Yet another study found that women were rated more highly than men in all but one area of leadership—visioning.[45] A possible explanation is that women aren't considered as visionaries because they are perceived as acting less directive as leaders.

{ ONLY 37% OF WORKERS IN A HARRIS SURVEY BELIEVE THEIR MANAGERS DISPLAY "INTEGRITY AND MORALITY."

Facts to **Consider**

■ Workers Report Shortcomings of Leaders and Top Managers

Harris Interactive periodically conducts surveys of workers' attitudes toward their jobs and employers. The results for a query about how workers view "leaders" and "top managers" reveal lots of shortcomings:

- 37% believe their top managers display integrity and morality.
- 39% believe leaders most often act in the best interest of organization.
- 22% see leaders as ready to admit mistakes.
- 46% believe their organizations give them freedom to do their jobs.

- 25% of women and 16% of men believe their organizations pick the best people for leadership.
- 33% of managers are perceived by followers as "strong leaders."

YOUR THOUGHTS?

How do the leaders you have experienced stack up—"strong or weak," "moral or immoral"? What makes the most difference in the ways leaders are viewed in the eyes of followers?

The pattern of behaviors associated with female leaders has been called **interactive leadership.**[46] Interactive leaders are democratic, participative, and inclusive, often approaching problems and decisions through teamwork.[47] They focus on building consensus and good interpersonal relations through emotional intelligence, communication, and involvement. They tend to get things done with personal power, seeking influence over others through support and interpersonal relationships.

Rosabeth Moss Kanter says that in many ways, "Women get high ratings on exactly those skills required to succeed in the Global Information Age, where teamwork and partnering are so important."[48] Her observations are backed up by data that show firms with more female directors and executives outperform others.[49] But let's be careful. One of the risks here is placing individual men and women into boxes in which they don't necessarily belong.[50] It may be better to focus instead on the notion of interactive leadership. The likelihood is that this style is a very good fit with the needs of today's organizations and workers.[51] And, isn't there every reason to believe that both men and women can do interactive leadership equally well?

‖ Moral leadership builds trust from a foundation of personal integrity.

As discussed many times in this book, society expects organizations to be run with **moral leadership.** This is leadership by ethical standards that clearly meet the test of being "good" and "correct."[52] We should expect anyone in a leadership position to practice high ethical standards of behavior and help others to also behave ethically in their work. But the facts don't always support this aspiration.

Are you surprised by the Harris Poll reported in the Facts to Consider? Why are so few people willing to describe their top managers as acting with "integrity and morality"?[53] Based on that result, it may not surprise you that a *Business Week* survey found that just 13% of top executives at large U.S. firms rated "having strong ethical values" as a top leadership characteristic.[54]

Interactive leadership is strong on communicating, participation, and dealing with problems by teamwork.

Moral leadership has integrity and appears to others as "good" or "right" by ethical standards.

{ **IS DOING PERSONAL ERRANDS FOR THE BOSS PART OF THE JOB DESCRIPTION?**

Ethics Check

■ When the Boss Asks Too Much

Management scholars like to talk about the "zone of indifference" in leadership. It basically identifies the range of requests that a follower is willing to comply with just because someone is his or her boss. Inside the zone the answer to the "Would you do this for me?" question is a clear "Yes." Outside the zone it's supposed to be "No," but things can get tricky. Some bosses exploit their authority by asking us to do things that are on the borderline between appropriate and inappropriate. Sure we're getting paid to do them, but who benefits—the employer, or just the boss?

What if your boss wants to pay you overtime to make a set of presentation PowerPoints for a speech he is giving at a conference for his volunteer organization? Suppose the boss asks you to use your free time on the weekend to write a technology blog for the firm. What about a boss who views you as her personal assistant and consistently expects you to run personal errands—pick up dry cleaning, take the pet to the vet, make weekend dinner reservations, arrange vacation travel?

YOU DECIDE

By helping the boss with these and similar requests, you may benefit directly from pay and privileges. You may also benefit indirectly through ingratiating yourself and gaining a positive leader–follower relationship. And the boss gains as well. But when there is little or no benefit to the organization that is paying the bill, what is the ethical response on your part? Do you say, "Yes"? Do you say, "No"? Just where do you draw the line on your zone of indifference?

In contrast to the findings just described, is there any doubt that society today is demanding more ethical leadership? We want business, government, and non-profit leaders to act ethically and maintain ethical organizational cultures. We want them to help and require others to behave ethically in their work.[55] Such themes should be clear throughout this book. Hopefully too, you will agree that long-term success in your work and life can be built only on a foundation of solid ethical behavior.[56]

But how and where do we start when facing up to the challenge of building personal capacities for ethical leadership? A good answer is to focus on **integrity**.[57] You must start with honest, credible, and consistent behavior that puts your values into action. Words like "principled" and "fair" and "authentic" should come immediately to mind.

When a leader has integrity, he or she earns the trust of followers. And when followers believe that their leaders are trustworthy, they are more willing to try to live up to the leader's expectations. Southwest Airlines CEO Gary Kelly says: "Being a leader is about character . . . being straightforward and honest, having integrity, and treating people right." And there's a payoff. One of his co-workers says this about Kelly's leadership impact: "People are willing to run through walls for him."[58]

Dean Nitin Nohria of the Harvard Business School says: "The world isn't neatly divided into good people and bad people.[59] And, one of the risks we face in living up to the expectations of moral leadership is **moral overconfidence**. This occurs as an overly positive view of one's integrity and strength of character.[60] It may cause a leader to act unethically without recognizing it or while justifying it by inappropriate rationalizations. "I'm a good person, so I can't be wrong on this," a leader might say with moral overconfidence.

Integrity in leadership is honesty, credibility, and consistency in putting values into action.

Moral overconfidence is an overly positive view of one's integrity and strength of character.

■ Integrity

Even though we can get overly enamored with the notion of the "great" or "transformational" leader, it is just one among many leadership fundamentals that are enduring and important. This chapter covers a range of theories and models useful for leadership development. Each is best supported by a base of personal integrity.

Leaders with integrity are honest, credible, humble, and consistent in all that they do. They walk the talk by living up to personal values in all their actions. Transformational leadership operates on a foundation of integrity. The very concept of moral leadership is centered on integrity. And, servant leadership represents integrity in action. Why is it, then, that in the news and in everyday experiences we so often end up wondering where leadership integrity has gone?

> Get to know yourself better by taking the self-assessment on Least Preferred Co-Worker Scale and completing other activities in the *Exploring Management* Skill-Building Portfolio.

‖ Servant leadership is follower centered and empowering.

A classic observation about great leaders is that they view leadership as a responsibility, not a rank.[61] This is consistent with the notion of **servant leadership**. It means serving others and helping them use their talents to the fullest so that the organization benefits society.[62]

You might think of servant leadership by asking this question: Who is most important in leadership, the leader or the followers? For those who believe in servant leadership, there is no doubt about the correct answer: the followers. Servant leadership is "other centered" and not "self-centered." It shifts the leader's focus away from the self and toward others, and creates **empowerment** by giving people job freedom and opportunities to influence what happens in the organization.[63]

Max DePree, former CEO of Herman Miller and a noted leadership author, praises leaders who "permit others to share ownership of problems—to take possession of the situation."[64] Lorraine Monroe of the School Leadership Academy says: "The real leader is a servant of the people she leads . . . a really great boss is not afraid to hire smart people. You want people who are smart about things you are not smart about."[65] Robert Greenleaf, who is credited with coining the term "servant leadership," says: "Institutions function better when the idea, the dream, is to the fore, and the person, the leader, is seen as servant to the dream."[66]

Think about these ideas and then reach back and take a good look in the mirror. Is the leader in you capable of being a servant?

Servant leadership means serving others and helping them use their talents to help organizations benefit society.

Empowerment gives people job freedom and power to influence affairs in the organization.

STUDY GUIDE

Takeaway 11.3
What Are Current Issues and Directions in Leadership Development?

Terms to Define

Charismatic leader

Emotional intelligence (EI)

Emotional intelligence quotient (EQ)

Empowerment

Gender similarities hypothesis

Integrity

Interactive leadership

Moral leadership

Moral overconfidence

Servant leadership

Transactional leadership

Transformational leadership

Rapid Review

- Transformational leaders use charisma and emotion to inspire others toward extraordinary efforts to achieve performance excellence.
- Emotional intelligence, the ability to manage our emotions and relationships effectively, is an important leadership capability.
- The interactive leadership style, sometimes associated with women, emphasizes communication, involvement, and interpersonal respect.
- Moral or ethical leadership is built from a foundation of personal integrity, creating a basis for trust and respect between leaders and followers.
- A servant leader is follower-centered, not self-centered, and empowers others to unlock their personal talents in the quest for goals and accomplishments that help society.

Questions for Discussion

1. Should all managers be expected to excel at transformational leadership?
2. Do women lead differently than men?
3. Is servant leadership inevitably moral leadership?

Be Sure You Can

- differentiate transformational and transactional leadership
- list the personal qualities of transformational leaders
- explain how emotional intelligence contributes to leadership success
- discuss research findings on interactive leadership
- explain the role of integrity as a foundation for moral leadership
- explain the concept of servant leadership

Career Situation: What Would You Do?

Okay, so it's important to be "interactive" in leadership. By personality, though, you tend to be a bit withdrawn. If you could do things by yourself, that's the way you would behave. Yet here you are taking over as a team leader as the first upward career step in your present place of employment. How can you bend your personality to take advantage of interactive leadership and best master the challenges of your new role?

TestPrep 11

Answers to TestPrep questions can be found at the back of the book.

Multiple-Choice Questions

1. When managers use offers of rewards and threats of punishments to try to get others to do what they want them to do, they are using which type of power?
   (a) Formal authority
   (b) Position
   (c) Referent
   (d) Personal

2. When a manager says, "Because I am the boss, you must do what I ask," what power base is being put into play?
   (a) Reward
   (b) Legitimate
   (c) Moral
   (d) Referent

3. The personal traits that are now considered important for managerial success include _____.
   (a) self-confidence
   (b) gender
   (c) age
   (d) personality

4. In the research on leader behaviors, which style of leadership describes the preferred "high-high" combination?
   (a) Transformational
   (b) Transactional
   (c) Laissez-faire
   (d) Democratic

5. In Fiedler's contingency model, both highly favorable and highly unfavorable leadership situations are best dealt with by a _____-motivated leadership style.
   (a) task
   (b) vision
   (c) ethics
   (d) relationship

6. Which leadership theorist argues that one's leadership style is strongly anchored in personality and therefore very difficult to change?
   (a) Daniel Goleman
   (b) Peter Drucker
   (c) Fred Fiedler
   (d) Robert House

7. Vision, charisma, integrity, and symbolism are all attributes typically associated with _____ leaders.
   (a) people-oriented
   (b) democratic
   (c) transformational
   (d) transactional

8. In terms of leadership behaviors, someone who focuses on doing a very good job of planning work tasks, setting performance standards, and monitoring results would be described as _____.
   (a) task oriented
   (b) servant oriented
   (c) achievement oriented
   (d) transformational

9. In the discussion of gender and leadership, it was pointed out that some perceive women as having tendencies toward _____, a style that seems a good fit with developments in the new workplace.
   (a) interactive leadership
   (b) use of position power
   (c) command-and-control
   (d) transactional leadership

10. In House's path-goal theory, a leader who sets challenging goals for others would be described as using the _____ leadership style.
    (a) autocratic
    (b) achievement-oriented
    (c) transformational
    (d) directive

11. Someone who communicates a clear sense of the future and the actions needed to get there is considered a _____ leader.
    (a) task-oriented
    (b) people-oriented
    (c) transactional
    (d) visionary

12. Managerial Power = _____ Power × _____ Power.
    (a) Reward; Punishment
    (b) Reward; Expert
    (c) Legitimate; Position
    (d) Position; Personal

13. The interactive leadership style is characterized by _____.
    (a) inclusion and information sharing
    (b) use of rewards and punishments
    (c) command-and-control behavior
    (d) emphasis on position power

14. A leader whose actions indicate an attitude of "do as you want and don't bother me" would be described as having a(n) _____ leadership style.
    (a) autocratic
    (b) country club
    (c) democratic
    (d) laissez-faire

15. The critical contingency variable in the Hersey-Blanchard situational model of leadership is _____.
    (a) follower maturity
    (b) LPC
    (c) task structure
    (d) emotional intelligence

Short-Response Questions

16. Why are both position power and personal power essential in management?

17. Use Fiedler's terms to list the characteristics of situations that would be extremely favorable and extremely unfavorable to a leader.

18. Describe the situations in which House's path-goal theory would expect (a) a participative leadership style and (b) a directive leadership style to work best.

19. How do you sum up in two or three sentences the notion of servant leadership?

Integration and Application Question

20. When Marcel Henry took over as leader of a new product development team, he was both excited and apprehensive. "I wonder," he said to himself on the first day in his new assignment, "if I can meet the challenges of leadership." Later that day, Marcel shares this concern with you during a coffee break.

    Question: How would you describe to Marcel the personal implications of current thinking on transformational and moral leadership and how they might be applied to his handling of this team setting?

Steps *for* Further Learning

BUILD MARKETABLE SKILLS

DO A CASE ANALYSIS

GET AND STAY INFORMED

BUILD

MARKETABLE SKILLS.
EARN BIG CAREER
PAYOFFS!

Don't miss these
opportunities in the
**Skill-Building
Portfolio**

■ **SELF-ASSESSMENT 11:**
**Least-Preferred
Co-Worker Scale**
*Assess your leadership
personality . . . learn more
about leadership success.*

■ **CLASS EXERCISE 11:**
Leading by Participation
*There are different ways to
make decisions . . . great
leaders choose the right ones.*

■ **TEAM PROJECT 11:**
Leadership Believe-It-or-Not
*Not everyone knows how
to lead . . . sometimes the
mistakes are almost
unbelievable.*

**Many
learning
resources are
found at the end
of the book and
online within
WileyPLUS.**

Take advantage of **Cases for Critical Thinking**

■ **CHAPTER 11 CASE SNAPSHOT:**
Apple, Inc.—After the Torch was Passed/
Sidebar on Women, Leadership, and the "Double Bind"

Is Steve Jobs irreplaceable as CEO of Apple? His successor, Tim Cook, certainly thinks so. But does the company's record since Jobs's death back up the claim? Cook had been Apple's chief operating officer and, as a 13-year company veteran, seemed a natural successor to Jobs. But the industry is changing fast, competition is heating up, and many wonder if Cook can adequately fill his former boss's shoes. Jobs was viewed as abrasive by some and charismatic by others. Few would disagree that Apple's success story was crafted through his leadership. How can this company continue to excel in the absence of someone to answer the question: "What would Steve do?"

DO
A CASE ANALYSIS.
STRENGTHEN YOUR
CRITICAL THINKING!

Dig into this **Hot Topic**

■ **GOOD IDEA OR NOT?** When the boss says "Do it," consider saying "No!"

McDonald's Restaurant—A telephone caller claiming to be a police officer and having "corporate" on the line, directs the assistant store manager to take a female employee into the back room and interrogate her while he is on the line. The assistant manager does so for over three hours and follows "Officer Scott's" instructions to the point where the 18-year-old employee is naked and doing jumping jacks. The hoax was discovered only when the assistant manager called her boss to check out the story. The caller was later arrested and found to have tried similar tricks at over 70 McDonald's restaurants.

GET
AND STAY INFORMED.
MAKE YOURSELF
VALUABLE!

Managers are supposed to make decisions, and the rest of us are supposed to follow. Isn't that the conventional wisdom? But perhaps saying "Yes" to an authority figure isn't always the correct thing to do. There may be times when it's best to disobey.

Sooner or later someone in "authority" is going to ask us to do something that seems odd or incorrect or just plain suspicious. And if what we are being asked to do is wrong but we still comply, we'll share the blame. It can't be excused with the claim: "I was just following orders." But, who's prepared for the unexpected?

Final Take If obedience isn't always the right choice, how do we know when it's time to disobey? Should students get more training on both spotting bad directives and learning how to say "No"? Do management courses have enough to say about tendencies to obey, how to double-check decisions to make sure our obedience is justified, and even about the price of disobedience? Is it possible to educate and train students to be "principled" followers—ones who don't always follow orders and sometimes question them?

You don't have to look in a mirror to gain more self-awareness. What does your smart phone, tablet, or computer screen say about your personality?

Michel Gaillard/REA/ReduxPictures

Individual Behavior

There's Beauty in Individual Differences

Columbia Pictures/Photofest

Management Live

Ambition and *The Social Network*

At a time when social media seem to rule the online world, Sony's movie *The Social Network* is worth a look. Based on Facebook's visionary and controversial founder Mark Zuckerberg (Jesse Eisenberg), the movie raises ethical questions about his actions while developing the initial website, refining it, and eventually turning it into a global giant. Two former Harvard classmates, Cameron and Tyler Winklevoss, sued him, claiming the original idea was theirs. Another early collaborator and co-founder, Eduardo Saverin, was initially left out of the new firm's financial gains.

Entertainment Weekly asked: "Why did Zuckerberg betray these people? Or, in fact, did he really?" For his part, Zuckerberg called the movie pure "fiction." One thing that cannot be denied is Zuckerberg's **ambition,** the desire to succeed and reach for high goals. As the movie shows, ambition is one of those personality traits that can certainly have a big impact on individual behavior—both for the good and for the bad.

Watch *The Social Network* and discuss with your friends and classmates how different personalities and talents played out in creating the Facebook revolution. Are there lessons here that might help you deal with the ethics and intricacies of human behavior in work situations?

> ### YOUR CHAPTER 12 TAKEAWAYS
>
> 1. Understand how perceptions influence individual behavior.
> 2. Understand how personalities influence individual behavior.
> 3. Understand how attitudes, emotions, and moods influence individual behavior.

WHAT'S INSIDE

Explore Yourself
More on **ambition**

Role Models
Richard Branson leads with personality and flamboyance

Ethics Check
Is personality testing in your future?

Facts to Consider
Survey shows dissatisfaction and pessimism in lower economic classes

Manager's Library
Women Count: A Guide to Changing the World by Susan Bulkeley Butler

Takeaway 12.1
How Do Perceptions Influence Individual Behavior?

ANSWERS TO COME

- Perception filters information received from our environment.
- Perceptual distortions can obscure individual differences.
- Perception can cause attribution errors as we explain events and problems.
- Impression management is a way of influencing how others perceive us.

SOME YEARS AGO, KAREN NUSSBAUM FOUNDED AN ORGANIZATION CALLED 9 TO 5, devoted to improving women's salaries and promotion opportunities in the workplace. She had just left her job as a secretary at Harvard University. Describing what she calls "the incident that put her over the edge," Nussbaum says: "One day I was sitting at my desk at lunchtime, when most of the professors were out. A student walked into the office and looked me dead in the eye and said, 'Isn't anyone here'?" Nussbaum started 9 to 5 with a commitment to "remake the system so that it does not produce these individuals."[1]

⫾ Perception filters information received from our environment.

When people communicate with one another, everything passes through two silent but influential shields: the "perceptions" of the sender and the receiver. **Perception** is the process through which people receive and interpret information from the environment. It is the way we form impressions about ourselves, other people, and daily life experiences.

As suggested in **Figure 12.1**, you might think of perception as a bubble that surrounds us and significantly influences the way we receive, interpret, and process information received from our environments.[2] And because our individual idiosyncrasies, backgrounds, values, and experiences influence our perceptions, this means that people can and do view the same things quite differently. These differences in perceptions influence how we communicate and behave in relationship to one another.

Perception is the process through which people receive and interpret information from the environment.

FIGURE 12.1

How Does Perception Influence Communication? Perception is the process of receiving and interpreting information from our environment. It acts as a screen or filter through which we interpret messages in the communication process. Perceptions influence how we behave in response to information received. And, because people often perceive the same things quite differently, perception is an important issue in respect to individual behavior.

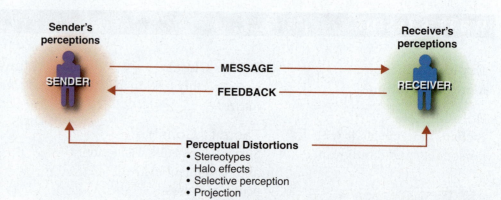

Perceptual distortions can obscure individual differences.

We live and work in an information and activity rich world that constantly bombards us with information. We deal with this complexity is by using various ways of simplifying and organizing our perceptions. One of the most common is the **stereotype**. This occurs when you identify someone with a group or category, and then use the attributes associated with the group or category to describe the individual. Although this makes things easier by reducing the need to deal with unique individual characteristics, it is an oversimplification. By relying on the stereotype, we end up missing the real individual.

A **stereotype** assigns attributes commonly associated with a group to an individual.

Consider how gender stereotyping might cause managers to misconstrue work behavior. Only a small portion, about 17%, of managers sent on international assignments are women. Do you wonder why? It's not lack of desire; there are as many women as men wanting those jobs. A Catalyst study of women in global business blames gender stereotypes that place women at a disadvantage to men for these jobs. The perception seems to be that women lack the abilities or willingness for working abroad.[3]

A **halo effect** occurs when we use one characteristic of a person or situation to form an overall impression. You probably do this quite often, as do I. When meeting someone new, for example, receiving a positive smile might create a halo effect that results in a positive impression. By contrast, the halo effect of an unfamiliar hairstyle or manner of dressing may create a negative impression.

Halo effects cause the same problems as stereotypes. They obscure individual differences. The person who smiles might have a very negative work attitude; the person with the unique hairstyle might be a top performer. Halo effects are especially significant in performance evaluations where one factor, such as a person's punctuality or lack of it, may become the halo that inaccurately determines the overall performance rating.

A **halo effect** uses one attribute to develop an overall impression of a person or situation.

Common Perceptual Distortions

- *Stereotypes*—put people into categories and then use attributes of the category to describe the individual. Example: He's close to retirement; too old to learn the new technology.
- *Halo Effects*—use one characteristic of a person or situation to form an overall impression. Example: She's always at work early; she's a great performer.
- *Selective Perception*—focuses attention on things consistent with existing beliefs, needs, and actions. Example: Sales are down; I knew the new product design was flawed.
- *Projection*—assumes others are just like us and assigns our attributes to them. Example: I'll schedule planning meetings for 7:30 a.m.; it feels good to get an early start.

Bias against Black Leaders Found on the Football Field

Are black leaders at a disadvantage when leadership success is evaluated? The answer is "yes" according to research reported in the *Academy of Management Journal*. Scholars Andrew M. Carton and Ashleigh Shelby Rosette studied how the performance of football quarterbacks was reported in the news. They found that successful performances by black quarterbacks were attributed less often to competence—such as "making decisions under pressure"—and more often to factors that made up for incompetence—such as having "the speed to get away." The researchers expressed concern that black leaders may suffer from poor career advancement because of biased evaluations.

Sportschrome/Newscom

Selective perception focuses attention on things consistent with existing beliefs, needs, or actions.

Selective perception is the tendency to focus attention on those aspects of a situation or person that reinforce or appear consistent with one's existing beliefs, needs, or actions.[4] We screen out the rest. This often happens in organizations when people from different departments or functions—such as marketing or information systems, for example—tend to see things only from their own point of view.

Like the other perceptual distortions, selective perception can bias our views of situations and individuals. One of the great benefits of teamwork and consultative decision making is the pooling of ideas and perceptions of many people, thus making it harder for selective perception to create problems.

Projection assigns personal attributes to other individuals.

Projection occurs when we assign our personal attributes to other individuals. Some call this the "similar-to-me" error. An example is to assume that other persons share our needs, desires, and values. Suppose you enjoy a lot of responsibility and challenge in your work as a team leader. You might try to increase responsibilities and challenges for team members, wanting them to experience the same satisfactions as you. But this involves projection. Instead of designing jobs to best fit their needs, you have designed their jobs to fit yours. An individual team member may be quite satisfied and productive doing his or her current job, one that

{ *Women Count: A Guide to Changing the World*
by Susan Bulkeley Butler

Manager's Library

A WOMAN'S WORK IS NOT YET DONE

Although women compose half of the workforce, they account for only 4.2% of *Fortune* 500 CEOs. Seventy percent of women with children work, and 40% are their family's primary breadwinner, yet women earn 78 cents for every dollar men earn.

Haven't women shown that these numbers are simply unacceptable?

In the book *Women Count: A Guide to Changing the World* (2010, Purdue University Press), author Susan Bulkeley Butler urges women to stop accepting statistics that underrepresent their leadership value and, instead, to take action. She says women can shift their paradigm of success and stop thinking about others first. Butler advises women to start by helping themselves, which may require rebalancing roles in their work, home, and personal life. She states that women can't master these roles separately and suffer from obligation guilt. They must redefine the roles with the help of employers.

An example is the attorney who relocated so her children's grandparents could assist with child care. The firm assigned her cases she could work on from home, and the flexibility in rebalancing her work, family, and personal roles was essential to her success.

In this book, Butler cites research that women are good for performance. Companies with the most women, either on their board of directors or in top management positions,

outperform those with the least women by 53% or 35%, respectively, measured by return on equity. She asserts that this is because women possess behavioral advantages over men—things like being more compassionate, less ego-driven, listening better, taking fewer risks, and tending to be consensus builders.

Butler advises organizations to appoint at least two women to the board, have women report directly to the CEO, and create mentoring programs for female leaders. Policies allowing women to rebalance life roles must also be commonplace. Butler herself mentors female executives and provides organizational resources through her Institute for the Development of Women Leaders.

The bottom line of *Women Count* is that action is needed to ensure the progress of more women into leadership roles. It may be that a woman's work is not done until the numbers reflect that women do really count.

REFLECT AND REACT

If women are good for performance, why don't more women lead large companies? Do you expect this situation to change substantially during your career? How can work, family, and personal roles of women conflict? What can organizations do in order to better accommodate professional females? What can a woman really do to "balance" multiple role expectations?

seems routine to you. We can control projection errors through self-awareness and a willingness to communicate and empathize with other persons, that is, to try to see things through their eyes.

‖ Perception can cause attribution errors as we explain events and problems.

One of the ways in which perception exerts its influence on behavior is through **attribution**. This is the process of developing explanations for events and their perceived causes. It is natural for people to try to explain what they observe and the things that happen to them. Suppose you perceive that someone else in a job or student group isn't performing up to expectations. How do you explain this? And, depending on the explanation, what do you do to try to correct things?

When considering so-called poor performance by someone else, we are likely to commit something called **fundamental attribution error**. This is a tendency to blame other people when things go wrong, whether or not this is really true. If I perceive that a student is doing poorly in my course, for example, this error pops up as a tendency to criticize the student's lack of ability or unwillingness to study hard enough. But that perception may not be accurate, as you may well agree. Perhaps there's something about the course design, its delivery, or my actions as an instructor that are contributing to the problem—a deficiency in the learning environment, not the individual.

Suppose you are having a performance problem—at school, at work, wherever. How do you explain it? Again, the likelihood of attribution error is high; this time it is called **self-serving bias**. It's the tendency for people to blame personal failures or problems on external causes rather than accept personal responsibility. This is the "It's not my fault!" error. The flip side is to claim personal responsibility for any successes—"It was me; I did it!"

The significance of these attribution errors can be quite substantial. When we perceive things incorrectly, we are likely to take the wrong actions and miss solving a lot of problems in the process. Think about self-serving bias the next time you hear someone blaming your instructor for a poor course grade. And think about the fundamental attribution error the next time you jump on a group member who didn't perform according to your standards. Our perceptions aren't always wrong, but they should always be double-checked and tested for accuracy. There are no safe assumptions when it comes to the power of attributions.

‖ Impression management is a way of influencing how others perceive us.

Richard Branson, CEO of the Virgin Group, may be one of the richest and most famous executives in the world. One of his early business accomplishments was the successful start-up of Virgin Airlines, which became a new competitive force in the airline industry. The former head of British Airways, Lord King, once said:

Attribution is the process of creating explanations for events.

The **fundamental attribution error** overestimates internal factors and underestimates external factors as influences on someone's behavior.

Self-serving bias underestimates internal factors and overestimates external factors as influences on someone's behavior.

"If Richard Branson had worn a shirt and tie instead of a goatee and jumper, I would not have underestimated him."[5] This is an example of how much our impressions count—both positive and negative. Knowing this, scholars now emphasize the importance of **impression management**, the systematic attempt to influence how others perceive us.[6]

You might notice that we often do bits and pieces of impression management as a matter of routine in everyday life. This is especially evident when we enter new situations—perhaps a college classroom or new work team, what we post on Facebook or Twitter, and as we prepare to meet people for the first time, such as going out with a new friend for a social occasion or heading off to a job interview. In these and other situations we tend to dress, talk, act, and surround ourselves with things that help convey a desirable self-image to other persons.

Impression management that is well done can help us advance in jobs and careers, form relationships with people we admire, and even create pathways to desired social memberships. Some basic tactics are worth remembering: knowing when to dress up and when to dress down to convey positive appeal in certain situations, using words to flatter other people in ways that generate positive feelings toward you, making eye contact and smiling when engaged in conversations to create a personal bond, and displaying a high level of energy that indicates work commitment and initiative.[7]

> **Impression management** tries to create desired perceptions in the eyes of others.

Chris Jackson/Getty Images

{ "HAVING A PERSONALITY OF CARING ABOUT PEOPLE IS IMPORTANT . . . YOU CAN'T BE A GOOD LEADER UNLESS YOU GENERALLY LIKE PEOPLE."

Role Models

■ Richard Branson Leads with Personality and Flamboyance

Could you imagine starting an airline? Richard Branson decided he would and called it Virgin Atlantic. It was another step in a career that began in his native England with a student literary magazine and small mail-order record business. Since then he's built Virgin Group into a global business conglomerate employing some 50,000 people in more than 30 countries. Its range of businesses spans music, financial services, Virgin Mobile, and even the space venture Virgin Galactic.

If you bump into Branson on the street, you might be surprised. He's casual, he's smiling, and he's fun. But, he's also creative, brilliant, and ambitious when it comes to business and leadership. As the man behind the Virgin brand, he's described as "flamboyant," something he doesn't deny and also considers a major business advantage that keeps him and his ventures in the public eye. Listed among the 25 most influential business leaders, Branson says: "I love to learn things I know little about," and "before I do anything I first get tons of feedback."

According to Branson, "Having a personality of caring about people is important. . . . You can't be a good leader unless you generally like people. That is how you bring out the best in them." His own style, he claims, was shaped by his family and childhood. At age 10 his mother put him on a 300-mile bike ride to build character and endurance. At 16, he started a student magazine. By the age of 22, he was launching Virgin record stores. And by the time he was 30, Virgin Group was running at high speed.

Now known as Sir Richard after being knighted by the Queen, he enjoys Virgin today "as a way of life." But he adds: "In the next stage of my life I want to use our business skills to tackle social issues around the world. . . . Malaria in Africa kills four million people a year. AIDS kills even more. . . . I don't want to waste this fabulous situation in which I've found myself."

WHAT'S THE LESSON HERE?

Do actions speak louder than impressions? Richard Branson succeeded while staying true to himself. How does this apply to you, or anyone seeking a rewarding career? Should those who aren't at the top be more or less worried about impression management?

STUDY GUIDE

Takeaway 12.1
How Do Perceptions Influence Individual Behavior?

Terms to Define

Attribution

Fundamental attribution error

Halo effect

Impression management

Perception

Projection

Selective perception

Self-serving bias

Stereotype

Rapid Review

- Perception acts as a filter through which all communication passes as it travels from one person to the next.
- Different people may perceive the same things differently.
- Stereotypes, projections, halo effects, and selective perception can distort perceptions and reduce communication effectiveness.
- Fundamental attribution error occurs when we blame others for their performance problems, without considering possible external causes.
- Self-serving bias occurs when, in judging our own performance, we take personal credit for successes and blame failures on external factors.
- Through impression management, we influence the way that others perceive us.

Questions for Discussion

1. How do advertising firms use stereotypes to influence consumer behavior?
2. Are there times when a self-serving bias is actually helpful?
3. Does the notion of impression management contradict the idea of personal integrity?

Be Sure You Can

- describe how perception influences behavior
- explain how stereotypes, halo effects, selective perceptions, and projection might operate in the workplace
- explain the concepts of attribution error and self-serving bias
- illustrate how someone might use impression management during a job interview

Career Situation: What Would You Do?

While standing in line at the office coffee machine, you overhear the person in front of you saying this to his friend: "I'm really tired of having to deal with the old-timers here. It's time for them to call it quits. There's no way they can keep up the pace and handle all the new technology we're getting these days." You can listen and forget, or you can listen and act. Take the action route. What would you do or say here, and why?

Takeaway 12.2

How Do Personalities Influence Individual Behavior?

ANSWERS TO COME

■ The Myers-Briggs Type Indicator is a popular approach to personality assessment.

■ The Big Five personality traits describe work-related individual differences.

■ Personalities vary on personal conception and emotional adjustment traits.

■ People with Type A personalities tend to stress themselves.

■ Stress has consequences for work performance and personal health.

■ Stress can be managed by good decisions and personal wellness.

THINK OF HOW MANY TIMES YOU'VE COMPLAINED ABOUT SOMEONE'S "BAD personality" or told a friend how much you like someone else because they had such a "nice personality." Well, the same holds true at work. Perhaps you have been part of or the subject of conversations like these: "I can't give him that job. He's a bad fit; with a personality like that, there's no way he can work with customers." Or "Put Erika on the project; her personality is perfect for the intensity that we expect from the team."

Personality is the profile of characteristics making a person unique from others.

The term **personality** describes the combination or overall profile of enduring characteristics that make each of us unique. And as the prior examples suggest, this uniqueness can have consequences for how we behave and how that behavior is regarded by others.

⫴ The Myers-Briggs Type Indicator is a popular approach to personality assessment.

Something known as the Myers-Briggs Type Indicator is a popular approach to personality assessment. It uses a sophisticated questionnaire to examine how people act or feel in various situations. Called the MBTI for short, it was developed by Katherine Briggs and her daughter Isabel Briggs-Myers from foundations set forth in the work of psychologist Carl Jung.[8]

Jung's model of personality differences included three main distinctions. First are personality differences in ways people relate with others—extraversion (being outgoing and sociable) or introversion (being shy and quiet). Second are how people vary in the way they gather information—by sensation (emphasizing details, facts, and routine) or by intuition (looking for the "big picture" and being willing to deal with various possibilities). Third, are differences in evaluating information—by thinking (using reason and analysis) or by feeling (responding to the feelings and desires of others).

Briggs and Briggs-Myers added a fourth dimension to Jung's personality model. It describes how people vary in the ways they relate to the outside world—judging (seeking order and control) or perceiving (acting with flexibility and spontaneity). What is now called the Myers-Briggs Type Indicator covers the following personality dimensions.[9]

- *Extraversion vs. introversion (E or I*—whether a person tends toward being outgoing and sociable or shy and quiet.
- *Sensing vs. intuitive (S or N)*—whether a person tends to focus on details or on the big picture in dealing with problems.
- *Thinking vs. feeling (T or F)*—whether a person tends to rely on logic or emotions in dealing with problems.
- *Judging vs. perceiving (J or P)*—whether a person prefers order and control or acts with flexibility and spontaneity.

The MBTI instrument can be easily found and completed online. A person's scores allow them to be categorized into one of 16 possible personality types, such as the sample personalities shown in the small box. This neat and understandable classification has made the MBTI very popular in management training and development, although it receives mixed reviews from researchers.[10] Employers and consultants tend to like it because once a person is "typed" on the Myers-Briggs, for example as an ESTJ or ISFJ, they can be trained to both understand their own styles and to learn how to better work with people having different styles.

Sample Myers-Briggs Personality Types

ESTJ (extraverted, sensing, thinking, judging)—practical, decisive, logical, and quick to dig in; common among managers.

ENTJ (extraverted, intuitive, thinking, judging)—analytical, strategic, forceful, quick to take charge; common for leaders.

ISFJ (introverted, sensing, feeling, judging)—conscientious, considerate, and helpful; common among team players.

INTJ (introverted, intuitive, thinking, judging)—insightful, free thinking, determined; common for visionaries.

Troels Graugaard/ iStockphoto

{ **WHEN IS PERSONALITY TESTING AN INVASION OF PERSONAL PRIVACY?**

Ethics Check

■ Is Personality Testing in Your Future?

Dear [your name goes here]:

I am very pleased to invite you to a second round of screening interviews with XYZ Corporation. Your online interview with our representative went very well, and we would like to consider you for a full-time position. Please contact me to arrange a visit date. We will need a full day. The schedule will include several meetings with executives and your potential team members, as well as a round of personality tests.

Thank you again for your interest in XYZ Corp. I look forward to meeting you during the next step in our recruiting process.

Sincerely,
[signed]
Human Resource Director

Getting a letter like this is great news. It's a nice confirmation of your hard work and performance in college. You obviously made a good first impression. But have you thought about this "personality test" thing? What do you know about them and how they are used for employment screening? Some people might consider their use an invasion of privacy.

YOU DECIDE

What are the ethical issues associated with personality testing for employment? In which situations might the use of personality tests be an invasion of privacy? Should employers have to provide evidence that the tests they use are good predictors of employee performance on the job?

⫼ The Big Five personality traits describe work-related individual differences.

We all know that variations among personalities are both real and consequential in our relationships with everyone from family to friends to co-workers. In addition to those personality traits in the MBTI, scholars have identified a list known as the Big Five: extraversion, agreeableness, conscientiousness, emotional stability, and openness to experience.[11]

Take a look at the descriptions in **Table 12.1**—How to Identify the Big Five Personality Traits. You can probably spot the Big Five pretty easily in people with whom you work, study, and socialize, as well as in yourself. And while you're at it, why not use the table as a quick check of your personality? Ask: What are the implications for my personal and work relationships?

Table 12.1 How to Identify the Big Five Personality Traits

Extraversion An extravert is talkative, comfortable, and confident in interpersonal relationships; an introvert is more private, withdrawn, and reserved.

Agreeableness An agreeable person is trusting, courteous, and helpful, getting along well with others; a disagreeable person is self-serving, skeptical, and tough, creating discomfort for others.

Conscientiousness A conscientious person is dependable, organized, and focused on getting things done; a person who lacks conscientiousness is careless, impulsive, and not achievement oriented.

Emotional stability A person who is emotionally stable is secure, calm, steady, and self-confident; a person lacking emotional stability is excitable, anxious, nervous, and tense.

Openness to experience A person open to experience is broad-minded, imaginative, and open to new ideas; and person who lacks openness is narrow-minded, has few interests, and resists change.

A considerable body of research links the Big Five personality traits with work and career outcomes. The expectation is that people with more extraverted, agreeable, conscientious, emotionally stable, and open personalities will have more positive relationships and experiences in organizations.[12] Conscientious persons tend to be highly motivated and high-performing in their work, whereas emotionally stable persons tend to handle change situations well. It's also likely that Big Five traits are implicit criteria used by managers when making judgments about people at work, handing out job assignments, building teams, and more. Psychologists even use the Big Five to steer people in the direction of career choices that may provide the best personality–job fits. Extraversion, for example, is a good predictor of success in management and sales positions.

⫼ Personalities vary on personal conception and self-monitoring traits.

A selection of additional personality traits that can influence how people behave and work together are shown in the nearby figure.[13] They include locus of control, authoritarianism, Machiavellianism, self-monitoring, and Type A orientation.

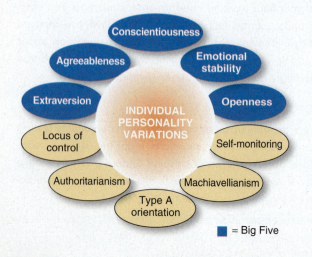

= Big Five

Scholars have a strong interest in **locus of control**, noting that some people believe they control their destinies, whereas others believe what happens is beyond their control.[14] "Internals" are more self-confident and accept responsibility for their own actions; "externals" are prone to blaming others and outside forces when bad things happen. Interestingly, research suggests that internals tend to be more satisfied and less alienated from their work.

Authoritarianism is the degree to which a person defers to authority and accepts status differences.[15] Someone with an authoritarian personality might act rigid and control-oriented as a leader. Yet, this same person is often subservient as a follower. People with an authoritarian personality tend to obey orders. Of course, this can create problems when their supervisors ask them to do unethical or even illegal things.

In his 16th-century book *The Prince*, Niccolo Machiavelli gained lasting fame for his advice on how to use power to achieve personal goals.[16] Today we use the term **Machiavellianism** to describe someone who acts manipulatively and emotionally detached when using power. We usually view a "high-Mach" personality as exploitative and unconcerned about others, seemingly guided only by a belief that the end justifies the means. Those with "low-Mach" personalities, by contrast, allow others to exert power over them.

Finally, **self-monitoring** reflects the degree to which someone is able to adjust and modify behavior in new situations.[17] Persons high in self-monitoring tend to be learners, comfortable with feedback, and both willing and able to change. Because they are flexible, however, others may perceive them as constantly shifting gears and hard to read. A person low in self-monitoring is predictable and tends to act consistently. But this consistency may not fit the unique needs of differing circumstances.

⦀ People with Type A personalities tend to stress themselves.

Stress is a state of tension experienced by individuals facing extraordinary demands, constraints, or opportunities.[18] As you consider stress in your life and in your work, you might think about how your personality deals with it. Researchers describe the **Type A personality**, also shown among the personality traits in the last figure, as someone who is oriented toward high achievement, impatience, and perfectionism. Because of this, Type A's are likely to bring stress on themselves even in circumstances that others find relatively stress-free.[19]

The work environment has enough potential *stressors*, or sources of stress, without this added burden of a stress-prone Type A personality. Some 87% of American workers in one survey said they experienced stress at work, whereas 34% of workers in another survey said that their jobs were so stressful that they were thinking of quitting.[20] The stress they were talking about comes from long hours of work, unreasonable workloads, low pay, difficult bosses or co-workers, and not working in desired career field.[21]

As if work stress isn't enough for Type A's to deal with, there's the added kicker of complicated personal lives. Things such as family events (e.g., the birth of a new child), economics (e.g., a sudden loss of extra income), and personal issues (e.g., a preoccupation with a bad relationship) are sources of potential emotional strain for most people, but especially for Type A's. Such personal stressors can spill over to negatively affect our behavior at work. Of course, the reverse also holds true; work stressors can spill over to affect our personal lives.

Locus of control is the extent to which one believes what happens is within one's control.

Authoritarianism is the degree to which a person defers to authority and accepts status differences.

Machiavellianism is the degree to which someone uses power manipulatively.

Self-monitoring is the degree to which someone is able to adjust behavior in response to external factors.

Stress is a state of tension experienced by individuals facing extraordinary demands, constraints, or opportunities.

A **Type A personality** is oriented toward extreme achievement, impatience, and perfectionism.

Stress has consequences for work performance and personal health.

It's tempting to view stress all in the negative. But don't forget that stress can have its positive side as well.[22]

Constructive stress is energizing and performance enhancing.[23] Take the analogy of a violin.[24] When a violin string is too loose, the sound produced by even the most skilled player is weak and raspy. When the string is too tight, the sound gets shrill and the string might even snap. But when the tension on the string is just right, it creates a beautiful sound.

You've probably felt constructive stress as a student. Don't you sometimes do better work "when the pressure is on," as we like to say? Moderate but not overwhelming stress can help us by encouraging effort, stimulating creativity, and enhancing diligence. But just like tuning a violin string, achieving the right balance of stress for each person and situation is difficult.

Destructive stress is dysfunctional because it is or seems so intense or long-lasting that it overloads and breaks down a person's physical and mental systems. One of its workplace outcomes is **job burnout**. This is a sense of physical and mental exhaustion that drains our energies both personally and professionally. Too much stress can also cause **flameout**, where someone expresses extreme agitation through words in interpersonal communication or electronic messages. Think of it as the e-mail message that you wish you'd thought twice about before hitting the "send" button.

Yet another possible outcome of excessive stress is **workplace rage** in the form of overly aggressive—even violent—behavior toward co-workers, bosses, or customers.[25] An extreme example called "bossnapping" made the news in France when workers at a Caterpillar plant held their manager hostage for 24 hours in protest of layoffs. A local sociologist said: "Kidnapping your boss is not legal. But it's a way workers have found to make their voices heard."[26]

Medical research also indicates that too much stress can be bad for health. It reduces resistance to disease and increases the likelihood of hypertension, ulcers, substance abuse, overeating, and depression.[27]

> **Constructive stress** is a positive influence on effort, creativity, and diligence in work.

> **Destructive stress** is a negative influence on one's performance.

> **Job burnout** is physical and mental exhaustion from work stress.

> A **flameout** occurs when we communicate extreme agitation in interpersonal communication or electronic messages.

> **Workplace rage** is aggressive behavior toward co-workers or the work setting.

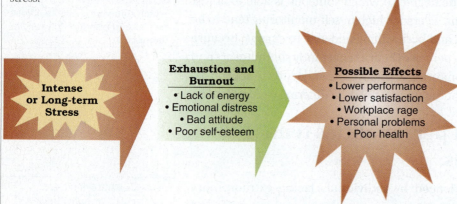

Intense or Long-term Stress → Exhaustion and Burnout
- Lack of energy
- Emotional distress
- Bad attitude
- Poor self-esteem

Possible Effects
- Lower performance
- Lower satisfaction
- Workplace rage
- Personal problems
- Poor health

Stress can be managed by good decisions and personal wellness.

So what can we do about stress—how can it be managed? The best strategy is to prevent it from reaching excessive levels in the first place. If we know we have a Type A personality and can identify our stressors, we can often take action to avoid or minimize their negative consequences. And as managers, we can take steps to help others who are showing stress symptoms. Things like temporary

Spanx Has Lots of Snap

Real People and Personalities Make Things Happen

The headline reads: "Spanx queen leads from the bottom line." The story goes: Woman unhappy with the way she looks in white pants cuts feet off panty hose, puts them on, and attends party. The result is: Sara Blakely founds a $250 million business called Spanx.

"I knew this could open up so many women's wardrobes," Blakely says. "All women have that clothing in the back of the closet that they don't wear because they don't like the way it looks." Taking $5,500 of her own money and the idea for "body shaping" underwear, she set out to start a business. Her unique blend of skills and personality made it all work.

When her first attempts to convince manufacturers to make product samples met with resistance—with one calling it "a stupid idea"—Blakely persisted until one agreed. She wanted to place Spanx in high-end department stores, but they kept turning her down. She kept at it until a buyer at Neiman Marcus gave Spanx its first big chance. Sales took off after Oprah voted Spanx "one of her favorite things."

About this time Blakely recognized her limits and realized additional skills were needed to handle the firm's fast-paced growth. "I was eager to delegate my weaknesses," she said after turning day-to-day operations over to a chief executive officer. This left her free to pursue creativity, new products, and brand development, as well as work with the Sara Blakely Foundation and its goal of "supporting and empowering women around the world."

Joe Kohen/Wireimage/GettyImages

Find Inspiration

Creative, outgoing, passionate, driven, persistent, and ambitious—these adjectives and more describe Sara Blakely and her personality. They can also go a long way in explaining how and why she was successful with Spanx. When you look in the mirror, what and whom do you see?

changes in work schedules, reduced performance expectations, long deadlines, and even reminders to take time off can all help.

When it comes to taking time off, the latest advice might be surprising—you may be able to work better by working less. A study by the Boston Consulting Group reports that requiring people to take time off from their work—by not skipping vacations or working too much overtime, for example—can pay off in more job satisfaction and better work-life balance. The professional services firm KPMG follows this advice almost to the letter. Its managers now use "wellness scorecards" to track and discuss with employees how well they are doing in taking their vacation days and not working excessive overtime. [28]

Finally, there is really no substitute for **personal wellness** in the form of a personal health-promotion program.[29] It begins by taking personal responsibility for your physical and mental health. It means getting rest, getting plenty of exercise, and eating a balanced diet. It means dealing with addictions to cigarettes, alcohol, or drugs. And it means committing to a healthy lifestyle, one that helps you deal with stress and the demands of life and work.

Personal wellness is the pursuit of a personal health-promotion program.

STUDY GUIDE

Takeaway 12.2
How Do Personalities Influence Individual Behavior?

Terms to Define

Agreeableness

Authoritarianism

Conscientiousness

Constructive stress

Destructive stress

Emotional stability

Extraversion

Flameout

Job burnout

Locus of control

Machiavellianism

Openness

Personal wellness

Personality

Self-monitoring

Stress

Type A personality

Workplace rage

Rapid Review

- The Big Five personality factors are extraversion, agreeableness, conscientiousness, emotional stability, and openness.
- The Myers-Briggs Type Indicator (MBTI) identifies personality types based on extraversion–introversion, sensing–intuitive, thinking–feeling, and judging–perceiving.
- Additional personality dimensions of work significance are locus of control, authoritarianism, Machiavellianism, self-monitoring, and Type A orientation.
- Stress is a state of tension that accompanies extraordinary demands, constraints, or opportunities.
- For some people, having a Type A personality creates stress as a result of continual feelings of impatience and pressure.
- Stress can be destructive or constructive; a moderate level of stress can have a positive impact on performance.

Questions for Discussion

1. Which personality trait would you add to the Big Five to make it the Big "Six"?
2. What are the advantages and disadvantages of having people of different MBTI types working on the same team?
3. Can you be an effective manager and not have a Type A personality?

Be Sure You Can

- list the Big Five personality traits and give work-related examples of each
- list five more personality traits and give work-related examples for each
- list and explain the four dimensions used to create personality types in the MBTI
- identify common stressors in work and personal life
- describe the Type A personality
- differentiate constructive and destructive stress
- explain personal wellness as a stress management strategy

Career Situation: What Would You Do?

You've noticed that one of your co-workers is always rushing, always uptight, and constantly criticizing herself while on the job. She never takes time for coffee with the rest of the team. Even at lunch it's hard to get her to sit and just talk for awhile. Your guess is that she's a Type A and fighting stress from some source or sources other than the nature of the job itself. How can you help her out?

Takeaway 12.3
How Do Attitudes, Emotions, and Moods Influence Individual Behavior?

ANSWERS TO COME

- Attitudes predispose people to act in certain ways.
- Job satisfaction is a positive attitude toward one's job and work experiences.
- Job satisfaction influences work behavior.
- Job satisfaction has a complex relationship with job performance.
- Emotions and moods are positive and negative states of mind that influence behavior.

TEACHING NOTE:
Discussion question 1: What causes a "bad" attitude and what can be done to change it—by the person or by someone who cares about them? Discussion question 2: What do you do to get yourself out of bad mood?

AT ONE TIME, CHALLIS M. LOWE WAS ONE OF ONLY TWO AFRICAN-AMERICAN women among the five highest-paid executives in over 400 U.S. corporations.[30] She attained this success after a 25-year career that included several changes of employers and lots of stressors—working-mother guilt, a failed marriage, gender bias on the job, and an MBA degree earned part-time. "I've never let being scared stop me from doing something," she said. "Just because you haven't done it before doesn't mean you shouldn't try." Would you agree that Lowe has what we often call a "can-do" attitude?

⫼ Attitudes predispose people to act in certain ways.

An **attitude** is a predisposition to act in a certain way toward people and environmental factors.[31] Challis Lowe seemed disposed to take risks and embrace challenges. This positive attitude influenced her behavior when dealing with the inevitable problems, choices, and opportunities of work and career.

The three components shown in the small figure help us understand attitudes. First is the *cognitive component* of the attitude. It reflects a belief or value. You might believe, for example, that your management course is very interesting. Second is the *affective* or *emotional component*, which reflects a specific feeling. For example, you might feel very good about being a management major. Third is the *behavioral component*, which reflects an intention to behave consistent with the belief and feeling. Using the same example again, you might say to yourself: "I am going to work hard and try to get As in all my management courses."

Have you noticed that attitudes don't always predict behavior? Despite pledging to work hard as a student, you might not. Despite wanting a more challenging job, you might keep the current one. In such cases we fail to live up to our own expectations. Usually it's not a good feeling.

The psychological concept of **cognitive dissonance** describes the discomfort we feel in situations where our attitude is inconsistent with our behavior.[32] Most of us manage this dissonance by modifying our attitude to better fit the behavior ("Oh well, work isn't really that important,

An **attitude** is a predisposition to act in a certain way.

Cognitive dissonance is discomfort felt when attitude and behavior are inconsistent.

Three Components of Attitudes

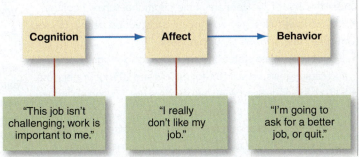

Cognition → Affect → Behavior

"This job isn't challenging; work is important to me."

"I really don't like my job."

"I'm going to ask for a better job, or quit."

anyway"), changing future behavior to fit the attitude (not putting extra time in at work; focusing more attention on leisure and personal hobbies), or rationalizing in ways that make the attitude and behavior seem compatible ("I'm in no hurry; there will be a lot of opportunities for better jobs in the future").

||| Job satisfaction is a positive attitude toward one's job and work experiences.

Job satisfaction is the degree to which an individual feels positive about a job and work experience.

People hold attitudes about many things in the workplace—bosses, each other, tasks, organizational policies, performance goals, paychecks, and more. A comprehensive or catch-all work attitude is **job satisfaction**, the degree to which an individual feels positive or negative about various aspects of his or her job and work experiences.[33]

Several things are usually at issue when researchers study and people talk about job satisfaction. Aspects of the work and social context that often affect job satisfaction include:

Aspects of Job Satisfaction ≫

- *Job tasks*—responsibility, interest, challenge.
- *Quality of supervision*—task help, social support.
- *Co-workers*—harmony, respect, friendliness.
- *Opportunities*—promotion, learning, growth.
- *Pay*—actual and comparative.
- *Work conditions*—comfort, safety, support.
- *Security*—job and employment.

If you watch or read the news, you'll regularly find reports on job satisfaction. You'll also find lots of job satisfaction studies in the academic literature. Interestingly, the majority of people tend to report being at least somewhat satisfied with

David Burton/Alamy

{ MORE AMERICANS ARE SELF-IDENTIFYING AS MEMBERS OF THE LOWER OR LOWER-MIDDLE CLASSES, AND REPORTING LESS JOB SATISFACTION

Facts to **Consider**

■ Survey Shows Dissatisfaction and Pessimism in Lower Economic Classes

More Americans are self-identifying as members of the lower or lower-middle classes. Pew Research data shows 32% of adults defining themselves in this economic category, an increase of 7% between 2008 and 2012. The largest proportion of them, 39%, is under the age of 30. Here are some additional survey findings.

- 28% of lower class reports job dissatisfaction versus 6% for middle class and 7% for upper class.
- 39% of lower class state they are not making progress on work and career goals, versus 18% for middle and 10% for upper class.
- 53% of lower-class women say they are not advancing in their careers, versus 26% of lower-class men.
- 3% of lower classes feel less financially secure than 10 years ago, versus 42% for middle and 24% for upper classes.

- 58% of lower classes lack confidence that they will have enough money to retire, versus 32% for middle and 18% for upper classes.

YOUR THOUGHTS

Are these data consistent with what you hear in conversations with family and friends? What's the mood among those who are seeking jobs? How does the current economy affect job satisfaction and satisfaction with life overall? When people are stuck in jobs that don't provide career satisfaction, how can they deal with the situation? Is there anything an existing employer can do to help improve their job satisfaction?

their jobs. But the trend is down.[34] The least satisfying things about people's jobs often relate to feeling underpaid, not having good career advancement opportunities, and being trapped in the current job. And in respect to things that create job satisfaction, a global study finds pay, contrary to what you might expect, is less important than things like opportunities to do interesting work, recognition for performance, work-life balance, chances for advancement, and job security.[35]

▌ Job satisfaction influences work behavior.

Researchers tell us that there is a strong relationship between job satisfaction and the **withdrawal behaviors** of *absenteeism*—not showing up for work—and *turnover*—quitting one's job. In respect to absenteeism, workers who are more satisfied with their jobs are absent less often than those who are dissatisfied. In respect to turnover, satisfied workers are more likely to stay and dissatisfied workers are more likely to quit their jobs. The consequences of these withdrawal behaviors can be significant. Both absenteeism and excessive turnover are expensive for employers. In fact, one study found that changing retention rates—up or down—results in similar changes to corporate earnings.[36]

Researchers also identify a relationship between job satisfaction and **organizational citizenship behaviors**.[37] They show up as a willingness to "go beyond the call of duty" or "go the extra mile" in one's work.[38] A person who is a good organizational citizen does things that, although not required, help advance the performance of the organization. You might observe this as a service worker who takes especially good care of a customer, a team member who always takes on extra tasks, or a friend who is works extra hours without pay just to make sure things are done right for his employer.

Job satisfaction is also tied with **employee engagement**, a strong sense of belonging or connection with one's job and employer. It shows up both in *high involvement*—being willing to help others and always trying to do something extra to improve performance, and *in high commitment*—feeling and speaking positively about the organization. A survey of American workers by the Gallup Organization suggests that more engaged workforces generate higher profits for employers.[39] Things that counted most toward employee engagement in this research were believing one has the opportunity to do the best every day, believing one's opinions are valued, believing fellow workers are committed to quality, and believing there is a direct connection between one's work and the company's mission.

Withdrawal behaviors include absenteeism (not showing up for work) and turnover (quitting one's job).

Organizational citizenship behaviors are things people do to go the extra mile in their work.

Employee engagement is a strong sense of belonging and connection with one's work and employer.

If You Want Job Satisfaction, You Might Consider Being Your Own Boss.

Are you working for money alone, or will you be? If so, perhaps you might try self-employment. A survey from the Pew Research Center found the self-employed to be more satisfied and less prone to work for a paycheck alone. On pay, 50% of those not self-employed said they worked because they needed the money versus only 38% of the self-employed. Results for job satisfaction showed 39% of the self-employed reporting "complete satisfaction" versus 28% of the not self-employed.

Job satisfaction has a complex relationship with job performance.

We know that job satisfaction influences withdrawal, citizenship, and engagement. But, does it influence performance? The data are, as you might expect, somewhat complicated.[40] Consider a sign that once hung in a tavern near a Ford plant in Michigan: "I spend 40 hours a week here, am I supposed to work too?" Three different arguments on the satisfaction and performance relationship are shown in the small figure. Can you make a case for each argument based on your personal experiences?

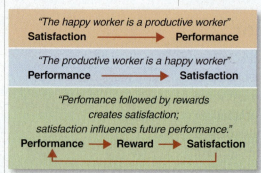

There is probably a modest link between job satisfaction and performance.[41] But emphasize the word "modest." We can't conclude that making people happy is a surefire way to improve their job performance. The reality is that some people will like their jobs, be very satisfied, and still not perform very well. That's part of the complexity of individual behavior.

It's also true that high-performing workers are likely to feel satisfied. But again, some people may work with high performance without experiencing high job satisfaction. Has this ever happened for you?

Finally, job satisfaction and job performance do influence each other. But the relationship depends a lot on rewards. High performance followed by rewards that are valued and perceived as fair is likely to create job satisfaction. This satisfaction, in turn, can be expected to increase motivation to work hard to achieve high performance in the future. The catch to this relationship, however, is difficulty making sure rewards are valued and perceived as fair by the recipient.

Emotions and moods are positive and negative states of mind that influence behavior.

Emotional intelligence, or EI, is an ability to understand emotions and manage relationships effectively.

Emotions are strong feelings directed toward someone or something.

Emotional intelligence is an important human skill for managers and an important leadership capability. Daniel Goleman defines "EI" as an ability to understand emotions in ourselves and in others and to use this understanding to manage relationships effectively.[42] His point in highlighting the importance of emotional intelligence is that we perform better in work and social situations when we are good at recognizing and dealing with emotions in ourselves and others. In other words, EI allows us to avoid having our emotions "get the better of us." But what is an "emotion"? And, how does it influence our behavior—positively and negatively?

An **emotion** is a strong feeling directed toward someone or something. For example, you might feel positive emotion or elation when an instructor congratulates you on a fine class presentation; you might feel negative emotion or anger when an instructor criticizes you in front of the class. In both cases the object of your emotion is the instructor, but in each case the impact of the instructor's behavior on your feelings is quite different. And your behavior in response to the aroused emotions is likely to differ as well—perhaps

Understanding Emotions

"I was really mad when Prof. Nitpicker criticized my presentation."

- Linked with a specific cause
- Tends to be brief or episodic
- Specific effect on attitude, behavior
- Might turn into a mood

breaking into a wide smile with the compliment or making a nasty side comment in response to criticism.

Whereas emotions tend to be short-term and clearly targeted, **moods** are generalized positive and negative feelings or states of mind that may persist for some time. Everyone seems to have occasional moods, and we each know the full range of possibilities they represent. How often do you wake up in the morning and feel excited, refreshed, and just happy? . . . or, wake up feeling low, depressed, and generally unhappy? How do these different moods affect your behavior with friends and family, and at work or school?

> **Moods** are generalized positive and negative feelings or states of mind.

When it comes to moods in the workplace, a *Business Week* article claims that it pays to be likable.[43] Harsh now seems out and caring is in. Some CEOs are even hiring executive coaches to help them manage emotions and moods so as to come across as more personable and friendly in relationships with others. There's a bit of impression management to consider here. If a CEO goes to a meeting in a good mood and gets described as "cheerful," "charming," "humorous," "friendly," and "candid," she or he may be viewed as on the upswing. But if the CEO is in a bad mood and comes away perceived as "prickly," "impatient," "remote," "tough," "acrimonious," or even "ruthless," she or he may be seen as on the downhill slope.

Researchers are very interested in **mood contagion**, the spillover effects of one's mood onto others.[44] It turns out that positive emotions of leaders can be "contagious," causing followers to display more positive moods and also be both more attracted to the leaders and willing to rate the leaders more highly. As you might expect, such mood contagion can also have positive and negative effects on the moods of co-workers and teammates, as well as family and friends.[45]

> **Mood contagion** is the spillover of one's positive or negative moods onto others.

Understanding Moods

"I just feel lousy today and don't have any energy. I've been down all week."

- Hard to identify cause
- Tends to linger, be long-lasting
- General effect on attitude, behavior
- Can be "negative" or "positive"

{ AMBITION SHOWS UP IN PERSONALITY AS COMPETITIVENESS AND A DESIRE TO BE THE BEST.

Explore **Yourself**

■ Ambition

People are different; our styles vary in the way we work, the way we relate to others, and even in how we view ourselves. One of the differences you might observe when interacting with other people is in **ambition**, or the desire to succeed and reach for high goals.

Ambition is one of those traits that can certainly have a big impact on individual behavior. It is evident in how we act and what we try to achieve at work, at home, and in leisure pursuits. It comes out in personality as competitiveness and desire to be the best at something. The more we understand ambition in our lives, and the more we understand how personality traits influence our behavior, the more successful we're likely to be in accomplishing our goals and helping others do the same.

> Get to know yourself better by taking the **Stress Test** self-assessment and completing other activities in the *Exploring Management* **Skill-Building Portfolio.**

STUDY GUIDE

Takeaway 12.3
How Do Attitudes, Emotions, and Moods Influence Individual Behavior?

Terms to Define

Attitude

Cognitive dissonance

Emotion

Emotional intelligence

Employee engagement

Job satisfaction

Mood

Mood contagion

Organizational citizenship behaviors

Withdrawal behaviors

Rapid Review

- An attitude is a predisposition to respond in a certain way to people and things.
- Cognitive dissonance occurs when a person's attitude and behavior are inconsistent.
- Job satisfaction is an important work attitude, reflecting a person's evaluation of the job, co-workers, and other aspects of the work setting.
- Job satisfaction influences withdrawal behaviors of absenteeism and turnover, and organizational citizenship behaviors.
- Job satisfaction has a complex and reciprocal relationship with job performance.
- Emotions are strong feelings that are directed at someone or something; they influence behavior, often with intensity and for short periods of time.
- Moods are generalized positive or negative states of mind that can be persistent influences on one's behavior.

Questions for Discussion

1. Is cognitive dissonance a good or bad influence on us?
2. How can a manager deal with someone who has high job satisfaction but is a low performer?
3. What are the lessons of mood contagion for how a new team leader should behave?

Be Sure You Can

- identify the three components of an attitude
- explain cognitive dissonance
- describe possible measures of job satisfaction
- explain the consequences of job satisfaction for absenteeism and turnover
- explain the link between job satisfaction, organizational citizenship, and employee engagement
- list and describe three alternative explanations in the job satisfaction–performance relationship
- explain how emotions and moods influence work behavior

Career Situation: What Would You Do?

Your team leader has just told you that some of your teammates have complained that you have been in a really bad mood lately and it is rubbing off on the others. They like you and point out that this isn't characteristic of you at all. They don't know what to do about it. Can they do anything to help? Is there anything your team leader might do? What is your responsibility here, and how can you best handle the situation?

TestPrep 12

Answers to TestPrep questions can be found at the back of the book.

Multiple-Choice Questions

1. Among the Big Five personality traits, _____ indicates someone who tends to be responsible, dependable, and careful in respect to tasks.
   - (a) authoritarian
   - (b) agreeable
   - (c) conscientious
   - (d) emotionally stable

2. A person with a/an _____ personality would most likely act unemotional and manipulative when trying to influence others to achieve personal goals.
   - (a) extroverted
   - (b) sensation-thinking
   - (c) self-monitoring
   - (d) Machiavellian

3. When a person tends to believe that he or she has little influence over things that happen in life, this indicates a/an _____ personality.
   - (a) low emotional stability
   - (b) external locus of control
   - (c) high self-monitoring
   - (d) intuitive-thinker

4. How is a person with an authoritarian personality expected to act?
   - (a) Strong tendency to obey orders
   - (b) Challenges the authority of others
   - (c) Tries to play down status differences
   - (d) Always flexible in personal behavior

5. A new team leader who designs jobs for persons on her work team mainly "because I would prefer to work the new way rather than the old," is committing a perceptual error known as _____.
   - (a) the halo effect
   - (b) stereotyping
   - (c) impression management
   - (d) projection

6. If a manager allows one characteristic of a person—say, a pleasant personality—to bias performance ratings of that individual overall, the manager is falling prey to a perceptual distortion known as _____.
   - (a) the halo effect
   - (b) impression management
   - (c) stereotyping
   - (d) projection

7. Use of special dress, manners, gestures, and vocabulary words when meeting a prospective employer in a job interview are all examples of how people use _____ in daily life.
   - (a) the halo effect
   - (b) impression management
   - (c) introversion
   - (d) mood contagion

8. _____ is a form of attribution error that involves blaming the environment for problems that we may have caused ourselves.
   - (a) Self-serving bias
   - (b) Fundamental attribution error
   - (c) Projection
   - (d) Self-monitoring

9. _____ is a form of attribution error that involves blaming others for problems that they may not have caused for themselves.
   - (a) Self-serving bias
   - (b) Fundamental attribution error
   - (c) Projection
   - (d) Self-monitoring

10. The _____ component of an attitude is what indicates a person's belief about something, whereas the _____ component indicates a specific positive or negative feeling about it.

    (a) cognitive; affective

    (b) emotional; affective

    (c) cognitive; attributional

    (d) behavioral; attributional

11. The term for the discomfort someone feels when his or her behavior is inconsistent with a previously expressed attitude is _____.

    (a) alienation

    (b) cognitive dissonance

    (c) job dissatisfaction

    (d) job burnout

12. Job satisfaction is known from research to be a strong predictor of _____.

    (a) personality

    (b) job burnout

    (c) conscientiousness

    (d) absenteeism

13. A person who is always willing to volunteer for extra work or to help someone else with his or her work is acting consistent with strong _____.

    (a) job performance

    (b) self-serving bias

    (c) emotional intelligence

    (d) organizational citizenship

14. A/an _____ represents a rather intense but short-lived feeling about a person or a situation, whereas a/an _____ describes a more generalized positive or negative state of mind.

    (a) attitude; emotion

    (b) external locus of control; internal locus of control

    (c) self-serving bias; halo effect

    (d) emotion; mood

15. Which statement about the job satisfaction–job performance relationship is most accurate based on research?

    (a) A happy worker will be a productive worker.

    (b) A productive worker will be a happy worker.

    (c) A productive worker well rewarded for performance will be a happy worker.

    (d) There is no relationship between being happy and being productive in a job.

Short-Response Questions

16. What is the most positive profile of Big Five personality traits in terms of positive impact on work behavior?

17. What is the relationship between personality and stress?

18. How does the halo effect differ from selective perception?

19. If you were going to develop a job satisfaction survey, exactly what would you try to measure?

Integration and Application Question

20. When Scott Tweedy picked up a magazine article on "How to Manage Health Care Workers," he was pleased to find some apparent advice. Scott was concerned about poor performance by several of the respiratory therapists in his clinic. The author of the article said that the "best way to improve performance is to make your workers happy." Well, Scott was happy on reading this and made a pledge to himself to start doing a much better job of "making the therapists happy in the future."

    Questions: Is Scott on the right track? Should he charge ahead as planned, or should he be concerned about this advice? What do we know about the relationship between job satisfaction and performance, and how can this understanding be used by Scott in this situation?

Steps *for* Further Learning

BUILD MARKETABLE SKILLS
DO A CASE ANALYSIS
GET AND STAY INFORMED

BUILD

MARKETABLE SKILLS.
EARN BIG CAREER PAYOFFS!

Don't miss these opportunities in the **Skill-Building Portfolio**

■ **SELF-ASSESSMENT 12:**
Stress Test

Stress can take its toll . . . learn how to recognize the symptoms.

■ **CLASS EXERCISE 12:**
Job Satisfaction Preferences

Not everyone wants the same things . . . it's important to understand individual differences.

■ **TEAM PROJECT 12:**
Difficult Personalities

Sometimes it's hard to get along . . . difficult personalities are a challenge.

Many learning resources are found at the end of the book and online within WileyPLUS.

Take advantage of **Cases for Critical Thinking**

■ **CHAPTER 12 CASE SNAPSHOT:**
Businesses in Trouble Pass the Buck on Blame/
Sidebar on The New Leadership IQ

What happened to Borders? Why did it fail? When McDonald's makes a mistake, who or what is to blame? If a CEO gets fired, was it her fault? How do executives explain failure in their companies, and how do others fix blame when things go wrong? Failure is ever-present. Letting it pass without proper reflection can be a huge loss of learning opportunity. But, it's quite common to deny responsibility for failure. Business executives do this all the time. Self-serving bias is the tendency to blame organizational and personal problems on external causes "beyond our control," rather than accepting responsibility, admitting fault, and hopefully avoiding similar mistakes in the future. Is there anything we can do about it?

DO

A CASE ANALYSIS.
STRENGTHEN YOUR CRITICAL THINKING!

Dig into this **Hot Topic**

■ **GOOD IDEA OR NOT? Some employers provide time for yoga and meditation.**

Situation 4 p.m.—large room on premises—50 or more smiling faces topping off loose-fitting clothes—lots of meditation cushions. Tibetan prayer bells are rung three times, and the session leader says to everyone: "Take a posture that for you in this moment embodies dignity and strength. Allow the body to rest, to step out of busyness, bringing attention to the sensation of each breath." A collective sigh rises from the room: Stress flows out as mindfulness settles in.

GET

AND STAY INFORMED.
MAKE YOURSELF VALUABLE!

Gone are the days when the only investment employers make in training is on "hard skills." It's a whole new world out there. The prior situation is a glimpse into what General Mills calls its Mindful Leadership Program. It's supported by senior management to the point where meditation and yoga are becoming part of the corporate culture. And evaluations back up the investment. Over 80% of participants say it helps them be productive, improves their decision making, and makes them better listeners.

Those in favor of yoga and meditation time are likely to say: "It relieves stress and allows better focus on the job" . . . "It's good for employee health" . . . "Workouts should be 'mental' and not just 'physical'." *Those against the practice are likely to say:* "No problem, just do it on your own time" . . . "I don't want to feel that I 'must' participate" . . . "It's just a fad and not worth the investment; tomorrow it'll be something else."

Final Take Is General Mills on to something that other employers, large and small alike, should be copying? Or, is this just a luxury approach that few employers can afford and few employees really want to bother with? Management scholars and consultants are paying a lot of attention to employee wellness. Should yoga be part of a wellness program? Just how far should organizations go in trying to encourage people to join in these types of activities?

When J. K. Rowling finished the first of her Harry Potter books, she was a single mother living on just over $100 a week. "You sort of start thinking anything's possible," she once said, "if you've got enough nerve."

Motivation

Respect Unlocks Human Potential

13

Disney/Pixar/Photofest

Management Live

Engagement and *The Incredibles*

Mr. Incredible (voiced by Craig T. Nelson) is no longer allowed to be a superhero. In his new life, he is Bob Parr, an ordinary claims adjuster for Insuricare.

Parr works in a cubicle in a massive office complex. He hates his monotonous job that doesn't use his special skills, and because he isn't allowed to help truly needy customers. When his boss Gilbert Huph (voiced by Wallace Shawn) calls Parr into his office for a lecture and threatens to fire him, it pushes Parr to the breaking point. He loses his temper and assaults the boss.

The difference between those who dislike their jobs and those who like them comes down to **engagement**—aspects of the work experience that create a sense of connection to the job and organization. Disengaged workers, like Bob Parr, experience negative emotions and attitudes. They become largely unmotivated to work hard. Workers who are engaged generally have positive attitudes toward their jobs, co-workers, and the organization.

The content, process, and reinforcement theories discussed in the chapter offer a variety of insights into motivation. Their usefulness isn't limited to the workplace. What about your classmates? Are they engaged or disengaged in academics? Which ones would you choose to work with on an important team project?

YOUR CHAPTER 13 TAKEAWAYS

1. Describe how human needs influence motivation to work.
2. Identify how thoughts and decisions affect motivation to work.
3. Understand how reinforcement influences motivation to work.

WHAT'S INSIDE

Explore Yourself
More on **engagement**

Role Models
Social entrepreneur finds rewards from helping those in need

Ethics Check
Information goldmine is an equity dilemma

Facts to Consider
Europe turns to quotas to increase female board members

Manager's Library
Drive: The Surprising Truth About What Motivates Us by Daniel H. Pink

Takeaway 13.1
How Do Human Needs Influence Motivation to Work?

ANSWERS TO COME

- Maslow described a hierarchy of needs topped by self-actualization.
- Alderfer's ERG theory deals with existence, relatedness, and growth needs.
- McClelland identified acquired needs for achievement, power, and affiliation.
- Herzberg's two-factor theory focuses on higher-order need satisfaction.
- The core characteristics model integrates motivation and job design.

Motivation accounts for the level, direction, and persistence of effort expended at work.

DID YOU KNOW THAT J. K. ROWLING'S FIRST *HARRY POTTER* BOOK WAS REJECTED by 12 publishers?[1] Thank goodness she didn't give up. In management we use the term **motivation** to describe forces within the individual that account for the level, direction, and persistence of effort expended at work. Simply put, a highly motivated person works hard at a job; an unmotivated person does not. A manager who leads through motivation creates conditions that consistently inspire other people to work hard.

Everyone wants highly motivated people on their teams. So how do we get there? Why do some people work enthusiastically, persevering in the face of difficulty, and often doing more than required to turn out an extraordinary performance? Why do others hold back, quit at the first negative feedback, and do the minimum needed to avoid reprimand or termination?

⫶ Maslow described a hierarchy of needs topped by self-actualization.

A **need** is an unfulfilled physiological or psychological desire.

One of the best starting points in exploring the issue of motivation are theories from psychology that deal with differences in individual **needs**—unfulfilled desires that stimulate people to behave in ways that will satisfy them. And as you might expect, there are different theories about human needs and how they may affect people at work.

Abraham Maslow's theory of human needs is an important foundation in the history of management thought. He described a hierarchy built on a foundation of **lower-order needs** (physiological, safety, and social concerns) and moving up to **higher-order needs** (esteem and self-actualization).[2] Whereas lower-order needs focus on physical well-being and companionship, the higher-order needs reflect psychological development and growth.

Lower-order needs are physiological, safety, and social needs in Maslow's hierarchy.

Higher-order needs are esteem and self-actualization needs in Maslow's hierarchy.

A key part of Maslow's thinking relies on two principles. The *deficit principle* states that a satisfied need is not a motivator of behavior. People act in ways that satisfy deprived needs, ones for which a "deficit" exists. We eat because we are hungry; we call a friend when we are lonely; we seek approval from others when we are feeling insecure. The *progression principle* states that people try to satisfy lower-level needs first and then move step-by-step up the hierarchy. This happens until the level of self-actualization is reached. The more these needs

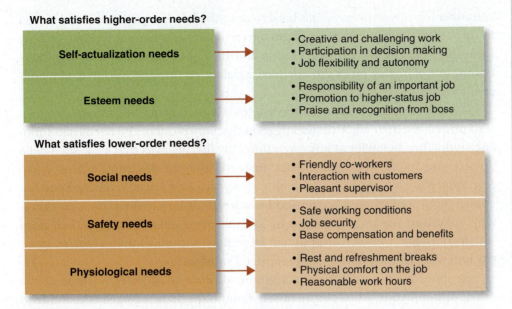

What satisfies higher-order needs?

Self-actualization needs
- Creative and challenging work
- Participation in decision making
- Job flexibility and autonomy

Esteem needs
- Responsibility of an important job
- Promotion to higher-status job
- Praise and recognition from boss

What satisfies lower-order needs?

Social needs
- Friendly co-workers
- Interaction with customers
- Pleasant supervisor

Safety needs
- Safe working conditions
- Job security
- Base compensation and benefits

Physiological needs
- Rest and refreshment breaks
- Physical comfort on the job
- Reasonable work hours

FIGURE 13.1 **What Are the Opportunities for Need Satisfaction in Maslow's Hierarchy?** For higher-order need satisfaction, people realize self-actualization by doing creative and challenging work and participating in important decisions; they boost self-esteem through promotions and praise and by having responsibility for an important job. For lower-order need satisfaction, people meet social needs through positive relationships with co-workers, supervisors, and customers; they achieve safety needs in healthy working conditions and a secure job with good pay and benefits; and they realize physiological needs by having reasonable work hours and comfortable work spaces.

are satisfied, the stronger they will grow. Maslow believes opportunities for self-fulfillment should continue to motivate a person as long as the other needs remain satisfied.

Maslow's theory is a good starting point for examining human needs and their potential influence on motivation. It seems to make sense, for example, that managers should try to understand the needs of people working with and for them. And isn't it a manager's job to help others find ways of satisfying their needs through work? **Figure 13.1** gives some suggestions along these lines.

‖ Alderfer's ERG theory deals with existence, relatedness, and growth needs.

A well-regarded alternative to Maslow's work is the ERG theory proposed by Clayton Alderfer.[3] His theory collapses Maslow's five needs into three. **Existence needs** are desires for physiological and material well-being. **Relatedness needs** are desires for satisfying interpersonal relationships. **Growth needs** are desires for continued psychological growth and development.

Growth needs are essentially the higher-order needs in Maslow's hierarchy. And they are important. Consider this example.[4] Laine Seator lost her management job and started volunteering during the recession. After putting in 35-hour weeks working for five different organizations, she realized her time helping others was well spent. She gained new skills in grant writing and strategic planning that strengthed her resume. "In a regular job," she says, "you'd need to be a director or management staff to be able to do these types of things, but on a volunteer basis they welcome the help." And at a United Way in Boise, Idaho,

Existence needs are desires for physiological and material well-being.

Relatedness needs are desires for satisfying interpersonal relationships.

Growth needs are desires for continued psychological growth and development.

volunteer Rick Overton says: "It's hard to describe how much better it feels to get to the end of the day and, even if you haven't made any money, feel like you did some good for the world." Don't Laine and Rick sound like motivated workers finding lots of higher-order growth need satisfaction through volunteer and non-profit work?

It's worth noting that ERG theory disagrees with Maslow's deficit and progression principles. Instead, Alderfer suggests that any or all of the needs can influence individual behavior at any given time. He also believes that a satisfied need doesn't lose its motivational impact. Instead, Alderfer describes a *frustration-regression principle* through which an already-satisfied lower-level need can become reactivated when a higher-level need cannot be satisfied. Perhaps this is why unionized workers frustrated by assembly-line jobs (lacking growth need satisfaction) give so much attention in labor negotiations to things like job security and wage levels (offering existence need satisfaction).

You shouldn't be quick to reject either Maslow or Alderfer in favor of the other. Although questions can be raised about both theories, each adds value to our understanding of how individual needs can influence motivation.[5] And, you should notice that Maslow's higher-order needs match up with Alderfer's growth needs.

‖ McClelland identified acquired needs for achievement, power, and affiliation.

In the late 1940s, David McClelland and his colleagues began experimenting with the Thematic Apperception Test (TAT) of human psychology.[6] The TAT asks people to view pictures and write stories about what they see. Researchers then analyze the stories, looking for themes that display individual needs.

From this research McClelland identified three acquired needs that he considers central to understanding human motivation. The **need for achievement** is the desire to do something better or more efficiently, to solve problems, or to master complex tasks. The **need for power** is the desire to control other people, to influence their behavior, or to be responsible for them. The **need for affiliation** is the desire to have friendly and warm relations with other people.

McClelland encourages managers to learn how to recognize the strength of these needs in themselves and in other people. Because each need can be associated with a distinct set of work preferences, his insights offer helpful ideas for designing jobs and creating work environments that are rich in potential motivation.

Consider someone high in the need for achievement. Do you, for example, like to put your competencies to work, take moderate risks in competitive situations, and often prefer to work alone? Need achievers are like this, and their work preferences usually follow a pattern. Persons high in need for achievement like work that offers challenging but achievable goals, feedback on performance, and individual responsibility. If you take one or more of these away, they are likely to become frustrated, and their performance may suffer. As a manager, these preferences offer pretty straightforward insights for dealing with a high need achiever. And if you are high in need for achievement, these are things you should be talking about with your manager.

Need for achievement is the desire to do something better, to solve problems, or to master complex tasks.

Need for power is the desire to control, influence, or be responsible for other people.

Need for affiliation is the desire to establish and maintain good relations with people.

Work Preferences of High Need Achievers

- Individual responsibilities
- Challenging but achievable goals
- Performance feedback

HopeLab Fights Disease with Fun

Video Games Motivates Kids to Take Medicine

Although many teens play video games just for fun, teens with cancer can now play ones that can help them beat the disease. Picture a teenager who has a tough time keeping up with cancer medication schedules. Now imagine him playing the video game called Re-Mission and maneuvering a nanobot called Roxxi through the body of a cancer patient to destroy cancer cells. And, then think about an article in the medical journal *Pediatrics* that says teen patients who play the game at least one hour a week do a better job of sticking to their medication schedules.

What's taking place is the brainchild of HopeLab, founded by Pam Omidyar. An immunology researcher and gaming enthusiast, she saw the possible link between games and fighting disease. The nonprofit's mission is combining "rigorous research with innovative solutions to improve the health and quality of life of young people with chronic illness."

One of HopeLabs' recent products is Zamzee, described as a "game-based website." It includes an activity meter where kids earn points for movement and activity. A research study using a control group concluded that "kids using Zamzee increased their moderate-to-vigorous physical activity (MVPA) by an average of 59%—or approximately 45 additional minutes of MVPA per week."

HopeLab/AP/Wide World Photos

Find Inspiration

Re-Mission is one positive step in the war against childhood cancer. One of HopeLab's current priorities is to use video gaming in the fight against childhood obesity. Think about how creative approaches to motivation might be used to improve lives in other ways as well.

McClelland's theory offers good insights about the other needs as well. People high in the need for affiliation prefer jobs offering companionship, social approval, and satisfying interpersonal relationships. People high in the need for power are motivated to behave in ways that have a clear impact on other people and events; they enjoy being in positions of control.

Importantly, McClelland distinguishes between two forms of the power need.[7] The need for *personal power* is exploitative and involves manipulation purely for the sake of personal gratification. As you might imagine, this type of power need is not respected in management. By contrast, the *need for social power* is the positive face of power. It involves the use of power in a socially responsible way, one that is directed toward group or organizational objectives rather than personal ones. This need for social power is essential to managerial leadership.

One interesting extension of McClelland's research found that successful senior executives often had high needs for social power that, in turn, were higher than their also strong needs for affiliation. Can you explain these results? It may be that managers high in the need for affiliation alone may let their desires for social approval interfere with business decisions. But with a higher need for power, they may be more willing to sometimes act in ways that other persons may disagree with. In other words, they'll do what is best for the organization, even if it makes some people unhappy. Does this make sense?

Two Types of Power Need

- *Need for Personal Power*—seeking power for personal gratification.
- *Need for Social Power*—seeking power to help people and groups achieve goals.

Herzberg's two-factor theory focuses on higher-order need satisfaction.

Frederick Herzberg's work on human needs took a slightly different route. He began with extensive interviews of people at work and then content-analyzed their answers. The result is known as the two-factor theory.[8]

When questioned about what "turned them on," Herzberg found that workers mainly talked about the nature of the job itself—such things as a sense of achievement, feelings of recognition, a sense of responsibility, the opportunity for advancement, and feelings of personal growth. In other words, they told him about what they did. Herzberg called these **satisfier factors**, or *motivator factors*, and described them as part of *job content*. They are consistent with the higher-order needs of Maslow, growth needs of Alderfer, and achievement and power needs of McClelland.

When questioned about what "turned them off," Herzberg found that his respondents talked about quite different things—working conditions, interpersonal relations, organizational policies and administration, technical quality of supervision, and base wage or salary. They were telling him about where they worked, not about what they did. Herzberg called these **hygiene factors** and described them as part of *job context*. They seem most associated with Maslow's lower-order needs, Alderfer's existence and relatedness needs, and McClelland's affiliation need.

Herzberg's two-factor theory is shown in **Figure 13.2**. Hygiene factors influence job dissatisfaction, whereas satisfier factors influence job satisfaction. The distinction is important. Herzberg is saying that you can't increase job satisfaction by improving the hygiene factors. You will only get less dissatisfaction. Although minimizing dissatisfaction is a worthy goal, you can't expect much by way of increased motivation. At least that's his theory.

*A **satisfier factor** is found in job content, such as a sense of achievement, recognition, responsibility, advancement, or personal growth.*

*A **hygiene factor** is found in the job context, such as working conditions, interpersonal relations, organizational policies, and salary.*

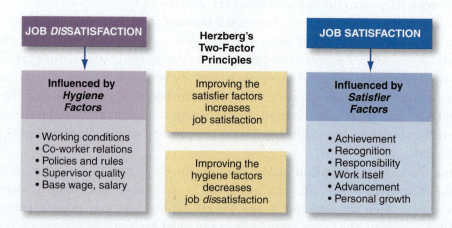

FIGURE 13.2 What Are the Motivational Implications of Job Content and Job Context in Herzberg's Two-Factor Theory?
Scholars criticize this theory because of its research foundations. However, Herzberg makes an interesting and useful distinction between the motivational implications of job content and job context. He believes that you can't increase job satisfaction and motivation by improving hygiene factors in the job context, for example, by increasing wages. This only reduces levels of dissatisfaction. Instead, he argues in favor of improving satisfier factors in the job content, things like responsibility and recognition. In the two-factor theory, such changes are pathways to higher job satisfaction and motivation.

Scholars have criticized Herzberg's research as method-bound and difficult to replicate. But still, the two-factor theory makes us think about both job content and job context.[9] It's a reminder that managers shouldn't expect too much by way of motivational gains from investments in things like pleasant work spaces and even high base salaries. Instead, it focuses our attention on building jobs to provide opportunities for responsibility, growth, and other sources of higher-order need satisfactions. And to create these high-content jobs, Herzberg suggests allowing people to manage themselves and exercise self-control over their work.

The core characteristics model integrates motivation and job design.

If you really think about it, you should see that for a job to be highly motivational there has to be a good fit between the needs and talents of the individual and tasks to be performed. And as you might expect, just what constitutes a good fit is going to vary from one individual and situation to the next. **Job design** is the allocation of specific work tasks to individuals and groups.[10] Its goal is a good person–job fit.

Herzberg, known for the two-factor theory just discussed, poses the job design challenge this way: "If you want people to do a good job, give them a good job to do."[11] He goes on to argue that this is best done through **job enrichment**, the practice of designing jobs rich in content that offers opportunities for higher-order need satisfaction. For him, an enriched job allows the individual to perform planning and controlling duties normally done by supervisors. In other words, job enrichment involves a lot of self-management.

Modern management theory values job enrichment and its motivating potential. In true contingency fashion, however, it recognizes that not everyone wants or needs an enriched job. The core characteristics model developed by J. Richard Hackman and his associates helps managers design jobs that best fit the needs of different people.[12]

Figure 13.3 shows that the core characteristics model approaches job design with a focus on five "core" job characteristics: skill variety, task identity, task

> **Job design** is the allocation of specific work tasks to individuals and groups.

> **Job enrichment** increases job content by adding work planning and evaluating duties normally performed by the supervisor.

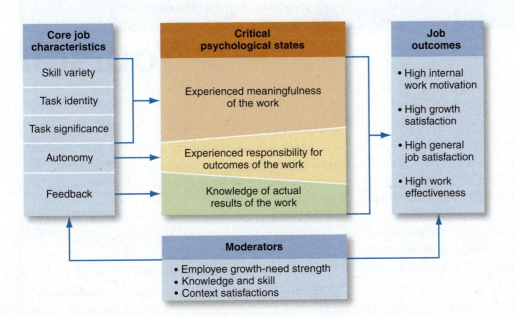

FIGURE 13.3

How Do Core Characteristics Influence Motivation Through Job Design?

This model shows how jobs can be designed according to five core characteristics—skill variety, task identity, task significance, autonomy, and feedback. Jobs that are high in these characteristics provide jobholders with experienced meaningfulness and responsibility as well as knowledge of results. Under the right contingency conditions—high growth need strength and satisfaction with job context—these critical psychological states are motivational and set the stage for positive job outcomes.

significance, autonomy, and job feedback. Can you think of specific jobs that might score high and low on these characteristics? Here's a bit more detail on them.

Five Core Job Characteristics ≫

1. *Skill variety*—the degree to which a job requires a variety of different activities to carry out the work and involves the use of a number of different skills and talents of the individual

2. *Task identity*—the degree to which the job requires completion of a "whole" and identifiable piece of work, one that involves doing a job from beginning to end with a visible outcome

3. *Task significance*—the degree to which the job has a substantial impact on the lives or work of other people elsewhere in the organization or in the external environment

4. *Autonomy*—the degree to which the job gives the individual freedom, independence, and discretion in scheduling work and in choosing procedures for carrying it out

5. *Feedback from the job itself*—the degree to which work activities required by the job result in the individual obtaining direct and clear information on his or her performance

The higher a job scores on the five core characteristics, the more enriched it is. But as you consider this model, don't forget the contingency logic. It recognizes that not everyone will be a good fit for a highly enriched job. Whether they do fit or not depends on the presence of three "moderators," also shown Figure 13.3. People are expected to respond most favorably to job enrichment when they have strong growth needs, have appropriate job knowledge and skills, and are otherwise satisfied with the job context. When these conditions are weak or absent, the fit between the individual and an enriched job may turn out less favorably than expected.

{ LOOK AROUND THE CLASSROOM. WHO WOULD YOU WANT TO HIRE FOR AN IMPORTANT JOB SOMEDAY?

Explore **Yourself**

■ Engagement

There's a lot of attention being given these days to the levels of **engagement** displayed by people at work. Differences in job engagement are evident in a variety of ways. Is someone enthusiastic or lethargic, diligent or lazy, willing to do more than expected or at best willing to do only what is expected?

Managers want high engagement by members of their work units and teams, and the ideas of this chapter offer many insights on how to create engagement by using the different theories of motivation.

Take a look around the classroom. What do you see and what would you predict for the futures of your classmates based on the engagement they now show as students? Who might you want to hire for an important job someday, and who would you pass on?

Get to know yourself better by taking the **Two-Factor Profile** self-assessment and completing other activities in the *Exploring Management* Skill-Building Portfolio.

STUDY GUIDE

Takeaway 13.1
How Do Human Needs Influence Motivation to Work?

Terms to Define

Existence needs

Growth needs

Higher-order needs

Hygiene factors

Job design

Job enrichment

Lower-order needs

Motivation

Need

Need for achievement

Need for affiliation

Need for power

Relatedness needs

Satisfier factors

Rapid Review

- Motivation involves the level, direction, and persistence of effort expended at work; a highly motivated person can be expected to work hard.
- Maslow's hierarchy of human needs moves from lower-order physiological, safety, and social needs up to higher-order ego and self-actualization needs.
- Alderfer's ERG theory identifies existence, relatedness, and growth needs.
- McClelland's acquired needs theory identifies the needs for achievement, affiliation, and power, all of which may influence what a person desires from work.
- Herzberg's two-factor theory identifies satisfier factors in job content as influences on job satisfaction; hygiene factors in job context are viewed as influences on job dissatisfaction.
- The core characteristics model of job design focuses on skill variety, task identity, task significance, autonomy, and feedback.

Questions for Discussion

1. Was Maslow right in suggesting we each have tendencies toward self-actualization?
2. Is high need for achievement always good for managers?
3. Why can't job enrichment work for everyone?

Be Sure You Can

- describe work practices that can satisfy higher-order needs in Maslow's hierarchy
- contrast Maslow's hierarchy with ERG theory
- explain needs for achievement, affiliation, and power in McClelland's theory
- differentiate the needs for personal and social power
- describe work preferences for a person with a high need for achievement
- describe differences in hygiene and satisfier factors in Herzberg's theory
- explain how a person's growth needs and job skills might affect his or her responses to job enrichment

Career Situation: What Would You Do?

Two student workers are being considered for promotions at a campus recreation center that you manage. One works really well with people and seems to thrive on teamwork and social interaction. The other tackles tough jobs with enthusiasm and always wants to do her best, while preferring to do things alone rather than with others. The center's staff is expanding and you have flexibility to design jobs to best fit each student. What jobs might you create for them, and why?

TEACHING NOTE: Ask students to use expectancy theory to explain their motivation to work hard to achieve an "A" grade in a course of their choosing. After discussing some examples, ask them to be the course instructor. Have them describe—using their own examples, how an instructor could use this understanding to boost a student's motivation in the course.

Takeaway 13.2
How Do Thoughts and Decisions Affect Motivation to Work?

ANSWERS TO COME

- Equity theory explains how social comparisons motivate individual behavior.
- Expectancy theory considers Motivation = Expectancy × Instrumentality × Valence.
- Goal-setting theory shows that well-chosen and well-set goals can be motivating.

HAVE YOU EVER RECEIVED AN EXAM OR PROJECT GRADE AND FELT GOOD ABOUT IT, only to get discouraged when you hear about someone who didn't work as hard getting the same or a better grade? Or, have you ever suffered a loss of motivation when the goal set by your boss or instructor seems so high that you don't see any chance at all of succeeding?

My guess is that most of us have had these types of experiences, and perhaps fairly often. They raise the question of exactly what influences decisions to work hard or not in various situations. The equity, expectancy, and goal-setting theories of motivation offer possible answers.

⦀ Equity theory explains how social comparisons motivate individual behavior.

The equity theory of motivation is best known in management through the work of J. Stacy Adams.[13] Based on the logic of social comparisons, it pictures us continually checking our rewards for work accomplished against those of others. Any perceived inequities in these comparisons are uncomfortable. This makes us motivated to act in ways that restore a sense of equity to the situation. Think of it this way.

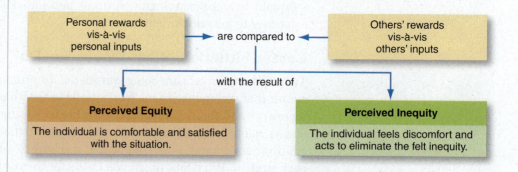

Check these equity dynamics against your own experiences. How have you reacted when your grade seems unfair compared with others? Did you reduce your efforts in the future ... drop the course ... rationalize that you really didn't work that hard ... complain to the instructor and request a higher grade? All of these are ways to reduce the perceived grading inequity. And they are the same types of behaviors that perceived inequity can motivate people to engage in at work. Only instead of grades, the sources of inequity are more likely to be pay raises, job assignments, work schedules, office "perks," and the like. Pay, of course, is the really big one!

Research on equity theory has largely occurred in the laboratory. It is most conclusive with respect to **perceived negative inequity**—feeling uncomfortable at being unfairly treated. People who feel underpaid, for example, may experience disappointment or even a sense of anger. They will be motivated to try to restore perceived equity to the situation. This might be done by reducing work efforts to compensate for the missing rewards, asking for more rewards or better treatment, or even by quitting the job.[14]

Interestingly, there is also some evidence for an equity dynamic among people who feel overpaid. This **perceived positive inequity** is associated with a sense of guilt. It is discomfort felt over benefitting from unfair treatment. The individual is motivated to restore perceived equity by doing such things as increasing the quantity or quality of work, taking on more difficult assignments, or working overtime. Do you think this really happens? What if one of your instructors decides to inflate the grades of students on early assignments, thinking that perceived positive inequities will motivate them to study harder for the rest of the course? Would you work harder or perhaps work less?

> **Perceived negative inequity** is discomfort felt over being harmed by unfair treatment.

> **Perceived positive inequity** is discomfort felt over benefitting from unfair treatment.

Image Source/Getty Images

{ **"SHOULD I PASS THIS INFORMATION AROUND ANONYMOUSLY SO THAT EVERYONE KNOWS WHAT'S GOING ON?"**

Ethics **Check**

■ Information Goldmine is an Equity Dilemma

A worker opens the top of the office photocopier and finds a document someone has left behind. It's a list of performance evaluations, pay, and bonuses for 80 co-workers. She reads the document. Lo and behold, someone she considers a "non-starter" is getting paid more than others regarded as "super workers." New hires are also being brought in at much higher pay and bonuses than those of existing staff. And to make matters worse, she's in the middle of the list and not near the top, where she would have expected to be. The fact is she makes a lot less money than many others.

Looking at the data, she begins to question why she is spending extra hours working on her laptop evenings and weekends at home, trying to do a really great job for the firm. She wonders to herself: "Should I pass this information around anonymously so that everyone knows what's going on? Or should I quit and find another employer who fully values me for my talents and hard work?"

In the end she decided to quit, saying: "I just couldn't stand the inequity." She also decided not to distribute the information to others in the office because "it would make them depressed, like it made me depressed."

YOU DECIDE

What would you do in this situation? You're going to be concerned and perhaps upset. Would you hit "print," make about 80 copies, and put them in everyone's mailboxes—or even just leave them stacked in a couple of convenient locations? That would get the information out into the gossip chains pretty quickly. But is this ethical? If you don't send out the information on the other hand, is it ethical to let other workers go about their days with inaccurate assumptions about the firm's pay practices? By quitting and not sharing the information, did this worker commit an ethics mistake?

Although there are no clear answers available in equity theory, there are some very good insights. The theory is a reminder that rewards perceived as equitable should positively affect satisfaction and performance; those perceived as inequitable may create dissatisfaction and cause performance problems.[15] Probably the best advice is to anticipate potential equity problems from social comparisons whenever rewards of any type are being allocated. It's important to recognize that people may compare themselves not only with co-workers but also with others elsewhere in the organization, including senior executives, and even persons employed by other organizations. And, we should always remember that people behave according to their perceptions. If someone perceives inequity in a work situation, it is likely to affect his or her behavior whether the manager sees things the same way or not.

⦀ Expectancy theory considers Motivation = Expectancy × Instrumentality × Valence.

Victor Vroom offers another approach to understanding motivation. His expectancy theory asks: What determines the willingness of an individual to work hard at tasks important to the organization?[16] Vroom answers this question with an equation:

$$\text{Motivation} = \text{Expectancy} \times \text{Instrumentality} \times \text{Valence}$$

Expectancy is a person's belief that working hard will result in high task performance.

Instrumentality is a person's belief that various outcomes will occur as a result of task performance.

Valence is the value a person assigns to work-related outcomes.

The terms in this expectancy equation are defined as follows. **Expectancy** is a person's belief that working hard will result in achieving a desired level of task performance (sometimes called *effort-performance expectancy*). **Instrumentality** is a person's belief that successful performance will lead to rewards and other potential outcomes (sometimes called *performance-outcome expectancy*). **Valence** is the value a person assigns to the possible rewards and other work-related outcomes. Think of them this way.

Person exerts work effort	→ to achieve →	task performance	→ and realize →	work-related outcomes

Expectancy	**Instrumentality**	**Valence**
"Can I achieve the desired level of task performance?"	"What work outcomes will be received as a result of the performance?"	"How highly do I value work outcomes?"

The use of multiplication signs in the expectancy equation ($M = E \times I \times V$) has important implications. Mathematically speaking, a zero at any location on the right side of the equation will result in zero motivation. This means that we cannot neglect any of the three factors—expectancy, instrumentality, or valence. For motivation to be high, all three must be positive.

Are you ready to test this theory? Most of us assume that people will work hard to get promoted. But is this necessarily true? Expectancy theory predicts that motivation to work hard for a promotion will be low if any one or more of three conditions apply. If *expectancy is low*, motivation suffers. The person feels that he or she cannot achieve the performance level necessary to get promoted. So why try? If *instrumentality is low*, motivation suffers. The person lacks confidence that high performance will actually result in being promoted. So why try? If *valence is low*, motivation suffers. The person doesn't want a promotion, preferring less responsibility in the present job. So, if it isn't a valued outcome, why work hard to get it?

Figure 13.4 summarizes the management implications of expectancy theory. It is a reminder that different people are likely to come up with different answers to the question: Why should I work hard today? Knowing that their answers will differ, Vroom's point is that each person must be respected as an individual with unique work needs, preferences, and concerns. His theory identifies the following ways to do this while creating work environments that are high in motivating potential.

To have high expectancies, people must believe in their abilities; they must believe that if they try hard to do something, they can perform well at it. Managers can help build these expectancies by selecting workers with the right abilities for the jobs to be done, providing them with the best training and development, and supporting them with resources so that the jobs can be done very well. All these factors stimulate motivation based on something called **self-efficacy**, a person's belief that they are capable of performing a task.

To have high instrumentalities, people must perceive that their performance accomplishments will be followed by desired work outcomes. In others words, they believe that performance will lead to valued rewards. Managers can create positive instrumentalities by taking care to clarify the rewards to be gained by high performance. They must also continually confirm this "promise," so to speak,

Self-efficacy is a person's belief that they are capable of performing a task.

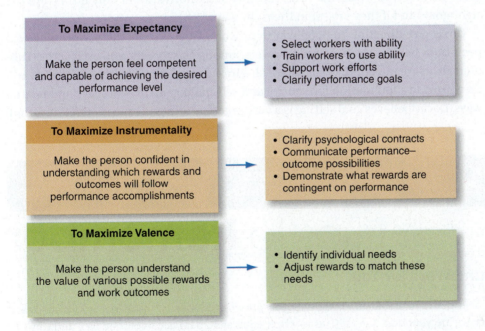

FIGURE 13.4 How Can Managers Use the Insights of the Expectancy Theory of Motivation?
Managers should act in ways that maximize expectancies, instrumentalities, and valences for others. To maximize expectancy, they need to hire capable workers, train and develop them continuously, and communicate goals and confidence in their skills. To maximize instrumentality, managers must clarify and stand by performance-reward linkages. Finally, to maximize valence, they need to understand individual needs and try to tie work outcomes to important sources of need satisfaction.

by actually delivering the expected results. Any disconfirmation or failure to deliver will diminish the instrumentality.

To have high and positive valences, people must value the outcomes associated with high performance. This means that the reward being offered is what they really want. Of course, this is a major source of individual differences. But managers should be able to use insights of the content theories—Maslow, Alderfer, and McClelland, for example—to best match important individual needs with the rewards and outcomes that can be earned through high performance.

||| Goal-setting theory shows that well-chosen and well-set goals can be motivating.

Listed by *Black Enterprise* as one of America's most powerful CEOs, Steven A. Davis's pathway to success began as a a child who grew up with a lot of encouragement from his parents. "They never said that because you are an African American you can only go this far or do only this or that," he says, "they just said 'go for it.'" Davis also says that when he graduated from college, he set goals—to be corporate vice president in 10 years and a president in 20. He made it; Davis rose through a variety of management jobs to become president of Long John Silver's, part of Yum! Brands, Inc. He is now chairman of the board and CEO of Bob Evans Farms in Columbus, Ohio.[17]

If asked to comment on this example, scholar Edwin Locke would likely point out that Davis found lots of motivation through the goals he set as a college graduate. The basic premise of Locke's goal-setting theory is that task goals can be a great source of motivation.[18] But, they become motivational only if they are the right goals and if they are set in the right ways.[19]

Goals give direction to people in their work. Goals clarify the performance expectations between leaders and followers, among co-workers, and even across subunits in an organization. Goals establish a frame of reference for task feedback, and they provide a foundation for control and self-management.[20] In these and related ways, Locke believes goal setting is a very practical and powerful motivational tool.

{ TELLING YOURSELF OR SOMEONE ELSE TO "DO YOUR BEST" ISN'T GOOD ENOUGH WHEN IT COMES TO GOAL SETTING.

Tips to **Remember**

■ How to Make Goal Setting Work for You

- *Set specific goals:* They lead to higher performance than do more generally stated ones, such as "do your best."
- *Set challenging goals:* When viewed as realistic and attainable, more difficult goals lead to higher performance than do easy goals.
- *Build goal acceptance and commitment:* People work harder for goals they accept and believe in; they resist goals forced on them.

- *Clarify goal priorities:* Make sure that expectations are clear as to which goals should be accomplished first, and why.
- *Provide feedback on goal accomplishment:* Make sure that people know how well they are doing with respect to goal accomplishment.
- *Reward goal accomplishment:* Don't let positive accomplishments pass unnoticed; reward people for doing what they set out to do.

{ **"SOME MEN OVER 60 THINK SUITABLE FEMALES DON'T EXIST BECAUSE THEY HAVE NEVER HAD WOMEN AS THEIR PEERS."**

Facts to **Consider**

■ Europe Turns to Quotas to Increase Female Board Members

The consulting firm McKinsey & Company reports that women are hired to fill more than 50% of professional jobs in America's large corporations. But then they start leaking from the career pipeline. They hold 3% of CEO positions, 14% of C-suite jobs, and 28% of director positions on corporate boards. Data from the rest of the world are worse. Women hold just 13.7% of seats on corporate boards in Europe and 7.1% elsewhere. Diane Segalen, senior executive at a Paris-based executive search company, says: "Some men over 60 think suitable females don't exist because they have never had women as their peers. They think women can't take the pressure involved in serving on a board."

- British firms are under threat of mandatory quotas unless the proportion of nonexecutive board seats filled by females rises to 25% by 2015, versus 12.5% at present.
- Norway, Spain, Iceland, and France have adopted a mandatory quota of 40% female board members.

- When legislation was proposed to the European Commission requiring all EU-listed companies to appoint women to 40% of nonexecutive board seats by 2020, it was later pulled for lack of support. Some member countries say they plan to file it again in the future.
- A Heidrick & Struggles survey in the United States showed 51% of women directors supporting quotas like those appearing in Europe. Only 25% of men directors voiced similar support.

YOUR THOUGHTS?

Is underrepresentation of women on boards a "pipeline" problem—not enough qualified women available for these senior positions at this point in time? Or, is it a "discrimination" problem—men at the top still aren't ready to open the doors to female candidates? And when it comes to correcting the problem, is it enough to sit back and wait for change? Or, are quotas like ones used in Europe the way to motivate positive action?

So, what makes a goal motivational? Research by Locke and his associates answer this question by advising managers and team leaders to focus on goal *specificity*—the more specific the better, and on goal *difficulty*—challenging but not impossible. They also point out that people are more likely to accept and commit to accomplishing goals when they participate in setting them.[21]

Although these findings sound ideal and good, we have to be realistic. We can't always choose our own goals. There are many times in work when goals come to us from above, and we are expected to help accomplish them. Does this mean that the motivational properties of goal setting are lost? Not necessarily. Even when the goals are set, there may be opportunities to create motivation by allowing people to participate in choosing how to best pursue them. It is also true that a lack of time may make participation hard or impossible. But, Locke's research also suggests that workers will respond positively to externally imposed goals if they trust the supervisors assigning them and they believe the supervisors will adequately support them.

As you might suspect, the goal setting ideas presented in Tips to Remember can be a tall order. It is no easy task for managers to work with others to set the right goals in the right ways, including the element of participation.

STUDY GUIDE

Takeaway 13.2
How Do Thoughts and Decisions Affect Motivation to Work?

Terms to Define

Expectancy

Instrumentality

Perceived negative inequity

Perceived positive inequity

Self-efficacy

Valence

Rapid Review

- Adams's equity theory recognizes that social comparisons take place when rewards are distributed in the workplace.
- In equity theory, any sense of perceived inequity is considered a motivating state that causes a person to behave in ways that restore equity to the situation.
- Vroom's expectancy theory states that Motivation = Expectancy × Instrumentality × Valence.
- Managers using expectancy theory are advised to make sure rewards are achievable (maximizing expectancies), predictable (maximizing instrumentalities), and individually valued (maximizing valence).
- Locke's goal-setting theory emphasizes the motivational power of goals that are specific and challenging as well as set through participatory means.

Questions for Discussion

1. Is it against human nature to work harder as a result of perceived positive inequity?
2. Can a person with low expectancy ever be motivated to work hard at a task?
3. Will goal-setting theory work if the goals are fixed and only the means for achieving them are open for discussion?

Be Sure You Can

- explain the role of social comparison in Adams's equity theory
- list possible ways people with felt negative inequity may behave
- differentiate the terms "expectancy," "instrumentality," and "valence"
- explain the reason for "3" signs in Vroom's expectancy equation, $M = E \times I \times V$
- explain Locke's goal-setting theory
- describe the link between goal-setting theory and MBO

Career Situation: What Would You Do?

It's apparent that something is wrong with Kate. Her great performance as a Web designer got her promoted to team leader for Web Design Services. But you notice that she now appears anxious, stressed, and generally unhappy in the new assignment. This is quite a contrast from the highly motivated and happy Kate you knew in her old job. What might be wrong here, and what can you, as her supervisor, do to help fix it?

Takeaway 13.3
How Does Reinforcement Influence Motivation to Work?

ANSWERS TO COME

- Operant conditioning influences behavior by controlling its consequences.
- Positive reinforcement connects desirable behavior with pleasant consequences.
- Punishment connects undesirable behavior with unpleasant consequences.

THE THEORIES DISCUSSED SO FAR FOCUS ON PEOPLE SATISFYING NEEDS, RESOLVING felt inequities, and/or pursuing positive expectancies and task goals. Instead of looking within the individual to explain motivation in these ways, reinforcement theory takes a different approach. It views human behavior as determined by its environmental consequences.

⦀ Operant conditioning influences behavior by controlling its consequences.

The premises of reinforcement theory rely on what E. L. Thorndike called the **law of effect**: People repeat behavior that results in a pleasant outcome and avoid behavior that results in an unpleasant outcome.[22] Psychologist B. F. Skinner used this notion to popularize the concept of **operant conditioning**. This is the process of influencing behavior by manipulating its consequences.[23] You may think of operant conditioning as learning by reinforcement, and Figure 13.5 shows how managers stimulate it through four reinforcement strategies.[24]

The **law of effect** states that behavior followed by pleasant consequences is likely to be repeated; behavior followed by unpleasant consequences is not.

Operant conditioning is the control of behavior by manipulating its consequences.

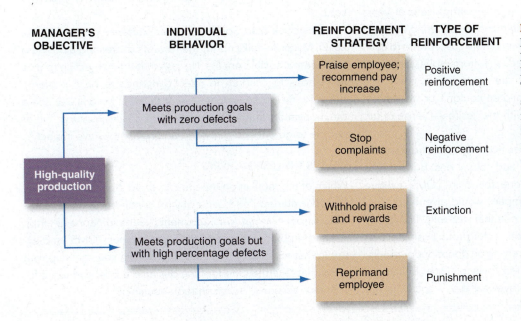

MANAGER'S OBJECTIVE	INDIVIDUAL BEHAVIOR	REINFORCEMENT STRATEGY	TYPE OF REINFORCEMENT
High-quality production	Meets production goals with zero defects	Praise employee; recommend pay increase	Positive reinforcement
		Stop complaints	Negative reinforcement
	Meets production goals but with high percentage defects	Withhold praise and rewards	Extinction
		Reprimand employee	Punishment

FIGURE 13.5

How Can Managers Use Reinforcement Strategies to Influence Work Behavior? To strengthen quality work, a supervisor might use positive reinforcement by praising the individual or negative reinforcement by no longer complaining to him about poor-quality work. To discourage poor-quality work, a supervisor might use extinction (withholding things that are positively reinforcing, such as outcomes) or punishment (associating the poor-quality work with unpleasant results for the individual).

Positive reinforcement strengthens a behavior by making a desirable consequence contingent on its occurrence.

Negative reinforcement strengthens a behavior by making the avoidance of an undesirable consequence contingent on its occurrence.

Punishment discourages a behavior by making an unpleasant consequence contingent on its occurrence.

Extinction discourages a behavior by making the removal of a desirable consequence contingent on its occurrence.

Positive reinforcement strengthens or increases the frequency of desirable behavior by making a pleasant consequence contingent on its occurrence. *Example:* A manager nods to express approval to someone who makes a useful comment during a staff meeting. **Negative reinforcement** increases the frequency of or strengthens desirable behavior by making the avoidance of an unpleasant consequence contingent on its occurrence. *Example:* A manager who has nagged a worker every day about tardiness does not nag when the worker comes to work on time.

Punishment decreases the frequency of or eliminates an undesirable behavior by making an unpleasant consequence contingent on its occurrence. *Example:* A manager issues a written reprimand to an employee whose careless work creates quality problems. **Extinction** decreases the frequency of or eliminates an undesirable behavior by making the removal of a pleasant consequence contingent on its occurrence. *Example:* After observing that co-workers are providing social approval to a disruptive employee, a manager counsels co-workers to stop giving this approval.

If you look again at the case described in Figure 13.5, you'll see that the supervisor's goal is to improve work quality by an individual performer as part of a total quality management program. This goal can be reached if she can get the individual to show more positive quality behaviors and stop engaging in those that harm or disregard quality goals. Notice that both the positive and negative reinforcement strategies are used to strengthen desirable behavior when it occurs. The punishment and extinction strategies are used to weaken or eliminate undesirable behaviors.

Michael Kovac/Getty Images

{ AFTER SEEING THE SUFFERING OF POOR CHILDREN WITHOUT SHOES, MYCOSKIE WAS "INSTANTLY STRUCK WITH THE DESIRE—A SENSE OF FELT RESPONSIBILITY, TO DO MORE."

Role Models

■ Social Entrepreneur Finds Rewards from Helping Those in Need

Have you ever associated having a pair of shoes with access to education? While traveling through Argentina several years ago, Blake Mycoskie witnessed firsthand the suffering endured by children without shoes. They were more susceptible to cuts, scrapes, sores, and even infections from soil-transmitted diseases. And because shoes are required as part of a school uniform, some of the children couldn't go to school. Mycoskie was "instantly struck with the desire—a sense of felt responsibility—to do more."

When Mycoskie returned home from his travels he started a for-profit business that sourced and sold shoes. But it was a shoe seller with a difference, one found in TOMS' unique pledge to its customers: the company would give needy children one pair of shoes for every one that was sold. TOMS was social entrepreneurship in action, a for-profit business that supported social action without relying on donations or grants. The social business model, called One for One, became a TOMS hallmark. It now includes eyewear that is sold with the same pledge—one free pair given to the needy for each pair sold.

In his book *Start Something that Matters* (Speigel & Grau, 2012), Mycoskie talks about the rewards of creating a business that has real social benefits. He says that the "objective to give new shoes to children in need continues to be a powerful driver for me and everyone else at TOMS." He'd like to share the motivation, stating that his current goal is inspiring "other people to go out into the world and have a positive impact."

WHAT'S THE LESSON HERE?

Which of the motivation theories do good jobs explaining why Mycoskie started TOMS and why he continues to derive satisfaction from it? What "reinforcements" does someone get from social entrepreneurship like this? How about TOMS employees? What most likely motivates them? Can you come up with ideas that take the One for One business model and use it for your own version of social entrepreneurship?

Positive reinforcement connects desirable behavior with pleasant consequences.

Among the reinforcement strategies, positive reinforcement deserves special attention. It should be part of any manager's motivational strategy. In fact, it should be part of our personal life strategies as well—as parents working with children, for example. One of the ways to mobilize the power of positive reinforcement is through **shaping**. This is the creation of a new behavior by the positive reinforcement of successive approximations to it.

Sir Richard Branson, well-known founder of Virgin Group, is a believer in positive reinforcement. "For the people who work for you or with you, you must lavish praise on them at all times," he says. "If a flower is watered, it flourishes. If not, it shrivels up and dies."[25] David Novak, CEO of Yum! Brands, Inc., is another believer. He claims "you can never underestimate the power of telling someone he's doing a good job."[26] And Zappos takes all this one step further. If an employee spots someone doing a good thing they can immediately give them a "Wow" award—it's worth an immediate $50.[27]

Whether we are talking about verbal praise, a pay raise, or any other forms of positive reinforcement, two laws govern the process. The **law of contingent reinforcement** states: For a reward to have maximum reinforcing value, it must be delivered only if the desired behavior is exhibited. The **law of immediate reinforcement** states: The more immediate the delivery of a reward after the occurrence of a desirable behavior, the greater the reinforcing value of the reward. Table 13.1—Guidelines for Positive Reinforcement and Punishment—presents several useful guidelines for using these two laws.

> **Shaping** is positive reinforcement of successive approximations to the desired behavior.

> **Law of contingent reinforcement**—deliver the reward only when desired behavior occurs.

> **Law of immediate reinforcement**—deliver the reward as soon as possible after the desired behavior occurs.

Table 13.1 Guidelines for Positive Reinforcement and Punishment

Positive Reinforcement
- Clearly identify desired work behaviors.
- Maintain a diverse inventory of rewards.
- Inform everyone what must be done to get rewards.
- Recognize individual differences when allocating rewards.
- Follow the laws of immediate and contingent reinforcement.

Punishment
- Tell the person what is being done wrong.
- Tell the person what is being done right.
- Make sure the punishment matches the behavior.
- Administer the punishment in private.
- Follow the laws of immediate and contingent reinforcement.

Punishment connects undesirable behavior with unpleasant consequences.

As a reinforcement strategy, punishment tries to eliminate undesirable behavior by making an unpleasant consequence contingent with its occurrence. To punish an employee, for example, a manager may deny a valued reward—such as verbal

{ *Drive: The Surprising Truth About What Motivates Us*
By Daniel H. Pink

Manager's **Library**

WHAT DRIVES YOU?

Two human drives are well described in motivation theory. One is our self-guided biological drive for food, water, and sex—motivation to survive and procreate. The second is our drive to respond to rewards and punishment from external sources, or "extrinsic motivation." For example, you may get a job to buy groceries and provide for your family, work overtime if offered bonus pay, and avoid errors if threatened with termination.

In the book *Drive: The Surprising Truth About What Motivates Us* (2009, Riverhead Books), author Daniel Pink argues that more attention should be given to a third drive he calls "intrinsic motivation." It includes our desire to do activities because we enjoy and are gratified by them. They give us purpose and satisfy our need to do what we choose and value without others telling us. We do them not because we need to (buy groceries), or have to (avoid errors), but because we want to (enjoy work).

Pink uses the term "Motivation 3.0" to reflect this third drive and recommends that managers change reward systems to improve opportunities for intrinsic motivation. He points out that the economy has shifted from algorithmic work—routine, ruled-based work like product assembly, toward heuristic work—knowledge-driven, creative work that requires intuition and self-direction. Reward systems need to shift too.

Extrinsic rewards like pay that drive algorithmic work might appeal to heuristic workers initially. But once a "baseline" level of security is achieved, motivation becomes more linked to things that excite and give them purpose. That's where intrinsic motivation kicks in.

REFLECT AND REACT

Make two lists, one of things you do because you have to and the other of things you do because you want to. How do the lists differ in the activities represented? How do they differ in motivational impact on you? Can you spend a whole day doing only what you have to? Do the "have to's" sometimes make it difficult to find motivation and satisfaction from the "want to's"? What does this exercise say about what drives you and . . . about what should drive you?

---

praise or merit pay, or deliver an unpleasant outcome—such as a verbal reprimand or pay reduction.

Like positive reinforcement, punishment can be done poorly or it can be done well. All too often, it is done both too frequently and poorly. If you look again at Table 13.1, you'll find advice on how to best handle punishment when it is necessary.

Whether talking about using punishment or positive reinforcement, some people complain about the underlying reinforcement principles. They believe that any use of operant conditioning techniques ignores the individuality of people, restricts their freedom of choice, and fails to recognize they can be motivated by things other than extrinsic rewards. Critics view this as inappropriate manipulation and control of human behavior. Others agree that reinforcement involves the control of behavior but argue that control is part of every manager's job. The ethical issue, they say, isn't whether to use reinforcement principles, but whether or not we use them well—in the performance context of the organization and in everyday living.[28] How about you? Do you see reinforcement theory as full of useful insights, or as something to be feared?

STUDY GUIDE

Takeaway 13.3
How Does Reinforcement Influence Motivation to Work?

Terms to Define

Extinction

Law of contingent reinforcement

Law of effect

Law of immediate reinforcement

Negative reinforcement

Operant conditioning

Positive reinforcement

Punishment

Shaping

Rapid Review

- Reinforcement theory views human behavior as determined by its environmental consequences.
- The law of effect states that behavior followed by a pleasant consequence is likely to be repeated; behavior followed by an unpleasant consequence is unlikely to be repeated.
- Managers use strategies of positive reinforcement and negative reinforcement to strengthen desirable behaviors.
- Managers use strategies of punishment and extinction to weaken undesirable work behaviors.
- Positive reinforcement and punishment both work best when applied according to the laws of contingent and immediate reinforcement.

Questions for Discussion

1. Is operant conditioning a manipulative way to influence human behavior?
2. When is punishment justifiable as a reinforcement strategy?
3. Is it possible for a manager, or parent, to only use positive reinforcement?

Be Sure You Can

- explain the law of effect and operant conditioning
- illustrate how positive reinforcement, negative reinforcement, punishment, and extinction can influence work behavior
- explain the reinforcement technique of shaping
- describe how managers can use the laws of immediate and contingent reinforcement when allocating rewards
- list ways to make punishment effective

Career Situation: What Would You Do?

You can predict with great confidence that when Jason comes to a meeting of your student team, he will spend most of his time cracking jokes, telling stories, and otherwise entertaining other team members. He doesn't do any real work. In fact, his behavior makes it hard for the team to accomplish much in its meetings. But Jason's also a talented guy. How can you put reinforcement theory to work here and turn Jason the mischief maker into a solid team contributor?

TestPrep 13

Answers to TestPrep questions can be found at the back of the book.

Multiple-Choice Questions

1. Maslow's progression principle stops working at the level of _____ needs.
   (a) growth
   (b) self-actualization
   (c) achievement
   (d) self-esteem

2. Lower-order needs in Maslow's hierarchy correspond to _____ needs in ERG theory.
   (a) growth
   (b) affiliation
   (c) existence
   (d) achievement

3. A worker high in need for _____ power in McClelland's theory tries to use power for the good of the organization.
   (a) position   (b) expert   (c) personal   (d) social

4. In the _____ theory of motivation, an individual who feels underrewarded relative to a co-worker might be expected to reduce his or her work efforts in the future.
   (a) ERG
   (b) acquired needs
   (c) two-factor
   (d) equity

5. Which of the following is a correct match?
   (a) McClelland–ERG theory
   (b) Skinner–reinforcement theory
   (c) Vroom–equity theory
   (d) Locke–expectancy theory

6. In Herzberg's two-factor theory, base pay is considered a/an _____ factor.
   (a) hygiene
   (b) satisfier
   (c) equity
   (d) higher-order

7. The expectancy theory of motivation says that Motivation = Expectancy × Instrumentality × _____.
   (a) Rewards   (b) Valence   (c) Equity   (d) Growth

8. When a team member shows strong ego needs in Maslow's hierarchy, the team leader should find ways to _____.
   (a) link this person's compensation with team performance
   (b) provide the individual with praise and recognition for good work
   (c) encourage more social interaction with other team members
   (d) assign challenging individual performance goals

9. When someone has a high and positive "expectancy" in expectancy theory of motivation, this means that the person _____.
   (a) believes he can achieve performance expectations
   (b) highly values the rewards being offered
   (c) sees a performance–reward link
   (d) believes rewards are equitable

10. The law of _____ states that behavior followed by a positive consequence is likely to be repeated, whereas behavior followed by an undesirable consequence is not likely to be repeated.
    (a) reinforcement
    (b) contingency
    (c) goal setting
    (d) effect

11. When a job allows a person to do a complete unit of work, it is high on which core characteristic?
    (a) Task identity
    (b) Task significance
    (c) Task autonomy
    (d) Feedback

12. _____ is a positive reinforcement strategy that rewards successive approximations to a desirable behavior.
    (a) Extinction
    (b) Negative reinforcement
    (c) Shaping
    (d) Merit pay

13. The purpose of negative reinforcement as an operant conditioning technique is to _____.
    (a) punish bad behavior
    (b) discourage bad behavior
    (c) encourage desirable behavior
    (d) cancel the effects of shaping

14. The basic premise of reinforcement theory is that : _____.
    (a) behavior is a function of environment
    (b) motivation comes from positive expectancy
    (c) higher-order needs stimulate hard work
    (d) rewards considered unfair are demotivators

15. Both Barry and Marissa are highly motivated students. Knowing this, an instructor can expect them to be _____ in the management course.
    (a) hard working
    (b) high performing
    (c) highly satisfied
    (d) highly dissatisfied

Short-Response Questions

16. What preferences does a person high in the need for achievement bring to the workplace?

17. How can a team leader use goal-setting theory in working with individual team members?

18. What are three ways a worker might react to perceived negative inequity over a pay raise?

19. How can shaping be used to encourage desirable work behaviors?

Integration and Application Question

20. I once overheard a conversation between two Executive MBA students. One was telling the other: "My firm just contracted with Muzak to have mood music piped into the offices at various times of the workday." The other replied: "That's a waste of money; there should be things to spend money on if the firm is really interested in increasing motivation and performance." **Question:** Is the second student right or wrong, and why?

Steps *for* Further Learning

BUILD MARKETABLE SKILLS
DO A CASE ANALYSIS
GET AND STAY INFORMED

BUILD

MARKETABLE SKILLS.
EARN BIG CAREER
PAYOFFS!

Don't miss these
opportunities in the
**Skill-Building
Portfolio**

■ **SELF-ASSESSMENT 13:**
Two-Factor Profile

Motivation is complicated . . . it helps to know the difference between job content and job context.

■ **CLASS EXERCISE 13:**
Why We Work

Work means different things to different people . . . practice finding each person's story.

■ **TEAM PROJECT 13:**
CEO Pay

CEOs often earn quite a lot, some think too much . . . are CEOs paid what they are worth?

Many learning resources are found at the end of the book and online within WileyPLUS.

Take advantage of **Cases for Critical Thinking**

■ **CHAPTER 13 CASE SNAPSHOT:**
Salesforce.com: Instant Praise, Instant Criticism / Sidebar on Digging in to a Free Lunch

DO

A CASE ANALYSIS.
STRENGTHEN YOUR
CRITICAL THINKING!

Snapshot Instead of waiting a year for a performance review, how would you like to know where you stand and always get immediate feedback about how you're doing? The annual performance review can feel like an archaic, inaccurate, time-warped, boss-administered feedback session. Some human resource professionals call it "little more than a dysfunctional pretense." It can be a case of information overload, covering everything from past performance, to goal setting, to pay, to improvement needs.

For goals accomplished today, how valuable and motivating is recognition and feedback received 12 months from now? Things could be different. What if, in real time, you were able to get feedback by asking colleagues, managers, and peers online questions like: "What did you think of my presentation?" or "What can be done better?" Salesforce.com is one employer that believes such new directions are not only possible, but necessary.

"*The way a team plays as a whole determines its success. You may have the greatest bunch of individual stars in the world, but if they don't play together, the club won't be worth a dime.*"
Former UCLA coach John Wooden

Teams and Teamwork

Two Heads Really Can Be Better Than One

ABC/Photofest

Team Contributions and *Lost*

Picture a mysterious island and a group of random strangers brought together by a plane crash. There is little hope of rescue. You've probably been there before, at least vicariously. It's the setting for the hit television series *Lost*.

In episode 5 of season 1 a doctor, Jack Shephard (Matthew Fox), strikes off on his own to deal with personal demons. He ends up discovering a source of clean water and realizes it is the key to keeping everyone alive.

Upon returning to the crash site, Jack finds several of the survivors fighting for control of the remaining bottled water. He interrupts the fight and delivers what becomes the guiding mantra of the series—"live together, die alone." Jack implores each person to figure out what they can contribute to the good of all, and then make the commitment to everyone else that they'll really do it.

If you watch old *Lost* episodes, you'll find quite a bit going on about the lessons of teamwork and **team contributions**. Team success always depends on members contributing in a wide variety of ways to help the team reach its goals. Most teams underperform not because they lack talent and energy. They do poorly because members can't overcome the difficulties of working together.

Pick a recent team experience of yours. Make a good realistic assessment of what took place—the good parts and the rough spots, including your contributions. This chapter has lots of ideas on teamwork and team success. Make becoming a strong team contributor a personal development goal.

YOUR CHAPTER 14 TAKEAWAYS

1. Understand the importance of teams and teamwork.

2. Identify the building blocks of successful teamwork.

3. Understand how managers create and lead high-performance teams.

WHAT'S INSIDE

Explore Yourself
More on **team contributions**

Role Models
Amazon's Jeff Bezos bets on two-pizza teams

Ethics Check
Danger! Social loafing may be closer than you think

Facts to Consider
Unproductive meetings are major time wasters

Manager's Library
Crowdsourcing: Why the Power of the Cloud is Driving the Future of Business
by Jeff Howe

Takeaway 14.1
Why Is It Important to Understand Teams and Teamwork?

ANSWERS TO COME

■ Teams offer synergy and other benefits to organizations and their members.
■ Teams often suffer from common performance problems.
■ Organizations are networks of formal teams and informal groups.
■ Organizations use committees, task forces, and cross-functional teams.
■ Virtual teams are increasingly common in organizations.
■ Self-managing teams are a form of job enrichment for groups.

WE ARE ALL PART OF TEAMS EVERY DAY, AND IT'S TIME TO RECOGNIZE A BASIC FACT: Teams are hard work, but they are mostly worth it. The beauty of teams is accomplishing something far greater than what's possible for an individual alone. But even though two heads can be better than one, the key word is "can." Have you ever heard someone say, "Too many cooks spoil the broth" or "A camel is an elephant put together by a committee"? There are good reasons why such sayings are well used.

Let's start this discussion realistically. On one level there seems little to debate. Groups and teams have a lot to offer organizations. But at another level you have to sometimes wonder if the extra effort is really worth it. Sometimes teams can be more pain than gain. There's a lot to learn about them, their roles in organizations, and how we participate in and help lead them for real performance gains.[1]

‖ Teams offer synergy and other benefits to organizations and their members.

A **team** is a collection of people who regularly interact to pursue common goals.

Teamwork is the process of people actively working together to accomplish common goals.

Synergy is the creation of a whole greater than the sum of its individual parts.

A **team** is a small group of people with complementary skills who work together to accomplish shared goals while holding each other mutually accountable for performance results.[2] Teams are essential to organizations of all types and sizes. Many tasks are well beyond the capabilities of individuals alone.[3] And in this sense, **teamwork**, people actually working together to accomplish a shared goal, is a major performance asset.[4]

The term **synergy** means the creation of a whole that exceeds the sum of its parts. When teams perform well, it's because of synergy that pools many diverse talents and efforts to create extraordinary results. *Check synergy and team success in the NBA.* Scholars find that both good and bad basketball teams win more the longer the players have been together. Why? A "teamwork effect" creates wins because players know one another's moves and playing tendencies. *Check synergy and team success in the hospital operating room.* Scholars notice the same heart surgeons have lower death rates for similar procedures performed in hospitals where the surgeons did more operations. Why? A teamwork effect—the doctors had more time working together with the surgery teams—anesthesiologists, nurses, and other surgical technicians. They say it's not only the surgeon's skills that count; the skills of the team and the time spent working together count too.[5]

Don't forget—teams are not only good for performance, they're also good for their members.[6] Just as in life overall, being part of a work team or informal group can strongly influence our attitudes and behaviors. The personal relationships can help with job performance—making contacts, sharing ideas, responding to favors, and bypassing roadblocks. And being part of a team often helps satisfy important needs that are unfulfilled in the regular work setting or life overall. Teams provide members with social relationships, security, a sense of belonging, and emotional support.

Teams often suffer from common performance problems.

We all know that working in teams isn't always easy or productive. Problems not only happen; they are common.[7] Teams often suffer from personality conflicts and work style differences that disrupt relationships and accomplishments. Sometimes group members battle over goals or competing visions. Sometimes they withdraw from active participation due to uncertainty over tasks and relationships. Ambiguous agendas or ill-defined problems can cause teamwork fatigue. Motivation can fall when teams work too long on the wrong things and end up having little to show for it. And, not everyone is always ready to jump in and do a great job on a team. These and other difficulties can easily turn the great potential of teams into frustration and failure.

One of the most troublesome team problems is **social loafing**—the presence of one or more "free-riders" who slack off and allow other team members to do most of the work.[8] For whatever reason, perhaps the absence of spotlight on personal performance, individuals sometimes work less hard, not harder, when they are part of a group.

What can a team leader do when someone is free-riding? The possibilities include a variety of actions to make individual contributions more visible—rewarding individuals for their contributions, making task assignments more interesting, and keeping group size small so that free-riders are more noticeable. This makes the loafers more susceptible to pressures from peers and to critical leader evaluations. And if you've ever considered free-riding as a team member, think again. You may get away with it in the short term, but your reputation will suffer, and sooner or later it will be "payback" time.

Why Teams Are Good for Organizations

- More resources for problem solving
- Improved creativity and innovation
- Improved quality of decision making
- Greater commitment to tasks
- Increased motivation of members
- Better control and work discipline
- More individual need satisfaction

Social loafing is the tendency of some people to avoid responsibility by free-riding in groups.

How to Handle Social Loafing

- Reward individuals for contributions.
- Make individuals visible by keeping team size small.
- Encourage peer pressure to perform.
- Make task assignments more interesting.

{ **"I'LL BE ACTIVE IN DISCUSSIONS, BUT I CAN'T BE A LEADER OR VOLUNTEER FOR ANY EXTRA WORK."**

Ethics **Check**

■ Danger! Social Loafing May Be Closer Than You Think

Psychology study: A German researcher asks people to pull on a rope as hard as they can. First, individuals pull alone. Second, they pull as part of a group. Results show people pull harder when working alone than when working as part of a team. Such social loafing is the tendency to reduce effort when working in groups.

Faculty office: A student wants to speak with the instructor about his team's performance on the last group project. There were four members, but two did almost all the work. The two loafers largely disappeared, showing up only at the last minute to be part of the formal presentation. His point is that the team was disadvantaged because the two free-riders caused a loss of performance capacity.

Telephone call from the boss: "John, I really need you to serve on this committee. Will you do it? Let me know tomorrow." In thinking about this, I ponder: I'm overloaded, but I don't want to turn down the boss. I'll accept but let the committee members know about my situation. I'll be active in discussions and try to offer viewpoints and perspectives that are helpful. However, I'll let them know up front that I can't be a leader or volunteer for any extra work.

YOU DECIDE

Whether you call it social loafing, free-riding, or just plain old slacking off, the issue is the same. What right do some people have to sit back in team situations and let other people do all or most of the work? Is this ethical? Does everyone in a group have an ethical obligation to do his or her fair share of the work? Does the fact that John is going to be honest with the other committee members make any difference? Won't he still be a loafer that gets credit with the boss for serving on the committee? Would it be more ethical for him to decline the boss's request?

‖ Organizations are networks of formal teams and informal groups.

> A **formal team** is officially recognized and supported by the organization.

A **formal team** is officially designated for a specific organizational purpose. You'll find such teams described by different labels on organization charts—examples are *departments* (e.g., market research department), *work units* (e.g., audit unit), *teams* (e.g., customer service team), or *divisions* (e.g., office products division).

Formal teams are headed by supervisors, managers, department heads, team leaders, and the like. It is common, in fact, to describe organizations as interlocking networks of teams in which managers and leaders play "linking pin" roles.[9] This means that they serve both as head of one work team and as a regular member in the next-higher-level one. It's also important to recognize, as shown here, that managers play more than one role in groups and teams. In addition to serving as the supervisor or team leader, they also act as network facilitators, helpful participants, and external coaches.

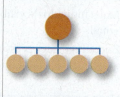

Supervisor

Network facilitator

Helpful participant

External coach

© Leontura/iStockphoto

Facts to **Consider**

■ Unproductive Meetings Are Major Time Wasters

A survey of some 38,000 workers around the world links low productivity with bad meetings, poor communication, and unclear goals.

- 69% of meetings attended are considered ineffective.
- 32% of workers complain about team communication.
- 31% complain about unclear objectives and priorities.

YOUR THOUGHTS?

Do these data match your experiences with team meetings? Given the common complaints about meetings, what can a team leader do to improve them? Think about the recent meetings you have attended. In what ways were the best meetings different from the worst ones? Did your behavior play a significant role in both these cases?

The informal structure of an organization also consists of **informal groups**. They emerge from natural or spontaneous relationships and offer members opportunities for social satisfactions as well as contacts for getting work done. Some are *interest groups,* whose members pursue a common cause, such as a women's career network. Some are *friendship groups* that develop for a wide variety of personal reasons, including shared hobbies and other nonwork interests. Others are *support groups* in which members basically help one another out in work and personal affairs.

> An **informal group** is unofficial and emerges from relationships and shared interests among members.

‖ Organizations use committees, task forces, and cross-functional teams.

Among the formal teams and groups in organizations, a **committee** brings together people outside their daily job assignments to work in a small team for a specific purpose.[10] A designated head or chairperson typically leads the committee and is held accountable for the task agenda. Organizations, for example, often have committees dealing with issues like diversity, quality, and compensation.[11]

> A **committee** is designated to work on a special task on a continuing basis.

Project teams or **task forces** put people together to work on common problems, but on a temporary rather than a continuing basis. Project teams, for example, might be formed to develop a new product or service, redesign workflows, or provide specialized consulting for a client.[12] A task force might be formed to address employee retention problems or come up with ideas for improving work schedules.[13]

> A **project team** or **task force** is convened for a specific purpose and disbands after completing its task.

The **cross-functional team** brings together members from different functional units.[14] They are supposed to work together on specific problems or tasks, sharing information and exploring new ideas. They are expected to help knock down the "functional chimneys" or "walls" that otherwise separate departments and people in the organization. For example, Target CEO Gregg Steinhafel says that his firm uses cross-functional teams from "merchandising, marketing, design,

> A **cross-functional team** operates with members who come from different functional units of an organization.

An **employee involvement team** meets on a regular basis to help achieve continuous improvement.

A **quality circle** is a team of employees who meet periodically to discuss ways of improving work quality.

Members of a **virtual team** work together and solve problems through computer-based interactions.

communications, presentation, supply chain and stores" to create and bring to customers new limited edition fashions.[15]

Some organizations also use **employee involvement teams**. These groups of workers meet on a regular basis with the goal of using their expertise and experience for continuous improvement. The **quality circle**, for example, is a team that meets regularly to discuss and plan specific ways to improve work quality.[16]

||| Virtual teams are increasingly common in organizations.

A vice president for human resources at Marriott once called electronic meetings "the quietest, least stressful, most productive meetings you've ever had."[17] She was talking about a type of group that is increasingly common in today's organizations—the **virtual team**.[18] Sometimes called a *distributed team*, its members work together and solve problems through computer-mediated rather than face-to-face interactions. The constant emergence of new technologies is making virtual collaboration both easier and more common. At home it may be Skype or Facebook; at the office it's likely to be any number of in-house or other Web-based meeting resources.[19]

As you probably realize already from working in college study teams, virtual teamwork has many advantages. It allows teamwork by people who may be located at great distances from one another, offering cost and time efficiencies. It makes it easy to widely share lots of information, keep records of team activities, and maintain databases. And, virtual teamwork can help reduce interpersonal problems that might otherwise occur when team members are dealing face-to-face with controversial issues.[20]

{ VIRTUAL TEAMS NEED THE RIGHT MEMBERS, GOALS, FEEDBACK, AND TECHNOLOGY. }

Tips to **Remember**

■ **Steps to Successful Virtual Teams**

- *Select team members high in initiative and capable of self-starting.*
- *Select members who will join and engage the team with positive attitudes.*
- *Select members known for working hard to meet team goals.*
- *Begin with social messaging that allows members to exchange information about one another to personalize the process.*

- *Assign clear goals and roles so that members can focus while working alone and also know what others are doing.*
- *Gather regular feedback from members about how they think the team is doing and how it might do better.*
- *Provide regular feedback to team members about team accomplishments.*
- *Make sure the team has the best virtual meeting technology.*

Are there any downsides to virtual teams? Yes, for sure, and often they're the same as in other groups.[21] Social loafing can still occur, goals may be unclear, meeting requests may be too frequent. Members of virtual teams can also have difficulties establishing good working relationships. The lack of face-to-face interaction limits the role of emotions and nonverbal cues in the communication and may depersonalize member relations.[22] Even with these potential problems, however, teams working in virtual space rather than face-to-face are proving their performance potential.[23] In fact, they're becoming a way of organizational life.

⦀ Self-managing teams are a form of job enrichment for groups.

In a growing number of organizations, traditional work units of supervisors and subordinates are being replaced with **self-managing teams**. Sometimes called *autonomous work groups*, these are teams whose members have been given collective authority to make many decisions about how they work, ones previously made by higher-level managers.[24] The expected advantages include better performance, decreased costs, and higher morale.

Members of a **self-managing team** have the authority to make decisions about how they share and complete their work.

As shown in **Figure 14.1**, the "self-management" responsibilities of self-managing teams include planning and scheduling work, training members in various tasks, distributing tasks, meeting performance goals, ensuring high quality, and solving day-to-day operating problems. In some settings the team's authority may even extend to "hiring" and "firing" its members when necessary. A key feature is multitasking, in which team members each have the skills to perform several different jobs.

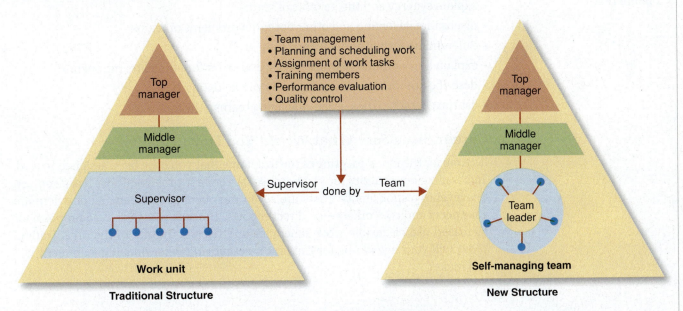

FIGURE 14.1 What Are the Management Implications of Self-Managing Teams?
Members of self-managing teams make decisions together on team membership, task plans and job assignments, training and performance evaluations, and quality control. Because they essentially manage themselves in these ways, they no longer need a traditional supervisor or department head. Instead, the team leader performs this role with the support of team members. The team leader and team as a whole report to the next higher level of management and are held accountable for performance results.

STUDY GUIDE

Takeaway 14.1
Why Is It Important to Understand Teams and Teamwork?

Terms to Define

Committee

Cross-functional team

Employee involvement team

Formal team

Informal group

Project team

Quality circle

Self-managing team

Social loafing

Synergy

Task force

Team

Teamwork

Virtual team

Rapid Review

- A team consists of people with complementary skills working together for shared goals and holding one another accountable for performance.
- Teams benefit organizations by providing for synergy that allows the accomplishment of tasks that are beyond individual capabilities alone.
- Social loafing and other problems can limit the performance of teams.
- Organizations use a variety of formal teams in the form of committees, task forces, project teams, cross-functional teams, and virtual teams.
- Self-managing teams allow team members to perform many tasks previously done by supervisors.

Questions for Discussion

1. Do committees and task forces work better when they are given short deadlines?
2. Are there some things that should be done only by face-to-face teams, not virtual ones?
3. Why do people in teams often tolerate social loafers?

Be Sure You Can

- define "team" and "teamwork"
- describe the roles managers play in teams
- explain synergy and the benefits of teams
- discuss social loafing and other potential problems of teams
- differentiate formal and informal groups
- explain how committees, task forces, and cross-functional teams operate
- describe potential problems faced by virtual teams
- list the characteristics of self-managing teams

Career Situation: What Would You Do?

It's time for the initial meeting of the task force that you have been assigned to lead. This is a big opportunity for you because it's the first time your boss has given you this level of responsibility. There are seven members of the team, all of whom are your peers and co-workers—no direct reports. The task is to develop a proposal for increased use of flexible work schedules and telecommuting in the organization. What will your agenda be for the first meeting, and what opening statement will you make?

Takeaway 14.2
What Are the Building Blocks of Successful Teamwork?

ANSWERS TO COME

■ Teams need the right members for the tasks to be accomplished.

■ Teams need the right setting and size to be effective.

■ Teams need the right processes to be effective.

■ Teams move through different stages of development.

■ Team performance is affected by norms and cohesiveness.

■ Team performance is affected by task and maintenance roles.

■ Team performance is affected by communication networks.

AFTER TALKING ABOUT THE TYPES OF TEAMS IN ORGANIZATIONS, IT'S TIME TO focus on the teamwork that can make them successful.[25] Look at **Figure 14.2**. It diagrams a team as an open system that, like the organization itself, transforms a variety of inputs into outputs.[26] It also shows that an **effective team** should be accomplishing three output goals—task performance, member satisfaction, and team viability.[27]

The first outcome of an effective team is high *task performance*. When you are on a team, ask: Did we accomplish our tasks and meet expectations? The second

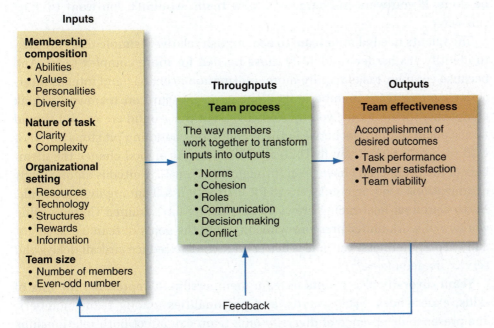

FIGURE 14.2 **What Are the Foundations of Team Effectiveness?**
An effective team achieves high levels of task performance and member satisfaction and remains viable for the future. The foundations of effectiveness begin with inputs— things such as membership composition, nature of the task, resources and support in the organizational setting, and team size. The foundations of effectiveness further rest with team process—how well the members utilize their talents and other inputs to create the desired outputs. Key process factors on any team include the stages of development, norms and cohesion, task and maintenance activities, communication, and decision making.

An **effective team** achieves high levels of task performance, membership satisfaction, and future viability.

outcome of an effective team is *member satisfaction*. Ask: Are we individually and collectively pleased with our participation in the process? The third outcome of an effective team is *viability for future action*. Ask: Can this team be successful again in the future?[28]

You might hear an effective team described as one that has "the right players in the right seats on the same bus, headed in the same direction."[29] The open-systems model in Figure 14.2 shows this thinking. A team's effectiveness is influenced by inputs—getting the right players and putting them in the right seats, and by process—making sure everyone knows they're on the same bus and headed in the same direction. You can remember the implications with this **team effectiveness equation**.

$$\text{Team Effectiveness} = \text{Quality of Inputs} + (\text{Process Gains} - \text{Process Losses})$$

⦀ Teams need the right members for the tasks to be accomplished.

The foundations for team effectiveness are set when a team is formed. The better or worse the inputs, you might say, the more or less likely are good teamwork and performance success.[30] And when it comes to optimizing inputs for team success, the starting point is membership composition. In other words, just who should you select as team members?

Ability counts in team membership. You want talent available to accomplish the task at hand. In an ideal world, managers carefully form teams by choosing team members whose talents and interests fit well with the job to be done. If you were in charge of a new team, wouldn't you want to start this way?

The talents needed for a team to accomplish relatively simple tasks are easy to identify. It's harder to identify those needed for more complex tasks. And because complex tasks require more information exchange and intense interaction among team members, they put more pressure on teamwork. Think complexity the next time you fly. And check out the ground crews. You should notice some similarities between them and teams handling pit stops for NASCAR racers. In fact, if you fly United Airlines, there's a good chance the members of the ramp crews have been through "Pit Crew U." United is among many organizations sending employees to Pit Instruction & Training in Mooresville, North Carolina. Real racing crews at this facility have trained United's ramp workers to work under pressure while meeting the goals of teamwork, safety, and job preparedness. The goal is better teamwork to reduce aircraft delays and service inadequacies.[31]

Team diversity is the mix of skills, experiences, backgrounds, and personalities of team members.

Team diversity also counts in team membership. It represents the mix of skills, experiences, backgrounds, and personalities among team members. The presence or absence of diversity on a team can affect both relationships among members and team performance. And when diversity is present, just how well it is managed can make the difference between a team that struggles between failure or modest success and one that achieves something truly great.

Homogeneous teams have members with similar personal characteristics.

It is easier to manage relationships among members of **homogeneous teams**—those whose members share similar characteristics. But this sense of harmony can come at a price. Researchers warn about risks when team members are too similar in background, training, and experience. Such teams may underperform, especially on complex or creative tasks, even though the members may feel very comfortable with one another.[32]

It is harder to manage relationships among members of more **heterogeneous teams**—those whose members are quite dissimilar to one another.[33] But, the potential complications of membership diversity also come with special performance opportunities. When heterogeneous teams are well managed, the variety of ideas, perspectives, and experiences within them can be helpful for problem solving. Highly creative teams, for example, are often ones that mix experienced people with those who haven't worked together before.[34] The experienced members have the connections, whereas the newcomers add fresh thinking.

What are your experiences with diversity in team membership? Do you get along better in teams whose members are pretty much all alike? Have you encountered problems on teams whose members are quite different from one another?

> ### Input Foundations for Team Effectiveness
>
> - *Membership composition*—diversity of skills, experiences, backgrounds, personalities
> - *Nature of task*—clear and defined versus open-ended and complex
> - *Organizational setting*—information, resources, technology, space
> - *Team size*—smaller versus larger, odd/even count

Heterogeneous teams have members with diverse personal characteristics.

‖ Teams need the right setting and size to be effective.

As you might expect, the *organizational setting* influences team outputs. A key issue here is how well the organization supports the team in terms of information, material resources, technology, organization structures, available rewards, and even physical space. Teams are much more likely to perform well when they are given the right support than when they lack it.

Team size also makes a difference. The number of potential interactions increases exponentially as teams increase in size. This affects how members communicate, work together, handle disagreements, and reach agreements. So, just how big should a team be? The general answer is five to seven members for creative tasks. The more members, the harder it is to engage in the interactions needed for good problem solving. And, when voting is required, teams should have odd numbers of members to prevent ties.

‖ Teams need the right processes to be effective.

Although having the right team inputs in respect to membership composition, task, setting, and size is important, it's no guarantee of team success. **Team process** counts, too. Think of it as the way the members of any team actually work together as they transform inputs into outputs. This team effectiveness equation is also worth remembering.

Team process is the way team members work together to accomplish tasks.

Team Effectiveness = Quality of Inputs + (Process Gains − Process Losses).

Emmanuel Dunand/AFP/
Getty Images

{ AMAZON'S INNOVATIONS DON'T JUST COME OUT OF THE BLUE.... TEAMS ARE A CENTRAL INGREDIENT.... CEO JEFF BEZOS SAYS IF TWO PIZZAS AREN'T ENOUGH TO FEED A TEAM, IT'S TOO BIG

Role Models

■ Amazon's Jeff Bezos Bets on Two-Pizza Teams

Amazon.com's founder and CEO Jeff Bezos is one of America's top businesspersons and a technology visionary. He's also a great fan of teams. Bezos coined a simple rule when it comes to sizing the firm's product development teams: If two pizzas aren't enough to feed a team, it's too big.

Don't expect to spot a stereotyped corporate CEO in Jeff Bezos. His standard office attire is still blue jeans and a blue-collared shirt. But, this attire comes with a unique personality and a great business mind.

If you go to Amazon.com and click on the "Gold Box" at the top, you'll be tuning in to Bezos's vision. It's a place for special deals, lasting only an hour and offering everything from a power tool to a new pair of shoes. If you join Amazon Prime and "One-Click" your way to free shipping and a hassle-free checkout, you're benefiting from his vision as well. And, of course, there's the Kindle. Not only has it become Amazon's best-selling product ever, but it also made electronic books an everyday reality—one that competitors have been racing to also take advantage of.

Amazon's innovations don't just come out of the blue. They're part and parcel of the management philosophy Bezos has instilled at the firm. And teams are a central ingredient. He believes Amazon's small two-pizza teams are "innovation engines." He's also betting they'll help fight creeping bureaucracy as the company keeps growing larger and more complex.

WHAT'S THE LESSON HERE?

Is Bezos on to a great management lesson with his notion of the two-pizza team? What difference does team size make in your experience? Can you come up with an example of a team with over a dozen members that performed really well? If so, how can you explain its success? On the other hand, can a team be too small? What example can you give of a team that would have done better if it was just a bit bigger?

Team IQ is the ability of a team to perform well by using talent and emotional intelligence.

The process aspects of any team, also called *group dynamics*, include how members get to know one another, develop expectations and loyalty, communicate, handle conflicts, and make decisions. And, the simple fact is that group dynamics aren't always pretty. Haven't you been on teams where people seemed to spend more time dealing with personality conflicts than with the task? How often have you read or heard about high-talent college sports teams where a lack of the right "chemistry" among players meant subpar team performance?

A positive team process takes full advantage of group inputs in ways that raise team effectiveness. These are process gains in the team effectiveness equation. But any problems with process can quickly drain energies and create process losses that reduce team effectiveness. Scholar and consultant Daniel Goleman says process failures show a lack of **team IQ** or "the ability of teams to perform well."[35] He points out that "champion" teams excel because their members know how to use their talents in cooperation with others and are able to handle occasional disharmony and interpersonal conflicts. In other words, great teams combine talent with emotional intelligence and positive team processes to create a winning performance combination.

Teams move through different stages of development.

Teams tend to change as they age. Things are often very different for a newly formed team than one whose members have been together for a long time. It turns out that one of the factors determining the success or failure of a team is how well problems and opportunities are handled over different phases of its life cycle. Scholars like to talk about this issue in terms of the five stages of team development listed here.[36]

1. *Forming*—a stage of initial orientation and interpersonal testing
2. *Storming*—a stage of conflict over tasks and working as a team
3. *Norming*—a stage of consolidation around task and operating agendas
4. *Performing*—a stage of teamwork and focused task performance
5. *Adjourning*—a stage of task completion and disengagement

≪ **5 Stages of Team Development**

An effective team meets and masters key process challenges as it moves through each of the prior stages. An example using membership diversity is shown in the nearby figure. We know that team diversity can expand the talents, ideas, perspectives, and experiences useful in problem solving.[37] But we also know that relationships and processes can get more complicated as diversity grows. It's important to not let process losses overwhelm the opportunity for performance gains. When team leaders and members do well at managing diversity across the stages of team development, especially through the critical zone of storming and norming, the chances for real team success are greatly increased.

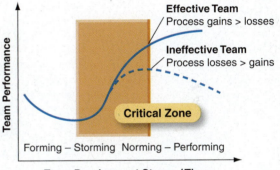

The *forming stage of team development* is one of initial task orientation and interpersonal testing. New members are likely to ask: What can or does the team offer me? What will they ask me to contribute? Can my efforts serve team needs while also meeting my needs? In this stage, people begin to identify with other members and with the team itself. They focus on getting acquainted, establishing interpersonal relationships, discovering what is considered acceptable behavior, and learning how others perceive the team's task. Difficulties in the forming stage tend to be greater in more culturally and demographically diverse teams.

The *storming stage of team development* is a period of high emotionality. Tension often emerges between members over tasks and interpersonal concerns. There may be periods of conflict, outright hostility, and even infighting as some individuals try to impose their preferences on others. But this is also the stage where members start to clarify task agendas and understand one another. Attention begins to shift toward mastering obstacles, and team members start looking for ways to meet team goals while also satisfying individual needs. As the prior figure shows, the storming stage is part of a "critical zone" in team development where process failures cause lasting problems but process successes set the foundations for future effectiveness.

Cooperation is an important issue for teams in the *norming stage of team development*. At this point, members of the team begin to better coordinate their efforts as a working unit and operate with shared rules of conduct. The team feels a sense of leadership, with each member starting to play a useful role. Most interpersonal hostilities give way to a precarious balancing of forces as norming builds initial integration. Norming is also part of the critical zone of team development. When it is well managed, team members are likely to develop initial feelings of closeness and a sense of shared expectations. This helps protect the team from disintegration while members continue their efforts to work well together.

Teams in the *performing stage of team development* are mature, organized, and well functioning. This is a stage of total integration in which team members are able to creatively deal with complex tasks and interpersonal conflicts. The team has a clear and stable structure, members are motivated by team goals, and the process scores high on the criteria of team maturity shown in **Figure 14.3**.[38]

	Very poor			Very good	
1. Trust among members	1	2	3	4	5
2. Feedback mechanisms	1	2	3	4	5
3. Open communications	1	2	3	4	5
4. Approach to decisions	1	2	3	4	5
5. Leadership sharing	1	2	3	4	5
6. Acceptance of goals	1	2	3	4	5
7. Valuing diversity	1	2	3	4	5
8. Member cohesiveness	1	2	3	4	5
9. Support for each other	1	2	3	4	5
10. Performance norms	1	2	3	4	5

FIGURE 14.3   What Are the Criteria for Assessing the Process Maturity of a Team?
Teams vary greatly in the degree of maturity they achieve and demonstrate in day-to-day behavior. These criteria are helpful for assessing the development and maturity of a team as it moves through various phases—from forming to storming to norming to performing. We would expect that teams would start to show strong positives on these criteria as members gain experience with one another in the norming stage of team development. We would expect teams to have consistently strong positive scores in the performing stage.

The *adjourning stage of team development* is the final stage for temporary committees, task forces, and project teams. Here, team members prepare to achieve closure and disband, ideally with a sense that they have accomplished important goals.

||| Team performance is affected by norms and cohesiveness.

Have you ever felt pressure from other group members when you do something wrong—come late to a meeting, fail to complete an assigned task, or act out of character? What you are experiencing is related to group **norms**, or

A **norm** is a behavior, rule, or standard expected to be followed by team members.

Explore **Yourself**

■ Team Contributions

If teams and teamwork are a major part of how organizations operate today, **team contributions** have to be considered one of the most essential career skills.

We need to be able to contribute in as many different ways team members so that our teams can reach their performance potential. But experience proves time and time again that teams often underperform or, at least, lose time and effectiveness as members struggle with a variety of process difficulties.

Take a good, hard look at the teams that you participate in. While so doing, make a realistic self-assessment of your team contributions as well as those of other members. Ask: How can the insights of this chapter help me build team skills so that I can help turn teamwork potential into real team achievements?

> Get to know yourself better by taking the self-assessment on **Team Leader Skills** and completing other activities in the *Exploring Management* **Skill-Building Portfolio**.

behaviors expected of team members.[39] A norm is a rule or standard that guides behavior. And when a norm is violated, team members are usually pressured to conform. In the extreme, violating a norm can result in expulsion from the group or social ostracism.

Any number of norms can be operating in a group at any given time. During the forming and storming stages of development, norms often focus on expected attendance and levels of commitment. By the time the team reaches the performing stage, norms have formed around adaptability, change, and desired levels of achievement. And without a doubt, one of the most important norms for any team is the **performance norm**. It defines the level of work effort and performance that team members are expected to contribute.

It shouldn't surprise you that teams with positive performance norms are more successful than those with negative ones. But how do you build teams with the right norms? Actually, there are a number of things leaders can do.[40]

- Act as a positive role model.
- Reinforce the desired behaviors with rewards.
- Control results by performance reviews and regular feedback.
- Train and orient new members to adopt desired behaviors.
- Recruit and select new members who exhibit the desired behaviors.
- Hold regular meetings to discuss progress and ways of improving.
- Use team decision-making methods to reach agreement.

Whether the team members will accept and conform to norms is largely determined by **cohesiveness**, the degree to which members are attracted to and motivated to remain part of a team.[41] Members of a highly cohesive team value their membership. They try to conform to norms and behave in ways that meet the expectations of other members, and they get satisfaction from doing so. In this way, at least, a highly cohesive team is good for its members. But does the same hold true for team performance?

The **performance norm** defines the effort and performance contributions expected of team members.

 **How Leaders Build Positive Team Norms**

Cohesiveness is the degree to which members are attracted to and motivated to remain part of a team.

Figure 14.4 shows that teams perform best when the performance norm is positive and cohesiveness is high. In this best-case scenario, cohesion results in conformity to the positive norm, which ultimately benefits team performance. When the performance norm is negative in a cohesive team, however, high conformity to the norm creates a worst-case scenario. In this situation, members join together in restricting their efforts and performance contributions.

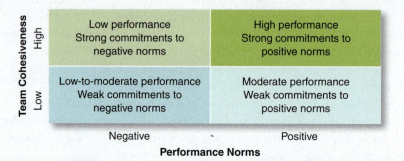

FIGURE 14.4   How Do Norms and Cohesiveness Influence Team Performance?
Group norms are expected behaviors for team members; cohesiveness is the strength of attraction members feel toward the team. When cohesiveness is high, conformity to norms is high. Positive performance norms in a highly cohesive group create a desirable situation, with high-performance outcomes likely. However, negative performance norms in a highly cohesive group can be troublesome; conformity by members to the negative norms creates low-performance outcomes.

What are the implications of this relationship between norms and cohesiveness? Basically it boils down to this: Each of us should be aware of what can be done to build both positive norms and high cohesiveness in our teams. In respect to cohesiveness, this means such things as keeping team size as small as possible, working to gain agreements on team goals, increasing interaction among members, rewarding team outcomes rather than individual performance, introducing competition with other teams, and putting together team members who are very similar to one another.

||| Team performance is affected by task and maintenance roles.

Research on the group process identifies two types of activities that are essential if team members are to work well together over time.[42] **Task activities** contribute directly to the team's performance purpose; **maintenance activities** support the emotional life of the team as an ongoing social system. Although you might expect that these are things that team leaders or managers should be doing, this is only partially correct. In fact, all team members should share the responsibilities for task and maintenance leadership.

The concept of **distributed leadership** in teams makes every member continually responsible for both recognizing when task or maintenance activities are needed and taking actions to provide them. Leading through task activities involves making an effort to define and solve problems and advance work toward performance results. Without task activities, such as initiating

A **task activity** is an action taken by a team member that directly contributes to the group's performance purpose.

A **maintenance activity** is an action taken by a team member that supports the emotional life of the group.

Distributed leadership is when any and all members contribute helpful task and maintenance activities to the team.

agendas and sharing information, teams have difficulty accomplishing their objectives. Leading through maintenance activities, such as encouraging others and reducing tensions, helps strengthen and perpetuate the team as a social system.

As shown below, both task and maintenance activities stand in distinct contrast to dysfunctional or **disruptive behaviors.** These include obvious self-serving behaviors that you often see and perhaps even engage in yourself—things such as aggressiveness, excessive joking, and nonparticipation. Think about this the next time one of your groups is drifting toward ineffectiveness. Think also what you and other members can do to correct things by fulfilling distributed leadership responsibilities.

> **Disruptive behaviors** are self-serving and cause problems for team effectiveness.

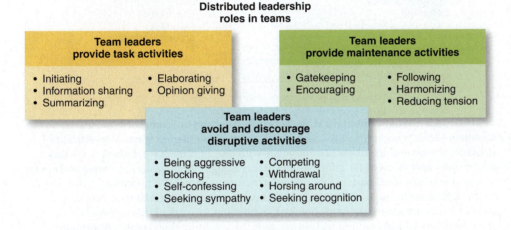

Team performance is affected by communication networks.

Teams use the different communication networks shown in **Figure 14.5** as they work and interact together.[43] In a **decentralized communication network**, all members communicate directly with one another. Sometimes called the *all-channel* or *star* structure, this arrangement works well for tasks that require lots of creativity, information processing, and problem solving. Use of a decentralized communication network creates an *interacting team* in which all members actively work together and share information. Member satisfaction on successful interacting teams is usually high.

> A **decentralized communication network** allows all members to communicate directly with one another.

When tasks are more routine and less demanding, team members can often divide up the work and then simply coordinate the final results. This is best done with a **centralized communication network**, sometimes called the *wheel* or *chain* structure. It has a central "hub" through which one member, often the team leader, collects information from and distributes information to all others. This creates a *coacting team* whose members work independently and pass completed tasks to the hub. There, they are put together into a finished product. The hub member often experiences the most satisfaction on successful coacting teams.

> In a **centralized communication network**, communication flows only between individual members and a hub or center point.

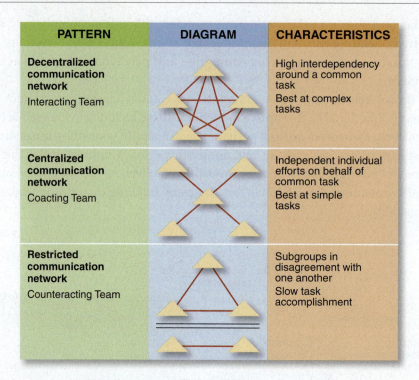

PATTERN	DIAGRAM	CHARACTERISTICS
Decentralized communication network Interacting Team		High interdependency around a common task Best at complex tasks
Centralized communication network Coaching Team		Independent individual efforts on behalf of common task Best at simple tasks
Restricted communication network Counteracting Team		Subgroups in disagreement with one another Slow task accomplishment

FIGURE 14.5 **What Communication Networks Are Used in Teams?**
Members of teams communicate and interact together in different ways. A decentralized structure is where all members communicate with one another. It works best when tasks are complex and the need for information sharing is high. When tasks are simple and easily broken down into small parts, a centralized structure works well. It coordinates members' communications through one central point. A restricted communication network sometimes forms when subgroups break off to do separate work or due to member alienation. Any lack of communication between the subgroups can create performance problems.

When teams break into subgroups, either on purpose or because members are experiencing issue-specific disagreements, this may create a **restricted communication network**. Left unmanaged, this *counteracting team* environment can deteriorate to the point where subgroups fail to adequately communicate with one another and even engage in outwardly antagonistic relations. Although these situations create problems, there are times when counteracting teams might be intentionally set up to encourage conflict, increase creativity, and help double-check the quality of specific decisions or chosen courses of action.

In summary, the best teams use all three communication networks—decentralized, centralized, and restricted. But, they use them in the right ways and at the right times. When the task is simple and routine, organize as a coaching team using a centralized network. When things are getting complicated and unclear, go with an interacting team and the decentralized network. And when there isn't enough critical discussion or you're worried that too much harmony is limiting team creativity, it may be time to form a counteracting team where subgroups in a restricted network engage in a bit of conflict.

Subgroups in a **restricted communication network** contest one anothers' positions and restrict interactions with one another.

STUDY GUIDE

Takeaway 14.2
What Are the Building Blocks of Successful Teamwork?

Rapid Review

- An effective team achieves high levels of task performance, member satisfaction, and team viability.
- Important team input factors include the membership characteristics, nature of the task, organizational setting, and group size.
- A team matures through various stages of development, including forming, storming, norming, performing, and adjourning.
- Norms are the standards or rules of conduct that influence the behavior of team members; cohesion is the attractiveness of the team to its members.
- In highly cohesive teams, members tend to conform to norms; the best situation is a team with positive performance norms and high cohesiveness.
- Distributed leadership occurs when team members step in to provide helpful task and maintenance activities and discourage disruptive activities.
- Effective teams make use of alternative communication networks and interaction patterns to best complete tasks.

Questions for Discussion

1. What happens if a team can't get past the storming stage?

2. What can a manager do to build positive performance norms on a work team?

3. Why would a manager ever want to reduce the cohesion of a work group?

Be Sure You Can

- list the outputs of an effective team
- identify inputs that influence team effectiveness
- discuss how diversity influences team effectiveness
- list five stages of group development
- explain how norms and cohesion influence team performance
- list ways to build positive norms and change team cohesiveness
- illustrate task, maintenance, and disruptive activities in teams
- describe how groups use decentralized and centralized communication networks

Career Situation: What Would You Do?

For quite some time you've been watching the performance of your work team slowly deteriorate. Although everyone seems to like one another, the "numbers" in terms of measured daily accomplishments have now fallen to an unacceptable level. It's time to act. What will you look at to identify likely problem issues? What steps might you take to get this team back on track and improve its overall effectiveness?

Team building involves activities to gather and analyze data on a team and make changes to increase its effectiveness.

Takeaway 14.3
How Can Managers Create and Lead High-Performance Teams?

ANSWERS TO COME

- Team building helps team members learn to better work together.
- Team performance benefits from good use of decision methods.
- Team performance suffers when groupthink leads to bad decisions.
- Team performance benefits from good conflict management.

THERE'S QUITE A BIT OF AGREEMENT ABOUT THE CHARACTERISTICS OF HIGH-performance teams.[44] They have clear and elevating goals. They are results-oriented, and their members are hardworking. They have high standards of excellence in a collaborative team culture. They get solid external support and recognition for their accomplishments. And they have strong and principled leaders. It's a great list, isn't it? But how do we get and stay there?

Although we know that high-performance teams generally share the characteristics just noted, not all teams reach this level of excellence. Just as in the world of sports, there are many things that can go wrong and cause problems for teams in the workplace.

‖ Team building helps team members learn to better work together.

One of the ways to grow capacity for long-term team effectiveness is a practice known as **team building**. This is a set of planned activities used to analyze the functioning of a team and then make changes to increase its operating effectiveness.[45] Most systematic approaches to team building begin with awareness that a problem may exist or may develop within the team. Members then work together to gather data and fully understand the problem. Action plans are made and implemented. Results are evaluated by team members. As difficulties or new problems are discovered, the team-building process recycles.

There are many methods for gathering data on team functioning, including structured and unstructured interviews, questionnaires, team meetings, and reality experiences. Regardless of the method used, the basic principle of team building remains the same—a careful and collaborative assessment of data on team inputs, processes, and results. It works best when all members participate in data gathering and analysis and then collectively decide on actions to be taken.

Team building can be done with or without the help of outside consultants. It can also be done in the workplace or in off-site locations. It is increasingly popular, for example, to engage in outdoor activities—obstacle courses or special events like Geocaching—to create enthusiasm for a team building experience. As one outdoor team-building expert points out, these outdoor team activities "focus on building trust, increasing productivity and emphasizing the importance of being a team player, as well as improving communication and listening skills while learning about group dynamics."[46] It's quite a statement, but the power of team building cannot be denied.

Fast Lanes for NASCAR Teams

The Beauty Is in the Teamwork

When a NASCAR driver pulls in for a pit stop, the pit crew must jump in to perform multiple tasks flawlessly and in perfect order and unison. A second gained or lost can be crucial to a NASCAR driver's performance. "You can't win a race with a 12-second stop, but you can lose it with an 18-second stop," says pit crew coach Trent Cherry.

Pit crew members execute intricate maneuvers while taking care of tire changes, car adjustments, fueling, and related matters on a crowded pit lane. Each crew member is an expert at one task but fully aware of how it fits with every other. Duties are carefully scripted for each peak individual performance and choreographed to fit together seamlessly at the team level. If the jacker is late, for example, the wheel changer can't pull the wheel.

The best crews plan and practice over and over again, getting ready for the big test of race day performance. The crew chief makes sure that everyone is in shape, well trained, and ready to go. "I don't want seven all-stars," Trent Cherry says, "I want seven guys who work as a team."

Christian Petersen/Getty Images, Inc.

Find Inspiration

NASCAR pit crews don't just get together and "wing it" on race days. Members are carefully selected for their skills and attitudes. Teams practice, practice, and practice. And, the pit crew leader doesn't hesitate to make changes when things aren't going well. Is this a model for teams everywhere?

⦀ Team performance benefits from good use of decision methods.

The best teams don't limit themselves to just one **decision-making** method. Edgar Schein, a respected scholar and consultant, describes six ways teams make decisions.[47] He and other scholars note that teams ideally choose and use methods that best fit the problems at hand.[48] But mistakes are often made.

In *decision by lack of response*, one idea after another is suggested without any discussion taking place. When the team finally accepts an idea, all alternatives have been bypassed and discarded by simple lack of response rather than by critical evaluation. In *decision by authority rule*, the leader, manager, committee head, or some other authority figure makes a decision for the team. Although time-efficient, the quality of the decision depends on whether the authority figure has the necessary information. Its implementation depends on how well other team members accept the top-down approach. In *decision by minority rule*, two or three people dominate by "railroading" the team into a decision. How often have you heard: "Does anyone object? Okay, let's go ahead with it."

One of the most common ways teams make decisions, especially when early signs of disagreement arise, is *decision by majority rule*. Although consistent with democratic methods, it is often used without awareness of potential downsides. When votes are taken some people will be "winners" and others will be "losers." In all likelihood, you've been on the losing side at times. How did it feel? If you're like me, it may have made you feel left out,

Decision making is the process of making choices among alternative courses of action.

Keys to Consensus Decisions

- Don't argue blindly; consider others' reactions to your points.
- Don't change your mind just to reach quick agreement.
- Avoid conflict reduction by voting, coin tossing, bargaining.
- Keep everyone involved in the decision process.
- Allow disagreements to surface so that things can be deliberated.
- Don't focus on winning versus losing; seek acceptable alternatives.
- Discuss assumptions, listen carefully, and encourage inputs by all.

unenthusiastic about supporting the majority decision, and even hoping for a future chance to win.

Consensus is reached when all parties believe they have had their say and been listened to, and they agree to support the group's final decision.

Teams are often encouraged to try for *decision by* **consensus**. This is where full discussion leads to most members favoring one alternative, with the other members agreeing to support it. Even those opposed to the decision know that the others listened to their concerns. Consensus doesn't require unanimity, but it does require that team members be able to argue, debate, and engage in reasonable conflict, while still listening to and getting along with one another.[49]

A *decision by unanimity* means all team members agree on the course of action to take. This is the ideal state of affairs but it is also very difficult to reach. One of the reasons that teams sometimes turn to authority decisions, majority voting, or even minority decisions is the difficulty of managing team processes to achieve consensus or unanimity.

||| Team performance suffers when groupthink leads to bad decisions.

How often have you held back stating your views in a meeting, agreed to someone else's position when it really seemed wrong, or gone along with a boss's suggestions even though you disagreed?[50] If and when you do these things, you are likely trapped by **groupthink**, the tendency for members of highly cohesive groups to lose their critical evaluative capabilities.[51] It occurs when teams strive so hard to reach agreement and avoid disagreement that they end up making bad decisions.[52]

Groupthink is a tendency for highly cohesive teams to lose their evaluative capabilities.

Psychologist Irving Janis first described groupthink using well-known historical blunders—the lack of preparedness of U.S. naval forces for the Japanese attack on Pearl Harbor and the failed Bay of Pigs invasion under President Kennedy.[53] It has also been linked to flawed U.S. decision making during the Vietnam war, events leading up to the NASA space shuttle disasters, and failures of intelligence agencies regarding the presence of weapons of mass destruction in Iraq. But be aware, groupthink isn't limited to big government or big corporate decision making. It appears all too often in any team, at any level, in all sorts of organizations. Hasn't it been part of your experience?

Teams suffering groupthink often fit the description shown in **Table 14.1**— Symptoms of Groupthink. They engage in things like rationalizing disconfirming data, stereotyping competitors as weak, and assuming the team is too good for criticism. They do this because members are trying to hold the group together and maintain harmony at all costs. They avoid doing anything that might detract from feelings of goodwill, such as communicating disagreement about a proposed course of action or pointing out that the team is moving too fast toward consensus. The problem is that whenever concerns like these are kept private and not shared, the team runs the risk of making a bad decision because of groupthink.

When you are leading or are part of team heading toward groupthink, don't assume there's no way out. Janis noted, for example, that after suffering the Bay of Pigs fiasco, President Kennedy approached the Cuban missile crisis quite differently. He purposely did not attend some cabinet discussions and allowed the group to deliberate without him. His absence helped the cabinet members

Table 14.1 Symptoms of Groupthink

Illusions of invulnerability—Members assume that the team is too good for criticism or is beyond attack.

Rationalizing unpleasant and disconfirming data—Members refuse to accept contradictory data or to thoroughly consider alternatives.

Belief in inherent group morality—Members act as though the group is inherently right and above reproach.

Stereotyping competitors as weak, evil, and stupid—Members refuse to look realistically at other groups.

Applying direct pressure to deviants to conform to group wishes—Members refuse to tolerate anyone who suggests the team may be wrong.

Self-censorship by members—Members refuse to communicate personal concerns to the whole team.

Illusions of unanimity—Members accept consensus prematurely, without testing its completeness.

Mind guarding—Members protect the team from hearing disturbing ideas or outside viewpoints.

talk more openly and be less inclined to try and say things consistent with his own thinking. When a decision was finally reached, the crisis was successfully resolved.

In addition to having the leader stay absent for some team discussions, Janis has other advice on how to get a team that is moving toward groupthink back on track.[54] You can assign one member to act as a critical evaluator or "devil's advocate" during each meeting. Subgroups can be assigned to work on issues and then share their findings with the team as a whole. Outsiders can be brought in to observe and participate in team meetings and offer their advice and viewpoints on both team processes and tentative decisions. And, the team can hold a "second chance" meeting after an initial decision is made to review, change, and even cancel it. With actions like these available, there's no reason to let groupthink lead a team down the wrong pathways.

▮ Team performance benefits from good conflict management.

The ability to deal with conflicts in interpersonal relationships and on a team is critical. But "conflict" is one of those words like "communication" or "power." We use it a lot, but rarely think it through to the specifics.

At its core **conflict** involves disagreements among people. And in our experiences, it appears in two quite different forms.[55] **Substantive conflict** involves disagreements over such things as goals and tasks, the allocation of resources, the distribution of rewards, policies and procedures, and job assignments. You are in a substantive conflict with a teammate when, for example, each of you wants to solve a problem by following a different strategy. **Emotional conflict** results from feelings of anger, distrust, dislike, fear, and resentment as well as relationship problems. You know this form of conflict as a clash of personalities or emotions—when you don't want to agree with another person just because you don't like or are angry with him or her.

Conflict is a disagreement over issues of substance and/or an emotional antagonism.

Substantive conflict involves disagreements over goals, resources, rewards, policies, procedures, and job assignments.

Emotional conflict results from feelings of anger, distrust, dislike, fear, and resentment as well as from personality clashes.

Manager's **Library**

WHAT'S NEXT IN THE WORLD OF "CROWDSOURCING"?

Test: What is a collection of individuals working together to achieve a common purpose? Digital immigrant's answer—an organization. Digital native's answer—an online community.

In the book *Crowdsourcing: Why the Power of the Cloud is Driving the Future of Business* (2008, Crown Business), author Jeff Howe discusses how the Internet has shifted the paradigm of organizations, teamwork, and innovation. He believes past generations of workers viewed teamwork as physical actions of paid experts, guided by managers telling them what to do. But new generations may view teamwork as primarily a virtual effort of unpaid volunteers, guided by popular opinion that permits them to do what they enjoy. In the past, newspaper editors gathered staffs to determine the news. Today, online "bloggers," "discussion boards," and "trending now" topics provide much of the news content that is consumed.

Howe defines "crowdsourcing" as Internet teamwork that draws on talents of amateurs to create value comparable to companies of paid experts. There are many variations. Digg.com uses "crowd voting" of six million user ratings to promote top news stories. Kiva.org relies on "crowd funding" to gather financing from individuals for small business loans. Wikipedia uses "crowd creation" to create and update an online encyclopedia.

Howe believes crowdsourcing is shifting how organizations approach intellectual capital. It allows large audiences of diverse hobbyists to generate ideas in digital transparency and accelerate innovations quickly in open examination.

REFLECT AND REACT

How do you use crowdsourcing in everyday life? What work and career applications do you see for it? Should contributors to crowdsourcing be paid? Should members of the crowd remain anonymous or be identified? Should a crowd be led or guided? And, is there any risk of groupthink in crowdsourcing?

Avoidance pretends that a conflict doesn't really exist.

Accommodation, or smoothing, plays down differences and highlights similarities to reduce conflict.

Competition, or authoritative command, uses force, superior skill, or domination to win a conflict.

Compromise occurs when each party to the conflict gives up something of value to the other.

With all this potential for conflict in and around teams, how do you and others deal with it? Most people respond to conflict through different combinations of cooperative and assertive behaviors.[56] **Figure 14.6** shows how this results in five conflict management styles—avoidance, accommodation, competition, compromise, and collaboration.[57]

In **avoidance**, everyone withdraws and pretends that conflict doesn't really exist, hoping that it will simply go away. You might think of this as teammates mad about a missed deadline and each unwilling to mention it to the other. In **accommodation**, peaceful coexistence is the goal. Differences are played down, and areas of agreement are highlighted, even though the real cause for the conflict doesn't get addressed. Both avoidance and accommodation are forms of *lose-lose conflict*. No one achieves her or his true desires, and the underlying conflict remains unresolved, often to recur in the future.

In **competition**, one party wins through superior skill or outright domination. Although the first example that may come to mind is sports, competition is common in work teams. It occurs as authoritative command by team leaders and as railroading or minority domination by team members. In **compromise**, trade-offs are made, with each party giving up and gaining something of value. Both competition and compromise are forms of *win-lose conflict*. Each party strives to gain at the other's expense. But whenever one party loses something, seeds for future conflict remain in place.

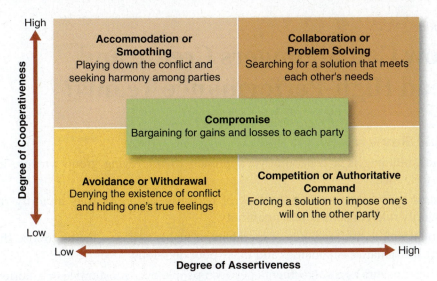

FIGURE 14.6 **What Are the Five Common Styles of Conflict Management?**
In conflict situations, a combination of cooperative and aggressive behaviors results in five possible conflict management styles. Competition occurs when aggression dominates our behavior, and accommodation occurs when cooperation dominates. Avoidance occurs with both low aggression and cooperation, whereas compromise occurs with moderate amounts of both. When both cooperation and aggression are high, true collaboration and problem solving are more likely to occur.

Collaboration, or problem solving, involves working through conflict differences and solving problems so everyone wins.

Unlike the prior methods, **collaboration** tries to find and address the problem and reconcile the real differences underlying a conflict. As you would expect, it is often time-consuming and stressful. But it's also the most effective conflict management style in terms of real conflict resolution. Collaboration turns a difficult situation into a *win-win conflict.* Things are resolved to everyone's mutual benefit—no avoiding, no smoothing, no domination, and no compromising. A real agreement is reached. From experience, you should recognize that this approach depends on the willingness of everyone to dig in, confront the issues, and openly and honestly discuss them. When it works, collaboration eliminates the underlying causes of a conflict and creates positive conditions for future teamwork.

The small box is a reminder that each of the five conflict management styles can be useful.[58] Most of us probably use each at least some of the time. But we should make good choices, being sure to fit our style to the requirements of each unique conflict situation. It's also worth remembering that unresolved or suppressed conflicts often sow the seeds for future conflicts. Only true **conflict resolution,** characteristic of the collaborative style, eliminates the underlying causes of a conflict in ways that should prevent similar conflicts in the future.

When to Use Alternative Conflict Management Strategies

- *Collaboration, or problem solving,* is the preferred way to gain true conflict resolution when time and cost permit.
- *Avoidance, or withdrawal,* may be used when an issue is trivial, when more important issues are pressing, or when people need to cool down temporarily and regain perspective.
- *Competition, or authoritative command,* may be used when quick and decisive action is vital or when unpopular actions must be taken.
- *Accommodation, or smoothing,* may be used when issues are more important to others than to yourself or when you want to build "credits" for use in later disagreements.
- *Compromise* may be used to arrive at temporary settlements of complex issues or to arrive at expedient solutions when time is limited.

Conflict resolution is the removal of the substantive and/or emotional reasons for a conflict.

STUDY GUIDE

Takeaway 14.3
How Can Managers Create and Lead High-Performance Teams?

Terms to Define

Accommodation

Avoidance

Collaboration

Competition

Compromise

Conflict

Conflict resolution

Consensus

Decision making

Emotional conflict

Groupthink

Substantive conflict

Team building

Rapid Review

- Team building is a collaborative approach to improving group process and performance.
- Teams can make decisions by lack of response, authority rule, minority rule, majority rule, consensus, and unanimity.
- Groupthink is the tendency of members of highly cohesive teams to lose their critical evaluative capabilities and make poor decisions.
- Conflict occurs as disagreements between people over substantive or emotional issues.
- Tendencies toward cooperativeness and assertiveness create the interpersonal conflict management styles of avoidance, accommodation, compromise, competition, and collaboration.

Questions for Discussion

1. How does consensus differ from unanimity in group decision making?
2. Is groupthink found only in highly cohesive teams, or could it exist in precohesive ones?
3. When is it better to avoid conflict rather than directly engage in it?

Be Sure You Can

- describe how team building might help one of your groups
- list and discuss the different ways groups make decisions
- define the term "groupthink" and identify its symptoms
- list at least four ways teams can avoid groupthink
- differentiate substantive and emotional conflict
- explain the conflict management styles of avoidance, accommodation, competition, compromise, and collaboration

Career Situation: What Would You Do?

The members of the executive compensation committee that you are chairing show a high level of cohesiveness. It's obvious that they enjoy being part of the committee and are proud to be on the organization's board of directors. But the committee is about to approve extraordinarily high pay bonuses for the CEO and five other senior executives. This is occurring at a time when executive pay is getting lots of criticism from the press, unions, and the public at large. What can you do to make sure groupthink doesn't cause this committee to make a bad decision?

Answers to TestPrep questions can be found at the back of the book.

Multiple-Choice Questions

1. _____ occurs when a group of people is able to achieve more than its members could by working individually.
   - (a) Distributed leadership
   - (b) Consensus
   - (c) Team viability
   - (d) Synergy

2. One of the recommended strategies for dealing with a group member who engages in social loafing is to _____.
   - (a) redefine tasks to make individual contributions more visible
   - (b) ask another member to encourage this person to work harder
   - (c) give the person extra rewards and hope he or she will feel guilty
   - (d) just forget about it

3. An effective team is defined as one that achieves high levels of task performance, high member satisfaction, and _____.
   - (a) resource efficiency
   - (b) team viability
   - (c) group consensus
   - (d) creativity

4. In the open-systems model of teams, the _____ is an important input factor.
   - (a) communication network
   - (b) decision-making method
   - (c) performance norm
   - (d) diversity of membership

5. A basic rule of team dynamics might be stated this way: The greater the _____ in a team, the greater the conformity to norms.
   - (a) membership diversity
   - (b) cohesiveness
   - (c) task clarity
   - (d) competition among members

6. The team effectiveness equation states the following: Team Effectiveness = Quality of Inputs × (_____ – Process Losses).
   - (a) Process Gains
   - (b) Leadership Impact
   - (c) Membership Ability
   - (d) Problem Complexity

7. Members of a team become more motivated and better able to deal with conflict during the _____ stage of team development.
   - (a) forming
   - (b) norming
   - (c) performing
   - (d) adjourning

8. A team member who does a good job at summarizing discussion, offering new ideas, and clarifying points made by others is providing leadership by contributing _____ activities to the group process.
   - (a) required
   - (b) task
   - (c) disruptive
   - (d) maintenance

9. A team performing very creative and unstructured tasks is most likely to succeed using _____.
   - (a) a decentralized communication network
   - (b) decisions by majority rule
   - (c) decisions by minority rule
   - (d) more task than maintenance activities

10. One way for a manager to build positive norms within a team is to _____.
    - (a) act as a positive role model
    - (b) increase group size
    - (c) introduce groupthink
    - (d) isolate the team

11. The best way to try to increase the cohesiveness of a team would be to _____.
    (a) start competition with other groups
    (b) add more members
    (c) reduce isolation from other groups
    (d) increase the diversity of members

12. A _____ decision is one in which all members agree on the course of action to be taken.
    (a) consensus
    (b) unanimous
    (c) majority
    (d) synergy

13. Groupthink is most likely to occur in teams that are _____.
    (a) large in size
    (b) diverse in membership
    (c) high performing
    (d) highly cohesive

14. When people are highly cooperative but not very assertive in a conflict situation, the likelihood is that they will be using which conflict management style?
    (a) Avoidance
    (b) Authoritative
    (c) Accommodation
    (d) Collaboration

15. The interpersonal conflict management style with the greatest potential for true conflict resolution is _____.
    (a) compromise
    (b) competition
    (c) avoidance
    (d) collaboration

Short-Response Questions

16. What are the major differences among a task force, an employee involvement group, and a self-managing team?

17. How can a manager influence team performance by modifying group inputs?

18. How do cohesiveness and performance norms together influence team performance?

19. What are two symptoms of groupthink and two possible remedies for them?

Integration and Application Question

20. Valeria Martínez has just been appointed manager of a production team operating the 11 p.m. to 7 a.m. shift in a large manufacturing firm. An experienced manager, Valeria is pleased that the team members seem to really like and get along well with one another, but she notices that they also appear to be restricting their task outputs to the minimum acceptable levels.

    Question: How might Valeria improve this situation?

Steps *for* Further Learning

BUILD MARKETABLE SKILLS
DO A CASE ANALYSIS
GET AND STAY INFORMED

BUILD

MARKETABLE SKILLS.
EARN BIG CAREER PAYOFFS!

Don't miss these opportunities in the **Skill-Building Portfolio**

■ **SELF-ASSESSMENT 14:**
Team Leader Skills

Team leadership is coming your way ... know your strengths and weaknesses.

■ **CLASS EXERCISE 14:**
Understanding Team Dynamics

Teams are great ... understanding how they work can make them better.

■ **TEAM PROJECT 14:**
Superstars on the Team

It helps to have a star on the team ... what happens when the star causes problems?

Many learning resources are found at the end of the book and online within WileyPLUS.

Take advantage of **Cases for Critical Thinking**

■ **CHAPTER 14 CASE SNAPSHOT:**
Whole Foods—Teamwork the Natural Way/
Sidebar on Decision Making at the Federal Reserve

The culture of Whole Foods Market, included in *Fortune* magazine's annual list of the "100 Best Companies to Work For" every year since the list began, epitomizes decentralized teamwork. Company values identify the team, not the hierarchy, as the "defining unit of activity." Each Whole Foods store has an average of ten self-managed teams. Within the team members work together to accomplish a shared goal, and the same holds true across teams. Goals are not only clearly defined; they are also celebrated when reached. A produce team leader in Chicago is quoted as saying, "Without our people, we are just four walls and food."

DO

A CASE ANALYSIS.
STRENGTHEN YOUR CRITICAL THINKING!

Dig into this **Hot Topic**

■ **PRO AND CON DEBATE** **Can disharmony build a better team?**

"There is no 'I' in team,!" is a common cry. But basketball superstar Michael Jordan once responded: "There is an 'I' in win." What's the point here? Jordan is suggesting that someone as expert as him at a task shouldn't always be subordinated to the team. Rather, the team's job may be to support his or her talents so that they shine to their brightest.

GET

AND STAY INFORMED.
MAKE YOURSELF VALUABLE!

In his book, *There Is an I in Team: What Elite Athletes and Coaches Really Know About High Performance* (Harvard Business Review Press, 2012), Cambridge scholar Mark de Rond notes that sports metaphors abound in the workplace. We talk about "heavy hitters" and ask teammates to "step up to the plate." The real world of teamwork is dominated by the quest for cooperation, perhaps at the cost of needed friction. And that, according to du Rond, is a potential performance problem. "When teams work well," du Rond says, "it is because, not in spite, of individual differences."

Those in favor of du Rond's views are likely to argue that even if superstars bring a bit of conflict to the situation, the result may well be added creativity and a performance boost. Instead of trying to make everyone happy, perhaps it's time for managers and team leaders to accept that disharmony can be functional. A bit of team tension may be a price worth paying for high performance. *Those worried about du Rond's views* might say there's a fine line between a superstar's real performance contribution and collateral damage or negative impact caused by personality and temperament clashes. And, that line is a hard one to spot and to manage.

Final Faceoff   Given what we know about teams and your personal experiences with them, should we be finding ways to accommodate the superstar on a team . . . or avoid them?

Kayak.com's chief technology officer Paul English placed a two-foot-tall toy elephant, Annabelle, in the conference room where it can't be ignored. "So often at work," he says, "people have issues that they can't resolve because they won't talk about it."

Communication

Listening Is the Key to Understanding

Management Live

Communication/Networking and *The Devil Wears Prada*

20th Century Fox/Photofest

Who wears Prada? In the hit movie *The Devil Wears Prada* there is no doubt that it is Miranda Priestly (Meryl Streep). She's quite a contrast to her new assistant Andrea Sachs (Anne Hathway). "Andy" is clearly out of her element when it comes to working in the fashion industry. As an assistant to the demanding Miranda, editor-in-chief of *Runway* magazine, she frequently finds herself assigned to impossible tasks.

In one scene Andy is sent to retrieve sketches from designer James Holt (Daniel Sunjata) and gets buried in a party. She meets famed writer Christian Thompson (Simon Baker), and their conversation centers on career talk. But it's easy to see that Thompson has other motives. Although Andy recognizes this to a degree, she also realizes this relationship could have real value in terms of helping her meet Miranda's "impossible demands."

There are many work themes in this movie, from good boss/bad boss issues to everyday "How do you get along in a tough job?" insights. The next time you watch it check how the various players use **communication and networking** skills—not the kind you do on Facebook or Twitter, but the face-to-face variety.

Management consultant William C. Byham says it is important to forge "deliberate connections" on the job. These connections become networks for learning, collaboration, and work accomplishment. They help us build social capital, the all-important capacity to enlist the help and support of others when it is needed.

YOUR CHAPTER 15 TAKEAWAYS

1. Understand the nature of communication and when it is effective.

2. Identify the major barriers to effective communication.

3. Discuss ways to improve communication with people at work.

WHAT'S INSIDE

Explore Yourself
More on **communication and networking**

Role Models
The Limited's Linda Heasley gives others reasons to work with her

Ethics Check
Blogging is easy, but bloggers beware

Facts to Consider
Employees should worry about electronic monitoring

Manager's Library
Collaboration: How Leaders Avoid the Traps, Build Common Ground, and Reap Big Results by Morten Hansen

Takeaway 15.1

What Is Communication, and When Is It Effective?

ANSWERS TO COME

- Communication helps people build social capital.
- Communication is a process of sending and receiving messages with meanings attached.
- Communication is effective when the receiver understands the sender's messages.
- Communication is efficient when it is delivered at low cost to the sender.
- Communication is persuasive when the receiver acts as the sender intends.

COMMUNICATION IS AT THE HEART OF THE MANAGEMENT PROCESS. YOU MIGHT think of it as the glue that binds together the four functions of planning, organizing, leading, and controlling.[1] Planning is accomplished and plans are shared through the communication of information. Organizing identifies and structures communication linkages among people and positions. Leading uses communication to achieve positive influence over organization members and stakeholders. And, controlling relies on communication to process information to assess and measure performance results.

⦀ Communication helps people build social capital.

Social capital is the capacity to attract support and help from others to get things done.

In many ways communication by managers is all about building something everyone needs—**social capital**. It is the capacity to attract support and help from others to get things done. Whereas intellectual capital is basically what you know, social capital comes from who you know and how well you relate to them.

Managers need social capital to get things done while working with other people. They are always entwined in complex webs of interpersonal networks through which they work with others to implement work priorities and agendas. And in these networks managers serve as information nerve centers, continually gathering information, processing it, using it for problem solving, and sharing it with others.[2]

Given all this, would it surprise you that when the American Management Association asked members to rate the communication skills of their managers, only 22.1% rated them "high"?[3] The respondents also rated their bosses only slightly above average on transforming ideas into words, credibility, listening and asking questions, and written and oral presentations.[4] And even though communication skills regularly top the lists of characteristics looked for by corporate recruiters, why is it that 81% of college professors in one survey rated high school graduates as "fair" or "poor" in writing clearly? Take a quick self-check. Can you convince a recruiter that you have the communication skills necessary for success in your career field?

- Convey positive image in all communications
- Use e-mail and social media well
- Write concise memos, letters, reports
- Network with peers and mentors
- Run meetings, contribute to meetings
- Give persuasive presentations
- Give and receive constructive feedback

⫴ Communication is a process of sending and receiving messages with meanings attached.

Communication is an interpersonal process of sending and receiving symbols with messages attached to them. Although the definition sounds simple and commonsense enough, there is a lot of room for error when we actually implement the process. There are many places where things can go wrong and our communications end up misunderstood or poorly received.

Figure 15.1 summarizes the key elements in the communication process. A *sender* encodes an intended message into meaningful symbols, both verbal and nonverbal. He or she sends the *message* through a *communication channel* to a *receiver*, who then decodes or interprets its meaning. This *interpretation* may or may not match the sender's original intentions. When present, *feedback* reverses the process and conveys the receiver's response back to the sender.

Communication is the process of sending and receiving symbols with meanings attached.

FIGURE 15.1
What Are the Major Elements in the Process of Interpersonal Communication?
The communication process begins when a sender encodes an intended meaning into a message. This message is then transmitted through a channel to a receiver. The receiver next decodes the message into perceived meaning. Finally, the receiver may transmit feedback back to the sender. The communication process is effective when the perceived meaning of the receiver is the same as the intended meaning of the sender.

A useful way to describe the communication process shown in the figure is as a series of questions. "Who?" (sender) "says what?" (message) "in what way?" (channel) "to whom?" (receiver) "with what result?" (interpreted meaning). To check the outcome it's important to ask yet another important question: Do receiver and sender understand things in the same ways?

⫴ Communication is effective when the receiver understands the sender's messages.

The ability to communicate well both orally and in writing is a critical managerial skill and the foundation of effective leadership. Through communication, people exchange and share information and influence one another's attitudes, behaviors, and understandings. Communication allows managers to establish and maintain interpersonal relationships, listen to others, deal with conflicts, negotiate, and otherwise gain the information needed to make decisions. But all this assumes that the communication goes as intended.

As much as communication is part of our everyday lives, we often fail in using it to our best advantage. One problem is that we take our abilities for granted and end up being disappointed when the process breaks down. Another is that we are too busy, or too lazy, to invest enough time in making sure that the process really works. These problems point to issues of "effectiveness" and "efficiency" in the communication process.

In management, we say that **effective communication** occurs when the receiver fully understands the sender's intended message. In other words, the intended meaning matches the received meaning. As you well know, this outcome doesn't always happen.

How often have you wondered what an instructor really wants in an assignment or struggled to understand a point during class lecture? How often have you been angry when a friend or loved one just "didn't seem to get" your message and, unfortunately, didn't respond in the desired way? And, how often have you sent an SMS or e-mail, or left a voice message, only to receive back a confused or even angry reply that wasn't at all appropriate to your intended message? These are all examples of well-intentioned communications that weren't effective. Things don't have to be this way. But it does take effort to achieve effective communication in work and personal affairs.

‖ Communication is efficient when it is delivered at low cost to the sender.

One reason why communication is not always effective—and the prior examples are good cases in point—is a trade-off between effectiveness and efficiency. **Efficient communication** occurs at minimum cost in terms of resources

In **effective communication** the receiver fully understands the intended meaning.

Efficient communication occurs at minimum cost to the sender.

Marilynn K. Yee/Redux Pictures

{ "I LIKE TO KNOW THE BAD NEWS AS SOON AS YOU KNOW IT . . . I PROMISE NO RECRIMINATIONS."

Role Models

■ The Limited's Linda Heasley Gives Others Reasons to Work With Her

Would you like to work for a boss who encourages you to keep your eyes open for other job opportunities? Well, that's the message heard by Linda Heasley's team at The Limited. As president and CEO, she says it's her job to "re-recruit them every day and give them a reason to choose to work for us and for me as opposed to anyone else." She describes this approach as part of a leadership philosophy based on the belief that "it's not about me . . . it's very much about the team."

Newcomers to Heasley's team are advised to follow a 90-day rule when it comes to communication. She believes in taking the first 90 days to "watch and listen," trying "not to talk at meetings" and working to build relationships. She also says: "I like to know the bad news as soon as you know it—I promise no recriminations—but I will expect to know what we could've avoided so it doesn't happen again."

Heasley is focused on recruiting staff who will find excitement in the challenges ahead. When asked what she looks for in hiring, Heasley highlights things like passion, curiosity, energy, willingness to take risks, and a sense of humor. During interviews she uses proven questions to try to draw out job candidates and discover their capabilities. She might ask "What books have you read lately?" or "Can you describe a challenging situation you've been in and where you took a controversial position?"

WHAT'S THE LESSON HERE?

Linda Heasley seems very comfortable with herself and her role as president and CEO of this major company. Can you see where communication is one of her strengths? Would you respond well to a leader like this? In what respects might Heasley become a role model for your personal leadership approach someday?

expended. These costs, time and convenience, in particular, often become very influential in how we choose to communicate.

Picture your instructor speaking individually, face-to-face, with each student about this chapter. Although most likely very effective, it would certainly be inefficient in terms of the cost of his or her time. This is why we often use chat apps, send text messages, leave voice-mail messages, and use e-mail rather than speak directly with other people. These alternatives are more efficient than one-on-one and face-to-face communications. They may also allow us to avoid the discomfort of dealing with a difficult matter face-to-face. But although quick and easy, are these efficient communications always effective?

The next time you have something important to communicate, you might pause and consider the trade-offs between effectiveness and efficiency. A low-cost approach such as a text message may save time, but it may not result in the other party getting the real intended meaning. By the same token, an effective communication may not always be efficient. If a team leader visits each team member individually to explain a new change in procedures, this may guarantee that everyone truly understands the change. It will also take a lot of the leader's time. A team meeting is much more efficient. In these and other ways, potential give and take between effectiveness and efficiency must be recognized in communication.

⫴ Communication is persuasive when the receiver acts as the sender intends.

In personal life and at work we often want not just to be heard, but to be followed. We want our communication to "persuade" the other party to believe or behave in a specific way that we intend. **Persuasive communication** gets someone else to accept, support, and act consistent with the sender's message.[5]

If you agree that managers get most things done through other people, you should also agree that managers must be very good at persuasive communication.

Persuasive communication presents a message in a manner that causes others to accept and support it.

{ RECRUITERS GIVE COMMUNICATION AND NETWORKING SKILLS HIGH PRIORITY WHEN SCREENING CANDIDATES FOR COLLEGE INTERNSHIPS AND FIRST JOBS.

Explore **Yourself**

■ Communication and Networking

Effective **communication and networking** skills are essential for turning ideas into actions, being credible, listening and asking questions, and giving written and oral presentations. You might think that the attention given to them as critical management and career skills is overdone. But such attention is warranted.

Recruiters give these skills high priority when screening candidates for college internships and first jobs. Employers consider it essential that workers be able to communicate well both orally and in writing and be able to network with others for collaboration and work accomplishment.

This chapter offers many insights to help you develop communication and networking skills. They are key foundations of one's social capital, or capacity to enlist the help and support of others when needed. Communication and networking are ways of getting work done with the support of other people.

> Get to know yourself better by taking the self-assessment on **Feedback and Assertiveness** and completing other activities in the *Exploring Management* **Skill-Building Portfolio**.

Kevin Mazur/WireImage/GettyImages

Jay-Z Raps to a Business Empire

Talent Points Way to Corporate Power

Decisions . . . hunches . . . achievements? It's all about being tuned into the environment.

That's a message well learned years ago by a young rapper just breaking into the music scene and calling himself Jay-Z. He could have been doing something else with his time, but he wasn't; he could have stopped with the music, but he didn't. As his lyrics state: "No lie, just know I chose my own fate. I drove by the fork in the road and went straight." Now past the age of 40, he's still rapping, but his rare talent with communication is serving him well in more ways than this one.

Born Shawn Carter, Jay-Z started as a street busker, went on to get his own label, Roc-A-Fella Records, made lots more music, won 10 Grammy awards, and became CEO of Def Jam Records. But the Jay-Z story doesn't end with hip-hop. He turned a talent for communication into shrewd entrepreneurship that includes not only Roc Nation, the latest incarnation of Roc-A-Fella Records, but also part ownership of the New Jersey Nets, the marketing firm Translation, and brand partnerships with the likes of Hewlett-Packard and Microsoft. His hard work and success have led to a listing as one of *Forbes* magazine's "Richest People in America."

Was it luck that moved him toward fame and fortune or something else? Raw talent alone isn't enough to succeed in any business. Success happens when talent is partnered with insight, intuition, and an ability to make the right decisions. Jay-Z obviously made the connections and uses his communication skills to great business advantage.

Find Inspiration

"This guy from out in the projects who didn't graduate from high school is now living this sort of life," Jay-Z says about himself. "And this is how he got there." His lyrics don't always tell an easy story or recommend a solution. But they do make the case for how communication, other talents, and positive goals can help create career success.

Credible communication earns trust, respect, and integrity in the eyes of others.

Charisma is the ability to inspirationally persuade and motivate others.

Charismatic leadership tactics are communication techniques people use to make themselves more "leaderlike" and be perceived by others as influential and trustworthy.

Yet scholar and consultant Jay Conger believes that many managers "confuse persuasion with bold stands and aggressive arguing."[6] This sounds a lot like the so-called "debates" that we watch on television as advocates of different political viewpoints face off against one another. A lot is said, some of it quite aggressively, but little in the way of influence on the other speaker or the listening audience really takes place. An overly confrontational or uncompromising approach can also raise questions about one's credibility.

Conger goes on to define **credible communication** as that which earns trust, respect, and integrity in the eyes of others. He says it is a learned skill, one based on the personal powers of expertise and reference. And without credibility, he claims there is little chance for successful persuasion.

Speaking about learning, the link between communication and leadership charisma is a hot topic again. The latest thinking is that people can learn **charisma**— the ability to inspirationally persuade and motivate others—by mastering and successfully using basic communication skills. Called **charismatic leadership tactics**, these are communication techniques people use to make themselves more "leaderlike" and be perceived by others as influential and trustworthy.[7] They include techniques of *ethos*—using words and phrases common to your audience, *logos*—using clear logic that separates the good from the bad, and *pathos*— displaying emotions through facial gestures and voice intonations and cadence.

STUDY GUIDE

Takeaway 15.1
What Is Communication, and When Is It Effective?

Terms to Define

Charisma

Charismatic leadership tactics

Communication

Credible communication

Effective communication

Efficient communication

Persuasive communication

Social capital

Rapid Review

- Communication is the interpersonal process of sending and receiving symbols with messages attached to them.
- Effective communication occurs when the sender and the receiver of a message both interpret it in the same way.
- Efficient communication occurs when the sender conveys the message at low cost.
- Persuasive communication results in the recipient acting as the sender intends.
- Credibility earned by expertise and good relationships is essential to persuasive communication.

Questions for Discussion

1. Why do recruiters place so much emphasis on the communications skills of job candidates?
2. Can you describe a work situation where it's okay to accept less communication effectiveness to gain communication efficiency?
3. What can a manager do to gain the credibility needed for truly persuasive communication?

Be Sure You Can

- describe the communication process and identify its key components
- define and give an example of effective communication
- define and give an example of efficient communication
- explain why an effective communication is not always efficient
- explain the role of credibility in persuasive communication

Career Situation: What Would You Do?

Your boss just sent a text message that he wants you at a meeting starting at 3 p.m. Your daughter is performing a music program at her elementary school at 2:45 p.m., and she wants you to attend. You're out of the office making sales calls and have scheduled appointments to put you close to the school in the early afternoon. The office is a long way across town. Do you call the boss, text him, or send him an e-mail? What exactly will you say in your response to his message?

Takeaway 15.2
What Are the Major Barriers to Effective Communication?

ANSWERS TO COME

- Poor use of channels makes it hard to communicate effectively.
- Poor written or oral expression makes it hard to communicate effectively.
- Failure to spot nonverbal signals makes it hard to communicate effectively.
- Status differences make it hard to communicate effectively.
- Physical distractions make it hard to communicate effectively.

JOB INTERVIEW SCENE A COLLEGE SENIOR PAUSES ABOUT 15 MINUTES INTO A JOB interview to answer a call on his smart phone. It lasted a minute and wasn't an emergency. *Salary negotiation scene* A candidate has been offered a job, but doesn't like the salary offer. She has her father call the recruiter to negotiate a higher salary. *Another job interview scene* A college student brings her cat to a job interview and puts the carrier on the interviewer's desk. She played with the cat several times while speaking with the interviewer. *What happened next* None of these candidates were successful.[8]

One of the HR executives in the prior situations remarked: "Why would you think that's okay?" Others blame the missteps on a millennial generation that grew up with text messaging, smart phones, and social media, and ended up with poor communication skills. "Life has gotten more casual," says one recruiter. "They don't realize the interview is a sales event."[9]

Whatever the situation—interviewing for a job, giving directions to a team member, asking a boss for help, or even building a personal relationship, everyone needs the ability to communicate well. Now is a good time for you to think about improving this important career skill.

Look at **Figure 15.2.** It updates our description of the communication process to include **noise**—anything that interferes with the effectiveness of communication. Common sources of noise to guard against are poor choice of communication channels, poor written or oral expression, failure to recognize nonverbal signals, physical distractions, and status differences.

Noise is anything that interferes with the communication process.

FIGURE 15.2
How Does Noise Interfere with the Communication Process? Among the types of noise that can interfere with the effectiveness of communication, the following are well worth noting: Semantic problems in the forms of poor written or oral expression, the absence of feedback, improper choice and use of communication channels, physical distractions, status differences between senders and receivers, and cultural differences can all in one way or another complicate the communication process. Unless these factors are given attention, they can reduce communication effectiveness.

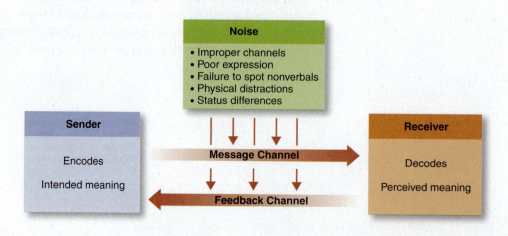

⫼ Poor use of channels makes it hard to communicate effectively.

People communicate with one another using a variety of **communication channels**, or pathways used to carry the message. A poor choice of channel often causes problems because of differences in **channel richness**, the capacity to carry information in an effective manner.[10] Good communicators choose the right channel or combination of channels to accomplish their intended purpose.

The small figure shows that face-to-face communication is very high in richness. These channels are personal and can help create a supportive, even inspirational, relationship between sender and receiver. They work especially well when we need to convey complex or difficult messages, and when we need immediate feedback. Written channels like memos, e-mails, and text messages are much less rich. They are impersonal, one-way interactions with limited opportunity for feedback.

> A **communication channel** is the pathway used to carry a message.
>
> **Channel richness** is the capacity of a communication channel to effectively carry information.

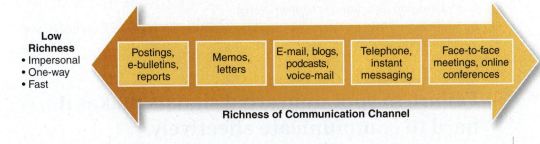

Low Richness
- Impersonal
- One-way
- Fast

| Postings, e-bulletins, reports | Memos, letters | E-mail, blogs, podcasts, voice-mail | Telephone, instant messaging | Face-to-face meetings, online conferences |

High Richness
- Personal
- Two-way
- Slow

Richness of Communication Channel

⫼ Poor written or oral expression makes it hard to communicate effectively.

A survey of 150 companies by the National Commission on Writing found that over one-third of their employees were considered deficient in writing skills and that employers were spending over $3 billion each year on remedial training.[11] As an example, consider the following "bafflegab" found among some executive communications.

> *A business report said:* "Consumer elements are continuing to stress the fundamental necessity of a stabilization of the price structure at a lower level than exists at the present time." *Why couldn't the report say:* "Consumers want prices to come down and stay down."?
>
> *A manager said:* "Substantial economies were affected in this division by increasing the time interval between distributions of data-eliciting forms to business entities." *Why couldn't the manager say:* "The division saved money by sending out fewer surveys."?

It takes a lot of practice to write a concise letter or report, or deliver a great oral presentation. There's no getting around it, good writing and good speaking are products of plain old hard work.[12] But it's well worth the investment. How many drafts do you write for memos, letters, and reports? Are you getting so used to texting that you can't write a proper sentence? How often do you practice for an oral presentation? Are you well informed on the tips shown next in **Table 15.1**?

Table 15.1 Essential Ingredients of Successful Presentations

Be prepared—Know what you want to say; know how you want to say it; rehearse saying it.

Set the right tone—Focus on your audience; make eye contact and act pleasantly and confidently.

Sequence your points—State your purpose, make important points, follow with details, and then summarize.

Support your points—Give specific reasons for your points; state them in understandable terms.

Accent the presentation—Use good visual aids; provide supporting handouts when possible.

Add the right amount of polish—Attend to details; have room, materials, and arrangements ready to go.

Check the technology—Check everything ahead of time; make sure it works, and know how to use it.

Don't bet on the Internet—Beware of plans to make real-time Internet visits; save sites on a disk and use a browser to open the file.

Be professional—Be on time; wear appropriate attire; act organized, confident, and enthusiastic.

‖ Failure to spot nonverbal signals makes it hard to communicate effectively.

Nonverbal communication takes place through gestures, expressions, posture, and even use of interpersonal space.

The ways we use **nonverbal communication** can also work for or against our communication effectiveness. It takes place through hand movements, facial expressions, body posture, eye contact, and the use of interpersonal space.[13] And it can be a powerful means of transmitting messages.

Research shows that up to 55% of a message's impact comes through nonverbal communication.[14] A good listener, for example, knows how to read the "body language" of a speaker while listening to the words being spoken. In fact, a potential side effect of the growing use of electronic media is that the added value of reading nonverbal signals, such as gestures, voice intonation, or eye movements, gets lost.

Think of how nonverbal signals play out in your own communications. A simple hand gesture can show whether someone is positive or negative, excited or bored, or even engaged or disengaged while interacting with you.[15] Sometimes our body may be "talking" even as we otherwise maintain silence. One rule-of-thumb, for example, is that people tend to lean forward when they like something or someone, and lean back when they don't.[16] And when we do speak, our body may be saying different things than our words. This is called a **mixed message**, when a person's words communicate one thing while his or her nonverbal actions communicate something else.

A **mixed message** results when words communicate one message while actions, body language, or appearance communicates something else.

‖ Status differences make it hard to communicate effectively.

The risk of ineffective communication is high when people are communicating upward in organizations—with their boss in particular. Haven't you heard people say things like this? "Criticize my boss? I'd get fired." "It's her company, not mine." "I can't tell him that; he'll just get mad at me."

We have to be realistic; status differences in the hierarchy of authority are always potential barriers to effective communication between lower and higher levels in organizations. They cause a tendency known as **information filtering**—the intentional distortion of information to make it appear favorable to the recipient. You know this as "telling the boss or instructor what he or she wants to hear." And it's more common than many people think. Consultant Tom Peters calls it "Management Enemy Number 1." He also says that "once you become a boss you will never hear the unadulterated truth again."[17]

Whether caused by fear of retribution for bringing bad news, an unwillingness to identify personal mistakes, or just a general desire to please, the end result of filtering is the same. Lower levels "cleanse" the information sent to higher levels. Then the higher levels, although well intentioned, make poor decisions because the information used is inaccurate or incomplete.

> **Information filtering** is the intentional distortion of information to make it more favorable to the recipient.

‖ Physical distractions make it hard to communicate effectively.

Don't neglect how physical distractions can disrupt communication. Have you ever tried to talk with someone—perhaps an interviewer or your boss—about an important matter, only to have that conversation interrupted by phone calls? Any number of distractions, from drop-in visitors to instant messages to beeping smart phones, can interfere with the effectiveness of a communication attempt. Some of these distractions are evident in the following conversation between an employee, George, and his manager.[18]

Okay, George, let's hear your problem . . . [phone rings, manager answers and promises to deliver a report "just as soon as I can get it done"]. Uh, now, where were we—oh, you're having a problem with your technician. She's . . . [manager's secretary walks in with papers he pauses to sign]—you say she's overstressed lately, wants to leave. I tell you what, George, . . . [lunch partner drops by]—look, uh, let's get back on this later. Send me a note with your open times on Thursday.

Besides what may have been poor intentions in the first place, the manager in this example did a very poor job communicating with George. It's something that could easily have been avoided or at least minimized with awareness and planning. Adequate time should have been set aside for the meeting; instructions should have been given or a better location chosen to avoid interruptions. The big lesson here is: Good communication takes work. Plan ahead. When someone needs to communicate with you, set aside adequate time, choose the right location, and take steps to avoid interruptions—including turning off the smart phone.

STUDY GUIDE

Takeaway 15.2
What Are the Major Barriers to Effective Communication?

Rapid Review

- Noise interferes with the effectiveness of communication.
- Poor choice of channels can reduce communication effectiveness.
- Poor written or oral expression can reduce communication effectiveness.
- Failure to accurately read nonverbal signals can reduce communication effectiveness.
- Filtering caused by status differences can reduce communication effectiveness.

Questions for Discussion

1. When is texting not an appropriate way to convey a message in a work situation?
2. If someone just isn't a good writer or speaker, what can he or she do to improve communication skills?
3. How can a higher-level manager avoid the problem of filtering when lower-level staffers pass information upward to her?

Be Sure You Can

- list common sources of noise that can interfere with effective communication
- discuss how the choice of channels influences communication effectiveness
- give examples of poor language choices in written and oral expression
- clarify the notion of mixed messages and how nonverbals affect communication
- explain how filtering operates in upward communication

Career Situation: What Would You Do?

As the leader of your work team, some members have come to you and pointed out that there is no way they can complete the current project on time. In fact, they expect to be at least two weeks late. This is a "pet" project for your boss, and your understanding is that she has a lot riding on its success for her career advancement. She is aloof and very formal in her dealings with you. Now you're stuck in the middle between her and your team. What actions will you take, and why?

Takeaway 15.3
How Can We Improve Communication with People at Work?

ANSWERS TO COME

■ Active listening helps people say what they really mean.

■ Constructive feedback is specific, timely, and relevant.

■ Office spaces can be designed to encourage interaction and communication.

■ Transparency and openness ensure that accurate information is shared.

■ Appropriate online behavior can facilitate better communication.

■ Sensitivity and etiquette can improve cross-cultural communication.

TEACHING NOTE: Ask students if they a) have a right to know their instructor's salaries, and b) what difference this information would make to them? Ask if instructor's have rights to know students' academic histories. Frame discussion around the broader issue of information transparency in organizations. Can openness and transparency go too far? Are there limits on transparency from an ethics perspective?

COMMUNICATION! MOST OF US PROBABLY GET IT RIGHT SOME OF THE TIME BUT also make our fair share of mistakes. That's what happened to Richard Herlich. Before participating in workshops held at the Center for Creative Leadership, or CCL,[19] he said: "I thought I had the perfect style." But in feedback sessions following role-playing exercises, he learned that wasn't how others saw him. He was actually perceived as aloof and a poor communicator. Back on his new job as a director of marketing, Richard made it a point to meet with his team, discuss his style, and become more involved in their projects.

With so much room for error, don't you wonder how we ever communicate effectively? Fortunately, there are a number of things we can do to give things the best possible chance. They include active listening, constructive use of feedback, opening upward communication channels, understanding the use of space, utilizing technology, and valuing diversity.

⦀ Active listening helps people say what they really mean.

When people talk, they are trying to communicate something. That "something" may or may not be what they are saying. This is why managers must be so good at listening. According to the late John Wooden, legendary UCLA men's basketball coach, "Many leaders don't listen. We'd all be a lot wiser if we listened more—not just hearing the words, but listening and not thinking about what you are going to say."[20]

Active listening is the process of taking action to help others say what they really mean.[21] It requires being sincere while listening to someone and trying to find the full meaning of a message. It also involves being disciplined, controlling one's emotions, and withholding premature evaluations that turn off rather than turn on the other party's willingness to communicate.

Check these alternative workplace conversations. They show the contrast in how a "passive" listener and an "active" listener might act.

Questioner: "Don't you think employees should be promoted on the basis of seniority?"

Passive listener's response: "No, I don't!"

Active listener's response: "It seems to you that they should, I take it?"

Active listening helps the source of a message say what he or she really means.

Questioner: "What does the supervisor expect us to do about these out-of-date computers?"

> *Passive listener's response:* "Do the best you can, I guess."

> *Active listener's response:* "You're pretty disgusted with those machines, aren't you?"

The prior examples help show how active listening can facilitate communication in difficult circumstances, rather than discourage it. But it isn't easy to do. As you think further about active listening skills, keep these rules in mind.[22]

Rules for Active Listening »

1. *Listen for message content:* Try to hear exactly what content is being conveyed in the message.
2. *Listen for feelings:* Try to identify how the source feels about the content in the message.
3. *Respond to feelings:* Let the source know that her or his feelings are being recognized.
4. *Note all cues:* Be sensitive to nonverbal and verbal messages; be alert for mixed messages.
5. *Paraphrase and restate:* State back to the source what you think you are hearing.

⦀ Constructive feedback is specific, timely, and relevant.

> **Feedback** is the process of telling someone else how you feel about something that person did or said.

Feedback is the process of telling other people how you feel about something they did or said, or about the situation in general. Like active listening, the art of giving feedback is an indispensable skill. Feedback that is poorly given can easily come off as threatening and create more resentment than positive action. But when well delivered, the recipient is more likely to listen and carefully consider the message.[23] See Tips to Remember for advice on making feedback constructive.[24]

Consider someone who comes late to meetings. Feedback from the meeting chair might be *evaluative*—"You are unreliable and always late for everything." It

---

{ WHEN WE TRY TO GIVE FEEDBACK, NOT EVERYONE WANTS TO LISTEN.

Tips to **Remember**

■ How to Give Constructive Feedback

- *Choose the right time*—Give feedback at a time when the receiver seems most willing or able to accept it.
- *Be genuine*—Give feedback directly and with real feeling, based on trust between you and the receiver.
- *Be specific*—Make feedback specific rather than general; use clear and recent examples to make points.

- *Stick to the essentials*—Make sure the feedback is valid; limit it to things the receiver can be expected to do something about.
- *Keep it manageable*—Give feedback in small doses; never give more than the receiver can handle at any particular time.

might be *interpretive*—"You're coming late to meetings; you might be spreading yourself too thin and have trouble meeting your obligations." And it might be *descriptive*—"You were 30 minutes late for today's meeting and missed a lot of the context for our discussion."[25] The descriptive feedback might be better received and have the more lasting positive impact.

Office spaces can be designed to encourage interaction and communication.

Look at the figure below and think about office spaces, yours and those of persons you visit. What messages do the layouts and furnishings send to visitors? Do they help or hinder communication? These are issues of **proxemics,** the study of the ways people use and communicate with space.[26] We know that physical distance between people conveys varying intentions in terms of intimacy, openness, and status as they communicate with one another. But we might not be as sensitive to how the physical layout of work and leisure spaces can do the same things.

Proxemics is the study of the way we use and communicate with space.

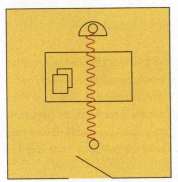

"I am the boss!"

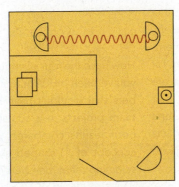
"I am the boss, but let's talk"

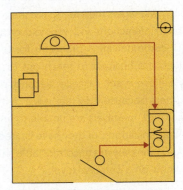
"Forget I'm the boss, let's talk"

Today's organizations are being run with the premise that the better people communicate with one another, the better the organization will perform. We live in an increasingly connected world and the same levels of connectedness are sought in the workplace. Google, for example, thrives and depends on high levels of innovation. So, the company's new headquarters is designed to make it easy for employees to have casual, not just formal, communications. "We want it to be easy [for] Googlers to bump into one another," says a spokeswoman.[27]

Part of the push toward greater connectedness and more casual conversations is found in what might be called the demise of the office cubicle. It's been popular for quite awhile to design office spaces with small cubicles for individual workers and larger meeting rooms where they can hold meetings. The new trend is toward smaller teams, less formal meetings, and more frequent casual interaction. Architects and office supply firms are responding with designs that up open up or eliminate cubicles by giving them shorter walls or no walls at all. They are also creating lots of small "focus rooms" where two or just a few people can huddle up while exchanging ideas, working on a project, or just having a chat. Martha Clarkson heads Microsoft's global workplace strategy. She says it's based on a postcubical model because "Work is really getting done in smaller teams." And at Campbell Foods, a spokesperson says that breaking down cubicle walls at the firm resulted in people "collaborating more."[28]

Manager's **Library**

IS THE SUM OF THE PARTS GREATER THAN THE WHOLE?

In the book *Collaboration: How Leaders Avoid the Traps, Build Common Ground, and Reap Big Results* (2009, Harvard Business Press), author Morten Hansen admits that group efforts often fail and are more costly than their results justify. He suggests managers may assign collaborative projects too frivolously because they believe teamwork is always better than individual assignment. But it isn't, and misdirected teamwork can be costly to organizations in terms of time, expense, and lost productivity. Hansen's research finds that "good collaboration" is possible under the proper conditions and can improve sales, reduce costs, and enhance efficiency in organizations. Managers must recognize the barriers that prevent beneficial team interactions and work to overcome them.

Hansen lists four communication problems for team members. First, individuals are hesitant to reach out to others for help because they believe in self-reliance. Second, people are unwilling to help others because they fear it will diminish their power of expertise. Third, members are unable to find experts in large or complex organizations, or they have limited contacts in their networks. And four, they are uncomfortable sharing with people they don't know on a personal level.

To solve this Hansen believes managers must appreciate how difficult collaboration is and limit its use. He thinks improved organizational sharing begins with recruiting and hiring members who can overcome communication barriers. These types of individuals are able to unify with others in common goals because they possess "T-shaped" skills—they work well within their discipline (the vertical bar), but also across other disciplines (the horizontal bar). Managers can also encourage members to build and use personal networks within the organization to alleviate discomfort. Collaborative results should then sum to greater values than individual outcomes.

REFLECT AND REACT

How have the four communication barriers affected teams that you've been on? Would it have been possible to select members that wouldn't have had these problems? Why is it that team projects in a course can create problems or generate poor results compared with individual projects? Does this concept of "T-shaped skills" make sense as a criterion for selecting team members?

Communication transparency involves being honest and openly sharing accurate and complete information.

In **open-book management** managers provide employees with essential financial information about their employers.

‖ Transparency and openness ensure that accurate and timely information is shared.

CEO Vineet Nayar believes that one of his most important tasks at the technology outsourcing firm HCL Industries is to create a "culture of trust." And to do that, he says, you have to create transparency. Nayar posts HCL's financial information on the internal Web site, saying "We put all the dirty linen on the table." Results of 360° feedback reviews for HCL's 3,800 managers, including Nayar's, are posted there as well. And when managers present plans to top executives, they also get posted because Nayar wants others to read and comment on them. Why? By the time a plan is approved, it's likely to be a good one he says because of the "massive collaborative learning that took place."[29]

Communication transparency involves being honest and openly sharing accurate and complete information about the organization and workplace affairs. Its absence is evident when managers try to hide information and restrict the access of organizational members to it. Whereas lack of transparency creates conditions for distrust and harmful rumor, full transparency can have a positive impact on trust and employee engagement.

Transparency and openness in communication is a characteristic of **open-book management,** where managers provide employees with essential financial

Underground Boss Opens Communication Channels

CEO Stephen Martin "went underground" at a firm in England for two weeks. He posed with an assumed name as an office worker and kept his ears and eyes open wide while going about his daily work. After the experience, Martin said: "They (workers) said things to me that they never would have told their manager". . . . "Our key messages were just not getting through to people" . . . "We were asking the impossible of some of them." But when he shared these concerns with the firm's managers, the response was: "They never told us that!"

information about their companies. This willingness to open the books was evident in the HCL Industries example. At Bailard, Inc., a private investment firm, openness extends to salaries. If you want to know what others are making at the firm, all you need to do is ask the chief financial officer. The firm's co-founder and CEO, Thomas Bailard, believes this approach is a good way to defeat office politics. "As a manager," he says, "if you know that your compensation decisions are essentially going to be public, you have to have pretty strong convictions about any decision you make."[30]

||| Appropriate online behavior can facilitate better communication.

Knowing how and when to use e-mail, text messaging, and social media is now a top issue in workplace communications. But the goal must always be appropriate—not inappropriate—use. "Thnx for the IView! I Wud Luv to Work 4 U!!;)" may be understandable "textspeak" for some people, but it isn't the follow-up message that most employers like to receive from job candidates.[31]

When Tory Johnson, President of Women for Hire Inc., received a thank-you note by e-mail from an intern candidate, it included "hiya," "thanx," three exclamation points—"!!!," and two emoticons. She says: "That e-mail just ruined it for me." The risk of everyday shorthand in chats and texting is that we become too casual overall in its use, forgetting that how a message is received is in large part determined by the receiver. Even though textspeak and emoticons are the norm in social networks, staffing executives at KPMG, which hires hundreds of new college grads and interns each year, consider them "not professional."

Millennial text to Baby Boomer:
Omg sry abt mtg nbd 4 nw b rdy nxt time g2g ttul

Baby Boomer text to Millennial:
Missed you at meeting. It was important. Don't forget next one. Stop by my office.

It's not only what a job applicant says or sends directly to a recruiter that counts. Every comment and photo that we post on the Web, or that others post about us, becomes part of our public profile. And, this profile communicates a "personal brand." CareerBuilder points out that close to 40% of recruiters browse social media to check up on job applicants.[32] If what they find fits the impression they are looking for, the personal brand revealed in the online profile works in the applicant's favor. But if it gives the wrong impression, a rejection is likely.

Dmitriy Shironosov/
iStockphoto

Facts to **Consider**

■ Employees Should Worry About Electronic Monitoring

An American Management Association survey of 304 U.S. companies found the following:

- 66% monitor Internet connections.
- 65% block Web sites: pornography (96%), games (61%), social networking (61%), shopping/auction (27%), and sports (21%).
- 45% track keystrokes and keyboard time.
- 43% store and review computer files.
- 43% monitor e-mail.

YOUR THOUGHTS?

Is this type of employer "snooping" justified? What boundaries should be set on employer invasion of employee privacy? Is there anything special about the fact that in the advertising industry the majority of executives thought personal Web surfing was alright?

The point is to engage in appropriate online behavior, making technology work for rather than against us. The first step is editing what we put on the Web to minimize negative impressions and maximize positive ones. This might mean something as simple as exercising good judgment on Facebook postings for friends and building another professional profile on LinkedIn. It might also mean crafting a Web presence that backs up your resume and career goals, such as by posting links to relevant newspaper and magazine articles along with intelligent comments about them. The second step, of course, is to stay vigilant and be Web smart. The founder of reputation.com, Michael Fertik, says: "Assume that every employer is constantly looking at your profile. Just because you don't get negative feedback doesn't mean it's not there."[33]

Even though Facebook's CEO Mark Zuckerberg says that privacy is "no longer a social norm," we have to take the issue very seriously in personal affairs and at work. Technology makes it easy for employers to monitor what employees do, and when, on the Internet. They get concerned when too much work time gets spent with personal e-mail, texting, Web browsing, and social networking. Employees are concerned that employers are or may be electronically eavesdropping. But, they can also be casual in time spent on the Web and inappropriate in how they use it. Consider this tweet that became an Internet sensation: "Cisco just offered me a job! Now I have to weigh the utility of a fatty paycheck against the daily commute to San Jose and hating the work."[34] What would you do if you were the recruiter who had just made this job offer?

⫼ Sensitivity and etiquette can improve cross-cultural communication.

Nancy McKinstry initiated major changes when taking over as the first American CEO of the Dutch publisher Wolters Kluwer. She cut staff, restructured divisions, and invested in new business areas. She described the new strategy as "aggressive" to her management team. When the word wasn't well received by Europeans, she switched to "decisive."[35] "I was coming across as too harsh, too much of a results-driven American to the people I needed to get on board," says McKinstry.

Cultural differences are a ready source of potential problems in communication. But keep in mind that you don't have be doing international business or taking a foreign vacation for this point to be relevant. Think about it—going to work, to class, and out to shop can be a cross-cultural journey for most of us today.

You should recall that **ethnocentrism** is a major source of intercultural difficulties. It is the tendency to consider one's culture superior to any and all others. Any such tendencies can hurt cross-cultural communication in at least three ways. First, they may cause someone to not listen well to what others have to say. Second, they may cause someone to address or speak with others in ways that alienate them. And third, they may involve use of inappropriate stereotypes.

Just recognizing tendencies toward ethnocentrism is helpful. You can spot it in conversations as arrogance in tone, manners, gestures, and words. But success in cross-cultural communication also takes sensitivity and a willingness to learn about how different people see, do, and interpret things. This involves **cultural etiquette**, the use of appropriate manners, language, and behaviors when communicating with people from other cultures.

Knowing the etiquette helps us avoid basic cross-cultural mistakes. Messages can easily get lost in translation, as advertising miscues often demonstrate. A Pepsi ad in Taiwan that intended to say "the Pepsi generation" came out as "Pepsi will bring your ancestors back from the dead." A KFC ad in China intended to convey "finger lickin' good" came out as "eat your fingers off."[36] Nonverbals are important too. The American "thumbs-up" sign is an insult in Ghana and Australia. Signaling "okay" with thumb and forefinger circled together is not okay in parts of Europe. Whereas we wave "hello" with an open palm, in West Africa it's an insult suggesting the other person has five fathers.[37]

> **Ethnocentrism** is the tendency to consider one's culture superior to any and all others.

> **Cultural etiquette** is use of appropriate manners and behaviors in cross-cultural situations.

PhotoEdi/Alamy

{ SHE SAYS THAT SHE WAS "DOOCED"—A TERM USED TO DESCRIBE BEING FIRED FOR WHAT ONE WRITES IN A BLOG.

Ethics **Check**

Blogging is Easy, But Bloggers Beware

It is easy and tempting to set up your own blog, write about your experiences and impressions, and then share your thoughts with others online. So, why not do it?

Catherine Sanderson, a British citizen living and working in Paris, might have asked this question before launching her blog, *Le Petite Anglaise*. At one point it was so "successful" that she had 3,000 readers. But, the Internet diary included reports on her experiences at work—and her employer wasn't happy when it became public knowledge.

Even though Sanderson was blogging anonymously, her photo was on the site, and the connection was eventually discovered. Noticed, too, was her running commentary about bosses, colleagues, and life at the office. A Christmas party was described in detail, including an executive's "unforgivable faux pas."

When her blog came to management attention, Sanderson says that she was "dooced"—a term used to describe being fired for what one writes in a blog. She sued for financial damages and confirmation of her rights, on principle, to have a private blog. The court awarded her a year's salary.

YOU DECIDE

Just what are the ethics issues here—from the blogger's and the employer's perspectives? What rights do workers have when it comes to communicating in public about their work experiences and impressions? How about employers? Should they be protected from disgruntled employee-bloggers?

STUDY GUIDE

Takeaway 15.3
How Can We Improve Communication with People at Work?

Terms to Define

Active listening

Communication transparency

Cultural etiquette

Electronic grapevine

Ethnocentrism

Feedback

Open-book management

Proxemics

Rapid Review

- Active listening, through reflecting back and paraphrasing, can help overcome barriers and improve communication.
- Organizations can design and use office architecture and physical space to improve communication.
- Information technology, such as e-mail, instant messaging, and intranets, can improve communication in organizations, but it must be well used.
- Ethnocentrism, a feeling of cultural superiority, can interfere with cross-cultural communication; with sensitivity and cultural etiquette it can be improved.

Questions for Discussion

1. Which rules for active listening do you think most people break?
2. Is transparency in communications a sure winner, or could a manager have problems with it?
3. How could you redesign your office space, or that of your instructor or boss, to make it more communication-friendly?

Be Sure You Can

- role-play the practice of active listening
- list the rules for giving constructive feedback
- explain how space design influences communication
- identify ways technology utilization influences communication
- explain the concept of cultural etiquette

Career Situation: What Would You Do?

The restaurant you own and manage is being hit hard by a bad economy. The number of customers is down, as is the amount of the average dinner bill. You employ a staff of 12, but you're going to have to cut back or go to job sharing so that the payroll covers no more than 8. One of the servers just told you that someone is tweeting that the restaurant is going to close its doors after the coming weekend. Loyal customers and staff are "buzzing" about the news and it's starting to travel more widely. How do you deal with this situation?

Answers to TestPrep questions can be found at the back of the book.

Multiple-Choice Questions

1. Who is responsible for encoding a message in the communication process?
   - (a) Sender
   - (b) Receiver
   - (c) Observer
   - (d) Consultant

2. Issues of "respect" and "integrity" are associated with _____ in communication.
   - (a) noise
   - (b) filtering
   - (c) credibility
   - (d) ethnocentrism

3. Which is the best example of a team leader providing descriptive rather than evaluative feedback to a team member?
   - (a) You are a slacker.
   - (b) You are not responsible.
   - (c) You cause me lots of problems.
   - (d) You have been late to meetings three times this month.

4. When interacting with an angry co-worker who is complaining about a work problem, a manager skilled at active listening would most likely try to _____.
   - (a) delay the conversation until a better time
   - (b) point out that the conversation would be better held at another location
   - (c) express displeasure in agreement with the co-worker's complaint
   - (d) rephrase the co-worker's complaint to encourage him to say more

5. When the intended meaning of the sender and the interpreted meaning of the receiver are the same, communication is _____.
   - (a) effective
   - (b) persuasive
   - (c) passive
   - (d) efficient

6. What happens when a communication is persuasive?
   - (a) The receiver understands the message.
   - (b) The sender feels good about the message.
   - (c) The receiver acts as the sender intended.
   - (d) The sender becomes a passive listener.

7. How can a manager build the credibility needed for persuasive communications?
   - (a) Offer rewards for compliance with requests.
   - (b) Clarify penalties for noncompliance with requests.
   - (c) Remind everyone that she or he is the boss.
   - (d) Work hard to establish good relationships with others.

8. One of the rules for giving constructive feedback is to make sure that it is always _____.
   - (a) general rather than specific
   - (b) indirect rather than direct
   - (c) given in small doses
   - (d) delivered at a time convenient for the sender

9. When a worker receives an e-mail memo from the boss with information about changes to his job assignment and ends up confused because he doesn't understand it, the boss has erred by making a bad choice of _____ for communicating the message.
   - (a) words
   - (b) channels
   - (c) nonverbals
   - (d) filters

10. The safest conclusion about privacy in electronic communications is _____.
    - (a) it's guaranteed by law
    - (b) it's not a problem
    - (c) it really doesn't exist
    - (d) it can be password protected

11. A/An _____ is higher in channel richness than a/an _____.
    (a) memo; voice mail
    (b) letter; video conference
    (c) chat message; e-mail
    (d) voice mail; telephone conversation

12. The negative effects of status differences on communication between lower and higher levels in organizations show up in the form of _____.
    (a) filtering
    (b) MBWA
    (c) ethnocentrism
    (d) passive listening

13. A manager who understands the influence of proxemics in communication is likely to _____.
    (a) avoid sending mixed messages
    (b) arrange work spaces to encourage interaction
    (c) be very careful choosing written words
    (d) send frequent e-mail messages to team members

14. When a person's words say one thing but his or her body language suggests something quite different, the person is sending _____.
    (a) a mixed message
    (b) noise
    (c) social capital
    (d) destructive feedback

15. If a visitor to a foreign culture makes gestures commonly used at home even after learning that they are offensive to locals, the visitor can be described as _____.
    (a) a passive listener
    (b) ethnocentric
    (c) more efficient than effective
    (d) an active listener

Short-Response Questions

16. What is the goal of active listening?

17. Why do managers sometimes make bad decisions based on information received from their subordinates?

18. What are four errors team leaders might make when trying to give constructive feedback to team members?

19. How does ethnocentrism influence cross-cultural communication?

Integration and Application Questions

20. Glenn was recently promoted to be the manager of a new store being opened by a large department store chain. He wants to start out right by making sure that communications are always good between him, the six department heads, and the 50 full-time and part-time sales associates. He knows he'll be making a lot of decisions in the new job, and he wants to be sure that he is always well informed about store operations. He also wants to make sure everyone is always "on the same page" about important priorities. Put yourself in Glenn's shoes.

    Questions: What should Glenn do right from the start to ensure that he and the department managers communicate well with one another? How can he open up and maintain good channels of communication with the sales associates?

Steps *for* Further Learning

BUILD MARKETABLE SKILLS
DO A CASE ANALYSIS
GET AND STAY INFORMED

BUILD

MARKETABLE SKILLS.
EARN BIG CAREER PAYOFFS!

Don't miss these opportunities in the Skill-Building Portfolio

■ **SELF-ASSESSMENT 15:**
Feedback and Assertiveness

Stress can take its toll . . . learn how to recognize the symptoms.

■ **CLASS EXERCISE 15:**
Communication and Teamwork Dilemmas

Not everyone wants the same things . . . it's important to understand individual differences.

■ **TEAM PROJECT 15:**
How Words Count

Sometimes it's often others . . . handling difficult personalities are a management challenge.

Many learning resources are found at the end of the book and online within WileyPLUS.

Take advantage of **Cases for Critical Thinking**

■ **CHAPTER 15 CASE SNAPSHOT:**
Twitter—Rewriting Communication/
Sidebar on Technology across Generations

Whether or not you tweet, there's no denying that Twitter's having a profound effect on the way we communicate with each other and the outside world. But is the popular microblogging service reinventing communication or just abbreviating it? Do tweets contribute to the conversation or dumb it down? Many social media researchers, sociologists, and corporate marketing experts are asking themselves the same questions. Co-founder Evan Williams believes, "It adds a layer of information and connection to people's lives that wasn't there before. "It has the potential to be a really substantial part of how people keep in touch with each other." Nicely said. But really, is a tweet in 140 characters or less effective communication . . . or just a distraction?

DO

A CASE ANALYSIS.
STRENGTHEN YOUR CRITICAL THINKING!

Dig into this **Hot Topic**

■ **GOOD IDEA OR NOT?** Gain influence by tapping the science of persuading.

Scene 1. Hoteliers want to wash fewer towels. So how do they get their customers to reuse more of them? The science of persuading says it's best to identify the request with a social norm. Researchers found that guests reused 33% more towels when left a message card that said "75% of customers who stay in this room reuse their towels." *Lesson:* Want to persuade? Identify with the social norm.

GET

AND STAY INFORMED.
MAKE YOURSELF VALUABLE!

Scene 2. Restaurant servers want to maximize tips. How can they get more customers to leave bigger ones? The science of persuading says it's best to create a sense of reciprocity in the server–customer relationship. Researchers found that tip giving increased when servers gave customers a piece of candy when presenting the bill. *Lesson:* Want to persuade? Create a sense of reciprocity.

Final Take. Can these lessons be turned into advice for leaders? Leadership is complicated in any setting. But, it ultimately requires success at influencing other people. Do a self-check of your success in leadership situations: To what extent is "persuasion" part of your leadership skill portfolio? How about the leaders you work with: Do they pass or fail as masters of the science of persuasion? And if persuasion is so important, should we spend more time learning and practicing how to do it really well?

A day at work, a trip to the store, a visit with friends—all bring diversity into our lives. Even a walk across the college campus can be a trip around the world, if you're willing to take it.

Jerry Horbert/Shutterstock

Diversity and Global Cultures

16

There Are New Faces in the Neighborhood

Management Live

Diversity Maturity and *Finding Forrester*

Columbia Pictures/Photofest

Finding Forrester is an intriguing story about the relationship between an aging and reclusive Caucasian writer—William Forrester (Sean Connery), and a young African American from the projects—Jamal Wallace (Rob Brown). Jamal first enters Forrester's apartment through a fire escape window. It is the fulfillment of a dare by friends. Forrester catches Wallace, who escapes by running out the front door. Later, they come face-to-face in the apartment when Wallace writes a 5,000-word essay to appease the reclusive tenant.

The two become fast friends, but only after Forrester tests Wallace's mettle by pretending to be racist. He is anything but that. But Wallace's literature professor, Robert Crawford (F. Murray Abraham), is racist. He finds it hard to believe that Wallace, a star athlete, can perform in the class as well as he does on the basketball court.

The roles of Forrester and Crawford provide excellent examples of differing levels of **diversity maturity,** the ability to respect and work with others who may be ethnically and culturally different. When Forrester invites Wallace into his apartment, it is clear he already trusts the young man. When Crawford refers to Wallace's "previous education" and "background," it is evident that he is biased.

Most of us have inherent bias. Give yourself a good honest self-check on diversity maturity. If the results are not what you hoped, begin to think about what you can do to improve.

YOUR CHAPTER 16 TAKEAWAYS

1. Understand what we need to know about diversity in the workplace.

2. Understand what we need to know about diversity among global cultures.

WHAT'S INSIDE

Explore Yourself
More on **diversity maturity**

Role Models
Salman Khan crosses borders to foster learning

Ethics Check
Fair-trade fashion

Facts to Consider
Employee morale varies around the world.

Manager's Library
Half the Sky: Turning Oppression into Opportunity for Women Worldwide
by Nicholas D. Kristof and Sheryl WuDunn

Takeaway 16.1
What Should We Know About Diversity in the Workplace?

ANSWERS TO COME

- Inclusion drives the business case for diversity.
- Multicultural organizations value and support diversity.
- Minorities and women suffer diversity bias in many situations.
- Organizational subcultures can create diversity challenges.
- Managing diversity should be a top leadership priority.

FACT! THE U.S. POPULATION IS GETTING OLDER AND MORE ETHNICALLY DIVERSE. That shouldn't surprise you. But did you know that more than half of newborn children in the United States come from what the *Wall Street Journal* calls "racial and ethnic groups that in previous generations would have been considered minorities," or that by 2043 whites will constitute less than 50% of the U.S. population?[1] Such facts and projections are just one window into our changing social fabric.

Issues of **diversity** are often discussed in respect to age, race, ethnicity, gender, physical ability, and sexual orientation. An even broader definition includes differences in religious beliefs, education, experience, family status, national cultures, and perhaps more.[2] In his book *Beyond Race and Gender,* diversity consultant R. Roosevelt Thomas Jr. says that "diversity includes everyone . . . white males are as diverse as their colleagues."[3] He also says that diversity is good for organizations, offering a source of competitive advantage. Picture an organization whose diverse employees possess a mix of talents and perspectives and reflect the firm's customers and clients. Wouldn't this be good for the organization and its members?

Diversity describes race, gender, age, and other individual differences.

||| Inclusion drives the business case for diversity.

Many organizations seem to be good or relatively good at attracting new employees of diverse backgrounds to join. But they aren't always successful in keeping them for the long term. This problem of high employee turnover among minorities and women has been called the **revolving door syndrome.**[4] It can reflect a lack of **inclusivity** in the employing organizations—the degree to which they are open to anyone who can perform a job, regardless of race, sexual preference, gender, or other diversity attribute.[5]

The **revolving door syndrome** is high turnover among minorities and women.

Research reported in the *Gallup Management Journal* shows that having a diverse and inclusive workplace is good for morale. In a study of 2,014 American workers, those who felt a sense of inclusion were more likely to stay with their employers and recommend them to others. Survey questions asked such things as "Do you always trust your company to be fair to all employees?" "At work, are all employees always treated with respect?" "Does your supervisor always make the best use of employees' skills?"[6] The New York research group Catalyst also reports that companies with a greater percentage of women on their boards outperform those whose boards have the lowest female representation.[7]

Inclusivity is how open the organization is to anyone who can perform a job.

Studies like those just cited back what some call a strong "business case for diversity."[8] But, Thomas Kochan and his colleagues at MIT point out that the hoped-for advantages are gained only when managers make diversity a priority by investing in training and supportive human resource practices. They say:[9]

To be successful in working with and gaining value from diversity requires a sustained, systemic approach and long-term commitment. Success is facilitated by a perspective that considers diversity to be an opportunity for everyone in an organization to learn from each other how better to accomplish their work and an occasion that requires a supportive and cooperative organizational culture as well as group leadership and process skills that can facilitate effective group functioning.

Multicultural organizations value and support diversity.

Look around. Think about how people are treating those who differ from themselves. What about your experiences at school and at work? Are you and others always treated with respect and inclusion? Or do you sense at times disrespect and exclusion?

The model for inclusivity is a **multicultural organization** that displays commitments to diversity like those in Table 16.1—Characteristics of Multicultural Organizations.[10] One such organization is Xerox, the first *Fortune* 500 firm to have an African-American woman, Ursula Burns, as CEO and also the first to have one woman succeed another as CEO. When praising Burns's appointment, Ilene Lang, head of the nonprofit Catalyst, which supports women in business, said: "Most companies have one woman who might be a possibility to become CEO; Xerox has a range of them." The firm has an Executive Diversity Council, runs diversity leadership programs, and evaluates managers on how well they recruit and develop employees from underrepresented groups. Harvard professor David Thomas says Xerox has "a culture where having women and people of color as candidates for powerful jobs has been going on for two decades."[11]

A **multicultural organization** is based on pluralism and operates with inclusivity and respect for diversity.

Table 16.1 Characteristics of Multicultural Organizations

Pluralism—Members of minority and majority cultures influence key values and policies.

Structural integration—Minority-culture members are well represented at all levels and in all responsibilities.

Informal network integration—Mentoring and support groups assist career development of minority-culture members.

Absence of prejudice and discrimination—Training and task force activities support the goal of eliminating culture-group biases.

Minimum intergroup conflict—Members of minority and majority cultures avoid destructive conflicts.

Minorities and women suffer diversity bias in many situations.

We have to be realistic in facing up to the challenges of creating inclusive and multicultural organizations. It isn't always easy to get the members of a workforce to really respect and work well with one another. The term "diversity" basically means the presence of differences, and that's potentially challenging in its own right. But

FIGURE 16.1

How Do Glass Ceilings Constrain Career Advancement for Women and Minorities? Organizations consist of a majority culture (often white males) and minority cultures (including women, people of color, and other minorities). It is likely that members of the majority culture will dominate higher management levels. One of the potential consequences is a "glass ceiling" effect that, although not publicized, acts as a barrier that sometimes makes it hard for women and minorities to advance and gain entry into higher-management ranks.

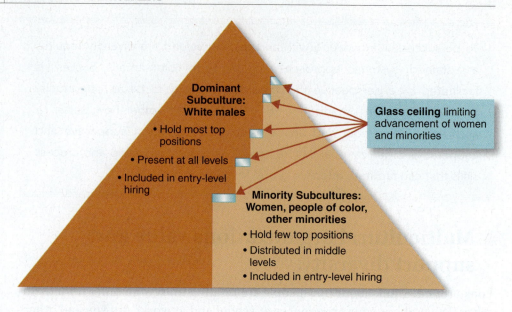

Dominant Subculture: White males
- Hold most top positions
- Present at all levels
- Included in entry-level hiring

Glass ceiling limiting advancement of women and minorities

Minority Subcultures: Women, people of color, other minorities
- Hold few top positions
- Distributed in middle levels
- Included in entry-level hiring

The **glass ceiling** is a hidden barrier to the advancement of women and minorities.

The **leaking pipeline problem** occurs when women leave careers because employers lack family-friendly policies and practices.

Biculturalism is when minority members adopt characteristics of majority cultures in order to succeed.

diversity issues in organizations are further complicated because such differences and subcultures are often distributed unequally in the power structure. Let's be honest. Most senior executives in large businesses are still older, white, and male. There is more diversity among lower and middle levels of most organizations than at the top. And for some women and minority workers, the **glass ceiling** depicted in **Figure 16.1** can be a real—albeit hidden—barrier to career advancement.

Minorities and women can face diversity challenges that range from misunderstandings, to lack of sensitivity, to glass ceiling limitations, to outright job discrimination and various types of harassment. One senior executive expressed her surprise on finding that the top performer in her work group, an African-American male, was paid 25% less than anyone else. This wasn't because his pay had been cut to that level; it was because his pay increases had always trailed those given to white co-workers. The differences added up significantly over time, but no one noticed or stepped forward to make the adjustment.[12]

Something called the **leaking pipeline problem** shows up in male-dominant organizational cultures. It occurs as women leave careers because their employer lacks family-friendly human resource policies and practices.[13] The EEOC, for example, reports an increase in pregnancy and pay discrimination complaints.[14] Data from the U.S. Equal Employment Opportunity Commission (EEOC) show that sex discrimination is behind an increasing number of bias suits filed by workers. And sexual harassment is another problem.[15] It takes the form of unwanted sexual advances, requests for sexual favors, and sexually laced communications.

People respond to bad treatment at work in different ways. Some may challenge the system by filing internal complaints or taking outside legal action. Some may quit to look for better positions elsewhere or to pursue self-employment opportunities. Some may try to "fit in" by adapting through **biculturalism**, attempting to display majority culture characteristics that seem necessary to succeed in the work environment. For example, gays, lesbians, bisexuals, and transgendered might hide their sexual orientations and gender identities; an African-American or Hispanic manager might avoid using words or phrases that white colleagues would consider slang; a woman might use football or baseball metaphors in conversations with men to gain acceptance into their career networks.

Big Continent Attracts a Global Giant

Dear Wal-Mart: "Welcome to South Africa."

When Wal-Mart bought 51% ownership of South Africa's Massmart, it joined forces with an established and successful retailer. And the decision was strategic. "The more we learn about South Africa and the surrounding countries, the more we are convinced that this is an important region with attractive growth characteristics," said Doug McMillon, head of Wal-Mart International. It's a belief confirmed by Massmart's local record. "Yeah, people here love it," says one of the store's salespersons, "by midday there is a stampede through the doors."

Massmart operates close to 400 stores, mostly in South Africa but also in 12 other sub-Saharan African countries. The firm has prospered from a growing middle class and an acceptance of the "shopping mall" experience. Wal-Mart hopes to find the right fit with African cultures with the assistance of its local partner.

CEO Grant Pattison says Massmart will operate with regional sensitivity. This means that Wal-Mart's corporate culture, which originated in founder Sam Walton's hometown of Bentonville, Arkansas, will have to do some adapting. "Not everyone comes in the morning and does the rah-rah thing," says Pattison. "Not everyone does the Wal-Mart cheer."

Denis Farrell/AP

Find Inspiration

It's a long way from Arkansas to South Africa, and it's a big step across cultures. But that's the nature of business these days, and we all have to be prepared to work well across diverse cultural boundaries. How experienced are you at cross-cultural relationships, whether in the neighborhood or while traveling? What do you need to know to succeed in a globally connected world of work?

⫼ Organizational subcultures can create diversity challenges.

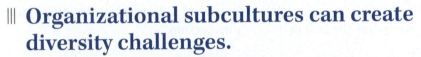

Another reason that the truly multicultural organization is hard to find is the existence of **organizational subcultures**. These are informal groupings of persons that form around such things as gender, age, race and ethnicity, and even job functions. People can get so caught up in their subcultures that they identify and interact mostly with others who are like themselves. Although perhaps unintentional, they can develop tendencies toward **ethnocentrism**, and act in ways that suggest their subculture is superior to all others.

Occupational subcultures develop as people form shared identities around the work that they do. Some employees may consider themselves "systems people" who are very different from "those marketing people" and even more different still from "those finance people." Even at school, in course project groups, have you noticed how students tend to identify with their majors? Don't some look down on others they consider to be pursuing "easy" majors and view their majors as the superior ones?

Differences in **ethnic or national subcultures** exist among people from various races, language groups, regions, and countries. And as we all know, it can be difficult for some to work together across these boundaries. Although one may speak in everyday conversations about "African-American" or "Latino" or "Anglo" cultures, one has to wonder: Do members of these subcultures really understand one another?[16] **Cultural intelligence**, sometimes called CQ, is defined as a "person's capability to function effectively in situations characterized by cultural diversity."[17] It's a concept often used in the context of global business and travel. But shouldn't CQ skills be part of subculture relationships right here at home—at work and in everyday living?

It's common for **gender subcultures** to form among persons that share the same gender identities. Although common ground creates lots of comfort for those inside these subcultures, it may create distance between them and outsiders. Women, for

Organizational subcultures are groupings of people based on shared demographic and job identities.

Ethnocentrism is the belief that one's membership group or subculture is superior to all others.

Occupational subcultures form among people doing the same kinds of work.

Ethnic or national subcultures form among people from the same races, language groupings, regions, and nations.

Cultural intelligence is the ability to work well in situations of cultural diversity.

example, might feel a sense of exclusion in an environment of men who talk with lots of sports metaphors focused on winning and losing.[18] Men might feel similar exclusion in an environment of women whose conversations and interactions emphasize relationships and collaboration.[19] And what about persons with transgender identities? How do they fit in, how do they feel, and how do they adapt in work settings dominated by men and women who identify along traditional gender lines?

Generational subcultures form among people in similar age groups.

Age is the basis for **generational subcultures** in organizations. Harris and Conference Board polls report that younger workers tend to be more dissatisfied than older workers.[20] They are also described as more short-term oriented, giving higher priority to work-life balance, and expecting to hold several jobs during their careers.[21] Imagine the conflicts that can occur when members of today's college generation go to work for older managers who grew up with quite different life experiences and even values. Have you had a conflict with a parent, perhaps over a lifestyle or authority issue, that might foreshadow similar ones you might encounter at work someday?

||| Managing diversity should be a top leadership priority.

What can leaders and managers do so that people under their care are treated inclusively? The answer begins with a willingness to recognize that, most workers want the same things regardless of their backgrounds. They want respect for their talents; they want to be fairly treated; they want to be able to work to the best of their abilities; they want to achieve their full potential. Meeting these expectations requires the best in diversity leadership.

CLAYTON DE SOUZA/ ESTADAOCONTEUDO/AP

{ "WHEN YOU COMBINE MOBILE DEVICES, FREE CONTENT AND AN INEXPENSIVE, BLENDED LEARNING MODEL, YOU CAN SERVE KIDS IN NAIROBI FOR $4 A MONTH. . . ."

Role Models

■ Salman Khan Crosses Borders to Foster Learning

The idea for the nonprofit Khan Academy was born when Salman Khan used Yahoo's Doodle online notepad to help his cousin Nadia with her math. He soon began to create tutorials which he uploaded to YouTube. Khan, a graduate of MIT and Harvard Business School, created his academy so that users could engage in free online learning of content they wanted, when they wanted, and how they wanted.

With a mission of "providing a high quality education to anyone, anywhere," Khan Academy provides free "micro-lectures" (there are close to 4,000 to date), in a ten-minute video tutorial format in subjects such as math, finance, physics, history, biology, astronomy, economics, and computer science. The result has made quality secondary education available to students in every corner of the earth. With inexpensive tablet devices, accessibility to secondary education was opened up to rural and urban populations most in need.

"When you combine mobile devices, free content and an inexpensive, blended learning model, you can serve kids in the slums of Nairobi for $4 a month and you can start to imagine a $100-a-year high school that is quite high quality," says Tom Vander Ark, CEO of Open Education Foundation and author of *Getting Smart: How Personal Digital Learning Is Changing the World*.

WHAT'S THE LESSON HERE?

Some praise the Khan Academy as "the future of education" and "game-changing." Skeptics are less sure. But it's hard to question the benefits of "flipping the classroom" and using the Internet so that students can study from anywhere and at their own time and at their own pace. What's your take on supplementing traditional in-class learning with online learning? When you're struggling in a course, are you ready to engage a tutor who might be reaching out to you from India, the Phillippines, or some other country?

The small figure describes what R. Roosevelt Thomas calls a continuum of leadership approaches to diversity.[22] At one end is *affirmative action*. Here, leadership commits the organization to hiring and advancing minorities and women. You might think of this as advancing diversity by increasing the representation of diverse members in the organization's workforce. But this is only a partial solution, and the revolving door syndrome may even negate some of its positive impact. Thomas says it's a mistake to assume "that once you get representation, people will assimilate." He describes *valuing diversity* as a step beyond affirmative action. Here, a leader commits the organization to educate its workforce so that people better understand and respect differences. The training goal is to help them better deal with "similarities, differences and tensions" by answering a fundamental question: "Can I work with people who are qualified that are not like me?"[23]

Affirmative Action
Create upward mobility for minorities and women

Valuing Differences
Build quality relationships with respect for diversity

Managing Diveristy
Achieve full utilization of diverse human resources

The final step in Thomas's continuum is **managing diversity**. A leader who actively manages diversity is always seeking ways to make an organization truly multicultural and inclusive—and keep it that way. For example, Eastman Kodak has been praised by *Business Ethics* magazine for "leading-edge anti-discrimination policies toward gay, bisexual, and transgender employees." It has also received a perfect score from the Human Rights Campaign for its efforts to end sexual discrimination.[24]

> **Managing diversity** is building an inclusive work environment that allows everyone to reach his or her potential.

As pointed out earlier, Thomas argues quite forcibly that leaders have a performance incentive to embrace managing diversity.[25] A diverse workforce offers a rich pool of talents, ideas, and viewpoints that can help solve complex problems. A diverse workforce also aligns well with needs and expectations of diverse customers and stakeholders.[26] Michael R. Losey, former president of the Society for Human Resource Management (SHRM), says, "Companies must realize that the talent pool includes people of all types, including older workers; persons with disabilities; persons of various religious, cultural, and national backgrounds; persons who are not heterosexual; minorities; and women."[27]

{ ARE YOU WILLING TO COPE WITH TENSIONS IN ADDRESSING DIVERSITY?

Explore **Yourself**

■ Diversity Maturity

Today's organizations and the nature of our global workforce demand **diversity maturity** from anyone who is serious about career success. Being mature about diversity means being able to answer a confident "yes" to questions such as these:

- Do you understand diversity concepts?
- Do you make decisions about others based on their abilities?
- Do you understand that diversity issues are complex?
- Are you able to cope with tensions in addressing diversity?
- Are you willing to challenge the way things are?

Be honest; admit where you still have work left to do. Use your answers to help set future goals to ensure that your actions, not just your words, consistently display positive diversity values.

> Get to know yourself better by taking the self-assessment on **Diversity Awareness** and completing other activities in the *Exploring Management* Skill-Building Portfolio.

STUDY GUIDE

Takeaway 16.1
What Should We Know About Diversity in the Workplace?

Terms to Define

Biculturalism

Cultural intelligence

Diversity

Ethnic or national subcultures

Ethnocentrism

Gender subcultures

Generational subcultures

Glass ceiling

Inclusivity

Leaking pipeline problem

Managing diversity

Multicultural organization

Occupational subcultures

Organizational subcultures

Revolving door syndrome

Rapid Review

- Workforce diversity can improve business performance by expanding the talent pool of the organization and establishing better understandings of customers and stakeholders.
- Inclusivity is a characteristic of multicultural organizations that values and respects diversity of their members.
- Minorities and women can suffer diversity bias in such forms as job and pay discrimination, sexual harassment, and the glass ceiling effect.
- Organizational subcultures, including those based on occupational, functional, ethnicity, nationality, age, and gender differences, can create diversity challenges.
- A top leadership priority should be managing diversity to develop an inclusive work environment within which everyone is able to reach their full potential.

Questions for Discussion

1. What subcultures do you see operating at work and/or in school, and how do they affect relationships and daily events?
2. What are some of the things organizations and leaders can do to reduce diversity bias faced by minorities and women in the workplace?
3. What does the existence of an affirmative action policy say about an organization's commitment to diversity?

Be Sure You Can

- identify major diversity trends in American society
- explain the business case for diversity
- explain the concept of inclusivity
- list characteristics of multicultural organizations
- identify subcultures common to organizations
- discuss the types of employment problems faced by minorities and women
- explain Thomas's concept of managing diversity

Career Situation: What Would You Do?

One of your co-workers brought along his friend to lunch. When discussing his new female boss, the friend says: "Yeh, she got the job just because she's a Hispanic woman. There's no way that someone like me had a chance given her pedigree. And she now has the gall to act as if we're all one big happy team and the rest of us should accept her leadership. I'm doing my best to make it hard for her to succeed." It was uncomfortable for you just to hear this. Your co-worker looks dismayed but isn't saying anything. What do you do or say? Will you just let the comment go, or do something more?

Takeaway 16.2
What Should We Know About Diversity Among Global Cultures?

ANSWERS TO COME

- Culture shock comes from discomfort in cross-cultural situations.
- Cultural intelligence is the capacity to adapt to foreign cultures.
- The "silent" languages of cultures include context, time, and space.
- Cultural tightness and looseness varies around the world.
- Hofstede's model identifies five value differences among national cultures.
- Intercultural competencies are essential career skills.

A TRIP TO THE GROCERY STORE, A DAY SPENT AT WORK, A VISIT TO OUR CHILDREN'S schools—all are possible opportunities for us to have cross-cultural experiences. And you have to admit, there are a lot of new faces in the neighborhood. At my university even a walk across campus can be a trip around the world, but we have to be willing to take it. How about you? Do you greet, speak with, and actively engage people of other cultures? Or are you shy, hesitant, and even inclined to avoid them?

⦀ Culture shock comes from discomfort in cross-cultural situations.

Maybe it is a bit awkward to introduce yourself to an international student or foreign visitor to your community. Maybe the appearance of a Muslim woman in a headscarf or a Nigerian man in a long overblouse is unusual to the point of being intimidating. Maybe, too, meeting or working with someone from another culture, causes us to experience something known to international travelers as **culture shock**. This is a feeling of confusion and discomfort when in or dealing with an unfamiliar culture.[28]

Global businesses are concerned about culture shock because they need their employees to be successful as they travel and work around the world. Perhaps this understanding might also be applied at home to our everyday cross-cultural experiences. Listed here are stages that are often encountered as someone adjusts to the unfamiliar setting of a new culture. The assumption is that knowing about the stages can help us better deal with them.[29]

Culture shock is the confusion and discomfort that a person experiences when in an unfamiliar culture.

- *Confusion*—First contacts with the new culture leave you anxious, uncomfortable, and in need of information and advice.
- *Small victories*—Continued interactions bring some "successes," and your confidence grows in handling daily affairs.
- *Honeymoon*—This is a time of wonderment, cultural immersion, and even infatuation, with local ways viewed positively.
- *Irritation and anger*—This is a time when the "negatives" overwhelm the "positives" and the new culture becomes a target of your criticism.
- *Reality*—This is a time of rebalancing; you are able to enjoy the new culture while accommodating its less-desirable elements.

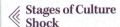

Stages of Culture Shock

{ **SURVEYS SHOWS HIGHEST MORALE AMONG WORKERS IN THE NETHERLANDS**

Facts to **Consider**

■ Employee Morale Varies Around the World

A worldwide study shows that the morale of workers varies from one country to the next. FDS International of the United Kingdom surveyed 13,832 workers in 23 countries. Here is how selected countries ranked based on employee reports of job satisfaction, quality of employer-employee relations, and work-life balance.

  Top-Ranked—1. Netherlands, 2. Ireland and Thailand, 3. Switzerland, 4. Denmark, 5. United Kingdom.

  Some Others—10. United States, 11. Canada, 12. Poland, 13. Korea, 14. Australia, 15. Japan.

YOUR THOUGHTS?

Why do you think employee morale in the United States and Canada trails that of other countries such as the Netherlands, Ireland, and Switzerland? Why might one Asian country such as Thailand score very high in employee morale and another such as Korea score much lower? Are there cultural factors that might make a difference in how employees respond to a survey about their workplace morale?

‖ Cultural intelligence is the capacity to adapt to foreign cultures.

A U.S. businessman once went to meet a Saudi Arabian official. He sat in the office with crossed legs and the sole of his shoe exposed. He didn't know this is a sign of disrespect in the local culture. He passed documents to the host using his left hand, which Muslims consider unclean. And, he declined when coffee was offered. This suggested criticism of the Saudi's hospitality. What was the price for these cultural miscues? A $10 million contract was lost to a Korean executive better versed in Saudi ways.[30]

Some might say that this American's behavior was ethnocentric, so self-centered that he ignored and showed no concern for the culture of his Arab host. Others might excuse him as suffering from culture shock. Maybe he was so uncomfortable on arrival in Saudi Arabia that all he could think about was offering his contract and leaving as quickly as possible. Still others might give him the benefit of the doubt. It could have been that he was well intentioned but didn't have time to learn about Saudi culture before making the trip.

Regardless of the possible reasons for the cultural miscues, they still worked to the businessman's disadvantage. There is also no doubt that he failed to show **cultural intelligence**—the ability to adapt and adjust to new cultures.[31] This was also called "CQ" in our discussion of diversity among organizational subcultures and described as an ability to work well in situations of cultural diversity. In the context of global management, people with high CQ have high cultural self-awareness and are flexible in dealing with cultural differences. They are willing to learn from unfamiliar cross-cultural situations and modify their behaviors to act with sensitivity toward another culture's ways. In other words, someone high in cultural intelligence views cultural differences not as threats but as learning opportunities.

Cultural intelligence is probably a good indicator of someone's capacity for success in international assignments and in relationships with persons of different cultures. How would you rate yourself? Could cultural intelligence be one of your important personal assets?

Cultural intelligence is the ability to adapt to new cultures and work well in situations of cultural diversity.

Silent Language Skills Do Lots of Talking in China

What are the silent language lessons for meeting a Chinese counterpart? Be sure to initiate the handshake when you are the lower-ranking person. Act impressed when receiving a business card and don't quickly tuck it away. Don't point with your finger; use a folded hand with thumb on top. Mind your alcohol, but be ready to mix drinks with business during dinner. Speaking of dinner, get ready. There will be many new and interesting things on the menu. And don't eat too much too fast, new dishes may keep arriving well past your "I'm full" point.

Igor Demchenkov/iStockphoto

⦀ The "silent" languages of cultures include context, time, and space.

Hanoi, Vietnam   Visiting former U.S. Secretary of Defense Leon Panetta exchanged war relics with his counterpart, General Phung Quang Thanh. During a short ceremony Thanh presented letters found on a dead U. S serviceman during the war. The letters were placed on top of a red cloth with yellow fringe. Secretary Panetta presented a diary found on a dead North Vietnamese soldier. He presented the diary in a Fedex envelop.[32]

It is easy to recognize differences in the spoken and written languages used by people around the world. And foreign-language skills can open many doors to cultural understanding. But anthropologist Edward T. Hall points out that there are other "silent" languages of culture that are also very significant.[32] If we look and listen carefully, he believes we should recognize how cultures differ in the ways their members use language in communication.[33] Whether Secretary Panetta realized it or not in the prior example, it wasn't only his words that were communicating to the Vietnamese. The Fedex envelop was too.

In **high-context cultures** such as Vietnam, what is actually said or written may convey only part, sometimes a very small part, of a message. The rest must be interpreted from nonverbal signals and the situation as a whole—things such as body language, physical setting, and even past relationships among the people involved. Context counts, and cultures and ceremonies are carefully interpreted. Things like dinner parties and social gatherings are also important. They allow potential business partners to get to know one another. It is only after the relationships are established that it becomes possible to discuss and hopefully make business deals.

In **low-context cultures** most communication takes place via the written or spoken word. This is common in the United States, Canada, and Germany, for example. We rely on words to communicate messages. And as the saying goes: "We say (or write) what we mean, and we mean what we say."

Hall also notes that the way people approach and deal with time varies across cultures.[34] He describes a **monochronic culture** as one in which people tend to do one thing at a time. This is typical of the United States, where most businesspeople schedule a meeting for one person or group to focus on one issue for an allotted time period. And if someone is late for one of those meetings or brings an uninvited guest, we tend not to like it.

High-context cultures rely on nonverbal and situational cues as well as spoken or written words in communication.

Low-context cultures emphasize communication via spoken or written words.

In **monochronic cultures** people tend to do one thing at a time.

{ **"WE WILL THEREFORE GUARANTEE THAT EVERY EMPLOYEE WHO MAKES OUR CLOTHING IS PAID A FAIR WAGE, NOT JUST A LEGAL MINIMUM WAGE . . ."**

Ethics **Check**

■ Fair-Trade Fashion

Are you someone who likes to shop "fair trade." Do you feel good when buying coffee, for example, that is certified as grown by persons who were paid fairly for their labor?

The clothing retailer Fair Indigo wants to be known for selling fair-trade fashion. It presents itself as "a new clothing company with a different way of doing business" that wants to "create stylish, high-quality clothes while paying a fair and meaningful wage to the people who produce them." Pointing out that there is no certifying body for fair-trade apparel, Fair Indigo offers its own guarantee: "We will therefore guarantee that every employee who makes our clothing is paid a fair wage, not just a legal minimum wage, as is the benchmark in the industry."

Fair Indigo's representatives travel the globe searching for small factories and work cooperatives that meet their standards. CEO Bill Bass says: "The whole evolution of the clothing and manufacturing industry has been to drive prices and wages down, shut factories and move work to countries with lower wages. We said, 'we're going to reverse this and push wages up.'"

YOU DECIDE

Are you willing to pay a bit more for a fair-trade product? And what do you think about Fair Indigo's business model? Is it "fashion" that sells apparel, or fashion plus conditions of origin? Is Fair Indigo at the forefront of the next new wave of value creation in retailing—fair-trade fashion?

> In **polychronic cultures** people accomplish many different things at once.

Members of a **polychronic culture** are more flexible about time and who uses it. They often try to work on many different things at once, perhaps not in any particular order. An American visitor (monochronic culture) to an Egyptian client (polychronic culture) may be frustrated, for example, by interruptions as the client deals with people continually flowing in and out of his office.

> **Proxemics** is the study of how people use interpersonal space.

In addition, Hall points out that cultures vary in how they value and use space. He describes cultural tendencies in terms of **proxemics**, or how people use space to communicate. If you visit Japan you'll notice the difference in proxemics very quickly. Space is precious in Japan; it is respected, and its use is carefully planned. Small, tidy homes, offices, and shops are the norm; gardens are tiny but immaculate; public spaces are carefully organized for most efficient use. Americans, by contrast tend to like as much space as they can get. We like big offices, big homes, big yards. We also like personal space and get uncomfortable, for example, if others stand too close to us in lines. When someone "talks right in our face," we don't like it; the behavior may even be interpreted as an expression of anger.

⫼ Cultural tightness and looseness varies around the world.

The nail that sticks up will be hammered down.   Asian Proverb
The squeaking wheel gets the grease.   American Idiom

Two sayings; two different cultural settings. What are their implications? Picture young children listening to parents and elders as they offer these words of wisdom. One child grows up being careful to not speak out, stand out, or attract attention. The other grows up trying to speak up and stand out in order to get attention.

This contrast in childhoods introduces the concept of cultural tightness-looseness. Scholars Michele J. Gelfand, Lisa H. Nishii, and Jana L. Raver describe it as "the strength of social norms and degree of sanctioning within societies."[35] Two things are

Manager's **Library**

WOMAN AREN'T THE PROBLEM: THEY'RE THE SOLUTION

An ancient Chinese proverb claims that "women hold up half the sky." But the harsh reality is that women are oppressed throughout the developing world. Sex trafficking, rape, and death after childbirth are but a few gender-specific human rights violations.

In the book *Half the Sky: Turning Oppression into Opportunity for Women Worldwide.*, authors Nicolas Kristof and Sheryl WuDunn outline the prevalence of indignities suffered by poor, uneducated women around the globe. They offer well-thought-out ideas for eliminating that injustice, and equate the modern oppression of women worldwide to that of slavery. They argue that because slavery was legal, it was readily identified and defeated. Yet inhumane treatments of underprivileged women continue despite the rule of law.

Kristof and WuDunn, both Pulitzer Prize–winning journalists, state that "gendercide"—the daily slaughter of girls in the developing world—takes more lives in one decade than any genocide did in the entire 20th century. They travel the world writing and working to fight oppressive practices, but are resigned to harsh realities. Victimized women are poor, uneducated, and powerless in their societies. Crimes against them are hidden from the developing world and often tolerated in their male-dominated cultures.

This book offers practical solutions framed as a moral and political movement to emancipate women. The authors suggest that we first recognize injustices, then speak against them. Ordinary citizens can initiate change by volunteering with global organizations that fight oppression or joining e-mail lists. Educating maltreated women about their moral rights and the economic means to maintain independence is a key. Female leadership is needed in countries with masculine power structures.

REFLECT AND REACT

Are our diversity initiatives toward women properly focused on a global scale? For example, is it more important to increase the ranks of female executives in *Fortune* 500 corporations, or to stop global "gendercide"? Do you agree that moral and economic education can empower poor, uneducated women to stand against injustice? Does the plight of victimized women get lost sometimes when we are too quick to embrace and accept so-called cultural differences?

---

at issue in this definition: (1) the strength of norms that govern social behavior, and (2) the tolerance that exists for any deviations from the norms. Empirical studies have classified 33 societal cultures around the world on their tightness and looseness.[36]

In a **tight culture**, such as ones found in Korea, Japan, or Malaysia, social norms are strong and clear. People know the prevailing norms and let them guide their behavior. They self-govern and try to conform. They also understand that any deviations are likely to be noticed, discouraged, and even sanctioned. The goal in tight cultures, as suggested in the Asian proverb, is to fit in with society's expectations and not stand out.

In a **loose culture**, such as ones found in Australia, Brazil, or Hungary, social norms are mixed and less clear cut. People may be more or less concerned with them, and conformity will vary a good deal. Deviations from norms tend to be tolerated unless they take the form of criminal behavior or reach toward the extremes of morality. It is quite acceptable for individuals in loose cultures, as suggested in the American idiom, to show unique identities and express themselves independent from the masses.

It can be challenging to go from a tight to a loose-culture, or vice versa, for travel or work. This calls for lots of cultural awareness to understand differences and a similar amount of self-management to handle the differences well. One of the most common settings where the dynamics of tight and loose cultures play out is a course group or work team whose members come from different cultures. You've probably been there; what did you see and what might you expect?

In **tight cultures** social norms are rigid and clear, and members try to conform.

In **loose cultures** social norms are mixed and ambiguous, and conformity varies.

A mix of tightness and looseness on a cross-cultural team may result in soft or unstated conflict and missed performance opportunity. Members from tight cultures may look toward formal authority for direction while trying to always be on time and prepared. They may be slow to volunteer, criticize, show emotion, or seek praise. Members from loose cultures may not show much respect for authority, and punctuality may be a hit-or-miss proposition. They may be quick to voice opinions, criticize others, display emotions, and look for recognition. It takes a lot of cultural awareness for a team leader and team members to spot these culturally derived behaviors. And, it takes a lot of skill to create a team environment where everyone gets their chance to both contribute to team performance and take satisfaction from the experience.

‖ Hofstede's model identifies five value differences among national cultures.

Understanding the ideas just discussed is a good place to start in cultural appreciation, but cultures are still more complex. Scholars offer many models and useful perspectives.[37] One of the most discussed is Geert Hofstede, who explores value differences among national cultures.[38] His work began with a study of employees of a U.S.-based corporation operating in 40 countries. Hofstede identified the four cultural dimensions of power distance, uncertainty avoidance, individualism-collectivism, and masculinity-femininity. Later studies resulted in the addition of a fifth dimension, time orientation.[39] **Figure 16.2** shows a sample of how national cultures varied in his research. Can you see why Hofstede's cultural dimensions can be significant in business and management?

Power distance is the degree to which a society accepts or rejects the unequal distribution of power in organizations and society. In high power distance cultures such as Japan, we expect to find great respect for age, status, and titles. Could this create problems for an American visitor used to the informalities of a more moderate power distance culture, and perhaps accustomed to first names and casual dress in the office?

Uncertainty avoidance is the degree to which a society tolerates or is uncomfortable with risk, change, and situational uncertainty. In high uncertainty avoidance cultures, such as France, one would expect to find a preference for structure, order, and predictability. Could this be one of the reasons why the French seem to favor employment practices that provide job security?

Power distance is the degree to which a society accepts unequal distribution of power.

Uncertainty avoidance is the degree to which a society tolerates risk and uncertainty.

FIGURE 16.2

How Do Countries Compare on Hofstede's Five Dimensions of National Cultures?
Countries vary on Hofstede's five dimensions of value differences in national cultures. For example, Japan scores high on uncertainty avoidance and masculinity; the United States scores high on individualism and short-term thinking. Imagine what this might mean when international business executives try to make deals or when representatives of national governments try to work across these cultural boundaries.

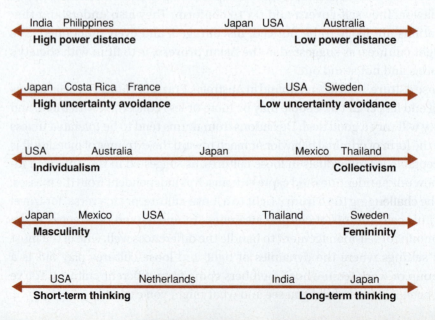

| India Philippines | Japan USA | Australia |
| High power distance | | Low power distance |

| Japan Costa Rica France | USA Sweden |
| High uncertainty avoidance | Low uncertainty avoidance |

| USA Australia | Japan | Mexico Thailand |
| Individualism | | Collectivism |

| Japan Mexico USA | Thailand Sweden |
| Masculinity | Femininity |

| USA Netherlands | India Japan |
| Short-term thinking | Long-term thinking |

Individualism-collectivism is the degree to which a society emphasizes individual accomplishments and self-interests, versus collective accomplishments and the interests of groups. In Hofstede's data the United States had the highest individualism score of any country. Don't you find the "I" and "me" words used a lot in our conversations and meetings? I'm always surprised how often they occur in student team presentations. What are the implications of our cultural tendency toward individualism when we try to work with people from more collectivist national cultures?

Masculinity-femininity is the degree to which a society values assertiveness and materialism, versus feelings, relationships, and quality of life.[40] You might think of it as a tendency to emphasize stereotypical masculine or feminine traits and attitudes toward gender roles. Visitors to Japan, with the highest masculinity score in Hofstede's research, may be surprised at how restricted career opportunities can be for women. The *Wall Street Journal* comments: "In Japan, professional women face a set of socially complex issues—from overt sexism to deep-seated attitudes about the division of labor." One female Japanese manager says: "Men tend to have very fixed ideas about what women are like.[41]

Time orientation is the degree to which a society emphasizes short-term or long-term goals and gratifications.[42] Americans are notorious for being impatient and wanting quick, even instantaneous, gratification. Even our companies are expected to achieve short-term results; those failing to meet quarterly financial targets often suffer immediate stock price declines. Many Asian cultures are quite the opposite, valuing persistence and thrift, and being patient and willing to work for long-term success.

Although Hofstede's ideas are insightful, his five value dimensions offer only a ballpark look at national cultures. They're a starting point at best. Hofstede himself even warns that we must avoid the **ecological fallacy**.[43] This is acting with the mistaken assumption that a generalized cultural value, such as individualism in American culture or masculinity in Japanese culture, applies always and equally to all members of the culture.

⫴ Intercultural competencies are essential career skills.

The many complications of cultures place a premium on **intercultural competencies**, skills and personal characteristics that help us function successfully in cross-cultural situations. Think of them as "must-haves" for career success today. These intercultural competencies focus us on acting competent when working in another culture or in culturally mixed settings. Scholars describe them as the three pillars of perception management, relationship management, and self-management.[44]

In terms of *perception management* a person must be inquisitive and curious about cultural differences and be flexible and nonjudgmental when interpreting and dealing with situations in which differences are at play. In terms of *relationship management* a person must be genuinely interested in others, sensitive to their emotions and feelings, and able to make personal adjustments while engaging in cross-cultural interactions. In terms of *self-management* a person must have a strong sense of personal identity, understand their own emotions and values, and be able to stay self-confident even in situations that call for personal adaptations because of cultural differences.

Individualism-collectivism is the degree to which a society emphasizes individuals and their self-interests.

Masculinity-femininity is the degree to which a society values assertiveness and materialism.

Time orientation is the degree to which a society emphasizes short-term or long-term goals.

The **ecological fallacy** assumes that a generalized cultural value applies equally well to all members of the culture.

Intercultural competencies are skills and personal characteristics that help us be successful in cross-cultural situations.

Foundations for Global Management Success

Goal: Global Knowledge
Goal: Intercultral Competency
Goal: Management Skills

STUDY GUIDE

Takeaway 16.2
What Should We Know About Diversity Among Global Cultures?

Terms to Define

Cultural intelligence

Culture shock

Ecological fallacy

High-context culture

Individualism-collectivism

Intercultural competencies

Loose culture

Low-context culture

Masculinity-femininity

Monochronic culture

Polychronic culture

Power distance

Proxemics

Tight culture

Time orientation

Uncertainty avoidance

Rapid Review

- People can experience culture shock due to the discomfort experienced in cross-cultural situations.
- Cultural intelligence is an individual capacity to understand, respect, and adapt to cultural differences.
- Hall's silent languages of culture include the role of context in communication, time orientation, and use of interpersonal space.
- Hofstede's five dimensions of value differences in national cultures are power distance, uncertainty avoidance, individualism-collectivism, masculinity-femininity, and time orientation.
- The foundations for intercultural competency are found in perception management, relationship management, and self-management.

Questions for Discussion

1. Should religion be included on Hall's list of the silent languages of culture?
2. Which of Hofstede's cultural dimensions might pose the greatest challenges to U.S. managers working in Asia, the Middle East, or Latin America?
3. Even though cultural differences are readily apparent around the world, is the trend today for cultures to converge and become more like one another?

Be Sure You Can

- explain culture shock and how people may respond to it
- differentiate low-context and high-context cultures, monochronic and polychronic cultures
- explain what makes cultures "tight" and "loose"
- list Hofstede's five dimensions of value differences among national cultures
- contrast American culture with that of other countries on each of Hofstede's dimensions

Career Situation: What Would You Do?

You've just been asked to join a team being sent to China for 10 days to discuss a new software development project with your firm's Chinese engineers. It's your first trip to China or Asia. In fact, you've only been to Europe as part of a study tour when in college. The trip is scheduled four weeks from today. What can you do to prepare for the trip and for your work with Chinese colleagues? What worries you the most about the trip and how well you'll do in the unfamiliar cultural circumstances?

TestPrep 16

Answers to TestPrep questions can be found at the back of the book.

Multiple-Choice Questions

1. Which statement is most consistent with arguments that diversity is good for organizations?
   (a) Having a diverse workforce guarantees success.
   (b) Diversity is easy to manage because it is already valued by all people.
   (c) Diverse workforces help organizations deal with diverse customers.
   (d) When workforces are diverse, organizations can spend less on training.

2. When members of minority cultures feel that they have to behave similar to the ways of the majority culture, this tendency is called _____.
   (a) biculturalism
   (b) particularism
   (c) the glass ceiling effect
   (d) multiculturalism

3. The beliefs that older workers are not creative and prefer routine, low-stress jobs are stereotypes that might create bad feelings among members of different _____ subcultures in organizations.
   (a) gender
   (b) generational
   (c) functional
   (d) ethnic

4. Among the three leadership approaches to diversity identified by Thomas, which one is primarily directed at making sure that enough minorities and women are hired by the organization?
   (a) Equal employment opportunity
   (b) Affirmative action
   (c) Valuing diversity
   (d) Managing diversity

5. Pluralism and the absence of discrimination and prejudice in policies and practices are two important hallmarks of _____.
   (a) the glass ceiling effect
   (b) a multicultural organization
   (c) exclusive organizational cultures
   (d) affirmative action

6. The term _____ helps describe an organization that fully integrates members of minority cultures and majority cultures.
   (a) equal employment opportunity
   (b) affirmative action
   (c) revolving door syndrome
   (d) pluralism

7. When members of the marketing department stick close to one another, as well as share jokes and even a slang language, the likelihood is that a/an _____ subculture is forming.
   (a) occupational
   (b) generational
   (c) gender
   (d) ethnic

8. When someone experiences culture shock on a study abroad trip, the first stage is likely to be one of anxiety caused by confusion in the new cultural setting. What is the next stage in culture shock?
   (a) Experiencing a sense of confidence from small victories in dealing with differences.
   (b) Displaying outright irritation and anger at the ways of this new culture.
   (c) Wanting to give up and go home immediately.
   (d) Accepting reality and enjoying the good and bad aspects.

9. When dealing with proxemics as a silent language of culture, what is the issue of most concern?

   (a) How people use the spoken word to communicate

   (b) How people use nonverbal to communicate

   (c) How people use time to communicate

   (d) How people use space to communicate

10. In _____ cultures, members tend to do one thing at a time; in _____ cultures, members tend to do many things at once.

   (a) monochronic; polychronic

   (b) universal; particular

   (c) collectivist; individualist

   (d) neutral; affective

11. When a foreign visitor to India attends a dinner and criticizes as "primitive" the local custom of eating with one's fingers, he or she can be described as acting in a/an _____ way.

   (a) culturally intelligent

   (b) polychronic

   (c) monochronic

   (d) ethnocentric

12. In a high-context culture we would expect to find _____.

   (a) low uncertainty avoidance

   (b) high power distance

   (c) monochronic time orientation

   (d) strong emphasis on nonverbal communication

13. It is common in Malaysian culture for people to value teamwork and to display great respect for authority. Hofstede would describe this culture as high in both _____.

   (a) uncertainty avoidance and feminism

   (b) universalism and particularism

   (c) collectivism and power distance

   (d) long-term orientation and masculinity

14. On which dimension of national culture did the United States score highest and Japan score highest in Hofstede's original survey research?

   (a) Masculinity, femininity

   (b) Long-term, short-term

   (c) Individualism, masculinity

   (d) High uncertainty avoidance, collectivism

15. If someone commits what Hofstede calls the "ecological fallacy," what are they likely to be doing?

   (a) Disregarding monochronic behavior

   (b) Assuming all members of a culture fit the popular stereotype

   (c) Emphasizing proxemics over time orientation

   (d) Forgetting that cultural intelligence can be learned

Short-Response Questions

16. What is the difference between valuing diversity and managing diversity?

17. How can subculture differences create diversity challenges in organizations?

18. If you were asked to give a short class presentation on the "silent languages" of culture, what cultural issues would you talk about and what examples would you give?

19. In what ways can the power distance dimension of national culture become an important issue in management?

Integration and Application Questions

20. A friend in West Virginia owns a small manufacturing firm employing about 50 workers. His son spent a semester in Japan as an exchange student. Upon return, he said to his dad: "Boy, the Japanese really do things right; everything is organized in teams; decisions are made by consensus, with everyone participating; no one seems to disagree with anything the bosses say. I think we should immediately start more teamwork and consensus decision making in our factory."

   Questions: The friend asks you for advice. Using insights from Hofstede's framework, what would you say to him? What differences in the Japanese and American cultures should be considered in this situation, and why?

BUILD MARKETABLE SKILLS
DO A CASE ANALYSIS
GET AND STAY INFORMED

Steps *for* Further Learning

BUILD

MARKETABLE SKILLS.
EARN BIG CAREER
PAYOFFS!

Don't miss these opportunities in the **Skill-Building Portfolio**

■ **SELF-ASSESSMENT 16:**
Diversity Awareness

It's easy to talk about diversity . . . where do you stand in day-to-day behavior?

■ **CLASS EXERCISE 16:**
Alligator River Story

Ambiguous situations can highlight diversity differences . . . compare values with your peers.

■ **TEAM PROJECT 16:**
Job Satisfaction Around the World

Discover how the world's workers view job satisfaction . . . consider cultural differences in work expectations.

Many learning resources are found at the end of the book and online within WileyPLUS.

Take advantage of **Cases for Critical Thinking**

■ **CHAPTER 16 CASE SNAPSHOT:**
Cultural Charades in Business Process Outsourcing/ *Sidebar on Beyond Race and Gender*

When you call a toll-free number for customer service assistance, possibly pertaining to finance or banking, an airline reservation, an insurance claim or technical support for one of your gadgets, there is a good possibility that the person on the other end of the line is a half-world away. India and the Philippines are two of the biggest players. Your experience as a caller is part of the quest of multinational companies (think: Dell, American Express, and Verizon) to realize significant cost savings in customer service by outsourcing the work to lower-wage countries. The name for this industry is business process outsourcing, or BPO for short. Its critics worry not just about how customers react. They also worry about its impact on the personalities, lifestyle, careers, and culture of local workers across the world.

DO

A CASE ANALYSIS.
STRENGTHEN YOUR
CRITICAL THINKING!

Dig into this **Hot Topic**

■ **GOOD IDEA OR NOT?** **Use punishment to sting incivility in the workplace**

Rudeness isn't a good thing under any circumstance. But a recent study of workplace incivility found that it has many adverse effects on work attitudes and performance. Among workers that have been the targets or rude comments or uncivil behavior:

GET

AND STAY INFORMED.
MAKE YOURSELF
VALUABLE!

- 8% said they decreased work efforts and 66% say their performance suffered.
- 80% said the incident caused them to lose work time through worry.
- 12% said they quit because of the incivility.

Those in favor of making incivility subject to work punishment might say it is too important from just a "bottom line" perspective to ignore. Some of them might also add it deserves sanction because it goes contrary to social norms. *Those against making incivility subject to work punishment* might say that it's too hard to judge. What one person considers "uncivil" or "rude" might mean something else to another person. If you can't agree on describing the bad behavior, you really can't sanction it.

Final Take It's a fair guess that diversity and cultural differences are sometimes—perhaps often—at the core of rude and uncivil comments and behavior. Given all the complexities of human behavior, and individual and cultural differences, can you draw a line that would help identify a specific comment or behavior as "unacceptable" in a work setting? What examples of across-the-line incivility can you give? Should incivility of any form be subject to meaningful penalties at work?

The International Labour Organization reports there are 215 million child laborers worldwide; 115 million of them work in hazardous conditions.

Reuters/Corbis

Globalization and International Business

Going Global Isn't Just for Travelers

Photo by Jeffrey R. Staab/CBS/GettyImages

Management Live

Cultural Awareness and *The Amazing Race*

The popular reality series *The Amazing Race* pits teams of players in an around-the-world competition. Each week, contestants race to complete cultural and physical challenges. They face grueling travel demands within and between countries and face unfamiliar languages and customs. Sleep and eating schedules are thrown off by global time differences. And, one thing becomes painfully clear as the race episodes unfold. Many of the participants do not know a lot about other countries in the world.

Like most of us, race contestants have grown used to the values and patterns of home. And that's understandable. But, if you watch closely, you'll see that their lack of **cultural awareness** sometimes reflects attitudes of superiority. As the race teams come face-to-face with one new culture after another, however, they learn a lot about themselves in the process.

When Nat Strand and Kat Chang won the $1 million prize, they were the first female team to do so. Their journey took them to 30 cities across four continents for a total of 32,000 miles. They crossed a lot of national and cultural boundaries along the way, much as today's global organizations do.

There's no better time to check your cultural awareness than now. This chapter discusses many ways you can put it to work in today's global economy. And there may well be a million dollar payoff for success in your future—measured in career success!

YOUR CHAPTER 17 TAKEAWAYS

1. Discuss ways that globalization affects international business.

2. Understand what global corporations are and how they work.

WHAT'S INSIDE

Explore Yourself
More on **cultural awareness**

Role Models
Nobel peace prize winner asks global firms to fight poverty

Ethics Check
Nationalism and protectionism

Facts to Consider
Corruption and bribes haunt global business

Manager's Library
The New Digital Age: Reshaping the Future of People, Nations and Business
by Eric Schmidt and Jared Cohen

Takeaway 17.1
How Does Globalization Affect International Business?

ANSWERS TO COME

- Globalization involves the growing interdependence of the world's economies.
- Global sourcing is a common international business activity.
- Export/import, licensing, and franchising are market entry approaches to international business.
- Joint ventures and wholly owned subsidiaries are direct investment approaches to international business.
- International business is complicated by different legal and political systems.
- International businesses must navigate regional economic alliances

OUR GLOBAL COMMUNITY IS RICH WITH INFORMATION, OPPORTUNITIES, controversies, and complications. We get on-the-spot news delivered from around the world right to our smart phones. When crises like the Japanese tsunami or civil strife in Syria happen, Twitter, Facebook, and other social media get the news out instantaneously. You can board a plane in New York and fly nonstop to Beijing, China, or Mumbai, India, or Johannesburg, South Africa. Colleges offer a growing variety of study-abroad programs. And, an MBA earned from a globally ranked school is an increasingly desirable credential.

Here are some conversation starters on the business side of things. Ben & Jerry's Ice Cream is owned by the British-Dutch firm Unilever; Anheuser-Busch is owned by the Belgian firm InBev; Mercedes builds M-class vehicles in Alabama; and India's Tata Group owns Jaguar, Land Rover, and Tetley Tea. Japan's Honda, Nissan, and Toyota get 80% to 90% of their profits from sales in America, IBM employs more than 40,000 software developers in India. Components for Boeing planes come from 5,400 suppliers in 40 countries, and Nike has manufacturing contracts with over 120 factories in China alone.[1]

The growing power of global businesses affects all of us in roles as citizens, consumers, and career-seekers. If in doubt, take a look at what you are wearing. It's hard to find a garment or a shoe that is really "Made in America." What about your T-shirt? Where did you buy it? Where was it made? Where will it end up?

In a fascinating book called *The Travels of a T-Shirt in the Global Economy*, economist Pietra Rivoli tracks the origins and disposition of a T-shirt that she bought while on a vacation to Florida.[2] As shown in **Figure 17.1**, the common T-shirt lives a complicated global life. The life of Rivoli's T-shirt begins with cotton grown in Texas. It moves to China, where the cotton is processed and white T-shirts are manufactured. These are imported by a U.S. firm that silk-screens them and sells them to retail shops for resale to American customers. When customers like Rivoli donate used T-shirts to charity, they're sold to a recycler. In this case the recycler sells them to a vendor in Africa, who distributes them to local markets, where they are sold yet again to new customers.

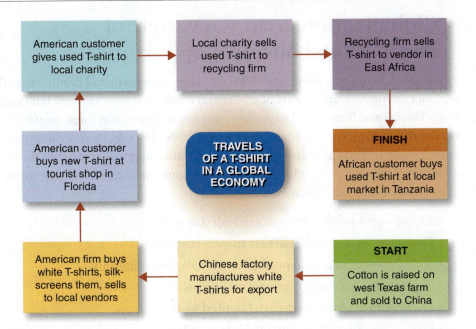

American customer gives used T-shirt to local charity

Local charity sells used T-shirt to recycling firm

Recycling firm sells T-shirt to vendor in East Africa

American customer buys new T-shirt at tourist shop in Florida

TRAVELS OF A T-SHIRT IN A GLOBAL ECONOMY

FINISH

African customer buys used T-shirt at local market in Tanzania

American firm buys white T-shirts, silk-screens them, sells to local vendors

Chinese factory manufactures white T-shirts for export

START

Cotton is raised on west Texas farm and sold to China

FIGURE 17.1

How Does a T-Shirt Travel Through the World's Global Economy?
This sketch shows the T-shirt beginning as cotton grown in Texas that is shipped to China, where it is processed and white T-shirts are manufactured. The white shirts come back to the United States, where they are silk-screened and sold to retail shops for resale to customers. If customers donate used T-shirts to a charity, they may go to a recycler, who sells them to vendors in other countries, where the used T-shirts get sold again to local customers.

‖ Globalization involves the growing interdependence of the world's economies.

We live and work in a **global economy** where labor and resource supplies, capital and product markets, and business competition are worldwide in scope.[3] Pretty much everything we do—from the things we buy to the food we eat to the investments we make, is influenced by the forces of **globalization**. Think of it as the process of growing interconnections among the components of the global economy.[4] Harvard scholar and consultant Rosabeth Moss Kanter describes globalization as "one of the most powerful and pervasive influences on nations, businesses, workplaces, communities, and lives."[5]

Do you have a good idea of how globalization affects your life? It's not just an issue of what you buy and how you invest. What about your work and career plans? If you come to Ohio, where I live, you'll find over 180,000 people working for foreign-owned firms.[6] They hold jobs created by **insourcing** where a foreign investor, say Honda, establishes business operations in America and hires local workers to staff it. Some 5.65 million U.S. jobs are linked to such inward foreign investment and, interestingly, these jobs pay 33% more on the average than ones locally created.[7]

Outsourcing is the other side of the jobs story in the global economy. It shifts them to foreign locations to save costs by taking advantage of lower-wage skilled labor. John Chambers, CEO of Cisco Systems Inc., pretty much lays it on the line for all of us when he says: "I will put my jobs anywhere in the world where the right infrastructure is, with the right educated workforce, with the right supportive government."[8] Although investors might favor outsourcing as a cost-reduction strategy, not everyone is pleased to hear this message. How would you like to be told that your job was being eliminated and outsourced to another country? Should you be thinking about how this possibility might affect future job opportunities in your chosen career?

In the **global economy**, resources, markets, and competition are worldwide in scope.

Globalization is the process of growing interdependence among elements of the global economy.

Insourcing is the creation of domestic jobs by foreign employers.

Outsourcing shifts local jobs to foreign locations to take advantage of lower-wage labor in other countries.

Globalization creates a variety of international business opportunities.

An **international business** conducts commercial transactions across national boundaries.

Firms like Cisco, Sony, Ford, and IKEA are large **international businesses**. They conduct for-profit transactions of goods and services across national boundaries. Such businesses, from small exporters and importers to the huge multinational corporations, form the foundations of world trade. They move raw materials, finished products, and specialized services from one country to another in the global economy. And, they all "go global" for good reasons—profits, customers, suppliers, capital, labor, and risk management.[9]

Why Businesses Go Global »

- *Profits*—gain profits through expanded operations.
- *Customers*—enter new markets to gain customers.
- *Suppliers*—get access to products, services, and materials.
- *Capital*—get access to financial resources.
- *Labor*—get access to low-cost, talented workers.
- *Risk*—spread assets among multiple countries.

Nike's swoosh is one of the world's most globally recognized brands. But did you know that Nike, headquartered in Beaverton, Oregon, does no domestic manufacturing? All its products come from sources abroad. New Balance, by contrast, still produces at a few factories in the United States even while making extensive use of global suppliers in China and elsewhere.[10] Although competing in the same industry, Nike and New Balance are pursuing somewhat different global strategies. But both are also seeking the international business advantages listed above.

Today you can also add *economic development* to the list of reasons why some businesses go global. An example is found in Rwanda, where coffee giants Green Mountain Coffee Roasters, Peet's Coffee & Tea, and Starbucks work with the non-profit TechnoServe. Its goal is to help raise the incomes for African coffee farmers by improving their production and marketing methods. The global firms send advisors to teach coffee growers how to meet their international standards. It's a win-win. The global firm gets a quality product at a good price, the growers gain skills and market opportunities, and the local economy improves.[11]

Global sourcing is a common international business activity.

In **global sourcing**, firms purchase materials, manufacturing, or services around the world for local use.

Just as there more is than one reason for getting into international business, there are several ways of doing it. A mainstay approach is **global sourcing**, where a business purchases materials, manufacturing, or services from around the world. It basically takes advantage of international wage gaps by contracting for low-cost goods and services in foreign locations. You see lots of it in manufacturing. Boeing's new 787 Dreamliner, for example, has wings and center fuselage from Japan, engines from the U.K. and Canada, and doors from Sweden and France. You also see it in services, such as when

Mainstay and market entry approaches			Direct investment approaches	
Global sourcing	Exporting and importing	Licensing and franchising	Joint ventures	Foreign subsidiaries

Increasing involvement in ownership and control of foreign operations

Micheline Pelletier/Corbis

{ **WE CAN CREATE A WORLD WHERE POVERTY DOESN'T EXIST . . . NOW EVERY TIME I WANT TO ADDRESS A PROBLEM, I CREATE A BUSINESS**

Role **Models**

■ **Nobel Peace Prize Winner Asks Global Firms to Fight Poverty**

Should global businesses balance the pursuit of profit with genuine efforts to do public good? A strong and positive "Yes!" is the answer given by Nobel Peace Prize winner Muhammad Yunus. The Bangladeshi economist gained fame for creating the Grameen Bank to offer microcredit loans to help fight poverty in his home country. The bank loans small amounts (as low as $30) to poor applicants (96% women) so that they can start their own small businesses and gain financial independence.

The Grameen Bank model of microfinance has spread around the world to serve some 200 million borrowers. Now Yunus is asking global firms to join in a transformational approach that unlocks the power of business to tackle poverty and other enduring social problems. In his book *Creating a World Without Poverty*, Yunus advocates a social business model in which a company's products or services are targeted to benefit those suffering from social ills. "Now every time I want to address a problem, I create a business," he says. "These businesses are all focused on problem solving, not on money making."

Yunus's call to the global business community was heard by the German yogurt maker Danone. It joined with him to start Grameen Danone as the world's first multinational social business. The firm manufactures nutritional yogurt and sells it at low cost in an attempt to help the 46% of Bangladesh's children that are undernourished. Profits in this "new class of business" are reinvested rather than being paid out as dividends, says Yunus. As profits grow, they are used to provide even cheaper and better goods and services to customers.

"We can create a world where poverty doesn't exist," claims Yunus, while hoping that within five years "at least 1 percent of the world economy be made up with social business." In recognition of his efforts "to combat global poverty," he was awarded the Congressional Gold Medal in 2013.

WHAT'S THE LESSON HERE?

When a multinational company travels into countries where social problems like poverty, disease, and illiteracy are present, should it find a way to help? Can the social business model really take off in the global business context? Or, is this something most likely to remain the "unusual" case rather than the "common" one in the future? Do you agree, or not, that global corporations can become powerful tools for eliminating social problems?

---

speaking with a customer-support call center in the Philippines or having medical X-rays read by physicians in India.

The network of outsourcing suppliers and contractors is called a firm's **global supply chain.** And this chain can get very complex and risky as it extends around the world. Automakers suffered when the Japanese tsunami knocked many parts suppliers offline. Computer makers suffered when massive flooding in Thailand shut down their supply of hard drives. Apple suffered when complaints surfaced that some of its Chinese suppliers used inappropriate work practices, and an internal audit by the firm revealed problems with work hours (62%), worker safety (35%), and hazardous substance practices (32%).[12]

The garment industry largely runs on a global sourcing model that is quite notorious for controversy. Benetton, for example, contracts with a shifting mix of some 700 suppliers to support a fast fashion strategy. Its garments, along with those from other Western retailers, were linked to several outsourcing factories destroyed when a building collapsed in Bangladesh killing over 1100 people. The tragedy focused public attention on how well global firms were monitoring safety conditions and work practices at their Bangladeshi suppliers. The *Wall Street Journal* used this case to say that many global supply chains are "tangled networks" where it is "difficult to assess blame when something goes wrong."[13]

A **global supply chain** is a network of a firm's outsourcing suppliers and contractors.

Problems with sketchy suppliers, rising labor costs in places like China, high transportation costs, cheaper energy at home, and good public relations are all reasons why some firms are now modifying their outsourcing strategies. You'll notice an increasing number of news reports about **reshoring** that shifts foreign production—and jobs—back to the domestic locations. A survey of large U.S.-based manufacturers by the Boston Consulting Group, for example, found that almost one-half had plans to return some foreign manufacturing to the United States. The report concluded that "Companies are realizing that the economics of manufacturing are swinging in favor of the U.S."[14]

Reshoring moves foreign production and jobs back to domestic locations.

||| Export/Import, licensing, and franchising are market entry approaches to international business.

A lot of international business involves **exporting**—selling locally made products in foreign markets, and **importing**—buying foreign-made products and selling them in domestic markets. Because the growth of export industries creates local jobs, you'll often read and hear about governments supporting these types of business initiatives.

In **exporting**, local products are sold abroad.

Importing is the process of acquiring products abroad and selling them in domestic markets.

Another form of international business is the **licensing** agreement, where foreign firms pay a fee for rights to make or sell another company's products in a specified region. The license typically grants access to a unique manufacturing technology, special patent, or trademark. One of the business risks of licensing is counterfeiting.[15] New Balance, for example, licensed a Chinese supplier to produce one of its brands. Even after New Balance revoked the license, the supplier continued to produce and distribute "New Barlun" shoes around Asia. New Balance ended up facing costly and complex litigation in China's courts.[16]

In **licensing**, one firm pays a fee for rights to make or sell another company's products.

In **franchising**, a foreign firm buys the rights to use another's name and operating methods in its home country. When companies such as McDonald's or Subway franchise internationally, they sell facility designs, equipment, product ingredients, recipes, and management systems to foreign investors. They also typically retain certain product and operating controls to protect their brand's image.

In **franchising**, a firm pays a fee for rights to use another company's name and operating methods.

||| Joint ventures and wholly owned subsidiaries are direct investment approaches to international business.

Sooner or later, some firms that are active in international business decide to make costly direct investments in operations in foreign countries. One way to do this is by a **joint venture**. This is a co-ownership arrangement in which the foreign and local partners agree to pool resources, share risks, and jointly operate the new business. Sometimes the joint venture is formed when a foreign partner buys part ownership in an existing local firm. In other cases it is formed when the foreign and local partners start an entirely new operation together.

A **joint venture** operates in a foreign country through co-ownership with local partners.

Tips to **Remember**

■ Checklist for Choosing a Good Joint Venture Partner

- *Familiar with your firm's major business*
- *Employs a strong local workforce*
- *Values its customers*
- *Values its employees*
- *Has strong local market for its own products*

- *Has record of good management*
- *Has good profit potential*
- *Has sound financial standing*
- *Has reputation for ethical decision making*
- *Has reputation for socially responsible practices*

International joint ventures are types of **global strategic alliances** in which foreign and domestic partners cooperate for mutual gains. Each partner hopes to get from the alliance things they couldn't do or would have a hard time doing alone. For the local partner an alliance may bring access to technology and opportunities to learn new skills. For the outside partner an alliance may bring access to new markets and customers, and the expert assistance of locals that understand them.[17]

Joint ventures were the business forms of choice for the world's large automakers when they decided to pursue major operations in China. Recognizing the local complexities, they decided it was better to cooperate with local partners than try to enter the Chinese markets on their own. Of course, such joint venture deals pose potential risks. And loss of technology is a big one. Not long ago, GM executives noticed that a new car from a fast-growing local competitor looked very similar to one of their models. This competitor was partially owned by GM's Chinese joint venture partner, and GM claimed its design was copied. The competitor denied it, and Chery Automobile, Ltd., has grown to be China's largest exporter for cars.[18]

In contrast to the international joint venture, which is a cross-border partnership, a **foreign subsidiary** is a local operation completely owned and controlled by a foreign firm. It might be a local firm that was purchased in its entirety or it might be a brand-new operation built from start as a **greenfield venture**. Decisions to set up foreign subsidiaries are most often made only after foreign firms have gained experience in the local environment through earlier joint ventures.

> In a **global strategic alliance**, each partner hopes to achieve through cooperation things they couldn't do alone.

> A **foreign subsidiary** is a local operation completely owned by a foreign firm.

> A **greenfield venture** establishes a foreign subsidiary by building an entirely new operation in a foreign country.

⫼ International business is complicated by different legal and political systems.

As you might imagine, the more home-country and host-country laws differ, the more difficult and complex it is for international businesses to operate successfully. And the greater the depth of foreign involvement, the more complex it becomes to understand and adapt to local ways. Common legal problems faced by international businesses involve incorporation practices and business ownership; negotiation and implementation of contracts with foreign parties; handling of foreign exchange; and intellectual property—patents, trademarks, and copyrights.

The issue of intellectual property is particularly sensitive these days. You might know this best in terms of concerns about movie and music downloads, photocopying of books and journals, and sale of fake designer fashions. Many Western businesses know it as lost profits due to their products or designs being copied and sold as imitations by foreign firms. After a lengthy and complex legal battle, for example, Starbucks won a major intellectual property case it had taken to the Chinese courts. A local firm was using Starbucks' Chinese name, "Xingbake" (*Xing* means "star" and *bake* is pronounced "bah kuh"), and was also copying its café designs.[19]

When international businesses believe they are being mistreated in foreign countries, or when local companies believe foreign competitors are disadvantaging them, their respective governments might take the cases to the **World Trade Organization (WTO)**. The 140 members of the WTO give one another **most favored nation status**—the most favorable treatment for imports and exports. Members also agree to work together within its framework to try to resolve some international business problems.

Even though WTO members are supposed to give one another most favored nation status, trade barriers are still common. They include outright **tariffs** or taxes that governments impose on imports. They also include **nontariff barriers** that discourage imports in nontax ways such as quotas and government import restrictions.

Yet another trade barrier emerges as outright **protectionism**—the attempt by governments to protect local firms from foreign competition and save jobs for local workers. You will see such issues reflected in many political campaigns and debates. And the issues aren't easy. Government leaders face internal political dilemmas involving the often-conflicting goals of seeking freer international trade while still protecting domestic industries. Such dilemmas can make it difficult for countries to reach international agreements on trade matters and hard for the WTO to act as a global arbiter of trade issues.

The **World Trade Organization (WTO)** is a global institution established to promote free trade and open markets around the world.

Most favored nation status gives a trading partner the most favorable treatment for imports and exports.

Tariffs are taxes governments levy on imports from abroad.

Nontariff barriers are nontax policies that governments enact to discourage imports, such as quotas and import restrictions.

Protectionism is a call for tariffs and favorable treatments to protect domestic firms from foreign competition.

{ BOLIVIA'S PRESIDENT TELLS GLOBAL FIRMS THE COUNTRY'S NATURAL RESOURCES BELONG TO ITS PEOPLE.

Ethics **Check**

■ Nationalism and Protectionism

The headline read "Bolivia Seizes Control of Oil and Gas Fields." The announcement said: "We are beginning by nationalizing oil and gas; tomorrow we will add mining, forestry, and all natural resources, what our ancestors fought for."

The country's president, Evo Morales, set forth new terms that gave a state-owned firm 82% of all revenues, leaving 18% for the foreign firms. He said: "Only those firms that respect these new terms will be allowed to operate in the country." The implicit threat was that any firms not willing to sign new contracts would be sent home.

Although foreign governments described this nationalization as an "unfriendly move," Morales considered it patriotic.

His position was that any existing contracts with the state were in violation of the constitution, and that Bolivia's natural resources belonged to its people.

YOU DECIDE

If you were the CEO at one of these global firms, do you resist and raise the ethics of honoring your "old" contracts with the Bolivian government? Or do you comply with the new terms being offered? And as an everyday citizen of the world, can you disagree that a country has a right to protect its natural resources from exploitation by foreigners? Just what are the ethics of Morales's decision?

‖ International businessess must navigate regional economic alliances.

Globalization has brought with it the growth of regional economic alliances, where nations agree to work together for economic gains. **NAFTA**, the **North American Free Trade Agreement**, creates a trade zone that frees the flows of goods and services, workers, and investments among the United States, Canada, and Mexico. Many firms have taken advantage of NAFTA by moving production facilities to Mexico and benefit from lower wages paid to skilled Mexican workers. These job shifts have pros and cons, and NAFTA is still a hot topic in some political debates. Arguments on the positive side credit NAFTA with greater cross-border trade and strengthening of the Mexican business environment. Arguments on the negative side blame NAFTA for substantial job losses to Mexico and lower wages being paid to American workers wanting to keep their jobs.

The **European Union** or **EU** is both a regional economic and political alliance. The EU now comprises 28 countries that are integrating politically with a European Parliament and economically by removing barriers to cross-border trade and business development. Seventeen EU members use a common currency—the *euro*—that is a major competitor to the U.S. dollar in the global economy.

APEC, Asia-Pacific Economic Cooperation, links 21 nations to promote free trade and investment in the Pacific region. Its members include some of the world's fastest growing economies such as China, Republic of Korea, Indonesia, Russia, and Australia.

Africa is also moving center stage in world business headlines. The region's economies are growing, the middle class is expanding, and regional economic alliances are gaining strength. Among them, the **Southern Africa Development Community, SADC**, links 14 southern African countries in trade and economic development efforts to improve prosperity and living standards for their citizens.

> **NAFTA** is the North American Free Trade Agreement linking Canada, the United States, and Mexico in an economic alliance.

> The **EU** or **European Union** is a political and economic alliance of 28 European countries.

> **APEC** is the **Asia-Pacific Economic Cooperation** that links 21 nations to promote free trade and investment in the Pacific region.

> **SADC** is the **Southern Africa Development Community** that links 14 southern African countries in trade and economic development efforts.

{ NATIONAL ECONOMIES ARE NOW GLOBAL; BUSINESS IS NOW GLOBAL; OUR PERSONAL THINKING MUST BE GLOBAL AS WELL.

Explore **Yourself**

■ Cultural Awareness

The forces of globalization are often discussed in respect to job migration, outsourcing, currency fluctuations, and the fortunes of global corporations. Yet it is important to remember that globalization is best understood and dealt with in a context of **cultural awareness**.

We become used to the ways of our culture. But many of these same values and patterns of behavior can be called into question when we work and interact with persons from different cultures. Our ways of doing things may seem strange and even, at the extreme, offensive to others who come from different cultural backgrounds. It's only natural, too, for cultural differences to be frustrating and even threatening when we come face-to-face with them. National economies are now global; business is now global; our personal thinking must be global as well.

Get to know yourself better by taking the **Global Intelligence** self-assessment and completing other activities in the *Exploring Management* **Skill-Building Portfolio**.

STUDY GUIDE

Takeaway 17.1
How Does Globalization Affect International Business?

Terms to Define

APEC

EU

Exporting

Foreign subsidiary

Franchising

Global economy

Global sourcing

Global strategic alliance

Globalization

Greenfield venture

Importing

Insourcing

International business

Joint venture

Licensing

Most favored nation status

NAFTA

Nontariff barriers

Outsourcing

Protectionism

Reshoring

SADC

Tariffs

World Trade Organization (WTO)

Rapid Review

- The forces of globalization create international business opportunities to pursue profits, customers, capital, and low-cost suppliers and labor in different countries.
- The least costly ways of doing business internationally are to use global sourcing, exporting and importing, and licensing and franchising.
- Direct investment strategies to establish joint ventures or wholly owned subsidiaries in foreign countries represent substantial commitments to international operations.
- Environmental differences, particularly in legal and political systems, can complicate international business activities.
- The World Trade Organization (WTO) is a global institution established to promote free trade and open markets around the world.
- Regional economic alliances link member nations for cooperation in economic and trade development.

Questions for Discussion

1. Why would a government want to prohibit a foreign firm from owning more than 49% of a local joint venture?
2. Are joint ventures worth the risk of being taken advantage of by foreign partners, as with GM's "Chery" case in China?
3. What aspects of the U.S. legal environment might prove complicated for a Russian firm starting new operations in the United States?

Be Sure You Can

- explain how globalization affects our lives
- list five reasons that companies pursue international business opportunities
- describe and give examples of how firms do international business by global sourcing, exporting/importing, franchising/licensing, joint ventures, and foreign subsidiaries
- discuss how differences in legal environments can affect businesses operating internationally
- explain the purpose of the World Trade Organization

Career Situation: What Would You Do?

Your new design for a revolutionary golf putter has turned out to be a big hit with friends and players on the local golf courses. So, you decide to have some made, start selling them, and see if you can make a business out it. A friend says: "Go to China, someone there will build it cheap and to your quality standard." But you're not sure. Sending your design to China for manufacturing is worrisome, and there's a side of you that would really like to have "Made in America" stamped on the clubs. Make a list of positives and negatives of manufacturing in each place. What factors are likely to drive your final decision on global versus local sourcing?

Takeaway 17.2
What Are Global Corporations, and How Do They Work?

ANSWERS TO COME

- Global corporations or MNCs do substantial business in many countries.
- The actions of global corporations can be controversial at home and abroad.
- Managers of global corporations face a variety of ethical challenges.
- Planning and controlling are complicated in global corporations.
- Organizing can be difficult in global corporations.
- Leading is challenging in global corporations.
- Technology is a global game changer.

TEACHING NOTE: Call for a debate on the "globalization gap." Have one set of students come up with arguments why global firms are mostly at fault for any such gap. Have another set come up with arguments why blame can't be placed on global firms alone. Ask both sides for proposals for how the gap might be reduced.

IF YOU TRAVEL ABROAD THESE DAYS, MANY OF YOUR FAVORITE BRANDS AND products will travel with you. You can have a McDonald's sandwich in over 100 countries, enjoy Häagen-Dazs ice cream in 50, and brush up with Procter & Gamble's Crest in 180. Economists even use the "Big Mac" index to track purchasing power parity among the world's currencies. A recent index listed $4.37 in the U.S., $2.57 in China, and $4.88 in the Euro area.[20]

⫶ Global corporations or MNCs do substantial business in many countries.

A **global corporation** or **multinational corporation (MNC)** has extensive international operations in many foreign countries and derives a substantial portion of its sales and profits from international sources.[21] The world's largest MNCs are identified in annual listings such as *Fortune* magazine's Global 500 and the *Financial Times'* FT Global 500. They include names very familiar to consumers, such as Wal-Mart, BP, Toyota, Nestlé, BMW, Hitachi, Caterpillar, Sony, and Samsung. Also on the list are some you might not recognize such as big oil and gas producers like PetroChina (China), Gazprom (Russia), Total (France), and Petrobas (Brazil).[22]

Top managers of some multinationals are trying to move their firms toward becoming **transnational corporations**. That is, they would like to operate worldwide without being identified with one national home.[23] When you buy Nestlé's products, for example, do you have any idea that it is a registered Swiss company? The firm's executives view the entire world as their domain for acquiring resources, locating production facilities, marketing goods and services, and establishing brand image. They seek total integration of global operations, try to make major decisions from a global perspective, and have top managers from many different countries.

Most MNCs still retain strong national identifications even while operating around the world. Is there any doubt in your mind that Wal-Mart and HP are "American" firms, whereas Nissan and Sony are "Japanese"? Most likely not, but that may not be the way their executives would like the firms viewed. And by the way, which company is really more American—the Indian giant Tata Group,

A **global corporation** or **multinational corporation (MNC)** has extensive international business dealings in many foreign countries.

A **transnational corporation** is an MNC that operates worldwide on a borderless basis.

which gets more than 50% of its revenues from North America, or IBM, which gets 65% of its revenues outside the United States?[24]

||| The actions of global corporations can be controversial at home and abroad.

What difference does a company's nationality really make? Does it matter to an American whether local jobs come from a domestic giant such as Verizon or a foreign one such as Honda?[25] What about the power global firms wield in the world economy? Is this a problem? The United Nations reports that multinationals hold one-third of the world's productive assets and control 70% of world trade. Revenues of Exxon/Mobil, for example, are equivalent to Egypt's GDP; Finland's budget is 20% less than the annual sales of its large multinational Nokia.[26] And how about what some call the **globalization gap**? This is where large multinationals gain disproportionately from the forces of globalization, versus smaller firms and many countries that do not.[27]

The **globalization gap** is where large global firms gain disproportionately from the global economy versus smaller firms.

Global corporations and the countries that host their foreign operations should all benefit. But as **Figure 17.2** shows, things can go both right and wrong in MNC–host country relationships. Although the economic power of global firms is undoubtedly good for business leaders and investors, it can be threatening to small and less-developed countries and their domestic industries.

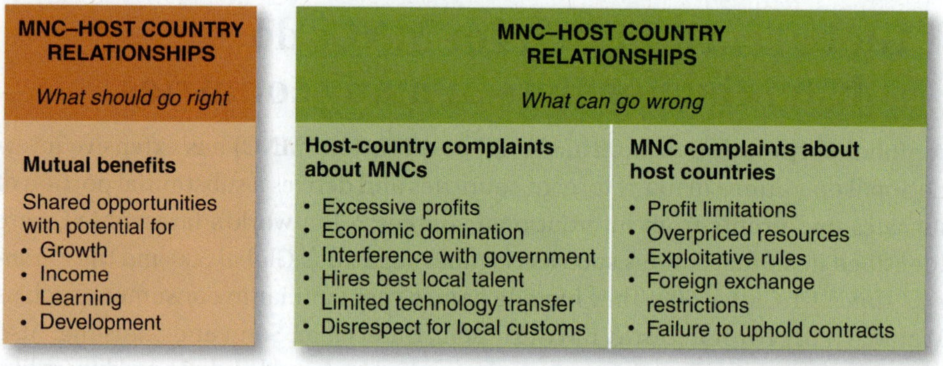

FIGURE 17.2

What Can Go Right and Wrong in Relationships Between Global Corporations and Their Host Countries? When things go right, both the global corporation, or MNC, and its host country gain. The global firm gets profits or resources, and the host country often sees more jobs and employment opportunities, higher tax revenues, and useful technology transfers. But when things go wrong, each finds ways to blame the other.

MNC–HOST COUNTRY RELATIONSHIPS *What should go right*
Mutual benefits
Shared opportunities with potential for • Growth • Income • Learning • Development

MNC–HOST COUNTRY RELATIONSHIPS *What can go wrong*	
Host-country complaints about MNCs	**MNC complaints about host countries**
• Excessive profits • Economic domination • Interference with government • Hires best local talent • Limited technology transfer • Disrespect for local customs	• Profit limitations • Overpriced resources • Exploitative rules • Foreign exchange restrictions • Failure to uphold contracts

MNCs may complain that a host country bars it from taking profits out of the country, overprices local resources, and imposes restrictive government rules. Host countries may accuse that an MNC hires the best local talent, fails to respect local customs, makes too much profit, and doesn't transfer really useful technology.[28] Another complaint is that MNCs use unfair practices, such as below-cost pricing, to drive local competitors out of business. This is one of the arguments in favor of *protectionism*, discussed earlier as the use of laws and practices to protect a country's domestic businesses from foreign competitors.

MNCs can also run into difficulties in their home or headquarter countries. If a multinational cuts local jobs and then moves or outsources the work to another country, local government and community leaders will quickly criticize the firm for its lack of social responsibility. After all, they will say, shouldn't you be creating local jobs and building the local economy? Perhaps you might agree with this view. But can you see why business executives might disagree?

‖ Managers of global corporations face a variety of ethical challenges.

"Avon Products Says It Fired Four Executives Over Bribes" . . . "Mexico starts Investigation in Wal-Mart Bribery Case."[29] The ethical aspects of international business are often in the news, and sometimes the report involves outright **corruption**. This occurs when employees or representatives of MNCs resort to illegal practices such as bribes to further their business interests in foreign countries. The **Foreign Corrupt Practices Act** (FCPA) makes it illegal for U.S. firms and their representatives to engage in corrupt practices overseas. This prohibits them from paying or offering bribes or excessive commissions, including nonmonetary gifts, to foreign officials or employees of state-run companies in return for business favors.[30]

Critics of the FCPA claim that it fails to recognize the realities of business as practiced in many foreign nations. They believe it puts U.S. companies at a competitive disadvantage because they can't offer the same "deals" as businesses from other nations—deals that the locals may regard as standard business practices. And, to some at least, the issues aren't always clear cut. An American executive, for example, says that payoffs are needed to get shipments through customs in Russia even though all legal taxes and tariffs are already paid. "We use customs brokers," he says, "and they build bribes into the invoice."[31] What do you think? Should U.S. legal standards apply to American companies operating abroad? Or should they be allowed to do whatever is locally acceptable?

We noted earlier that even the most well-intentioned MNCs can end up in troublesome relationships with global suppliers. One risk is that the local firms are **sweatshops**, places in which employees work at low wages for long hours and in poor, even unsafe, conditions. A notorious example was the collapse of a building in Bangladesh that housed outsourcing suppliers to global clothing retailers. The tragedy killed over 1100 people and exposed unsafe buildings and sweatshop conditions in factories throughout the country. The local garment industry runs on workers, often female and illiterate, trying to shed lives of poverty. One says her workplace has blocked elevators, filthy tap water, and unclean overflowing toilets.[32] The nonprofit Institute for Global Labour and Human Rights is dedicated to exposing sweatshops as part of its mission "to promote and defend human, women's and workers' rights in the global economy."[33]

Another global business risk is working with contractors who use **child labor**, the full-time employment of children for work otherwise done by adults.[34] And, the facts are startling: 215 million child laborers worldwide and 115 million of them work in hazardous conditions.[35] As you might guess, factories employing children might be in a good position to offer low prices to foreign companies buying their products. Even if the practice is legal by local standards, does this justify doing business with such a place? One Apple audit discovered that three of its foreign contractors had used underage workers.[36] Steve Dowling, an Apple spokesperson, says the firm regularly audits suppliers "to make sure they comply with Apple's

Corruption involves illegal practices to further one's business interests.

The **Foreign Corrupt Practices Act** makes it illegal for U.S. firms and their representatives to engage in corrupt practices overseas.

Sweatshops employ workers at very low wages, for long hours, and in poor working conditions.

Des Willie/Alamy

Child labor is the full-time employment of children for work otherwise done by adults.

Daniel Laflor/iStockphoto

{ **TRANSPARENCY INTERNATIONAL SEEKS A WORLD FREE OF CORRUPTION AND BRIBES.**

Facts to **Consider**

■ Corruption and Bribes Haunt Global Business

If you want a world free of corruption and bribes, you have a lot in common with the nonprofit activist organization Transparency International. Its mission is to "create change for a world free of corruption." The organization publishes regular surveys and reports on corruption and bribery around the world. Here are some recent data.

Corruption: Best and worst out of 178 countries in perceived public sector corruption. (Note: & = ties)

Best—Denmark, Finland, & New Zealand (#1), Sweden (#4), Singapore, (#5)

Worst—Afghanistan, North Korea, Somalia (# 174), Sudan (#173), Myanmar (#172)

In-Betweens—United States (#19), Costa Rica (#48), Italy (#72), India (#94), Vietnam (#123)

Bribery: Best and worst of 20 countries in likelihood of home-country firms' willingness to pay bribes abroad.

Best—Netherlands & Switzerland (#1), Belgium (#3), Germany & Japan (#4)

Worst—Russia (#28), China (#27), Mexico (#26), Indonesia (#25)

In Betweens—Canada (#6), United States (#10), Brazil (#14), Turkey (#19)

YOUR THOUGHTS?

What patterns do you detect in these data, if any? Does it surprise you that the United States didn't make the "best" lists? How would you differentiate between the terms "corruption" and "bribery" as they apply in international business?

---

strict standards" and that the firm also conducts "extensive training programs to educate workers about their right to a safe and respectful work environment."

||| Planning and controlling are complicated in global corporations.

Setting goals, making plans, controlling results—all of these standard management functions can become quite complicated in the international arena. Picture a home office somewhere in the United States, say, Chicago, and foreign operations scattered in Asia, Africa, South America, and Europe. Planning and controlling must somehow span all locations, meeting both home office needs and those of foreign affiliates.

One planning issue in international business is **currency risk**, or profit loss due to fluctuations in foreign exchange rates. Companies such as McDonald's and HP, for example, make a lot of sales abroad. These sales are in foreign currencies. But as exchange rates vary, the dollar value of sales revenues goes up and down and profits are affected. Companies have to plan for the potential positive and negative impacts of exchange rate fluctuations on their profits.

When the dollar is weak against the euro, it takes more dollars to buy one euro. This is bad for American consumers, who must pay more to buy European products. But it's good for European consumers, who pay less for American ones. A weak dollar is also good for American companies who make lots of sales in euros and then get more when exchanging them for dollars. But suppose the dollar

Currency risk is possible profit loss because of fluctuating exchange rates.

Scenario 1: Weak dollar

1 $US = 0.75 euro

Euro sales = €100,000

U.S. take-home revenue = $133,000

Scenario 2: Strong dollar

1 $US = 1.25 euros

Euro sales = €100,000

U.S. take-home revenue = $80,000

strengthens against the euro? Is this good or bad for firms with large sales in euro-zone countries? The boxed example shows that it's bad.

Global businesses must also deal with **political risk**, potential losses because of instability and political changes in foreign countries. The major threats of political risk today come from terrorism, civil wars, armed conflicts, shifting government systems through elections or forced takeovers, and new laws and economic policies. An example is the surprise nationalization of Bolivia's oil and gas industries as described in the earlier ethics check. Although such things can't be prevented, they can be anticipated to some extent by a planning technique called **political-risk analysis**. It tries to forecast the probability of disruptive events that can threaten the security of a foreign investment. Given the world we now live in, can you see the high stakes of such analysis?

Political risk is possible loss because of instability and political changes in foreign countries.

Political-risk analysis forecasts how political events may have an impact on foreign investments.

‖ Organizing can be difficult in global corporations.

Even after plans are in place, it isn't easy to organize for international operations. In the early stages of international activities, businesses often appoint someone or a specific unit to handle them. But as global business expands, a more complex arrangement is usually necessary.

One possible choice for organizing an MNC is the *global area structure* shown in **Figure 17.3**. It arranges production and sales functions into separate geographical units and puts top managers in charge—such as Area Manager Africa or Area Manager Europe. This allows business in major areas of the world to be run by executives with special local expertise.

Another organizing option is the *global product structure*, also shown in the figure. It gives worldwide responsibilities to product group managers who are assisted by area specialists who work as part of the corporate staff. These specialists provide expert guidance on the cultures, markets, and unique conditions of various countries or regions.

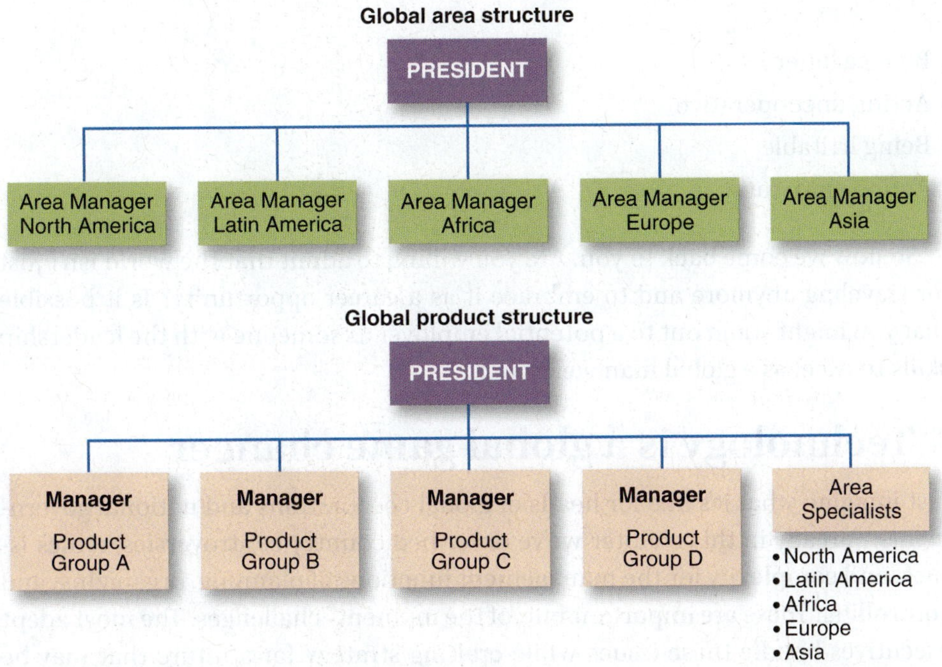

Global area structure

Global product structure

FIGURE 17.3
How Can Multinational Corporations Organize for Success in Their Global Operations?
When the international side of a business grows, the structure often gets complicated. One approach is a global area structure, which assigns senior managers to oversee all product operations in major parts of the world. Another is the global product structure, in which area specialists advise other senior managers on business practices in their parts of the world.

⫴ Leading is challenging in global corporations.

As executives in businesses and other types of organizations press forward with global initiatives, the challenges of leading diverse workforces and dealing with customers across national and cultural borders have to be mastered. Globalization and the growth of international businesses are creating needs for more **global managers**, ones aware of international developments and competent in working across cultures.[37] The *Wall Street Journal* says that global companies need managers who "understand different countries and cultures" and "intuitively understand the markets they are trying to penetrate."[38]

A truly global manager is always inquisitive and informed of international events and complexity in our ever-changing world, such as those featured throughout this book.[39] A truly global manager is also culturally sensitive and aware. And, a truly global manager is highly skilled in leadership competencies that travel well across cultural boundaries.

Some evidence-based findings on global leadership skills are shown in the following lists.[40] It turns out that universal facilitators of leadership success are things like being trustworthy, informed, communicative, and inspiring. Regardless of where they live and work, people tend to like leaders who give them confidence and are good with teamwork. But things like being a loner and acting irritable, uncooperative, and autocratic are viewed negatively across cultures. They are universal inhibitors of leadership success.

A **global manager** is culturally aware and informed on international affairs.

Universal *Facilitators* of Leadership Success ⟫

- Acting trustworthy, just, honest
- Showing foresight, planning
- Being positive, dynamic, motivating
- Inspiring confidence
- Being informed and communicative
- Being a coordinator and team builder

Universal *Inhibitors* of Leadership Success ⟫

- Being a loner
- Acting uncooperative
- Being irritable
- Acting autocratic

So now we come back to you. Are you willing to admit that the world isn't just for traveling anymore and to embrace it as a career opportunity? Is it possible that you might stand out to a potential employer as someone with the leadership skills to excel as a global manager?

⫴ Technology is a global game changer.

Just imagine what it's like for heads of global corporations and national governments. Already in this chapter we've described country controversies, ethics issues, and complexity for the management functions of planning, organizing, and controlling. These are important but "of the moment" challenges. The most adept executives handle these issues while crafting strategy for a future that may be

Manager's **Library**

"THERE IS A CANYON DIVIDING PEOPLE WHO UNDERSTAND TECHNOLOGY AND PEOPLE CHARGED WITH ADDRESSING THE WORLD'S TOUGHEST GEOPOLITICAL ISSUES. . . ."

When the executive chairman of Google, Eric Schmidt, visits North Korea and Myanmar, you know something has to be up. Were the visits business or diplomacy? A combination is the best answer. And if you read *The New Digital Age: Reshaping the Future of People, Nations and Business* (Knopf, 2013) by Schmidt and foreign relations expert Jared Cohen, you'll understand why.

The book challenges all of us, but especially business and government leaders, to get on top of the "new digital age" of intense global connectivity driven by an ever-developing Internet. Right now, say the authors: "There is a canyon dividing people who understand technology and people charged with addressing the world's toughest geopolitical issues, and no one has built a bridge." In other words, leaders aren't keeping up with what the rest of us are finding out about the utility of changing technology. Schmidt and Cohen believe it's in everyone's best interests to close this divide.

War and conflict—physical and in cyberspace, citizen journalists, high-tech gadgets and lifestyle apps, science and health, big data, digital manufacturing, and more are all at issues in a book that claims "technology is natural, people aren't." The authors point toward extreme planning challenges the new digital age poses for executives trying to do business around the world and for those who run or even try to conquer nations. "Authoritarian governments will find their newly connected populations more difficult to control, repress and influence," say Schmidt and Cohen, "while democratic states will be forced to include many more voices (individuals, organizations and companies), in their affairs."

REFLECT AND REACT

How is technological change affecting global firms like IBM, Nike, Samsung, and others? What do executives in multinationals have to gain and fear as technology keeps evolving? When the authors say "technology is neutral, but people aren't," what are the implications for you, for your organizations, and for your government? And when it comes to the "new digital age," can politicians afford not to listen to what business executives have to say?

---

very different from the present. One of the most important considerations in this regard is technology and the implications of where it's headed.

We tend to think of global business technology in communication terms—ease of linking a firm's customers with overseas call centers, ease of staying in touch with global supply chains, or risk of losing privileged information and intellectual property through security breaches and outright theft. All such things are important. But there's another, emerging side to technology that has important ramifications for global firms—the growth of digital manufacturing.

Companies like General Electric are building factories that run with lots of technology and a few highly skilled people. Entrepreneurs use similar technologies to start small firms that spin out customized products on demand and at low cost. The *Wall Street Journal* calls it a "new industrial revolution" that might fuel a resurgence of "Made in America" labels.[41]

The huge global outsourcer Nike, for example, has eliminated substantial waste and labor costs by making its Flyknit shoe with new digital manufacturing technology. A project consultant says: "It's a hugely significant advance, not the least because, once you start doing things this way it obviously takes a lot of the labor cost out of the equation."[42] In other words, if Nike and others can build something quickly and efficiently using new technology at home, why take the risks of going abroad to find cheap labor?

STUDY GUIDE

Takeaway 17.2
What Are Global Corporations, and How Do They Work?

Terms to Define

Child labor

Corruption

Currency risk

Foreign Corrupt Practices Act

Global corporation or multinational corporation (MNC)

Global manager

Globalization gap

Political risk

Political risk analysis

Sweatshop

Transnational corporation

Rapid Review

- A global business or multinational corporation (MNC) has extensive operations in several foreign countries; a transnational corporation attempts to operate without national identity and with a worldwide strategy.
- Global firms benefit host countries by paying taxes, bringing in new technologies, and creating employment opportunities; they can also harm host countries by interfering with local government and politics, extracting excessive profits, and dominating the local economy.
- The Foreign Corrupt Practices Act prohibits representatives of U.S. international businesses from engaging in corrupt practices abroad.
- Planning and controlling global operations must take into account such things as currency risk and political risk in changing environmental conditions.
- Organizing for global operations often involves use of a global product structure or a global area structure.
- Leading global operations requires universal leadership skills and global managers who are capable of working in different cultures and countries.

Questions for Discussion

1. Should becoming a transnational corporation be the goal of all MNCs?
2. Is there anything that global firms and host governments can do to avoid conflicts and bad feelings with one another?
3. Are laws such as the Foreign Corrupt Practices Act unfair to American companies trying to compete around the world?

Be Sure You Can

- differentiate a multinational corporation from a transnational corporation
- list common host-country complaints and three home-country complaints about MNC operations
- explain the international business challenges of corruption, sweatshops, and child labor
- discuss the implications of political risk for global businesses
- differentiate the global area structure and global product structure
- list possible competencies of global managers

Career Situation: What Would You Do?

You've just read in the newspaper that one of your favorite brands of sports shoes is being investigated for being made in sweatshop conditions at factories in Asia. It really disturbs you, but the shoes are great. A student group on campus has a campaign to boycott the brand. Will you join the boycott, or not, and why? How effective are such consumer threats? Is it still too easy for global firms to get away with bad behaviors? If so, what can and should be done about it?

TestPrep 17

Answers to TestPrep questions can be found at the back of the book.

Multiple-Choice Questions

1. In addition to gaining new markets, businesses often go international in the search for _____.
   (a) political risk
   (b) protectionism
   (c) lower labor costs
   (d) most favored nation status

2. When boot-maker Rocky Brands bought 70% ownership of a manufacturing company in the Dominican Republic, Rocky was engaging in which form of international business?
   (a) Import/export
   (b) Licensing
   (c) Foreign subsidiary
   (d) Joint venture

3. When Limited Brands buys cotton in Egypt and has tops sewn from it in Sri Lanka according to designs made in Italy and then sells the tops at Victoria's Secret stores in the United States, this is a form of international business known as _____.
   (a) licensing
   (b) importing
   (c) joint venturing
   (d) global sourcing

4. When foreign investment creates new jobs in the U.S., this is a form of _____ that is welcomed by the local economy.
   (a) globalization
   (b) insourcing
   (c) joint venturing
   (d) licensing

5. When a Hong Kong firm makes an agreement with the Walt Disney Company to use the Disney logo and legally make jewelry in the shape of Disney cartoon characters, Disney is engaging in a form of international business known as _____.
   (a) exporting
   (b) licensing
   (c) joint venturing
   (d) franchising

6. One major difference between an international business and a transnational corporation is that the transnational tries to operate _____.
   (a) without a strong national identity
   (b) in at least six foreign countries
   (c) with only domestic managers at the top
   (d) without corruption

7. The Foreign Corrupt Practices Act makes it illegal for _____.
   (a) U.S. businesses to work with subcontractors running foreign sweatshop operations
   (b) foreign businesses to pay bribes to U.S. government officials
   (c) U.S. businesses to make "payoffs" abroad to gain international business contracts
   (d) foreign businesses to steal intellectual property from U.S. firms operating in their countries

8. The World Trade Organization, or WTO, would most likely become involved in disputes between countries over _____.
   (a) exchange rates
   (b) ethnocentrism
   (c) nationalisation
   (d) tariffs and protectionism

9. The athletic footwear maker New Balance discovered that exact copies of its running shoe designs were on sale in China under the name "New Barlun." This is an example of a/an _____ problem in international business.
   (a) most favored nation
   (b) global strategic alliance
   (c) joint venture
   (d) intellectual property rights

10. When the profits of large international businesses are disproportionately high relative to those of smaller firms and even the economies of some countries, this is called _____.
    (a) return on risk for business investment
    (b) the globalization gap
    (c) protectionism
    (d) most favored nations status

11. If a government seizes all foreign assets of global firms operating in the country, the loss to foreign firms is considered a _____ risk of international business.
    (a) franchise
    (b) political
    (c) currency
    (d) corruption

12. Who gains most when the dollar weakens versus a foreign currency such as the Brazilian real?
    (a) American consumers of Brazilian products
    (b) Brazilian firms selling products in Europe
    (c) American firms selling products in Brazil
    (d) Brazilian consumers of European products

13. Which of the following is identified by researchers as a universal inhibitor of leadership success across cultures?
    (a) Inspiring confidence
    (b) Acting autocratic
    (c) Being a good planner
    (d) Acting trustworthy

14. If an international business firm has separate vice presidents in charge of its Asian, African, and European divisions, it is most likely using a global _____ structure.
    (a) product   (b) functional
    (c) area   (d) matrix

15. Which is the best definition of a truly "global manager?"
    (a) A manager who is competent working across cultures
    (b) A manager who travels internationally on business at least once a year
    (c) A manager who lives and works in a foreign country
    (d) A manager who is employed by a transnational corporation

Short-Response Questions

16. What is the difference between a joint venture and a wholly owned subsidiary?

17. List three reasons why host countries sometimes complain about MNCs.

18. What does it mean in an international business sense if a U.S. senator says she favors "protectionism"?

19. What is the difference between currency risk and political risk in international business?

Integration and Application Question

20. Picture yourself sitting in a discussion group at the local bookstore and proudly signing copies of your newly published book, *Business Transitions in the New Global Economy*. A book buyer invites a comment from you by stating: "I am interested in your point regarding the emergence of transnational corporations. But, try as I might, a company like Ford or Procter & Gamble will always be 'as American as Apple pie' for me."

    Questions: How would you respond in a way that both (a) clarifies the difference between a multinational and a transnational corporation, and (b) explains reasons why Ford or P&G may wish not to operate as or be viewed as "American" companies?

Steps*for* FurtherLearning

BUILD

MARKETABLE SKILLS.
EARN BIG CAREER PAYOFFS!

Don't miss these opportunities in the **Skill-Building Portfolio**

■ **SELF-ASSESSMENT 17:**
Global Intelligence

The world's a complex place . . . are you really up to date?

■ **CLASS EXERCISE 17:**
American Football

Cultures are different . . . let sports open your window to the view.

■ **TEAM PROJECT 17:**
Globalization Pros and Cons

Coins have two sides . . . getting a handle on globalization may be harder than you think.

Many learning resources are found at the end of the book and online within WileyPLUS.

Take advantage of **Cases for Critical Thinking**

■ **CHAPTER 17 CASE SNAPSHOT:**
Harley-Davidson—Style and Strategy with a Global Reach/
Sidebar on NOT Made in China

Harley-Davidson is an American success story. It was started in 1903 when two friends since boyhood, William Harley and Arthur Davidson, decided to design a motorized bicycle in a machine shop in Milwaukee, Wisconsin. The Harley-Davidson brand was born when the prototype bike was used to compete in a 1904 motorcycle race. Harley now designs, manufactures, and sells heavyweight motorcycles in the United States, Canada, Europe, and Asia. After facing a near-death experience from global competition some years ago, the firm has roared back to reap profits and position itself for strong global growth.

DO

A CASE ANALYSIS.
STRENGTHEN YOUR CRITICAL THINKING!

Dig into this **Hot Topic**

■ **GOOD IDEA OR NOT? Avoid China problems by reshoring our manufacturing**

If you were a manufacturer in days past you went to China, at least as a first stop on your global scouting trip. But things have changed a bit. A San Diego-based CEO says: "Now people are trying to come back."

Why so?

LightSaver Technologies tried for two years to get things done in China. Now its work is back in California. CEO Jerry Anderson says China lost its allure: "It's probably 30 percent cheaper to manufacture in China. But factor in shipping and all the other B.S. that you have to endure."

GET

AND STAY INFORMED.
MAKE YOURSELF VALUABLE!

Transportation costs and time are up for goods moved from China to the U.S. and other world markets. Labor costs are up; rising about 20% a year. Business risks in China, if not up, are at least more visible. Theft of intellectual property is a problem. One small manufacturer says: "They're infamous over there for knocking [products] off." Poor labor standards and work practices are a problem. Just ask Apple CEO Tim Cook about negative publicity over its use of China-based manufacturing.

Final Take   What's a manufacturing executive to do? The *Economist* says China "is still a manufacturing power." With super-efficient plants and supply chains it remains a bargain in labor costs. So, are you on the reshoring side or the offshoring side of the issue? What facts are available to support or deny your position? Think of things from a consumer's perspective. If you can buy a child's toy made in China for $8.00, will you be willing to pay $12.00 so that it could be labeled "Made in America"? Should more of America's businesses, large and small, say "Not worth the trouble!" when Chinese manufacturers come calling with offers?

Nick D'Aloisio—17 years old . . . writes Summly app while in high school . . . puts $30 million in the bank. He says: "My parents at first were a bit concerned . . . . You shouldn't be keeping these hours."

Matt Dunham/AP Photo

Entrepreneurship and Small Business

18

Taking Risks Can Make Dreams Come True

Photofest

Management Live

Risk Taking and *The Bourne Ultimatum*

In *The Bourne Ultimatum*, FBI chief Pamela Landy (Joan Allen) is trying to track down someone who leaked highly classified intelligence information to a British newspaper reporter. The reporter is dead and was last seen with rogue CIA operative Jason Bourne (Matt Damon). Bourne is a highly trained killer who is looking for Neil Daniels (Colin Stinton), the individual responsible for the leak.

Landy's team makes contact with Daniels's assistant, Nicky Parsons (Julia Stiles), while Bourne is in the office. In a play to put Bourne at ease, Landy reveals to Parsons that the CIA is looking for him but that she doesn't believe he has anything to do with the leak. She has taken a gamble that Bourne will trust her and make contact. Does the gamble pay off? That's the ultimate question for anyone who's just taken a risk.

Successful entrepreneurs have a tendency toward **risk taking**, but this does not mean they charge blindly into situations. They're not gamblers. They take calculated risks using information and experience to guide them. But taking risks does mean there is always a chance for failure. The true mark of an accomplished entrepreneur is the ability to learn from mistakes and continue trying.

Your career will have its share of risks. Think about the many complexities of the present job environment and your plans for career success. Could your ability to deal with risk be a personal strength and competency?

YOUR CHAPTER 18 TAKEAWAYS

1. Understand the nature of entrepreneurship and entrepreneurs.
2. Discuss small business and how to start one.

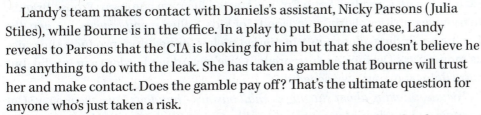

WHAT'S INSIDE

Explore Yourself
More on **risk taking**

Role Models
Grad school start-up takes on global competitors

Ethics Check
Entrepreneurship and social good

Facts to Consider
Minority entrepreneurs are on the move

Manager's Library
In-N-Out Burger: A Behind the Counter Look at the Fast-food Chain that Breaks all the Rules by Stacy Perman

Takeaway 18.1

What Is Entrepreneurship, and Who Are Entrepreneurs?

ANSWERS TO COME

- Entrepreneurs are risk takers who spot and pursue opportunities.
- Entrepreneurs often share similar backgrounds and experiences.
- Entrepreneurs often share similar personality traits.
- Women and minority entrepreneurs are growing in numbers.
- Social entrepreneurs seek novel solutions to pressing social problems.

JUST OUT OF THE MILITARY AND GETTING RESTARTED? WHY NOT CREATE YOUR own job? John Raftery did. After a four-year tour with the Marines—including two on deployment—he earned an accounting degree with help from the G I Bill. But after being disappointed with slow advancement at an accounting firm, he answered an e-mail about a free Entrepreneurship Bootcamp for Veterans with Disabilities at Syracuse Unversity. Raftery went and ended up with a business plan to start his own firm, Patriot Contractors, in Waxahachie, Texas.[1]

Struggling with work-life balance as a mother? An interest like child nutrition can become a business proposition. It was for Denise Devine. A former financial executive with Campbell Soup Co., she started her own company, Froose Brands, to provide nutritional drinks and foods for kids. Called *mompreneurs,* women like Devine are finding opportunity in market niches for healthier products they spot as moms. Says Devine: "As entrepreneurs we're working harder than we did, but we're doing it on our own schedules."

Female, thinking about starting a small business, but don't have the money? Get creative and reach out to organizations like Count-Me-In. Started by co-founders Nell Merlino and Iris Burnett, it provides microcredit loans from $500 to $10,000 to help women start and expand small businesses. Things such as a divorce, time off to raise a family, or age aren't held against applicants, contrary to practices by some conventional lenders. Merlino says: "Women own 38% of all businesses in this country, but still have far less access to capital than men because of today's process."[2]

Retired, feeling a bit old, and want to do more? Not to worry. People aged 55–64 are the most entrepreneurially active in the United States. Realizing that he needed "someplace to go and something to do" after retirement, Art Koff, now 74, started RetiredBrains.com. It's a job board for retirees and gets thousands of hits a day. It also employs seven people and keeps Koff as busy as he wants to be.

These examples should be inspiring. Each shows a personal quality that is much valued in today's challenging economic times—**entrepreneurship.** Think of it as risk taking to achieve business success. People like John Raftery, Nell Merlino and Iris Burnett, Denise Devine, and Art Koff acted on their ideas to create something new for society. They are **entrepreneurs,** persons who are willing to take risks to pursue opportunities that others either fail to recognize or view as problems or threats.

Entrepreneurship is risk-taking behavior in pursuit of business success.

An **entrepreneur** is willing to pursue opportunities in situations that others view as problems or threats.

⫼ Entrepreneurs are risk takers who spot and pursue opportunities.

H. Wayne Huizenga, former owner of AutoNation, Blockbuster Video, and the Miami Dolphins, and a member of the Entrepreneurs' Hall of Fame, describes being an entrepreneur this way: "An important part of being an entrepreneur is a gut instinct that allows you to believe in your heart that something will work even though everyone else says it will not." You say, "I am going to make sure it works. I am going to go out there and make it happen."[3]

A **classic entrepreneur** is a risk-taking individual who takes action to pursue opportunities others fail to recognize, or even view as problems or threats. Some people become **serial entrepreneurs** that start and run new ventures over and over again, moving from one interest and opportunity to the next. We find such entrepreneurs both in business and nonprofit settings.

On the business side, serial entrepreneur H. Wayne Huizenga made his fortune founding and selling companies like Blockbuster Entertainment, Waste Management, and AutoNation. A member of the Entrepreneurs' Hall of Fame, he describes being an entrepreneur this way: "We're looking for something where we can make something happen: an industry where the competition is asleep, hasn't taken advantage. The point is, we're going to be busy."[4]

On the nonprofit side, classic entrepreneur Scott Beale quit his job with the U.S. State Department to start Atlas Corps, something he calls a "Peace Corps in reverse." The organization brings nonprofit managers from developing countries to the United States to work with local nonprofits while improving their management skills. After a year they return home. "I am just like a business entrepreneur," Beale says, "but instead of making a big paycheck I try to make a big impact."[5]

A common pattern among successful entrepreneurs is **first-mover advantage**. They move quickly to spot, exploit, and deliver a product or service to a new market or an unrecognized niche in an existing one. Consider the following brief examples of entrepreneurs who built successful long-term businesses from good ideas and hard work.[6] As you read about these creative and confident individuals, think about how you might apply their experiences to your own life and career. After all, it might be nice to be your own boss someday.

Caterina Fake

From idea to buyout it only took 16 months. That's quite a benchmark for would-be Internet entrepreneurs. Welcome to the world of Flickr, co-founded by Caterina Fake. Flickr took the notion of online photo sharing and turned it into an almost viral Internet phenomenon. Start-up capital came from families, friends, and angel investors. The payoff came when Yahoo! bought them out for $30 million. Fake then started Hunch.com, a Web site designed to help people make decisions (e.g., Should I buy that Porsche?). She sold it to eBay for $80 million. She says: "You pick a big, ambitious problem, and look for great people to solve it."

Peter Foley/Bloomberg/GettyImages

A **classic entrepreneur** is someone willing to pursue opportunities in situations others view as problems or threats.

A **serial entrepreneur** starts and runs businesses and nonprofits over and over again, moving from one interest and opportunity to the next.

A **first-mover advantage** comes from being first to exploit a niche or enter a market.

Earl Graves

With a vision and a $175,000 loan, Earl G. Graves Sr. started *Black Enterprise* magazine in 1970. That success grew into the diversified business information company Earl G. Graves Ltd.—a multimedia company covering television, radio, and digital media including BlackEnterprise. com. Among his many accomplishments— named by *Fortune* magazine as one of the 50 most powerful and influential African Americans in corporate America, recipient of the Lifetime Achievement Award from the National Association of Black Journalists, and selection for

Louis Johnny/SIPA/NewsCom

the Junior Achievement Worldwide U.S. Business Hall of Fame. He has written a best-selling book, *How to Succeed in Business Without Being White,* and is a member of many business and nonprofit boards. The business school at his college alma mater, Baltimore's Morgan State University, is named after him. Graves says: "I feel that a large part of my role as publisher of *Black Enterprise* is to be a catalyst for black economic development in this country."

Anita Roddick

In 1973, Anita Roddick was a 33-year-old housewife looking for a way to support herself and her two children. She spotted a niche for natural-based skin and health care products and started mixing and selling them from a small shop in Brighton, England. The Body Shop PLC has grown to some 1,500 outlets in 47 countries with 24 languages, selling a product every half-second

NewsCom

to one of its 86 million customers. Known for her commitment to human rights, the environment, and economic development, the late Roddick believed in business social responsibility, saying: "If you think you're too small to have an impact, try going to bed with a mosquito."

Shawn Corey Carter

You probably know him as Jay Z, and there's an entrepreneurial story behind the name. Carter began rapping on the streets of Brooklyn, where he lived with his single mom and three brothers. Hip-hop turned into his ticket to travel. "When I left the block," he told an interviewer, "everyone was saying I was crazy, I was doing well for myself on the streets, and cats

Andrew Milligan/PA Photos/Landov

around me were like, these rappers . . . just record, tour, and get separated from their families, while some white person takes all their money. I was determined to do it differently." He sure did. Carter used his music millions to found the media firm Roc Nation, co-found the apparel firm Rocawear, and become part owner of the New Jersey Nets.

||| Entrepreneurs often share similar backgrounds and experiences.

Is there something in your experience that could be a pathway to business or nonprofit entrepreneurship? As you ponder this question, don't be dissuaded by the common misconceptions in Table 18.1, Debunking Common Myths about Entrepreneurs.[7] There are real people behind all acts of entrepreneurship, and you could quite possibly become one of them.

With the myths out of the way, researchers tell us that most entrepreneurs are self-confident, determined, self-directing, resilient, adaptable, and driven by excellence.[8] A report in the *Harvard Business Review* suggests that they have strong interests in both "creative production" and "enterprise control." *Entrepreneurs like to start things*—creative production. They enjoy working with the unknown and finding unique solutions to problems. *Entrepreneurs also like to run things*—enterprise control. They enjoy making progress toward a goal. They thrive on independence and the sense of mastery that comes with success.[9]

Evidence shows that many entrepreneurs tend to have unique backgrounds.[10] *Childhood experiences and family environment* seem to make a difference. Evidence links entrepreneurs with parents who were entrepreneurial and self-employed. Similarly, entrepreneurs are often raised in families that encourage responsibility, initiative, and independence. Another pattern is found in *career or work history*. Entrepreneurs who try one venture often go on to others, and prior work experience in the same business area or industry is helpful.

Entrepreneurs also tend to blossom during certain *windows of career opportunity*. It seems to make sense that the risk-taking required by entrepreneurship

Table 18.1 Debunking Common Myths About Entrepreneurs

Entrepreneurs are born, not made—Not true! Talent gained and enhanced by experience is a foundation for entrepreneurial success.

Entrepreneurs are gamblers—Not true! Entrepreneurs are risk takers, but the risks are informed and calculated.

Money is the key to entrepreneurial success—Not true! Money is no guarantee of success. There's a lot more to it than that; many entrepreneurs start with very little.

You have to be young to be an entrepreneur—Not true! Age is no barrier to entrepreneurship; with age often come experience, contacts, and other useful resources.

You have to have a degree in business to be an entrepreneur—Not true! But it helps to study and understand business fundamentals.

{ THERE'S PROBABLY A BIT OF ENTREPRENEUR IN EACH OF US.

Explore **Yourself**

■ Risk Taking

Entrepreneurship plays an important role in local economies and the nation as a whole. It can also be a pathway to personal success. There's probably a bit of entrepreneur in each of us. Just how much probably depends on our tendency toward **risk taking**. This is a willingness to take action to achieve a goal even in the face of uncertainty. How would others describe you in this regard? How would you describe yourself?

Get to know yourself better by taking the self-assessment on **Entrepreneurship Orientation** and completing other activities in the *Exploring Management* Skill-Building Portfolio.

favors the younger set. And indeed, there is lots of entrepreneurship in the college and a bit older age groups. But research by the Kauffman foundation points out that the average age of entrepreneurs starting "high growth" companies is 40, and that the fastest-growing group is actually the 55- to 64-year-olds.[11]

A study by the U.S. Small Business Administration has also found that active-duty military veterans are 45% more likely to start their own businesses than those without military experience. The so-called **veteran's advantage** that fosters entrepreneurship includes strong organizational skills and tolerance for risk.[12]

The **veteran's advantage** in entrepreneurship is strong organizational skills and tolerance for risk.

Entrepreneurs often share similar personality traits.

Although we can't say that there is bona fide entrepreneurial personality, we can say that entrepreneurs often share similar personality traits and characteristics.

How about it, is it possible that your personality has aspects in common with those of successful entrepreneurs?

Take a moment to look at the figure. How many of the boxes could you put a check next to and say with confidence—"yes, that's me for sure"?[13] Perhaps it's time to further explore the entrepreneur that may reside within you.

Here's some more detail on the personality traits and characteristics often shared by entrepreneurs. Although the list isn't definitive or limiting, we can be confident in assuming that the more of these traits someone has, the more likely they will try entrepreneurship at some point in their careers.[14]

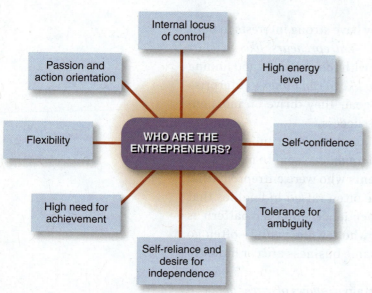

Personality Traits and Characteristics Shared by Many Entrepreneurs

- *Internal locus of control:* Entrepreneurs believe that they are in control of their own destiny; they are self-directing and like autonomy.

- *High energy level:* Entrepreneurs are persistent, hardworking, and willing to exert extraordinary efforts to succeed.

- *High need for achievement:* Entrepreneurs are motivated to accomplish challenging goals; they thrive on performance feedback.

- *Tolerance for ambiguity:* Entrepreneurs are risk takers; they tolerate situations with high degrees of uncertainty.

- *Self-confidence:* Entrepreneurs feel competent, believe in themselves, and are willing to make decisions.

- *Passion and action orientation:* Entrepreneurs try to act ahead of problems; they want to get things done and not waste valuable time.

- *Self-reliance and desire for independence:* Entrepreneurs want independence; they are self-reliant; they want to be their own bosses, not work for others.

- *Flexibility:* Entrepreneurs are willing to admit problems and errors, and willing to change a course of action when plans aren't working.

||| Women and minority entrepreneurs are growing in numbers.

Although background and personality help set the stage, it sometimes takes an outside stimulus or a special set of circumstances to kick-start one's entrepreneurial tendencies. And while some entrepreneurs are driven by the desire for new opportunities, others are driven by **necessity-based entrepreneurship**. They start new ventures because they see no other employment options or they find career doors closed, perhaps due to hitting glass ceilings of discrimination. The fact is that some women and minorities find entrepreneurship a way to strike out on their own and gain economic independence. Anita Roddick, featured earlier, once said that she started the first Body Shop store because she needed "to create a livelihood for myself and my two daughters, while my husband, Gordon, was trekking across the Americas."[15]

> **Necessity-based entrepreneurship** occurs when people start new ventures because they have few or no other employment options.

One survey of women leaving private-sector employment to pursue entrepreneurship found 33% believing they were not being taken seriously by their prior employer and 29% having experienced what they called "glass ceiling" issues. Another report, *Women Business Owners of Color: Challenges and Accomplishments*, identifies the motivations for entrepreneurship by women of color as including not being recognized or valued by their prior employers, not being taken seriously, and seeing others promoted ahead of them.[16] Still, women own just over 8 million businesses in the United States, and their firms are expected to create one-third of all new jobs by 2018. And, many women business owners say they started their firms after realizing they could do for themselves what they were already doing for other employers.[17]

The last U.S. small business census identified almost 2 million small firms owned by African Americans, a growth of 60% over prior numbers and representing 7% of total businesses. Among new start-ups in 2010, 9% were led by African-American entrepreneurs and 23% by Latinos.[18] Yet even with this record of accomplishment, the obstacles to minority entrepreneurship are real and

Jacob Wackerhausen/ iStockphoto

{ **MINORITY ENTREPRENEURS PROVIDE 6 MILLION JOBS BUT ATTRACT LESS THAN 1% OF VENTURE CAPITAL.**

Facts to **Consider**

■ Minority Entrepreneurs are on the Move

Minority entrepreneurship is one of the fastest-growing sectors of our economy. Consider these facts and trends:

- There are close to 6 million minority-owned firms in America (29% of all business), and they contribute $1 trillion annually to the economy.
- Minority-owned firms employ some 6 million workers, with the largest employers Asian-owned (2.9 million jobs), Hispanic-owned (1.9 million jobs), and African-American-owned (921,000 jobs).
- In the last census of small businesses, those owned by African Americans had grown by 45%, by Hispanics 31%, and by Asians 24%.

- If minority business ownership was proportionate to their share of the U. S. population, they would number more than 8 million firms and provide more than 17 million jobs.
- Minority businesses export to 41 countries on six continents and generate twice the export activity of nonminority firms.

YOUR THOUGHTS?

How can we explain the growth of minority-owned businesses? Is minority entrepreneurship a way to fight economic disparities in society? What special obstacles do minorities and women face on their pathways toward entrepreneurship? What can be done about it?

Manager's Library

THE ALL-AMERICAN BURGER NEVER GOES OUT OF STYLE

In 1948, Harry and Esther Snyder opened a small hamburger stand beside a busy road in Los Angeles, California. They were eager to make ends meet, and after years of sacrifice during the depression and war, people were in the mood to get about and enjoy life. Driving cars to roadside stands was a novel idea. Their restaurant, In-N-Out Burger, is now a successful family-owned chain of 250 drive-through stores.

In the book *In-N-Out Burger: A Behind-the-Counter Look at the Fast-food Chain that Breaks All the Rules* (2009, HarperCollins), author Stacy Perman profiles the Snyder's values and the investment they put into every In-N-Out burger, employee, and customer. She claims their dedication to quality, reinvestment in employees, and joy in delighting customers has generated an "uncopyable" competitive advantage. In-N-Out stores meet McDonald's stores revenues but do so without advertising, franchising, financing debt, paying minimum wage, or sacrificing quality for volume, speed, and price.

Part of the In-N-Out difference is a focus on quality—right from the beef to the service. Another part is genuine interest in employees: Called associates, they are paid well above minimum wage and train at In-N-Out University. New stores open only after managers have been groomed. Perman says In-N-Out has unrivaled loyal customers and a "cult-like" following.

REFLECT AND REACT

Do you agree with Perman that In-N-Out Burger is doing things in ways that create an "uncopyable" advantage in its industry? Are these things that could be copied by entrepreneurs setting out to gain success in other industries?

---

shouldn't be underestimated. Consider the critical area of start-up financing. Less than 1% of the available venture capital in the U.S. goes to minority entrepreneurs. The Minority Business Development Agency of the Department of Commerce is well aware of this and related problems. As part of its mission to support the development of minority-owned small and medium-sized firms, the MBDA has set up a nationwide network of 40 business development centers with the goal of helping them grow in "size, scale, and capacity."[19]

⫴ Social entrepreneurs seek novel solutions to pressing social problems.

A **social entrepreneur** takes risks to find new ways to solve pressing social problems.

Social entrepreneurs are a growing force in entrepreneurship today. They are persons whose entrepreneurial ventures pursue novel ways to help solve pressing social problems.[20] You can think of these problems as the likes of poverty, illiteracy, poor health, and even social oppression. Social entrepreneurs share many characteristics with other entrepreneurs, including backgrounds and personalities. But there is one big difference. Instead of the profit motive, they are driven by a social mission.[21] They want to start and run social enterprises, whose missions are to help make lives better for people who are disadvantaged.[22]

Fast Company magazine says social entrepreneurs run enterprises with "innovative thinking that can transform lives and change the world." It celebrates them with its prestigious Honor Roll of Social Enterprises of the Year. Here are two recent winners.[23]

- Chip Ransler and Manoj Sinha tackled the lack of power faced by many of India's poor villagers. As University of Virginia business students, they realized that 350 million of the people without reliable electricity lived in the country's rice-growing regions. And in those regions, tons of rice husks were being discarded with every harvest. Ransler and Sinha sought a way to create biogas from the husks and use the gas to fuel small power plants. They succeeded, and Husk Power Systems is a reality. But with more than 125,000 villages suffering a lack of power, Ransler says, "There's a lot of work to be done."

- Rose Donna and Joel Selanikio were concerned about public health problems in sub-Saharan Africa. After noting that developing nations are often bogged down in the paperwork of public health, they created software to make the process quicker and more efficient. The UN, the World Health Organization, and the Vodafone Foundation are now helping their firm, DataDyne, move the program into 22 more African nations.

There's probably quite a bit of social entrepreneurship taking place in your community. Sadly, it may get little notice. Most attention often goes to business entrepreneurs making lots of money—or trying to do so. Yet there are many examples you can find of local people who have made the commitment to social entrepreneurship. Deborah Sardone, for example, owns a housekeeping service in Texas. After noticing that her clients with cancer really struggled with everyday household chores, she started Cleaning for a Reason. It's a nonprofit that networks with cleaning firms around the country that are willing to offer free home cleaning to cancer patients.[24]

How about it? Can you think of ideas that could turn social entrepreneurship by yourself and others into a positive impact on your community?

MTC/NewsCom

{ CAN SMALL BUSINESSES BUILT ON CARING CAPITALISM SURVIVE BIG BUSINESS BUYOUTS?

Ethics Check

■ Entrepreneurship and Social Good

Would you buy shoes just because their maker is pledged to philanthropy? Blake Mycoskie wants you to. Back in 2002, he was participating with his sister in the reality TV show *The Amazing Race*. It whetted his appetite for travel, and he visited Argentina in 2006. There he came face-to-face with lots of young children without shoes, and he had a revelation: He would return home and start a sustainable business that would help address the problem.

Mycoskie launched TOMS (short, he says, for "better tomorrow") to sell shoes made in a classic Argentinean style. But there's a twist—for each pair of shoes it sells, the firm donates a pair to needy children. Blake calls this One for One, a "movement" that involves "people making everyday choices that improve the lives of children." After giving away its one-millionth pair of shoes, Mycoskie renamed the company One for One.

One for One's business model can be described as caring capitalism or profits with principles. Two other names associated with this approach are Ben & Jerry's Ice Cream and Tom's of Maine. But each of these firms was sold to a global enterprise—Unilever for Ben & Jerry's and Colgate-Palmolive for Tom's of Maine. The expectation was that the corporate buyers wouldn't compromise on the founders' core values and social goals. Who knows what the future holds if One for One grows to the point where corporate buyers loom.

Several states have passed laws creating the "benefit corporation" as a new legal entity. The "B-Corp" is designed to protect the missions of firms like One for One for the long term. It also requires them to report their social benefit activities and impact.

YOU DECIDE

What about it? Is Blake's business model one that others should adopt? Is it ethical to link personal philanthropic goals with the products that your business sells? And if an entrepreneurial firm is founded on a caring capitalism model, is it ethical for a future corporate buyer to reduce or limit the emphasis on social benefits? Should more states get behind the B-Corp concept?

STUDY GUIDE

Takeaway 18.1
What Is Entrepreneurship, and Who Are Entrepreneurs?

Terms to Define

Classic entrepreneur

Entrepreneur

Entrepreneurship

First-mover advantage

Necessity-based entrepreneurship

Serial entrepreneur

Social entrepreneur

Veteran's advantage

Rapid Review

- Entrepreneurship is original thinking that creates value for people, organizations, and society.
- Entrepreneurs take risks to pursue opportunities others may fail to recognize.
- Entrepreneurs tend to be creative people who are self-confident, determined, resilient, adaptable, and driven to excel; they like to be masters of their own destinies.
- Women and minorities are well represented among entrepreneurs, with some of their motivation driven by necessity or the lack of alternative career options.
- Social entrepreneurs apply their energies to create innovations that help to solve important problems in society.

Questions for Discussion

1. Does an entrepreneur always need to have first-mover advantage to succeed?
2. Are there any items on the list of entrepreneurial characteristics that are "must-haves" for someone to succeed in any career, not just entrepreneurship?
3. Could growth of necessity-driven entrepreneurship be an indicator of some deeper problems in our society?

Be Sure You Can

- explain the concept of entrepreneurship
- explain the concept of first-mover advantage
- explain why people such as Caterina Fake and Earl Graves might become entrepreneurs
- list personal characteristics often associated with entrepreneurs
- explain trends in entrepreneurship by women and minorities
- explain what makes social entrepreneurs unique

Career Situation: What Would You Do?

After reading the examples in this chapter, you're struck by the potential to try entrepreneurship. You're thinking now that it would be very nice to be your own boss, do your own thing, and make a decent living in the process. But how do you get started? One possibility is to start with ideas passed around among your friends and family. Or perhaps there's something that has already been on your mind as a great possible business idea. And then there's the notion of tackling a social problem like poverty or illiteracy. So, tell us about it. What ideas do you have? What would you like to pursue as an entrepreneur and why?

Takeaway 18.2
What Should We Know About Small Businesses and How to Start One?

ANSWERS TO COME

■ Small businesses are mainstays of the economy.

■ Small businesses must master three life-cycle stages.

■ Family-owned businesses can face unique challenges.

■ Many small businesses fail within five years.

■ Assistance is available to help small businesses get started.

■ A small business should start with a sound business plan.

■ There are different forms of small business ownership.

■ There are different ways of financing a small business.

THE U.S. SMALL BUSINESS ADMINISTRATION (SBA) DEFINES A **SMALL BUSINESS** AS one that is independently owned and operated and that does not dominate its industry.[25] It also has 500 or fewer employees, with the number varying a bit by industry. Almost 99% of U.S. businesses meet this definition.

How does owning a small business stack up in terms of satisfaction? Pretty well. Data from the Gallup-Healthways Well-Being Index show that business owners rank highest among 10 other occupations in terms of contentment. This includes things like physical and mental health, job satisfaction, and quality of life overall.[26] "I'm still excited to get up and go to work every day," says Roger Peugot, who owns a 14-employee plumbing firm. He goes on to add: "Even when things get tough, I'm still in control."[27]

A **small business** has fewer than 500 employees, is independently owned and operated, and does not dominate its industry.

⦀ Small businesses are mainstays of the economy.

Most nations rely on their small business sector. Why? Among other things, small businesses offer major economic advantages. In the United States, for example, small businesses employ some 55% of private workers and provide as many as 6 out of every 10 new jobs in the economy.[28] The vast majority employ fewer than 20 persons, and over half are home based. The most common small business areas are restaurants, skilled professions such as craftspeople and doctors, general services such as hairdressers and repair shops, and independent retailers.[29]

Once a decision is made to go the small business route, the most common ways to get involved are to start one, buy an existing one, or buy and run a **franchise**—where a business owner sells to another the right to operate the same business in another location. A franchise such as Subway, Quiznos, or Domino's Pizza runs under the original owner's business name and guidance. In return, the franchise parent receives a share of income or a flat fee from the franchisee.

Any business—large or small, franchise or startup, needs a solid underlying **business model.** Think of this as a plan for making a profit by generating revenues that are greater than the costs of doing business. Serial entrepreneur

A **franchise** is when one business owner sells to another the right to operate the same business in another location.

A **business model** is a plan for making a profit by generating revenues that are greater than costs.

Kathy Willens/AP

{ "... FOUNDED WITH A REBELLIOUS SPIRIT AND A LOFTY OBJECTIVE: TO CREATE BOUTIQUE-QUALITY, CLASSICALLY CRAFTED EYEWEAR AT A REVOLUTIONARY PRICE POINT."

Role Models

■ Grad School Start-up Takes on Global Competitors

Did you ever wonder why prescription eyeglasses are so expensive? That's a question four MBA students at Wharton asked. And they found the answer was due to an oligopoly situation in the industry that was controlled by just a few firms.

Spotting both business opportunity and a social calling, they decided to start a company to do what they felt was only right—make eyeglasses available to people at a reasonable price. Their creation is WarbyParker, described as being "founded with a rebellious spirit and a lofty objective: to create boutique-quality, classically crafted eyewear at a revolutionary price point."

The founders—David Gilboa, Niel Blumenthal, Andrew Hunt, and Jeffrey Raider—wrote a Web-driven business plan that many questioned at first. Could eyeglasses be sold over the Internet? The Warby Parker answer was: "Of course!" The start-up is now in a growth phase, having attracted close to $40 million in venture funding since its inception.

If you're in doubt, and especially if you wear glasses, check out the offerings on warbyparker.com. You can buy stylish glasses for as low as $95—frames with Rx lenses and free shipping. They are e-commerce and customer friendly—letting you have free home try-ons of up to five "loaner" pairs. And if you end up buying, you're helping someone else who can't afford to buy new glasses for themselves. Warby Parker donates a pair of glasses to someone in need for every pair it sells. That adds up quickly when you consider they are already selling over 250,000 pairs a year.

The company's Web site proudly announces: "Let's do good. We're building a company to do good in the world. . . . We think it's good business to do good." They call their business model "eyewear with a purpose." That purpose is anchored in the fact that over a billion people in the world don't have the glasses they need for school, work, and everyday living. It's a social problem that Warby Parker aims to help solve through business.

All this is made possible by the founders' careful analysis of the industry and its supply chains. They source directly from the manufacturers and then sell direct to customers, cutting out a lot of costs and profit-taking in the middle of the chain.

WHAT'S THE LESSON HERE?

Warby Parker's founders discovered that prescription eyeglasses could be sold for less. And by selling for less they created more value for society at large. Instead of buying glasses at a boutique for $695 you can buy a stylish pair online from Warby Parker for $95. And your purchase sends a free pair to someone in need. Why aren't there more businesses like this? Why aren't there more entrepreneurs that try to match social problems and business opportunities? How about you—any good ideas here?

A **start-up** is a new and temporary venture that is trying to discover a profitable business model for future success.

Steven Blank calls business **start-ups** temporary organizations that are trying "to discover a profitable, scalable business model."[30] In other words, a start-up is just that—a "start"; it's a new venture that the entrepreneur is hoping will take shape and prove successful as things move forward.

‖ Small businesses must master three life-cycle stages.

The typical small business moves through recognizable life-cycle stages.[31] The new firm begins with the *birth stage*, where the entrepreneur struggles to get the new venture established and survive long enough to really test the marketplace. The firm then passes into the *breakthrough stage*, where the business model begins to work well, growth takes place, and the complexity of the business expands significantly. Next is the *maturity stage*, where the entrepreneur experiences market success and financial stability but also has to face competitive challenges in a dynamic environment.

BIRTH STAGE	BREAKTHROUGH STAGE	MATURITY STAGE
• Establishing the firm • Getting customers • Finding the money	• Working on finances • Becoming profitable • Growing	• Refining the strategy • Continuing growth • Managing for success
Fighting for existence and survival	*Coping with growth and takeoff*	*Investing wisely and staying flexible*

FIGURE 18.1 **What Are the Stages in the Life Cycle of an Entrepreneurial Firm?** It is typical for small businesses to move through three life-cycle stages. During the *birth* stage, the entrepreneur focuses on getting things started—bringing a product to market, finding initial customers, and earning enough money to survive. *Breakthrough* is a time of rapid growth when the business model really starts working well. Growth often slows in the *maturity* stage, where financial success is realized but also where the entrepreneur often needs to make adjustments to stay successful in a dynamic marketplace.

As shown in **Figure 18.1**, small business owners often face somewhat different management dilemmas as their firms move through these life-cycle stages. When they experience growth, including possible diversification or global expansion, they can encounter problems making the transition from entrepreneurial leadership to professional strategic leadership. The entrepreneur brings the venture into being and sees it through the early stages of life; the professional manages and leads the venture into maturity as an ever-evolving and perhaps still-growing corporate enterprise. If the entrepreneur is incapable of meeting or unwilling to meet the firm's leadership needs in later life-cycle stages, continued business survival and success may well depend on the business being sold or management control being passed to professionals.

⦀ Family-owned businesses can face unique challenges.

Among the reasons given for getting started in small businesses, you'll find the owners saying they were motivated to be their own bosses, be in control of their own futures, fulfill dreams, and become part of a family-owned business.[32] Indeed, **family businesses**, those owned and financially controlled by family members, represent the largest percentage of businesses operating worldwide. The Family Firm Institute reports that family businesses account for 70 to 90% of global domestic product. They create 78% of new jobs in the United States and provide 60% of the nation's employment.[33]

Family businesses must master the same challenges as other small or large businesses, such as devising strategy, achieving competitive advantage, and ensuring operational excellence. When everything goes right, the family firm can be an ideal situation. Everyone works together, sharing values and a common goal: doing well to support the family. But things don't always turn out this way or stay this way. Changes and complications often test the family bonds, especially as a business changes hands over successive generations.

"Okay, Dad, so he's your brother. But does that mean we have to put up with inferior work and an erratic schedule that we would never tolerate from anyone else in the business?"[34] Welcome to the **family business feud**, a problem that can

Family businesses are owned and financially controlled by family members.

A **family business feud** can lead to small business failure.

Etsy Turns "Handmade" into Entrepreneurship

Etsy's mission is described as empowering people and creating "a world in which very-very small businesses have much-much more sway in shaping the economy. . . ." The original idea came from painter and photographer Rob Kalin, who wanted an online market for his works. Along with Chris Maguire and Haim Schoppik, he founded Etsy as an online marketplace where artisans could showcase their work and link with customers. The business model was as neat as a hand-stitched quilt: take a 3.5% transaction fee and 20¢ listing charge, and sell ads to artists. And it worked. Etsy now has 14 million members.

The **succession problem** is the issue of who will run the business when the current head leaves.

A **succession plan** describes how the leadership transition and related financial matters will be handled.

---

lead to small business failure. The feud can be about jobs and who does what, business strategy, operating approaches, finances, or other matters. It can be between spouses, among siblings, between parents and children. It really doesn't matter. Unless family business feuds are resolved satisfactorily, the firm may not survive.

A survey of small and midsized family businesses indicated that 66% planned on keeping the business within the family.[35] The management question is: Upon leaving, how will the current head of the company distribute assets and determine who will run the business? This introduces the **succession problem**, how to handle the transfer of leadership from one generation to the next. The data on succession are eye-opening. About 30% of family firms survive to the second generation; 12% survive to the third generation; only 3% are expected to survive beyond that.[36]

If you were the owner of a successful family business, what would you do? Wouldn't you want to have a **succession plan** that clearly spells out how leadership transition and related matters, including financial ones, are to be handled when the time for changeover occurs?

‖ Many small businesses fail within five years.

Does the prospect of starting your own small business sound good? It should, but a word of caution is called for as well. What the last figure on life-cycle stages didn't show is a very common event—small business failure.

Small businesses have a high failure rate. The SBA reports that as many as 60% to 80% of new businesses fail in their first five years of operation.[37] Part of this might be explained as a "counting" issue. The government counts as a "failure" any business that closes, whether it is due to the death or retirement of an owner, the sale to someone else, or the inability to earn a profit.[38] Nevertheless, the fact remains: A lot of small business start-ups just don't make it. Small business failures are many times due to poor judgment and basic mistakes that could be avoided or overcome with proper planning and good management. Most such business failures are the result of problems like the following.[39]

- *Insufficient financing*—not having enough money available to maintain operations while still building the business and gaining access to customers and markets.
- *Lack of experience*—not having sufficient know-how to run a business in the chosen market or geographical area.
- *Lack of expertise*—not having expertise in the essentials of business operations, including finance, purchasing, selling, and production.
- *Lack of strategy and strategic leadership*—not taking the time to craft a vision and mission, nor to formulate and properly implement a strategy.
- *Poor financial control*—not keeping track of the numbers, and failure to control business finances and use existing monies to best advantage.
- *Growing too fast*—not taking the time to consolidate a position, fine-tune the organization, and systematically meet the challenges of growth.
- *Lack of commitment*—not devoting enough time to the requirements of running a competitive business.
- *Ethical failure*—falling prey to the temptations of fraud, deception, and embezzlement.

Look at the nearby figure and consider again the many possible causes of small business failures. Many of the failures may be preventable. So if you decide to launch your own venture someday, you'll need to learn from the mistakes of others.

⫴ Assistance is available to help small businesses get started.

Individuals who start small businesses face a variety of challenges. And even though the prospect of being part of a new venture is exciting, the realities of working through complex problems during setup and the early life of the business can be especially daunting. Fortunately, there is often some assistance available to help entrepreneurs and owners of small businesses get started.

A **business incubator** is a facility that offers services to help new businesses get established.

One way that start-up difficulties can be managed is through participation in a **business incubator**. These are special facilities that offer space, shared administrative services, and management advice at reduced costs with the goal of helping new businesses get successfully established. Some incubators are focused on specific business areas such as technology, light manufacturing, or professional services; some are located in rural areas, whereas others are urban based; some focus only on socially responsible businesses.

Regardless of their focus or location, business incubators share the common goal of increasing the survival rates for new business start-ups. They want to help build new businesses that will create new jobs and expand economic opportunities in their local communities. In the incubators, small businesses are nurtured and assisted so that they can grow quickly and become healthy enough to survive on their own. An example is the Y Combinator in Mountain View, California. It focuses on nurturing Web start-ups. Members get offices, regular meetings with business experts, access to potential investors, and $15,000 start-up investments.[40]

Small Business Development Centers offer guidance to entrepreneurs and small business owners on how to set up and manage business operations.

Another source of assistance for small business development is the U. S. Small Business Administration. Because small businesses play such significant roles in the economy, the SBA works with state and local agencies as well as the private sector to support a network of over 1,100 **Small Business Development Centers** nationwide.[41] These SBDCs offer guidance to entrepreneurs and small business owners, actual and prospective, on how to set up and manage business operations. They are often associated with colleges and universities, and they give students a chance to work as consultants with small businesses at the same time that they pursue their academic programs. If you are inclined toward small business, why not check out your local SBDC?

⫼ A small business should start with a sound business plan.

A **business plan** describes the direction for a new business and the financing needed to operate it.

When people start new businesses or even start new units within existing ones, they can greatly benefit from another type of plan—a sound **business plan**. This plan describes the goals of the business and the way it intends to operate, ideally in ways that can help obtain any needed start-up financing.[42] Although there is no single template for a successful business plan, most would agree on the general framework presented in Tips to Remember.[43]

Banks and other financiers want to see a business plan before they loan money or invest in a new venture. Senior managers want to see a business plan before they allocate scarce organizational resources to support a new entrepreneurial project. You should also want a small business plan. The detailed and disciplined thinking helps sort out your ideas, map strategies, and pin down your business model. Says Ed Federkeil, who founded a small business called California Custom Sport Trucks: "It gives you direction instead of haphazardly sticking your key in the door every day and saying—'What are we going to do?'"[44]

⫼ There are different forms of small business ownership.

One of the important choices when starting a new venture is the legal form of ownership. There are a number of alternatives, and each has its own advantages and disadvantages.

Tips to **Remember**

■ What to Include in a Business Plan

- *Executive summary*—business purpose, highlights of plan
- *Industry analysis*—nature of industry, economic trends, legal or regulatory issues, risks
- *Company description*—mission, owners, legal form
- *Products and services*—major goods or services, uniqueness vis-à -vis competition
- *Market description*—size, competitor strengths and weaknesses, five-year sales goals
- *Marketing strategy*—product characteristics, distribution, promotion, pricing

- *Operations description*—manufacturing or service methods, suppliers, controls
- *Staffing*—management and worker skills needed and available, compensation, human resource systems
- *Financial projection*—cash flow projections 1–5 years, breakeven points
- *Capital needs*—amount needed, amount available, amount being requested
- *Milestones*—timetable for completing key stages of new venture

A **sole proprietorship** is simply an individual or a married couple that pursues business for a profit. The business often operates under a personal name, such as "Tiaña Lopez Designs." Because a sole proprietorship is simple to start, run, and terminate, it is the most common form of U.S. small business ownership. If you choose this form, however, you have to remember—any owner of a sole proprietorship is personally liable for all business debts and claims.

A **partnership** is formed when two or more people contribute resources to start and operate a business together. Most are set up with legal and written agreements that document what each party contributes as well as how profits and losses are to be shared. You would be ill advised to enter into a serious partnership without such an agreement. But once the choice is made to go the partnership route, there are two alternatives.

In a **general partnership**, the simplest and most common form, the owners share day-to-day management and responsibilities for debts and losses. This differs from a **limited partnership**, consisting of a general partner and one or more "limited" partners. The general partner runs the business; the limited partners do not participate in day-to-day management. All partners share in profits, but their losses are limited to the amounts of their investments. This limit to one's liabilities is a major advantage. You'll notice that many professionals, such as accountants and attorneys, work in *limited liability partnerships*—designated as LLP—because they limit the liability of one partner in case of negligence by any others.

A **corporation**, commonly identified by the "Inc." designation in a name, is a legal entity that exists separately from its owners. Corporations are legally chartered by the states in which they are registered, and they can be for-profit, such as Microsoft Inc., or not-for-profit, such as Count-Me-In, Inc.—a firm featured early in the chapter as helping women entrepreneurs get started with small loans. There are two major advantages in choosing to incorporate: (1) it grants the organization certain legal rights—for example, to engage in contracts, and (2) the corporation is responsible for its own liabilities. This gives the firm a life of its own and separates the owners from personal liability. The major disadvantages

A **sole proprietorship** is an individual pursuing business for a profit.

A **partnership** is when two or more people agree to contribute resources to start and operate a business together.

In a **general partnership**, owners share management and responsibility for debts and losses.

In a **limited partnership** owners shares profits, but responsibility for losses is limited to original investments.

A **corporation** is a legal entity that exists separately from its owners.

are the legal costs of setting up the corporation and the complex documentation required to operate as one.

The **benefit corporation** is a new corporate form for businesses whose stated goals are to benefit society while making a profit.[45] Businesses that choose this ownership type formally adopt the goals of social entrepreneurship and social enterprises to help solve social and environmental problems. Often called "B-Corps" for short, these goals must be stated in the firm's bylaws or rules of corporation. Each B-Corp is then required to file an annual "benefit report" as well as an annual financial report so that both social and financial performance can be properly assessed against stated goals. The adoption of this form by a number of larger and well-recognized businesses—Ben & Jerry's and Patagonia, for example—are giving it public visibility. So far 12 states have legalized the B-Corp, but it is being considered by many others.[46]

The **limited liability corporation (LLC)** has gained popularity as an ownership form. It combines the advantages of sole proprietorship, partnership, and corporation. It functions as a corporation for liability purposes and protects the assets of owners against claims made against the company. For tax purposes, it functions as a partnership in the case of multiple owners and as a sole proprietorship in the case of a single owner.

⦀ There are different ways of financing a small business.

Starting a new venture takes money. Unless you possess personal wealth that you are willing to risk, that money has to be raised. The two most common ways to raise it are debt financing and equity financing.

Debt financing involves borrowing money from another person, a bank, or a financial institution. This is a loan that must be paid back over time with interest. A loan also requires collateral that pledges business assets or personal assets, such as a home, as security in case of default. You borrow money with a promise to repay both the loan amount and interest. If you can't pay, the security is lost up to the amount of the outstanding loan.

Equity financing gives ownership shares to outsiders in return for their financial investments. In contrast to debt financing, this money does not need to be paid back. Instead, the investor assumes the risk of potential gains and losses based on the performance of the business. But in return for taking that risk, the equity investor gains something—part of your original ownership. The amount of ownership and control given up is represented in the number and proportion of ownership shares transferred to the equity investors.

When businesses need equity financing in fairly large amounts, from the tens of thousands to the millions of dollars, they often turn to **venture capitalists**. These are individuals and companies that pool capital to invest in new ventures. The hope is that their equity stakes rise in value and can be sold for a profit when the business becomes successful. Venture capitalists can sometimes be quite aggressive in wanting active management roles to make sure the business grows in value as soon as possible. This value is often tapped by an **initial public offering (IPO)**. This is when shares in the business are sold to the public at large, most likely beginning to trade on a major stock exchange.

The **benefit corporation**, or B-Corp, is a corporate form for businesses whose stated goals are to combine making a profit with benefiting society and the environment.

A **limited liability corporation (LLC)** combines the advantages of the sole proprietorship, partnership, and corporation.

Debt financing involves borrowing money from another person, a bank, or a financial institution.

Equity financing gives ownership shares to outsiders in return for their financial investments.

Venture capitalists make large investments in new ventures in return for an equity stake in the business.

An **initial public offering (IPO)** is an initial selling of shares of stock to the public at large.

When venture capital isn't available or isn't yet interested, entrepreneurs may try to find an **angel investor**. This is a wealthy individual who invests in return for equity in a new venture. Angel investors are especially helpful in the late birth and early breakthrough stages of a new venture. Once they jump in, it can raise the confidence and interests of the venture capitalists, thus making it easier to attract even more funding. When Liz Cobb wanted to start her sales compensation firm, Incentive Systems, for example, she contacted 15 to 20 venture capital firms. Only 10 interviewed her, and all of those turned her down. However, after she located $250,000 from two angel investors, the venture capital firms renewed their interest, allowing her to obtain her first $2 million in financing. Her firm grew to employ over 70 workers.[47]

An **angel investor** is a wealthy individual willing to invest in return for equity in a new venture.

The rise of social media has given birth to **crowdfunding**, where those starting new ventures go online to obtain startup funds from a "crowd" of willing providers. Many options already exist and more are appearing all the time. Kickstarter, for example, focuses on fundraising for innovative and imaginative projects from software to literature to films and more. Investors get no ownership rights in return for their funding support, but they do get the satisfaction of sponsorship and in some cases early access to the results. An option offering equity participation is AngleList which bills itself as the place "Where startups meet investors." The site matches entrepreneurs with pools of potential investors willing to put up as little as $1,000 to back a new venture.[48]

In **crowdfunding** new ventures go online to get start-up financing for their businesses from crowds of investors.

The JOBS Act—Jumpstart our Business Startups—made it easier for small U.S. companies to sell equity on the Internet. President Obama called crowdfunding a "game changer" when he signed the act in 2012.[49] But, the U.S. Securities and Exchange Commission which oversees the practice has been cautious in developing and implementing guidelines. Crowdfunding has both advocates and skeptics. Advocates claim it spurs entrepreneurship by giving small start-ups a better shot at raising investment capital and helps small investors join the venture capital game. Skeptics worry that small investors in a crowd may be easy prey for fraudsters because they won't do enough analysis or have the financial expertise to ensure they are making good investments.[50]

Would-be Entrepreneurs Dive for Dollars in the Shark Tank

Have you seen the reality TV show, Shark Tank? It pits entrepreneurs against potential investors called "sharks." The entrepreneurs present their ideas, and the sharks, people with money to invest, debate the worthwhileness of investing in their businesses. Brian Duggan went on the show to pitch his Element Bars, a custom energy bar he developed as an MBA student. He previously tried to get a bank loan, but failed. His presentation impressed the sharks. By show's end they had given him $150,000 to help turn his energy bars into a popular product. But it came at a price. He gave them in return 30% ownership in his business.

Michael Ansell/Getty Images

STUDY GUIDE

Takeaway 18.2

What Should We Know About Small Businesses and How to Start One?

Terms to Define

Angel investor

Benefit corporation

Business incubator

Business model

Business plan

Corporation

Crowdfunding

Debt financing

Equity financing

Family business

Family business feud

Franchise

General partnership

Initial public offering (IPO)

Limited liability corporation (LLC)

Limited partnership

Partnership

Small business

Small business development centers

Sole proprietorship

Start-ups

Succession plan

Succession problem

Venture capitalists

Rapid Review

- Small businesses constitute the vast majority of businesses in the United States and create 7 out of every 10 new jobs in the economy.
- Small businesses have a high failure rate; as many as 60% to 80% of new businesses fail in their first five years of operation.
- Small businesses owned by family members can suffer from the succession problem of transferring leadership from one generation to the next.
- A business plan describes the intended nature of a proposed new business, how it will operate, and how it will obtain financing.
- Proprietorships, partnerships, and corporations are different forms of business ownership, with each offering advantages and disadvantages.
- New ventures can be financed through debt financing in the form of loans and through equity financing, which involves the exchange of ownership shares in return for outside investment.
- Venture capitalists and angel investors invest in new ventures in return for an equity stake in the business.

Questions for Discussion

1. Given the economic importance of small businesses, what could local, state, and federal governments do to make it easier for them to prosper?
2. If you were asked to join a small company, what would you look for as potential success indicators in its business plan?
3. Why might the owner of a small but growing business want to be careful when accepting big investments from venture capitalists?

Be Sure You Can

- state the SBA definition of small business
- list the life-cycle stages of a small business
- list several reasons why many small businesses fail
- discuss the succession problem in family-owned businesses
- list the major elements in a business plan
- differentiate the common forms of small business ownership
- differentiate debt financing and equity financing
- explain the roles of venture capitalists and angel investors in new venture financing

Career Situation: What Would You Do?

Your start-up e-textbook rating Web site is attracting potential investors. One angel is willing to put up $50,000 to help move things to the next level. But you and your two co-founders haven't done anything to legally structure the business. You've operated so far on personal resources and a "handshake" agreement among friends. What's the best choice to legally set up the company? What's your best option for getting the financing needed for future growth while still protecting your ownership?

TestPrep 18

Answers to TestPrep questions can be found at the back of the book.

Multiple-Choice Questions

1. An entrepreneur who thrives on uncertainty displays _____.
   - (a) high tolerance for ambiguity
   - (b) internal locus of control
   - (c) need for achievement
   - (d) action orientation

2. _____ is a personality characteristic common among entrepreneurs.
   - (a) External locus of control
   - (b) Inflexibility
   - (c) Self-confidence
   - (d) Low self-reliance

3. When a new business is quick to capture a market niche before competitors, this is _____.
   - (a) intrapreneurship
   - (b) an initial public offering
   - (c) succession planning
   - (d) first-mover advantage

4. Almost_____% of U.S. businesses meet the definition of "small business."
   - (a) 40
   - (b) 99
   - (c) 75
   - (d) 81

5. A small business owner who wants to pass the business to other family members after retirement or death should prepare a _____ plan.
   - (a) retirement
   - (b) succession
   - (c) partnership
   - (d) liquidation

6. A common reason small business start-ups often fail is _____.
   - (a) the owner lacks experience and business skills
   - (b) there is too much government regulation
   - (c) the owner tightly controls money and finances
   - (d) the business grows too slowly

7. A pressing problem faced by a small business in the birth or start-up stage is _____.
   - (a) gaining acceptance in the marketplace
   - (b) finding partners for expansion
   - (c) preparing the initial public offering
   - (d) getting management professional skills

8. A venture capitalist that receives an ownership share in return for investing in a new business is providing _____ financing.
   - (a) debt
   - (b) equity
   - (c) limited
   - (d) corporate

9. In _____ financing, the business owner borrows money as a loan that must be repaid.
   - (a) debt
   - (b) equity
   - (c) partnership
   - (d) limited

10. If you start a small business and want to avoid losing any more than the original investment, what form of ownership is best?
   - (a) Sole proprietorship
   - (b) General partnership
   - (c) Limited partnership
   - (d) Corporation

11. The first element in a good business plan is
_____.

(a) an industry analysis

(b) a marketing strategy

(c) an executive summary

(d) a set of performance milestones

12. Trends in U.S. small businesses show
_____.

(a) a growing number owned by minorities

(b) fewer of them using the Internet for business

(c) more small businesses leaving small communities for the big city

(d) fewer of them being family owned

13. A _____ protects small business owners from personal liabilities for losses.

(a) sole proprietorship

(b) franchise

(c) limited partnership

(d) corporation

14. _____ take ownership shares in a new venture in return for start-up funds.

(a) Business incubators

(b) Angel investors

(c) SBDCs

(d) Intrapreneurs

15. _____ makes social entrepreneurship unique.

(a) Lack of other career options

(b) Focus on international markets

(c) Refusal to finance by loans

(d) Commitment to solving social problems

Short-Response Questions

16. What is the relationship between diversity and entrepreneurship?

17. What major challenges are faced at each life-cycle stage of an entrepreneurial firm?

18. What are the advantages of a limited partnership form of ownership?

19. What is the difference, if any, between a venture capitalist and an angel investor?

Integration and Application Question

20. You have a great idea for an Internet-based start-up business. A friend advises you to clearly link your business idea to potential customers and then describe it well in a business plan. "You won't succeed without customers, she says, and you'll never get a chance if you can't attract financial backers with a good business plan."

Questions: What questions will you ask and answer to ensure that you are customer focused in this business? What are the major areas that you would address in your initial business plan?

Steps *for* Further Learning

BUILD

MARKETABLE SKILLS.
EARN BIG CAREER
PAYOFFS!

Don't miss these opportunities in the **Skill-Building Portfolio**

■ **SELF-ASSESSMENT 18:**
Entrepreneurship Orientation

Lots of people can do it . . . find out if entrepreneurship fits you.

■ **CLASS EXERCISE 18:**
Entrepreneurs Among Us

Entrepreneurs are all around us . . . find out who are the best role models.

■ **TEAM PROJECT 18:**
Community Entrepreneurs

Many of them fly below the radar . . . find out how entrepreneurs help build your community.

Many learning resources are found at the end of the book and online within WileyPLUS.

Take advantage of **Cases for Critical Thinking**

■ **CHAPTER 18 CASE SNAPSHOT:**
The new mother of angel investors/
Sidebar on Accidental Entrepreneurs

"How do I get financing?" Answering this fundamental question presents one of the greatest challenges to entrepreneurs intent on following their dream of business independence. Never easy, start-up financing is even harder to get now after banks shrunk their small business loan portfolios in the recent financial crisis. Many owners of existing small businesses as well as those launching new start-ups are finding it hard to come up with timely and solid business funding options. But, as with so many things, the Web is offering some help. Crowdfunding is an emerging field of financing built around a social media platform. It's still developing, and it's not without controversy; but it's also here to stay.

DO

A CASE ANALYSIS.
STRENGTHEN YOUR
CRITICAL THINKING!

Dig into this **Hot Topic**

■ **PRO AND CON DEBATE?** **Is it right for students to crowdfund their human capital?**

Crowdfunding is an interesting option for entrepreneurs. But how far should the practice go?

Situation An undergraduate student at an art and design school needs money to pay back student loans and fund ideas for a startup company. He goes online at Upstart.com and finds investors willing to give him upfront money in return for a portion of what he earns in the future. He signs on and takes in $38,500.

GET

AND STAY INFORMED.
MAKE YOURSELF
VALUABLE!

The idea here is to sell equity stakes in your human capital. In other words, get money now from people willing to invest in you while hoping for good paybacks from rights to a percentage of your future pre-tax earnings. Terms used to describe this form of crowdfunding are "human-capital contracts" or "social financial agreements."

Those in favor of students' crowdfunding their human capital are likely to say that it helps them get the education or resources they need to succeed. It's also a way of avoiding interest on debt; if the student fails to earn enough or the project fails, the investor loses. And, the investors may turn out to be good mentors and motivators that drive the student to high levels of achievement.

Those against students' crowdfunding their human capital are likely say that it's a form of servitude. It's not right for one person to indenture themselves to another in this way. Young students, furthermore, may not be mature or insightful enough to make good decisions that commit them to long-term financial contracts. And if the student's "back is to the wall," she or he might make a really bad decision.

Final Faceoff   How about it? Is crowdfunding human capital something that sounds attractive to you? What are the possible risks and returns as you see them? If you were a parent, would you let your child do this? If you were an investor, would you consider this a legitimate way to earn a return on your money?

Great jobs aren't easy to get. Career success today requires lots of initiative, self-awareness, and continuous personal improvement. The question is: "Are you ready?"

Self-Assessments **Class Exercises** **Team Projects**

Self-Assessment 1: Personal Career Readiness

Instructions

Use this scale to rate yourself on the following list of personal characteristics.[1]

- **S** = Strong, I am very confident with this one.
- **G** = Good, but I still have room to grow.
- **W** = Weak, I really need work on this one.
- **U** = Unsure, I just don't know.

_____ **1.** *Resistance to stress:* The ability to get work done even under stressful conditions

_____ **2.** *Tolerance for uncertainty:* The ability to get work done even under ambiguous and uncertain conditions

_____ **3.** *Social objectivity:* The ability to act free of racial, ethnic, gender, and other prejudices or biases

_____ **4.** *Inner work standards:* The ability to personally set and work to high performance standards

_____ **5.** *Stamina:* The ability to sustain long work hours

_____ **6.** *Adaptability:* The ability to be flexible and adapt to changes

_____ **7.** *Self-confidence:* The ability to be consistently decisive and display one's personal presence

_____ **8.** *Self-objectivity:* The ability to evaluate personal strengths and weaknesses and to understand one's motives and skills relative to a job

_____ **9.** *Introspection:* The ability to learn from experience, awareness, and self-study

_____ **10.** *Entrepreneurism:* The ability to address problems and take advantage of opportunities for constructive change

Scoring

Give yourself 1 point for each S, and 1/2 point for each G. Do not give yourself points for W or U responses. Total your points and enter the result here: _____.

Interpretation

This assessment offers a self-described *profile of your management foundations*. Are you a perfect 10 or something less? There shouldn't be too many 10s around. Also ask someone else to assess you on this instrument. You may be surprised at the results, but the insights are well worth thinking about. The items on the list are skills and personal characteristics that should be nurtured now and throughout your career.

Self-Assessment 2: Managerial Assumptions

Instructions

Use the space in the left margin to write "Yes" if you agree with the statement or "No" if you disagree with it. Force yourself to take a "yes" or "no" position for every statement.

1. Are good pay and a secure job enough to satisfy most workers?
2. Should a manager help and coach subordinates in their work?
3. Do most people like real responsibility in their jobs?
4. Are most people afraid to learn new things in their jobs?
5. Should managers let subordinates control the quality of their work?
6. Do most people dislike work?
7. Are most people creative?
8. Should a manager closely supervise and direct the work of subordinates?
9. Do most people tend to resist change?
10. Do most people work only as hard as they have to?
11. Should workers be allowed to set their own job goals?
12. Are most people happiest off the job?
13. Do most workers really care about the organization they work for?
14. Should a manager help subordinates advance and grow in their jobs?

Scoring

Count the number of "yes" responses to items 1, 4, 6, 8, 9, 10, 12; write that number here as [**X** = _____].

Count the number of "yes" responses to items 2, 3, 5, 7, 11, 13, 14; write that score here as [**Y** = _____].

Interpretation

This assessment examines your orientation toward Douglas McGregor's Theory X (your "X" score) and Theory Y (your "Y" score) assumptions. Consider how your X/Y assumptions might influence how you behave toward other people at work. What self-fulfilling prophecies are you likely to create?

Self-Assessment 3: Terminal Values Survey

Instructions

1. Read the following list of things people value.[2] Think about the importance of each value as a guiding principle in your life.

A comfortable life	An exciting life	A sense of accomplishment
A world at peace	A world of beauty	Equality
Family security	Freedom	Happiness
Inner harmony	Mature love	National security
Pleasure	Salvation	Self-respect
Social recognition	True friendship	Wisdom

2. *Circle* six of these 18 values to indicate that they are *most important* to you. If you can, rank-order these most important values by writing a number above them—with "1" the most important value in my life, and so on through "6."

3. *Underline* the six of these 18 values that are *least important* to you.

Interpretation

Terminal values reflect a person's preferences concerning the ends to be achieved. They are the goals individuals would like to achieve in their lifetimes. As you look at the items you have selected as most and least important, what major differences exist among the items in the two sets? Think about this and then answer the following questions.

A) What does your selection of most and least important values say about you as a person?

B) What does your selection of most and least important values suggest about the type of work and career that might be best for you?

C) Which values among your most and least important selections might cause problems for you in the future—at work and/or in your personal life? What problems might they cause, and why? How might you prepare now to best deal with these problems in the future?

D) How might your choices of most and least important values turn out to be major strengths or assets for you—at work and/or in your personal life, and why?

Self-Assessment 4: Intuitive Ability

Instructions

Answer each of the following questions.[3]

1. Do you prefer to: **(a)** be given a problem and left free to do it?   **(b)** get clear instructions on how to solve a problem before starting?

2. Do you prefer to work with colleagues who are: **(a)** realistic?   **(b)** imaginative?

3. Do you most admire: **(a)** creative people?   **(b)** careful people?

4. Do your friends tend to be: **(a)** serious and hardworking?   **(b)** exciting and emotional?

5. When you ask for advice on a problem, do you: **(a)** seldom or never get upset if your basic assumptions are questioned?   **(b)** often get upset with such questions?

6. When you start your day, do you: **(a)** seldom make or follow a specific plan?   **(b)** usually make and follow a plan?

7. When working with numbers, do you make factual errors: **(a)** seldom or never?   **(b)** often?

8. Do you: **(a)** seldom daydream and really not enjoy it?   **(b)** often daydream and enjoy it?

9. When working on a problem, do you: **(a)** prefer to follow instructions or rules?   **(b)** often enjoy bypassing instructions or rules?

10. When trying to put something together, do you prefer: **(a)** step-by-step assembly instructions?   **(b)** a picture of the assembled item?

11. Do you find that people who irritate you most appear to be: **(a)** disorganized?   **(b)** organized?

12. When an unexpected crisis comes up, do you: **(a)** feel anxious?   **(b)** feel excited by the challenge?

Scoring

Total the a responses for 1, 3, 5, 6, 11; [**A** = _____].

Total the b responses for 2, 4, 7, 8, 9, 10, 12; [**B** = _____].

Your *intuitive score* is A + B. The highest score is 12.

Self-Assessment 5: Time Management Profile

Instructions

Indicate Y (yes) or N (no) for each item. Be frank; let your responses describe an accurate picture of how you tend to respond to these kinds of situations.[4]

1. When confronted with several items of similar urgency and importance, I tend to do the easiest one first.
2. I do the most important things during that part of the day when I know I perform best.
3. Most of the time I don't do things someone else can do; I delegate this type of work to others.
4. Even though meetings without a clear and useful purpose upset me, I put up with them.
5. I skim documents before reading them and don't complete any that offer a low return on my time investment.
6. I don't worry much if I don't accomplish at least one significant task each day.
7. I save the most trivial tasks for that time of day when my creative energy is lowest.
8. My workspace is neat and organized.
9. My office door is always "open"; I never work in complete privacy.
10. I schedule my time completely from start to finish every workday.
11. I don't like "to-do" lists, preferring to respond to daily events as they occur.
12. I "block" a certain amount of time each day or week to be dedicated to high-priority activities.

Scoring

Count the number of Y responses to items 2, 3, 5, 7, 8, 12. [Enter that score here _____]. Count the number of N responses to items 1, 4, 6, 9, 10, 11. [Enter that score here _____]. Add together the two scores.

Interpretation

The higher the total score, the closer your behavior matches recommended time management guidelines. Reread those items where your response did not match the desired one. Why don't they match? Are there reasons for your action tendencies? Think about what you can do to be more consistent with time management guidelines.

Self-Assessment 6: Internal/External Control

Instructions

Circle either a or b to indicate the item you most agree with in each pair of the following statements.[5]

1. (a) Promotions are earned through hard work and persistence.
   (b) Making a lot of money is largely a matter of breaks.
2. (a) Many times the reactions of teachers seem haphazard to me.
   (b) In my experience I have noticed that there is usually a direct connection between how hard I study and the grades I get.
3. (a) The number of divorces indicates that more and more people are not trying to make their marriages work.
   (b) Marriage is largely a gamble.
4. (a) It is silly to think that one can really change another person's basic attitudes.
   (b) When I am right, I can convince others.
5. (a) Getting promoted is really a matter of being a little luckier than the next guy.
   (b) In our society, an individual's future earning power is dependent on his or her ability.
6. (a) If one knows how to deal with people, they are really quite easily led.
   (b) I have little influence over the way other people behave.
7. (a) In my case, the grades I make are the results of my own efforts; luck has little or nothing to do with it.
   (b) Sometimes I feel that I have little to do with the grades I get.
8. (a) People such as I can change the course of world affairs if we make ourselves heard.
   (b) It is only wishful thinking to believe that one can really influence what happens in society at large.
9. (a) Much of what happens to me is probably a matter of chance.
   (b) I am the master of my fate.
10. (a) Getting along with people is a skill that must be practiced.
    (b) It is almost impossible to figure out how to please some people.

Scoring

Give yourself 1 point for 1b, 2a, 3a, 4b, 5b, 6a, 7a, 8a, 9b, 10a. Total scores of: 8–10 = high *internal* locus of control, 6–7 = moderate *internal* locus of control, 5 = *mixed* locus of control, 3–4 = moderate *external* locus of control, 0–2 = high *external* locus of control.

Interpretation

This instrument offers an impression of your tendency toward an *internal locus of control or external locus of control*. Persons with a high internal locus of control tend to believe they have control over their own destinies. They may be most responsive to opportunities for greater self-control in the workplace. Persons with a high external locus of control tend to believe that what happens to them is largely in the hands of external people or forces. They may be less comfortable with self-control and more responsive to external controls in the workplace.

Self-Assessment 7: Handling Facts and Inferences

Instructions

1. Read the following report.[6]

   A well-liked college instructor had just completed making up the final examination and had turned off the lights in the office. Just then a tall, broad figure with dark glasses appeared and demanded the examination. The professor opened the drawer. Everything in the drawer was picked up, and the individual ran down the corridor. The president was notified immediately.

2. Indicate whether you think the following observations are true (T), false (F), or doubtful in that it may be either true or false (?). Judge each observation in order. Do not reread the observations after you have indicated your judgment, and do not change any of your answers.

   1. The thief was tall, broad, and wore dark glasses.
   2. The professor turned off the lights.
   3. A tall figure demanded the examination.
   4. The examination was picked up by someone.
   5. The examination was picked up by the professor.
   6. A tall, broad figure appeared after the professor turned off the lights in the office.
   7. The man who opened the drawer was the professor.
   8. The professor ran down the corridor.
   9. The drawer was never actually opened.
   10. Three persons are referred to in this report.

Scoring

The correct answers in reverse order (starting with 10) are: ?, F, ?, ?, T, ?, ?, T, T, ?.

Interpretation

To begin, ask yourself if there was a difference between your answers and the correct ones. If so, why? Why do you think people, individually or in groups, may answer these questions incorrectly? Good planning depends on good decision making by the people doing the planning. Being able to distinguish "facts" and understand one's "inferences" are important steps toward improving the planning process. Involving others to help do the same can frequently assist in this process.

Self-Assessment 8: Empowering Others

Instructions

Think of times when you have been in charge of a group—this could be a full-time or part-time work situation, a student work group, or whatever. Complete the following questionnaire by recording how you feel about each statement according to this scale.[7]

   1 = Strongly disagree   2 = Disagree   3 = Neutral   4 = Agree   5 = Strongly agree

When in charge of a team, I find that

1. Most of the time other people are too inexperienced to do things, so I prefer to do them myself.
2. It often takes more time to explain things to others than to just do them myself.
3. Mistakes made by others are costly, so I don't assign much work to them.
4. Some things simply should not be delegated to others.
5. I often get quicker action by doing a job myself.
6. Many people are good only at very specific tasks, so they can't be assigned additional responsibilities.
7. Many people are too busy to take on additional work.
8. Most people just aren't ready to handle additional responsibilities.
9. In my position, I should be entitled to make my own decisions.

Scoring

Total your responses and enter the score here [_____].

Interpretation

This instrument gives an impression of your willingness to delegate. Possible scores range from 9 to 45. The lower your score, the more willing you appear to be to delegate to others. Willingness to delegate is an important managerial characteristic: It is how you—as a manager—can empower others and give them opportunities to assume responsibility and exercise self-control in their work. With the growing importance of horizontal organizations and empowerment in the new workplace, your willingness to delegate is worth thinking about seriously.

Self-Assessment 9: Tolerance for Ambiguity

Instructions

Rate each of the following items on this seven-point scale.[8]

strongly agree   1   2   3   4   5   6   7   strongly disagree

_____ 1. An expert who doesn't come up with a definite answer probably doesn't know too much.

_____ 2. There is really no such thing as a problem that can't be solved.

_____ 3. I would like to live in a foreign country for a while.

_____ 4. People who fit their lives to a schedule probably miss the joy of living.

_____ 5. A good job is one where what is to be done and how it is to be done are always clear.

_____ 6. In the long run it is possible to get more done by tackling small, simple problems rather than large, complicated ones.

_____ 7. It is more fun to tackle a complicated problem than it is to solve a simple one.

_____ 8. Often the most interesting and stimulating people are those who don't mind being different and original.

_____ 9. What we are used to is always preferable to what is unfamiliar.

_____ 10. A person who leads an even, regular life in which few surprises or unexpected happenings arise really has a lot to be grateful for.

_____ 11. People who insist upon a yes or no answer just don't know how complicated things really are.

_____ 12. Many of our most important decisions are based on insufficient information.

_____ 13. I like parties where I know most of the people more than ones where most of the people are complete strangers.

_____ 14. The sooner we all acquire ideals, the better.

_____ 15. Teachers or supervisors who hand out vague assignments give a chance for one to show initiative and originality.

_____ 16. A good teacher is one who makes you wonder about your way of looking at things.

Scoring

To obtain a score, first *reverse* your scores for items 3, 4, 7, 8, 11, 12, 15, and 16 (i.e., a rating of 1 = 7, 2 = 6, 3 = 5, etc.).

Next add up your scores for all 16 items. The higher your total, the higher your indicated tolerance for ambiguity.

Self-Assessment 10: Performance Review Assumptions

Instructions

In each of the following pairs of statements, check the one that best reflects your assumptions about performance evaluation.[9]

1. **(a)** a formal process that is done annually
   (b) an informal process done continuously

2. **(a)** a process that is planned for subordinates
   (b) a process that is planned with subordinates

3. **(a)** a required organizational procedure
   (b) a process done regardless of requirements

4. **(a)** a time to evaluate subordinates' performance
   (b) a time for subordinates to evaluate their manager

5. **(a)** a time to clarify standards
   (b) a time to clarify the subordinate's career needs

6. **(a)** a time to confront poor performance

   (b) a time to express appreciation

7. **(a)** an opportunity to clarify issues and provide direction and control

   (b) an opportunity to increase enthusiasm and commitment

8. **(a)** only as good as the organization's forms

   (b) only as good as the manager's coaching skills

Interpretation

In general, the (a) responses show more emphasis on the *evaluation* function of performance appraisal. This largely puts the supervisor in the role of documenting a subordinate's performance for control and administrative purposes. The (b) responses show a stronger emphasis on the *counseling* or *development* function. Here, the supervisor is concerned with helping the subordinate do better and with learning from the subordinate what he or she needs to be able to do better.

Self-Assessment 11: Least Preferred Co-Worker Scale

Instructions

Think of all the different people with whom you have ever worked—in jobs, in social clubs, in student projects, or whatever. Next, think of the one person with whom you could work least well—that is, the person with whom you had the most difficulty getting a job done. This is the one person—a peer, boss, or subordinate—with whom you would least want to work. Describe this person by circling numbers at the appropriate points on each of the following pairs of bipolar adjectives. Work rapidly. There is no right or wrong answer.[10]

Pleasant	8 7 6 5 4 3 2 1	Unpleasant
Friendly	8 7 6 5 4 3 2 1	Unfriendly
Rejecting	1 2 3 4 5 6 7 8	Accepting
Tense	1 2 3 4 5 6 7 8	Relaxed
Distant	1 2 3 4 5 6 7 8	Close
Cold	1 2 3 4 5 6 7 8	Warm
Supportive	8 7 6 5 4 3 2 1	Hostile
Boring	1 2 3 4 5 6 7 8	Interesting
Quarrelsome	1 2 3 4 5 6 7 8	Harmonious
Gloomy	1 2 3 4 5 6 7 8	Cheerful
Open	8 7 6 5 4 3 2 1	Guarded
Backbiting	1 2 3 4 5 6 7 8	Loyal
Untrustworthy	1 2 3 4 5 6 7 8	Trustworthy
Considerate	8 7 6 5 4 3 2 1	Inconsiderate
Nasty	1 2 3 4 5 6 7 8	Nice
Agreeable	8 7 6 5 4 3 2 1	Disagreeable
Insincere	1 2 3 4 5 6 7 8	Sincere
Kind	8 7 6 5 4 3 2 1	Unkind

Scoring

This is called the "least-preferred co-worker scale" (LPC). Compute your LPC score by totaling all the numbers you circled; enter that score here [LPC = _____].

Interpretation

The LPC scale is used by Fred Fiedler to identify a person's dominant leadership style. Fiedler believes that this style is a relatively fixed part of one's personality and is therefore difficult to change. This leads Fiedler to his contingency views, which suggest that the key to leadership success is finding (or creating) good "matches" between style and situation.

If your score is 73 or above on the LPC scale, Fiedler considers you a "relationship-motivated" leader; if it is 64 or below on the scale, he considers you a "task-motivated" leader. If your score is between 65 and 72, Fiedler leaves it up to you to determine which leadership style is most accurate.

Self-Assessment 12: Stress Test

Instructions

Complete the following questionnaire. Circle the number that best represents your tendency to behave on each bipolar dimension.[11]

Am casual about appointments	1	2	3	4	5	6	7	8	Am never late for appointments
Am not competitive	1	2	3	4	5	6	7	8	Am very competitive
Never feel rushed	1	2	3	4	5	6	7	8	Always feel rushed
Take things one at a time	1	2	3	4	5	6	7	8	Try to do many things at once
Do things slowly	1	2	3	4	5	6	7	8	Do things fast
Express feelings	1	2	3	4	5	6	7	8	"Sit on" feelings
Have many interests	1	2	3	4	5	6	7	8	Have few interests but work

Scoring

Total the numbers circled for all items, and multiply this by 3; enter the result here [_____].

Points	Personality Type
120+	A+
106–119	A
100–105	A−
90–99	B+
below 90	B

Self-Assessment 13: Two-Factor Profile

Instructions

On each of the following dimensions, distribute a total of 10 points to indicate your preference between the two options. For example:

Summer weather	(7)	(3)	Winter weather
1. Very responsible job	(__)	(__)	Job security
2. Recognition for work accomplishments	(__)	(__)	Good relations with co-workers
3. Advancement opportunities at work	(__)	(__)	A boss who knows his/her job well
4. Opportunities to grow and learn on the job	(__)	(__)	Good working conditions
5. A job that I can do well	(__)	(__)	Supportive rules, policies of employer
6. A prestigious or high-status job	(__)	(__)	A high base wage or salary

Scoring

Summarize your total score for all items in the *left-hand column* and write it here. MF = _____

Summarize your total score for all items in the *right-hand column* and write it here. HF = _____

Interpretation

The MF score indicates the relative importance that you place on the motivating, or satisfier, factors in Herzberg's two-factor theory. This shows how important job content is to you. The HF score indicates the relative importance that you place on hygiene, or dissatisfier, factors in Herzberg's two-factor theory. This shows how important job context is to you.

Self-Assessment 14: Team Leader Skills

Instructions

Consider your experiences in groups and work teams. Ask: "What skills do I bring to team leadership situations?" Then complete the following inventory by rating yourself on each item using this scale.[12]

1 = Almost never   2 = Seldom   3 = Sometimes   4 = Usually   5 = Almost always

_____ 1. I facilitate communications with and among team members between team meetings.

_____ 2. I provide feedback/coaching to individual team members on their performance.

_____ 3. I encourage creative and out-of-the-box thinking.

_____ **4.** I continue to clarify stakeholder needs/expectations.

_____ **5.** I keep team members' responsibilities and activities focused within the team's objectives and goals.

_____ **6.** I organize and run effective and productive team meetings.

_____ **7.** I demonstrate integrity and personal commitment.

_____ **8.** I have excellent persuasive and influence skills.

_____ **9.** I respect and leverage the team's cross-functional diversity.

_____ **10.** I recognize and reward individual contributions to team performance.

_____ **11.** I use the appropriate decision-making style for specific issues.

_____ **12.** I facilitate and encourage border management with the team's key stakeholders.

_____ **13.** I ensure that the team meets its team commitments.

_____ **14.** I bring team issues and problems to the team's attention and focus on constructive problem solving.

_____ **15.** I provide a clear vision and direction for the team.

Scoring and Interpretation

Add your scores for the items listed next to each dimension below to get an indication of your potential strengths and weaknesses on seven dimensions of team leadership. The higher the score, the more confident you are on the particular skill and leadership capability. When considering the score, ask yourself if others would rate you the same way.

1, 9	Building the team
2, 10	Developing people
3, 11	Team problem solving/decision making
4, 12	Stakeholder relations
5, 13	Team performance
6, 14	Team process
7, 8, 15	Providing personal leadership

Self-Assessment 15: Feedback and Assertiveness

Instructions

For each statement below, decide which of the following answers best fits you.[13]

1 = Never true   2 = Sometimes true   3 = Often true   4 = Always true

_____ **1.** I respond with more modesty than I really feel when my work is complimented.

_____ **2.** If people are rude, I will be rude right back.

_____ **3.** Other people find me interesting.

_____ **4.** I find it difficult to speak up in a group of strangers.

_____ **5.** I don't mind using sarcasm if it helps me make a point.

_____ **6.** I ask for a raise when I feel I really deserve it.

_____ **7.** If others interrupt me when I am talking, I suffer in silence.

_____ **8.** If people criticize my work, I find a way to make them back down.

_____ **9.** I can express pride in my accomplishments without being boastful.

_____ **10.** People take advantage of me.

_____ **11.** I tell people what they want to hear if it helps me get what I want.

_____ **12.** I find it easy to ask for help.

_____ **13.** I lend things to others even when I don't really want to.

_____ **14.** I win arguments by dominating the discussion.

_____ **15.** I can express my true feelings to someone I really care for.

_____ **16.** When I feel angry with other people, I bottle it up rather than express it.

_____ **17.** When I criticize someone else's work, they get mad.

_____ **18.** I feel confident in my ability to stand up for my rights.

Scoring and Interpretation

Aggressiveness tendency score—Add items 2, 5, 8, 11, 14, and 17.

Passiveness tendency score—Add items 1, 4, 7, 10, 13, and 16.

Assertiveness tendency score—Add items 3, 6, 9, 12, 15, and 18.

The maximum score in any single area is 24. The minimum score is 6. Try to find someone who knows you well. Have this person complete the instrument also as it relates to you. Compare his or her impression of you with your own score. What is this telling you about your behavior tendencies in social situations?

Self-Assessment 16: Diversity Awareness

Instructions

Indicate O for often, S for sometimes, and N for never in response to each of the following questions as they pertain to where you work or go to school.

1. How often have you heard jokes or remarks about other people that you consider offensive?
2. How often do you hear men "talk down" to women in an attempt to keep them in an inferior status?
3. How often have you felt personal discomfort as the object of sexual harassment?
4. How often do you work or study with persons of different ethnic or national cultures?
5. How often have you felt disadvantaged because members of ethnic groups other than yours were given special treatment?
6. How often have you seen a woman put in an uncomfortable situation because of unwelcome advances by a man?
7. How often does it seem that African Americans, Hispanics, Caucasians, women, men, and members of other minority demographic groups seem to "stick together" during work breaks or other leisure situations?
8. How often do you feel uncomfortable about something you did and/or said to someone of the opposite sex or a member of an ethnic or racial group other than yours?
9. How often do you feel efforts are made in this setting to raise the level of cross-cultural understanding among people who work and/or study together?
10. How often do you step in to communicate concerns to others when you feel actions and/or words are used to the disadvantage of minorities?

Interpretation

There are no correct answers for the Diversity Awareness Checklist. The key issue is the extent to which you are sensitive to diversity issues in the workplace or university. Are you comfortable with your responses? How do you think others in your class responded? Why not share your responses with others and examine different viewpoints on this important issue?

Self-Assessment 17: Global Intelligence

Instructions

Use the following scale to rate yourself on these 10 items.[14]

   1 = Very poor   2 = Poor   3 = Acceptable   4 = Good   5 = Very good

1. I understand my own culture in terms of its expectations, values, and influence on communication and relationships.
2. When someone presents me with a different point of view, I try to understand it rather than attack it.
3. I am comfortable dealing with situations where the available information is incomplete and the outcomes unpredictable.
4. I am open to new situations and am always looking for new information and learning opportunities.
5. I have a good understanding of the attitudes and perceptions toward my culture as they are held by people from other cultures.
6. I am always gathering information about other countries and cultures and trying to learn from them.
7. I am well informed regarding the major differences in the government, political, and economic systems around the world.
8. I work hard to increase my understanding of people from other cultures.
9. I am able to adjust my communication style to work effectively with people from different cultures.
10. I can recognize when cultural differences are influencing working relationships, and I adjust my attitudes and behavior accordingly.

Scoring

The goal is to score as close to a perfect 5 as possible on each of the three dimensions of global intelligence. Develop your scores as follows:

• Items (1 + 2 + 3 + 4)/4 = _____ **Global Mindset Score**—The extent to which you are receptive to and respectful of cultural differences.

- Items $(5 + 6 + 7)/3 =$ **Global Knowledge Score**—Your openness to know and learn more about other nations and cultures.
- Items $(8 + 9 + 10)/3 =$ **Global Work Skills Score**—Your capacity to work effectively across cultures.

Interpretation

To be successful in the global economy, you must be comfortable with the cultural diversity that it holds. This requires a global mindset that is receptive to and respectful of cultural differences, global knowledge that includes the continuing quest to know and learn more about other nations and cultures, and global work skills that allow you to work effectively across cultures.

Self-Assessment 18: Entrepreneurship Orientation

Instructions

Answer each of the following questions.[15]

1. What portion of your college expenses did you earn (or are you earning)?

   (a) 50% or more **(b)** Less than 50% **(c)** None

2. In college, your academic performance was/is

   (a) above average. **(b)** average. **(c)** below average.

3. What is your basic reason for considering opening a business?

   (a) I want to make money. **(b)** I want to control my own destiny. **(c)** I hate the frustration of working for someone else.

4. Which phrase best describes your attitude toward work?

   (a) I can keep going as long as I need to; I don't mind working for something I want. **(b)** I can work hard for a while, but when I've had enough, I quit. **(c)** Hard work really doesn't get you anywhere.

5. How would you rate your organizing skills?

   (a) Superorganized **(b)** Above average **(c)** Average **(d)** I do well to find half the things I look for.

6. You are primarily a(n)

   (a) optimist. **(b)** pessimist. **(c)** neither.

7. You are faced with a challenging problem. As you work, you realize you are stuck. You will most likely

   (a) give up. **(b)** ask for help. **(c)** keep plugging; you'll figure it out.

8. You are playing a game with a group of friends. You are most interested in

   (a) winning. **(b)** playing well. **(c)** making sure that everyone has a good time. **(d)** cheating as much as possible.

9. How would you describe your feelings toward failure?

   (a) Fear of failure paralyzes me. **(b)** Failure can be a good learning experience. **(c)** Knowing that I might fail motivates me to work even harder. **(d)** "Damn the torpedoes! Full speed ahead."

10. Which phrase best describes you?

    (a) I need constant encouragement to get anything done. **(b)** If someone gets me started, I can keep going. **(c)** I am energetic and hardworking—a self-starter.

11. Which bet would you most likely accept?

    (a) A wager on a dog race **(b)** A wager on a racquetball game in which you play an opponent **(c)** Neither. I never make wagers.

12. At the Kentucky Derby, you would bet on

    (a) the 100-to-1 long shot. **(b)** the odds-on favorite. **(c)** the 3-to-1 shot. **(d)** none of the above.

Scoring

Give yourself 10 points each for answers 1a, 2a, 3c, 4a, 5a, 6a, 7c, 8a, 9c, 10c, 11b, 12c; total the scores and enter the result here [I = _____].

Give yourself 8 points each for answers 3b, 8b, 9b; enter total here [II = _____].

Give yourself 6 points each for answers 2b, 5b; enter total here [III = _____].

Give yourself 5 points for answer 1b; enter result here [IV = _____].

Give yourself 4 points for answer 5c; enter result here [V = _____].

Give yourself 2 points each for answers 2c, 3a, 4b, 6c, 9d, 10b, 11a, 12b; enter total here [VI = _____].

The other answers are worth 0 points.

Total your summary scores for I + II + III + IV + V + VI and enter the result here: My Entrepreneurship Potential Score is _____.

Interpretation

This assessment offers an impression of your *entrepreneurial profile (EP)*. It compares your characteristics with those of typical entrepreneurs, according to this profile: 100+ = Entrepreneur extraordinaire; 80–99 = Entrepreneur; 60–79 = Potential entrepreneur; 0–59 = Entrepreneur in the rough.

Class Exercise 1: My Best Manager

Preparation

Working alone, make a list of the *behavioral attributes* that describe the "best" manager you have ever had.[1] This could be someone you worked for in a full-time or part-time job, summer job, volunteer job, student organization, or elsewhere. If you have trouble identifying an actual manager, make a list of behavioral attributes of the manager you would most like to work for in your next job.

Instructions

Form into teams as assigned by your instructor, or work with a nearby classmate. Share your list of attributes and listen to the lists of others. Be sure to ask questions and make comments on items of special interest. Work together in your team to create a master list that combines the unique attributes of the "best" managers experienced by members of your group. Have a spokesperson share that list with the rest of the class for further discussion.

Class Exercise 2: Evidence-Based Management Quiz

Instructions

1. For each of the following questions, answer T (true) if you believe the statement is backed by solid research evidence or F (false) if you do not believe it is an evidence-based statement.[2]

    1. Intelligence is a better predictor of job performance than having a conscientious personality.
    2. Screening job candidates for values results in higher job performance than screening for intelligence.
    3. A highly intelligent person will have a hard time performing well in a low-skill job.
    4. "Integrity tests" are good predictors of whether employees will steal, be absent, or take advantage of their employers in other ways.
    5. Goal setting is more likely to result in improved performance than is participation in decision making.
    6. Errors in performance appraisals can be reduced through proper training.
    7. People behave in ways that show pay is more important to them than what they indicate on surveys.

2. Share your answers with others in your assigned group. Discuss the reasons members chose the answers they did; arrive at a final answer to each question for the group as a whole.

3. Compare your results with these answers "from the evidence."

4. Engage in a class discussion of how "commonsense" answers can sometimes differ from answers provided by "evidence." Ask: What are the implications of this discussion for management practice?

Class Exercise 3: Confronting Ethical Dilemmas

Preparation

Read and indicate your response to each of the following situations.

1. Ron Jones, vice president of a large construction firm, receives in the mail a large envelope marked "personal." It contains a competitor's cost data for a project that both firms will be bidding on shortly. The data are accompanied by a note from one of Ron's subordinates saying: "This is the real thing!" Ron knows that the data could be a major advantage to his firm in preparing a bid that can win the contract. What should he do?

2. Kay Smith is one of your top-performing team members. She has shared with you her desire to apply for promotion to a new position just announced in a different division of the company. This will be tough on you because recent budget cuts mean you will be unable to replace anyone who leaves, at least for quite some time. Kay knows this and, in all fairness, has asked your permission before she submits an application. It is rumored that the son of a good friend of your boss is going to apply for the job. Although his credentials are less impressive than Kay's, the likelihood is that he will get the job if she doesn't apply. What will you do?

3. Marty José got caught in a bind. She was pleased to represent her firm as head of the local community development committee. In fact, her supervisor's boss once held this position and told her in a hallway conversation, "Do your best and give them every support possible." Going along with this, Marty agreed to pick up the bill (several hundred dollars) for a dinner meeting with local civic and business leaders. Shortly thereafter, her supervisor informed everyone that the entertainment budget was being eliminated in a cost-saving effort. Marty, not wanting to renege on supporting the community development committee, was able to charge the dinner bill to an advertising budget. Eventually, an internal auditor discovered the charge and reported it to you, the personnel director. Marty is scheduled to meet with you in a few minutes. What will you do?

Instructions

Working alone, make the requested decisions in each of these incidents. Think carefully about your justification for the decision. Meet in a group assigned by your instructor. Share your decisions and justifications in each case with other group members. Listen to theirs. Try to reach a group consensus on what to do in each situation and why. Be prepared to share the group decisions, and any dissenting views, in general class discussion.

Class Exercise 4: Lost at Sea

Preparation

Consider This Situation: You are adrift on a private yacht in the South Pacific when a fire of unknown origin destroys the yacht and most of its contents.[3] You and a small group of survivors are now in a large raft with oars. Your location is unclear, but you estimate that you are about 1,000 miles south-southwest of the nearest land. One person has just found in her pockets five $1 bills and a packet of matches. Everyone else's pockets are empty. The following items are available to you on the raft.

	Individual ranking	Team ranking	Expert ranking
Sextant	_____	_____	_____
Shaving mirror	_____	_____	_____
5 gallons water	_____	_____	_____
Mosquito netting	_____	_____	_____
1 survival meal	_____	_____	_____
Maps of Pacific Ocean	_____	_____	_____
Floatable seat cushion	_____	_____	_____
2 gallons oil-gas mix	_____	_____	_____
Small transistor radio	_____	_____	_____
Shark repellent	_____	_____	_____
20 square feet black plastic	_____	_____	_____
1 quart 20-proof rum	_____	_____	_____
15 feet nylon rope	_____	_____	_____
24 chocolate bars	_____	_____	_____
Fishing kit	_____	_____	_____

Instructions

1. *Working alone,* rank the 15 items in order of their importance to your survival (1 is most important and 15 is least important).
2. *Working in an assigned group,* arrive at a "team" ranking of the 15 items. Appoint one person as team spokesperson to report your team ranking to the class.
3. *Do not write in column* 3 until your instructor provides the "expert" ranking.

Class Exercise 5: The Future Workplace

Instructions

Form groups as assigned by the instructor. Brainstorm to develop a master list of the major characteristics you expect to find in the workplace in the year 2020. Use this list as background for completing the following tasks:

1. Write a one-paragraph description of what the typical "Workplace 2020" manager's workday will be like.
2. Draw a "picture" representing what the "Workplace 2020" organization will look like.
3. Summarize in list form what you consider to be the major planning implications of your future workplace scenario for management students today. That is, explain what this means in terms of using academic and extracurricular activities to best prepare for success in this future scenario.
4. Choose a spokesperson to share your results with the class as a whole and explain their implications for the class members.

Class Exercise 6: Stakeholder Maps

Preparation

Review the discussion of organizational stakeholders in the textbook. (1) Make a list of the stakeholders that would apply to all organizations—for example, local communities, employees, and customers. What others would you add to this starter listing? (2) Choose one organization that you are familiar with from each list that follows. (3) Draw a map of key stakeholders for each organization. (4) For each stakeholder, indicate its major interest in the organization. (5) For each organization, make a list of possible conflicts among stakeholders that the top manager should recognize.

Nonprofit	Government	Business
Elementary school	Local mayor's office	Convenience store
Community hospital	State police	Movie theater
Church	U.S. Senator	National retailer
University	Internal Revenue Service	Local pizza shop
United Way	Homeland Security agency	Urgent care medical clinic

Instructions

In groups assigned by your instructor, choose one organization from each list. Create "master" stakeholder maps for each organization, along with statements of stakeholder interests and lists of potential stakeholder conflicts. Assume the position of top manager for each organization. Prepare a "stakeholder management plan" that represents the high-priority issues the manager should be addressing with respect to the stakeholders. Make a presentation to the class for each of your organizations and engage in discussion about the importance and complexity of stakeholder analysis.

Class Exercise 7: Strategic Scenarios

Preparation

In today's turbulent economic climate, it is no longer safe to assume that an organization that was highly successful yesterday will continue to be so tomorrow—or that it will even be in existence.[4] Changing times exact the best from strategic planners. Think about the situations currently facing the following well-known organizations. Think, too, about the futures they may face.

McDonald's	Ford	Sony
Apple Computer	Nordstrom	United Airlines
Yahoo!	National Public Radio	AT&T
Ann Taylor	*The New York Times*	Federal Express

Instructions

Form into groups as assigned by your instructor. Choose one or more organizations from the prior list (or as assigned) and answer the following questions for the organization:

1. What in the future might seriously threaten the success, perhaps the very existence, of this organization? As a group, develop at least three such *future scenarios*.
2. Estimate the probability (0 to 100%) of each future scenario occurring.
3. Develop a strategy for each scenario that will enable the organization to successfully deal with it.
4. Thoroughly discuss these questions within the group and arrive at your best possible consensus answers. Be prepared to share and defend your answers in general class discussion.

Class Exercise 8: Organizational Metaphors

Instructions

1. Start by answering the following questions using this scale:

   5 = strongly agree   4 = agree somewhat   3 = undecided   2 = disagree somewhat   1 = strongly disagree

   I prefer to work in an organization where:

   _____ 1. Goals are defined by those in higher levels.

   _____ 2. Work methods and procedures are specified.

   _____ 3. Top management makes important decisions.

Class Exercise 12: Job Satisfaction Preferences

Preparation

Rank the following items from 1 = least important to 9 = most important to your future job satisfaction.[6]

My job will be satisfying when:

_____ **1.** It is respected by other people.

_____ **2.** It encourages continued development of knowledge and skills.

_____ **3.** It provides job security.

_____ **4.** It provides a feeling of accomplishment.

_____ **5.** It provides the opportunity to earn a high income.

_____ **6.** It is intellectually stimulating.

_____ **7.** It rewards good performance with recognition.

_____ **8.** It provides comfortable working conditions.

_____ **9.** It permits advancement to high administrative responsibility.

Instructions

Form into groups as designated by your instructor. Within each group, the men should develop a consensus ranking of the items as they think women ranked them. The reasons for the rankings should be shared and discussed so they are clear to everyone. The women in the group should not participate in this ranking task. They should listen to the discussion and be prepared to comment later in class discussions. A spokesperson for the men in the group should share the group's rankings with the class.

Optional Instructions

Form into groups consisting entirely of men or women. Each group should meet and decide which of the work values members of the opposite sex will rank first. Do this again for the work value ranked last. The reasons should be discussed, along with the reasons why each of the other values probably was not ranked first—or last. A spokesperson for each group should share group results with the rest of the class.

Class Exercise 13: Why We Work

Preparation

Read this "ancient story."[7]

In days of old, a wandering youth happened upon a group of men working in a quarry. Stopping by the first man, he said: "What are you doing?" The worker grimaced and groaned as he replied: "I am trying to shape this stone, and it is backbreaking work." Moving to the next man, the youth repeated the question. This man showed little emotion as he answered: "I am shaping a stone for a building." Moving to the third man, our traveler heard him singing as he worked. "What are you doing?" asked the youth. "I am helping to build a cathedral," the man proudly replied.

Instructions

In groups assigned by your instructor, discuss this short story. (1) Ask and answer the question: "What are the motivation and job design lessons of this ancient story?" (2) Have members of the group role-play each of the stonecutters as they are answering this additional question: "Why are you working?" Have someone in the group be prepared to report and share the group's responses with the class as a whole.

Class Exercise 14: Understanding Team Dynamics

Preparation

Think about your course work team, a team you are involved with in another campus activity, or any other team situation suggested by your instructor. Use this scale to indicate how often each of the following statements accurately reflects your experience in the group.[8]

   1 = always   2 = frequently   3 = sometimes   4 = never

_____ **1.** My ideas get a fair hearing.
_____ **2.** I am encouraged to offer innovative ideas and take risks.
_____ **3.** Diverse opinions within the group are encouraged.
_____ **4.** I have all the responsibility I want.
_____ **5.** There is a lot of favoritism shown in the group.
_____ **6.** Members trust one another to do their assigned work.
_____ **7.** The group sets high standards of performance excellence.
_____ **8.** People share and change jobs a lot in the group.
_____ **9.** You can make mistakes and learn from them in this group.
_____ **10.** This group has good operating rules.

Instructions

Form groups as assigned by your instructor. Ideally, this will be the group you have just rated. Have all group members share their ratings, and then make one master rating for the group as a whole. Circle the items for which there are the biggest differences of opinion. Discuss those items and try to find out why they exist. In general, the better a group scores on this instrument, the higher its creative potential. If everyone has rated the same group, make a list of the five most important things members can do to improve its operations in the future. Nominate a spokesperson to summarize the group discussion for the class as a whole.

Class Exercise 15: Communication and Teamwork Dilemmas

Instructions

1. Identify from the list below the three activities that you find most uncomfortable when part of a team.[9]
   (a) Telling a friend that she or he must stop coming late to team meetings
   (b) Pointing out to a team member that his or her poor performance is hurting the team
   (c) Asking teammates to comment on your criticism of the consensus that seems to be emerging on a particular issue
   (d) Telling a teammate who has problems working with others on the team that he or she has to do something about it
   (e) Responding to a team member who has just criticized your performance
   (f) Responding to a team member who has just criticized your attitude toward the team
   (g) Responding to a team member who becomes emotional and defensive when you criticize his or her performance
   (h) Having a teammate challenge you to justify your contributions to a discussion
2. Form three-person teams as assigned by your instructor. Identify the three behaviors with which each person indicates the most discomfort.
3. Have each team member practice performing these behaviors with another member, while the third member acts as an observer. Be direct, but try to perform the behavior in an appropriate way. Listen to feedback from the observer, and try the behaviors again, perhaps with different members of the group practicing each behavior.
4. When finished, discuss the overall exercise, and be prepared to share highlights of the exercise with the rest of the class.

Class Exercise 16: Alligator River Story

Preparation

Read this story.[10]

There lived a woman named Abigail who was in love with a man named Gregory. Gregory lived on the shore of a river. Abigail lived on the opposite shore of the same river. The river that separated the two lovers was teeming with dangerous alligators. Abigail wanted to cross the river to be with Gregory. Unfortunately, the bridge had been washed out by a heavy flood the previous week. So she went to ask Sinbad, a riverboat captain, to take her across. He said he would be glad to if she would consent to go to bed with him prior to the voyage. She promptly refused and went to a friend named Ivan to explain her plight. Ivan did not want to get involved at all in the situation. Abigail felt her only alternative was to accept Sinbad's terms. Sinbad fulfilled his promise to Abigail and delivered her into the arms of Gregory. When Abigail told Gregory about her amorous escapade in order to cross the river, Gregory cast her aside with disdain. Heartsick and rejected, Abigail turned to Slug with her tale of woe. Slug, feeling compassion for Abigail, sought out Gregory and beat him brutally. Abigail was overjoyed at the sight of Gregory getting his due. As the sun set on the horizon, people heard Abigail laughing at Gregory.

Instructions

1. After reading the story, rank the five characters in the story beginning with the one you consider the most offensive and ending with the one you consider the least objectionable. That is, the character who seems to be the most reprehensible to you should be entered first in the list, then the second most reprehensible, and so on, with the least reprehensible or objectionable being entered fifth. Of course, you will have your own reasons for why you rank them in the order that you do. Very briefly note these, too.

2. Form groups as assigned by your instructor (at least four persons per group with gender mixed). Each group should

   (a) Elect a spokesperson for the group

   (b) Compare how the group members have ranked the characters

   (c) Examine the reasons used by each of the members for their rankings

   (d) Seek consensus on a final group ranking

3. After completing the prior steps, discuss in the group the outcomes and reasons for agreement or disagreement on the rankings. Pay particular attention to any patterns that emerge.

4. Have a spokesperson be prepared to discuss the results of the exercise and the discussion within your group with the rest of the class.

Class Exercise 17: American Football

Instructions

Form into groups as assigned by the instructor. In the group, do the following:

1. Discuss American football—the rules, the way the game is played, the way players and coaches behave, and the roles of owners and fans.

2. Use American football as a metaphor to explain the way U.S. corporations run and how they tend to behave in terms of strategies and goals.

3. Prepare a class presentation for a group of visiting Japanese business executives. In this presentation, use the metaphor of American football to (1) explain American business strategies and practices to the Japanese and (2) critique the potential strengths and weaknesses of the American business approach in terms of success in the global marketplace.

Class Exercise 18: Entrepreneurs Among Us

Preparation

Michael Gerber, author and entrepreneur, says: "The entrepreneur in us sees opportunities everywhere we look, but many people see only problems everywhere they look."[11]

Instructions

1. Think about the people you know and deal with. Who among them is the best example of a successful entrepreneur? Write down their name and also a brief justification for your choice.

2. Think about your personal experiences, interests, and ideas that might be sources of personal entrepreneurship. Jot down a few notes that set forth some tentative plans for turning at least one into an actual accomplishment.

3. Form teams as assigned by the instructor. Within the team share both (a) your example of a successful entrepreneur and (b) your personal entrepreneurship plan.

4. Choose one as your team's "exemplar" entrepreneur to share with the class at large. Focus on the entrepreneur as a person, the entrepreneur's business or nonprofit venture, what factors account for success and/or failure in this case, and what the entrepreneur contributes to the local community.

5. Choose one of the entrepreneurship plans from among your teammates, and be prepared to share and explain it as well with the class at large.

Team Project 1: Managing Millennials

Question

What should baby boomers know about members of the Millennial generation to best manage them in the workplace?

Instructions

- Gather insights regarding the work and career preferences, values, and expectations of members of these different generational subcultures—specifically, baby boomers, Generation Xers, and Millennials.
- Analyze the points of potential difference between baby boomers and Millennials. What advice can you give to a baby boomer manager on how to best deal with a Millennial worker? What advice can you give the Millennial on how to best deal with a baby boomer boss?
- Analyze the points of potential difference between baby boomers and Generation Xers. What advice can you give to a baby boomer manager on how to best deal with a Generation X worker? What advice can you give the Generation Xer on how to best deal with a baby boomer boss?
- Analyze the points of potential difference between Millennials and Generation Xers. What advice can you give to a Generation X manager on how to best deal with a Millennial worker? What advice can you give the Millennial on how to best deal with a Generation X boss?

Team Project 2: Management in Popular Culture

You'll notice that the Management Live chapter openers in this book bring in movies and television shows from our popular culture. Lots of them have situations and themes that deal with things like leadership, team dynamics, attitudes, personalities—all the major topics of this textbook. The point is: Management learning is everywhere in our popular culture, we just have to look for it.

Question

What management insights are available in various elements of our popular culture and reflected in our everyday living?

Instructions

- Listen to music. Pick out themes that reflect important management concepts and theories. Put them together in a multimedia report that presents your music choices and describes their messages about management and working today.
- Watch television. Look again for the management themes. In a report, describe what popular television programs have to say about management and working. Also consider TV advertisements. How do they use and present workplace themes to help communicate their messages?
- Read the comics. Compare and contrast management and working themes in two or three popular comic strips.
- Read a best-selling novel. Find examples of management and work themes in the novel. Report on what the author's characters and their experiences say about people at work.
- Create your own alternative to the above suggestions.
- Share results with your class and instructor.

Team Project 3: Organizational Commitment to Sustainability

Instructions

In your assigned work teams do the following.

1. Agree on a definition of "sustainability" that should fit the operations of any organization.
2. Brainstorm audit criteria that can be used to create a Commitment to Sustainability Scorecard (CSS) that can be used to assess the sustainability practices of an organization.
3. Formalize your list of criteria, and then create a formal CSS worksheet that can be used to conduct an actual audit. Be sure that an organization being audited would not only receive scores on individual dimensions or categories of sustainability performance but also receive a total overall "Sustainability Score" that can be compared with results for other organizations.
4. Present and defend your CSS to the class at large.
5. Use feedback received from the class presentation to revise your CSS to be used in an actual organizational sustainability audit.
6. Use your CSS to conduct a sustainability audit for a local organization.

Team Project 4: Crisis Management Realities

Question

What types of crises do business leaders face, and how do they deal with them?

Instructions

- Identify three crisis events from the recent local, national, and international business news.

- Read at least three different news reports on each crisis, trying to learn as much as possible about its specifics, how it was dealt with, what the results were, and the aftermath of the crisis.
- For each crisis, use a balance sheet approach to list sources or causes of the conflict and management responses to it. Analyze the lists to see if there are any differences based on the nature of the crisis faced in each situation. Also look for any patterns in the responses to them by the business executives.
- Score each crisis (from 1 = low to 5 = high) in terms of how successfully it was handled. Be sure to identify the criteria that you use to describe "success" in handling a crisis situation. Make a master list of "Done Rights" and "Done Wrongs" in crisis management.
- Summarize the results of your study into a report on "Realities of Crisis Management."

Team Project 5: Personal Career Planning

Instructions

1. Complete the following activities and bring the results to class. Your work should be in a written form suitable for grading.[1]

   Activity 1: Strengths and Weaknesses Inventory   Different occupations require special talents, abilities, and skills. Each of us, you included, has a repertoire of existing strengths and weaknesses that are "raw materials" we presently offer a potential employer. Actions can (and should!) be taken over time to further develop current strengths and to turn weaknesses into strengths. Make a list identifying your most important strengths and weaknesses in relation to the career direction you are likely to pursue upon graduation. Place a * next to each item you consider most important to focus on for continued personal development.

   Activity 2: Five-Year Career Objectives   Make a list of three career objectives that you hope to accomplish within five years of graduation. Be sure they are appropriate given your list of personal strengths and weaknesses.

   Activity 3: Five-Year Career Action Plans   Write a specific action plan for accomplishing each of the five objectives. State exactly what you will do, and by when, in order to meet each objective. If you will need special support or assistance, identify what it is and state how you will obtain it. An outside observer should be able to read your action plan for each objective and end up feeling confident that he or she knows exactly what you are going to do and why.

2. In class, form into groups as assigned by the instructor. Share your career-planning analysis with the group and listen to those of others. Participate in a discussion that examines any common patterns and major differences among group members. Take advantage of any opportunities to gather feedback and advice from others. Have one group member be prepared to summarize the group discussion for the class as a whole.

Team Project 6: After Meeting/Project Review

Instructions

1. Complete the following assessment after participating in a meeting or a group project.[2]

   1. How satisfied are *you* with the outcome of the meeting project?

   Not at all satisfied   1   2   3   4   5   6   7   Totally satisfied

   2. How do you think *other members of the meeting/project group would rate you* in terms of your *influence* on what took place?

   No influence   1   2   3   4   5   6   7   Very high influence

   3. In your opinion, how *ethical* was any decision that was reached?

   Highly *un*ethical   1   2   3   4   5   6   7   Highly ethical

   4. To what extent did you feel *"pushed into"* going along with the decision?

   Not pushed into it at all   1   2   3   4   5   6   7   Very pushed into it

   5. How *committed* are *you* to the agreements reached?

   Not at all committed   1   2   3   4   5   6   7   Highly committed

   6. Did you understand what was expected of you as a member of the meeting or project group?

   Not at all clear   1   2   3   4   5   6   7   Perfectly clear

   7. Were participants in the meeting/project group discussion listening to each other?

   Never   1   2   3   4   5   6   7   Always

   8. Were participants in the meeting/project group discussion honest and open in communicating with one another?

   Never   1   2   3   4   5   6   7   Always

   9. Was the meeting/project completed efficiently?

   Not at all   1   2   3   4   5   6   7   Very much

   10. Was the outcome of the meeting/project something that you felt proud to be a part of?

   Not at all   1   2   3   4   5   6   7   Very much

2. Make sure that everyone in your group completed this assessment for the same team project.

3. Each person in the group should then take the "mirror test." They should ask: (a) What are my thoughts about my team and my contributions to the team, now that the project is finished? (b) What could I do in future situations to end up with a "perfect" score after a meeting or after a project review?

4. Share results of both the assessment and mirror test with one another. Discuss their implications: (a) for the future success of the group on another project and (b) for the members as they go forward to work with other groups on other projects in the future.

5. Be prepared to share your team project results with the class as a whole.

Team Project 7: Contrasting Strategies

Starbucks is the dominant name among coffee kiosks—how does Dunkin Donuts compete? Google has become the world's search engine of choice—can Bing ever catch up? Does it make a difference to you whether you shop for books at Amazon or Barnes & Noble, or buy gasoline from BP, Shell, or the local convenience store?

Question

How do organizations in the same industry fare when they pursue somewhat or very different strategies?

Instructions

1. Look up recent news reports and analyst summaries for each of the following organizations:
   - Coach and Kate Spade
   - Southwest Airlines and Delta Airlines
   - New York Times and USA Today
   - UnderArmour and Lululemon
   - National Public Radio and Sirius Satellite Radio
   - Coca-Cola and PepsiCo

2. Use this information to write a short description of the strategies that each seems to be following in the quest for performance success.

3. Compare the strategies for each organizational pair, with the goal of identifying whether or not one organization has a strategic advantage in the industry.

4. Try to identify other pairs of organizations and do similar strategic comparisons for them.

5. Prepare a summary report highlighting (a) the strategy comparisons and (b) those organizations whose strategies seem best positioned for competitive advantage.

Team Project 8: Network "U"

Instructions

Form into groups as assigned by the instructor. In the group do the following:

1. Discuss the concept of the network organization structure as described in the textbook.

2. Create a network organization structure for your college or university. Identify the "core staffing" and what will be outsourced. Identify how outsourcing will be managed.

3. Draw a diagram depicting the various elements in your Network "U."

4. Identify why Network "U" will be able to meet two major goals: (a) create high levels of student learning and (b) operate with cost efficiency.

5. Present and justify your design for Network "U" to the class.

Team Project 9: Organizational Culture Walk

Question

What organizational cultures do we encounter and deal with every day, and what are their implications for employees, customers, and organizational performance?

Instructions

1. In your team make two lists. List A should identify the things that represent the core cultures of organizations. List B should identify the things that represent the observable cultures of organizations. For each item on the two lists, identify one or more indicators that you might use to describe this aspect of the culture for an actual organization.

2. Take an *organizational culture walk* through a major shopping area of your local community. Choose at least three business establishments. Visit each as customers. As you approach, put your "organizational culture senses" to work. Start gathering data on your Lists A and B. Keep gathering it while you are at the business and right through your departure. Take good notes, and gather your thoughts together after leaving. Do this for each of the three organizations you choose.

3. Analyze and compare your data to identify the major cultural attributes of the three organizations and how they influence customers and organizational performance.

4. Use your results to make some general observations and report on the relationship between organizational cultures and performance as well as among organizational cultures, employee motivation, and customer satisfaction.

Team Project 10: The Future of Labor Unions

Question

What is the future for labor unions in America?

Instructions

1. Perform library research to identify trends in labor union membership in the United States.
2. Analyze the trends to identify where unions are gaining and losing strength; develop possible explanations.
3. Consider talking with members of labor unions in your community to gather their viewpoints.
4. Consider examining data on labor union trends in other countries.
5. Prepare a report that uses the results of your research to answer the project question.

Team Project 11: Leadership Believe-It-or-Not

You would think leaders would spend lots of time talking with the people who make products and deliver services, trying to understand problems and asking for advice. But Business Week reports a survey that shows quite the opposite. Persons with a high school education or less are asked for advice by only 24% of their bosses; for those with a college degree, the number jumps to 54%.

Question

What stories do your friends, acquaintances, family members, and you tell about their bosses that are truly hard to believe?

Instructions

1. Listen to others and ask others to talk about the leaders they have had or presently do have. What strange-but-true stories are they telling?
2. Create a journal that can be shared with class members that summarizes, role-plays, or otherwise communicates the real-life experiences of people whose bosses sometimes behave in ways that are hard to believe.
3. For each of the situations in your report, try to explain the boss's behaviors.
4. Also for each of the situations, assume that you observed or heard about it as the boss's supervisor. Describe how you would "coach" or "counsel" the boss to turn the situation into a "learning moment" for positive leadership development.

Team Project 12: Difficult Personalities

Question

What personalities cause the most problems when people work together in teams, and what can be done to best deal with them?

Instructions

1. Do a survey of friends, family, co-workers, and even the public-at-large to get answers to these questions:
   1. When you work in a team, what personalities do you have the most difficulty dealing with?
   2. How do these personalities affect you, and how do they affect the team as a whole?
   3. In your experience and for each of the "difficult personalities" that you have described, what have you found to be the best way of dealing with them?
   4. How would you describe your personality, and are there any circumstances or situations in which you believe others could consider your personality "difficult" to deal with?
   5. Do you engage in any self-management when it comes to your personality and how it fits when you are part of a team?
2. Gather the results of your survey, organize them for analysis, and then analyze them to see what patterns and insights your study has uncovered.
3. Prepare a report to share your study with the rest of your class.

Team Project 13: CEO Pay

Question

What is happening in the area of executive compensation, and what do you think about it?

Instructions

1. Check the latest reports on CEO pay. Get the facts and prepare a brief report as if you were writing a short, informative article for *Fortune* magazine. The title of your article should be "Status Report: Where We Stand Today on CEO Pay."
2. Address the equity issue: Are CEOs paid too much, especially relative to the pay of average workers?
3. Address the pay-for-performance issue: Do corporate CEOs get paid for performance or for something else? What do the researchers say? What do the business periodicals say? Find some examples to explain and defend your answers to these questions.
4. Address the social responsibility issue: Should CEOs accept pay that is many times the amounts that workers receive?
5. Take a position: Should a limit be set on CEO pay? If not, why not? If yes, what type of limit should be set? Who, if anyone, should set these limits—the government, company boards of directors, or someone else?

Team Project 14: Superstars on the Team

During a period of reflection following a down cycle for his teams, Sasho Cirovski, head coach of the University of Maryland's men's soccer, came to a realization. "I was recruiting talent," he said. "I wasn't doing a very good job of recruiting leaders." With a change of strategy, his teams moved back to top-ranked national competition.

Question

What do you do with a "superstar" on your team?

Instructions

1. Everywhere you look—in entertainment, in sports, and in business—a lot of attention these days goes to the superstars. What is the record of teams and groups with superstars? Do they really outperform the rest?
2. What is the real impact of a superstar's presence on a team or in the workplace? What do they add? What do they cost? Consider the potential cost of having a superstar on a team in the equation Benefits − Cost = Value. What is the bottom line of having a superstar on the team?
3. Interview the athletic coaches on your campus. Ask them the previous questions about superstars. Compare and contrast their answers. Interview players from various teams. Ask them the same questions.
4. Develop a set of guidelines for creating team effectiveness in a situation where a superstar is present. Be thorough and practical.

Team Project 15: How Words Count

Question

What words do people use in organizations that carry meanings that create unintended consequences for the speaker?

Instructions

1. Brainstorm with others to make a list of words that you have used or heard used by people and that cause other persons to react or respond negatively and even with anger toward the person speaking them.
2. For each word on the list, write its "positive" meaning and "negative" meaning.
3. Choose two or three of the words that seem especially significant. Write role-plays that display speakers using each word in the positive sense in conversations and in which the words are interpreted positively by the receivers.
4. For these same words, write role-plays that display speakers using each word conversationally with positive intentions but in which they are interpreted negatively by the receiver.
5. Explain the things that make a difference in how the same words are interpreted by receivers.
6. Draft a report that explains how people in organizations can avoid getting trapped unintentionally in problems caused by poor choice and/or use of words in their conversations.

Team Project 16: Job Satisfaction Around the World

Question

Does job satisfaction vary around the world, and does it reflect differences in national cultures?

Instructions

1. Gather together recent reports on job satisfaction among workers in the United States.
2. Gather similar data on workers in other countries—for example, Canada, the United Kingdom, Germany, Brazil, Mexico, Japan, India.
3. Compare the job satisfaction data across countries to answer the project question.
4. Consider pursuing your results further by researching how the various countries compare on working conditions, labor laws, and related matters. Use this information to add context to your findings.
5. Prepare a report to share your study with the rest of your class.

Team Project 17: Globalization Pros and Cons

Question

"Globalization" is frequently in the news. You can easily read or listen to both advocates and opponents. What is the bottom line? Is globalization good or bad, and for whom?

Instructions

1. What does the term "globalization" mean? Review various definitions, and find the common ground.
2. Read and study the scholarly arguments about globalization. Summarize what the scholars say about the forces and consequences of globalization in the past, present, and future.
3. Examine current events relating to globalization. Summarize the issues and arguments. What is the positive side of globalization? What are the negatives that some might call its "dark" side?
4. Consider globalization from the perspective of your local community or one of its major employers. From their perspectives, is globalization a threat or an opportunity, and why?
5. Take a position on globalization. State what you believe to be the best course for government and business leaders to take. Justify your position.

Team Project 18: Community Entrepreneurs

Entrepreneurs are everywhere. Some might live next door, many own and operate the small businesses of your community, and you might even be one.

Question

Who are the entrepreneurs in your community and what are they accomplishing?

Instructions

1. Read the local news, talk to your friends and other locals, and think about where you shop. Make a list of the businesses and other organizations that have an entrepreneurial character. Be as complete as possible—look at both businesses and nonprofits.
2. For each of the organizations, do further research to identify the persons who are the entrepreneurs responsible for them.
3. Contact as many of the entrepreneurs as possible and interview them. Try to learn how they got started, why, what they encountered as obstacles or problems, and what they learned about entrepreneurship that could be passed along to others. Add to these questions a list of your own: What do you want to know about entrepreneurship?
4. Analyze your results for class presentation and discussion. Look for patterns and differences in terms of entrepreneurs as persons, the entrepreneurial experience, and potential insights into business versus social entrepreneurship.
5. Consider writing short cases that summarize the "founding stories" of the entrepreneurs you find especially interesting.

Today's problems and opportunities—career and personal—are often complex and unstructured. It takes lots of wisdom and good analytic skills to master them. How about it: Are you developing the critical thinking skills needed for future success?

Cases for Critical Thinking

Case 1: Trader Joe's—Managing Less to Gain More

dashingstock/Shutterstock

In a space one-fourth the size of its competitors, the average Trader Joe's stocks approximately 4,500 products—a mere ten percent of those typically found in a supermarket. Affectionately nicknamed "TJ's" by its loyal customers, the retail grocery chain of 365+ U.S. stores spends less than one-half of 1% of sales on advertising compared to 4% by competitors.

The company stands for unique quality items like Greek olives, brie, and baguettes, all at peanut butter and jelly prices. Well known for its wine, Trader Joe's is also the exclusive distributor of the iconic and cheap Charles Shaw wine. After more than a decade at $2 per bottle, the price of "Two-and-a-half-Buck Chuck" increased to $2.49.

Take a walk down any Trader Joe's aisle and you'll see the fundamentals of management at work—planning, organizing, leading, and controlling. It's one reason TJ's has become more than just the "average Joe" of food retailers.

From Corner Store to Hundreds More

In 1958, Joe Coulombe, an MBA from Stanford Business School, started a "7-11 style" corner store in the Los Angeles area, which soon grew into a chain. While on vacation in the Caribbean, the Trader Joe South Seas motif resonated with Coulombe, particularly when he witnessed firsthand tourists proudly returning home from their travels with hard-to-find food delights. In 1967, he opened the first Trader Joe's store. Twelve years later, he

sold the chain to the Albrecht family, billionaires and owners of discount supermarket chain Aldi's, based in Germany.

How did this retail grocer attract an obsessive and diverse cult following of foodies, hipsters, and recessionistas? Much has to do with its corporate culture, which includes everything from how the company meticulously plans its store locations, manages its employees, and purchasing and branding strategies, and more. Planning for new stores is premised on offbeat strip mall locations. Purchasing is direct from manufacturers. Distribution centers minimize "the number of hands that touch a product."

Trader Joe's Upside-Down Pyramid

The notion of an upside-down pyramid well describes the mindset at Trader Joe's. Rather than being given orders, crew members—nonmanagerial employees—are coached. They're also given the go-ahead to open up a bag of goodies for customer sampling and taste tests. At the top of its pyramid, stockers and checkers interact with customers to provide a unique shopping experience. They are supported by "mates" who assist the "captain" or store manager.

The attitude and culture is customer-focused, yet laid back. Crew members make placement decisions solely on customer wants and needs. Shoppers are led by cheerful guides in Hawaiian print shirts to culinary discoveries such as lime and chili cashews, salmon jerky, ginger almond and cashew granola, and baked jalapeño cheese crunchies.

Knowledgeable, friendly and enthusiastic employees leave no doubt that Trader Joe's exists to serve its customers.

Aligning People and Culture

Trader Joe's aggressively courts friendly, customer-oriented employees by writing job descriptions highlighting desired soft skills—such as "ambitious and adventurous, enjoy smiling and have a strong sense of values"—as much as actual retail experience.

Employees earn more than their counterparts at other chain grocers. In California, Trader Joe's pays almost 20% more than counterparts at supermarket giants Albertsons or Safeway. Store managers, hired only from within the company, are highly compensated, partly because they know the Trader Joe's culture and system inside and out. Future leaders enroll in training programs such as Trader Joe's University that foster the loyalty necessary to run stores. To fulfill company and customer expectations, managers teach and role model the customer-focused attitude shoppers have come to expect.

Going Direct with Private-Label House Brands

Approximately 80% of Trader Joe's products are their own private label goods. Most Trader Joe's products are sold under a variant of their house brand—Italian food under the "Trader Giotto's" moniker, Mexican food under the "Trader Jose's" label, vitamins and health supplements under "Trader Darwin's," and Chinese food under the "Trader Ming's" label. The house brand success is no accident. According to now-retired Trader Joe's President Doug Rauch, the company pursued the strategy to "put our destiny in our own hands."

You won't find mass marketed brands (think Coca-Cola or Doritos) at Trader Joe's. But this weapon to keep costs low may also create its greatest appeal to customers—unique products. The company follows a deliciously simple approach to stocking stores. (1) Search out tasty, unusual foods across the globe; (2) contract directly with manufacturers; (3) label each product under one of several catchy house brands or private labels; and (4) maintain a small stock, making each product fight for its place on the shelf.

By limiting its stock and selling quality products at low prices, Trader Joe's sells

Planning Tops Chobani's Recipe for Success

Mike Okoniewski/newscast/NewsCom

"I think I learned from my father the unspoken business language or instincts that go back thousands of years."

Can you feel the difference between traditional and Greek-style yogurt? Greek-style yogurt is tangier and creamier, strained to remove much of the whey and sugar and bring out a dense and creamy texture. Many health-conscious consumers are pushing aside traditional sugar-filled yogurt and reaching for the alternative.

The popular Greek-Style yogurt brand Chobani was started in 2005 by Hamdi Ulukaya in a former Kraft food dairy plant in upstate New York. Ulukaya began by bringing in an expert yogurt maker and spending 18 months perfecting the Chobani recipe. With good planning, he says, "You are less likely to launch a premature business ridden with flaws." Planning has clearly paid off—in less than a decade, Chobani is ranked among major yogurt makers Yoplait and Dannon.

Collaboration is deeply rooted in Ulukaya's management style. Chobani aired the following commercial during the last Olympic Games: "The Chobani story is a community story. We started with a handful of local employees and a whole lot of heart. The community came together, got stronger. The dairy farmers, the plant workers, the truck drivers. Like our Olympians, all worked hard to fulfill a dream."

Rather than go the traditional route of paying fees for shelf space Ulukaya convinced major retailers to allow product samplings of his bold flavors—like pomegranate and pineapple. But the overriding secret to Ulukaya's success is leading by example. "If you make yogurt, go to the plant," he advises. "Work with your people; if you want people to work on Sunday, be there next to them." Calling himself an "accidental entrepreneur," Ulukaya credits his company's success to its people and "not knowing the old way of doing business."

twice as much per square foot than other supermarkets—customers trade value for selection. Most of its research and development dollars are spent on travel by its four top buyers or "product developers." They go on "product finding missions" to bring back the most unique products at the best value. There are another dozen or so buyers, called category leaders, who manage hoards of vendors and food suppliers eager to land their products on the shelves of Trader Joe's.

Economic Food Democracy

Ten to 15 new products debut each week at Trader Joe's—and the company maintains a strict "one in, one out" policy so as to not increase the total number of unique products it sells. Items that sell poorly or whose costs go up get the heave-ho in favor of new blood, something the company calls the "gangway factor." If the company hears that customers don't like a product, out it goes.

Discontinued items may be brought back if customers are vocal enough, making Trader Joe's control function the model of an open crowd-sourcing system. "We feel really close to our customers," says Audrey Dumper, vice president of marketing for Trader Joe's East. "When we want to know what's on their minds, we don't need to put

them in a sterile room with a swinging bulb. We like to think of Trader Joe's as an economic food democracy."

The Secret World of TJ's

Shares of Trader Joe's stock are owned by the Albrecht family and not sold to the public. This helps the company stay hyperprivate and media-shy, and executives do not grant interviews. It's very guarded about revealing producers of their store brand manufacturer relationships to customers and competitors. Suppliers operate under a Trader Joe's "cloak of secrecy."

What does the future hold? Critics claim that as Trader Joe's expands, it risks losing "entrepreneurial zeal" and cozy, intimate "quirky cool." But the company keeps its growing. Will Trader Joe's quest to tempt customers with cosmopolitan food at provincial prices keep customers coming?

CASE ANALYSIS QUESTIONS

1. DISCUSSION Review the six "must-have" management skills in Table 1.1. How is each important to the management and culture of Trader Joe's? Are any of these skills more critical than others to implementing an "upside-down pyramid" management approach?

2. DISCUSSION Hamdi Ulukaya achieved his entrepreneurial dream to sell Greek-style yogurt in America. Could he have achieved this success without the commitment to planning and collaboration suggested in this case? What, if anything, seems to be a management lesson worth remembering by other aspiring entrepreneurs?

3. PROBLEM SOLVING Mates and captains are the managers at a Trader Joe's. Suppose you were being hired in as a "mate" right from college. How could you make your efforts with planning, organizing, leading, and controlling fit well with the Trader Joe's culture?

3. FURTHER RESEARCH Study recent news reports to find additional information on Trader Joe's management and organization practices. Look for comparisons with its competitors, and try to identify whether Trader Joe's has the right management approach and business model for continued success. Are there any internal weaknesses, or external competitors, or industry forces that might create future challenges?

Case 2: Zara International—Fast Fashion's Style Maker

Pascal Sittler/REA / Redux Pictures

Welcome to fast fashion, a trend that sees clothing retailers frequently purchasing small quantities of merchandise to stay on top of emerging trends. In this world of "hot today, gauche tomorrow," no company does fast fashion better than Zara International. Fans value Zara's art of bringing the latest styles from sketchbook to clothing rack at lightning speed and reasonable prices. Zara ties what is sold on the floor of its stores to in-house designers and in-house manufacturing facilities as quickly as a teenager, or adult for that matter, can change their mind.

Defying the recession with its "cheap-and-chic" clothing, the company continues to post strong sales and global growth. Louis Vuitton fashion director Daniel Piette described Zara as "possibly the most innovative and devastating retailer in the world."

In Fast Fashion, Moments Matter

Because style-savvy customers expect shorter and shorter delays from runway to store, Zara launches 12,000 designs annually and employs a creative team of 250 designers to keep up with the latest fashions. It takes just two weeks for the company to update existing garments and get them into its stores.

Most retailers have their clothes inexpensively manufactured in China. But managing a long supply chain is difficult, time consuming and costly. By the time the goods arrive "hemlines may have risen an inch and its cargo will be as popular as geriatric haddock," says a writer for *Economist* magazine.

Efficient Operations Management

Spain-based Inditex Group, owner of Zara and the world's largest retailer, shortens the time from order to arrival by a complex system of just-in-time production and intensive inventory reporting. Their distribution centers can have items in stores within 24 to 48 hours of receiving an order. "They're a fantastic [operations management] case study in terms of how they manage to get product to their stores so quick," says a retail competitor. Inditex Group chooses the location of their manufacturing facilities carefully. Its successful approach to operations management is evident in the way the company manages and plans its work, production, just-in-time inventory, and quality control.

Design, production, distribution, and retail sales are all controlled to optimize the flow of goods, without having to share profits with wholesalers or intermediary partners. Twice a week, Zara's finished garments are shipped to logistical centers that all simultaneously distribute product to stores worldwide. These small production batches help the company avoid the risk of oversupply. Zara's stores perpetually energize their inventories with new products from these batches. Most clothing lines are not replenished. Instead they are replaced with new designs to create scarcity value—shoppers cannot be sure that designs in stores one day will be available the next.

Using Data to Solve Problems

Analytics are a top priority for Zara. Store managers track sales data with handheld computers, complex logistics systems, and information technology. This helps solve problems and make informed decisions. They know what's selling and what's not, and can reorder hot items in less than an hour. When a look doesn't pan out, designers promptly put together new products. Shoppers who are in "the know" recognize these designs as the newest of the new.

Zara stores sit on some of the world's glitziest shopping streets—including New York's Fifth Avenue. They locate near the flagship stores of leading international fashion brands so their reasonable prices stand out. "Inditex gives people the most up-to-date fashion at accessible prices, so it is a real alternative to high-end fashion lines," said Luca Solca, senior research analyst with Sanford C. Bernstein in London. That is good news for Zara, as many shoppers trade down from higher-priced chains.

Continuous Improvement

H&M, one of Zara's top competitors, uses a slightly different strategy. Around one-quarter of its stock is made up of fast-fashion items that are designed in-house and farmed out to independent factories. As at Zara, these items move quickly through the stores and are replaced often by fresh designs. But H&M also keeps a large inventory of basic, everyday items sourced from inexpensive Asian factories.

Frugality rules Zara's CEO Pablo Isla, who loathes markdowns and sales—and believes in cutting expenses wherever and whenever possible. Zara spends just 0.3% of sales on ads, making the 3 to 4% typically spent by rivals seem excessive in comparison. The company's sales have increased by 30% over the last three years. Perhaps most important in an industry based on image, Inditex is currently Europe's largest fashion retailer—taking the reigns from H&M.

Supply Chain Pressures

Essential to Zara's growth and success are Inditex's 100-plus textile design, manu-

Change-Driven Manager Crafts Uniqlo's Success

Bloomberg/Contributor/Getty

"... unless top managers are fully committed to paying attention to the details, I don't think you can call such people good business managers."

Japanese retailer Uniqlo's lofty corporate mission is: "Changing clothes. Changing conventional wisdom. Changing the world." Headed by an uber-confident CEO, Tadashi Yanai, willing to take bold risks, the firm is an aggressive player in an increasingly intense battlefield among rival retailers Zara, Hennes & Mauritz (H & M), Gap,

Aeropostle, and even Abercrombie. Yanai says: "We cannot win a dominant position in global markets simply by imitating other companies. Instead, true to our unique clothing concept, we seek to create clothes of the future with the potential to change the world." As Japan's biggest retailer, with close to 800 stores in Japan and 1,000 worldwide, the company may be positioned to do just that.

Although "changing the world" in the cutthroat retail sector may seem like an overly ambitious goal, Yanai is committed to taking market share away from competitors. Uniqlo, which stands for "unique clothing" has no intention of following its fast fashion rivals by cranking out the latest styles at rock-bottom prices. Instead, Uniqlo is committed to high quality, functional clothing at reasonable prices. Uniqlo sells basics and essentials like socks, underwear, jeans, dresses, and blazers.

As American retailers feel the pains of competitors, Uniqlo has plans to open flagship stores in the United States—with goals to increase revenues fivefold to $20 billion

by 2020. "We are not a fashion company. We are a technology company," Yanai proclaims. "We realize contemporary Japanese culture in our clothing," he says.

The change-driven Yanai is sometimes criticized for being overly involved, too hands-on and an insufficient delegator. But it's all part of his belief that managers and great employees create success, or failure, for companies. "Unless they look at the details of day-to-day operations, I don't think you can call them real managers," he says. "People often say that the details are everything—that everything shows up in details. So unless top managers are fully committed to paying attention to the details, I don't think you can call such people good business managers."

Tadashi Yanai has built Uniqlo into a fashion superstar in a highly competitive industry, and he's become Japan's richest man in the process. Soon he'll most likely turn the business over to his two sons. But one has to wonder, can they can follow their father's management footsteps and keep this fast-growing firm as successful in the future as it is today?

facturing, and distribution companies that employ close to 110,000 workers. Inditex, Zara's parent company, farms out much of its garment production to specialist companies, which it often supplies with its own fabrics.

Although Inditex's dominance of fast fashion seems virtually complete, it isn't without its challenges. For instance, keeping production so close to home becomes difficult when an increasing number of Zara stores are far-flung across the globe. "The efficiency of the supply chain is coming under more pressure the farther abroad they go," notes a London Business School professor.

Analysts worry that Inditex's rapid expansion may harm its business. The rising number of overseas stores and China in particular, they warn, adds cost and complexity and is straining its operations. Inditex may no longer be able to manage everything from Spain, where consumer spending has been weak. But Isla isn't worried. Consumers have become more demanding and

more arbitrary, he says—and fast fashion is better suited to these changes.

Does Zara International have what it takes to succeed in the hypercompetitive world of fast fashion? Or is the company's hyperexpansion going to create challenges?

CASE ANALYSIS QUESTIONS

1. **DISCUSSION** In what ways are elements of the behavioral or human resource approaches to management evident at Zara International? Provide specific examples.

2. **DISCUSSION** One of Zara's major competencies is producing goods and services efficiently and effectively. In what ways does this competency require strength with the quantitative management approaches?

3. **PROBLEM SOLVING** How would you describe CEO Tadashi Tanai's management style? Does he tend more toward

Theory X or more toward Theory Y? Looking toward the future of the company as an expanding global player in a cutthroat industry, should Tanai' expect his sons to follow a similar style to achieve success? Or, will the challenges of competition require a change in management style at the top?

4. **FURTHER RESEARCH** Zara, intent on making small batches in facilities located close to its distribution headquarters and rarely marking items down, is remarkably different than Uniqlo. It produces garments on a steady basis year-round without chasing every trend. Uniqlo keeps its factory costs reined in by booking in advance. Gather the latest information about Zara and Uniqlo and discuss the differences in their supply chain management approaches, and the implications of these differences for their future success.

Cases for Critical Thinking

Case 3: Patagonia—Leading a Green Revolution

Ray Mickshaw/PictureGroup / AP

How has Patagonia managed to stay both green and profitable? Are Patagonia's business practices-good for outdoor enthusiasts and good for the environment-sustainable?

Twelve hundred Wal-Mart buyers, a group legendary for their tough-as-nails negotiating tactics, sit in rapt attention in the company's Bentonville, Arkansas, headquarters. They're listening to a small man in a mustard-yellow corduroy sport coat lecture them on the environmental impact of Wal-Mart's purchasing choices. He's not criticizing the company, per se—*he's criticizing them*. Yet when he finishes speaking, the buyers leap to their feet and applaud enthusiastically.

Such is the authenticity of Yvon Chouinard. Since founding Patagonia in 1972, he's built it into one of the most successful outdoor clothing companies, and one that is steadfastly committed to environmental sustainability.

It's hard to discuss Patagonia without constantly referencing Chouinard because for all practical purposes, the two are one. Where Chouinard ends, Patagonia begins. He breathes life into the company, espousing the outdoorsy athleticism of Patagonia's customers. In turn, Patagonia's business practices reflect Chouinard's insistence on minimizing environmental impact, even at the expense of the bottom line.

Taking Risks to Succeed

For decades, Patagonia has been at the forefront of a cozy niche: high-quality, performance-oriented outdoor clothes and gear sold at top price points. Derided as *Pradagonia* or *Patagucci* by critics, the brand

is aligned with top-shelf labels like North Face and Royal Robbins. Patagonia clothes are designed for fly fishermen, rock climbers, and surfers. They are durable, comfortable, and sustainably produced. And they are not cheap.

It seems counterintuitive, almost dangerous, to market a $400 raincoat in a down economy. But the first thing you learn about Yvon Chouinard is that he's a risk taker. The second thing you learn is that he's usually right.

"Corporations are real weenies," he says. "They are scared to death of everything. My company exists, basically, to take those risks and prove that it's a good business."

And it is a good business. Patagonia succeeds by staying true to Chouinard's vision. "They've become the Rolls-Royce of their product category," says Marshal Cohen, chief industry analyst with market research firm NPD Group. "When people were stepping back, and the industry became copycat, Chouinard didn't sell out, lower prices, and dilute the brand. Sometimes, the less you do, the more provocative and true of a leader you are."

Ideal Corporate Behavior

Chouinard is not shy about espousing the environmentalist ideals intertwined with Patagonia's business model. "It's good business to make a great product, and do it with the least amount of damage to the planet," he says. "If Patagonia wasn't profitable or successful, we'd be an environmental organization."

In many ways, Patagonia is an environmental organization. The company publishes online a library of working documents, *The Footprint Chronicles*, that guides employees in making sustainable decisions in even the most mundane office scenarios. Its mission statement: "Build the best product, cause no unnecessary harm, use business to inspire and implement solutions to the environmental crisis." Patagonia has long contributed 10% of pretax profits or 1% of sales—whichever is *greater*—to environmental groups each year. Whatever you do, don't call it a handout. "It's not a charity," Chouinard flatly states. "It's a cost of doing business. We use it to support civil democracy."

A core value at Patagonia is providing opportunities for motivated volunteers to devote themselves to sustainable causes. Employees can leave their jobs for up to two months to volunteer full-time for the

environmental cause of their choice, while continuing to receive full pay and benefits from Patagonia.

Growing Green

Patagonia grew from small start-up into a booming manufacturer of outdoor clothing. Along the way they achieved success with products woven with synthetic threads, although the majority of their items were still spun with natural fibers like cotton and wool. The firm commissioned an external audit of the environmental impact of their four major fibers, anticipating bad news about petroleum-derived nylon and polyester.

Instead, they were shocked to learn that the production of cotton, a mainstay of the American textile market for hundreds of years, had a more negative impact on the environment than any of their other fibers. The evidence was clear: destructive soil and water pollution, unproven but apparent health consequences for field-workers, and the astounding statistic that 25% of all toxic pesticides used in agriculture are spent in the cultivation of cotton.

To Chouinard and Patagonia, the appropriate response was equally clear: Source organic fibers for all 66 of their cotton clothing products. Company representatives went directly to organic cotton farmers, ginners, and spinners, seeking pledges from them to increase production, dust off dormant processing equipment, and do whatever it would take to line up enough raw materials to fulfill the company's promise to its customers and the environment. Not surprisingly, Patagonia met its goal, and every cotton garment made since has been spun from organic cotton.

Sustaining Momentum

Now in his seventies, Chouinard can't lead Patagonia forever. But that's not to say he isn't continuing to find better ways for Patagonia to do business. "I think entrepreneurs are like juvenile delinquents who say, 'This sucks. I'll do it my own way,'" he says. "I'm an innovator because I see things and think I can make it better. So I try it. That's what entrepreneurs do."

It's doubtful that Chouinard will ever stop thinking about how Patagonia can responsibly innovate and improve. "Right now, we're trying to convince zipper companies to make

Billionaires and the Growing Business of Philanthrocapitalism

Peter Macdiarmid/Getty Images

Philanthrocapitalism refers to billionaires "trying to apply the rudiments of their business success—defining goals, monitoring investments, implementing programs, measuring results—to charitable giving."

Philanthrocapitalism is a name given to the trend of newly rich business billionaires intent on using their fortunes to help solve social problems and change the world. It is the focus of the book *Philanthrocapitalism: How Giving Can Change the World*

co-authored by Matthew Bishop, a chief business writer for the *Economist,* and Michael Green, an expert in international development. The authors describe philanthropic billionaires as "trying to apply the rudiments of their business success—defining goals, monitoring investments, implementing programs, measuring results—to charitable giving." They discuss how billionaires get into the business of philanthropy, but also question whether it has all been for the best.

America's early charities were founded by wealthy entrepreneurial families like the Carnegies (fortune from steel) and Rockefellers (fortune from oil), who set up what they hoped would be transformative organizations, also called private foundations. Their legacy foundations still exist, and their early impact was found in a cure for yellow fever, expansion of public libraries, and increased agricultural output and production to help feed the hungry.

Andrew Carnegie is quoted as urging his rich counterparts to give away "Surplus wealth," stop "hoarding great sums," and not "die in disgrace" with undistributed wealth. Today's "rock-star" philanthropists who have listened to this message include such notables as Bill and Melinda Gates (fortune from Microsoft) and Warren Buffet (fortune from Berkshire Hathaway).

After stepping down from the helm at Microsoft, Bill Gates has achieved remarkable results through his Bill and Melinda Gates Foundation. Started with a pledge of $54 million, the foundation's endowment now exceeds $36 billion. Its stated goal is to "help all people lead healthy, productive lives." The foundation's grants aim to address problems of hunger and poverty, health and disease, education, and vulnerable children.

Critics of philanthrocapitalism believe that attempts to take lessons from the pages of business books and apply them to social issues have fundamental flaws and weaknesses. They believe that results might be short term and not based on "deep-rooted" social and political change. "The principles that would make you successful in business don't translate easily into the practice of what makes you successful outside that world," says Robert Frank, author of *Just Another Emperor: The Myths and Realities of Philanthrocapitalism."* Some also argue that charitable giving allows wealthy individuals entirely too much influence in terms of allocation public funds, thus creating a tension between "participatory citizenship and elitism."

Like so many other things philanthrocapitalism is full of opportunities and potential pitfalls. Where do you stand on the concept and its future?

---

teeth out of polyester or nylon synths, which can be recycled infinitely," he says. "Then we can take a jacket and melt the whole thing down back to its original polymer to make more jackets."

Despite his boundless enthusiasm for all things green, Chouinard admits that no process is truly sustainable. "I avoid using that word as much as I can," he says. He pauses for a moment and adds: "I keep at it, because it's the right thing to do."

CASE ANALYSIS QUESTIONS

1. DISCUSSION Patagonia has a history of putting sustainability ahead of profits. But it also has to face up to everyday business realities and the need for operating capital. How do you think the company decides which products to offer so

that the outcomes will be both business practical and environmentally friendly? And, with Chouinard such an important influence on company ideals and values, what can be done now to ensure that his positive impact is still felt long after he leaves the company?

2. DISCUSSION Philanthrocapitalism is here to stay. Is it reasonable to assume that someone's capacity to solve social problems increases with the amount of their personal wealth? What are the possible downsides as today's business billionaires tackle societal ills?

3. PROBLEM SOLVING Let's suppose Yvon Chouinard comes to you, a new employee, and asks for a proposal on a timely and "forward looking" sustainability agenda for the firm. In other

words, he wants a program that can drive Patagonia's future and not just celebrate its past. What would you include in this agenda and why?

4. FURTHER RESEARCH Could ethics lose out to greed even in a company with the idealism of Patagonia? See if you can find examples of decisions that forced people in the firm to make difficult choices between ethics and profitability. Look for examples of decisions made at other companies that may have resulted in different ethics versus profitability choices. Try to explain through the examples what makes the difference between organizations where ethics and social responsibility are part of core values and those where they are more superficial issues.

Case 4: Amazon.com—Keeping the Fire Hot

© J. Emilio Flores/Corbis

Amazon.com has gained the No. 1 spot as the world's largest Internet retailer. But never content to rest on past laurels, CEO Jeff Bezos keeps introducing and upgrading Amazon products and services. It's hard to keep pace with new versions of the Amazon Kindle Fire e-book reader, Prime Instant Video TV and movie content streamed on demand, and a variety of cloud computer services. A *New York Times* article states: "Within a few years, Amazon's creative destruction of both traditional book publishing and retailing may be footnotes to the company's larger and more secretive goal: giving anyone on the planet access to an almost unimaginable amount of computing power through its cloud services." But will the investments pay off?

Creative Decision Making in Action

From its modest beginning in Jeff Bezos's garage in 1995, Amazon.com has quickly grown into the most megalithic online retailer. Once Bezos saw that Amazon could outgrow its role as an immense book retailer, he began to sell CDs and DVDs. Even its logo was updated to symbolize that Amazon.com sells almost anything you can think of, from A to Z. And that only takes into account Amazon's U.S. presence. The count of customers with access to Amazon sister sites in other countries keeps growing.

Bezos continues to diversify Amazon's product offerings and broaden its brand by partnering with existing retailers (third-party sellers) to add new product lines. It's a win-win proposition for a multitude of retail companies who use the world's most trusted site's loyal customer base to sell its items.

Some retailers report selling greater volume on Amazon's site than their own—and even with a 15% cut to Amazon, for many retailers, this makes more sense than selling in a retail store environment. Amazon spends lots on marketing to draw customers to its site, and on technology and content to convert them once they get there. Without undercutting their existing business, third-party sellers profit from the additional exposure and sales, and Amazon's brand thrives from the opportunity to expand its selection and buying options for customers who might otherwise shop elsewhere.

Continuous Innovation

Beyond simply finding more and more products and services to offer, Bezos knows that to prevent his brand from becoming stagnant he has to innovate, creating new levels of service to complement existing products. He says the key question is: 'What kind of innovation can we layer on top of that that will be meaningful for our customers?'

Amazon's Kindle almost single handedly launched the e-book revolution. Bezos sees it as a natural evolution of technology.

"Books are the last bastion of analog," he said to *Newsweek*. "Music and video have been digital for a long time, and short-form reading has been digitized, beginning with the early Web. But long-form reading really hasn't."

Amazon Prime is another great example. Prime members get free two-day shipping and discounted one-day shipping as well as access to Amazon Instant Video, movie, and TV streaming at no additional cost. It also includes access to Kindle Owners' Lending Library, which allows Kindle owners to borrow up to one book a month for free.

Bezos calls Amazon Prime "the best bargain in the history of shopping, and it's going to keep getting better." So far, much of this innovation has come from the depth of the free content available to Amazon Prime members. Far from being a loss leader, Amazon's free content spurs sales and reinforces customers' perception of Amazon's commitment to customer service.

Amazon versus the Rest

In recent years, Amazon has found itself squaring off against Netflix, Apple, and Google in realms of both hardware and digital entertainment. Amazon launched its Amazon MP3 music downloading service and, in a move of digital one-upmanship, offered all its tracks from the Big 4 record labels without proprietary digital rights management (DRM) software, allowing the files to be played on any MP3 player.

Amazon also bought top-shelf audio book vendor Audible.com for $300 million, adding more than 85,000 audio titles to its arsenal. It later added shoe and clothing merchant Zappos.com for $928 million. Then came acquisition of Boston-based Kiva Systems. Kiva's automated guided robots deliver product to workers at pick stations, allowing Amazon increased efficiency (and reduced labor costs) in its worldwide distribution centers.

A recent multiyear licensing deal with cable channel Epix signals Amazon's commitment to online movie viewing. Epix is owned by Lions Gate Entertainment, Viacom Inc.'s Paramount Pictures, and Metro-Goldwyn-Mayer Studios Inc. Amazon has invested hundreds of millions of dollars to expand its Prime Instant Video Library for its customers and is now moving into original content programming.

Netflix CEO Makes and Remakes a Decision

MIKE CASSESE/REUTERS/NewsCom

Some call the move by Hastings "the worst self-inflicted corporate wound since Coca-Cola introduced New Coke, in 1985."

It seemed almost routine for a growth company when Netflix CEO Reed Hastings announced he was splitting the firm into two unique units. But his decision caused an uproar.

Hastings's plan was that one unit would consist of its longstanding DVD-by-mail business and the other would be an online streaming unit for movies and TV shows. The DVD business would be renamed "Qwikster." The Netflix name would go to the online streaming business unit. Customers would have two accounts, and there would be two separate Web sites. As more customers moved from the DVD-by-mail model to instant streaming, Qwikster was expected to eventually go away in the future.

Hastings, who has been quoted as saying "make tough decisions without agonizing," made these changes in face of competition from Google, Amazon, Wal-Mart, Dish Network, and Apple. To push customers away from the mail-in model to now view content by streaming, Hastings announced a 60% price hike in the popular combination DVD plus streaming plan.

Customers were quick to complain, and many subscriptions were cancelled. And, Netflix's stock price fell.

Some called Hastings's move "the worst self-inflicted corporate wound since Coca-Cola introduced New Coke, in 1985." But, he stood up and took the blame. He admitted to "messing up" and "sliding into arrogance" while underestimating the "unquantifiable emotions of subscribers who still want those little red envelopes."

Hastings believes his biggest mistake was the decision to phase out Netflix's DVD-by-mail rental service more quickly than customers were ready. But maybe his self-criticism was premature. Netflix seems on top of its game again. Was Hastings wrong, or just early in his strategic thinking?

Information Competency to Make Decisions

The Amazon's Kindle almost single handedly launched the e-book revolution. Bezos sees it as a natural evolution of technology. "Books are the last bastion of analog," he said to *Newsweek*. "Music and video have been digital for a long time, and short-form reading has been digitized, beginning with the early Web. But long-form reading really hasn't." He must be right, because Amazon now sells more Kindle books than paperback books.

Bezos as a Decision Maker

Rather than sticking to just the analytical step-by-step process, Bezos isn't afraid of informed intuition. He uses creativity, flexibility, and spontaneity when making key decisions. He seems comfortable with abstraction and lack of structure when making decisions and also isn't afraid to fail.

Even as Amazon's stock values fluctuate, Bezos still believes that customer service, not the stock ticker, defines the Amazon experience. "I think one of the things people don't understand is we can build more shareholder value by lowering product prices than we can by trying to raise margins," he says. "It's a more patient approach, but we think it leads to a stronger, healthier company. It also serves customers much, much better."

Amazon.com has quickly—not quietly—grown from a home operation into a global e-commerce giant. By forging alliances to ensure that he has what customers want and making astute purchases, Jeff Bezos has made Amazon the go-to brand for online shopping. After its significant investments in new media and services, does the company risk losing its original appeal? Will customers continue to flock to Amazon, the go-to company for their each and every need?

CASE ANALYSIS QUESTIONS

1. **DISCUSSION** Bezos once said: "Amazon may break even or even lose money on the sale of its devices." The company expects to recoup the money later through the sale of products, with a further boost from its annual $79 Prime fast-shipping membership. In what ways does this strategy show Bezos as a systematic and intuitive thinker?

2. **DISCUSSION** Would you describe the digital entertainment market as certain, risky, or uncertain for Amazon's decision makers? Discuss.

3. **PROBLEM SOLVING** How would you describe Netflix CEO's "bad" decision and how he handled the aftermath? Could he be a role model for others in crisis situations? What three lessons can this example provide to help you handle future crises?

4. **FURTHER RESEARCH** What are the latest initiatives coming out of Amazon? How do they stack up in relation to actual or potential competition? How have the Kiva and Zappos acquisitions worked out? Is Bezos making the right decisions as he is guides the firm through today's many business and management challenges?

Case 5: Nordstrom—"High Touch" with "High Tech"

Raymond Boyd/Getty Images

How has Nordstrom managed to stay profitable despite dips in consumer spending, changing fashion trends, and intense competition among retailers? One answer: The fourth generation of family members running this business have brought time-honored retail practices into a new era.

Nordstrom provides a quality customer experience via personalized service, a compelling merchandise offering, a pleasant shopping environment, and now, even better management of its inventory. Acute attention to detail and well-laid plans have allowed the company to navigate the recession far better than its rivals during a time when most people have purchased fewer clothes.

Creating a Vision

Nordstrom has over 100 full-line stores, an e-commerce website, and another 100+ off-price Nordstrom Rack stores, through which it sells high-quality shoes, clothing, accessories, handbags, jewelry, cosmetics, fragrances, and in some locations, home furnishings. "Nordstrom, it seems, is that rarity in American business: an enterprise run by a founding family that hasn't wrecked it," says one business writer.

Since its inception in 1901 by Swedish immigrant John W. Nordstrom, the Nordstrom name has been synonymous with customer service *par excellence*. Some industry observers cite Nordstrom's success

at selling "customer service" as its primary good. And for decades, having top-notch salespeople, carrying the right brands, and developing lasting relationships with customers did the trick. Employees are valued, well trained, respected, and they thrive—which is primarily why Nordstrom has spent 15 consecutive years on *Fortune's* "100 Best Workplaces" List.

Secret of Success

The secret of this company's success lies in its strategic planning efforts and the ability of its management team to set broad, comprehensive, and longer-term action directions—all of which are focused on the customer experience.

The current generation of Nordstrom family members was quick to spearhead an ultramodern $150+ million Web-based inventory management system upgrade, which allowed the company to "sell more without buying more inventory," according to the *New York Times*.

The upgrade accomplished two key goals: correlate purchasing with demand to keep inventory as lean as possible, and present both customers and sales associates with a comprehensive view of Nordstrom's entire inventory, including every store and warehouse.

Items don't stay in stock very long. The chain turns inventory about twice as fast as its competitors, thanks to strong help from

Web sales. Nordstrom's all-time-best inventory turnover—the ratio that shows how many times a company's inventory is sold and replaced over a period—to date is 5.6 times annually, which they attribute to their merchant selections.

Demand Planning

Instead of relying on one-day sales, coupon blitzes, or marking down entire lines of product, Nordstrom prefers to discount only certain items. "Markdown optimization" software assists in planning more profitable sale prices. According to retail analyst, Patricia Edwards, this helps Nordstrom calculate what will sell better at different discounts and forecast which single items should be marked down. If a style is no longer in demand, the company can ship it off to its Nordstrom Rack outlet stores.

This kind of demand planning is part of Nordstrom's long-term investment in efficiency. "If we can identify what is not performing and move it out to bring in fresh merchandise," says Pete Nordstrom, "that's a decision we want to make."

Inventory Planning

There was a time when a customer who fell in love with a red Marc Jacobs satchel handbag one day might return 24 hours later to find her Nordstrom store out of her color. Although inventory naturally fluctuates, Nordstrom associates couldn't easily locate the same item in another store or verify when it would return to stock. And in an era of booming online sales, Nordstrom realized they were likely to lose such a customer faster than you could say, "I'll just Google that."

That changed when Nordstrom integrated the inventory of each of its stores into its Web site. After an immense overhaul of the chain's inventory management processes, customers at their laptops and associates behind sales counters see the same thing—the entire inventory of Nordstrom's stores presented as one selection, which the company refers to as "perpetual inventory."

The upgrade was an immediate hit. As of launch day, Nordstrom found that the percentage of customers who purchased products after searching the Web site for an item doubled. It also learned that multi-

Contingency Planning and Global Supply Chain Management

ITAR-TASS/Yuri Smityuk/Corbis

"Japan's disaster will have a lasting impact on how global manufacturers manage their operations."

"Even before the extent of the [tsunami] disruption becomes clear," said a business writer for the *Economist*, "it seems certain that Japan's disaster will have a lasting impact on how global manufacturers manage their operations." Each of Japan's big-three automakers—Toyota, Honda, and Nissan—is heavily reliant on parts from suppliers in Japan for its vehicle production. When the massive earthquake and tsunami hit, it was a stark reminder of the vulnerability to each automaker's just-in-time (JIT) inventory system and the risks of global supply chain management.

Implementation of just-in-time inventory planning allows parts and supplies to be delivered "just-in-time" and making "only what is needed, when it is needed, and in the amount needed." Essentially, the system allows for supply to be synchronized with production demand so that tying up precious cash resources by holding in-process inventory (storage costs) is eliminated.

But does this work in all situations? Global companies can be hit hard when parts supplies become interrupted. Natural disasters are a worst-case scenario.

It soon became clear in the Tsunami crisis that Japan's automakers did not have contingency plans in place. Because they were highly dependent on parts from just a few key Japanese parts suppliers whose business was disrupted, their production was disrupted for over one month. Many other elements critical to each automaker's distribution were also affected, things like electrical power, fuel supplies, and rail and highway transportation.

JIT is not without its flaws—and the number and location of suppliers is even more crucial. It's not effective if suppliers can't locate close by or make deliveries on time or otherwise meet the ever-changing demands and whims of their clients.

The lessons of the Tsunami disaster extend beyond JIT practices alone. Does it take a tragic occurrence like this for companies to realize the importance of contingency planning efforts—particularly global manufacturers who rely on the shipment of parts worldwide?

---

channel customers—those who shop from Nordstrom in more than one way—spend on average four times more than one-source customers. This profit more than offsets the cost of hiring additional shipping employees to wrap and mail items from each store. Now Nordstrom doesn't have to turn away the customer who spied that red Marc Jacobs handbag; she can buy it online or in her local store, and it will be shipped to her door directly from a store that has it in stock, even if it's located across the country. By displaying stock on both its Web warehouse and in its stores, Nordstrom has realized some very meaningful results.

"Customer service is not just a friendly, helpful, knowledgeable salesperson helping you buy something," says Robert Spector, retail expert and author of *The Nordstrom Way*. "Part of customer service is having the right item at the right size at the right price at the right time. And that's something perpetual inventory will help with."

Better yet, Nordstrom is finding that after integrating store inventory into its Web site, inventory is selling faster, and more profitably, than before. "If we're out of something on the Web site, it's probably late in the season and the stores are try- ing to clear it out," says Jaime Nordstrom, president of Nordstrom Direct. "By pulling merchandise from the store, you've now dramatically lessened the likelihood that you'll take a markdown."

Keeping It Lean and Staying Step Ahead of the Competition

Fast-turning inventories are a sign a retailer is well managed, making it more attractive to investors, especially in an uncertain economy. "The old, classic Nordstrom way is that if you sell more stuff, that compensates for any deficiency you may have in terms of technology," says Robert Spector. "They didn't want to replace the high touch with the high-tech," and they faced striking "that balance between having up-to-date systems and giving that personal service."

"Traditional retailers have traditional ways of doing things," echoes Adrianne Shapira, Goldman Sachs retail analyst, "and sometimes those barriers are hard to break down." But Nordstrom's investments in inventory planning and tracking have paid handsome dividends. "If I am going to put my money behind a retailer in this rocky economic environment, I want it to be one of the best-run companies out there," Patricia Edwards says. "Nordstrom is one of those."

CASE ANALYSIS QUESTIONS

1. **DISCUSSION** How might a firm as large as Nordstrom apply the concept of participatory planning to areas like product purchasing and floor displays?

2. **DISCUSSION** What objectives and measures could Nordstrom use to assess the success of its Web-based inventory integration?

3. **PROBLEM SOLVING** How can global firms prepare to deal with inevitable problems in their global supply chains? What alternatives to JIT are there? If Toyota and Nissan, for example, were willing to give up some of the cost efficiencies and savings from JIT, would a reduction in the practice be justifiable?

4. **FURTHER RESEARCH** Nordstrom wants to grow in a number of different areas. Research one of its strategies, and project it into the future. What changes, revisions, or updates would you plan for the company? What stretch goals come to mind?

Case 6: Chipotle—Control Keeps Everything Fresh

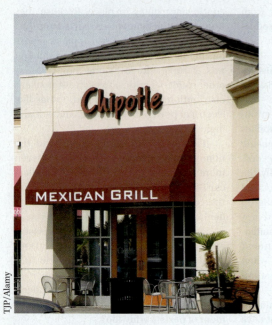

TJP/Alamy

Since its humble beginnings in Denver, Colorado, Chipotle has implemented the control process with fervor—catapulting the company to where it is today. Whether reviewing sales to cost ratios, same-store sales figures to gauge growth, payment initiatives to speed checkout during peak lunch hours, or tracking stock performance, management control is deeply entrenched in the firm's culture of performance.

In 1993, Steve Ells, trained in classical French cooking, opened his first Chipotle in Denver, Colorado. He wasn't your average chain-restaurant mogul. After spending time in San Francisco working for famous Chef Jeremiah Tower at the once-famous Stars Restaurant, Ells saw the need for a similar format using high-quality ingredients and classic cooking methods he had learned in culinary school.

With a loan of $85,000 from his father and inspiration from the vast number of taquerias found in San Francisco's Mission district, Ells took over an old Dolly Madison ice cream store near the University of Denver campus. He calculated his first store needed to sell 107 burritos per day to break even. After one month, sales of 1,000 burritos a day far exceeded his projections and his wildest dreams. Chipotle was an instant success, and Ells knew he was onto something big.

Culture Clash in a McDonalds Umbrella

After getting 16 stores up and running in Colorado, Ells thought it timely to bring the McDonald's burger empire on board as a minority owner and help fuel his company's growth toward being a national brand. The strategy was for Chipotle to leverage the buying power and supplier networks enjoyed by the burger empire's economies of scale.

During critical growth years, McDonald's invested over $360 million into Chipotle and at one time owned more than 80% of the company. With McDonald's as their partner, Chipotle's store locations skyrocketed. But, the two companies eventually parted ways. McDonald's was eager to return its focus to its core business. During that time, McDonald's also divested a few other companies, including Donato Pizza and Boston Market.

Thinking back on the union, Ells laments that the two cultures could not have been more different. "We just didn't see eye to eye," he said. McDonald's wanted Chipotle to follow its growth model using franchising. Ells wanted to grow the firm through internal expansion and without the use of other people's money as franchise owners. "We wanted to own the economic model. You franchise if you want money and people. We had plenty of money for our growth rate, and we had great people," he said.

Chipotle went public in an initial public offering (IPO) to settle the McDonald's breakup. It turned out to be the second-best restaurant IPO of all time, opening at $22 and closing at $44 per share. From its initial investment of $360 million, McDonald's walked away with a cool $1.5 billion.

"Fast-Casual" Dining with a Difference

Chipotle is classified in its industry as "fast-casual." This is a fusion of a fast-food and fine dining restaurant. More and more customers have come to expect higher food quality and service that is more in line with casual dining over that of a fast-food experience. Chipotle

is also known for its "less is more" philosophy when it comes to its limited number of menu items, which include burritos, burrito bowls (a burrito without the tortilla), tacos, and salads. Another hallmark is its generous-size burritos and all high-quality, natural, fresh, sustainable ingredients.

Technology with Caution

At some of its most efficient restaurants, Chipotle averages more than 350 transactions during the lunch hour alone, or on average, one transaction about every 11 seconds. Executives pay close attention to its customers getting through the line quickly, which results in greater sales revenues and a higher-quality customer experience. But discouragingly long lunch and dinner lines still cause problems. "We've come a long way, but there is still a long line, and there is people turning away at the end," says a Chipotle operations executive. In some stores, Chipotle has experimented with portable credit card swipers, additional cash registers, and handheld ordering systems.

Chipotle executives remain hesitant about the impact of technology on the personalization of their business. It becomes a balancing act, and the company is working to increase efficiency within its organization. This means being better organized during rush times with more workers on the floor and advance preparation. With technology comes the risk of speed, which introduces a potential for sloppiness that Chipotle wants to avoid.

Sourcing Sustainable Ingredients

Chipotle Mexican Grill's vision and mission statement in a recent annual report reads: "to change the way people think about and eat fast food." A threefold value philosophy, called "Food with Integrity" includes "finding and sourcing the very best ingredients raised with respect for the animals, the environment and the farmers."

Whenever possible, the company uses meat from animals raised without the use of added hormones or antibiotics and dairy from cows raised without the use of synthetic hormones or recombinant bovine growth hormone (rBGH). As an advocate of animal rights, Steve Ells has tirelessly

Mint.com Makes Personal Financial Management Easy

Chris Mueller/Redux Pictures

"Measuring financial performance and taking action to meet desired results is as crucial for personal success as it is for business success."

Financial management is an important control mechanism in any organization. But it isn't always done well. Effective financial control is facilitated by using financial ratios such as liquidity—money to pay bills—leverage—measure of debt, asset management—managing inventory, and profitability—revenues greater than expenses. Business executives are supposed to be good at understanding these things. How about you?

Measuring financial performance and taking action to meet desired results is as crucial for personal success as it is for business success. But if you're like many others, you may at times neglect the task. Aaron Patzer, founder of personal finance Web site, Mint.com with some 10 million users, is out to change all that.

A quintessential computer geek, Patzer—at the age of 26, became frustrated with using traditional personal finance software programs. The long, cumbersome task of inputting numbers into spreadsheets, categorizing and deciding where each should go, and ultimately, not getting meaningful information to make informed decisions was frustrating. So, he started Mint.com.

"I wanted something you could set up and that would get your finances organized in five minutes or less," says Patzer. His target market is young people between the ages of 18 and 29, many of whom are burdened with both credit card debt and high student loan debt.

A free Web-based service, Mint.com grew out of Patzer's realization that his target market knew very little about financial controls for their personal finances. Mint.com automatically pulls in transactional and balance information from financial institutions to provide an accurate financial picture using lots of visuals like charts and graphs. It offers personal finance recommendations, analysis of financial transactions, and e-mail updates and alerts when bills become due or account balances run low. And, its planning tool encourages users to meet debt pay-off and savings goals.

Two years after Patzer started Mint.com, Intuit bought the company for $170 million. This sale certainly changed Patzer's personal finances and financial plans. Luckily, Mint.com was right there when he needed it most.

---

committed himself to change the way pork is raised in the United States.

He learned of the horrific conditions to which pigs were subjected in factory farm settings, and that approximately 99% of the pork consumed in the United States was produced in "confined animal feeding operations."

As a big enough buyer of pork, Ells knew he was in a position to create change, saying: "I knew at that moment I did not want my success to be based on this kind of exploitation, so we started buying all naturally raised meat." His initial curiosity about the meat supply was actually prompted by the fact that he was unimpressed with the quality. By switching sources, he wound up with a product produced by humane animal treatment and tasting better to customers. Despite a price increase, Ells happily reports: "We started selling twice as many carnitas as before."

A Fickle Industry

Chipotle is a company that commits itself to constantly seeking new ways to improve performance. But its high stock price and the fickle nature of the industry raise some questions about future growth. Should Chipotle's record of sound management be enough to quiet the naysayers?

CASE ANALYSIS QUESTIONS

1. DISCUSSION How did CEO Steve Ells use the control process to move Chipotle forward with success? Explain your answer using at least three examples based on the case.

2. DISCUSSION A balanced scorecard helps top managers exercise strategic control. The scorecard includes customer satisfaction and internal process improvement. Discuss how Chipotle might score on both.

3. PROBLEM SOLVING Could mint.com help you? Are you in control of your personal finances? What are your financial objectives? Can you show how a combination of internal and external controls could help you achieve them?

4. FURTHER RESEARCH Go online to find and analyze Chipotle's most recent annual report. Check and critique the company's recent financial performance. Review reports from competitors—e.g., Rubio, Baja Fresh, Qdoba, or Moe's Southwest Grill. How are they doing, and what threats, if any, do they pose to Chipotle? How about product extensions? Could the Chipotle model be copied with Indian or Caribbean food for example?

Case 7: Dunkin' Donuts—Growth Feeds a Sweet Tooth

Jessica Rinaldi/Reuters/NewsCom

Java giant Dunkin' Donuts is opening hundreds of stores and entering new markets appealing to a new generation of customers. But is the rest of the world ready for this upstart from the Northeast? Can Dunkin' stay on course with its rapid growth?

The firm's present global travels are a long step from its first coffee shops opened in the Boston, Massachusetts, area in 1950, a few decades before Starbucks appeared on the coffee scene. Now it's expanding internationally and broadening its food and coffee menus for a new generation of more health-conscious customers and to ride the wave of fresh trends.

Dunkin' Donuts is a nationally known brand with a long reputation for quality that has earned the trust of many loyal customers. With Starbucks rethinking its positioning strategy and McDonald's offering a great-tasting coffee at a reasonable price, Dunkin' Donuts is hoping that with careful strategic planning, consumers worldwide will, as its ad campaign purports, "Run on Dunkin."

Although Starbucks has driven the trend toward upscale coffee, Dunkin' Donuts is betting that consumers nationwide will embrace its reputation for good-tasting coffee, unpretentious value, simplicity, convenience, and delicious donuts.

Part of Dunkin' Donuts' strategic plan of action includes focusing on the sale of its core products—coffee and donuts. With 500 billion cups consumed every year, coffee is the most popular global beverage, and estimates are that Americans drink 400 million cups a day. Dunkin' Donuts serves close to 3 million of them. That equates to about 30 cups per second—and 65% of the company's annual store revenue.

Global Growth Strategy

Most Americans have had an encounter with the Dunkin' Donuts brand through its almost 7,000 domestic outlets. Over the next two decades, the company has plans to double the number to 14,000 stores. Because Dunkin' Donuts is a franchise system, access to capital from eager operators is easier than funding growth from within. Its parent company, Dunkin' Brands Group, Inc., also owns ice creamery Baskin-Robbins.

The Dunkin's brand has managed to carve out an international niche, not only in expected markets such as Canada and Brazil, but also in some unexpected ones like India, Brazil, Qatar, South Korea, Pakistan, and the Philippines. The company is betting big on emerging economies. "Emerging markets are attractive because

they are growing very quickly, they've a fast-growing middle-class [eating out more], and they love American brands," says CEO, Nigel Travis. The company's growth plans include opening between 80 and 100 outlets in India—with 500 stores there within 15 years. "The company plans to locate in Asia a 'disproportionate' number of the 350–450 outlets that it plans to open outside the U.S. this year," Travis said.

Related Diversification Strategy

For most of its existence, Dunkin' Donuts' main product focus has been expressed by its name: donuts and coffee in which to dunk them. Since Stan Frankenthaler became executive chef and vice president, Dunkin' has launched about 25 new products annually as a new product innovation initiative. It has stepped up to competition by offering a variety of espresso-based drinks complemented with a broad number of sugar-free flavorings, including caramel, vanilla, and mocha swirl.

Its related diversification strategy now includes entry into the crowded fast-growth breakfast market with a new line of products. Its sandwich offerings focus on combinations of eggs, cheese, ham, and sausage on Texas toast, English muffins, croissants, bagel sandwiches, and burritos. Considering that coffee is the most profitable item on the menu, it's a good bet that this gives the company room to experiment with new food offerings.

The update to Dunkin' Donuts' menu items was inevitable due to increased competition in the morning meal market. But, none of its strategic plans make much sense unless consumers buy into the notion that Dunkin' has the culinary skills to sell more than its name implies. If plans prove successful, more customers than ever may flock to the shops. However, it may take a while to convince them that Dunkin' Donuts is the place to go to for breakfast.

Customer Appeal and Strategic Partnerships

Sometimes called the "anti-Starbucks," Dunkin' Donuts has a rich history of offering

Jamba Juice Blends for Fruitful Growth

Timothy A. Clary/Getty Images

"We are going for an asset light business model with a focus on brand development"

Jamba Juice's humble beginnings started in 1990 in San Luis Obispo, California, when cycling enthusiast, Kirk Perron, opened his first store. Having now grown to over 760 locations, mostly in the United States, Jamba, Inc. plans to broaden its reach through franchising with a mix of 80–90% franchised stores with 10–20% company owned. The company sees potential for 2,700 domestic and 1,000 international store locations. "We are going for an asset-light business model, with a focus on brand development," says its CEO, James White.

Owners of the international chain of company-owned and franchised yogurt and smoothie stores, Yogen Früz, have invested $20 million in the firm. Its CEO Michael Serruya says his company's goal is to provide Jamba, Inc. with insights into global franchise operations. Jamba's accelerated growth plans include worldwide franchising, expanding in-store products beyond smoothies, complimentary acquisitions, and the sale of Jamba-branded consumer packaged goods beyond its stores—things like fruity coconut water, fruit cups, and even a frozen home-smoothie kit for kids.

Jamba's strategy is to diversify from a smoothie-only shop to a line of wraps, sandwiches, salads, and flatbreads. So far, so good. The company's expanded menu includes fruit and vegetable smoothies, Fit and Fruitful smoothies with a weight burner boost to support weight management goals, Whirl'ns Frozen Yogurt, Probiotic Yogurt blends, and coconut water infused smoothies. Nondairy, nongluten vegan items are included on its menu as well.

Viewing it as a natural fit to the breakfast market, Jamba acquired an Oprah Winfrey favorite—Talbott's Tea. The company believes premium, all-natural hot beverages will be a great complement to its existing lines. So far, with all of these growth strategies in place, same-store comparable sales at this cold beverage company are turning out to be very "hot." Is Jamba ready to take on the fast-developing market for beverage alternatives?

---

simplicity and straightforward morning snacks—earnest and without pretense—to the everyday working class. The company appeals to simple, modest, and quality- and cost-conscious customers.

Dunkin' Donuts is banking on strategic partnerships to help fuel its growth through widespread marketplace prominence. Although Dunkin' Donuts often partners with a select group of grocery retailers, such as Stop & Shop and Wal-Mart, to create a store-within-a-store concept, the company is very selective about where they choose to set up shop.

"We want to be situated in supermarkets that provide a superior overall customer experience," says a business development executive. "Of course, we also want to ensure that the supermarket is large enough to allow us to provide the full expression of our brand, . . . which includes hot and iced coffee, our line of high-quality espresso beverages, donuts, bagels, muffins, and even our breakfast sandwiches." Furthermore, the outlet's location within the supermarket is critical for a successful relationship. "We want to be accessible and visible to customers, because we feel that gives us the best chance to increase incremental traffic and help the supermarket to enhance their overall performance."

Finding the Sweet Spot

If Dunkin' Donuts can find the "sweet spot" by being within most consumers' reach without the feel of a mass-retail-like omnipresence, the company's growth strategy may prove fruitful. But this strategy is not without its risks.

In the quest to appeal to new customers, offering too many original products in too many locations could potentially dilute the essential brand appeal and alienate longtime customers who respect its history of simplicity. On the other hand, potential new customers and a younger demographic previously unexposed to Dunkin' Donuts might see it as uncool as "yesterday's brand." Some older franchises seem long overdue for a makeover, especially when compared to the trendy Italian feel of a nearby Starbucks café.

For the time being, Dunkin' Donuts seems determined in its quest for domination of the coffee and breakfast market. Will Dunkin' Donuts strike the right balance of products and placement needed to outserve its fierce competition?

CASE ANALYSIS QUESTIONS

1. **DISCUSSION** What does a Porter's Five Forces analysis reveal about the industry in which Dunkin' Donuts and Starbuck's compete? What are the strategic implications for Dunkin' Donuts?

2. **DISCUSSION** Discuss the pros and cons of Jamba Juice's strategy and how it compares to that of Dunkin' Donuts. What similarities are there between the two companies in terms of their growth strategies? Discuss.

3. **PROBLEM SOLVING** Gather information to build an up-to-date SWOT analysis for Dunkin' Donuts. If you were the CEO of the firm, what would you consider to be the strategic management implications of this SWOT analysis, and why?

4. **FURTHER RESEARCH** Research the latest moves by Starbucks and other Dunkin' Donuts' competitors. What is each doing that seems similar to and different from the approach of the other? Can you say that Dunkin' is on the right track? Is it carving out new market share? Or, is it going to be more of a copycat player in the industry?

Case 8: Law Firms Try the Case for New Structures

© Bariscan Celik/iStockphoto

The traditional structure of a large or mid-sized law firm had partners acting as owners, investors, and directors of its operations. Associates, often two-thirds or more of a firm's employees, were hired with the goal of earning their way up to partner level. Being a partner—or better yet, a named partner (a partner included in the official name of a firm)—brought with it an upside in earnings, prestige, and clout. But things are changing.

The economic downturn hit law firms with a drop-off in corporate, real estate, and finance deals. As revenues have fallen, some firms have teetered on the edge of collapse. For Dewey & LeBoeuf, this meant making the news as the largest law-firm failure in U.S. history. One business writer said this elite New York City law firm with as many as 1,300 lawyers at its peak, "pushed the notion of equity partnership to breaking point."

The demise of the firm, which was riddled with high debt, was blamed in part on its poaching of high flying or "rainmaker" partners from competing firms. Critical to most law firms, rainmakers are well connected and highly skilled at building relationships and courting and bringing in new clients.

Unsustainable Structure

The traditional partnership structure was a pyramid with large equity owners at the top and the associates at lower levels. But this became unsustainable at Dewey & LeBoeuf, where some partners were promised multi-million-dollar payments, whereas more junior partners were required to pay their way into the partnership. Its imbalanced partnership had some partners with reported earnings above $5 million a year, while others made a "mere" $300,000.

It isn't uncommon at traditional law firms to pass off work to associates while partners "play golf at clubs their clients are too poor to join," says one business writer. The ratio of partners to associates is often referred to as "leverage." When associates produce revenues during good times and big deals, this leverage pays off. However, it can be expensive to keep many associates on staff.

The past decade saw a 75% increase in fees for large law firms compared with a 20% increase in business costs. Clients fed up with being overcharged and high hourly rates have rebelled. And, decreased demand for legal services has created a need for restructuring. To survive, many law firms have been forced to realign their organiza-

tional structure with challenges of the new economic environment. Wharton management professor Olivier Chatain believes that recession exposed the "gross inefficiencies," but "There were signs before the crisis that the business model had to evolve. The crisis is just making it more urgent."

Enter Disruption

Axiom Legal is an example of "disruption" taking place in the legal services arena. *American Lawyer* magazine describes it as "attempting to pave a middle ground between legal process outsourcers (read: India) and law firms (both traditional and alternative) by providing solutions to legal challenges that may rise above mere document review tasks but don't require the bench strength and extensive talent infrastructure (read: cost) of a top-tier law firm."

Axiom's 800 attorneys are graduates of top-tier law schools and former stars from the elite grand firms. They have made a conscious career choice not to sacrifice their personal lives for professional advancement. They also work mostly from home and there is minimal office space at the firm.

Chief operating officer Paul Carr, says Axiom was founded with the "vague idea of using technology to cut costs and match corporate clients directly with lawyers outside a traditional law firm." "There is a lot of legal work which is semi repetitive," he claims, "where if you apply a process lens, technology tools, and work flow management [to it], you can deliver much better performance."

When Hewlett-Packard was in search of a more cost-effective way of negotiating, drafting, and executing contract agreements involving sales-related, licensing, and follow-on agreements, Axiom fit the bill. At the time, much of that routine work was being done by in-house lawyers. HP wanted to work with an on-shoring firm (or one close by) with whom their lawyers, staff, and customers could interact with more closely. The solution was Axiom Legal and its benefits of flexibility in scaling up or down without a large capital outlay.

Goodbye Office, Hello Unassigned Desks and Storage Lockers

View Pictures/Peter Cook/VIEW/
NewsCom

"They're more concerned about being around other people who do cool things than how big their desks are."

How would you feel if, upon showing up to work one day, your desk and personal work space were gone? As companies slash costs, go green, and accommodate increasingly more mobile workers, the free-flowing layout for roamers in an "officeless" office has evolved. Often called "free address" or "nonterritorial" offices, they're a growing trend.

At American Express, "club" or officeless employees represent 20% of its 5,000-person workforce. The company wants to reconfigure nontraditional offices worldwide throughout its various geographic locations.

Welcome to an office concept of communal tables and unassigned desks. Some employers use an online reservation system to reserved spots in advance, a practice called "hotelling." Others have a first-come, first-served policy. Storage lockers are provided for files and supplies.

For some organizations the officeless notion is the new norm. And it makes sense in a number of ways. Employees have reported greater creativity, collaboration, and idea exchange—and fewer e-mails. Surveys show that e-mail traffic at some companies has dropped by more than 50%. GlaxoSmithKline says it has saved an estimated $10 million in real estate costs.

"They're more concerned about being around other people who do cool things than how big their desks are," says a Zappos executive. "Our workspace has become our laptops." Open, collaborative, and shared space has also created less of a hierarchical corporate culture. For workers more interested in flexible work hours, telecommuting, creativity and collaboration than in office size or location as status symbols, technology has, once again deemed itself a game changer.

Technology Drives Restructuring

With 20 lawyers, Clearspire is another example of a law firm breaking from the conventional norm. Its lawyers work mostly from home "collaborating on a multi-million-dollar technology platform that mimics a virtual office," says a writer for the *Economist*. Clients can use the technology platform to collaboratively mark up, edit, and make changes to legal documents in the process of being drawn up. To allow for more predictable and accurate budget and cost forecasting, Clearspire quotes a flat fee for each phase of the job. If the work gets done in less time than quoted, both the client and Clearspire share in the savings. If it takes longer, Clearspire assumes responsibility for the difference.

In an *Economist* magazine article entitled, "50 Ways to Leave Your Lawyer," one writer stated: "If technology now helps cut gargantuan legal bills in America and elsewhere, it will be better late than never." But changing the costs of legal services isn't the only thing technology will be helping. Lifestyles count too.

An equity partner, onetime the dream of many at large elite law firms, may now be working directly with a client's legal and business teams or at a home computer while donning business attire above the waist and pajamas below. For many lawyers, this alternative structure has created a flexible work schedule, a choice of clients, and most important, happiness. Many lawyers are smiling as work-life balance travels with the new structures.

CASE ANALYSIS QUESTIONS

1. **DISCUSSION** What are the potential benefits, if any, to the traditional way law firms were structured? Can a case be made that instead of looking for new and radically different structures, it might be better to focus on getting the best out of the existing one? Explain.

2. **DISCUSSION** How would you compare the advantages and disadvantages of the new open and officeless environments— for employees, and for organizations? Would this fit well with you and your work preferences? How about an organization's culture, does an open office approach change things?

3. **PROBLEM SOLVING** If a law firm is struggling to do well, would it be helpful for a consultant to come in and analyze the informal structure? What might be learned that could help in designing with a new structure that better suits the firm's current needs? How could such an analysis be done?

4. **FURTHER RESEARCH** Check out the Axiom Legal website. Study its services and current approach to staffing and client services. Does Axiom seem to have the right structure for the moment? When you look at the legal services industry overall, is Axiom faring well versus competitors? Is it setting a new model for others to adopt in the future, or is it already behind the curve as technology keeps developing and the economy keeps changing?

Case 9: LinkedIn—Networking for Career Opportunities

Paul Sakuma/AP

We change jobs an average of seven times during our lifetime. Every time we do this, it's a rush to develop and find new contacts to assist in opening new doors. With a lot of uncertainty and insecurity about the future, both the employed and the unemployed feel a continued need to actively network. LinkedIn has created the perfect solution not only for recruiters in search of candidates, but also those in job search mode—or simply anyone wanting to make "connections." Driven by innovation, LinkedIn is the first social network to go public.

Need a Job? Have a Job, but Want a Better One?

LinkedIn is the place to be. It is a "freemium" social networking Web site for corporate and business professionals interested in networking. Although free to join, a premium subscription, which allows you, among other services, to see who has viewed your profile, is available for a fee. By building a profile that typically includes a resume, schools attended, and any other types of affiliations (think: volunteer or service work), users can self-promote and make old and new connections.

To pick job candidates the "old school" way, many firms relied on headhunters, job boards, and employee referrals. Now, LinkedIn has innovatively transformed the industry

for recruiters searching for qualified candidates to fill open positions. According to head of recruiting for Accenture, "You'd better be on the Web."

LinkedIn has built a business selling its rapidly expanding data to recruiters. More than half of its revenues come from "hiring solutions." As a tool for human resource professionals, employers can list and search for candidates. There are also hundreds of thousands of interest groups and forums on LinkedIn, the majority which are employment related. The groups are networks for professionals, academic or corporate alumni, and others. In addition, there is the ability to "create events" such as trade shows, conferences, and training courses.

LinkedIn vs. Facebook

Some might wonder how LinkedIn, a social media Web site, differentiates itself from social media giant Facebook. LinkedIn allows its registered users to "connect" with others through an "invitation" process (non-site users can be invited as well). Once an invitation is accepted, a "connection" is made. A contact network is built through direct connections and second-degree connections (or the connections of each of their connections). In essence, LinkedIn's innovation allows for "virtual introductions" through mutual contacts.

Whereas LinkedIn is used to keep up with work-related social interactions, Facebook is more for personal fun. Twitter, on the other hand, makes good sense for news updates and quickly sharing information. A business once said: "Facebook is for fun. Tweets have a short shelf life. If you're serious about managing your career, the only social site that really matters is LinkedIn." That's changing now as both Facebook and Twitter start to intrude on LinkedIn's space.

Culture of Innovation

Innovation has so far kept LinkedIn dominant. In voting it one of the 50 most innovative companies, *Fast Company* magazine said LinkedIn lets members "curate daily news roundups to showcase their expertise, transforming the professional network into a must-visit hub of information sharing." The firm's senior vice president, Deep Nishar, says the fact that "everybody wants to be better informed and better at their job" is a key driver of LinkedIn's and growth innovation.

The company hopes that users will keep profiles up-to-date and continue returning to the site. The goal according to *Fast Company* is to be an "indispensible tool for planning and managing careers." LinkedIn says it's all about "building the professional Web."

LinkedIn continues to innovate by providing new features. The endorsements feature is an online "letter of recommendation" of sorts. Companies can place a business page or profile page on LinkedIn with blog posts, Tweets, and even video. InMaps gives a visual of the connections within a network and detects relationships between them. Each network is then grouped into different clusters. It's easy for developers to access LinkedIn's data in the race to beat Facebook by creating a social network for the business world.

LinkedIn's values are a by-product of its founder, Reid Hoffman, who helped start the firm with former colleagues at PayPal and Socialnet, a dating Web site. In addition to his continued involvement at LinkedIn, Hoffman runs a $20 million venture fund for small technology startups.

Gamers Welcome in the New Corporate Culture

Monalyn Gracia/Corbis Corp.

"Adding gamification to the workplace drives performance, but it doesn't make up for bad management."

Would you be surprised if you approached a co-worker only to realize that they were playing a video game? Companies are increasingly using video games or "gamification" as a way to bring more happiness and levity into the workplace. Gaming is seen as a way to promote a culture of learning, individualism, and fun while still focusing on the company's goals and bottom line. However, "adding gamification to the workplace drives performance but it doesn't make up for bad management," says the chief executive of game maker Badgeville.com.

Approximately 40% of IBM's 40,000 employees work from home or travel. Gaming is used as a "way to help colleagues connect and stay engaged," explains an IBM executive. Software Company SAP uses a game that includes "assigning sales leads and environmental challenges that award points for tasks like carpooling," says its chief innovation strategist, Mario Herger. Retailer Target uses gaming to post a score measuring the speed and success of cashiers over multiple transactions.

Reports suggest that gaming helps employees feel more engaged and connected with others. In place of strategic planning sessions, gaming can be used to simulate various business scenarios. Rewards and competition, tactics commonly found in the gaming world, can be applied to boost mundane tasks like data entry and invoicing.

Employees can be rewarded with badges or points for on-time completion of assignments. Leaderboards can be posted for the competitive-at-heart, allowing participating workers to see who is in the lead. Although some fear that such competition could breed contempt, experts claim it's a motivator.

As the gamification trend continues to grow, employees may be asking themselves whether a virtual badge of accomplishment is truly better than a good old-fashioned pat on the back and verbal "job well done" from a manager. Which type of culture do you prefer?

Professional Matchmaking for Continued Growth

LinkedIn is heavily recruiting college graduates to add to its subscriber base. Growing up on Facebook and Twitter, they're already comfortable with the "hyper-sharing" aspect of the LinkedIn experience. Reportedly, the company grows its membership by two people every second. This growth is crucial, because LinkedIn makes money by selling its services to recruiters and advertisers interested in reaching white-collar professionals.

"Connecting talent to opportunity at massive scale," is what LinkedIn is all about, says CEO, Jeff Weiner. The company's success to date is consistent with its lofty mission statement: "Our vision is to create economic opportunity for every professional in the world." If that translates to lower unemployment, consider the company a game changer, to say the very least.

"The reason LinkedIn works so well for professional matchmaking is that most of its members already have jobs," says one business writer. A "cadre of happily employed people use it to research clients before sales calls, ask their connections for advice, and read up on where former colleagues are landing gigs."

Unemployed? Go to LinkedIn and you might find a good opportunity. Have a job? Want a better one? Create a profile on LinkedIn and "get connected."

CASE ANALYSIS QUESTIONS

1. **DISCUSSION** What type of corporate culture would you expect to find at LinkedIn? If you were to visit the firm's headquarters, what do you think you would see and hear around you as the observable culture? How about core values, what would you expect to be high on LinkedIn's list of priority values? Why?

2. **DISCUSSION** How has innovation by LinkedIn transformed the playing field for recruiters and hiring managers . . . and for job candidates? Is this an example of a disruptive innovation? Why or why not? What value can LinkedIn offer you?

3. **PROBLEM SOLVING** Consider yourself a gamer. Also consider yourself the go-to "idea person" for friends that head two local organizations—a fire department and a public library. Both complain about morale problems and ask you for advice on creating a positive organizational culture. They want to know how your interest in gaming can be used to improve staff morale and performance. What will you suggest and why?

4. **FURTHER RESEARCH** There's lots of public information available on LinkedIn, from its founding story to current performance. Study the company's history and current directions. Find out how it is handling competition. Check current statements to identify values, goals, and accomplishments. Then, prepare a summary report. Is this still the lead innovator and company to beat in the industry? Or, is LinkedIn's time starting to pass, and alternatives from Facebook, Google, Twitter, and others will be the hot choices for the future?

Case 10: Silicon Valley's "Chief Executive Mom"

Stephen Lam/Reuters/NewsCom

Prior to her appointment as CEO of Yahoo!, Marissa Mayer was best known as spokesperson and the public face of Google. She was Google's 20th employee and the company's first female engineer. She stayed 13 years. Then the offer that couldn't be refused came along. With compensation valued at over $100 million over five years, Mayer was appointed president and CEO of Yahoo!.

It was a great opportunity but a tough job. Yahoo! had gone through five CEOs over the prior five years. Mayer's challenge was to turn around the onetime Internet sweetheart which now trailed competitors in search and e-mail. Referred to by industry observers as a savior for Yahoo!, Mayer's arrival created some fairly interesting buzz, to say the least.

At age 37, Mayer became the youngest CEO of *any Fortune* 500 company. She is known for academic brilliance, and holds an advanced degree in computer science from Stanford University, where she performed in-depth research on artificial intelligence. The success of many of Google's blockbuster products, Web search and Gmail, were heavily influenced by her product leadership.

CEO on Maternity Leave

On the same day Yahoo! announced Mayer's hiring, she posted on Twitter an "unexpected" announcement—that she was expecting. She would give birth to her firstborn within 90 days. As Yahoo!'s newest and, at-the-time, pregnant CEO, the blogosphere immediately became crowded with frenetic posts regarding what might lie ahead for her and the company.

Although Yahoo!'s board supported and knew full well about Mayer's impending life event prior to appointing her as CEO, industry observers wondered how motherhood would coincide with the responsibility placed on her. As one writer put it: "What her pregnancy meant, and her new motherhood now means, remains a complicated question—for Yahoo!, for her hothouse-circuit Silicon Valley fame, and for the much broader interest in her among ambitious, ambivalent professional women across the country."

"My maternity leave will be a few weeks long, and I'll work throughout it," Mayer stated publicly. She has stuck to her word. *Time* magazine referred to her maternity leave as "blink-and-it's-over." But when she declared intent to limit her maternity leave some wondered about the impact this would have on working women. Mayer said that Yahoo!'s directors demonstrated "evolved thinking" in choosing to hire a pregnant chief executive. She also pointed out that her "few weeks and working through it" maternity leave was her own choice. "It is quite possible that she can do both effectively, but it is not un-'evolved' to express concern," says one business writer.

Legal Protection Against Pregnancy Discrimination

Most women are allowed 12 weeks unpaid, job-protected maternity leave under the Family Medical Leave Act (FMLA). However, Mayer is considered in legal language a "key employee"—in the top 10% of earn-

ers within a company. Key employees who become pregnant are not covered under the FMLA act of job protection. By law, a company is not required to reinstate a key employee back to her old job, nor do they have to cover maternity leave if she been there for less than 12 months.

Workplace issues and outcomes for pregnant women aren't always as sweet as a baby's arrival. As more women become empowered to break the silence about workplace bias, pregnancy discrimination claims have risen. Such cases are filed by women who believe they have been discriminated against, which includes being fired and not being hired, for either being pregnant or having the intent to become pregnant. Discrimination against working mothers includes prejudice and stigma stemming from management's fears of productivity loss from family and parenting distractions, and even fears new moms may demand unreasonable work adjustments and accommodations.

Pregnancy discrimination, an amendment to Title VII of the Civil Rights Act of 1964 (which outlawed major discrimination against racial, ethnic, national and religious minorities, and women), outlawed discrimination on the basis of pregnancy, childbirth, or related medical conditions. This constitutes unlawful sex discrimination under Title VII, which includes employers of 15 or more employees and state and local governments. All employees are to be treated equal regardless of pregnancy status. Employers, aware of laws covering pregnant employees, must provide the necessary documentation and justification of any action against a pregnant employee. They must also be able to prove, if necessary, that men are being held to the same standards.

Back to The Real World

Some believe Mayer's "rock star" status in the tech industry places her in a different position than that faced by most lower-paid new mothers. Lisa Miller of *New York Magazine* says Mayer "will work out her conflicts, however difficult, with the luxury of more-than-ample resources."

Not every woman has Mayer's privileges. Once their pregnancy becomes public, many

New Workplace Perks—Free Lunch Followed by a Nap

Stan Honda/Getty Images

"As Americans sleep fewer hours at night and work longer hours than ever, companies are . . . 'cozying up' to the idea of at-work napping."

The workplace of yesteryear has undergone transformation, and it's barely recognizable today. With the lifestyles of today's employees, the demand for flexibility and work-life balance has become well publicized.

Technology companies rich with cash and chasing scarce talent offer perks like on-site haircuts, a bring your pet to work policy, dry cleaning, lactation rooms, laundry rooms, and of course free food.

But, is legitimating the afternoon nap taking things too far? Some employee-centric companies have taken this step and are, as one business writer puts it, "cozying up" to the idea of "sleeping on the job."

At tech companies, long hours—and sometimes, all-night hackathons—are the norm. So too is the power nap. As Americans sleep fewer hours at night and work longer hours, more employers are experimenting with the idea of at-work napping.

An employee benefits survey of 600 American companies conducted by the Society for Human Resource Management, found 6% of workplaces had nap rooms, and the number is growing. Another poll conducted by the Sleep Foundation found that 34% of respondents say that their employer allows a workplace nap in designated nap areas.

The good news for employers is that a power nap reenergizes employees and increases productivity. Letting employees take naps isn't just nice; it can be productive. Sleep-deprived employees on average lose a few days of productivity each month. Studies show that a 26-minute nap can improve output by at least one-third and alertness by 25%.

So, liberal at-work sleeping policies are starting to appear along with perks like free food, child care, pets-at-work, laundry rooms, on-site haircuts, lactation rooms, fitness facilities, social activities, and more. It's no longer taboo at some places to take an afternoon snooze. In fact, the nap may become the new coffee break. Think about how refreshed it might make you.

---

women have to fight for ample maternity leave and rights to get their jobs back. Some employers have been known to force an unpaid leave of absence, says Sharon Terman, an attorney at the Legal Aid Society Employment Law Center in San Francisco. "The leave," she stated, is based not on medical need, but on the "unfounded assumption about the woman's capacity to do her job."

One disgruntled employee at Bayer quotes her boss as saying, "I need to stop hiring women of reproductive age." After being fired while on maternity leave, she joined a $100 million class-action lawsuit against the pharmaceutical giant.

Some employers invest in pregnancy discrimination training sessions. But, the attitude around pregnant women at work is, even in today's environment, perpetuated by archaic thinking about their worth and value to the organization.

Marissa Mayer's decided to shorten her maternity leave and get back to business at Yahoo!. Does this set a bad precedent for women in all ranks of organizations? Or, does it help make the case that new moms are to be welcomed, not feared, in the workplace?

CASE ANALYSIS QUESTIONS

1. **DISCUSSION** Yahoo! pays Mayer a base salary of $1 million a year, cash performance bonuses, stock grants, and other retention and equity awards should she stay. The total comes to $70 to $120 million. Does this compensation package ensure high performance for the firm? Should lower-level employees be celebrating her pay package, or be concerned about disparities between it and their own? Just what difference does it make how much a CEO gets paid? Explain.

2. **DISCUSSION** Has there ever been a time when you wished to take a nap at work? If so, where did you go, and did others know about it? Were you violating policy? What is your take on legitimating naps in the workplace? What is high on your list of desperate-to-have employee "perks"?

3. **PROBLEM SOLVING** As an executive just hired to overhaul human resource policies and practices at your new firm, how would you deal with the issue of pregnancy? Will you advocate anything special for new mothers? How about new fathers? Make a list of actions you would like to take and the programs you would like to implement. For each item, jot notes on how you will justify your proposals to the top executive team.

4. **FURTHER RESEARCH** Research current news related to Marissa Mayer and Yahoo!. How is the company doing, and how has it evolved since Mayer was appointed CEO? Does her performance justify her pay package? What major human resource management decisions has she made, and have they been good or bad for the employees? Based on what your find, would you consider Yahoo! a benchmark for great human resource management? Why or why not?

Case 11: Apple, Inc.—After the Torch Was Passed

Glenn Chapman/AFP/Getty Images

Is Steve Jobs Irreplaceable? Upon his death, Tim Cook, then Apple's Chief Operating Officer and a 13-year company veteran, was chosen as a natural successor. How has Apple fared without its founder, leader, and "irreplaceable" icon? When it was time to give up the helm, Jobs's resignation letter to the Apple Board of Directors and Apple Community read as follows: "I have always said if there ever came a day when I could no longer meet my duties and expectations as Apple's CEO, I would be the first to let you know. Unfortunately, that day has come. I hereby resign as CEO of Apple. I would like to serve, if the Board sees fit, as Chairman of the Board, director and Apple employee. As far as my successor goes, I strongly recommend that we execute our succession plan and name Tim Cook as CEO of Apple."

The Leader Becomes Ill

From 2004 until 2011, Steve Jobs took three medical leaves of absence while battling cancer. Pressured by various labor groups and industry watchers to publicize its succession plan, Apple confirmed in a regulatory filing that it had a confidential succession plan in place. In its usual veil of secrecy, the company did not wish to dis-

close any such information to competitors, nor did they wish to cause unrest among company insiders interested in being considered for the top post.

During Jobs's multiple health leaves, technology industry insiders and those within Apple deliberated and prepared for the day to come when Steve Jobs, a genius would no longer by synonymous with Apple. During this time of uncertainty, Tim Cook, then Apple's chief operating officer and at the time a 13-year company veteran respected by Jobs, emerged as a natural successor.

Cook filled in when Jobs took his first medical leave and delivered some of Apple's best results to date. He earned respect from Wall Street and was even referred to as the best "try-before-you-buy" successor a company could experience.

Charismatic Legacy

Charismatic leadership is the ability to inspire others in exceptional ways. Some have referred to Jobs's charisma as "superhuman," and Apple as an organization that developed its prominence as a result of such charisma.

Apple fanatics, called "Apple Fanboys or Girls," reflect on the inspiration of Jobs and how he was perceived, respected,

valued, and by some, even worshipped. There is even a "Mac Inspired" dating Web site, Cupidtino—a combination of words "Cupid" and "Cupertino," where Apple is headquartered. It was created for fans of Apple products because they often have so much in common—personalities, creative professions, a similar sense of style and aesthetics, taste, and a love for technology."

The Baton Gets Passed

A human resources expert and professor at the University of Michigan's Ross School of Business, Dave Ulrich, explains: "In a logical CEO succession, Steve Jobs would have gone out with him, let Tim [Cook] begin to do the speaking, and then that 'relationship equity' is transferred." Because Apple remained shrouded in secrecy, this type of succession plan and transition did not happen.

"In some sense, with the charismatic person, it's difficult to prepare a successor, because they are bigger than life," says John Larrere, general manager at the Hay Group, a management consulting firm. Microsoft worked diligently to groom Steve Ballmer as a successor to Bill Gates, who remained with the firm in a high-profile position for eight years prior to leaving to pursue his foundation's initiatives on a full-time basis.

Still, some argue that leaders like Jobs, are simply irreplaceable. Has Tim Cook created an Apple different than his predecessor and iconic co-founder, Steve Jobs?

As with any management transition, and particularly one of this high-profile magnitude, differences in leadership styles are bound to be "compared and contrasted." Over time, differences become apparent—with Cook, however, the vision of Apple seems to have remained much the same as what Steve instilled. As one writer put it, "It's not as simple as Cook will be either like Jobs or he won't."

Challenges of Change

Although Tim Cook promised that the company would not change when he assumed the helm, there have been more than a few, yet significant, differences between decisions and actions taken by Cook and those implemented during Jobs's

Women, Leadership, and the "Double-Bind"

If they assert themselves forcefully, people may perceive them as not acting feminine enough, triggering a backlash. But if they act in a stereotypically feminine way, they aren't seen as strong leaders.

For a woman, the leadership development process is a challenge and a balancing act.

Early in their careers, some women may resort to, "trying on" different styles to see what fits and what feels appropriate, rather than adopting one that "meets the needs of the moment," although this is not always the best approach. Others may adopt a style from a mentor, watching others or by reading leadership books written by thought leaders. Still others may simply use experience, gut, and intuition. How does a woman go about developing her own effective style of leadership?

The *Wall Street Journal* states, "Leadership experts say women must navigate a 'double-bind': If they assert themselves forcefully, people may perceive them as not acting feminine enough, triggering a backlash. But if they act in a stereotypically feminine way, they aren't seen as strong leaders." When developing a leadership style, the issue for a young woman has much to do with what still persists as

a lack of female role models for women. Although much can be learned from male counterparts, knowledge of the sensitivity around navigating the perception of female stereotypes within the workplace is largely missing.

One leadership expert says: "They shouldn't be content simply that their name is on an important report. Instead, they should actively engage colleagues and superiors, and talk frequently about their ideas and research." This may be difficult for women who find self-promotion unnatural. Another suggestion for young female managers is to "ask superiors to back them up when others second-guess them." The challenges faced by women in the workplace may be further solved by joining outside groups and associations with other like-minded women. In this type of setting, there will be those who can assist in the nuances of developing as a leader.

tenure. They include a cash dividend, the first in 30 years, a response and trip to China to address complaints about worker conditions in supplier factories, more attention given to administrative matters, a greater level of communication with employees and Wall Street, greater transparency with product strategy and planning, and even a greater commitment to social responsibility. Apple agreed to match an employee's contributions to nonprofits of up to $10,000.

Cook has even been known to apologize, express empathy, and reveal his feelings, something very new to the scene for an Apple CEO. One writer puts it like this: "It will be years, perhaps a decade, before we can look back on Apple and decide whether Tim Cook was able to provide the needed product inspiration and evolution. Steve Jobs was driven by demons that Tim Cook doesn't have, yet Mr. Cook can draw upon that legacy and draw upon the best spirit of Apple without necessarily being driven by the same demons. Time will tell."

What Comes Next?

Indeed, it will take some time until it is determined whether or not Apple's cre-

ative and high performance foundation will remain for years to come—the Steve Jobs legacy. Not many people can say they have changed the world the way he did. Many wonder what else he would have done. Now, at least for the time being, it's up to Tim Cook to show the world that even though Steve Jobs set the foundations, Apple's best is yet to come.

CASE ANALYSIS QUESTIONS

1. DISCUSSION If leading builds commitments and enthusiasm for people to apply their talents to put an organization's plans into action, what special qualities of Steve Jobs seem to have contributed to his leadership success as Apple's CEO?

2. DISCUSSION Suppose the successor to Steve Jobs was not Tim Cook, but Tamara Cook. Would the leadership challenge have been any different? What might make it hard or easy for a female leader to take over from a very successful male predecessor?

3. PROBLEM SOLVING There is always a tendency to compare a successor, such

as Tim Cook, to a predecessor, like Steve Jobs. This happens at all levels and in all types of organizations when there is a leadership transition. How important are the leadership styles of the successor and predecessor to the latter's eventual success or failure? Should the styles of each be the same or different, or does it depend on the situation? If you were taking over from someone who had successfully led a team for quite a while, how would you address this issue of leadership styles, and what would you do in the first weeks to make sure that your tenure as team leader would be a good one?

4. FURTHER RESEARCH There's a lot to the Apple story and how Tim Cook fared as he took over the helm. Dig into the news and see what the latest reports are saying. How has Cook done? What changes has he made? How is the company doing? Does it appear that Cook had what it would take to move Jobs's great legacy forward in a dynamic industry environment of copycatting and competition? How can you account for Cook's successes and failures at this point in time?

Case 12: Businesses in Trouble Pass the Buck on Blame

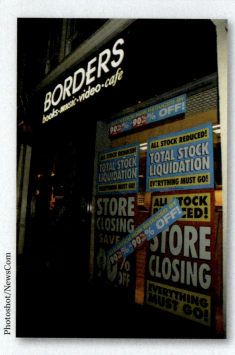

Photoshot/NewsCom

How do the leaders of now defunct companies, including those that were once industry stalwarts, explain failure? It's not uncommon to deny responsibility and blame the environment or other factors when a business goes bad.

When Borders Group, Inc., an international retailer of books and music, filed for Chapter 11 bankruptcy its leadership blamed failure in part on external causes such as the "eReading revolution and the turbulent economy." If this was truly the case, industry insiders ask, why didn't Barnes and Noble fail as well?

Executives have different reactions when it comes to mistakes and failures. Depending on a company's culture, some see failure as a reason to place blame, whereas others may see it as a learning opportunity and a chance to do better in the future.

Fear Failure-Find Fault Workplace Cultures

Finding fault and assigning blame is part of the dominant culture at some workplaces. When something goes wrong, the immediate response is to discover who was at fault. Rather than accepting personal responsibility, employees tend to find fault and place blame for personal failures on external causes. This can create a situation where employees fear failure. They become stuck, complacent, and paralyzed. A workplace culture that fears failure can create workers who are risk-averse and afraid to make mistakes. They play it safe rather than seek innovation and try new ideas.

Self-serving bias is the tendency to blame personal workplace failures or problems on external causes rather than accept personal responsibility and admit fault. External causes can include an unrealistic or demanding boss, annoying co-workers or working conditions, low pay and long hours. Leaders of organizations can blame poor results or failure on a variety of external factors ranging in everything from a poor economy to changing consumer purchasing patterns to price wars by competitors.

Conversely, the opposite can also be true when dealing with success and positive results. There may be a tendency, when judging our own performance, to take personal credit for any successes. When judging or explaining superior company performance, for example, there is often a tendency for executives to claim personal responsibility for any success. Some call such behavior self-enhancement bias—to wit, "Yes, it's all me."

Back to Borders

Yes, increased online book sales, digital downloads, and the Great Recession surely hurt. But the company's failure was also a result of internal causes: inability to develop an online presence, management's decision to allow Amazon to handle its digital book business, and taking on massive amounts of debt to expand its large superstores too quickly.

A decision to ramp up DVD and CD sales in its superstores just as the digital revolution of movies and books had begun didn't help matters. Six CEOs in less than a decade, none of whom had retail book experience, also contributed to Borders's string of poor decisions.

How About Fast Food?

Fast-food companies are common targets of blame for the cause of childhood obesity and rising rates of childhood diabetes. A 2002 lawsuit was filed against the Golden Arches by parents of two girls, one of whom is 19 years old, 5-foot-6 and 270 pounds, and the other, age 14, 4-foot-10 and 170 pounds. Their daily meals included an egg McMuffin for breakfast and a Big Mac meal for dinner for one and Happy Meals three to four times weekly for the other. The girls' father claims that he was never informed by McDonald's about the food's ingredients and potential health issues associated with its consumption.

Should McDonald's be held responsible for childhood obesity? What about parental guidance and sedentary lifestyles among children?

Lawyers for McDonald's in the prior lawsuit argued that the matter was really about "common sense and individual responsibility." In their motion to dismiss, the lawyers wrote: "Every responsible person understands what is in products such as hamburgers and fries, as well as the consequences to one's waistline, and potentially to one's health, of excessively eating those foods over a prolonged period of time."

Others argue that McDonald's multi-billion-dollar advertising efforts target children who are not in a position to make rational food choices. Ronald McDonald, its longtime clown mascot has been urged by many to "retire." But CEO Don Thompson says: "Ronald is not a bad guy. He's about fun. He's a clown. I'd urge you to let your kids have fun too."

Poor Exam Grades-Bad Teaching or Lack of Study?

Self-serving bias is often evident in a classroom or school environment. Have you ever found yourself with a grade on an exam that was lower than what you expected? Who was at fault? Was it due to a lack of time spent studying? Or was it due to the teacher's poor teaching?

If you've ever overlooked your own personal study habits and instead placed blame on the teacher for your test result, you are not alone. Check your self-serving bias the next time a test is returned with a lower grade than expected. Think also how you would have reacted to an A on the test. Would you have attributed it to diligent studying, brilliance, and intelligence?

The New Leadership IQ—Empathy, Self-Awareness, and Social Skills

Richard Lewis/WireImage/GettyImages

If your class valedictorian did not become the soaring success everyone predicted, perhaps it's a case of IQ exceeding EI.

Psychologist Daniel Goleman writes frequently about the importance of emotional intelligence in defining one's character and destiny. Although temperaments are a function of neurochemistry, Goleman argues that "they can be altered." But this ability to control and manage reactions is contingent on first recognizing emotions.

Simply put, emotional intelligence means having the skill set to deal with emotions rather than "becoming emotional." It includes the competencies of self-awareness, self-regulation, self-management, empathy, and social skills.

Emotional intelligence is an important human skill for managers and an important leadership capability. Being able to manage emotions leads to better and more enhanced relationships, and potentially, more effective leadership. The ongoing development of these skills gives executives and professionals an edge when dealing with others—particularly when relationships can make or break a deal.

When senior-level executives are able to manage themselves emotionally, they are able to set themselves apart. In other words, according to Goleman, "the higher the rank of the person considered a star performer, the more emotional intelligence capabilities showed up as the reason for his or her effectiveness."

There are some highly intelligent executives possessing high IQs who, when promoted to senior-level positions, simply cannot make it as leaders. Conversely, there are those with extraordinary empathy, self-awareness, and social skills who command the respect of others while subsequently becoming wildly successful leaders.

What is your ability to understand others emotionally, control your impulses, or refrain from judgment? How would you rank your emotional intelligence?

Breaking Away from Self-Serving Bias

Shifting the blame from oneself to external forces doesn't help much in trying to change the course of one's fate through behavior modification. So, what's the solution? Experts advise us to accept responsibility for moving forward and learning from mistakes and circumstances. Shouldn't CEOs and top executives take the same advice?

Now may be a good time to check your attitude toward mistakes. If you've made a few lately, who or what did you blame, and what have you learned? Do the inevitable mistakes help create a more adaptive and innovative you?

CASE ANALYSIS QUESTIONS

1. DISCUSSION This case opened with the example of Borders and questioned the placement of blame for its performance failures. It may be easy to criticize executives for self-serving bias in such situations. But, how do you draw the line between blaming the environment correctly and incorrectly for problems, even the most devastating ones? What case can you make that what happened to Borders was really out of top management control?

2. DISCUSSION Emotions are everywhere, including the workplace. No doubt leaders should be good at dealing with emotions. But, can a concern for emotions reach the point where it gets in the way of making timely and performance-driven decisions? Are there any limits on emotional intelligence as an executive or team leader skill?

3. PROBLEM SOLVING Fast food, sugary drinks . . . they're under attack these days. But should the companies that make and sell them be blamed for societal problems with obesity and unhealthy habits? What about those who choose to consume them? Are lawsuits like the one filed against McDonald's justified? If you were CEO of McDonald's, Wendy's, Coca-Cola, or PepsiCo, what would worry you about such issues? What steps could you take to manage perceptions of your company while still meeting customer demands for tasty drinks and fast foods?

4. FURTHER RESEARCH Research examples of three recently failed companies—large or small—and examine their causes can reasons for failure. Look for quotes from company executives that might explain why the company failed. Check what outside observers and former employees have to say. How is self-serving bias at play in each situation and on the parts of the different observers? What lessons can be learned here on managing perceptions for better decision making?

Case 13: Salesforce.com—Instant Praise. Instant Criticism.

David Paul Morris/Bloomberg/GettyImages

Instead of waiting a year for your annual performance review, how would you like to know where you stand by getting immediate feedback about how you're doing? After all, the once-a-year version might be what some human resource professionals call "little more than a dysfunctional pretense." In other words, it becomes a boss-administered exercise in unhelpful feedback.

The typical annual review can present information overload for many—including past performance, goal setting, pay, and improvement needs. For goals accomplished today, how valuable and motivating is recognition and feedback six months from now? What if, you were able to get real-time feedback and coaching by asking colleagues, managers, and peers pointed questions like: "What did you think of my presentation?" or "What can be done better?"

Forget Old School Ways

Forget old formal chains of command, deeply entrenched hierarchies, and traditional top-down management. Welcome to today's "instant feedback gratification system" using Web-based social network programs. They give employees timely and meaningful feedback of their work performance. "Performance management has become disconnected from real performance. Today, we move faster. We're more connected. This requires a new approach

to performance," say executives at Rypple, a maker of Web-based social performance management software.

Meaningful Recognition

Rypple's founder Daniel Debow says: "I decided to start a new company, and we came up with its first really basic feature—the ability to ask anonymously for feedback at work." Rather than waiting a year to learn what managers think of them, employees using the Rypple platform can send out a quick (50 words or less) pointed question to folks ranging from managers to peers to customers to suppliers. Some call this just-in-time performance improvement. And in today's business environment of rapid speed, employers are beginning to realize its true value for employee recognition, control, performance, and motivation.

Rypple was acquired by the software-as-service firm Salesforce.com. It was the company's first-time entry into the human capital management (HCM) market. Chairman and CEO of Salesforce.com, Mark Benioff, says that "the next generation of HCM is not just about a cloud delivery model; it's about a fundamentally better way to recruit, manage and empower employees in a social world."

The rebranded Salesforce Rypple provides real-time coaching and 1:1 feedback. Its Web site proclaims: "Watch teams rally

around organizational goals and driving results."

Constant Learning and Growing

A Mozilla Firefox employee explains that with Salesforce Rypple, she is able to constantly "learn, adjust and grow without having to wait until the next review cycle." In a single place, on completion of a goal, project, or quarter, the application provides a real-time snapshot of employee performance. Benefits include the ability to give public thanks and solicit meaningful feedback in a timely manner.

A coaching interface allows workers to build coaching networks to spot needed improvements. This helps resolve problems and issues as they arise rather than after the fact. It also means quicker implementation of needed changes.

More or Less Motivation?

How does this affect motivation? When efforts are recognized in a public way, workers are motivated to continue their efforts and, in some cases, work even harder. Social goals allow for greater collaboration for input and advice—and the ability to see what each team member is working on. Painful annual reviews become less significant.

Some drawbacks to Salesforce Rypple might include its anonymity. Although users choose which peers or managers to provide anonymous feedback, with only a few solicitations, anonymity may get lost. Some users also argue that with the ability to pick and choose, the software turns into a tool used to solicit positive strokes. The level of honest of feedback may be questionable.

Still others ask if too much feedback becomes a bad thing. Reliance on so much feedback and what other people say can be a detriment to learning the hard way—by making mistakes.

Change Coming Your Way?

Although the way people work has changed dramatically, feedback and performance management tools had not, until recently. In today's connected workplace, more employers are embracing tools like Salesforce Rypple to allow continuous and ongoing dialogue between employees and their managers.

Digging in to a Free Lunch

© Britta Pedersen/dpa/Getty Images

The free food perk may bring an increase in employee morale and productivity, while also encouraging more healthy eating habits.

How influential would a daily "free lunch" be when you're considering a job offer? Long a tradition of technology firms, free food as a work perk has been widely used to lure young engineers and, of course, others, who are hungry for more than just career success. If you're one of many workers who look forward to the midday lunch break with a meal outside the office, you know all too well how quickly the daily ritual can add to your monthly personal expenses.

Greg Casella, owner of a Silicon Valley San Jose-based catering company, has coined a term for the free food work perk. He calls it the "Google Effect." Catering companies report a brisk increase in business as more companies realize the benefits of a Google-like free lunch.

Employers say that "they now need to do the same to attract employees who are used to hearing about these perks from their friends in tech jobs." Although the free food perk may seem like a significant investment for a company, the increase in employee morale and productivity, along with the encouragement to eat healthy foods at work, more than offset its cost.

The trend of food emporium-type cafeterias was sparked by Google in an effort to both lure employee talent and make it convenient for employees to get a quick bite and return back to coding. In place of cafeteria-style food like burgers and fries, pasta, and pizza, Google's offering includes sushi, fresh-ground espresso, smoothies, and a range of international delicacies as well. Facebook is said to offer "gourmet grub" such as fettuccine, fish, baby beets, and celery root puree, alongside a daily selection of pizzas. And, save room for swirled homemade frozen yogurt for desert.

To attract high caliber employees, more businesses, including small and nontechnology companies, are following suit by offering the on-site free food perk—some on a Friday or occasional basis, and others on a daily schedule.

How big a deal is free food as a perk? If you had to decide between two employers—one with and one without free lunches—would the cost of lunch be a deal breaker? And once on the job, just how long will a free lunch be a performance motivator?

So, are you willing to wait a year until your next performance review to get some of that much-needed positive feedback? Or would you like to work in an environment where real-time report cards of your progress are common?

CASE ANALYSIS QUESTIONS

1. DISCUSSION What is your position on the annual performance review—past its "sell by" date, or just in need of some modest revisions? Even if real-time reviews are available using software like Salesforce Rypple, is there a need for a good annual performance review? In other words, does the annual review offer something that real-time reviews can't?

2. DISCUSSION In addition to having a healthy and free lunch as an employment perk, what other unique incentives and motivators are of interest to today's high-talent college graduates? Other than a good salary, what incentives might cause you to choose one job offer over another? What's on your list of top "must-have" perks, and why?

3. PROBLEM SOLVING You've just taken a new job in human resource management and the organization's president gave you this high-priority task: Give us a plan that can make performance reviews motivating to the recipients and their bosses alike. "I' m tired," she says, "of hearing everyone complain that annual reviews are demotivating. We need to review performance. Surely there are ways that we can make ours more valuable." As you sit down to think about this assignment, make a few notes on what you believe the major issues are and the types of things you might recommend. Use insights from motivation theories to justify what's on your list.

4. FURTHER RESEARCH How about the real-time and Web-based approach to performance reviews offered by software such as Salesforce Ryyple? Do some research and identify the latest developments with it and others like it. Is this online approach to performance assessment the right pathway to a more motivated workforce? What does the evidence say about benefits? What downsides are users reporting? Overall, what's the current verdict on Salesforce Rypple and similar products—good for bosses, good for employers, good for employees?

Case 14: Whole Foods—Teamwork the Natural Way

© Brooks Kraft/Corbis

Whole Foods Market, emulated and imitated, is the sweetheart of the supermarket industry. With revenue exceeding $10 billion, and growth of 26% over the last decade, the Austin, Texas-based company's management philosophies leave no room for complacency.

In a $560-billion grocery industry with profit margins described as "slimmer than angel-hair pasta," the high-end retail grocer has survived a squeamish economy and cutbacks in discretionary consumer spending. If you're wondering about the company's survival tactics, much of it has to do with its basic organizational unit—the team. Add to that its culture of "open books, open doors, and open people," and what you get is a real formula for prolific growth.

With over 300 retail stores, Whole Foods operates as a "high trust organization" with small teams, referred to by insiders as a "tribal setting." It is within the teams that empowered workers perpetuate this trust and fulfill a quality mission. The firm's Web site states the following: "Achieving unity of vision about the future of our company, and building trust between Team Members is a goal of Whole Foods Market." One of the company's core values is excellence and team member happiness—for all 68,000 of them.

The Team as Defining Unit of Activity

Included in *Fortune* magazine's annual list of the "100 Best Companies to Work For" every year since the list began in 1998, the Whole Foods culture epitomizes decentralized teamwork. The team, not the hierarchy, is the "defining unit of activity," and each of its stores is comprised of an average of ten self-managed teams epitomizing the true definition of teamwork. They include produce, grocery, prepared foods, seafood, bakery, floral, and wine, among others.

Teams work together to accomplish a shared goal. Goals are not only clearly defined, but they are also celebrated when reached. A produce team leader in Chicago is quoted as saying, "Without our people, we are just four walls and food."

No Room for Free Riders or Social Loafers

Whole Foods sets itself apart from other retailers with its democratic peer-based selection process. Because teams can suffer from common performance problems, every new "associate" is assigned to a team, and after a four-week trial period, it is the team's two-thirds vote that determines whether the associate will make it to the full-time ranks and earn a spot on the team. If performance issues are detected, the team member is voted off the team,

because, as one team member says, "there is no room for free-riders or social loafers." This peer-based selection process is in effect not only in retail stores, but also at the company's corporate headquarters in areas ranging from marketing to IT to finance.

To increase communication, team member forums and advisory groups are prevalent throughout the company. Its "open book, open door, and open people" practices further encourage communication. To build positive relationships among team members, Whole Foods pushes the philosophy that there is no room for an "us versus them" mentality. Participation among team members is deeply encouraged, and this is achieved by team meetings. Self-directed teams meet regularly to discuss and resolve problems. Members reward and commend the contributions of one another.

Employees Are Everything

Co-CEO Walter Robb believes deeply that "employees are everything." One of the company's core values is team member happiness and excellence, and that is something we believe in our hearts and something that guides our actions every day as a company, he says. "If we're taking care of one another the customers are going to feel that."

The team members of Whole Foods are a diverse bunch, making *Fortune* magazine's "Most Diverse" list. Its workforce is comprised of up to 44% women and 43% minorities. The company's culture is one of inclusiveness. Employees feel as if they're not only being taken care of, but that they are supposed to take care of one another.

There's a reason why Whole Foods has some of the nation's happiest workers. "Our Team Members are the heart and soul of this company: that's our not-so-secret sauce," says Robb.

Promoting from Within

Whole Foods' policy is to encourage employees to apply for jobs for which they are qualified. Once chosen, training consists of a new team member orientation, department-specific training, and customer service training.

Promoting from within fits the company's focus on team member development. This results in better trained and more highly skilled employees who require less supervision. Many believe that this

Decision Making at the Federal Reserve Board

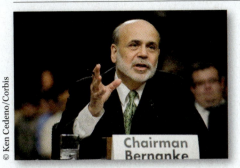

© Ken Cedeno/Corbis

Ben Bernanke, Chairman of the Federal Reserve Board, acknowledged "deep divisions at the central bank about how to handle today's complex economic problems."

Group decision making has both advantages and disadvantages. As chairman of the Federal Reserve Board, Ben Bernanke, a former professor of economics at Princeton University, has acknowledged "deep divisions at the central bank about how to handle today's complex economic problems." He practices a consensus-driven leadership style, but acknowledges the "divide" among members of the FOMC (Federal Open Market Committee) when it comes to resolving the country's slow economic recovery.

The FOMC is the Fed's policy-making body, which consists of its seven board of governors in Washington, DC, and 12 regional Fed bank presidents. A prolonged slump led to different views about what to do to heal the economy. Some opted for the central bank to increase its purchases of U.S. Treasury bonds to drive down interest rates—though some fear this tool lacks effectiveness. Others feared inflation or the creation of "asset bubbles," created when too much money is injected into the financial system.

Predecessors of Bernanke made individual decisions with far less, if any, input and collaboration from board members. Bernanke has taken two bold steps in his attempt to create more consensus. The first is publishing detailed interest-rate projections of each of the 17 officials who participate in policy meetings. The information is published anonymously and does not identify the official by name. Second, the Fed has spelled out its goals for inflation and unemployment in ways far more explicit and open than the prior administration.

Bernanke welcomed disagreement and dissent among the committee members. He stated that: "Disagreement is a good thing. It creates new ideas. It forces people to look at all sides of the question."

---

is one of the key reasons the company's team structure works so seamlessly and successfully.

Key Decisions Made by Teams

At traditional large supermarket chains, key decisions are made primarily by national buyers who have the power to dictate what all stores will carry. Competition for shelf space among suppliers results in "slotting fees" paid by national brands to get their products on store shelves.

Decentralization is at work at Whole Foods as team leaders and their managers collaborate on stocking decisions of products that they feel will appeal to local customer tastes by store location. Teams are also given the responsibility for operating decisions like pricing, ordering, and in-store promotion.

Living by the Same Rules

Long before the financial meltdown and recession hit, Whole Foods' governance implemented a salary cap for top executives, which is 19 times the average worker pay every year. "It helps us keep faith with one another," says Robb, who emphasizes the importance of "all living by the same rules." He disparages the insanity of traditional CEO salaries, which can run to 400 times that of average worker pay. For several years co-founder John Mackey's pay has been $1 a year.

Although most companies constantly seek ways to improve performance, Whole Foods Market seems to have found the key in teams and teamwork, and happy employees.

CASE ANALYSIS QUESTIONS

1. DISCUSSION What seems to be the prevailing performance norm at Whole Foods Market? How is it conveyed to team members? What, if anything, seems to make it stick? What other norms might support and encourage high-performance work by members of Whole Foods teams?

2. DISCUSSION The Federal Reserve is a complex and important institution in the U.S. government. Is it an appropriate place for leaders to seek consensus-style decisions given all the complications of economic recession and turmoil around the world? Or, should other decision-making methods come into play?

3. PROBLEM SOLVING What risk is there that teams at Whole Foods might find themselves in groupthink? Are the conditions ripe for it, or do the culture and practices of the firm make this an unlikely outcome? If you were on one of the teams, how might you suggest dealing with a recommendation by a member to start stocking a so-called hot new product—carbonated carrot juice?

4. FURTHER RESEARCH Check out some of Whole Foods competitors. How do they operate...how are they structured...how do they use teams...what's the culture? Does Whole Foods have much to fear? Is there anything Whole Foods executives could learn from others to further improve their existing practices? How is Whole Foods' commitment to teams and decentralization holding up in face of competition?

Case 15: Twitter—Rewriting Communication

NICHOLAS KAMM/AFP/GettyImages

Whether or not you tweet, there's no denying that Twitter's having a profound effect on the way we communicate with each other. The online social networking service is now well known for its 140-character text-based messages, or "Twitter-speak." But as it permeates everyday life, the questions become: Is Twitter reinventing communication or just abbreviating it? Do tweets create meaningful conversation or dumbing down in the form of quick blasts?

Tweets, RTs (retweets, or a reposting of someone else's tweet), and DMs (direct messages) were conceived on a playground slide during a burrito-fueled brainstorming session by employees of podcasting company Odeo. Co-founder Jack Dorsey, now Twitter's executive chairman, suggested the idea of using short, SMS-like messages to connect with a small group. "[W]e came across the word *twitter*, and it was just perfect," Dorsey says. "The definition was 'a short burst of inconsequential information' and 'chirps from birds.' And that's exactly what the product was."

Dorsey, also CEO and founder of Square, a mobile payments company, developed a working prototype. It was initially used internally by Odeo employees. He then refined the concept before releasing the first public version. Within three months and sensing the magnitude of the invention, Dorsey and other members of Odeo, including current product strategist Evan Williams and creative director Biz Stone, acquired Odeo and gained Twitter.com in the process.

A Communication Channel with Capacity

Channel richness is the capacity of a communication channel to effectively carry information. And for organizations, celebrities, athletes, sports teams, and thought leaders intent on creating and enforcing brand image or a message, Twitter has provided a channel par excellence. It has become a vehicle for communicating carefully crafted messages of self-promotion and branding by the likes of Whole Foods, Nike, Coca-Cola, American Express, McDonald's, Starbucks, General Motors, and JetBlue Airways.

Frequent or heavy Twitter users include politicians (*@BarackObama*), social causes and nonprofits (*@amnesty*), actors, athletes, and musicians (*@beyonce*). Top Twitter topics or "trends" driving tweets include sports, politics, and music as well as natural disasters, human conflicts, and crises.

According to a recent Internet study by Pew Research, Twitter usage is pervasive among technology early adopters. The male–female ratio is almost equal, with women making up 53% of its users. Approximately 26% of all Internet users aged 18 to 29 use Twitter, nearly double the usage rate of 14% for the age group of 30- to 49-year-olds. Those in the 50- to 64-year-old age range comprise 9% of Twitter users, and 4% are 65+. The increase among younger adults can be attributed to the increased smart phone usage.

Messages with Meanings

Twitter's 140-character limit keeps messages terse and to the point. However, there's no guarantee they'll be pertinent, or that each message will have meaning attached.

Market research firm Pear Analytics captured 2,000 U.S. and British tweets sent during daytime hours over two weeks. Its two largest categories, pointless babble (small talk) and conversation comprised 78% of all tweets. "For many people, the idea of describing your blow-by-blow activities in such detail is absurd," concurs writer Clive Thompson. "Why would you subject your friends to your daily minutiae?"

Avid Twitter users argue that although not all tweets are gems, the service has its place in digital culture. Social network researcher Danah Boyd criticized Pear Analytics' results, pointing out that pointless babble could be better characterized as *social grooming*, where tweeters "want to know what the people around them are thinking and doing and feeling."

Tweets Travel Faster

Twitter's low overhead translates into instantaneous broadcast communication, and for some users, that's part of the appeal. "Twitter lets me hear from a lot of people in a very short period of time," says tech evangelist Robert Scoble. In addition, Twitter has become a de facto emergency communication "broadcast network" for vital, real-time, breaking news. Its Web site reads: "Twitter is without a doubt the best way to share and discover what is happening right now."

During recent conflicts in Iran, Tunisia, Egypt, and Syria, residents tweeted instantaneous reports of fast-moving situations. "A Twitter Revolution" refers to various revolutions and protests coordinated using Twitter. Examples include the Egyptian revolution, Tunisian protests, Iranian election protests, and Moldova civil unrest.

Changing Communication

Twitter may be paving the way to the next era of communication. But many social

Yammer Makes Microblogging Corporate

Courtesy of Yammer Inc.

"Companies that use Yammer have employees that feel more connected to their co-workers."

Microblogging tool Yammer, oftentimes called "Twitter for companies," was originally developed for internal use by David Sacks in a Silicon Valley start-up. It, too, was spun into its own company.

Whereas Twitter lets users blast bite-sized comments openly across the Internet, Yammer is enterprise social software. It is used for private internal communications or between organizational members and predesignated stockholders. Users can only see posts by co-workers within their own company or designated outsiders.

Yammer's Web site reads: "Yammer is as easy to use as great consumer software like Facebook and Twitter, but is designed for company collaboration, file sharing, knowledge exchange and team efficiency."

"Companies that use Yammer have employees that feel more engaged," says co-founder David Sacks. "They feel more connected to their co-workers; they feel more connected to the company's mission."

Microsoft bought Yammer for $1.2 billion. The two companies have integrated well with Yammer taking advantage of the large Microsoft salesforce. Over 85% of *Fortune* 500 companies already use Yammer. More are likely to come as the value of internal Tweets gains ground.

---

media researchers, sociologists, and corporate marketing experts are asking: Does Twitter enable effective communication, or is it a distraction?

Twitter's quick and short messages are creating more transparent communication. They're shortening the stages of communication—quick thoughts warrant a tweet. They're increasing the frequency of communication—more time efficient than a direct message or an e-mail.

Twitter is also used within organizations. Some managers are setting up Twitter accounts and encouraging employees to subscribe to it. It's a way to make announcements about upcoming events, rapid response items, and to share links. It is also being used in educational settings as a way to promote student interactions with both faculty and one another.

As you have probably read, a few well-known tweeters have been known to apologize and explain a tweet or two after it was misinterpreted. One downside of the immediacy of tweeting might be impulsive communication. With this in mind, organizations and individuals must be watchful that haphazard tweets don't cross any lines.

A Corporate Twitter Communications Strategy

Many corporations are using Twitter as a public relations tool, as kind of an instantaneous press release technology. In one survey, 81% of businesses queried responded that social media marketing generated exposure for their business. Although only 35% surveyed indicated that social media helped them close business deals, it's clear that tools like Twitter, when used properly, increase customer engagement. Dell's Twitter promotions (@DellOutlet) lets users know about incredible, yet brief, deals. JetBlue (@JetBlue) provides travel tips and answers customer questions. Some companies like Comcast (@ComcastCares) are using Twitter as an extension of its customer service. One Twitter user was able to lower his cable bill.

"Trust is the currency of social media," says consultant Joel Postman. "Without it, social media is worthless as a tool with which to engage customers." For a company less than a decade old, "there are as many ways to express yourself in 140 characters as there are people doing it," states the Twitter Web site.

CASE ANALYSIS QUESTIONS

1. **DISCUSSION** What are the advantages and disadvantages of trying to communicate via Twitter? How can a 140-character tweet really be effective? What guidelines would you recommend for maximizing the effectiveness of a tweet?

2. **DISCUSSION** Choose a national brand or entertainment personality, and discuss the ways Twitter might be used to create a following and desired brand image. How about a college course? In what ways could an instructor use Twitter to improve the classroom or online learning experience? Is Twitter more appropriate for the national brand and entertainment personality than for the college instructor? Why or why not?

3. **PROBLEM SOLVING** You've been given a first assignment as the new summer intern in the office of a corporate CEO. The task is to analyze Yammer and make a presentation to the CEO and her executive team recommending whether or not to adopt it's social media technology for corporate purposes. What points will you make in the presentation to summarize its potential uses, possible downsides, and overall strategic value to the firm?

4. **FURTHER RESEARCH** Focus on current developments with Twitter and Yammer. What is presently happening with each firm and its product? Are they still innovating, and if so, what new directions are evident for each firm? Is Twitter on a continued path of success, or is its 140-character appeal starting to fade? Is Yammer doing well as part of the Microsoft ownership umbrella? Or, has it suffered and lost momentum since being acquired by the big firm? Who are the major competitors faced by Twitter and Yammer at the moment? Are they real threats, or not?

Case 16: Cultural Charades in Business Process Outsourcing

© Terry Vine/Blend Images/Corbis

When you call a toll-free number for customer service assistance, possibly pertaining to finance or banking, an airline reservation, an insurance claim, or technical support for one of your gadgets, there is a good possibility that the person on the other end of the line is a half-world away. You end up speaking with a customer service agent in India, the Philippines, Ghana or some other location.

Your experience is part of an outsourcing arrangement made by multinational companies (think: Dell, American Express, and Verizon) with overseas service operators. The multinationals realize significant capital and cost savings due to lower wages.

This industry has a name—business process outsourcing, or BPO for short. And critics worry not only about customer satisfaction. They also worry about its impact on the personalities, lifestyle, careers, and culture of workers across the world—who assist in increasing your credit card limit or booking your airline reservation.

"How May I Help You?" India Style

India has a dominant stake in BPO services related to customer management, human resource outsourcing, finance and accounting, banking, financial services, billing, and supply chain management. The serviced industries include retail, insurance, mortgage, banking and finance, healthcare, telecommunications, technology, travel, and hospitality. High in transaction volume is found especially in payroll, recruiting, accounts payable, and customer data analytics and knowledge process outsourcing (KPO) activities.

The growing BPO industry has had, what some believe to be, both positive and negative effects on the culture and lifestyle of Indian workers. Americans are quick to share stories of call center experiences and in particular issues understanding the Indian English accent. However, what you might not have considered during your call is its cultural impact. Although India's BPO industry—highlighted by firms like Infosys and Tata—has given tremendous employment opportunities and a reduction in gender disparity, the result for some is a sociocultural shift.

Shehzad Nadeem, author of *Dead Ringers: How Outsourcing is Changing the Way Indians Understand Themselves* discusses concerns about "the damaging psychological effects on call-center employees who are expected to ape the Western employees they have replaced in terms of accents, slang, and even names." A popular Indian business magazine says: "Sanjay grew an alter ego as Sam, Nikhil turned into Nick, and Sulekha pretended to be Sally. Hours in training turned a Tamil accent into the Boston twang and the Punjabi gruffness into the Texan drawl."

De-Indianization by Culture Trainers

Call center training centers operate all over India, and for a fee, they teach Indians who wish to gain employment in a call center how to assimilate when speaking to U.S. callers. The training includes listening to pop music, audio and watching videos, CNN and Fox newscasts, and old TV shows like *Friends* and *Frazier*. Students try to learn U.S. accents and acquire a sense of what it's like to live a U.S. lifestyle. Those who aren't able to conform to a Western culture don't make the cut, which many see as a "financial necessity."

Vandana Raj Nath, who works as a call center worker, said: "I have to Americanize my accent so that my client is comfortable speaking with me and does not guess that I'm Indian. Some of them don't like dealing with Indians." In his opinion, the allure of making a wage significantly higher than average has caused the demise of Indian culture. Some of his co-workers, he states, "were way too disillusioned and 'too Westernized' to be happy in India." His conclusion: financial independence for call center employees comes with the risk of an identity crisis.

In a *Mother Jones* magazine article entitled "My Summer at an Indian Call Center," New York native Andrew Marantz recounts his experience as an undercover call center employee and trainee in Gurgaon, a suburb of Delhi in India. Marantz describes what he calls a process of "De-Indianization" by culture trainers, who encourage mostly Indian workers to adapt and "live" the Western culture. This includes eating fast food, taking on a Western name, listening to U.S. pop music, learning to use U.S. idioms, and of course, dealing with irate customers and the job hazard of racial abuse.

Chameleons at Work

Those who disagree with Marantz's claims about culture loss by BPO acknowledge that, to a certain degree, "we are all chameleons at work" and that what Marantz calls "De-Indianization" is overhyped. Has the impact of working in a call center created a sociocultural shift? While some may think so, others might disagree, claiming that those who work in this environment are already fairly Westernized and that the job doesn't necessarily create the perceived loss of a native culture.

The BPO industry's impact on its Indian call center workers may not be the only culprit of what many see as its risk of culture loss. Many young people in countries worldwide, and in particular, students studying abroad, find themselves influenced by cultures other than their own. Does the influence of Western culture for Indian call center workers necessarily mean that the

Beyond Race and Gender

Toby Talbot/AP

Employers are including sexual preference, disabilities, veteran status, working parent status, elderly parent care responsibilities, and even weight as diversity characteristics.

A National Public Radio (NPR) article entitled "Defining Diversity: Beyond Race and Gen-der" says today's workplace views diversity broadly and is moving beyond traditional race and gender lines. Employers are now including sexual preference, disabilities, veteran status, working parent status, elderly parent care responsibilities, and even weight, as diversity characteristics. As organizations both large and small up their commitments to a diverse and inclusive workplace, the diversity definition is evolving in accordance with the changing nature of its workplace inhabitants.

Traditional views of diversity tended to focus on those protected under landmark legislation—The Civil Rights Act of 1964—which outlawed major forms of discrimination against racial, ethnic, national and religious minorities, and women. Today, that diversity has been enlarged in scope by "moving beyond simple demographics."

Motorola defines diversity as including gay, lesbian, bisexual, or transgender status. Its Web site states: "We promote a workplace where differences are celebrated." The global pharmaceuticals and health care products company Abbott includes part-time and flexible work schedules as part of the way it defines diversity and inclusion. "Height, weight, the sport you play, socio-economic status—all of these are things we sort people by," says Laura Liswood, the secretary general of the Council of Women World Leaders and a senior adviser to Gold-man Sachs.

A culture and climate of inclusivity and diversity provides organizations a potential source of competitive advantage rich in beliefs, values, and expectations. What is your position and personal stake as the definition of "diversity" continues to expand? What challenges lie ahead for employers and employees alike?

---

pride and heritage of one's Indian culture is forgotten?

The next time you seek call center support of some kind, what will you think when "Nick" or "Sally" takes your call? Will you worry about their loss of cultural identity, or be pleased about their financial opportunities?

CASE ANALYSIS QUESTIONS

1. DISCUSSION What are the main arguments why the BPO industry contributes to a loss of cultural identity for workers who are asked to "act as Westerners" while serving customers of large multinational firms? How do you evaluate these arguments? If cultural identity loss is occurring, do financial benefits to the workers make its loss worthwhile? Should loss of cultural identity by BPO workers be a real social concern, or is it just a natural outcome of changes accompanying the global economy?

2. DISCUSSION How is diversity defined by your school, employer, or community group? What are major differences among these definitions? What are the implications of these differences for the organizations and their members? In what specific ways are these organizations moving (or not) beyond demographics in their approach to diversity? Do you think these shifts are good for the organization and its members? Why or why not?

3. PROBLEM SOLVING If you were leading a new diversity task force at your place of employment, what goal(s) would you present at the first meeting? What issues would you put on the agenda, and why? What disagreements or concerns among members might you expect to emerge at the first two or three meetings? What notes would you prepare ahead of time so that you could keep the discussion constructive when these arise?

4. FURTHER RESEARCH What is the current status of the business process outsourcing industry in India? Is it still a growth industry, or is it slowing down? What are the pros and cons being discussed on the Indian side . . . on the multinational contractor side? What other countries are big players in BPO? Is BPO in general a good thing for developing countries? How are multinationals responding to customer complaints about BPO? Are they paying any attention to criticisms that the BPO industry causes a loss of cultural identity for its employees? If so, what are they doing about it?

Case 17: Harley-Davidson—Style and Strategy with a Global Reach

Chuck Burton/AP

Harley-Davidson's American success story began in 1903 when two friends—William Harley and Arthur Davidson—built a motorized bicycle in a machine shop in Milwaukee, Wisconsin. That machine now travels the world. The Harley-Davidson brand was born in 1904 and then raced to success until the forces of global competition dealt it a near-death experience in the 1980s. Since then the company has overhauled its manufacturing facilities and production systems and positioned itself for global growth. Its 100+ year tradition of designing, manufacturing, and selling heavyweight motorcycles now encompasses North and South America, Europe, and Asia. Harley's success can be attributed to loyal customers and a brand built on history, personal relationships, satisfied customers, and a great ride.

Combating Foreign Competition

When Harley-Davidson began, it was one of more than 100 firms producing motorcycles in the United States. The U.S. government became an important customer for the company's high-powered, reliable bikes, using them in both world wars. By the 1950s, Harley-Davidson was the only remaining American manufacturer. But British competitors were entering the market with faster, lighter-weight bikes. And Honda Motor Company of Japan began marketing its light and middleweight bikes

in the United States. Harley initially tried to compete by manufacturing smaller bikes, but had difficulty making them profitably.

In 1983, Harley-Davidson asked the International Trade Commission (ITC) for tariff relief on the basis that Japanese manufacturers were stockpiling inventory in the United States and providing unfair competition. The request was granted, and a tariff relief for five years was placed on all imported Japanese motorcycles that were 700 cc or larger. By 1987 Harley was confident enough to petition the ITC to have the tariff lifted because the company had improved its ability to compete with foreign imports. Once Harley's image had been restored, the company began to increase production.

Harley-Davidson's U.S. Profile

Harley executives don't like the description of customers as "aging" baby boomers. A company statement says, "Our customers want the sense of adventure that they get on our bikes. . . . Harley-Davidson doesn't sell transportation, we sell transformation. We sell excitement, a way of life." The average age and income of Harley riders has continued to increase.

The Harley Owners Group (HOG) was formed so owners could share identities with other "fraternity-like" Harley enthusiasts. The name, originating in the 1920s among a group of Harley-riding farm boys whose mascot was a hog, has become a worldwide acronym.

The company has also created a line of jackets, caps, T-shirts, and other Harley-Davidson logoed accessories available through dealers or by catalog. The clothing and accessories are popular with nonbikers too and have a higher profit margin than motorcycles. Nonbike products make up as much as half of sales at some dealerships.

International Markets

Although the company had been exporting motorcycles ever since it was founded, it was not until the late 1980s that Harley-Davidson management began to seriously consider international markets. They did so by actively recruiting and developing dealers in Europe and Japan. The company purchased a Japanese distribution company and built a large parts warehouse in Germany. Recognizing, for example, that German motorcyclists rode at high speeds—often more than 100 mph—the company began studying ways to give Harleys a smoother ride and emphasizing accessories that would give riders more protection.

Although the recent global economic slowdown hurt Harley somewhat, the global thrust is paying off. Harley ranks #1 or #2 in the heavyweight motorcycle market across nine European countries. Some 40% of Harley's revenue comes from outside the United States.

Harley-Davidson in Asia

Harley motorcycles are among America's fastest-growing exports to Japan. Harley's Japanese subsidiary adapted the company's marketing approach to Japanese tastes, even producing shinier and more complete tool kits than those available in the United States. Harley bikes have long been considered symbols of prestige in Japan, and many Japanese enthusiasts see themselves as rebels on wheels.

The company continues to make inroads into the previously elusive Chinese market, which is anticipated to play an increasingly larger role in the future. The first official Chinese Harley-Davidson dealership opened its doors just outside downtown Beijing. To break into this emerging market, Harley partnered with China's Zongshen Motorcycle Group, which makes more than one million small-engine motorcycles each year.

Despite China's growing disposable income. Harley's top challenge in China remains improving its understanding of the market. Heavyweight leisure motorcycles are

NOT Made in China

Pigtronix

"Factor in shipping and all the other B.S. that you have to endure. It's a question of, 'How do I value my time at three in the morning when I have to talk to China?'"

For years companies eagerly flooded production to foreign outsourcing locations, especially China. Manufacturing a product overseas could be done at up to one-third the cost to produce the same product at home. The rise in global sourcing resulted in job shifts to foreign locations to take advantage of lower wages, less-stringent labor laws, and infrastructure. In recent years, however, things have changed. The gap in savings with overseas production has narrowed, and with that, there has been as increase in the amount of work returned to the United States through reshoring.

Brian Bethke, co-founder of Pigtronix, maker of pedals that create electric guitar sound effects, came to the realization that he couldn't "adequately monitor quality" at distant Chinese factories. After discovering technical glitches in as many as 30% of the overseas products, Bethke decided to move the production back home to a small nearby factory. A battery of tests, even those with a guitarist playing each of the pedals, can easily be performed on its products prior to shipping.

Lightsaver Technologies, like most other companies, assumed that China was a likely fit for outsourcing production of its emergency lights for homeowners. It worked for a few years. But now founders Sonja Zozula and Jerry Anderson claim: "Factor in shipping and all the other B.S. that you have to endure. It's a question of, 'How do I value my time at three in the morning when I have to talk to China?'" Lightsaver Technologies now produces in Carlsbad, California, about a half-hour drive from their offices.

Labor costs in China factories and other Asian locations are rising. Facing management issues and distance—12,000 miles and 12 times zones away—some companies are starting to abandon the "China price" and move back home. The attractions are greater quality control, better communication, and less management hassle.

Outsourcing production overseas can still make sense, especially for companies distributing products to foreign markets. But for those selling products at home—like Pigtronix and Lightsaver Technologies— keeping production local could be a better choice. "Made in America" offers not only a source of pride, it also helps control the risk of knockoffs, rising energy costs, and supply chain complexities.

still a rarity in China. Bans and riding restrictions in urban areas exist. But the China market is fast developing as road conditions, traffic management, and more mature rider profiles have evolved.

In 2011, the company completed its second complete knockdown assembly plant in India to further strengthen its position in the Asian-Pacific market. Harley seeks to grow its brand internationally and sees South Asian markets as crucial to achieving this goal. Despite the obvious cost of shipping parts halfway around the globe, it's still a win for Harley. Indian consumers pay nearly twice the normal international cost for fully assembled vehicles because India's import duties are so high.

From Recession to the Future

Amid a severe slump in sales during the brutal recession, Harley-Davidson significantly trimmed its costs by some $275 million. It eliminated inefficient practices and consolidated production previously scattered across 41 locations. It's paying off in better profits. But Harley's customer base is aging and it can still be difficult for loyal riders to get financing. Will the company's strong brand image and growth in oversea markets keep the scales topped in Harley's favor?

CASE ANALYSIS QUESTIONS

1. DISCUSSION What are the advantages and disadvantages to Harley of using exports, joint ventures, and wholly owned subsidiaries as ways of expanding its reach into new countries? Is one approach most often preferable to others? Or, can each be a good choice under certain circumstances? Explain.

2. DISCUSSION What is the major case in favor of global sourcing? What is the major case against it? Are rising labor costs, problems with intellectual property theft, and human tragedies in unsafe factories giving outsourcing a bad name that it doesn't deserve? Is the strategy flawed to the point where it should be used only sparingly? Or, is it more a case of making a good choice of outsourcing country locations and business partners?

3. PROBLEM SOLVING The countries of sub-Saharan Africa are among the world's emerging economies that are attracting international investors and global firms. If you were advising Harley's CEO on business expansion in this region, what would you recommend in terms of setting up sales centers and manufacturing sites in countries like South Africa, Kenya, and Zimbabwe? When a new location is set up, what would you suggest as the proper role for locals to play? Should they run everything, or should there be a mix of locals and expatriates? And if the CEO wants to send expatriates to some locations, what selection criteria would you recommend, and why?

4. FURTHER RESEARCH How is Harley doing today? Where is it operating in the world, and is it doing well in these global locations? What are the problems and opportunities of the moment in Harley's international operations? Who are its top competitors in other parts of the world, and how is Harley faring against them? Is there any risk that Harley will lose focus on its American customer base in the rush to expand even further as a global company?

Cases for Critical Thinking

Case 18: The New Mother of Angel Investors

Helder Almeida/Shutterstock

Financing is for sure the mother of all constraints on small businesses and new venture start-ups. But for those quick with the Web, social media may turn out to be the mother of all angel investors. Within the burgeoning domain of social media, some entrepreneurs are realizing their long-held dreams using a Web-based tool most had never imagined. It's called crowdfunding, and it's a force to be reckoned with.

Crowdfunding is an online fund-raising platform that utilizes the Internet as an intermediary to help entrepreneurs, artists, writers, filmmakers, and multitudes of others realize their dreams through less-traditional ways of raising seed money. By combining social media, electronic payment, and marketing campaigns, crowdfunding is becoming mainstream. As recently as a decade ago, the option did not exist. Today, many crowdfunding sites serve almost any type of project imaginable.

Green Light for Entrepreneurs

Traditional financing methods include debt financing, equity financing, an initial public offering, and venture capital or angel investors. With financing remaining the greatest challenge for both commercial and social entrepreneurs, crowdfunding is a growing and popular alternative.

Kiva.org was the first microlending site to appear on the Internet landscape. It allows individual lenders to browse through the profile of a borrower in a developing country and lend money through the Internet. Propser.com established the first peer-to-peer lending Web site. It offered a "micropatronage" system whereby the public could directly support the work of others by making online donations. These early movers led to the idea and rising popularity of today's crowdfunding sites.

Financing Models

"All or Nothing (AoN)" and Keep it All (KiA) are the two basic crowdfunding financing models. The all or nothing model allows pledged money to be kept after the collection period has ended only if the initial fundraising goal is met. If it is not met, then no money is collected. Keep it all, on the other hand, allows all collected funds to be kept, regardless of whether the fundraising goal is met or not.

"The People's National Endowment for the Arts"

The popular crowdfunding platform Kickstarter has raised pledges of close to $630 million for its projects, which range from software development to iPhone accesso-ries to graphic novels to indie films appearing at Sundance Film Festival. Its Web site reads: "Kickstarter is full of ambitious, innovative, and imaginative projects that are brought to life through the direct support of others."

In exchange for funding each project, investors receive no equity shares. They do get updates and the satisfaction of seeing their project get off the ground. Small tokens of appreciation, rewards, or perks include everything from Twitter Shout-outs, autographs, limited editions, and tickets to a film's premiere, to a T-shirt, a phone call, and in some cases, on completion, a discounted or free product. Kickstarter staff must approve the projects listed, and they must fit into one of its 13 art-related categories in the world of Art, Comics, Dance, Design, Fashion, Film, Food, Games, Music, Photography, Publishing, Technology, and Theater.

Backers, mostly friends and fans, fund each campaign on an altruistic basis—with the desire to help a cause, and/or as a value exchange—in return for something like an early release copy of the completed project. As Kickstarter's Web site says: "Backing a project is more than just giving someone money, it's supporting their dream to create something that they want to see exist in the world."

Pebble, an iPhone compatible "smart" watch is, to date, one of Kickstarter's greatest success stories. Starting with a goal of $100,000, the start-up raised over $10 million. Pebble connects to a smart phone using a Bluetooth device, which turns the $150 watch (backers purchase at a discount of $99) into a display for reading text messages, e-mails and any data imaginable.

Crowdfunding Pros and Cons

Those who support the growing crowdfunding phenomenon argue that ideas that don't fit traditional financing can successfully attract funding through the crowd. The initial crowdfunding financing then allows a project to gain traction for future backing from traditional sources.

A disadvantage of crowdfunding is the public disclosure required. Although this isn't a problem for charitable organizations and artists, firms in their early stages

Accidental Entrepreneurs

gorillaimages/Shutterstock

Want your canine companion's medicine in a chicken or bacon flavored capsule, or better yet, gel form?

Entrepreneurs often share similar backgrounds and experiences in terms of family environment. For Kenny Kramm, this indeed proved to be the case. A pharmacy technician, he launched FLAVORx out of love for his youngest daughter Hadley who was born with a seizure disorder and cerebral palsy. The medicine crucial to her existence had an intolerable taste that made it impossible for her to swallow. Without it Hadley would keep having seizures.

Kramm and his father owned a pharmacy and were aware of that flavoring medicine had been done for hundreds of years, but never in any sort of systematic way. As accidental entrepreneurs, the Kramms began mixing various concoctions with the goal of making the medicine palatable enough for her to swallow. After several weeks, they had an "aha moment" finding that Hadley preferred the banana flavor. Although she still didn't love taking her medication, she did so without resistance.

This was the start of FLAVORx, a company that now offers 18 sugar-free, nonallergenic, and inert pediatric flavors to over 35,000 pharmacies.

Kramm launched FLAVORx with $15,000 in savings and $200,000 from his father. Its formulary and refillable sets of flavorings allow pharmacists to safely turn any bitter or foul-tasting tablet, liquid, or capsule, into a readily accepted, flavored liquid.

Want your canine companion's medicine in a chicken or bacon flavored capsule or better yet, gel form? You can have it. In addition to a pediatric flavor offering, FLAVORx has expanded into flavoring systems for veterinarians with 17 flavors for animals, which can be added to prescription and over-the-counter medications. Kramm started Center Pet Pharmacy to partner with veterinarians' in-house pharmacies and retailers to offer medication exclusively for pets.

of product development can be compromised with well-financed competitors and copycats. Another possible downside is the time associated with managing communication to a broad base of investors and supporters.

President Obama has signed into law the Jumpstart our Business Startups (JOBS) Act, which permits backers who pledge money to projects on crowdfunding sites to earn an equity stake in the project. If the project becomes a success, the backer cashes in—similar to a venture capital firm.

The upside is that many more small businesses, challenged when it comes to financing, will be able to raise capital. But, critics of the act worry that this could be the start of fraudlent crowdsourcing sites and those interested solely in profiteering.

CASE ANALYSIS QUESTIONS

1. DISCUSSION   What are the pros and cons of crowdfunding? Look at it first from the perspective of the entrepreneur who needs the money. Look at it also from the side of the potential investor. What are the risks that each might face? Is crowdfunding a good option for them, or is it mainly a way for the owners of the crowdfunding sites to make money for themselves?

2. DISCUSSION   Kenny Kramm started FlavorX after solving a major personal problem out of necessity. He then made his solution available to others facing the same problem. Is necessity a good, perhaps the best, motivation for entrepreneurship? How can it increase the likelihood of success?

3. PROBLEM SOLVING   (a) As a potential investor, you want to take advantage of crowdfunding to put some excess cash to work. Investigate at least three possible crowdfunding sites that you might use. Which would you choose and why? (b) As an entre-preneur who needs money for a new start-up, you want to take advantage of crowdfunding. Investigate at least three possible crowdfunding sites that you might use. Which would you choose, and why?

4. FURTHER RESEARCH   Perform additional research to learn more about the status and implications of the Jumpstart our Business Startups (JOBS) Act. Who are its backers? Who are its opponents? What are the main arguments from each side? Review the major features of the act. Can you identify missing elements or loopholes that make it possible for investors and/or entrepreneurs to be taken advantage of by fraudsters and scammers? After considering the act and the crowdfunding industry as a whole, what advice would you offer to small investors attracted to crowdfunding as a way of becoming venture capitalists?

Test Prep 1

Multiple Choice

1. d.   **2.** c.   **3.** b.   **4.** b.   **5.** b.   **6.** d.   **7.** a.   **8.** d.
9. c.   **10.** a.   **11.** c.   **12.** a.   **13.** c.   **14.** c.   **15.** a.

Short Response

16. Prejudice involves holding a negative stereotype or irrational attitude toward a person who is different from one's self. Discrimination occurs when such prejudice leads to decisions that adversely affect the other person in his or her job, in advancement opportunities at work, or in his or her personal life.

17. The "free agent economy" is one in which there is a lot of job-hopping, and people work for several different employers over a career, rather than just one. This relates not only to the preferences of the individuals but also to the nature of organizational employment practices. As more organizations reduce the hiring of full-time workers in favor of more part-timers and independent contractors, this creates fewer long-term job opportunities for potential employees. Thus they become "free agents" who sell their services to different employers on a part-time and contract basis.

18. You will typically find that top managers are more oriented toward the external environment than the first-level or lower-level managers. This means that top managers must be alert to trends, problems, and opportunities that can affect the performance of the organization as a whole. The first-line or lower manager is most concerned with the performance of his or her immediate work unit and managing the people and resources of the unit on an operational day-to-day basis. Top management is likely to be more strategic and long term in orientation.

19. Planning sets the objectives or targets that one hopes to accomplish. Controlling measures actual results against the planning objectives or targets and makes any corrections necessary to better accomplish them. Thus, planning and controlling work together in the management process, with planning setting the stage for controlling.

Integration and Application

20. I consider myself "effective" as a manager if I can help my work unit achieve high performance and the persons in it to achieve job satisfaction. In terms of skills and personal development, the framework of essential management skills offered by Katz is a useful starting point. At the first level of management, technical skills are important, and I would feel capable in this respect. However, I would expect to learn and refine these skills even more through my work experiences. Human skills, the ability to work well with other people, will also be very important. Given the diversity anticipated for this team, I will need good human skills, and I will have to keep improving my capabilities in this area. One area of consideration here is emotional intelligence, or my ability to understand how the emotions of myself and others influence work relationships. I will also have a leadership responsibility to help others on the team develop and utilize these skills so that the team itself can function effectively. Finally, I would expect opportunities to develop my conceptual or analytical skills in anticipation of higher-level appointments. In terms of personal development I should recognize that the conceptual skills will increase in importance relative to the technical skills as I move upward in management responsibility, while the human skills are consistently important.

Test Prep 2

Multiple Choice

1. a.   **2.** b.   **3.** c.   **4.** a.   **5.** c.   **6.** b.   **7.** d.   **8.** b.
9. a.   **10.** a.   **11.** c.   **12.** a.   **13.** c   **14.** b.   **15.** b.

Short Response

16. You can see scientific management principles operating everywhere, from UPS delivery, to fast-food restaurants, to order-fulfillment centers. In each case, the workers are trained to perform highly specified job tasks that are carefully engineered to be the most efficient. Their supervisors try to keep the process and workers well supported. In some cases the workers may be paid on the basis of how much work they accomplish in a time period, such as a day or week. The basic principles are to study the job, identify the most efficient job tasks and train the workers, and then support and reward the workers for doing the tasks well.

17. According to the deficit principle, a satisfied need is not a motivator of behavior. The social need, for example, will motivate only if it is deprived or in deficit. According to the progression principle, people move step-by-step up Maslow's hierarchy as they strive to satisfy their needs. For example, the esteem need becomes activated only after the social need is satisfied. Maslow also suggested, however, that the progression principle stops operating at the level of self-actualization; the more this need is satisfied, the stronger it gets.

18. The Hawthorne effect occurs when people singled out for special attention tend to perform as expected. An example would be giving a student a lot of personal attention in class with the result that he or she ends up studying harder and performing better. This is really the same thing as McGregor's notion of the self-fulfilling prophesy with the exception that McGregor identified how it works to both the positive and the negative. When managers, for example, have positive assumptions about people, they tend to treat them well, and the people respond in ways that reinforce the original positive thinking. This is a form of the Hawthorne effect. McGregor also pointed out that negative self-fulfilling prophesies result when managers hold negative assumptions about people and behave accordingly.

19. Contingency thinking takes an "if–then" approach to situations. It seeks to modify or adapt management approaches to fit the needs of each situation. An example would be to give more customer contact responsibility to workers who want to satisfy social needs at work, while giving more supervisory responsibilities to those who want to satisfy their esteem or ego needs.

Integration and Application

20. A bureaucracy operates with a strict hierarchy of authority, promotion based on competency and performance, formal rules and procedures, and written documentation. Enrique can do all of these things in his store. However, he must be careful to meet the needs of the workers and not to make the mistake identified by Argyris—failing to treat them as mature adults. While remaining well organized, the store manager has room to help workers meet higher order esteem and self-fulfillment needs, as well as to exercise autonomy under Theory Y assumptions. Enrique must also be alert to the dysfunctions of bureaucracy that appear when changes are needed or when unique problems are posed or when customers want to be treated personally. The demands of these situations are difficult for traditional bureaucracies to handle, due to the fact that they are set up to handle routine work efficiently and impersonally, with an emphasis on rules, procedures, and authority.

Test Prep 3

Multiple Choice

1. a.　**2.** c.　**3.** d.　**4.** a.　**5.** c.　**6.** b.　**7.** c.　**8.** b.
9. a.　**10.** a.　**11.** b.　**12.** b.　**13.** d.　**14.** c.　**15.** d.

Short Response

16. Distributive justice means that everyone is treated the same, that there is no discrimination based on things like age, gender, or sexual orientation. An example would be a man and a woman who both apply for the same job. A manager violates distributive justice if he interviews only the man and not the woman as well, or vice versa. Procedural justice means that rules and procedures are fairly followed. For example, a manager violates distributive justice if he or she punishes one person for coming to work late while ignoring late behavior by another person with whom he or she regularly plays golf.

17. The "spotlight questions" for double-checking the ethics of a decision are "How would I feel if my family finds out?" "How would I feel if this were published in the local newspaper or on the Internet?" "What would the person you know or know of who has the strongest character and best ethical judgment do in this situation?"

18. The rationalizations include believing that (1) the behavior is not really illegal, (2) the behavior is really in everyone's best interests, (3) no one will find out, and (4) the organization will protect you.

19. The "virtuous circle" concept of social responsibility holds that social responsibility practices do not hurt the bottom line and often help it; when socially responsible actions result in improved financial performance, this encourages more of the same actions in the future—a virtuous circle being created.

Integration and Application

20. If the manager adopts a position of cultural relativism, there will be no perceived problem in working with the Tanzanian firm. The justification would be that as long as it is operating legally in Tanzania, that makes everything okay. The absolutist position would hold that the contract should not be taken because the factory conditions are unacceptable at home and therefore are unacceptable anywhere. The cultural relativism position can be criticized because it makes it easy to do business in places where people are not treated well; the absolutist position can be criticized as trying to impose one's values on people in a different cultural context.

Test Prep 4

Multiple Choice

1. b.　**2.** c.　**3.** a.　**4.** c.　**5.** d.　**6.** a.　**7.** b.　**8.** c.
9. c.　**10.** a.　**11.** a.　**12.** b.　**13.** c.　**14.** d.　**15.** b.

Short Response

16. An optimizing decision represents the absolute "best" choice of alternatives. It is selected from a set of all known alternatives. A satisficing decision selects the first alternative that offers a "satisfactory" choice, not necessarily the absolute best choice. It is selected from a limited or incomplete set of alternatives.

17. A risk environment is one in which things are not known for sure—all the possible decision alternatives, all the possible consequences for each alternative—but they can be estimated as probabilities. For example, if I take a new job with a new employer, I can't know for certain that it will turn out as I expect, but I could be 80% sure that I'd like the new responsibilities, or only 60% sure that I might get promoted within a year. In an uncertain environment, things are so speculative that it is hard to even assign such probabilities.

18. A manager using systematic thinking is going to approach problem solving in a logical and rational fashion. The tendency will be to proceed in a linear step-by-step manner, handling one issue at a time. A manager using intuitive thinking will be more spontaneous and open in problem solving. He or she may jump from one stage in the process to the other and deal with many different things at once.

19. Escalating commitment is the tendency of people to keep investing in a previously chosen course of action, continuing to pursue it, even though it is not working. This is a human tendency to try to make things work by trying harder, investing more time, effort, resources, and so on. In other words, I have decided in the past to pursue this major in college; I can't be wrong, can I? The feedback from my grades and course satisfaction suggests it isn't working, but I'm doing it now so I just need to make it work, right? I'll just stick with it and see if things eventually turn out okay. In this example, I am making a decision to continue with the major that is most likely an example of escalating commitment.

Integration and Application

20. This is what I would say. On the question of whether a group decision is best or an individual decision is best, the appropriate answer is probably: It all depends on the situation. Sometimes one is preferable to the other; each has its potential advantages and disadvantages. If you are in a situation where the problem being addressed is unclear, the information needed to solve it is uncertain, and you don't have a lot of personal expertise, the group approach to decision making is probably best. Group decisions offer advantages like bringing more information and ideas to bear on a problem; they often allow for more creativity; and they tend to build commitments among participants to work hard to implement any decisions reached. On the other hand, groups can be dominated by one or more members, and they can take a lot of time making decisions. Thus, when time is short, the individual decision is sometimes a better choice. However, it is important that you, as this individual, are confident that you have the information needed to solve the problem or can get it before making your decision.

Test Prep 5

Multiple Choice

1. d. **2.** a. **3.** b. **4.** b. **5.** d. **6.** c. **7.** a. **8.** d.
9. b. **10.** a. **11.** c. **12.** b. **13.** d. **14.** b. **15.** c.

Short Response

16. The five steps in the formal planning process are (1) define your objectives, (2) determine where you stand relative to objectives, (3) develop premises about future conditions, (4) identify and choose among action alternatives to accomplish objectives, and (5) implement action plans and evaluate results.

17. Planning facilitates controlling because the planning process sets the objectives and standards that become the basis for the control process. If you don't have objectives and standards, you have nothing to compare actual performance with; consequently, control lacks purpose and specificity.

18. Contingency planning essentially makes available optional plans that can be quickly implemented if things go wrong with the original plan. Scenario planning is a longer-term form of contingency planning that tries to project several future scenarios that might develop over time and to associate each scenario with plans for best dealing with it.

19. Participation is good for the planning process, in part because it brings to the process a lot more information, diverse viewpoints, and potential alternatives than would otherwise be available if just one person or a select group of top managers are doing the planning. Furthermore, and very importantly, through participation in the planning process, people develop an understanding of the final plans and the logic used to arrive at them, and they develop personal commitments to trying to follow through and work hard to make implementation of the plans successful.

Integration and Application

20. Benchmarking is the use of external standards to help evaluate one's own situation and develop ideas and directions for improvement. Curt and Rich are both right to a certain extent about its potential value for them. Rich is right in suggesting that there is much to learn by looking at what other bookstores are doing really well. The bookstore owner/manager might visit other bookstores in other towns that are known for their success. By observing and studying the operations of those stores and then comparing his store to them, the owner/manager can develop plans for future action. Curt is also right in suggesting that there is much to be learned potentially from looking outside the bookstore business. They should look at things like inventory management, customer service, and facilities in other settings—not just bookstores; they should also look outside their town as well as within it.

Test Prep 6

Multiple Choice

1. a. **2.** a. **3.** d. **4.** b. **5.** b. **6.** c. **7.** c. **8.** d.
9. a. **10.** b. **11.** c. **12.** a. **13.** a. **14.** b. **15.** c.

Short Response

16. The Army's "after-action review" takes place after an action or activity has been completed. This makes it a form of "feedback" control. The primary purpose is to critique the action/activity and try to learn from it so that similar things in the future can be done better and so that the people involved can be best trained.

17. One way to use clan control in a TQM context would be to set up small teams or task forces called "Quality Circles" that bring together persons from various parts of the workplace with a common commitment to quality improvements. You can ask these teams or QCs to meet regularly to discuss quality results and options and to try to maintain a continuous improvement momentum in their work areas. The members should ideally get special quality training. They should also be expected to actively serve as quality champions in their own work areas to implement continuous quality improvements and come up with ideas for new ones.

18. The just-in-time inventory approach reduces the carrying costs of inventories. It does this by trying to have materials arrive at a workstation just in time to be used. When this concept works perfectly, there are no inventory carrying costs. However, even if it is imperfect and some inventory ends up being stockpiled, it should still be less than that which would otherwise be the case. But as the recent tsunami and nuclear disaster in Japan showed, firms that are too reliant on JIT in their supply chains must prepare for the risk of disruptions when crises and natural disasters occur.

19. The four questions to ask when developing a balanced scorecard are (1) *Financial Performance*—To improve financially, how should we appear to our shareholders? (2) *Customer Satisfaction*—To achieve our vision, how should we appear to our customers? (3) *Internal Process Improvement*—To satisfy our customers and shareholders, at what internal business processes should we excel? (4) *Innovation and Learning*—To achieve our vision, how will we sustain our ability to change and improve?

Integration and Application

20. I would begin the speech by describing MBO as an integrated planning and control approach. I would also clarify that the key elements in MBO are objectives and participation. Any objectives should be clear, measurable, and time defined. In addition, these objectives should be set with the full involvement and participation of the employees; they should not be set by the manager and then told to the employees. Given this, I would describe how each business manager should jointly set objectives with each of his or her employees and jointly review progress toward their accomplishment. I would suggest that the employees should work on the required activities while staying in communication with their managers. The managers, in turn, should provide any needed support or assistance to their employees. This whole process could be formally recycled at least twice per year.

Test Prep Answers

Test Prep 7

Multiple Choice

1. a. **2.** b. **3.** b. **4.** c. **5.** a. **6.** c. **7.** d. **8.** a.
9. a. **10.** b. **11.** c. **12.** b. **13.** d. **14.** c. **15.** b.

Short Response

16. A corporate strategy sets long-term direction for an enterprise as a whole. Functional strategies set directions so that business functions such as marketing and manufacturing support the overall corporate strategy. A corporate strategy sets long-term direction for an enterprise as a whole. Functional strategies set directions so that business functions such as marketing and manufacturing support the overall corporate strategy.

17. If you want to sell at lower prices than competitors and still make a profit, you have to have lower operating costs (profit 5 revenues 2 costs). Also, you have to be able to operate at lower costs in ways that are hard for your competitors to copy. This is the point of a cost leadership strategy—always seeking ways to lower costs and operate with greater efficiency than anyone else.

18. A question mark in the BCG matrix has a low market share in a high-growth industry. This means that there is a lot of upside potential, but for now it is uncertain whether or not you will be able to capitalize on it. Thus, hard thinking is required. If you are confident, the recommended strategy is growth; if you aren't, it would be retrenchment, to allow resources to be deployed into more promising opportunities.

19. Strategic leadership is the ability to enthuse people to participate in continuous change, performance enhancement, and the implementation of organizational strategies. The special qualities of the successful strategic leader include the ability to make trade-offs, create a sense of urgency, communicate the strategy, and engage others in continuous learning about the strategy and its performance responsibilities.

Integration and Application

20. A SWOT analysis is useful during strategic planning. It involves the analysis of organizational strengths and weaknesses, and of environmental opportunities and threats. Such a SWOT analysis in this case would help frame Kim's thinking about the current and future positioning of her store, particularly in respect to possible core competencies and competitive opportunities and threats. Then she can use Porter's competitive strategy model for further strategic refinements. This involves the possible use of three alternative strategies: differentiation, cost leadership, and focus. In this situation, the larger department store seems better positioned to follow the cost leadership strategy. This means that Kim may want to consider the other two alternatives. A differentiation strategy would involve trying to distinguish Kim's products from those of the larger store. This might involve a "made in America" theme or an emphasis on leather or canvas or some other type of clothing material. A focus strategy might specifically target college students and try to respond to their tastes and needs rather than those of the larger community population. This might involve special orders and other types of individualized service for the college student market.

Test Prep 8

Multiple Choice

1. b. **2.** c. **3.** b. **4.** a. **5.** b. **6.** c. **7.** b. **8.** a.
9. c. **10.** b. **11.** c. **12.** b. **13.** c. **14.** b. **15.** c.

Short Response

16. An organization chart depicts the formal structure of the organization. This is the official picture of the way things are supposed to be. However, the likelihood is that an organization chart quickly becomes out of date in today's dynamic environments. So one issue is whether or not the chart one is viewing actually depicts the current official structure. Second, there is a lot more to the way things work in organizations than what is shown in the organization chart. People are involved in a variety of informal networks that create an informal structure. It operates as a shadow lying above or behind the formal structure and also influences operations. Both the formal structure and informal structure must be understood; at best, an organization chart helps with understanding the formal one.

17. There are two major ways that informal structures can be good for organizations. First, they can help get work done efficiently and well. When people know one another in informal relationships, they can and often do use these relationships as part of their jobs. Sometimes an informal contact makes it a lot easier to get something done or learn how to do something than the formal linkages displayed on an organization chart. Second, being part of informal groups is an important source of potential need satisfaction. Being in an informal network or group can satisfy needs in ways that one's job can't sometimes and can add considerably to the potential satisfactions of the work experience.

18. The matrix structure is organized in a traditional functional fashion in the vertical dimension. For example, a business might have marketing, human resources, finance, and manufacturing functions. On the horizontal dimension, however, it is organized divisionally in a product or project fashion, with a manager heading up each special product or project. Members from the functional departments are assigned to permanent cross-functional teams for each product or project. They report vertically to their functional bosses and horizontally to their product/project bosses. This two-boss system is the heart of the matrix organization.

19. An organic design tends to be quicker and more flexible because it is very strong in lateral communication and empowerment. People at all levels are talking to one another and interacting as they gather and process information and solve problems. They don't wait for the vertical structure and "bosses" to do these things for them. This means that as the environment changes, they are more likely to be on top of things quickly. It also means that when problems are complex and difficult to solve, they will work with multiple people in various parts of the organization to best deal with them.

Integration and Application

20. A network structure often involves one organization "contracting out" aspects of its operations to other organizations that

AN-4

specialize in these aspects. The example used in the text was of a company that contracted out its mailroom services. Through the formation of networks of contracts, the organization is reduced to a core of essential employees whose expertise is concentrated in the primary business areas. The contracts are monitored and maintained in the network to allow the overall operations of the organization to continue even though they are not directly accomplished by full-time employees. There are many possibilities for doing something similar in a university. In one model, the core staff would be the faculty. They would be supported by a few administrators who managed contracts with outsourcing firms for things such as facilities maintenance, mail, technology support, lawn maintenance, food services, housing services, and even things like development, registrar, and student affairs. Another model would have the administrators forming a small core staff who contract out for the above and, in addition, for faculty who would be hired "as needed" and on contracts for specific assignments.

Test Prep 9

Multiple Choice

1. a. **2.** c. **3.** d. **4.** b. **5.** b. **6.** c. **7.** a. **8.** c.
9. c. **10.** b. **11.** d. **12.** c. **13.** c. **14.** b. **15.** b.

Short Response

16. The core values that might be found in high-performance organizational cultures include such things as performance excellence, innovation, social responsibility, integrity, worker involvement, customer service, and teamwork.

17. First, process innovations result in better ways of doing things. Second, product innovations result in the creation of new or improved goods and services. Third, business model innovations result in new ways of making money for the firm.

18. Lewin's three phases of planned change are unfreezing, changing, and refreezing. In terms of the change leadership challenges, the major differences in attention would be as follows: unfreezing—preparing a system for change; changing—moving or creating change in a system; and refreezing—stabilizing and reinforcing change once it has occurred.

19. In general, managers can expect that others will be more committed and loyal to changes that are brought about through shared power strategies. Rational persuasion strategies can also create enduring effects if they are accepted. Force-coercion strategies tend to have temporary effects only.

Integration and Application

20. In any change situation, it is important to remember that successful planned change occurs only when all three phases of change—unfreezing, changing, and refreezing—have been taken care of. Thus, I would not rush into the changing phase. Rather, I would work with the people involved to develop a felt need for change based on their ideas and inputs as well as mine. Then I would proceed by supporting the changes and helping to stabilize them into everyday routines. I would also be sensitive to any resistance and respect that resistance as a signal that something

important is being threatened. By listening to resistance, I would be in a position to better modify the change to achieve a better fit with the people and the situation. Finally, I would want to take maximum advantage of the shared power strategy, supported by rational persuasion, and with limited use of force-coercion (if it is used at all). By doing all this, I would like my staff to feel empowered and committed to constructive improvement through planned change. Throughout all this I would strive to perform to the best of my ability and gain trust and credibility with everyone else; in this way I would be a positive role model for change.

Test Prep 10

Multiple Choice

1. a. **2.** b. **3.** c. **4.** b. **5.** b. **6.** d. **7.** a. **8.** b.
9. b. **10.** a. **11.** d. **12.** d. **13.** a. **14.** a. **15.** b.

Short Response

16. Orientation activities introduce a new employee to the organization and the work environment. This is a time when the individual may develop key attitudes and when performance expectations will also be established. Good orientation communicates positive attitudes and expectations and reinforces the desired organizational culture. It formally introduces the individual to important policies and procedures that everyone is expected to follow.

17. Mentoring is when a senior and experienced individual adopts a newcomer or more junior person with the goal of helping him or her develop into a successful worker. The mentor may or may not be the individual's immediate supervisor. The mentor meets with the individual and discusses problems, shares advice, and generally supports the individual's attempts to grow and perform. Mentors are considered very useful for persons newly appointed to management positions.

18. Any performance assessment approach should be both valid and reliable. To be valid it must measure accurately what it claims to measure—whether that is some aspect of job performance or personal behavior. To be reliable it must deliver the same results consistently—whether applied by different raters to the same person or when measuring the same person over time. Valid and reliable assessments are free from bias and as objective as possible.

19. The graphic rating scale simply asks a supervisor to rate an employee on an established set of criteria, such as quantity of work or attitude toward work. This leaves much room for subjectivity and debate. The behaviorally anchored rating scale asks the supervisor to rate the employee on specific behaviors that had been identified as positively or negatively affecting performance in a given job. This is a more specific appraisal approach and leaves less room for debate and disagreement.

Integration and Application

20. As Sy's supervisor, you face a difficult but perhaps expected human resource management problem. Not only is Sy influential as an informal leader, but he also has considerable experience on the job and in the company. Even though he is experiencing performance problems using the new computer system, there is no indication that he doesn't want to work hard and continue to perform for the company. Although retirement is an option, Sy may also be transferred, promoted, or simply terminated. The latter response seems unjustified and may cause legal problems. Transferring Sy, with his agreement, to another position could be a positive move; promoting Sy to a supervisory position in which his experience and networks would be useful is another possibility. The key in this situation seems to be moving Sy out so that a computer-literate person can take over the job, while continuing to utilize Sy in a job that better fits his talents. Transfer and/or promotion should be actively considered both in his and in the company's best interests.

Test Prep 11

Multiple Choice

1. b. **2.** b. **3.** a. **4.** d. **5.** a. **6.** c. **7.** c. **8.** a.
9. a. **10.** b. **11.** d. **12.** d. **13.** a. **14.** d. **15.** a.

Short Response

16. Position power is based on reward, coercion or punishment, and legitimacy or formal authority. Managers, however, need to have more power than that made available to them by the position alone. Thus, they have to develop personal power through expertise and reference. This personal power is essential in helping managers get things done beyond the scope of their position power alone.

17. Leadership situations are described by Fiedler according to: Position power—how much power the leader has in terms of rewards, punishments, and legitimacy; leader–member relations—the quality of relationships between the leader and followers; and task structure—the degree to which the task is clear and well defined, or open ended and more ambiguous. Highly favorable situations are high in position power, have good leader–member relations, and have structured tasks; highly unfavorable situations are low in position power, have poor leader–member relations, and have unstructured tasks.

18. According to House's path-goal theory, the following combinations are consistent with successful leadership. Participative leadership works well, for example, when performance incentives are low and people need to find other sources of need satisfaction. Through participation the leader gains knowledge that can help identify important needs and possible ways of satisfying them other than through the available performance incentives. Directive leadership works well, for example, when people aren't clear about their jobs or goals. In these cases the leader can step in and provide direction that channels their efforts toward desired activities and outcomes.

19. Servant leadership is basically other-centered and not self-centered. A servant leader is concerned with helping others to perform well so that the organization or group can ultimately do good things for society. The person who accepts the responsibilities of servant leadership is good at empowering others so that they can use their talents while acting independently to do their jobs in the best possible ways.

Integration and Application

20. In his new position, Marcel must understand that the transactional aspects of leadership are not sufficient enough to guarantee him long-term leadership effectiveness. He must move beyond the effective use of task-oriented and people-oriented behaviors—the "transactional" side of leadership, and demonstrate through his behavior and personal qualities the capacity to inspire others and lead with moral integrity—the "transformational" side. A transformational leader develops a unique relationship with followers in which they become enthusiastic, highly loyal, and high achievers. Marcel needs to work very hard to develop positive relationships with the team members. But he must add to this a moral and ethical dimension. He must emphasize in those relationships high aspirations for performance accomplishments, enthusiasm, ethical behavior, integrity and honesty in all dealings, and a clear vision of the future. By working hard with this agenda and by allowing his personality to positively express itself in the team setting, Marcel should make continuous progress as an effective and moral leader.

Test Prep 12

Multiple Choice

1. c. **2.** d. **3.** b. **4.** a. **5.** d. **6.** a. **7.** b. **8.** a.
9. b. **10.** a. **11.** b. **12.** d. **13.** d. **14.** d. **15.** c.

Short Response

16. All of the Big Five personality traits are relevant to the workplace. To give some basic examples, consider the following. Extroversion suggests whether or not a person will reach out to relate and work well with others. Agreeableness suggests whether or not a person is open to the ideas of others and willing to go along with group decisions. Conscientiousness suggests whether someone can be depended on to meet commitments and perform agreed-upon tasks. Emotional stability suggests whether or not someone will be relaxed and secure, or uptight and tense, in work situations. Openness suggests whether someone will be open to new ideas or resistant to change.

17. The Type A personality is characteristic of people who bring stress on themselves by virtue of personal characteristics. These tend to be compulsive individuals who are uncomfortable waiting for things to happen, who try to do many things at once, and who generally move fast and have difficulty slowing down. Type A personalities can be stressful for both the individuals and the people around them. Managers must be aware of Type A personality tendencies in their own behavior and among others with whom they work. Ideally, this awareness will help the manager take precautionary steps to best manage the stress caused by this personality type.

18. The halo effect occurs when a single attribute of a person, such as the way he or she dresses, is used to evaluate or form an overall impression of the person. Selective perception occurs when someone focuses in a situation on those aspects that reinforce or are most consistent with his or her existing values, beliefs, or experiences.

19. Job satisfaction is an attitude that reflects how people feel about their jobs, work settings, and the people with whom they work. A typical job satisfaction survey might ask people to respond to questions about their pay, co-worker relationships, quality of supervisor, nature of the work setting, and the type of work they are asked to do. These questions might be framed with a scale ranging from "very satisfied" to "not satisfied at all" for each question or job satisfaction dimension.

Integration and Application

20. Scott needs to be careful. Although there is modest research support for the relationship between job satisfaction and performance, there is no guarantee that simply doing things to make people happier at work will cause them to be higher performers. Scott needs to take a broader perspective on this issue and his responsibilities as a manager. He should be interested in job satisfaction for his therapists and do everything he can to help them to experience it. But he should also be performance oriented and understand that performance is achieved through a combination of skills, support, and motivation. He should be helping the therapists to achieve and maintain high levels of job competency. He should also work with them to find out what obstacles they are facing and what support they need—things that perhaps he can deal with in their behalf. All of this relates as well to research indications that performance can be a source of job satisfaction. And finally, Scott should make sure that the therapists believe they are being properly rewarded for their work because rewards are shown by research to have an influence on both job satisfaction and job performance.

18. When perceived negative inequity exists, an individual might (1) quit the job, (2) speak with the boss to try to increase rewards to the point where the inequity no longer exists, or (3) decide to reduce effort to the level that seems consistent with the rewards being received.

19. Shaping encourages the formation of desirable work behaviors by rewarding successive approximations to those behaviors. In this sense, the behavior doesn't have to be perfect to be rewarded—it just has to be moving in the right direction. Over time and with a change of reinforcement scheduling from continuous to intermittent, such rewards can end up drawing forth the desired behavior.

Integration and Application

20. The use of Muzak would be considered improvement in a hygiene factor under Herzberg's two-factor theory. Thus it would not be a source of greater work motivation and performance. Herzberg suggests that job content factors are the satisfiers or motivators. Based in the job itself, they represent such things as responsibility, sense of achievement, and feelings of growth. Job context factors are considered sources of dissatisfaction. They are found in the job environment and include such things as base pay, technical quality of supervision, and working conditions. Whereas improvements in job context such as introduction of Muzak make people less dissatisfied, improvements in job content are considered necessary to motivate them to high-performance levels.

Test Prep 13

Multiple Choice

1. b. **2.** c. **3.** d. **4.** d. **5.** b. **6.** a. **7.** b. **8.** b.
9. a. **10.** d. **11.** a. **12.** c. **13.** c. **14.** a. **15.** a.

Short Response

16. People high in need for achievement will prefer work settings and jobs in which they have (1) challenging but achievable goals, (2) individual responsibility, and (3) performance feedback.

17. One way for a team leader to use goal-setting principles in working with team members is to engage them in a process of joint goal-setting and performance review. In an earlier chapter on planning and controlling, this type of approach was described as "management by objectives." It is really a good application of goal-setting theory. Participation of both team leader and team member in goal setting offers an opportunity to choose goals to which the member will respond and which also will serve the team and organization as a whole. Furthermore, through goal setting, the team leader and team member can identify performance standards or targets. Progress toward these targets can be positively reinforced by the team leader. This type of approach harnesses the power of goal-setting theory by putting the team leader and team member together in a process where specific, challenging, and measureable goals can be set, and the team member can feel that he or she has helped set them.

Test Prep 14

Multiple Choice

1. d. **2.** a. **3.** b. **4.** d. **5.** b. **6.** a. **7.** c. **8.** b.
9. a. **10.** a. **11.** a. **12.** b. **13.** d. **14.** c. **15.** d.

Short Response

16. In a task force, members are brought together to work on a specific assignment. The task force usually disbands when the assignment is finished. In an employee involvement group, perhaps a quality circle, members are brought together to work on an issue or task over time. They meet regularly and always deal with the same issue/task. In a self-managing team, the members of a formal work group provide self-direction. They plan, organize, and evaluate their work, share tasks, and help one another develop skills; they may even make hiring decisions. A true self-managing team does not need the traditional "boss" or supervisor because the team as a whole takes on the supervisory responsibilities.

17. Input factors can have a major impact on group effectiveness. To best prepare a group to perform effectively, a manager should make sure that the right people are put in the group (maximize available talents and abilities), that these people are capable of working well together (membership characteristics should promote good relationships), that the tasks are clear, and that the group has the resources and environment needed to perform up to expectations.

18. A team's performance can be analyzed according to the interaction between cohesiveness and performance norms. In a highly cohesive team, members tend to conform to group norms. Thus, when the performance norm is positive and cohesion is high, we can expect everyone to work hard to support the norm—high performance is likely. By the same token, high cohesion and a low performance norm will act similarly—low performance is likely. With other combinations of norms and cohesion, the performance results will be more mixed.

19. The book lists several symptoms of groupthink along with various strategies for avoiding groupthink. For example, a group whose members censure themselves to refrain from contributing "contrary" or "different" opinions and/or whose members keep talking about outsiders as "weak" or the "enemy" may be suffering from groupthink. This may be avoided or corrected, for example, by asking someone to be the "devil's advocate" for a meeting and by inviting in an outside observer to help gather different viewpoints.

Integration and Application

20. Valeria is faced with a highly cohesive group whose members conform to a negative or low-performance norm. This is a difficult situation that is ideally resolved by changing the performance norm. To gain the group's commitment to a high-performance norm, Valeria should act as a positive role model for the norm. She must communicate the norm clearly and positively to the group. She should not assume that everyone knows what she expects of them. She may also talk to the informal leader and gain his or her commitment to the norm. She might carefully reward high-performance behaviors within the group. She may introduce new members with high-performance records and commitments. And she might hold group meetings in which performance standards and expectations are discussed, with an emphasis on committing to new high-performance directions. If attempts to introduce a high-performance norm fail, Valeria may have to take steps to reduce group cohesiveness so that individual members can pursue higher-performance results without feeling bound by group pressures to restrict their performance.

Test Prep 15

Multiple Choice

1. a.   2. c.   3. d.   4. d.   5. a.   6. c.   7. d.   8. c.
9. b.   10. c.   11. c.   12. a.   13. b.   14. a.   15. b.

Short Response

16. The manager's goal in active listening is to help the subordinate say what he or she really means. To do this, the manager should carefully listen for the content of what someone is saying, paraphrase or reflect back what the person appears to be saying, remain sensitive to nonverbal cues and feelings, and not be evaluative.

17. Well-intentioned managers can make bad decisions when they base decisions on bad information. Because of the manager's position of authority in the organization, those below him or

her may be reluctant to communicate upward information that they believe the manager doesn't want to hear. Thus, they may filter the information to make it as agreeable to the manager as possible. As a result of this filtering of upward communication, the manager may end up with poor or incomplete information and subsequently make bad decisions.

18. The four major errors in giving constructive feedback would be (1) being general rather than specific, (2) choosing a poor time, (3) including in the message irrelevant things, and (4) overwhelming the receiver with too much information at once.

19. Ethnocentrism is when a person views his or her own culture as superior to others. It can interfere with cross-cultural communication when the ethnocentrism leads the person to ignore cultural signals that indicate his or her behavior is inappropriate or offensive by local cultural standards. With the ethnocentric attitude of cultural superiority, the individual is inclined not to change personal ways or display the sensitivity to local cultural ways that are necessary to effective communication.

Integration and Application

20. Glenn can do a number of things to establish and maintain a system of communication with his employees and for his department store branch. To begin, he should, as much as possible, try to establish a highly interactive style of management based on credibility and trust. Credibility is earned through building personal power through expertise and reference. With credibility, he might set the tone for the department managers by using MBWA—"managing by wandering around." Once this pattern is established, trust will build between him and other store employees, and he should find that he learns a lot from interacting directly with them. Glenn should also set up a formal communication structure, such as bimonthly store meetings, where he communicates store goals, results, and other issues to the staff, and in which he listens to them in return. An e-mail system whereby Glenn and his staff could send messages to one another from their workstation computers would also be beneficial.

Test Prep 16

Multiple Choice

1. c.   2. a.   3. b.   4. b.   5. b.   6. d.   7. a.   8. a.
9. d.   10. a.   11. d.   12. d.   13. c.   14. c.   15. b.

Short Response

16. An approach of valuing diversity shows through leadership a commitment to helping people understand their differences, often through education and training programs. An approach of managing diversity, according to Roosevelt Thomas, is a step beyond in that it is where the leadership commits to changing the culture of the organization to empower everyone and create a fully inclusive environment where human resources are respected and fully utilized.

17. There are numbers of subcultures that form in organizations and can become the source of perceived differences as people

work with one another across subculture boundaries. Examples of common organizational subcultures include those based on age, gender, profession, and work function. If younger workers stereotype older workers as uncreative and less ambitious, a team consisting of an age mix of members might experience some difficulties. This illustrates an example of problems among generational subcultures.

18. The anthropologist Edward Hall identified communication context, time, and space as silent languages of culture. High-context cultures rely on nonverbal and situational cues as well as the spoken word to convey messages, whereas low-context cultures are more focused on what is being said. An American businessperson might press an Indonesian client to sign a contract immediately, whereas the body language of the client might say she doesn't want to, even though she is offering a reluctant "okay" in their conversation. Monochromic cultures deal with time in a linear fashion, whereas poly-chromic cultures view it as more nonlinear and dynamic. Whereas the American schedules time, saves time, and tries to meet time deadlines (monochromic behavior), a Mexican might be less concerned about time budgeting like this and more likely to act flexibly in terms of time schedules and engagements. Proxemics involves the use of space in communication. If you observe Americans in conversation, there is likely to be a modest amount of distance maintained between speakers. But in Italy the conversation is likely to take place in much closer face-to-face conditions, and this would likely make the American a bit uncomfortable.

19. Organizations are power structures, and the way people view and respond to power differences in organizations can be very significant in how they operate. In a national culture where power distance is high, there would be a tendency in organizations to respect persons of authority—perhaps defer to them, use job titles and formal greetings, and refrain from challenging their views in public meetings. In a low or moderate power distance culture, by contrast, there might be more informality in using first names without job titles and being more casual in relationships and even in public disagreements with views expressed by senior people.

Integration and Application

20. The friend must recognize that the cultural differences between the United States and Japan may affect the success of group-oriented work practices such as quality circles and work teams. The United States was the most individualistic culture in Hofstede's study of national cultures; Japan is much more collectivist. Group practices such as the quality circle and teams are natural and consistent with the Japanese culture. When introduced into a more individualistic culture, these same practices might cause difficulties or require some time for workers to get used to. At the very least, the friend should proceed with caution, discuss ideas for the new practices with the workers before making any changes, and then monitor the changes closely so that adjustments can be made to improve them as the workers gain familiarity with them and have suggestions of their own.

Test Prep 17

Multiple Choice

1. c. 2. d. 3. d. 4. b. 5. b. 6. a. 7. c. 8. d. 9. d. 10. b. 11. b. 12. c. 13. b. 14. c. 15. a.

Short Response

16. In a joint venture the foreign corporation and the local corporation each own a portion of the firm—e.g., 75% and 25%. In a wholly owned subsidiary the foreign firm owns the local subsidiary in its entirety.

17. The relationship between an MNC and a host country should be mutually beneficial. Sometimes, however, host countries complain that MNCs take unfair advantage of them and do not include them in the benefits of their international operations. The complaints against MNCs include taking excessive profits out of the host country, hiring the best local labor, not respecting local laws and customs, and dominating the local economy. Engaging in corrupt practices is another important concern.

18. If a senator says she favors "protectionism" in international trade, it basically means that she wants to make sure that domestic American firms are protected against foreign competitors. In other words, she doesn't want foreign companies coming into America and destroying through competition the local firms. Thus, she wants to protect them in some ways such as imposing import tariffs on the foreign firms' products or imposing legal restrictions on them setting up businesses in America.

19. Currency risk in international business involves the rise and fall of currencies in relationship with one another. For an American company operating in Japan, currency risk involves the value of the dollar vis-à-vis the yen. When the dollar falls relative to the yen (requiring more of them to buy 1 yen), it means that buying products and making investments in Japan will be more costly; the "risk" of this eventuality needs to be planned for when business relationships are entered in foreign countries. Political risk is the potential loss in one's investments in foreign countries due to wars or political changes that might threaten the assets. An example would be a Socialist government coming into power and deciding to "nationalize" or take over ownership of all foreign companies.

Integration and Application

20. This issue of MNC versus transnational is growing in importance. When a large global company such as Ford or IBM is strongly associated with a national identity, the firm might face risk in international business when foreign consumers or governments are angry at the firm's home country; they might stop buying its products or make it hard for them to operate. When the MNC has a strong national identity, its home constituents might express anger and create problems when the firm makes investments in creating jobs in other countries. Also, when the leadership of the MNC views itself as having one national home, it might have a more limited and even ethnocentric approach to international operations. When a firm such as Ford

or P&G operates as a transnational, by contrast, it becomes a global citizen and, theoretically at least, is freed from some potential problems identified here. Because a transnational views the world as its home, furthermore, its workforce and leadership are more likely to be globally diverse and have broad international perspectives on the company and its opportunities.

Test Prep 18

Multiple Choice

1. a.   **2.** c.   **3.** d.   **4.** b.   **5.** b.   **6.** a.   **7.** a.   **8.** b.
9. a.   **10.** c.   **11.** c.   **12.** a.   **13.** d.   **14.** b.   **15.** d.

Short Response

16. Entrepreneurship is rich with diversity. It is an avenue for business entry and career success that is pursued by many women and members of minority groups. Data show almost 40% of U.S. businesses are owned by women. Many report leaving other employment because they had limited opportunities. For them, entrepreneurship made available the opportunities for career success that they lacked. Minority-owned businesses are one of the fastest-growing sectors, with the growth rates highest for Hispanic-owned, Asian-owned, and African-American-owned businesses in that order.

17. The three stages in the life cycle of an entrepreneurial firm are birth, breakthrough, and maturity. In the birth stage, the leader is challenged to get customers, establish a market, and find the money needed to keep the business going. In the breakthrough stage, the challenges shift to becoming and staying profitable and managing growth. In the maturity stage, a leader is more focused on revising/maintaining a good business strategy and more generally managing the firm for continued success and possibly more future growth.

18. The limited partnership form of small business ownership consists of a general partner and one or more "limited partners."

The general partner(s) play an active role in managing and operating the business; the limited partners do not. All contribute resources of some value to the partnership for the conduct of the business. The advantage of any partnership form is that the partners may share in profits, but their potential for losses is limited by the size of their original investments.

19. A venture capitalist is an individual or group of individuals that invests money in new start-up companies and gets a portion of ownership in return. The goal is to sell their ownership stakes in the future for a profit. An angel investor is a type of venture capitalist, but on a smaller and individual scale. This is a person who invests in a new venture, taking a share of ownership, and also hoping to gain profit through a future sale of the ownership.

Integration and Application

20. The friend is right—it takes much forethought and planning to prepare the launch of a new business venture. In response to the question of how to ensure that you are really being customer-focused in the new start-up, I would ask and answer the following questions to frame my business model with a strong customer orientation. "Who are my potential customers? What market niche am I shooting for? What do the customers in this market really want? How do these customers make purchase decisions? How much will it cost to produce and distribute my product/service to these customers? How much will it cost to attract and retain customers?" Following an overall executive summary, which includes a commitment to this customer orientation, I would address the following areas in writing up my initial business plan. The plan would address such areas as company description—mission, owners, and legal form—as well as an industry analysis, product and services description, marketing description and strategy, staffing model, financial projections with cash flows, and capital needs.

Glossary

3 Ps of organizational performance The 3 Ps of organizational performance are profit, people, and planet.

360° feedback 360° feedback includes superiors, subordinates, peers, and even customers in the appraisal process.

A

accommodation Accommodation, or smoothing, plays down differences and highlights similarities to reduce conflict.

accountability Accountability is the requirement to show performance results to a supervisor.

active listening Active listening helps the source of a message say what he or she really means.

affirmative action Affirmative action is an effort to give preference in employment to women and minority group members.

after-action review After-action review is a structured review of lessons learned and results accomplished through a completed project, task force assignment, or special operation.

age discrimination Age discrimination penalizes an employee in a job or as a job applicant for being over the age of 40.

agenda setting Agenda setting identifies important action priorities.

amoral manager An amoral manager fails to consider the ethics of her or his behavior.

analytical competency Analytical competency is the ability to evaluate and analyze information to make actual decisions and solve real problems.

analytics Analytics is the systematic use and analysis of data to solve problems and make informed decisions.

anchoring and adjustment heuristic The anchoring and adjustment heuristic adjusts a previously existing value or starting point to make a decision.

angel investor An angel investor is a wealthy individual willing to invest in return for equity in a new venture.

assessment center An assessment center examines how job candidates handle simulated work situations.

attitude An attitude is a predisposition to act in a certain way.

attribution Attribution is the process of creating explanations for events.

authoritarianism Authoritarianism is the degree to which a person defers to authority and accepts status differences.

authority decision An authority decision is made by the leader and then communicated to the group.

autocratic leader An autocratic leader acts in unilateral command-and-control fashion.

availability heuristic The availability heuristic uses readily available information to assess a current situation.

avoidance Avoidance pretends that a conflict doesn't really exist.

B

B2B business strategy A B2B business strategy uses IT and Web portals to link organizations vertically in supply chains.

B2C business strategy A B2C business strategy uses IT and Web portals to link businesses with customers.

balanced scorecard A balanced scorecard measures performance on financial, customer service, internal process, and innovation and learning goals.

BCG Matrix The BCG Matrix analyzes business opportunities according to market growth rate and market share.

behavioral decision model The behavioral decision model describes decision making with limited information and bounded rationality.

behaviorally anchored rating scale (BARS) A behaviorally anchored rating scale (BARS) uses specific descriptions of actual behaviors to rate various levels of performance.

benchmarking Benchmarking uses external comparisons to gain insights for planning.

benefit corporation The benefit corporation, or B-Corp, is a corporate form for businesses whose stated goals are to combine making a profit with benefiting society and the environment.

best practices Best practices are methods that lead to superior performance.

biculturalism Biculturalism is when minority members adopt characteristics of majority cultures to succeed.

big-C creativity Big-C creativity occurs when extraordinary things are done by exceptional people.

board of directors Members of a board of directors are elected by stockholders to represent their ownership interests.

bona fide occupational qualifications Bona fide occupational qualifications are employment criteria justified by capacity to perform a job.

bonus pay Bonus pay plans provide one-time payments based on performance accomplishments.

breakeven analysis Breakeven analysis performs what-if calculations under different revenue and cost conditions.

breakeven point The breakeven point occurs where revenues just equal costs.

budget A budget is a plan that commits resources to projects or activities.

bureaucracy A bureaucracy is a rational and efficient form of organization founded on logic, order, and legitimate authority.

bureaucratic control Bureaucratic control influences behavior through authority, policies, procedures, job descriptions, budgets, and day-to-day supervision.

business incubator A business incubator is a facility that offers services to help new businesses get established.

business model A business model is a plan for making a profit by generating revenues that are greater than costs.

business model innovations Business model innovations result in ways for firms to make money.

business plan A business plan describes the direction for a new business and the financing needed to operate it.

business strategy A business strategy identifies how a division or strategic business unit will compete in its product or service domain.

C

career development Career development is the process of managing how a person grows and progresses in a career.

career planning Career planning is the process of matching career goals and individual capabilities with opportunities for their fulfillment.

centralization With centralization, top management keeps the power to make most decisions.

centralized communication network In a centralized communication network, communication flows only between individual members and a hub or center point.

certain environment A certain environment offers complete information on possible action alternatives and their consequences.

change leader A change leader tries to change the behavior of another person or social system.

changing Changing is the phase where a planned change actually takes place.

channel richness Channel richness is the capacity of a communication channel to effectively carry information.

Chapter 11 bankruptcy Chapter 11 bankruptcy protects an insolvent firm from creditors during a period of reorganization to restore profitability.

charisma Charisma is the ability to inspirationally persuade and motivate others.

charismatic leader A charismatic leader develops special leader–follower relationships and inspires followers in extraordinary ways.

charismastic leadership tactics Charismatic leadership tactics are communication techniques people use to make themselves more "leaderlike" and be perceived by others as influential and trustworthy.

child labor Child labor is the full-time employment of children for work otherwise done by adults.

clan control Clan control influences behavior through social norms and peer expectations.

classic entrepreneur A classic entrepreneur is someone willing to pursue opportunities in situations others view as problems or threats.

classical decision model The classical decision model describes decision making with complete information.

classical view of CSR The classical view of CSR is that business should focus on the pursuit of profits.

coaching Coaching occurs as an experienced person offers performance advice to a less-experienced person.

code of ethics A code of ethics is a formal statement of values and ethical standards.

coercive power Coercive power achieves influence by punishment.

cognitive dissonance Cognitive dissonance is discomfort felt when attitude and behavior are inconsistent.

cognitive style Cognitive style is the way an individual deals with information while making decisions.

cohesiveness Cohesiveness is the degree to which members are attracted to and motivated to remain part of a team.

collaboration Collaboration, or problem solving, involves working through conflict differences and solving problems so everyone wins.

collective bargaining Collective bargaining is the process of negotiating, administering, and interpreting a labor contract.

commercializing innovation Commercializing innovation is the process of turning new ideas into salable products.

committee A committee is designated to work on a special task on a continuing basis.

communication Communication is the process of sending and receiving symbols with meanings attached.

communication channel A communication channel is the medium used to carry a message.

communication transparency Communication transparency involves being honest and openly sharing accurate and complete information.

commutative justice Commutative justice focuses on the fairness of exchanges or transactions.

competition Competition, or authoritative command, uses force, superior skill, or domination to win a conflict.

competitive advantage A competitive advantage is an ability to outperform rivals.

complacency trap The complacency trap is being lulled into inaction by current successes or failures.

compressed workweek A compressed workweek allows a worker to complete a full-time job in less than five days.

compromise Compromise occurs when each party to the conflict gives up something of value to the other.

concentration Growth through concentration means expansion within an existing business area.

conceptual skill A conceptual skill is the ability to think analytically and solve complex problems.

concurrent control Concurrent control focuses on what happens during the work process.

confirmation error Confirmation error is when we attend only to information that confirms a decision already made.

conflict Conflict is a disagreement over issues of substance and/or an emotional antagonism.

conflict resolution Conflict resolution is the removal of the substantive and/or emotional reasons for a conflict.

consensus Consensus is reached when all parties believe they have had their say and been listened to, and agree to support the group's final decision.

constructive stress Constructive stress is a positive influence on effort, creativity, and diligence in work.

consultative decision A consultative decision is made by a leader after receiving information, advice, or opinions from group members.

contingency leadership perspective The contingency leadership perspective suggests that what is successful as a leadership style varies according to the situation and the people involved.

contingency planning Contingency planning identifies alternative courses of action to take when things go wrong.

contingency thinking Contingency thinking tries to match management practices with situational demands.

contingency workers Contingency workers or permatemps work part-time hours on a longer-term basis.

continuous improvement Continuous improvement involves always searching for new ways to improve work quality and performance.

control charts Control charts are graphical ways of displaying trends so that exceptions to quality standards can be identified.

controlling Controlling is the process of measuring performance and taking action to ensure desired results.

co-opetition Co-opetition is the strategy of working with rivals on projects of mutual benefit.

core competency A core competency is a special strength that gives an organization a competitive advantage.

core culture The core culture is found in the underlying values of the organization.

core values Core values are beliefs and values shared by organization members.

corporate governance Corporate governance is oversight of a company's management by a board of directors.

corporate social responsibility Corporate social responsibility is the obligation of an organization to serve its own interests and those of its stakeholders.

corporate strategy A corporate strategy sets long-term direction for the total enterprise.

corporation A corporation is a legal entity that exists separately from its owners.

corruption Corruption involves illegal practices to further one's business interests.

cost-benefit analysis Cost-benefit analysis involves comparing the costs and benefits of each potential course of action.

cost leadership strategy A cost leadership strategy seeks to operate with lower costs than competitors.

CPM/PERT CPM/PERT is a combination of the critical path method and the program evaluation and review technique.

creativity Creativity is the generation of a novel idea or unique approach that solves a problem or crafts an opportunity.

credible communication Credible communication earns trust, respect, and integrity in the eyes of others.

crisis A crisis is an unexpected problem that can lead to disaster if not resolved quickly and appropriately.

critical-incident technique The critical-incident technique keeps a log of someone's effective and ineffective job behaviors.

critical path The critical path is the pathway from project start to conclusion that involves activities with the longest completion times.

cross-functional team A cross-functional team operates with members who come from different functional units of an organization.

crowdfunding In equity crowdfunding, new ventures go online to get startup financing from crowds of investors.

crowdsourcing Crowdsourcing is strategic use of the Internet to engage customers and potential customers in providing opinions and suggestions on products and their designs.

cultural etiquette Cultural etiquette is use of appropriate manners and behaviors in cross-cultural situations.

cultural intelligence Cultural intelligence is the ability to adapt to new cultures.

cultural relativism Cultural relativism suggests there is no one right way to behave; cultural context determines ethical behavior.

culture shock Culture shock is the confusion and discomfort that a person experiences when in an unfamiliar culture.

currency risk Currency risk is possible loss because of fluctuating exchange rates.

customer structure A customer structure groups together people and jobs that serve the same customers or clients.

D

debt financing Debt financing involves borrowing money from another person, a bank, or a financial institution.

decentralization With decentralization, top management allows lower levels to help make many decisions.

decentralized communication network A decentralized communication network allows all members to communicate directly with one another.

decision A decision is a choice among possible alternative courses of action.

decision making Decision making is the process of making choices among alternative courses of action.

decision-making process The decision-making process begins with identification of a problem and ends with evaluation of implemented solutions.

deficit principle Maslow's deficit principle is that people act to satisfy needs for which a satisfaction deficit exists; a satisfied need doesn't motivate behavior.

delegation Delegation is the process of entrusting work to others.

democratic leader A democratic leader encourages participation with an emphasis on task and people.

departmentalization Departmentalization is the process of grouping together people and jobs into work units.

destructive stress Destructive stress is a negative influence on one's performance.

differentiation strategy A differentiation strategy offers products that are unique and different from those of the competition.

discrimination Discrimination actively denies women and minorities the full benefits of organizational membership.

disruptive behaviors Disruptive behaviors are self-serving and cause problems for team effectiveness.

disruptive innovation Disruptive innovation creates products or services that become so widely used that they largely replace prior practices and competitors.

distributed leadership Distributed leadership is when any and all members contribute helpful task and maintenance activities to the team.

distributive justice Distributive justice focuses on treating people the same regardless of personal characteristics.

diversification Growth through diversification means expansion by entering related or new business areas.

diversity Diversity describes race, gender, age, and other individual differences.

divestiture Divestiture involves selling off parts of the organization to refocus attention on core business areas.

division of labor The division of labor means that people and groups perform different jobs.

divisional structure A divisional structure groups together people working on the same product, in the same area, or with similar customers.

downsizing Downsizing decreases the size of operations.

E

e-business strategy An e-business strategy strategically uses the Internet to gain competitive advantage.

ecological fallacy The ecological fallacy assumes that a generalized cultural value applies equally well to all members of the culture.

economic order quantity The economic order quantity method places new orders when inventory levels fall to predetermined points.

effective communication In effective communication the receiver fully understands the intended meaning.

effective manager An effective manager successfully helps others achieve high performance and satisfaction in their work.

effective team An effective team achieves high levels of task performance, membership satisfaction, and future viability.

efficient communication Efficient communication occurs at minimum cost to the sender.

electronic grapevine The electronic grapevine uses computer technologies to transmit information around informal networks inside and outside organizations.

emotional conflict Emotional conflict results from feelings of anger, distrust, dislike, fear, and resentment as well as from personality clashes.

emotional intelligence (EI) Emotional intelligence (EI) is the ability to manage our emotions in leadership and social relationships.

emotions Emotions are strong feelings directed toward someone or something.

employee assistance programs Employee assistance programs help employees cope with personal stresses and problems.

employee engagement Employee engagement is a strong sense of belonging and connection with one's work and employer.

employee involvement team An employee involvement team meets on a regular basis to help achieve continuous improvement.

employee value proposition The employee value proposition, or EVP, is the exchange of value between what the individual and the employer offer each other as part of the employment relationship.

empowerment Empowerment gives people job freedom and power to influence affairs in the organization.

entrepreneur An entrepreneur is willing to pursue opportunities in situations that others view as problems or threats.

entrepreneurship Entrepreneurship is risk-taking behavior in pursuit of business success.

environmental capital or natural capital Environmental capital or natural capital is the storehouse of natural resources—atmosphere, land, water, and minerals—that we use to sustain life and produce goods and services for society.

equal employment opportunity (EEO) Equal employment opportunity (EEO) is the right to employment and advancement without regard to race, sex, religion, color, or national origin.

equity financing Equity financing gives ownership shares to outsiders in return for their financial investments.

escalating commitment Escalating commitment is the continuation of a course of action even though it is not working.

ethical behavior Ethical behavior is "right" or "good" in the context of a governing moral code.

ethical dilemma An ethical dilemma is a situation that, although offering potential benefit or gain, is also unethical.

ethical frameworks Ethical frameworks are well-thought-out personal rules and strategies for ethical decision making.

ethical imperialism Ethical imperialism is an attempt to impose one's ethical standards on other cultures.

ethics Ethics set moral standards of what is "good" and "right" behavior in organizations and in our personal lives.

ethics training Ethics training seeks to help people understand the ethical aspects of decision making and to incorporate high ethical standards into their daily behavior.

ethnic or national subcultures Ethnic or national subcultures form among people from the same races, language groupings, regions, and nations.

ethnocentrism Ethnocentrism is the belief that one's membership group or subculture is superior to all others.

evidence-based management Evidence-based management involves making decisions based on hard facts about what really works.

existence needs Existence needs are desires for physiological and material well-being.

expectancy Expectancy is a person's belief that working hard will result in high task performance.

expert power Expert power achieves influence by special knowledge.

exporting In exporting, local products are sold abroad.

external control External control occurs through direct supervision or administrative systems.

extinction Extinction discourages a behavior by making the removal of a desirable consequence contingent on its occurrence.

F

family business feud A family business feud can lead to small business failure.

family businesses Family businesses are owned and financially controlled by family members.

family-friendly benefits Family-friendly benefits help employees achieve better work-life balance.

feedback Feedback is the process of telling someone else how you feel about something that person did or said.

feedback control Feedback control takes place after completing an action.

feedforward control Feedforward control ensures clear directions and needed resources before the work begins.

first-line managers First-line managers supervise people who perform non-managerial duties.

first-mover advantage A first-mover advantage comes from being first to exploit a niche or enter a market.

flameout A flameout occurs when we communicate extreme agitation in interpersonal communication or electronic messages.

flexible benefits Flexible benefits programs allow choice to personalize benefits within a set dollar allowance.

flexible working hours Flexible working hours give employees some choice in daily work hours.

focused cost leadership strategy A focused cost leadership strategy seeks the lowest costs of operations within a special market segment.

focused differentiation strategy A focused differentiation strategy offers a unique product to a special market segment.

force-coercion strategy A force-coercion strategy pursues change through formal authority and/or the use of rewards or punishments.

forecasting Forecasting attempts to predict the future.

Foreign Corrupt Practices Act The Foreign Corrupt Practices Act makes it illegal for U.S. firms and their representatives to engage in corrupt practices overseas.

foreign subsidiary A foreign subsidiary is a local operation completely owned by a foreign firm.

formal structure Formal structure is the official structure of the organization.

formal team A formal team is officially recognized and supported by the organization.

framing error Framing error is solving a problem in the context perceived.

franchise A franchise is when one business owner sells to another the right to operate the same business in another location.

franchising In franchising, a firm pays a fee for rights to use another company's name and operating methods.

free-agent economy In a free-agent economy people change jobs more often, and many work on independent contracts with a shifting mix of employers.

fringe benefits Fringe benefits are nonmonetary forms of compensation such as health insurance and retirement plans.

functional chimneys, or functional silos, problem The functional chimneys, or functional silos, problem is a lack of communication and coordination across functions.

functional plan A functional plan identifies how different parts of an enterprise will contribute to accomplishing strategic plans.

functional strategy A functional strategy guides activities within one specific area of operations.

functional structure A functional structure groups together people with similar skills who perform similar tasks.

fundamental attribution error The fundamental attribution error overestimates internal factors and underestimates external factors as influences on someone's behavior.

G

gain sharing Gain sharing allows employees to share in cost savings or productivity gains realized by their efforts.

Gantt chart A Gantt chart graphically displays the scheduling of tasks required to complete a project.

gender similarities hypothesis The gender similarities hypothesis holds that males and females have similar psychological makeups.

gender subcultures Gender subcultures form among people of the same gender.

general partnership In a general partnership, owners share management responsibilities.

generational subcultures Generational subcultures form among people in similar age groups.

geographical structure A geographical structure brings together people and jobs performed in the same location.

glass ceiling The glass ceiling is a hidden barrier to the advancement of women and minorities.

glass ceiling effect The glass ceiling effect is an invisible barrier limiting career advancement of women and minorities.

global corporation or multinational corporation (MNC) A global corporation or multinational corporation (MNC) has extensive international business dealings in many foreign countries.

global economy In the global economy, resources, markets, and competition are worldwide in scope.

global manager A global manager is culturally aware and informed on international affairs.

global sourcing In global sourcing, firms purchase materials or services around the world for local use.

global strategic alliance In a global strategic alliance, each partner hopes to achieve through cooperation things they couldn't do alone.

globalization gap The globalization gap involves large global firms gaining disproportionately from the global economy versus smaller firms and many countries.

globalization Globalization is the worldwide interdependence of resource flows, product markets, and business competition.

globalization strategy A globalization strategy adopts standardized products and advertising for use worldwide.

governance Governance is oversight of top management by a board of directors or board of trustees.

graphic rating scale A graphic rating scale uses a checklist of traits or characteristics to evaluate performance.

green innovation or sustainable innovation Green innovation or sustainable innovation reduces the carbon footprint of an organization or its products.

greenfield venture A greenfield venture establishes a foreign subsidiary by building an entirely new operation in a foreign country.

group decision A group decision is made by group members themselves.

groupthink Groupthink is a tendency for highly cohesive teams to lose their evaluative capabilities.

growth needs Growth needs are desires for continued psychological growth and development.

growth strategy A growth strategy involves expansion of the organization's current operations.

H

halo effect A halo effect uses one attribute to develop an overall impression of a person or situation.

Hawthorne effect The Hawthorne effect is the tendency of persons singled out for special attention to perform as expected.

heterogeneous teams Heterogeneous teams have members with diverse personal characteristics.

hierarchy of objectives In a hierarchy of objectives, lower-level objectives help to accomplish higher-level ones.

high-context cultures High-context cultures rely on nonverbal and situational cues as well as spoken or written words in communication.

higher-order needs Higher-order needs are esteem and self-actualization needs in Maslow's hierarchy.

homogeneous teams Homogeneous teams have members with similar personal characteristics.

human capital Human capital is the economic value of people with job-relevant abilities, knowledge, ideas, energies, and commitments.

human relations A human relations leader emphasizes people over tasks.

human resource management (HRM) Human resource management (HRM) is the process of attracting, developing, and maintaining a high-quality workforce.

human skill A human skill is the ability to work well in cooperation with other people.

hygiene factor A hygiene factor is found in the job context, such as working conditions, interpersonal relations, organizational policies, and salary.

I

immoral manager An immoral manager chooses to behave unethically.

importing Importing is the process of acquiring products abroad and selling them in domestic markets.

impression management Impression management tries to create desired perceptions in the eyes of others.

improvement objectives Improvement objectives document intentions to improve performance in a specific way.

improvisational change Improvisational change makes continual adjustments as changes are being implemented.

inclusivity Inclusivity is how open the organization is to anyone who can perform a job.

incremental change Incremental change bends and adjusts existing ways to improve performance.

independent contractors Independent contractors are hired on temporary contracts and are not part of the organization's permanent workforce.

individualism view In the individualism view, ethical behavior advances long-term self-interests.

individualism-collectivism Individualism-collectivism is the degree to which a society emphasizes individuals and their self-interests.

informal group An informal group is unofficial and emerges from relationships and shared interests among members.

informal structure The informal structure is the set of unofficial relationships among an organization's members.

information competency Information competency is the ability to gather and use information to solve problems.

information filtering Information filtering is the intentional distortion of information to make it more favorable to the recipient.

initial public offering (IPO) An initial public offering (IPO) is an initial selling of shares of stock to the public at large.

innovation Innovation is the process of taking a new idea and putting it into practice.

input standard An input standard measures work efforts that go into a performance task.

insourcing Insourcing is the creation of domestic jobs by foreign employers.

instrumental values Instrumental values are preferences regarding the means to desired ends.

instrumentality Instrumentality is a person's belief that various outcomes will occur as a result of task performance.

integrity Integrity in leadership is honesty, credibility, and consistency in putting values into action.

intellectual capital Intellectual capital is the collective brainpower or shared knowledge of a workforce.

intellectual capital equation The intellectual capital equation is: IC = competency × commitment.

interactional justice Interactional justice is the degree to which others are treated with dignity and respect.

interactive leadership Interactive leadership is strong on communication, participation, and dealing with problems by teamwork.

intercultural competencies Intercultural competencies are skills and personal characteristics that help us be successful in cross-cultural situations.

internal control, or self-control Internal control, or self-control, occurs as people exercise self-discipline in fulfilling job expectations.

international business An international business conducts commercial transactions across national boundaries.

intrapreneurs Intrapreneurs display entrepreneurial behavior as employees of larger firms.

intuitive thinking Intuitive thinking approaches problems in a flexible and spontaneous fashion.

inventory control Inventory control ensures that inventory is only big enough to meet immediate needs.

ISO 14001 ISO 14001 is a global quality standard that certifies organizations that set environmental objectives and targets, account for the environmental impact of their activities, and continuously improve environmental performance.

J

job burnout Job burnout is physical and mental exhaustion from work stress.

job design Job design is the allocation of specific work tasks to individuals and groups.

job discrimination Job discrimination occurs when someone is denied a job or job assignment for non-job-relevant reasons.

job enrichment Job enrichment increases job content by adding work planning and evaluating duties normally performed by the supervisor.

job migration Job migration occurs when global outsourcing shifts from one country to another.

job satisfaction Job satisfaction is the degree to which an individual feels positive about a job and work experience.

job sharing Job sharing splits one job between two people.

joint venture A joint venture operates in a foreign country through co-ownership with local partners.

justice view In the justice view, ethical behavior treats people impartially and fairly.

Just-in-time scheduling (JIT) Just-in-time scheduling (JIT) routes materials to workstations just in time for use.

K

knowledge workers Knowledge workers add value to organizations through their intellectual capabilities.

L

labor contract A labor contract is a formal agreement between a union and an employer about the terms of work for union members.

labor union A labor union is an organization that deals with employers on the workers' collective behalf.

lack-of-participation error Lack-of-participation error is failure to include the right people in the decision-making process.

laissez-faire leader A laissez-faire leader is disengaged, showing low task and people concerns.

law of contingent reinforcement Law of contingent reinforcement—deliver the reward only when desired behavior occurs.

law of effect The law of effect states that behavior followed by pleasant consequences is likely to be repeated; behavior followed by unpleasant consequences is not.

law of immediate reinforcement Law of immediate reinforcement—deliver the reward as soon as possible after the desired behavior occurs.

leadership Leadership is the process of inspiring others to work hard to accomplish important tasks.

leadership style Leadership style is the recurring pattern of behaviors exhibited by a leader.

leading Leading is the process of arousing enthusiasm and inspiring efforts to achieve goals.

legitimate power Legitimate power achieves influence by formal authority.

licensing In licensing, one firm pays a fee for rights to make or sell another company's products.

lifelong learning Lifelong learning is continuous learning from daily experiences.

limited liability corporation (LLC) A limited liability corporation (LLC) combines the advantages of the sole proprietorship, partnership, and corporation.

limited partnership A limited partnership consists of a general partner who manages the business and one or more limited partners.

liquidation Liquidation occurs when a business closes and sells its assets to pay creditors.

little-C Creativity Little-C creativity occurs when average people come up with unique ways to deal with daily events and situations.

locus of control Locus of control is the extent to which one believes what happens is within one's control.

long-range plans Long-range plans usually cover three years or more.

loose culture In loose cultures social norms are mixed and ambiguous, and conformity varies.

low-context cultures Low-context cultures emphasize communication via spoken or written words.

lower-order needs Lower-order needs are physiological, safety, and social needs in Maslow's hierarchy.

M

machiavellianism Machiavellianism is the degree to which someone uses power manipulatively.

maintenance activity A maintenance activity is an action taken by a team member that supports the emotional life of the group.

management by exception Management by exception focuses attention on differences between actual and desired performance.

management process The management process is planning, organizing, leading, and controlling the use of resources to accomplish performance goals.

management science and operational research Management science and operational research apply mathematical techniques to solve management problems.

manager A manager is a person who supports and is responsible for the work of others.

managing by objectives Managing by objectives is a process of joint objective setting between a superior and a subordinate.

managing diversity Managing diversity is building an inclusive work environment that allows everyone to reach his or her potential.

market control Market control is essentially the influence of market competition on the behavior of organizations and their members.

masculinity-femininity Masculinity-femininity is the degree to which a society values assertiveness and materialism.

matrix structure A matrix structure combines functional and divisional approaches to emphasize project or program teams.

MBWA Managers using MBWA spend time out of their offices, meeting and talking with workers at all levels.

mechanistic designs Mechanistic designs are bureaucratic, using a centralized and vertical structure.

mentoring Mentoring assigns early-career employees as protégés to more senior ones.

merit pay Merit pay awards pay increases in proportion to performance contributions.

middle managers Middle managers oversee the work of large departments or divisions.

mission The mission is the organization's reason for existence in society.

mixed message A mixed message results when words communicate one message while actions, body language, or appearance communicate something else.

monochronic In monochronic cultures people tend to do one thing at a time.

mood contagion Mood contagion is the spillover of one's positive or negative moods onto others.

moods Moods are generalized positive and negative feelings or states of mind.

moral absolutism Moral absolutism suggests ethical standards apply universally across all cultures.

moral leadership Moral leadership has integrity and appears to others as "good" or "right" by ethical standards.

moral manager A moral manager makes ethical behavior a personal goal.

moral rights view In the moral rights view, ethical behavior respects and protects fundamental rights.

most favored nation status Most favored nation status gives a trading partner the most favorable treatment for imports and exports.

motion study Motion study is the science of reducing a job or task to its basic physical motions.

motivation Motivation accounts for the level, direction, and persistence of effort expended at work.

multicultural organization A multicultural organization is based on pluralism and operates with inclusivity and respect for diversity.

multiperson comparison A multiperson comparison compares one person's performance with that of others.

N

necessity-based entrepreneurship Necessity-based entrepreneurship occurs when people start new ventures because they have few or no other employment options.

need A need is a physiological or psychological deficiency that a person wants to satisfy.

need for achievement Need for achievement is the desire to do something better, to solve problems, or to master complex tasks.

need for affiliation Need for affiliation is the desire to establish and maintain good relations with people.

need for power Need for power is the desire to control, influence, or be responsible for other people.

negative reinforcement Negative reinforcement strengthens a behavior by making the avoidance of an undesirable consequence contingent on its occurrence.

network structure A network structure uses IT to link with networks of outside suppliers and service contractors.

networking Networking involves building and maintaining positive relationships with other people.

noise Noise is anything that interferes with the communication process.

nonprogrammed decision A nonprogrammed decision applies a specific solution that has been crafted to address a unique problem.

nontariff barriers Nontariff barriers are nontax policies that governments enact to discourage imports, such as quotas and import restrictions.

nonverbal communication Nonverbal communication takes place through gestures, expressions, posture, and even use of interpersonal space.

norm A norm is a behavior, rule, or standard expected to be followed by team members.

O

objectives Objectives are specific results that one wishes to achieve.

observable culture The observable culture is what you see and hear when walking around an organization.

occupational subcultures Occupational subcultures form among people doing the same kinds of work.

open-book management In open-book management managers provide employees with essential financial information about their employers.

open system An open system transforms resource inputs from the environment into product outputs.

operant conditioning Operant conditioning is the control of behavior by manipulating its consequences.

operating objectives Operating objectives are specific results that organizations try to accomplish.

operational plan or tactical plan An operational plan or tactical plan sets out ways to implement a strategic plan.

operations management Operations management is the study of how organizations produce goods and services.

optimizing decision An optimizing decision chooses the alternative providing the absolute best solution to a problem.

organic designs Organic designs are adaptive, using a decentralized and horizontal structure.

organization chart An organization chart describes the arrangement of work positions within an organization.

organization structure Organization structure is a system of tasks, reporting relationships, and communication linkages.

organizational citizenship behaviors Organizational citizenship behaviors are things people do to go the extra mile in their work.

organizational culture Organizational culture is a system of shared beliefs and values guiding behavior.

organizational design Organizational design is the process of configuring organizations to meet environmental challenges.

organizational subcultures Organizational subcultures are groupings of people based on shared demographic and job identities.

organizing Organizing is the process of assigning tasks, allocating resources, and coordinating work activities.

orientation Orientation familiarizes new employees with jobs, co-workers, and organizational policies and services.

output standard An output standard measures performance results in terms of quantity, quality, cost, or time.

outsourcing Outsourcing shifts local jobs to foreign locations to take advantage of lower-wage labor in other countries.

P

participatory planning Participatory planning includes the persons who will be affected by plans and/or who will be asked to implement them.

partnership A partnership is when two or more people agree to contribute resources to start and operate a business together.

pay discrimination Pay discrimination occurs when men and women are paid differently for doing equal work.

perceived negative inequity Perceived negative inequity is discomfort felt over being harmed by unfair treatment.

perceived positive inequity Perceived positive inequity is discomfort felt over benefitting from unfair treatment.

perception Perception is the process through which people receive and interpret information from the environment.

performance review or performance appraisal Performance appraisal is the process of formally evaluating performance and providing feedback to a jobholder.

performance norm The performance norm defines the effort and performance contributions expected of team members.

performance opportunity A performance opportunity is a situation that offers the possibility of a better future if the right steps are taken.

performance threat A performance threat is a situation where something is wrong or likely to be wrong.

person-job fit Person-job fit is the match of individual skills, interests, and personal characteristics with the job.

personal development objectives Personal development objectives document intentions to accomplish personal growth, such as expanded job knowledge or skills.

personal wellness Personal wellness is the pursuit of a personal health-promotion program.

personality Personality is the profile of characteristics making a person unique from others.

person-organization fit Person-organization fit is the match of individual values, interests, and behavior with the organizational culture.

persuasive communication Persuasive communication presents a message in a manner that causes others to accept and support it.

plan A plan is a statement of intended means for accomplishing objectives.

planning Planning is the process of setting performance objectives and determining how to accomplish them.

policy A policy is a standing plan that communicates broad guidelines for decisions and action.

political risk Political risk is possible loss because of instability and political changes in foreign countries.

political-risk analysis Political-risk analysis forecasts how political events may affect foreign investments.

polychronic cultures In polychronic cultures people accomplish many different things at once.

positive reinforcement Positive reinforcement strengthens a behavior by making a desirable consequence contingent on its occurrence.

power distance Power distance is the degree to which a society accepts unequal distribution of power.

power Power is the ability to get someone else to do something you want done.

pregnancy discrimination Pregnancy discrimination penalizes a woman in a job or as a job applicant for being pregnant.

prejudice Prejudice is the display of negative, irrational attitudes toward women or minorities.

problem solving Problem solving involves identifying and taking action to resolve problems.

procedural justice Procedural justice focuses on the fair application of policies and rules.

procedure A procedure or rule precisely describes actions to take in specific situations.

process innovations Process innovations result in better ways of doing things.

product innovations Product innovations result in new or improved goods or services.

product structure A product structure groups together people and jobs working on a single product or service.

profit sharing Profit sharing distributes to employees a proportion of net profits earned by the organization.

programmed decision A programmed decision applies a solution from past experience to a routine problem.

progression principle Maslow's progression principle is that a need at any level becomes activated only after the next-lower-level need is satisfied.

project management Project management makes sure that activities required to complete a project are planned well and accomplished on time.

project team or task force A project team or task force is convened for a specific purpose and disbands after completing its task.

projection Projection assigns personal attributes to other individuals.

projects Projects are one-time activities with many component tasks that must be completed in proper order and according to budget.

protectionism Protectionism is a call for tariffs and favorable treatments to protect domestic firms from foreign competition.

proxemics Proxemics is the study of the way we use space.

punishment Punishment discourages a behavior by making an unpleasant consequence contingent on its occurrence.

Q

quality circle A quality circle is a team of employees who meet periodically to discuss ways of improving work quality.

quality of work life Quality of work life is the overall quality of human experiences in the workplace.

R

rational persuasion strategy A rational persuasion strategy pursues change through empirical data and rational argument.

realistic job previews Realistic job previews provide job candidates with all pertinent information about a job and organization.

recruitment Recruitment is a set of activities designed to attract a qualified pool of job applicants.

referent power Referent power achieves influence by personal identification.

refreezing Refreezing is the phase at which change is stabilized.

relatedness needs Relatedness needs are desires for satisfying interpersonal relationships.

reliability Reliability means that a selection device gives consistent results over repeated measures.

representativeness heuristic The representativeness heuristic assesses the likelihood of an occurrence using a stereotyped set of similar events.

reshoring Reshoring moves job back from foreign to domestic locations.

restricted communication network Subgroups in a restricted communication network contest one anothers' positions and restrict interactions with one another.

restructuring Restructuring reduces the scale or mix of operations.

retrenchment strategy A retrenchment strategy changes operations to correct weaknesses.

reverse innovation Reverse innovation recognizes the potential for valuable innovations to be launched from lower organizational levels and diverse locations, including emerging markets.

reverse mentoring In reverse mentoring, younger and newly hired employees mentor senior executives, often on the latest developments with digital technologies.

reward power Reward power achieves influence by offering something of value.

revolving door syndrome The revolving door syndrome is high turnover among minorities and women.

risk environment A risk environment lacks complete information but offers probabilities of the likely outcomes for possible action alternatives.

S

satisficing decision A satisficing decision chooses the first satisfactory alternative that presents itself.

satisfier factor A satisfier factor is found in job content, such as a sense of achievement, recognition, responsibility, advancement, or personal growth.

scalar chain principle The scalar chain principle states that organizations should operate with clear and unbroken lines of communication top to bottom.

scenario planning Scenario planning identifies alternative future scenarios and makes plans to deal with each.

scientific management Scientific management emphasizes careful selection and training of workers and supervisory support.

selection Selection is choosing whom to hire from a pool of qualified job applicants.

selective perception Selective perception focuses attention on things consistent with existing beliefs, needs, actions.

self-efficacy Self-efficacy is a person's belief that they are capable of performing a task.

self-fulfilling prophecy A self-fulfilling prophecy occurs when a person acts in ways that confirm another's expectations.

self-management Self-management is the ability to understand oneself, exercise initiative, accept responsibility, and learn from experience.

self-managing team Members of a self-managing team have the authority to make decisions about how they share and complete their work.

self-monitoring Self-monitoring is the degree to which someone is able to adjust behavior in response to external factors.

self-serving bias Self-serving bias underestimates internal factors and overestimates external factors as influences on someone's behavior.

serial entrepreneur A serial entrepreneur starts and runs businesses and nonprofits over and over again, moving from one interest and opportunity to the next.

servant leadership Servant leadership means serving others and helping them use their talents to help organizations best serve society.

shamrock organization A shamrock organization operates with a core group of full-time long-term workers supported by others who work on contracts and part time.

shaping Shaping is positive reinforcement of successive approximations to the desired behavior.

shared power strategy A shared power strategy pursues change by participation in assessing change needs, values, and goals.

short-range plans Short-range plans usually cover a year or less.

Six Sigma Six Sigma is a quality standard of 3.4 defects or less per million products or service deliveries.

skunkworks Skunkworks are special creative units set free from the normal structure for the purpose of innovation.

small business A small business has fewer than 500 employees, is independently owned and operated, and does not dominate its industry.

Small Business Development Centers Small Business Development Centers offer guidance to entrepreneurs and small business owners on how to set up and manage business operations.

social business A social business is one in which the underlying business model directly addresses a social problem.

social capital Social capital is the capacity to attract support and help from others to get things done.

social entrepreneurs Social entrepreneurs take business risks to find novel ways to solve pressing social problems.

social innovation Social innovation is business innovation driven by a social conscience.

social loafing Social loafing is the tendency of some people to avoid responsibility by free-riding in groups.

social media strategy A social media strategy uses social media to better engage with an organization's customers, clients, and external audiences in general.

social network analysis Social network analysis identifies the informal structures and their embedded social relationships that are active in an organization.

social responsibility audit A social responsibility audit measures and reports on an organization's performance in various areas of corporate social responsibility.

socialization Socialization is the process through which new members learn the culture of an organization.

socioeconomic view of CSR The socioeconomic view of CSR is that business should focus on contributions to society, not just on making profits.

sole proprietorship A sole proprietorship is an individual pursuing business for a profit.

span of control Span of control is the number of persons directly reporting to a manager.

spotlight questions Spotlight questions highlight the risks of public disclosure of one's actions.

stakeholders Stakeholders are people and institutions most directly affected by an organization's performance.

start-up A start-up is a new and temporary venture that is trying to discover a profitable business model for future success.

stereotype A stereotype assigns attributes commonly associated with a group to an individual.

stock options Stock options give the right to purchase shares at a fixed price in the future.

strategic alliance In a strategic alliance, organizations join together in partnership to pursue an area of mutual interest.

strategic control Strategic control makes sure strategies are well implemented and that poor strategies are scrapped or changed.

strategic formulation Strategic formulation is the process of creating strategies.

strategic human resource management Strategic human resource management mobilizes human capital to implement organizational strategies.

strategic intent Strategic intent focuses organizational energies on achieving a compelling goal.

strategic leadership Strategic leadership inspires people to implement organizational strategies.

strategic management Strategic management is the process of formulating and implementing strategies.

strategic plan A strategic plan identifies long-term directions for the organization.

strategy A strategy is a comprehensive plan guiding resource allocation to achieve long-term organization goals.

strategy implementation Strategy implementation is the process of putting strategies into action.

stress Stress is a state of tension experienced by individuals facing extraordinary demands, constraints, or opportunities.

stretch goals Stretch goals are performance targets that we have to work extra hard and stretch to reach.

strong cultures Strong cultures are clear, well defined, and widely shared among members.

substantive conflict Substantive conflict involves disagreements over goals, resources, rewards, policies, procedures, and job assignments.

substitutes for leadership Substitutes for leadership are factors in the work setting that direct work efforts without the involvement of a leader.

subsystem A subsystem is a smaller component of a larger system.

succession plan A succession plan describes how the leadership transition and related financial matters will be handled.

succession problem The succession problem is the issue of who will run the business when the current head leaves.

sustainability Sustainability is a goal that addresses the rights of present and future generations as co-stakeholders of present-day natural resources.

sustainable business Sustainable business is where firms operate in ways that both meet the needs of customers and protect or advance the well-being of our natural environment.

sustainable competitive advantage A sustainable competitive advantage is achieved in ways that are difficult to imitate.

sustainable development Sustainable development is making use of natural resources to meet today's needs while also preserving and protecting the environment for use by future generations.

sweatshops Sweatshops employ workers at very low wages, for long hours, and in poor working conditions.

SWOT analysis A SWOT analysis examines organizational strengths and weaknesses, as well as environmental opportunities and threats.

symbolic leader A symbolic leader uses language, symbols, and actions to establish and maintain a desired organizational culture.

synergy Synergy is the creation of a whole greater than the sum of its individual parts.

systematic thinking Systematic thinking approaches problems in a rational and analytical fashion.

T

tariffs Tariffs are taxes governments levy on imports from abroad.

task activity A task activity is an action taken by a team member that directly contributes to the group's performance purpose.

team A team is a collection of people who regularly interact to pursue common goals.

team building Team building involves activities to gather and analyze data on a team and make changes to increase its effectiveness.

team diversity Team diversity is the mix of skills, experiences, backgrounds, and personalities of team members.

team IQ Team IQ is the ability of a team to perform well by using talent and emotional intelligence.

team process Team process is the way team members work together to accomplish tasks.

team structure A team structure uses permanent and temporary cross-functional teams to improve lateral relations.

teamwork Teamwork is the process of people actively working together to accomplish common goals.

technical skill A technical skill is the ability to use expertise to perform a task with proficiency.

technological competency Technological competency is the ability to understand new technologies and to use them to their best advantage.

telecommuting Telecommuting involves using IT to work at home or outside the office.

terminal values Terminal values are preferences about desired end states.

theory X Theory X assumes people dislike work, lack ambition, are irresponsible, and prefer to be led.

theory Y Theory Y assumes people are willing to work and accept responsibility, are self-directed, and are creative.

tight culture In tight cultures social norms are rigid and clear, and members try to conform.

time orientation Time orientation is the degree to which a society emphasizes short-term or long-term goals.

top managers Top managers guide the performance of the organization as a whole or of one of its major parts.

total quality management (TQM) Total quality management (TQM) commits to quality objectives, continuous improvement, and doing things right the first time.

transactional leadership Transactional leadership directs the efforts of others through tasks, rewards, and structures.

transformational change Transformational change results in a major and comprehensive redirection of the organization.

transformational leadership Transformational leadership is inspirational and arouses extraordinary effort and performance.

transnational corporation A transnational corporation is an MNC that operates worldwide on a borderless basis.

transnational firm A transnational firm tries to operate globally without having a strong national identity.

triple bottom line The triple bottom line of organizational performance includes financial, social, and environmental criteria.

two-tier wage systems Two-tier wage systems pay new hires less than workers already doing the same jobs with more seniority.

Type A personality A Type A personality is oriented toward extreme achievement, impatience, and perfectionism.

U

uncertain environment An uncertain environment lacks so much information that it is difficult to assign probabilities to the likely outcomes of alternatives.

uncertainty avoidance Uncertainty avoidance is the degree to which a society tolerates risk and uncertainty.

unfreezing Unfreezing is the phase during which a situation is prepared for change.

unity of command principle The unity of command principle states that a worker should receive orders from only one boss.

upside-down pyramid The upside-down pyramid view puts customers at the top of the organization being served by workers who are supported by managers below them.

utilitarian view In the utilitarian view, ethical behavior delivers the greatest good to the most people.

V

valence Valence is the value a person assigns to work-related outcomes.

validity Validity means that scores on a selection device have demonstrated links with future job performance.

value-based management Value-based management actively develops, communicates, and enacts shared values.

values Values are broad beliefs about what is appropriate behavior.

venture capitalists Venture capitalists make large investments in new ventures in return for an equity stake in the business.

vertical integration Growth through vertical integration occurs by acquiring suppliers or distributors.

veteran's advantage In entrepreneurship, strong organizational skills and tolerance for risk.

virtual organization A virtual organization uses information technologies to operate as a shifting network of alliances.

virtual team Members of a virtual team work together and solve problems through computer-based interactions.

virtuous circle A virtuous circle exists when corporate social responsibility leads to improved financial performance that leads to more social responsibility.

vision A vision clarifies the purpose of the organization and expresses what it hopes to be in the future.

visionary leadership Visionary leadership brings to the situation a clear sense of the future and an understanding of how to get there.

W

whistleblowers Whistleblowers expose misconduct of organizations and their members.

withdrawal behaviors Withdrawal behaviors include absenteeism (not showing up for work) and turnover (quitting one's job).

work sampling Work sampling evaluates applicants as they perform actual work tasks.

workforce diversity Workforce diversity describes differences among workers in gender, race, age, ethnicity, religion, sexual orientation, and able-bodiedness.

work-life balance Work-life balance involves balancing career demands with personal and family needs.

workplace privacy Workplace privacy is the right to privacy while at work.

workplace rage Workplace rage is aggressive behavior toward co-workers or the work setting.

workplace spirituality Workplace spirituality involves practices that create meaning and shared community among organizational members.

World Trade Organization (WTO) The World Trade Organization (WTO) is a global institution established to promote free trade and open markets around the world.

Z

zero-based budget A zero-based budget allocates resources as if each budget was brand new.

Endnotes

Feature Notes 1

Opening Quote—Wayne Niemi, "Zappos Milestone: Q&A With Tony Hsieh," *Footwear News*, (May 4, 2009). Accessed at: http://about.zappos.com/press-center/media-coverage/zappos-milestone-qa-tony-hsieh.

Slumdog Millionaire—Information and quotes from Manohla Dargis, "Orphan's Lifeline Out of Hell Could Be a Game Show in Mumbai," *New York Times* (November 12, 2008): movies.nytimes.com; and James Christopher, "Slumdog Millionaire," *The Times* (January 8, 2009): entertainment. timesonline.co.uk.

Role Models—Information and quotes from William M. Bulkeley, "Xerox Names Burns Chief as Mulcahy Retires Early," *Wall Street Journal* (May 22, 2009), pp. B1, B2; and Nanette Byrnes and Roger O. Crockett, "An Historic Succession at Xerox," *Business Week* (June 9, 2008), pp. 18–21 Ellen McGurt, "Fresh Copy," *Fast Company* (December 2011/January 2012), news.xerox.com (Accessed August 25, 2012); Drew Fitzgerald and Melodie Warner, Xerox Blames Economy for Lower Profit Outlook," *Wall Street Journal* (July 20, 2012); online.wsj.com (Accessed August 26, 2012); "Xerox Reports Second Quarter 2012 Earnings," Xerox Corporation Website, news.xerox.com (Accessed August 26, 2012); and "Game Changer in Business and Tech: Ursula Burns," *Huffington Post* (November 1, 2011), www.huffingtonpost.com.

Facts to Consider—Information from "The View from the Kitchen Table," *Newsweek* (January 26, 2009), p. 29; and Del Jones, "Women Slowly Gain on Men," *USA Today* (January 2, 2009), p. 6B; Catalyst research reports at www. Catalyst.org; "Nicking the Glass Ceiling," *Business Week* (June 9, 2009), p. 18; Francesco Guerrera and Alan Rappeport, "Women Still to Break Through 'Glass Ceiling' in U.S. Boardroom," *Financial Times*, Kindle Edition (October 19, 2010); "Women on Wall Street Fall Further Behind," *Bloomberg Business Week* (October 11–17, 2010), pp. 46–47.

Ethics Check— Jim Prevor, "Fraud at Your Local Farmer's Market," *Jim Prevor's Perishable Pundit* (February 2, 2011), www.perishablepundit.com (Accessed August 26, 2012); Associated Press, "NY Comptroller Notes Growth of Farmers' Markets," *Wall Street Journal* (August 11, 2012); online. wsj.com (Accessed August 26, 2012); Robert Strauss, "More Farms Vie for the $1 Billion Spent at Farmers' Markets," *BusinessWeek* (May 10, 2012), www. businessweek.com (Accessed August 26, 2011); and Tracie Cohn, "Number of U.S. Farmers Markets Surges," *BusinessWeek* (August 3, 2012), www. businessweek.com (Accessed August 26, 2012).

Hot Topic—Information and quote from Ashley Powers, "Quirky culture, good service attract Zappos.com tourists" *The Columbus Dispatch* (May 19, 2011), p. A12; and "Rhymer Rigby, "The Benefits of Workplace Levity," *Financial Times*, Kindle Edition (December 19, 2012).

Endnotes 1

[1] Quote from Philip Delves Broughton, "A Compelling Vision of a Dystopian Future for Workers and How to Avoid It," *Financial Times*, Kindle Edition (May 19, 2011). See also Lynda Gratton, *The Shift: The Future of Work is Already Here* (London: HarperCollins UK, 2011).

[2] See examples in Carol Hymowitz, "As Managers Climb, They Have to Learn How to Act the Parts," *Wall Street Journal* (November 14, 2005), p. B1.

[3] Information from *Wall Street Journal* (September 21, 2005), p. R4.

[4] For a perspective on the first-line manager's job, see Leonard A. Schlesinger and Janice A. Klein, "The First-Line Supervisor: Past, Present and Future," pp. 370–82, in Jay W. Lorsch (ed.), *Handbook of Organizational Behavior* (Englewood Cliffs, NJ: Prentice-Hall, 1987). Research reported in "Remember Us?" *Economist* (February 1, 1992), p. 71.

[5] For a discussion, see Marcus Buckingham, "What Great Managers Do," *Harvard Business Review* (March 2005). Reprint R0503D.

[6] Shelly Banjo, "Clutter Bluster's Next Foray," *Wall Street Journal* (March 21, 2013), p. B7.

[7] Ibid.

[8] See Alan M. Webber, "Danger: Toxic Company," *Fast Company* (November 1998), pp. 15–21; and Stewart D. Friedman, Perry Christensen, and Jessica De Groot, "Work and Life: The End of the Zero-Sum Game," *Harvard Business Review* (November/December 1998), pp. 119–29.

[9] See George Anders, "Overseeing More Employees—With Fewer Managers," *Wall Street Journal* (March 24, 2008), p. B6; and "Women Come on Board," *Business Week* (June 15, 2009), p. 24.

[10] Banjo, op cit.

[11] Henry Mintzberg, *The Nature of Managerial Work* (New York: Harper & Row, 1973, and HarperCollins, 1997), p. 60.

[12] Ibid., p. 30.

[13] See, for example, John R. Veiga and Kathleen Dechant, "Wired World Woes: www.Help," *Academy of Management Executive*, vol. 11 (August 1997), pp. 73–79.

[14] For a classic study, see Thomas A. Mahoney, Thomas H. Jerdee, and Stephen J. Carroll, "The Job(s) of Management," *Industrial Relations*, vol. 4 (February 1965), pp. 97–110.

[15] This running example is developed from information from "Accountants Have Lives, Too, You Know," *Business Week* (February 23, 1998), pp. 88–90; Silvia Ann Hewlett and Carolyn Buck Luce, "Off-Ramps and On-Ramps: Keeping Talented Women on the Road to Success," *Harvard Business Review* (March 2005), reprint R0503B; and the Ernst & Young Web site: www.Ey.com.

[16] Information on women and men leaving jobs from Hewlett and Luce, op. cit.

[17] See Mintzberg, op. cit. (1973/1997); Henry Mintzberg, "Covert Leadership: The Art of Managing Professionals," *Harvard Business Review* (November/December 1998), pp. 140–47; and Jonathan Gosling and Henry Mintzberg, "The Five Minds of a Manager," *Harvard Business Review* (November 2003), pp. 1–9.

[18] See Mintzberg, op. cit. (1973/1997); Mintzberg, op. cit. (1998); and Gosling and Mintzberg, op. cit. (2003).

[19] Mintzberg (1973/1997), op. cit

[20] Reported in Ray Fisman and Tim Sullivan, "In Defense of the CEO," *The Wall Street Journal* (January 12–13, 2013), pp. C. 3–4. See Oriana Bandiera, Luigi Guiso, Andrea Prat, and Raffaella Sadun, "What Do CEOs Do," Working Paper 11-1081, Harvard Business School (2011)

[21] For research on managerial work see Morgan W. McCall Jr., Ann M. Morrison, and Robert L. Hannan, *Studies of Managerial Work: Results and Methods. Technical Report #9* (Greensboro, NC: Center for Creative Leadership, 1978), pp. 7–9. See also John P. Kotter, "What Effective General Managers Really Do," *Harvard Business Review* (November–December 1982), pp. 156–57.

[22] This incident is taken from John P. Kotter, "What Effective General Managers Really Do," *Harvard Business Review* (November/December 1982), pp. 156–57.

[23] Ibid.

[24] Robert L. Katz, "Skills of an Effective Administrator," *Harvard Business Review* (September/October 1974), p. 94.

[25] See Daniel Goleman's books *Emotional Intelligence* (New York: Bantam, 1995) and *Working with Emotional Intelligence* (New York: Bantam, 1998); and his articles "What Makes a Leader," *Harvard Business Review* (November/December 1998), pp. 93–102, and "Leadership That Makes a Difference," *Harvard Business Review* (March/April 2000), pp. 79–90, quote from p. 80.

[26] Quote from "Insuring Success for the Road," *BizEd* (March/April 2005), p. 19.

[27] Henry Mintzberg, "The Manager's Job: Folklore and Fact," *Harvard Business Review*, vol. 53 (July/August 1975), p. 61. See also Mintzberg, op. cit. (1973/1997).

[28] Information from Micheline Maynard, "A Lifeline Not Made in the USA," *The New York Times* (October 18, 2009): nytimes.com (Accessed April 15, 2010)

[29] This example is updated from Thomas Friedman, *The World Is Flat: A Brief History of the 21st Century* (New York: Farrar, Straus & Giroux, 2005), pp. 208–09. See www8.hp.com/us/en/hp-information/facts.html (Accessed December 7, 2012).

[30]See Joseph E. Stiglitz, *Globalization and Its Discontents* (New York: W.W. Norton, 2003); and Joseph E. Stiglitz, *Making Globalization Work* (New York: W.W. Norton, 2007).

[31]Michael E. Porter, *The Competitive Advantage of Nations: With a New Introduction* (New York: Free Press, 1998).

[32]See for example, John Bussey, "Buck Up America: China is Getting Too Expensive," *The Wall Street Journal* (October 7, 2011), pp. B1,B2.

[33]An Internet search will turn up many news articles reporting the details of the Bernie Madoff scandal.

[34]Portions adapted from John W. Dienhart and Terry Thomas, "Ethical Leadership: A Primer on Ethical Responsibility in Management," in John R. Schermerhorn, Jr. (ed.), *Management*, 7th ed. (New York: Wiley, 2002).

[35]See Judith Burns, "Everything You Wanted to Know About Corporate Governance . . . But Didn't Know How to Ask," *Wall Street Journal* (October 27, 2003), pp. R1, R7.

[36]Daniel Akst, "Room at the Top for Improvement," *Wall Street Journal* (October 26, 2004), p. D8; and Herb Baum and Tammy King, *The Transparent Leader* (New York: HarperCollins, 2005).

[37]*Workforce 2000: Work and Workers for the 21st Century* (Indianapolis: Towers Perrin/Hudson Institute, 1987); Richard W. Judy and Carol D' Amico (eds.), *Work and Workers for the 21st Century* (Indianapolis: Hudson Institute, 1997). See Richard D. Bucher, *Diversity Consciousness: Opening Our Minds to People, Cultures, and Opportunities* (Upper Saddle River, NJ: Prentice-Hall, 2000); R. Roosevelt Thomas, "From Affirmative Action to Affirming Diversity," *Harvard Business Review* (March/April 1990), pp. 107–17; and *Beyond Race and Gender: Unleashing the Power of Your Total Workforce by Managing Diversity* (New York: AMACOM, 1992).

[38]June Kronholz, "Hispanics Gain in Census," *Wall Street Journal* (May 10, 2006), p. A6; Phillip Toledano, "Demographics: The Population Hourglass," *Fast Company* (March, 2006), p. 56; June Kronholz, "Racial Identity's Gray Area," *Wall Street Journal* (June 12, 2008), p. A10; "We're Getting Old," *Wall Street Journal* (March 26, 2009), p. D2; Les Christie, "Hispanic Population Boom Fuels Rising U.S. Diversity," *CnnMoney:* www.cnn.com; Betsy Towner, "The New Face of 501 America," *AARP Bulletin* (June 2009), p. 31; "Los U.S.A.: Latin Population Grows Faster, Spreads Wider," *Wall Street Journal* (March 25, 2011), p. A1; and, Laura Meckler, "Hispanic Future in the Cards," *The Wall Street Journal* (December 13, 2012), p. A3.

[39]Information from "Racism in Hiring Remains, Study Says," *Columbus Dispatch* (January 17, 2003), p. B2.

[40]For discussions of the glass ceiling effect, see Ann M. Morrison, Randall P. White, and Ellen Van Velso, *Breaking the Glass Ceiling* (Reading, MA: Addison-Wesley, 1987); Anne E. Weiss. *The Glass Ceiling: A Look at Women in the Workforce* (New York: Twenty First Century, 1999); and Debra E. Meyerson and Joyce K. Fletcher, "A Modest Manifesto for Shattering the Glass Ceiling," *Harvard Business Review* (January/February 2000).

[41]For background, see Taylor Cox, Jr., "The Multicultural Organization," *Academy of Management Executive*, vol. 5 (1991), pp. 34–47; and *Cultural Diversity in Organizations: Theory, Research and Practice* (San Francisco: Berrett-Koehler, 1993).

[42]See "Women Come on Board," *Business Week* (June 15, 2009), p. 24.

[43]Survey data reported in Sue Shellenbarger, "New Workplace Equalizer: Ambition," *Wall Street Journal* (March 26, 2009), p. D5.

[44]Judith B. Rosener, "Women Make Good Managers, So What?" *Business Week* (December 11, 2000), p. 24.

[45]*Business Week* (August 8, 1990), p. 50.

[46]Thomas, op. cit.

[47]See Tom Peters, "The Brand Called You," *Fast Company* (August/September 1997), p. 83.

[48]Charles Handy, *The Age of Unreason* (Cambridge, MA: Harvard Business School Press, 1990). See also Michael S. Malone, *The Future Arrived Yesterday: The Rise of the Protean Organization and What It Means for You* (New York: Crown Books, 2009).

[49]See Gareille Monaghan, "Don't Get a Job, Get a Portfolio Career," *The Sunday Times* (April 26, 2009), p. 15.

[50]Dave Ulrich, "Intellectual Capital = Competency × Commitment," *Harvard Business Review* (Winter, 1998), pp. 15–26.

[51]Max DePree's books include *Leadership Is an Art* (New York: Dell, 1990) and *Leadership Jazz* (New York: Dell, 1993). See also Herman Miller's home page at www.Hermanmiller.com.

[52]See Peter F. Drucker, *The Changing World of the Executive* (New York: T.T. Times Books, 1982), and *The Profession of Management* (Cambridge, MA: Harvard Business School Press, 1997); and Francis Horibe, *Managing Knowledge Workers: New Skills and Attitudes to Unlock the Intellectual Capital in Your Organization* (New York: Wiley, 1999).

[53]Daniel Pink, A Whole New Mind: Moving from the Information Age to the Conceptual Age (New York: Riverhead Books, 2005).

[54]Peters, op. cit.

Feature Notes 2

Role Models—Information from Marc Kielburger and Craig Kielburger. *From Me to We: Finding Meaning in a Material World* (New York, NY: John Wiley & Sons, 2006); "Oprah Winfrey," *TIME* (March 12, 2001), www.time.com (Accessed August 27, 2012); Oprah Website, "Oprah's Angel Network Fact Sheet," www.oprah.com; and Oprah Winfrey Leadership Academy for Girls Website. www.owla.co.za (Accessed August 27, 2012).

Facts to Consider—Information and quotes from "Generation Gap: On Their Bosses, Millennials Happier than Boomers," *Wall Street Journal* (November 15, 2010), p. B6.

Ethics Check—Heather Tooley. "Personal Internet Usage in the Workplace—a Serious Epidemic," January 17, 2010, Yahoo! Contributor Network; and, voices.yahoo.com (Accessed September 2, 2012).

Life Is Good—Information from Leigh Buchanan, "Life Lessons, Inc." (June 6, 2006): www.inc.com, "A Fortune Coined from Cheerfulness Entrepreneurship," *Financial Times* (May 20, 2009); and www.lifeisgood.com.

Photo Essays—Millennials—Information from "Why More Millennials Go Part-time for Full-time Pay," cnbc.com (accessed October 2, 2012). Crowdsourcing Grades—Adam F. Falk, "In Defense of the Living, Breathing Professor," *The Wall Street Journal*, Kindle Edition (August 29, 2012).

Hot Topic—Information and quote from Dan Ariely, "Coming to Grips with Chips and Dips," *The Wall Street Journal* (January 19-20, 2013), p. C12. See Dan Ariely, *The (Honest) Truth About Dishonesty: How We Lie to Everyone—Especially Ourselves* (New York: Harper, 2012).

Endnotes 2

[1]A thorough review and critique of the history of management thought, including management in ancient civilizations, is provided by Daniel A. Wren, *The Evolution of Management Thought*, 4th ed. (New York: Wiley, 1993).

[2]For a timeline of 20th-century management ideas, see "75 Years of Management Ideas and Practices: 1922–1997," *Harvard Business Review*, supplement (September/October 1997).

[3]For a sample of this work, see Henry L. Gantt, *Industrial Leadership* (Easton, MD: Hive, 1921; Hive edition published in 1974); Henry C. Metcalfe and Lyndall Urwick (eds.), *Dynamic Administration: The Collected Papers of Mary Parker Follett* (New York: Harper & Brothers, 1940); James D. Mooney, *The Principles of Administration*, rev. ed. (New York: Harper & Brothers, 1947); and Lyndall Urwick, *The Elements of Administration* (New York: Harper & Brothers, 1943) and *The Golden Book of Management* (London: N. Neame, 1956).

[4]References on Taylor's work are from Frederick W. Taylor, *The Principles of Scientific Management* (New York: W. W. Norton, 1967), originally published by Harper & Brothers in 1911. See Charles W. Wrege and Amedeo G. Perroni, "Taylor's Pig-Tale: A Historical Analysis of Frederick W. Taylor's Pig Iron Experiments," *Academy of Management Journal*, vol. 17 (March 1974), pp. 6–27, for a criticism; see Edwin A. Locke, "The Ideas of Frederick W. Taylor: An Evaluation," *Academy of Management Review*, vol. 7 (1982), p. 14, for an examination of the contemporary significance of Taylor's work. See also the biography by Robert Kanigel, *The One Best Way* (New York: Viking, 1997).

[5]Frank Gilbreth, *Motion Study* (New York: Van Nostrand, 1911).

[6]For current examples see Ben Worthen, "Do You Need to Work Faster? Get a Bigger Computer Monitor," *Wall Street Journal* (March 25, 2008), p. B8; and "Plant Seeks Savings with Shot-Clock Approach," *The Messenger*, Athens, Ohio (November 15, 2009), p. A3.

[7]Kanigel, op. cit.

[8]Opening quote from A. M. Henderson and Talcott Parsons (eds. and trans.), *Max Weber: The Theory of Social Economic Organization* (New York: Free Press, 1947), p. 337.

[9]Ibid.

[10]Available in the English language as Henri Fayol, *General and Industrial Administration* (London: Pitman, 1949); subsequent discussion relies on M. B. Brodie, *Fayol on Administration* (London: Pitman, 1949).

[11]M. P. Follett, *Freedom and Coordination* (London: Management Publications Trust, 1949).

[12]Pauline Graham, *Mary Parker Follett—Prophet of Management: A Celebration of Writings from the 1920s* (Boston: Harvard Business School Press, 1995).

[13]Information from "Honesty Top Trait for Chair," *Columbus Dispatch* (January 15, 2003), p. G1.

[14]See Peter F. Drucker, "Looking Ahead: Implications of the Present," *Harvard Business Review* (September/October, 1997), pp. 18–32.

[15]The Hawthorne studies are described in detail in F. J. Roethlisberger and William J. Dickson, *Management and the Worker* (Cambridge, MA: Harvard University Press, 1966); and G. Homans, *Fatigue of Workers* (New York: Reinhold, 1941). For an interview with three of the participants in the relay-assembly test-room studies, see R. G. Greenwood, A. A. Bolton, and R. A. Greenwood, "Hawthorne a Half Century Later: 'Relay Assembly Participants Remember,'" *Journal of Management*, vol. 9 (1983), pp. 217–31.

[16]The criticisms of the Hawthorne studies are detailed in Alex Carey, "The Hawthorne Studies: A Radical Criticism," *American Sociological Review*, vol. 32 (1967), pp. 403–16; H. M. Parsons, "What Happened at Hawthorne?" *Science*, vol. 183 (1974), pp. 922–32; and B. Rice, "The Hawthorne Defect: Persistence of a Flawed Theory," *Psychology Today*, vol. 16 (1982), pp. 70–74. See also Wren, op. cit.

[17]This discussion of Maslow's theory is based on Abraham H. Maslow, *Eupsychian Management* (Homewood, IL: Richard D. Irwin, 1965); and Abraham H. Maslow, *Motivation and Personality*, 2nd ed. (New York: Harper & Row, 1970).

[18]Douglas McGregor, *The Human Side of Enterprise* (New York: McGraw-Hill, 1960).

[19]See Gary Heil, Deborah F. Stevens, and Warren G. Bennis, *Douglas McGregor on Management: Revisiting the Human Side of Enterprise* (New York: Wiley, 2000).

[20]Chris Argyris, *Personality and Organization* (New York: Harper & Row, 1957).

[21]Information on attitude survey in the federal bureaucracy from David E. Rosenbaum, "Study Ranks Homeland Security Dept. Lowest in Morale," *New York Times* (October 16, 2005), p. 17.

[22]Scott Morrison, "Google Searches for Staffing Answers," *Wall Street Journal* (May 19, 2009), p. B1.

[23]Thomas H. Davenport, Jeanne G. Harris, and Robert Morison, *Analytics at Work: Smarter Decisions, Better Results* (Cambridge, MA: Harvard Business Press, 2010).

[24]The ideas of Ludwig von Bertalanffy contributed to the emergence of this systems perspective on organizations. See his article, "The History and Status of General Systems Theory," *Academy of Management Journal*, vol. 15 (1972), pp. 407–26. This viewpoint is further developed by Daniel Katz and Robert L. Kahn in their classic book, *The Social Psychology of Organizations* (New York: Wiley, 1978). For an integrated systems view, see Lane Tracy, *The Living Organization* (New York: Quorum Books, 1994). For an overview, see W. Richard Scott, *Organizations: Rational, Natural, and Open Systems*, 4th ed. (Upper Saddle River, NJ: Prentice Hall, 1998).

[25]See discussion by Scott, op. cit., pp. 66–68.

[26]For an overview, see ibid., pp. 95–97.

[27]W. Edwards Deming, *Quality, Productivity, and Competitive Position* (Cambridge, MA: MIT Press, 1982), and Rafael Aguay, *Dr. Deming: The American Who Taught the Japanese about Quality* (New York: Free Press, 1997).

[28]See Howard S. Gitlow and Shelly J. Gitlow, *The Deming Guide to Quality and Competitive Position* (Englewood Cliffs, NJ: Prentice-Hall, 1987).

[29]See Edward E. Lawler III, Susan Albers Mohrman, and Gerald E. Ledford, Jr., *Employee Involvement and Total Quality Management: Practices and Results in Fortune 1000 Companies* (San Francisco: Jossey-Bass, 1992).

[30]See William C. Bogner, "Tom Peters on the Real World of Business" and "Robert Waterman on Being Smart and Lucky," *Academy of Management Executive*, vol. 16 (2002), pp. 40–50.

[31]See Jim Collins and Jerry I. Porras, *Built to Last* (New York: HarperCollins, 1994); and Jim Collins, *Good to Great* (New York: HarperCollins, 2001). For recent research critical of Collins's work, see Bruce G. Resnick and Timothy L. Smunt, "From Good to Great to . . . ," *Academy of Management Perspectives* (November, 2008), pp. 6–12; and Bruce Niendorf and Kristine Beck, "Good to Great, or Just Good?" *Academy of Management Perspectives* (November, 2008), pp. 13–20.

[32]See Bruce G. Resnick and Timothy L. Smunt, "From Good to Great to . . ." *Academy of Management Perspectives* (November, 2008), pp. 6–12; and, "Bruce Niendorf and Kristine Beck, "Good to Great, or Just Good?" *Academy of Management Perspectives* (November, 2008), pp. 13–20.

[33]Jim Collins, *How the Mighty Fall: And Why Some Companies Never Give In* (New York: HarperCollins, 2009).

[34]Jeffrey Pfeffer and Robert I. Sutton, *Hard Facts, Dangerous Half-Truths, and Total Nonsense: Profiting from Evidence-Based Management* (Boston: Harvard Business School Press, 2006); Jeffrey Pfeffer and Robert I. Sutton, "Management Half-Truths and Nonsense," *California Management Review*, vol. 48 (2006), pp. 77–100; and Jeffrey Pfeffer and Robert I. Sutton, "Evidence-Based Management," *Harvard Business Review* (January, 2006), R0601E.

[35]Jeffrey Pfeffer, *The Human Equation: Building Profits by Putting People First* (Boston: Harvard Business School Press, 1998); and Z. Charles O'Reilly III and Jeffrey Pfeffer, *Hidden Value: How Great Companies Achieve Extraordinary Results with Ordinary People* (Boston: Harvard Business School Press, 2000).

[36]Denise M. Rousseau, "On Organizational Behavior," *BizEd* (May/June, 2008), pp. 30–31.

Feature Notes 3

Role Models—Information and quotes from stonyfieldfarms.com, notablebiographies.com, and "25 Rich Ass Greenies Who Made Their Fortune Saving the Environment," earthfirst.com (August 25, 2008).

Facts to Consider—Information from Deloitte LLP, "Leadership Counts: 2007 Deloitte & Touche USA Ethics & Workplace Survey Results," *Kiplinger Business Resource Center* (June, 2007): www.kiplinger.com

Ethics Check—Example and quote from Morice Mendoza, "How to Create a Green Supply Chain," *Financial Times*, Kindle Edition (November 11, 2010).

Find Inspiration—Information and quotes from Carolyn Y. Woo, "Lives, Not Just Livelihoods," *BizEd Magazine* (May/June, 2011), pp. 41–45; John Rivera, "CRS Names Carolyn Woo New President, CEO," crs.org (accessed February 21, 2012); and, "The Ten Principles," www.unglobalcompact.org.

Manager's Library—Information from Alan Murray, "Chicken Soup for a Davos Soul," *Wall Street Journal* (January 17, 2013), p. A15; and Anthony J. Sadar, "Book Review: *Conscious Capitalism*," *Washington Times* (March 20, 2013): washingtontimes.com (accessed March 22, 2013).

Photo Essays—Cheating—Pamela Engel, "Students Don't Cheat; They Collaborate?" *The Columbus Dispatch* (September 10, 2012): dispatch.com. Women on Board—Information from Rachel Soares Christopher Marquis and Mathew Lee, "Gender and Corporate Social Responsibility. It's a matter of Sustainability," *Catayst* (2011); Joseph Schumpeter, "The mommy track," *The Economist*, Kindle Edition (August 25, 2012); Jill Parkin, "Women at Director Level Help to Make a Marque, *Financial Times*, Kindle Edition (May 22, 2012); "Gender Politics," *The Economist*, Kindle Edition (September 7, 2012); Joann S. Lublin, "Europe's Boards Recruit U.S. Women," *The Wall Street Journal* (September 12, 2012), p. B8; James Fontanella-Khan, "EU Scraps Board Quotas for Women," *Financial Times*, Kindle Edition (October 24, 2012); and, Jeff Green, "The Boardroom's Still the Boys' Room," *Bloomberg BusinessWeek* (October 29–November 4, 2012), pp. 25–26.

Hot Topic—Data reported in Andrew Hill, "Business Leaders Focus on their Staff," *Financial Times* (January 9, 2013), Kindle Edition.

Endnotes 3

[1]See the discussion by Terry Thomas, John W. Dienhart, and John R. Schermerhorn, Jr., "Leading Toward Ethical Behavior in Business," *Academy of Management Executive*, vol. 18 (May 2004), pp. 56–66.

[2]See the discussion by Lynn Sharpe Paine, "Managing for Organizational Integrity," *Harvard Business Review* (March/April 1994), pp. 106–17.

[3]Desmond Tutu, "Do More Than Win," *Fortune* (December 30, 1991), p. 59.

[4]Ibid.

[5]For an overview, see Linda K. Trevino and Katherine A. Nelson, *Managing Business Ethics*, 3rd ed. (New York: Wiley, 2003).

[6]Information from Sue Shellenbarger, "How and Why We Lie at the Office: From Pilfered Pens to Padded Accounts," *Wall Street Journal* (March 24, 2005), p. D1.

[7]Milton Rokeach, *The Nature of Human Values* (New York: Free Press, 1973). See also W. C. Frederick and J. Weber, "The Values of Corporate Executives and Their Critics: An Empirical Description and Normative Implications," in W. C. Frederick and L. E. Preston (eds.), *Business Ethics: Research Issues and Empirical Studies* (Greenwich, CT: JAI Press, 1990).

[8]Case reported in Michelle Conlin, "Cheating—Or Postmodern Learning?" *Business Week* (May 14, 2007), p. 42.

[9]See Gerald F. Cavanagh, Dennis J. Moberg, and Manuel Velasquez, "The Ethics of Organizational Politics," *Academy of Management Review*, vol. 6 (1981), pp. 363–74; Justin G. Locknecker, Joseph A. McKinney, and Carlos W. Moore, "Egoism and Independence: Entrepreneurial Ethics," *Organizational Dynamics* (Winter 1988), pp. 64–72; and Justin G. Locknecker, Joseph A. McKinney, and Carlos W. Moore, "The Generation Gap in Business Ethics," *Business Horizons* (September/October 1989), pp. 9–14.

[10]Raymond L. Hilgert, "What Ever Happened to Ethics in Business and in Business Schools?" *The Diary of Alpha Kappa Psi* (April 1989), pp. 4–8.

[11]Jerald Greenburg, "Organizational Justice: Yesterday, Today, and Tomorrow," *Journal of Management*, vol. 16 (1990), pp. 399–432; and Mary A. Konovsky, "Understanding Procedural Justice and Its Impact on Business Organizations," *Journal of Management*, vol. 26 (2000), pp. 489–511.

[12]Interactional justice is described by Robert J. Bies, "The Predicament of Injustice: The Management of Moral Outrage," in L. L. Cummings & B. M. Staw (eds.), *Research in Organizational Behavior*, vol. 9 (Greenwich, CT: JAI Press, 1987), pp. 289–319. The example is from Carol T. Kulik & Robert L. Holbrook, "Demographics in Service Encounters: Effects of Racial and Gender Congruence on Perceived Fairness," *Social Justice Research*, vol. 13 (2000), pp. 375–402.

[13]See, for example, M. Fortin and M. R. Fellenz, 2008. "Hypocrisies of Fairness: Towards a More Reflexive Ethical Base in Organizational Justice Research and Practice," *Journal of Business Ethics*, vol. 78 (2008), pp. 415–433.

[14]The United Nations Universal Declaration of Human Rights is available online at: http://www.un.org/Overview/rights.html.

[15]Robert D. Haas, "Ethics—A Global Business Challenge," *Vital Speeches of the Day* (June 1, 1996), pp. 506–9.

[16]This discussion is based on Thomas Donaldson, "Values in Tension: Ethics Away from Home," *Harvard Business Review*, vol. 74 (September/October 1996), pp. 48–62.

[17]Ibid; Thomas Donaldson and Thomas W. Dunfee, "Towards a Unified Conception of Business Ethics: Integrative Social Contracts Theory," *Academy of Management Review*, vol. 19 (1994), pp. 252–85.

[18]Developed from Donaldson, op. cit.

[19]Reported in Barbara Ley Toffler, "Tough Choices: Managers Talk Ethics," *New Management*, vol. 4 (1987), pp. 34–39. See also Barbara Ley Toffler, *Tough Choices: Managers Talk Ethics* (New York: Wiley, 1986).

[20]See discussion by Trevino and Nelson, op. cit., pp. 47–62.

[21]Information from Steven N. Brenner and Earl A. Mollander, "Is the Ethics of Business Changing?" *Harvard Business Review*, vol. 55 (January/February 1977).

[22]Deloitte LLP, "Leadership Counts: 2007 Deloitte & Touche USA Ethics & Workplace Survey Results," *Kiplinger Business Resource Center* (June, 2007): www.kiplinger.com.

[23]"Who's to Blame: Washington or Wall Street?" *Newsweek* (March 30, 2009): www.newsweek.com.

[24]This research is summarized by Archie Carroll, "Pressure May Force Ethical Hand," *BGS International Exchange* (Fall 2004), p. 5.

[25]Ibid.

[26]Ibid.

[27]Saul W. Gellerman, "Why 'Good' Managers Make Bad Ethical Choices," *Harvard Business Review*, vol. 64 (July/August, 1986), pp. 85–90.

[28]Stephen Moore, "The Conscience of a Capitalist," *Wall Street Journal* (October 3–4, 2009), p. A11.

[29]Survey results from Del Jones, "48% of Workers Admit to Unethical or Illegal Acts," *USA Today* (April 4, 1997), p. A1.

[30]Lawrence Kohlberg, *The Psychology of Moral Development: The Nature and Validity of Moral Stages* (*Essays in Moral Development*, Volume 2) (New York: HarperCollins, 1984). See also the discussion by Linda K. Trevino, "Moral Reasoning and Business Ethics: Implications for Research, Education, and Management," *Journal of Business Ethics*, vol. 11 (1992), pp. 445–59.

[31]Information from "Gifts of Gab: A Start-Up's Social Conscience Pays Off," *Business Week* (February 5, 2001), p. F38.

[32]Developed from recommendations of the Government Accountability Project reported in "Blowing the Whistle without Paying the Piper," *Business Week* (June 3, 1991): businessweek.com/archives.

[33]Archie B. Carroll, "In Search of the Moral Manager," *Business Horizons* (March/April, 2001), pp. 7–15.

[34]Kohlberg, op. cit.

[35]See, for example, David Bielo, "MBA Programs for Social and Environmental Stewardship," *Business Ethics* (Fall 2005), pp. 22–28.

[36]See the Josephson model for ethical decision making: www. josephson-institute.org.

[37]Examples from "Whistle-Blowers on Trial," *Business Week* (March 24, 1997), pp. 172–78; and "NLRB Judge Rules for Massachusetts Nurses in Whistle-Blowing Case," *American Nurse* (January/February 1998), p. 7. For a review of whistleblowing, see Marcia P. Micelli and Janet P. Near, *Blowing the Whistle* (Lexington, MA: Lexington Books, 1992); Micelli and Near, "Whistleblowing: Reaping the Benefits," *Academy of Management Executive*, vol. 8 (August 1994), pp. 65–72; and Cynthia Cooper, *Extraordinary Circumstances* (Hoboken, NJ: Wiley, 2009).

[38]Information from Ethics Resource Center, "Major Survey of America's Workers Finds Substantial Improvements in Ethics": www.ethics.org/releases/nr_2003052l_nbes.html.

[39]Information from James A. Waters, "Catch 20.5: Mortality as an Organizational Phenomenon," *Organizational Dynamics*, vol. 6 (Spring 1978), pp. 3–15.

[40]Information from corporate Web site: www.gapinc.com/communitysourcing/vendor_conduct.htm.

[41]See Marc Gunther, "Can Factory Monitoring Ever Really Work?" *Business Ethics* (Fall 2005), p. 12.

[42]Information from corporate Web site: www.gapinc.com/communitysourcing/vendor_conduct.htm.

[43]See David Vogel, *The Market for Virtue: The Potential and Limits of Corporate Social Responsibility* (Washington, DC: Brookings Institution Press, 2006); and Thomas et al., op. cit.

[44]For more on this notion, see Alfred A. Marcus and Adam R. Fremeth, "Green Management Matters Regardless," *Academy of Management Perspectives*, vol. 23 (August, 2009), pp. 17–26; and Jeffrey Pfeffer, "Building Sustainable Organizations: The Human Factor," *Academy of Management Perspectives*, vol. 24 (February, 2010), pp. 34–45.

[45]Joe Biesecker, "What Today's College Graduates Want: It's Not All About Paychecks," *Central Penn Business Journal* (August 10, 2007).

[46]Sarah E. Needleman, "The Latest Office Perk: Getting Paid to Volunteer," *Wall Street Journal* (April 29, 2008), p. D1.

[47]The historical framework of this discussion is developed from Keith Davis, "The Case For and Against Business Assumption of Social Responsibility," *Academy of Management Journal* (June 1973), pp. 312–22; Keith Davis and William Frederick, *Business and Society: Management: Public Policy, Ethics*, 5th ed. (New York: McGraw-Hill, 1984). This debate is discussed by Joel Makower in *Putting Social Responsibility to Work for Your Business and the World* (New York: Simon & Schuster, 1994), pp. 28–33. See also Aneel Karnani, "The Case Against Social Responsibility," *Wall Street Journal* (August 23, 2010); www.usj.com.

[48]The Friedman quotation is from Milton Friedman, *Capitalism and Freedom* (Chicago: University of Chicago Press, 1962); the Samuelson quotation is from Paul A. Samuelson, "Love That Corporation," *Mountain Bell Magazine* (Spring 1971). Both are cited in Davis, op. cit.

[49]See James K. Glassman, "When Ethics Meet Earnings," *International Herald Tribune* (May 24–25, 2003), p. 15; Simon Zaydek, "The Path to Corporate Social Responsibility," *Harvard Business Review* (December 2004), pp. 125–32.

[50]See Makower, op. cit. (1994), pp. 71–75; Sandra A. Waddock and Samuel B. Graves, "The Corporate Social Performance–Financial Performance Link," *Strategic Management Journal* (1997), pp. 303–19: and Vogel, op. cit. (2006).

[51]Michael E. Porter and Mark R. Kramer, "Shared Value: How to Reinvent Capitalism and Unleash a Wave of Innovation and Growth," *Harvard Business Review* (January–February, 2011), pp. 62–77.

[52]Ibid, p. 64.

[53]Information and quotes from Mara Lemos-Stein, "Talking About Waste with P&G," *Wall Street Journal* (September 13, 2011), p. R8; and "Benefits Flow as Top People Join the Battle," *Financial Times*, Kindle edition (June 23, 2011); www.nestle.com/csv/ruraldevelopment/responsiblesourcing (retrieved February 18, 2012); "How to Create a Green Supply Chain," *Financial Times*, Kindle Edition (November 11, 2010); and Information from Steve Lohr, "First, Make Money. Also, Do Good." *New York Times* (August 13, 2011): nytimes.com

[54]Abuses of microcredit lending have been publicized in the press, and both the microfinance industry as a whole and the Grameen Bank in particular have been criticized by the Bangladesh government. Muhammad Yunus published his own criticism of the industry and defense of the Grameen Bank model in "Sacrificing Microcredit for Megaprofits," *The New York Times* (January 14, 2011): nytimes.com. A Norwegian documentary that aired criticisms of how Yunus and Grameen Bank handled funds has largely been refuted, but Yunus continues to be criticized by the Bangladesh government.

[55]David Bornstein, *How to Change the World—Social Entrepreneurs and the Power of New Ideas* (Oxford, UK: Oxford University Press, 2004).

[56]See Laura D'Andrea Tyson, "Good Works—With a Business Plan," *Business Week* (May 3, 2004), retrieved from Business Week Online (November 14, 2005) at www.Businessweek.com.

[57]Chip Fleiss, "Social Enterprise—the Fiegling Fourth Sector Soapbox," *Financial Times* (June 15, 2009).

[58]Drucker quote referenced and discussed at www.druckersociety.at/repository/newsletter/09/newsletter.html.

[59]Archie B. Carroll, "A Three-Dimensional Model of Corporate Performance," *Academy of Management Review*, vol. 4 (1979), pp. 497–505. Carroll's continuing work in this area is reported in Mark S. Schwartz and Archie B. Carroll, "Corporate Social Responsibility: A Three Domain Approach," *Business Ethics Quarterly*, vol. 13 (2003), pp. 503–30.

[60]See the discussion by Porter and Kramer, op. cit.

[61]Examples from Jim Phillips, "Business Leaders Say 'Green' Approach Doable," *Athens News* (March 27, 2008): www.athensnews.com; "The Bottom Line on Business and the Environment," Wall Street Journal (February 12, 2009), p. A7; and Alan G. Robinson and Dean M. Schroeder, "Greener and Cheaper," *Wall Street Journal* (March 23, 2009), p. R4.

[62]Information from Helen Jones, "CEOs Now Find that Principles and Profits Can Mix Well," *Wall Street Journal* (November 22, 2010), p. R5.

[63]Ibid.

[64]Ibid.

[65]Definition from www.sustainablebusiness.com.

[66]www.wbcsd.org.

[67]"Eco-nomics—Creating Environmental Capital," *Wall Street Journal* (March 8, 2010), p. R1.

[68]From www.iso.org.

[69]"Indra Nooyi of Pepsico, View from the Top," *Financial Times*: www.ft.com (February 1, 2010), retrieved March 11, 2010.

[70]Pfeffer, op cit. See also, Jeffrey Pfeffer, "Shareholders First? Not So Fast . . ." *Harvard Business Review* (July–August, 2009), pp. 89–91.

Feature Notes 4

Opening Quote—"Last Miner Out Hailed as a Shift Boss Who Kept Group Alive," news.blog.cnn.com (October 14, 2010).

Role Models—Information from Kate Klonick, "Pepsi's CEO a Refreshing Change" (August 15, 2006): www.abcnews.com; Diane Brady, "Indra Nooyi: Keeping Cool in Hot Water," *Business Week* (June 11, 2007), special report; Indra Nooyi, "The Best Advice I Ever Got," *CNNMoney* (April 30, 2008): www.cnnmoney.com; "Indra Nooyi," *Wall Street Journal* (November 10, 2008), p. R3; and "Indra Nooyi of PepsiCo," View from the Top, *Financial Times*: www.ft.com (February 1, 2010), retrieved March 11, 2010; Gary Burnison. "How Pepsi's Indra Nooyi Learned to be a CEO," *Fast Company* (April 29, 2011), http://www.fastcompany.com (Accessed September 6, 2012); and, Geoff Colvin, "Indra Nooyi's Pepsi Challenge," *Fortune* (May 29, 2012) http://management.fortune.cnn (Accessed September 5, 2012).

Facts to Consider—Information from Elizabeth G. Olson, "What are American Workers' Biggest Fears? *CNNMoney* (September 13, 2012): mNfwmwnr.doerunw.xnn.xom/2012/09/13 .

Ethics Check—Story reported in and quotes from *Economist* (June 17, 2006), vol. 379, issue 8482, pp. 65–66, 2p, 1c.

Hot Topic—Information and quotes from Claire Suddath, "Work-from-Home Truths, Half-Truths, and Myths," *Bloomberg BusinessWeek* (March 4–10, 2013), p. 75; and, Rick Hampson, "Boss vs. You: The Work-from-Home Tug of War," *USA Today* (March 13, 2013), pp. 2, 2A.

Endnotes 4

[1]Information and quotes from "Last Miner Out Hailed as a Shift Boss Who Kept Group Alive," news.blog.cnn.com (October 14, 2010); and Eva Bergara, "Chilean Miners Honored in Ceremony, Football Game," news.yahoo.com (October 25, 2010).

[2]Peter F. Drucker, "Looking Ahead: Implications of the Present," *Harvard Business Review* (September/October 1997), pp. 18–32. See also Shaker A. Zahra, "An Interview with Peter Drucker," *Academy of Management Executive*, vol. 17 (August 2003), pp. 9–12.

[3] For a good discussion see Michael S. Hopkins, Steve LaValle, Fred Balboni, Nina Kruschwitz, and Rebecca Shokley, "10 Insights: First Look at the New Intelligent Enterprise Survey on Winning with Data," *Sloan Management Review*, Vol. 52 (Fall, 2010), pp. 22–27.

[4]For a good discussion, see Watson H. Agor, *Intuition in Organizations: Leading and Managing Productively* (Newbury Park, CA: Sage, 1989); Herbert A. Simon, "Making Management Decisions: The Role of Intuition and Emotion," *Academy of Management Executive*, vol. 1 (1987), pp. 57–64; Orlando Behling and Norman L. Eckel, "Making Sense Out of Intuition," *Academy of Management Executive*, vol. 1 (1987), pp. 57–64; Orlando Behling and Norman L. Eckel, "Making Sense Out of Intuition," *Academy of Management Executive*, vol. 5 (1991), pp. 46–54.

[5]Alan Deutschman, "Inside the Mind of Jeff Bezos," *Fast Company*, Issue 85 (August, 2004); www.fastcompany.com.

[6]Quote from Susan Carey, "Pilot 'in Shock' as He Landed Jet in River," *Wall Street Journal* (February 9, 2009), p. A6.

[7]Based on Carl Jung's typology, as described in Donald Bowen, "Learning and Problem-Solving: You're Never Too Jung," in Donald D. Bowen, Roy J. Lewicki, Donald T. Hall, and Francine S. Hall, eds., *Experiences in Management and Organizational Behavior*, 4th ed. (New York: Wiley, 1997), pp. 7–13; and John W. Slocum Jr., "Cognitive Style in Learning and Problem Solving," in ibid., pp. 349–53.

[8]See Hugh Courtney, Jane Kirkland, and Patrick Viguerie, "Strategy Under Uncertainty," *Harvard Business Review* (November/December 1997), pp. 67–79.

[9]See George P. Huber, *Managerial Decision Making* (Glenview, IL: Scott, Foresman, 1975). For a comparison, see the steps in Xerox's problem-solving process, as described in David A. Garvin, "Building a Learning Organization," *Harvard Business Review* (July/August 1993), pp. 78–91; and the Josephson model for ethical decision making described at www.josephsoninstitute.org.

[10]Joseph B. White and Lee Hawkins Jr., "GM Cuts Deeper in North America," *Wall Street Journal* (November 22, 2005), p. A3. See also Rick Wagoner, "A Portrait of My Industry," *Wall Street Journal* (December 6, 2005), p. A20.

[11]See Herbert A. Simon, *Administrative Behavior* (New York: Free Press, 1947); James G. March and Herbert A. Simon, *Organizations* (New York: Wiley, 1958); and Herbert A. Simon, *The New Science of Management Decision* (New York: Harper, 1960).

[12]This figure and the related discussion is developed from conversations with Dr. Alma Acevedo of the University of Puerto Rico at Rio Piedras and her articles "Of Fallacies and Curricula: A Case of Business Ethics," *Teaching Business Ethics*, vol. 5 (2001), pp. 157–170; and "Business Ethics: An Introduction," working paper (2009).

[13]Based on Gerald F. Cavanagh, *American Business Values*, 4th ed. (Upper Saddle River, NJ: Prentice-Hall, 1998).

[14]The third spotlight question is based on the Josephson model for ethical decision making: www.josephsoninstitute.org.

[15]Example from Dayton Fandray, "Assumed Innocent: Hidden and Unexamined Assumptions Can Ruin your Day," *Continental.com/Magazine* (December 2007), p. 100.

[16]See, for example, Roger von Oech, *A Whack on the Side of the Head* (New York: Warner Books, 1983) and *A Kick in the Seat of the Pants* (New York: Harper & Row, 1986).

[17]For discussions of Big-C creativity and Little-C creativity see James C. Kaufman and Ronald A. Beghetto, "Beyond Big and Little: The Four C Model of Creativity," *Review of General Psychology*, vol. 13 (2009), pp. 1–12. My thanks go to Dr. Erin Fluge of Southeastern Missouri State University for bringing this useful distinction to my attention.

[18]Teresa M. Amabile, "Motivating Creativity in Organizations," *California Management Review*, vol. 40 (Fall, 1997), pp. 39–58.

[19]Developed from discussions by Edward DeBono, *Lateral Thinking: Creativity Step-by-Step* (New York: HarperCollins, 1970); John S. Dacey and Kathleen H. Lennon, *Understanding Creativity* (San Francisco: Jossey-Bass, 1998); and Bettina von Stamm, *Managing Innovation, Design & Creativity* (Chichester, England: Wiley, 2003).

[20]The classic work is Norman R. Maier, "Assets and Liabilities in Group Problem Solving," *Psychological Review*, vol. 74 (1967), pp. 239–49.

[21]This presentation is based on the work of R. H. Hogarth, D. Kahneman, A. Tversky, and others, as discussed in Max H. Bazerman, *Judgment in Managerial Decision Making*, 3rd ed. (New York: Wiley, 1994).

[22]Barry M. Staw, "The Escalation of Commitment to a Course of Action," *Academy of Management Review*, vol. 6 (1981), pp. 577–87; and Barry M. Staw and Jerry Ross, "Knowing When to Pull the Plug," *Harvard Business Review*, vol. 65 (March/April 1987), pp. 68–74.

[23] For a thorough literature review see Dustin J. Sleesman, Donald E. Conlon, Gerry McNamara, and Jonathan E. Miles," *Academy of Management Journal*, vol. 55, no. 3 (2012), pp. 541–562.

[24] Information and quotes from from "Response to Social Media Attack. Nestlé Faced Damage to Kit Kat Brand," *Financial Times*, Kindle Edition (Decembeer 4, 2012).

[25] For scholarly reviews, see Dean Tjosvold, "Effects of Crisis Orientation on Managers' Approach to Controversy in Decision Making," *Academy of Management Journal*, vol. 27 (1984), pp. 130–38; and Ian I. Mitroff, Paul Shrivastava, and Firdaus E. Udwadia, "Effective Crisis Management," *Academy of Management Executive*, vol. 1 (1987), pp. 283–92.

[26]Anna Muoio, "Where There's Smoke It Helps to Have a Smoke Jumper," *Fast Company*, vol. 33, p. 290.

Feature Notes 5

Opening photo—Quote from "Japan Widens Evacuation Zone Around Fukushima Nuclear Plant," www.dailytelegraph.com (May 15, 2011).

Role Models—Information from Julie Bennett, "Don Thompson Engineers Winning Role as McDonald's President," *Franchise Times* (February 2008), www.franchisetimes.com; Barbara Thau, "McDonald's Next CEO Don Thompson, the man Behind McCafe," *Daily Finance* AOL Original, (March 22, 2012), http://www.dailyfinance.com (Accessed September 12, 2012); and Julie Jargon, "Can McDonald's Keep Up the Pace? March 22, 2012, *Wall Street Journal*, http://online.wsj.com (Accessed September 12, 2012).

Facts to Consider—Information from Phred Dvorak, Baob Davis, and Louise Radnofsky, "Firms Confront Boss-Subordinate Love Affairs," *Wall Street Journal* (October 27, 2008), p. B5. Survey data from Society for Human Resource Management.

Ethics Check—See "Electronic Hazardous Waste (E-Waste)," California Department of Toxic Substances Control, www.dtsc.ca.gov (Accessed September 12, 2012); and "E-Cycling," United States Envriotional Protection Agency Website, www.epa.gov (Accessed September 12, 2012).

Photo Essay—Apple—Information from Kathrin Hille and Sarah Mishkin, "Foxconn Admits Employing 14-year old Interns," *Financial Times*, Kindle Edition (October 18, 2012); and Jessica E. Lessin and James R. Hagerty, "A Mac that's 'Made in U.S.A.'," *The Wall Street Journal* (December 7, 2012), pp. B1, B2.

Hot Topic—These viewpoints were found in the *Advanced Management Journal* (Summer, 1975), and reported in John R. Schermerhorn Jr., James G. Hunt, and Richard N. Osborn, *Managing Organizational Behavior* (New York: John Wiley & Sons, 1982, pp. 550—551.

Endnotes 5

[1]*Eaton Corporation Annual Report*, 1985.

[2]Henry Mintzberg, "The Manager's Job: Folklore and Fact," *Harvard Business Review*, vol. 53 (July/August 1975), pp. 54–67; and Henry Mintzberg, "Planning on the Left Side and Managing on the Right," *Harvard Business Review*, vol. 54 (July/August 1976), pp. 46–55.

[3]For a classic study, see Stanley Thune and Robert House, "Where Long-Range Planning Pays Off," *Business Horizons*, vol. 13 (1970), pp. 81–87. For a critical review of the literature, see Milton Leontiades and Ahmet Teel, "Planning Perceptions and Planning Results," *Strategic Management Journal*, vol. 1 (1980), pp. 65–75; and J. Scott Armstrong, "The Value of Formal Planning for Strategic Decisions," *Strategic Management Journal*, vol. 3 (1982), pp. 197–211.

For special attention to the small business setting, see Richard B. Robinson Jr., John A. Pearce II, George S. Vozikis, and Timothy S. Mescon, "The Relationship Between Stage of Development and Small Firm Planning and Performance," *Journal of Small Business Management*, vol. 22 (1984), pp. 45–52; and Christopher Orphen, "The Effects of Long–Range Planning on Small Business Performance: A Further Examination," *Journal of Small Business Management*, vol. 23 (1985), pp. 16–23. For an empirical study of large corporations, see Vasudevan Ramanujam and N. Venkatraman, "Planning and Performance: A New Look at an Old Question," *Business Horizons*, vol. 30 (1987), pp. 19–25.

[4]Quote from Stephen Covey and Roger Merrill, "New Ways to Get Organized at Work," *USA Weekend* (February 6/8, 1998), p. 18. Books by Stephen R. Covey include: *The 7 Habits of Highly Effective People: Powerful Lessons in Personal Change* (New York: Fireside, 1990), and Stephen R. Covey and Sandra Merril Covey, *The 7 Habits of Highly Effective Families: Building a Beautiful Family Culture in a Turbulent World* (New York: Golden Books, 1996).

[5]"McDonald's Tech Turnaround," *Harvard Business Review* (November 2004), p. 128.

[6]Information from Carol Hymowitz, "Packed Calendars Rule over Executives," *Wall Street Journal* (June 16, 2008), p. B1.

[7]Quotes from *Business Week* (August 8, 1994), pp. 78–86.

[8]See William Oncken Jr. and Donald L. Wass, "Management Time: Who's Got the Monkey?" *Harvard Business Review*, vol. 52 (September/October 1974), pp. 75–80, and featured as an HBR classic, *Harvard Business Review* (November/December 1999).

[9]For more on the long term, see Danny Miller and Isabelle Le Breton-Miller, *Managing for the Long Run* (Cambridge, MA: Harvard Business School Press, 2005).

[10]See Elliot Jaques, *The Form of Time* (New York: Russak & Co., 1982). For an executive commentary on his research, see Walter Kiechel III, "How Executives Think," *Fortune* (December 21, 1987), pp. 139–44.

[11]See Henry Mintzberg, "Rounding Out the Manager's Job," *Sloan Management Review* (Fall 1994), pp. 1–25.

[12]Excerpts in sample sexual harassment policy from American Express's advice to small businesses at www.americanexpress.com (retrieved November 21, 2005).

[13]Information from "Avoiding a Time Bomb: Sexual Harassment," *Business Week*, Enterprise issue (October 13, 1997), pp. ENT20–21.

[14]Information from "Climate Change is the Risk That Increases All Others," *Wall Street Journal* (March 26, 2013), p. R. 2

[15]Paul Glader, "GE's Immelt to Cite Lessons Learned," *Wall Street Journal* (December 15, 2009), p. B2.

[16]Forecasts in Stay Informed from "Long-Term Forecasts on EIU Country Data and Market Indicators & Forecasts," *The Economist* Intelligence Unit, www.eiu.com (retrieved November 21, 2005).

[17]Information and quotes from Guy Chazan and Neil King, "BP's Preparedness for Major Crisis Is Questioned," *Wall Street Journal* (May 10, 2010), p. A6; and Ben Casselman and Guy Chazan, "Disaster Plans Lacing at Deep Rigs," *Wall Street Journal* (May 18, 2010), p. A1.

[18]The scenario-planning approach is described in Peter Schwartz, *The Art of the Long View* (New York: Doubleday/Currency, 1991); and Arie de Geus, *The Living Company: Habits for Survival in a Turbulent Business Environment* (Boston, MA: Harvard Business School Press, 1997).

[19]Ibid.

[20]See, for example, Robert C. Camp, *Business Process Benchmarking* (Milwaukee: ASQ Quality Press 1994); Michael J. Spendolini, *The Benchmarking Book* (New York: AMACOM, 1992); and Christopher E. Bogan and Michael J. English, *Benchmarking for Best Practices: Winning Through Innovative Adaptation* (New York: McGraw-Hill, 1994).

[21]David Kiley, "One Ford for the Whole World," *Business Week* (June 15, 2009), pp. 58–59.

[22]See, for example, Cecile Rohwedder and Keith Johnson, "Pace-setting Zara Seeks More Speed to Fight Its Rising Cheap-Chic Rivals," *Wall Street Journal* (February 20, 2008), pp. B1, B6.

[23]"How Classy Can 7-Eleven Get?" *Business Week* (September 1, 1997), pp. 74–75; and Kellie B. Gormly, "7-Eleven Moving Up a Grade," *Columbus Dispatch* (August 3, 2000), pp. C1–C2.

[24]T. J. Rodgers, with William Taylor and Rick Foreman, "No Excuses Management," *World Executive's Digest* (May 1994), pp. 26–30.

[25]See Paul Ingrassia, "The Right Stuff," *Wall Street Journal* (April 8, 2005), p. D5.

Feature Notes 6

Opening Quote—"Here's Apple CEO Tim Cook's Apology Letter in China," *Wall Street Journal* (April 1, 2013): wsj.com (accessed April 2, 2013).

Role Models—Information from Bill Gates, "My Plan to Fix the World's Biggest Problems: Measure Them!" *Wall Street Journal* (January 26–27, 2013), pp. C1, C2.

Facts to Consider—Information and quotes from Rachel Emma Silverman, "Here's Why You Won't Finish This Article," *Wall Street Journal* (December 12, 2012), pp. B1, B6.

Ethics Check—Paul Davidson, "'Climate Has Changed' for Data Privacy," *USA Today* (May 12, 2006), p. B1; Ben Elgin, "The Great Firewall of China," *Business Week* (January 23, 2006), pp. 32–34; Alison Maitland, "Skype Says Text-Messages Censored by Partner in China," *Financial Times* (April 19, 2006), p. 15; and "Web Firms Criticized over China," CNN.com (July 20, 2006).

Manager's Library—Amazon.com Web site, "Lean In," amazon.com (accessed March 18, 2013); Colleen Taylor, "Sheryl Sandberg Launches 'Lean In' Organization as a Global Community for Workplace Equality," *TechCrunch* (March 6, 2013): techcrunch.com (accessed March 18, 2013); Ann Doyle, "It's Sheryl Sandberg's Courage to Raise her Voice That's Hot News. Not Leaning In," *Forbes* (March 15, 2013): forbes.com (accessed March 18, 2013); Sheryl Sandberg, "Why I Want Women to Lean In," *Time* (March 7, 2013): ideas.time.com/2013/03/07 (accessed March 18, 2013); Belinda Luscombe, "Confidence Woman," *Time* (March 7, 2013): http://ideas.time.com/2013/03/07 (accessed March 18, 2013); Todd Leopold, "Facebook's Sheryl Sandberg Suddenly in Crossfire," *CNN.com* (March 11, 2013): cnn.com/2013/03/11 (accessed March 18, 2013); and "Feminist Mystique What Must Change for Women to Make it to the Top," *Economist*, Kindle Edition (March 19, 2013).

Whole Foods—Lesley Patton and Bryan Gruley, "Whole Foods' Recession Lessons," *BusinessWeek* (August 9, 2012), http://www.businessweek.com (Accessed September 12, 2012); "Quality Standards," Whole Foods Market Website, http://www.wholefoodsmarket.com (Accessed September 12, 2012); and "Our Mission and Culture," Whole Foods Market Website, http://www.wholefoodsmarket.com (Accessed September 12, 2012).

Endnotes 6

[1]For an interesting commentary see Gates, op. cit.

[2]Information and quote on Toyota from Sharon Terlep and Josh Mitchell, "U.S. Widens Toyota Probe to Electronics," *Wall Street Journal* (February 4, 2010), pp. B1, B12; and "An Open Letter to Toyota Customers," *Columbus Dispatch* (February 4, 2010), p. A12. Information and quote on Apple from "Here's Apple CEO Tim Cook's Apology Letter in China," *Wall Street Journal* (April 1, 2013): wsj.com (accessed April 2, 2013); and Paul Mozur, "Apple's Chief: We're Sorry," *Wall Street Journal* (April 2, 2013), pp. B1, B4. Information and quote on Lululemon from Claire Suddath, "Lululemon, Exposed," *Bloomberg BusinessWeek* (April 1–April 7, 2013), p. 81.

[3]"The Renewal Factor: Friendly Fact, Congenial Controls," *Business Week* (September 14, 1987), p. 105.

[4]Rob Cross and Lloyd Baird, "Technology Is Not Enough: Improving Performance by Building Institutional Memory," *Sloan Management Review* (Spring 2000), p. 73.

[5]Information from Pep Sappal, "Integrated Inclusion Initiative," *Wall Street Journal* (October 3, 2006), p. A2.

[6]Example from George Anders, "Management Guru Turns Focus to Orchestras, Hospitals," *Wall Street Journal* (November 21, 2005), pp. B1, B5.

[7]Information from Leon E. Wynter, "Allstate Rates Managers on Handling Diversity," *Wall Street Journal* (October 1, 1997), p. B1.

[8]Information from Kathryn Kranhold, "U.S. Firms Raise Ethics Focus," *Wall Street Journal* (November 28, 2005), p. B4.

[9]Information from Raju Narisetti, "For IBM, a Groundbreaking Sales Chief," *Wall Street Journal* (January 19, 1998), pp. B1, B5; and "Linda S. Sanford: Senior Vice President for Enterprise Transformation," ibm.com (accessed April 1, 2013).

[10]Based on discussion by Harold Koontz and Cyril O'Donnell, *Essentials of Management* (New York: McGraw-Hill, 1974), pp. 362–65; see also Cross and Baird, op. cit.

[11]Information from Louis Lee, "I'm Proud of What I've Made Myself Into—What I've Created," *Wall Street Journal* (August 27, 1997), pp. B1, B5; and Jim Collins, "Bigger, Better, Faster," *Fast Company*, vol. 71 (June 2003), p. 74.

[12]See Sue Shellenbarger, "If You Need to Work Better, Maybe Try Working Less," *Wall Street Journal* (September 23, 2009), p. D1.

[13]Douglas McGregor, *The Human Side of Enterprise* (New York: McGraw-Hill, 1960).

[14]This distinction is made in William G. Ouchi, "Markets, Bureaucracies and Clans," *Administrative Science Quarterly*, vol. 25 (1980), pp. 129–41.

[15]Martin LaMonica, "Wal-Mart Readies Long-Term Move into Solar Power," *CNET News.com* (January 3, 2007).

[16]See Dale D. McConkey, *How to Manage by Results*, 3rd ed. (New York: AMACOM, 1976); Stephen J. Carroll Jr. and Henry J. Tosi Jr., *Management by Objectives: Applications and Research* (New York: Macmillan, 1973); and Anthony P. Raia, *Managing by Objectives* (Glenview, IL: Scott, Foresman, 1974).

[17]For a discussion of research on MBO, see Carroll and Tosi, op. cit.; Raia, op. cit.; and Steven Kerr, "Overcoming the Dysfunctions of MBO," *Management by Objectives*, vol. 5, no. 1 (1976). Information in part from Dylan Loeb McClain, "Job Forecast: Internet's Still Hot," *New York Times* (January 30, 2001), p. 9.

[18]The work on goal setting and motivation is summarized in Edwin A. Locke and Gary P. Latham, *Goal Setting: A Motivational Technique That Works!* (Englewood Cliffs, NJ: Prentice-Hall, 1984).

[19]McGregor, op. cit.

[20]The "hot stove rules" are developed from R. Bruce McAfee and William Poffenberger, *Productivity Strategies: Enhancing Employee Job Performance* (Englewood Cliffs, NJ: Prentice-Hall, 1982), pp. 54–55. They are originally attributed to Douglas McGregor, "Hot Stove Rules of Discipline," in G. Strauss and L. Sayles (eds.), *Personnel: The Human Problems of Management* (Englewood Cliffs, NJ: Prentice-Hall, 1967).

[21]For basic readings on quality control, see Joseph M. Juran, *Quality Control Handbook*, 3rd ed. (New York: McGraw-Hill, 1979); and "The Quality Trilogy: A Universal Approach to Managing for Quality," in H. Costin (ed.), *Total Quality Management* (New York: Dryden, 1994); W. Edwards Deming, *Out of Crisis* (Cambridge, MA: MIT Press, 1986) and "Deming's Quality Manifesto," *Best of Business Quarterly*, vol. 12 (Winter 1990–1991), pp. 6–101; Howard S. Gitlow and Shelly J. Gitlow, *The Deming Guide to Quality and Competitive Position* (Englewood Cliffs, NJ: Prentice-Hall, 1987); and Rafael Aguay, *Dr. Deming: The American Who Taught the Japanese About Quality* (New York: Free Press, 1997).

[22]Aguay, op. cit.; W. Edwards Deming, op. cit. (1986).

[23]Ibid.

[24]"See "Downsides of Just-In-Time Inventory," *Bloomberg BusinessWeek* (March 28–April 3, 2011), pp. 17–18.

[25]Information from Karen Carney, "Successful Performance Measurement: A Checklist," *Harvard Management Update* (No. U9911B), 1999.

[26]Robert S. Kaplan and David P. Norton, "The Balanced Scorecard: Measures That Drive Performance," *Harvard Business Review* (July/August, 2005); see also Robert S. Kaplan and David P. Norton, *The Balanced Scorecard* (Cambridge, MA: Harvard Business School Press, 1996).

Feature Notes 7

Opening Photo—Walter Mossberg, quoting Salman Khan, in "Changing the Economics of Education," *The Wall Street Journal* (June 4, 2012), p. R8.

Role Models—Information and quotes from Carmine Gallo, "The Seven Secrets of Inspiring Leaders," *Forbes* (July 6, 2011), http://www.forbes.com (Accessed September 29, 2012); Teach for America Website, "Our Mission," http://www.teachforamerica.org (Accessed September 29, 2012); and Nathaniel Popper, "Getting Brilliant Students to Seek Jobs Beyond Wall Street," *Los Angeles Times* (November 4, 2011), http://articles.latimes.com (Accessed September 30, 2012).

Facts to Consider—Information from Daniel Costello, "The Drought is Over (At Least for CEOs)," *The New York Times* (April 9, 2011); nytimes.com (accessed May 3, 2011); Joann S. Lublin, "CEO Pay in 2010 Jumped 11%," *Wall Street Journal* (May 9, 2011), p. 81; and, AFL-CIO, "2011 CEO Paywatch," http://www.aflcio.org/.

Ethics Check—Life and Death at an Outsourcing Factory: Information and quotes from "Life and Death at the iPad Factory," *Bloomberg BusinessWeek* (June 7–13, 2010), pp. 35–36; and Paul Mozur and Lorraine Luk, "Apple Contractor's Robots Hit a Glitch," *The Wall Street Journal* (December 13, 2012), p. B4.

Patagonia—Information and quotes from Yvon Chouinard, *Let My People Go Surfing: The Education of a Reluctant Businessman* (New York: Penguin Press HC, 2005); Steve Hamm, "A Passion for the Plan," *Business Week* (August 21/28, 2006), pp. 92–94; Hugo Martin, "Patagonia's Payoff," *The Columbus Dispatch* (June 9, 2012), p. A8; and www.patagonia.com.

Manager's Library—"Rebooting Work: Transform How you Work in the Age of Entrepreneurship," amazon.com (accessed March 25, 2013); "Rebooting Work," maynardwebb.com: (accessed March 25, 2013); Maynard Webb. "The Future of Mentorship in the Age of Entrepreneurs," *Fast Company* (December 13, 2012), fastcompany.com (accessed March 25, 2013); and, Dan Schwabel. "Maynard Webb: Rethink your Workplace Habits to Become Successful," *Forbes* (January 28, 2013): www.forbes.com (accessed March 25, 2013).

Hot Topic—This complex arrangement is described in the graphic "Double Irish with a Dutch Sandwich," *New York Times* (April 28, 2012), nytimes.com.

Endnotes 7

[1]Information and quote from Walter Mossberg, "Changing the Economics of Education," *The Wall Street Journal* (June 4, 2012), p. R8.

[2]Information and quotes from Marcia Stepanek, "How Fast Is Net Fast?" *Business Week E-Biz* (November 1, 1999), pp. EB52–54.

[3]Keith H. Hammonds, "Michael Porter's Big Ideas," *Fast Company* (March 2001), pp. 150–156.

[4]Gary Hamel and C. K. Prahalad, "Strategic Intent," *Harvard Business Review* (May/June 1989), pp. 63–76.

[5]Geoffrey A. Fowler and Nick Wingfield, "Apple's Showman Takes the Stage," *Wall Street Journal* (March 3, 2011), p. B1.

[6]Michael A. Hitt, R. Duane Ireland, and Robert E. Hoskisson, *Strategic Management: Competitiveness and Globalization* (Minneapolis: West, 1997), p. 197.

[7]See William McKinley, Carol M. Sanchez, and A. G. Schick, "Organizational Downsizing: Constraining, Cloning, Learning," *Academy of Management Executive*, vol. 9 (August 1995), pp. 32–44.

[8]Kim S. Cameron, Sara J. Freeman, and A. K. Mishra, "Best Practices in White-Collar Downsizing: Managing Contradictions," *Academy of Management Executive*, vol. 4 (August 1991), pp. 57–73.

[9]"Overheard," *Wall Street Journal* (April 16, 2009), p. C10; and Geoffrey A. Fowler and Evan Ramstad, "eBay Looks Abroad for Growth," *Wall Street Journal* (April 16, 2009), p. B2.

[10]This strategy classification is found in Hitt et al., op. cit.; the attitudes are from a discussion by Howard V. Perlmutter, "The Tortuous Evolution of the Multinational Corporation," *Columbia Journal of World Business*, vol. 4 (January/February 1969).

[11]Fowler and Ramstad, op. cit., 2009.

[12]Adam M. Brandenburger and Barry J. Nalebuff, *Co-Opetition: A Revolution Mindset that Combines Competition and Cooperation* (New York: Bantam, 1996).

[13]Jonathan Spiva, "BMW ActiveHybrid 7 Review," the dieseldriver.com (July 1, 2010).

[14]See Michael E. Porter, "Strategy and the Internet," *Harvard Business Review* (March 2001), pp. 63–78; and Michael Rappa, *Business Models on the Web* (www.ecommerce.ncsu.edu/business_models.html. February 6, 2001).

[15]See threadless.com.

[16]Peter F. Drucker, *Management: Tasks, Responsibilities, Practices* (New York: Harper & Row, 1973), p. 122.

[17]See Laura Nash, "Mission Statements—Mirrors and Windows," *Harvard Business Review* (March/April 1988), pp. 155–56; James C. Collins and Jerry I. Porras, "Building Your Company's Vision," *Harvard Business Review* (September/October 1996), pp. 65–77; and James C. Collins and Jerry I. Porras, *Built to Last: Successful Habits of Visionary Companies* (New York: Harper Business, 1997).

[18]Gary Hamel, *Leading the Revolution* (Boston, MA: Harvard Business School Press, 2000), pp. 72–73.

[19]Collins and Porras, op. cit., 1996 and 1997.

[20]See Peter F. Drucker's views on organizational objectives in his classic books *The Practice of Management* (New York: Harper & Row, 1954) and *Management: Tasks, Responsibilities, Practices* (New York: Harper & Row, 1973). For a more recent commentary, see his article "Management: The Problems of Success," *Academy of Management Executive*, vol. 1 (1987), pp. 13–19.

[21]C. K. Prahalad and Gary Hamel, "The Core Competencies of the Corporation," *Harvard Business Review* (May/June 1990), pp. 79–91; see also Hitt et al., op. cit., pp. 99–103.

[22]For a discussion of Michael Porter's approach to strategic planning, see his books, *Competitive Strategy: Techniques for Analyzing Industries and Competitors* (New York: Free Press, 1980) and *Competitive Advantage: Creating and Sustaining Superior Performance* (New York: Free Press, 1986) and his article, "What Is Strategy?" *Harvard Business Review* (November/December, 1996, pp. 61–78; and Richard M. Hodgetts's interview "A Conversation with Michael E. Porter: A Significant Extension Toward Operational Improvement and Positioning," *Organizational Dynamics* (Summer 1999), pp. 24–33.

[23]See Porter, op. cit. (1980 and 1986).

[24]Information from www.polo.com.

[25]Richard G. Hammermesh, "Making Planning Strategic," *Harvard Business Review*, vol. 64 (July/August 1986), pp. 115–20; and Richard G. Hammermesh, *Making Strategy Work* (New York: Wiley, 1986).

[26]See Gerald B. Allan, "A Note on the Boston Consulting Group Concept of Competitive Analysis and Corporate Strategy," Harvard Business School, Intercollegiate Case Clearing House, ICCH9-175-175 (Boston: Harvard Business School, June 1976).

[27]R. Duane Ireland and Michael A. Hitt, "Achieving and Maintaining Strategic Competitiveness in the 21st Century," *Academy of Management Executive*, vol. 13 (1999), pp. 43–57.

[28]www.patagonia.com/web/us/patagonia.go?assetid=3351.

[29]For a discussion see Paul J. H. Shoemaker, Steve Krupp, and Samantha Howland, "Strategic Leadership: The Essential Skills," *Harvard Business Review*, vol. 91 (January–February, 2013), pp. 131–134.

[30]Hammond, op. cit.

Feature Notes 8

Role Models—Information and quotes from David Kiley, "Ford's Savior?" *Business Week* (March 16, 2009), pp. 31–34; Alex Taylor III, "Fixing Up Ford," *Fortune* (May 14, 2009); and, Mike Ramsey, "Ford CEO Revs Up Auto Maker's China Role," *Wall Street Journal* (April 16, 2013), p. B7.

Facts to Consider—Information and quote from "Bosses Overestimate Their Managing Skills," *Wall Street Journal* (November 1, 2010), p. B10.

Build-A-Bear—Information and quotes from "Build-A-Bear Workshop, Inc., Funding Universe": www.fundinguniverse.com/company-histories/BuildABear-Workshop-Inc (accessed March 9, 2009); and www.buildabear.com; Maxine Clark and Amy Joyner, *The Bear Necessities of Business: Building a Company with Heart* (Hoboken, NJ: Wiley, 2007); and, Joan S. Lublin and Dana Mattoli, "Build-A-Bear Considers a New Face at the Top," *The Wall Street Journal* (December 14, 2012), p. B. 3.

Photo Essays—Creative People—Information and quote from Sue Shellenbarger, "Better Ideas through Failure," *The Wall Street Journal* (September 27, 2011), pp. D1, D4. Employee Engagement—"Employee Engagement: A Leading Indicator of Financial Performance," gallup.com/consulting (accessed June 24, 2012).

Hot Topic—Information from Rachel Emma Silverman and Leslie Kwoh, "Peer Performance Reviews Take Off," *The Wall Street Journal* (August 1, 2012), p. B6.

Endnotes 8

[1] Henry Mintzberg and Ludo Van der Heyden, "Organigraphs: Drawing How Companies Really Work," *Harvard Business Review* (September/October 1999), pp. 87–94.

[2] Ibid.

[3] See for example "Employee Engagement: A Leading Indicator of Financial Performance," gallup.com/consulting (Accessed June 24, 2012).

[4] The classic work is Alfred D. Chandler, *Strategy and Structure* (Cambridge, MA: MIT Press, 1962).

[5] See Alfred D. Chandler Jr., "Origins of the Organization Chart," *Harvard Business Review* (March/April 1988), pp. 156–57.

[6] "A Question of Management," *Wall Street Journal* (June 2, 2009), p. R4.

[7] See, for example, "Key Issues: CEO and Board Chair Roles," Center for Board Governance www.pwc.com/us/en/corporate-governance/board-leadership (accessed June 6, 2013).

[8] See David Krackhardt and Jeffrey R. Hanson, "Informal Networks: The Company Behind the Chart," *Harvard Business Review* (July/August 1993), pp. 104–11.

[9] Information from Jena McGregor, "The Office Chart That Really Counts," *Business Week* (February 27, 2006), pp. 48–49.

[10] See Phred Dvorak, "Engineering Firm Charts Ties," *Wall Street Journal* (January 26, 2009): www.wsj.com.

[11] See Kenneth Noble, "A Clash of Styles: Japanese Companies in the U.S.," *New York Times* (January 25, 1988), p. 7.

[12] Information from Ellen Byron, "A New Odd Couple: Google, P&G Swap Workers to Spur Innovation," *Wall Street Journal* (November 19, 2008), pp. A1, A18.

[13] For a discussion of departmentalization, see H. I. Ansoff and R. G. Bradenburg, "A Language for Organization Design," *Management Science*, vol. 17 (August 1971), pp. B705–B731; Mariann Jelinek, "Organization Structure: The Basic Conformations," in Mariann Jelinek, Joseph A. Litterer, and Raymond E. Miles (eds.), *Organizations by Design: Theory and Practice* (Plano, TX: Business Publications, 1981), pp. 293–302; Henry Mintzberg, "The Structuring of Organizations," in James Brian Quinn, Henry Mintzberg, and Robert M. James (eds.), *The Strategy Process: Concepts, Contexts, and Cases* (Englewood Cliffs, NJ: Prentice-Hall, 1988), pp. 276–304.

[14] "A Question of Management," op. cit.

[15] Example reported in "Top Business Teams: A Lesson Straight from Mars," *Time* (February 9, 2009), p. 40; and Howard M. Guttman, *Great Business Teams* (Hoboken, NJ: Wiley, 2009).

[16] These alternatives are well described by Mintzberg, op. cit.

[17] Norihiko Shirouzu, "Toyota Plans a Major Overhaul in U. S.," *Wall Street Journal* (April 10, 2009), p. B3.

[18] Information and quotes from "Management Shake-Up to Create 'Leaner Structure'," *Financial Times* (June 11, 2009).

[19] Information and quote from "Revamped GM Updates Image of Core Brands," *Financial Times* (June 18, 2009).

[20] Excellent reviews of matrix concepts are found in Stanley M. Davis and Paul R. Lawrence, *Matrix* (Reading, MA: Addison-Wesley, 1977); Paul R. Lawrence, Harvey F. Kolodny, and Stanley M. Davis, "The Human Side of the Matrix," *Organizational Dynamics,* vol. 6 (1977), pp. 43–61; and Harvey F. Kolodny, "Evolution to a Matrix Organization," *Academy of Management Review*, vol. 4 (1979), pp. 543–53.

[21] Davis and Lawrence, op. cit.

[22] Susan Albers Mohrman, Susan G. Cohen, and Allan M. Mohrman Jr., *Designing Team-Based Organizations* (San Francisco: Jossey-Bass, 1996).

[23] See Glenn M. Parker, *Cross-Functional Teams* (San Francisco: Jossey-Bass, 1995).

[24] Information from William Bridges, "The End of the Job," *Fortune* (September 19, 1994), pp. 62–74; and Alan Deutschman, "The Managing Wisdom of High-Tech Superstars," *Fortune* (October 17, 1994), pp. 197–206.

[25] See the discussion by Jay R. Galbraith, "Designing the Networked Organization: Leveraging Size and Competencies," in Susan Albers Mohrman, Jay R. Galbraith, Edward E. Lawler III, and Associates, *Tomorrow's Organizations: Crafting Winning Strategies in a Dynamic World* (San Francisco: Jossey-Bass, 1998), pp. 76–102. See also Rupert F. Chisholm, *Developing Network Organizations: Learning from Practice and Theory* (Reading, MA: Addison-Wesley, 1998); and Michael S. Malone, *The Future Arrived Yesterday: The Rise of the Protean Corporation and What It Means for You* (New York: Crown Books, 2009).

[26] See Jerome Barthelemy, "The Seven Deadly Sins of Outsourcing," *Academy of Management Executive*, vol. 17 (2003), pp. 87–98; and Paulo Prada and Jiraj Sheth, "Delta Air Ends Use of India Call Centers," *Wall Street Journal* (April 18–19, 2009), pp. B1, B5.

[27] See the collection of articles by Cary L. Cooper and Denise M. Rousseau (eds.), *The Virtual Organization: Vol. 6, Trends in Organizational Behavior* (New York: Wiley, 2000).

[28] For a discussion of organization theory, see W. Richard Scott, *Organizations: Rational, Natural, and Open Systems*, 4th ed. (Upper Saddle River, NJ: Prentice-Hall, 1998).

[29] For a classic work, see Jay R. Galbraith, *Organizational Design* (Reading, MA: Addison-Wesley, 1977).

[30] David Van Fleet, "Span of Management Research and Issues," *Academy of Management Journal*, vol. 26 (1983), pp. 546–52.

[31] Information from "The Troubling Dean-to-Professor Ratio," *Bloomberg BusinessWeek* (November 26 – December 2, 2012), p. 40.

[32] Information from Tim Stevens, "Winning the World Over," *Industry Week* (November 15, 1999).

[33] See George P. Huber, "A Theory of Effects of Advanced Information Technologies on Organizational Design, Intelligence, and Decision Making," *Academy of Management Review*, vol. 15 (1990), pp. 67–71.

[34] Developed from Roger Fritz, *Rate Your Executive Potential* (New York: Wiley, 1988), pp. 185–86; Roy J. Lewicki, Donald D. Bowen, Douglas T. Hall, and Francine S. Hall, *Experiences in Management and Organizational Behavior*, 3rd ed. (New York: Wiley, 1988), p. 144.

[35] Max Weber, *The Theory of Social and Economic Organization*, A. M. Henderson (trans.) and H. T. Parsons (ed.) (New York: Free Press, 1974). For classic treatments of bureaucracy, see also Alvin Gouldner, *Patterns of Industrial Bureaucracy* (New York: Free Press, 1954); and Robert K. Merton, *Social Theory and Social Structure* (New York: Free Press, 1957).

[36] Tom Burns and George M. Stalker, *The Management of Innovation* (London: Tavistock, 1961), republished (London: Oxford University Press, 1994). See also Wesley D. Sine, Hitoshi Mitsuhashi, and David A. Kirsch, "Revisiting Burns and Stalker: Formal Structure and New Venture Performance in Emerging Economic Sectors," *Academy of Management Journal*, vol. 49 (2006), pp. 121–32. The Burns and Stalker study was later extended by Paul R. Lawrence and Jay W. Lorsch, *Organizations and Environment* (Boston: Division of Research, Graduate School of Business Administration, Harvard University, 1967).

[37] See Henry Mintzberg, *Structure in Fives: Designing Effective Organizations* (Englewood Cliffs, NJ: Prentice-Hall, 1983).

[38] "What Ails Microsoft?" *Business Week* (September 26, 2005), p. 101.

[39] "Should Microsoft Break Up, on Its Own?" *Wall Street Journal* (November 26–27, 2005), p. B16.

[40] See, for example, Jay R. Galbraith, Edward E. Lawler III, and Associates, *Organizing for the Future* (San Francisco: Jossey-Bass, 1993); and Mohrman et al., op. cit.

[41] Peter Senge, *The Fifth Discipline: The Art and Practice of the Learning Organization* (New York: Doubleday, 1994).

[42] See Rosabeth Moss Kanter, *The Changing Masters* (New York: Simon & Schuster, 1983).

[43] Barney Olmsted and Suzanne Smith, *Creating a Flexible Workplace: How to Select and Manage Alternative Work Options* (New York: American Management Association, 1989).

[44] See Allen R. Cohen and Herman Gadon, *Alternative Work Schedules: Integrating Individual and Organizational Needs* (Reading, MA: Addison-Wesley, 1978), p. 125; Simcha Ronen and Sophia B. Primps, "The Compressed Work

Week as Organizational Change: Behavioral and Attitudinal Outcomes," *Academy of Management Review*, vol. 6 (1981), pp. 61–74.

[45]Information from Lesli Hicks, "Workers, Employers Praise Their Four-Day Workweek," *Columbus Dispatch* (August 22, 1994), p. 6.

[46]Business for Social Responsibility Resource Center: www.bsr.org/resourcecenter (January 24, 2001); Anusha Shrivastava, "Flextime Is Now Key Benefit for Mom-Friendly Employers," *Columbus Dispatch* (September 23, 2003), p. C2; Sue Shellenbarger, "Number of Women Managers Rises," *Wall Street Journal* (September 30, 2003), p. D2.

[47]"Networked Workers," *Business Week* (October 6, 1997), p. 8; and Diane E. Lewis, "Flexible Work Arrangements as Important as Salary to Some," *Columbus Dispatch* (May 25, 1998), p. 8.

[48]Christopher Rhoads and Sara Silver, "Working at Home Gets Easier," *Wall Street Journal* (December 29, 2005), p. B4.

[49]Information and quotes from Claire Suddath, "Work-from-Home Truths, Half-Truths, and Myths," *Bloomberg BusinessWeek* (March 4–10, 2013), p. 75; and Rick Hampson, "Boss vs. You: The Work-from-Home Tug of War," *USA Today* (March 13, 2013), pp. 2, 2A.

[50]For a review, see Wayne F. Cascio, "Managing a Virtual Workplace," *Academy of Management Executive*, vol. 14 (2000), pp. 81–90.

[51]Suddath, op cit.; Hampson, op cit.

[52]Ibid.

[53]Information and quotes from Emily Glazer, "Can't Afford an Office? Rent a Desk for $275," *The Wall Street Journal* (October 4, 2011), p. B4.

Feature Notes 9

Opening Photo—Quote from Shelly Banjo, "Clutter Buster's Next Foray," *Wall Street Journal* (March 21, 2013), p. B7.

Clif Bar—Information from Marnie Hanel, "CLif Bar's Offices Keep Employees Limber," *Bloomberg BusinessWeek* (November 21–27, 2011), pp. 104–105; and www.clifbar.com.

Role Models—Information from David A. Price, "From Dorm Room to Wal-Mart," *Wall Street Journal* (March 11, 2009), p. A13; "Huddler.com Interview with CEO and Founder Tom Szaky," www.greenhome.huddler.com; and Tom Szaky, *Revolution in a Bottle* (Knoxville, TN: Portfolio Trade, 2009).

Facts to Consider—Data reported in "A Saner Workplace," *Business Week* (June 1, 2009), pp. 66–69, and based on excerpt from Claire Shipman and Katty Kay, *Womenomics: Write Your Own Rules for Success* (New York: Harper Business, 2009); and "A to Z of Generation Y Attitudes," *Financial Times* (June 18, 2009).

Ethics Check—Information and examples from Joe O'Shea, "How a Facebook Update Can Cost You Your Job," *Irish Independent* (September 1, 2010), p. 34.

Photo Essay—Social Entrepreneur—Information and quotes from Aubrey Henvetty, "Seeds of Change," *Kellogg* (Summer, 2006), p. 13; "Amid Turmoil, Social Entrepreneur Sows Hope in Africa," *Kellogg* (Spring, 2008), p. 7; and Updates: Andrew Youn (KSM06), *Kellogg* (Winter, 2012), p. 57.

Hot Topic—Information and quotes from Leslie Kwoh, "More Firms Bow to Generation Y's Demands," *Wall Street Journal* (August 22, 2012), Kindle Edition.

Endnotes 9

[1]See the discussion of Anthropologie in William C. Taylor and Polly LaBarre, *Mavericks at Work: Why the Most Original Minds in Business Win* (New York: William Morrow, 2006).

[2]Edgar H. Schein, "Organizational Culture," *American Psychologist*, vol. 45 (1990), pp. 109–19. See also Schein's *Organizational Culture and Leadership*, 2nd ed. (San Francisco: Jossey-Bass, 1997); and *The Corporate Culture Survival Guide* (San Francisco: Jossey-Bass, 1999).

[3]Information and quotes from Christopher Palmeri, "Now for Sale, the Zappos Culture," *Business Week* (January 11, 2010), p. 57.

[4]Jena McGregor, "Zappos' Secret: It's an Open Book," *Business Week* (March 23 & 30, 2009), p. 62.

[5]James Collins and Jerry Porras, *Built to Last* (New York: Harper Business, 1994).

[6]Schein, op. cit. (1997); Terrence E. Deal and Alan A. Kennedy, *Corporate Cultures: The Rites and Rituals of Corporate Life* (Reading, MA: Addison-Wesley, 1982); and Ralph Kilmann, *Beyond the Quick Fix* (San Francisco: Jossey-Bass, 1984).

[7]Schein, op. cit. (1997).

[8]John P. Wanous, *Organizational Entry*, 2nd ed. (New York: Addison-Wesley, 1992).

[9]Scott Madison Patton, "Service Quality, Disney Style" (Lake Buena Vista, FL: Disney Institute, 1997).

[10] See Schein, op cit., 1990, 1997, 1999; Collins and Porras, op cit., Deal and Kennedy, op cit.

[11]This framework is described by Kim S. Cameron & Robert E. Quinn, *Diagnosing and Changing Organizational Culture: Based on the Competing Values Framework* (Reading, MA: Addison-Wesley, 1999).

[12]"Workplace Cultures Come in Four Kinds," *Wall Street Journal* (February 7, 2012), p. B6.

[13]This is a simplified model developed from Schein, op. cit. (1997).

[14]James C. Collins and Jerry I. Porras, "Building Your Company's Vision," *Harvard Business Review* (September/October 1996), pp. 65–77.

[15]See corporate Web sites.

[16]Tom's of Maine example is from Jenny C. McCune, "Making Lemonade," *Management Review* (June 1997), pp. 49–53.

[17]See, for example, Lee G. Bolman and Terrence E. Deal, *Reframing Organizations: Artistry, Choice, and Leadership*, 4th ed. (San Francisco: Jossey-Bass, 2008).

[18]See Robert A. Giacalone and Carol L. Jurkiewicz (Eds.), *Handbook of Workplace Spirituality and Organizational Performance* (Armonk, NY: M. E. Sharpe, 2003).

[19]See Peter F. Drucker, "The Discipline of Innovation," *Harvard Business Review* (November/December 1998), pp. 3–8.

[20]Peter F. Drucker, *Management: Tasks, Responsibilities, and Practices* (New York: Harper & Row, 1973), p. 797.

[21]See Cortis R. Carlson and William W. Wilmont, *Getting to "Aha"* (New York: Crown Business, 2006).

[22]See for example *Bloomberg Business Week* reports on "The World's Most Innovative Companies."

[23]See "Green Business Innovations" and "New Life for Old Threads," both in *Business Week* (April 28, 2008), special advertising section.

[24]David Bornstein, *How to Change the World: Social Entrepreneurs and the Power of New Ideas* (Oxford, U.K.: Oxford University Press, 2004).

[25]Peter F. Drucker, *Management: Tasks, Responsibilities, and Practices* (New York: Harper-Row, 1973), p. 797.

[26]Quote from "How to Measure Up," *Kellogg* (Summer, 2009), p. 17.

[27]See Gary Hamel, *Leading the Revolution* (Boston, MA: Harvard Business School Press, 2000).

[28]Based on Edward B. Roberts, "Managing Invention and Innovation," *Research Technology Management* (January/February 1988), pp. 1–19.

[29]"The Joys and Perils of 'Reverse Innovation'." *Business Week* (October 5, 2009), p. 12.

[30]Ibid. Also, example and quotes from "How to Compete in a World Turned Upside Down," *Financial Times*, Kindle edition (October 6, 2009).

[31]Clay Christensen, *The Innovator's Dilemma: When New Technologies Cause Great Firms to Fail*, Reprint Edition (New York: Harper Paperbacks, 2011); and Clay Christensen, Jeff Dyer, and Hal Gregersen, *The Innovator's DNA: Mastering the Five Skills of Disruptive Innovators* (Cambridge, MA: Harvard Business Press, 2011).

[32]See the chronicle of Steve Job's life and work in "Steve Jobs 1955–2011," Special Edition, *Bloomberg BusinessWeek* (October 10–16, 2011), pp. 1–65.

[33]Adam Lashinsky, "Jeff Bezos: The Ultimate Disrupter," *Fortune* (December 3, 2012), p. 42.

[34]Information and quotes from Nancy Gohring, "Microsoft: Stodgy or Innovative? It's All About Perception," *PC World* (July 25, 2008).

[35]This discussion is stimulated by James Brian Quinn, "Managing Innovation: Controlled Chaos," *Harvard Business Review*, vol. 63 (May/June 1985), 73–84.

[36]Quote from www.ideo.com (retrieved: March 11, 2009).

[37]"'Mosh Pits' of Creativity," *Business Week* (November 7, 2005), p. 99.

38"Innovation at Work," *Wall Street Journal* (January 22, 2013), p. B14.

39Quote from Brad Stone, "Amid the Gloom, an E-Commerce War," *New York Times* (October 12, 2008): www.nytimes.com.

40For a review of scholarly work on organizational change, see W. Warner Burke, *Organizational Change: Theory and Practice*, 2nd ed. (Thousand Oaks, CA: Sage, 2008).

41Quote from Pilita Clark, "Delayed, Not Cancelled," *Financial Times* (December 19, 2009).

42For an overview, see W. Warner Burke, *Organization Change: Theory and Practice* (Thousand Oaks, CA: Sage, 2002).

43For a discussion of alternative types of change, see David A. Nadler and Michael L. Tushman, *Strategic Organizational Design* (Glenview, II: Scott, Foresman, 1988); John P. Kotter, "Leading Change: Why Transformation Efforts Fail," *Harvard Business Review* (March/April 1995), pp. 59–67; and Burke, op. cit.

44Michael Beer and Nitin Nohria, "Cracking the Code of Change," *Harvard Business Review* (May–June 2000), pp. 138–141; "Change Management, An Inside Job," *Economist* (July 15, 2000), p. 61; and Mark Hughes, "Do 70 Per Cent of All Organizational Change Initiatives Really Fail?" *Journal of Change Management*, Vol. 11, No. 4 (2011), pp. 451–464.

45Ibid; Beer and Nohria, op. cit.; and "Change Management, An Inside Job," *Economist* (July 15, 2000), p. 61.

46Based on Kotter, op. cit.

47This is based on Rosabeth Moss Kanter's "Innovation Pyramid," *BusinessWeek* (March 2007), p. IN 3.

48Kurt Lewin, "Group Decision and Social Change," in G. E. Swanson, T. M. Newcomb, and E. L. Hartley (eds.), *Readings in Social Psychology* (New York: Holt, Rinehart, 1952), pp. 459–473.

49See Wanda J. Orlikowski and J. Debra Hofman, "An Improvisational Model for Change Management: The Case of Groupware Technologies," *Sloan Management Review* (Winter 1997), pp. 11–21.

50This discussion is based on Robert Chin and Kenneth D. Benne, General Strategies for Effecting Changes in Human Systems," in Warren G. Bennis, Kenneth D. Benne, Robert Chin, and Kenneth E. Corey (eds.), *The Planning of Change*, 3rd ed. (New York: Holt, Rinehart, 1969), pp. 22–45.

51The change agent descriptions here and following are developed from an exercise reported in J. William Pfeiffer and John E. Jones, *A Handbook of Structured Experiences for Human Relations Training*, vol. 2 (LaJolla, CA: University Associates, 1973).

52Ram N. Aditya, Robert J. House, and Steven Kerr, "Theory and Practice of Leadership: into the New Millennium," Chapter 6 in Cary L. Cooper and Edwin A. Locke, *Industrial and Organizational Psychology: Linking Theory with Practice* (Malden, MA: Blackwell, 2000).

53Information from Mike Schneider, "Disney Teaching Execs Magic of Customer Service," *Columbus Dispatch* (December 17, 2000), p. G9.

54Teresa M. Amabile, "How to Kill Creativity," *Harvard Business Review* (September/October 1998), pp. 77–87.

55See Jeffrey D. Ford and Laurie W. Ford, "Decoding Resistance to Change," *Harvard Business Review* (April, 2009), pp. 99–103.

56John P. Kotter and Leonard A. Schlesinger, "Choosing Strategies for Change," *Harvard Business Review*, vol. 57 (March/April 1979), pp. 109–112.

Feature Notes 10

Opening Quote—Information from "Men are People Too," *Bloomberg BusinessWeek* (June 3–June 6, 2013), pp. 59–63.

Working Mother—Information and quote from workingmother.com (retrieved September 29, 2006, and August 1, 2008); see also workingmother.com.

Role Models—Information and quotes from Matthew Lynley. "Survey Monkey Bucks the Trend—Picks up $100M in Debt Financing," *Venture Beat* (November 3, 2010), *http://venturebeat.com* (Accessed October 17, 2012); Diane Brady. "SurveyMonkey's Dave Goldberg on Managing Family Time," *Business Week* (Accessed October 17, 2012); Survey Monkey Management Team, Survey Monkey Website, *http://www.surveymonkey.com* (Accessed October 17, 2012); Aleron, Contributor, "Can You Only Really Work from 9 to 5?" *Forbes*, http://www.forbes.com (Accessed October 17, 2012).

Facts to Consider—Information from Joe Light, "Human-Resource Executives Say Reviews Are Off the Mark," *Wall Street Journal* (November 8, 2010), p. B8.

Ethics Check—Information from Jennifer Liberto, "CEOs Earn 354 Time More than Average Worker," *CNNMoney* (April 15, 2013): money.cnn.com (accessed April 15, 2013).

Manager's Library—Leslie Kwoh, "More Firms Bow to Generation Y's Demands." *Wall Street Journal* (August 22, 2012): online.wsj.com (accessed March 21, 2013); David Burstein, "TEDxNYU—David Burstein—Fast Future: The Rise of The Millennial Generation." Speech, May 11, 2012: YouTube.com; David Burstein Website, "About" and "Fast Future," davidburstein.com (accessed March 21, 2013).

Photo Essays—Online Job Searches—Information from "The Smart Way to Hire Workers," *The Economist*, Kindle edition (February 4, 2010). Zumba—Information from Bard Eagan, "Perks with a Payoff," *Wall Street Journal* (October 24, 2011), p. R3.

Hot Topic—Information and quotes from Rachel Emma Silverman, "My Colleague, My Paymaster," *The Wall Street Journal* (April 4, 2012), pp. B1, B8.

Endnotes 10

1See Jeffrey Pfeffer, *The Human Equation: Building Profits by Putting People First* (Boston: Harvard University Press, 1998).

2Jeffrey Pfeffer and John F. Veiga, "Putting People First for Organizational Success," *Academy of Management Executive*, vol. 13 (May 1999), pp. 37–48.

3Ibid. and Pfeffer, op. cit. See also James N. Baron and David M. Kreps, *Strategic Human Resources: Frameworks for General Managers* (New York: Wiley, 1999).

4Quote from William Bridges, "The End of the Job," *Fortune* (September 19, 1994), p. 68.

5Information from "New Face at Facebook Hopes to Map Out a Road to Growth," *Wall Street Journal* (April 15, 2008), pp. B1, B5.

6Baron and Kreps, op. cit.

7See also R. Roosevelt Thomas Jr.'s books, *Beyond Race and Gender* (New York: AMACOM, 1999) and (with Marjorie I. Woodruff) *Building a House for Diversity* (New York: AMACOM, 1999); and Richard D. Bucher, *Diversity Consciousness* (Englewood Cliffs, NJ: Prentice-Hall, 2000).

8Information from Courtney E. Martin, "Wal-Mart v. Dukes Ruling is Out of Synch with 21st Century Sex Discrimination," *The Christian Science Monitor* (June 22, 2011): csmonitor.com; Dahlia Lithwick, "Class Dismissed: The Supreme Court Decides That the Women of Wal-Mart Can't Have Their Day in Court," slate.com (June 20, 2011); and, "Walmart Statement Regarding Supreme Court Ruling in Dukes Case," corporate press release (June 20, 2011): walmartstores.com/pressromm.

9For a discussion of affirmative action, see R. Roosevelt Thomas Jr., "From 'Affirmative Action' to 'Affirming Diversity,' " *Harvard Business Review* (November/December 1990), pp. 107–117.

10See the discussion by David A. DeCenzo and Stephen P. Robbins, *Human Resource Management*, 6th ed. (New York: Wiley, 1999), pp. 66–68 and 81–83.

11Ibid., pp. 77–79.

12See, for example, Melanie Trottman, "Charges of Bias at Work Increase," *Wall Street Journal* (January 12, 2011), p. A2.

13Case reported in Sue Shellenbarger, "Work & Family Mailbox," *Wall Street Journal* (March 11, 2009), p. D6.

14See Frederick S. Lane, *The Naked Employee: How Technology Is Compromising Workplace Privacy* (New York: Amacom, 2003).

15This and other cases are described in Debra Cassens Weiss, "Companies Face 'Legal Potholes' as They Crack Down on Workers' Social Media Posts," ABAJournal.com (posted January 24, 2011).

16Information from Sheryl Gay Stolberg, "Obama Signs Equal-Pay Legislation," *New York Times* (January 30, 2009): www.nytimes.com.

17"What to Expect When You're Expecting," *Business Week* (May 26, 2008), p. 17.

18Ibid; and Madeline Heilman and Tyhler G. Okimoto, "Motherhood: A Potential Source of Bias in Employment Decisions," *Journal of Applied Psychology*, vol. 93, no. 1 (2008), pp. 189–98.

[19]Information and quotes from Jennifer Levitz and Philip Shiskin, "More Workers Cite Age Bias After Layoffs," *Wall Street Journal* (March 11, 2009), pp. D1, D2.

[20]For a good overview see Adrienne Fox, "Make a 'Deal,' " *HR Magazine* (January 2012), pp. 37–42.

[21]Information from Adam Lashinsky, "Zappos: Life After Acquisition," tech.fortune.cnn.com (November 24, 2010); Nicholas Boothman, "Will You be my Friend?" *Bloomberg BusinessWeek* (January 7 – January 13, 2013), pp. 63–65.

[22]Finding Job Candidates Who Aren't Looking," *Bloomberg BusinessWeek* (December 17–23, 2012), pp. 41–42; and, Rachel Emma Silverman and Lauren Weber, "The New Résumé: It's 140 Characters," *Wall Street Journal* (April 10, 2013), p. B8.

[23]"The Smart Way to Hire Hookers," *The Economist*, Kindle edition (February 4, 2010).

[24]Information and quote from Sarah E. Needleman, "The New Trouble on the Line," *Wall Street Journal* (June 2, 2009): www.wsj.com.

[25]See Sarah E. Needleman, "Initial Phone Interviews Do Count," *Wall Street Journal* (February 7, 2006), p. 29.

[26]Data reported in "At Work," *Wall Street Journal* (December 12, 2012), p. B6.

[27]See John P. Wanous, *Organizational Entry: Recruitment, Selection, and Socialization of Newcomers* (Reading, MA: Addison-Wesley, 1980), pp. 34–44.

[28]Josey Puliyenthuruthel, "How Google Searches for Talent," *Business Week* (April 11, 2005), p. 52.

[29]Quote from Ronald Henkoff, "Finding, Training, and Keeping the Best Service Workers," *Fortune* (October 3, 1994), pp. 110–122.

[30]Mina Kimes, "P&G's Leadership Machine," *Fortune* (May 20, 2009): money.cnn.com (accessed April 17, 2013).

[31]See Harry J. Martin, "Lessons Learned," *Wall Street Journal* (December 15, 2008), p. R11.

[32]"A to Z of Generation Y Attitudes," *Financial Times* (June 18, 2009); and "When Three Generations Can Work Better Than One," *Financial Times* (September 16, 2009).

[33]Dick Grote, "Performance Appraisal Reappraised," *Harvard Business Review Best Practice* (1999), Reprint F00105.

[34]See Larry L. Cummings and Donald P. Schwab, *Performance in Organizations: Determinants and Appraisal* (Glenview, IL: Scott, Foresman, 1973).

[35]For a good review, see Gary P. Latham, Joan Almost, Sara Mann, and Celia Moore, "New Developments in Performance Management," *Organizational Dynamics*, vol. 34, no. 1 (2005), pp. 77–87.

[36]See Mark R. Edwards and Ann J. Ewen, *360-Degree Feedback: The Powerful New Tool for Employee Feedback and Performance Improvement* (New York: Amacom, 1996).

[37]Examples are from Jena McGregor, "Job Review in 140 Keystrokes," *Business Week* (March 23 & 30, 2009), p. 58.

[38]Kimes, op. cit.

[39]Timothy Butler and James Waldroop, "Job Sculpting: The Art of Retaining Your Best People," *Harvard Business Review* (September/October 1999), pp. 144–52.

[40]Information from "What Are the Most Effective Retention Tools?" *Fortune* (October 9, 2000), p. S7.

[41]Quote from "Men are People Too," *Bloomberg BusinessWeek* (June 3–June 6, 2013), pp. 59–63.

[42]See Betty Friedan, *Beyond Gender: The New Politics of Work and the Family* (Washington, DC: Woodrow Wilson Center Press, 1997); and James A. Levine, *Working Fathers: New Strategies for Balancing Work and Family* (Reading, MA: Addison-Wesley, 1997).

[43]See Ravi S. Gajendran and David A. Harrison, "The Good, the Bad, and the Unknown about Telecommuting: Meta-Analysis of Psychological Mediators and Individual Consequences, "*Journal of Applied Psychology*, vol. 92 (2007), pp. 1524–1541.

[44]Claire Suddath, "Work-from-Home Truths, Half-Truths, and Myths," *Bloomberg BusinessWeek* (March 4–March 10, 2013), p. 75.

[45]Ibid.

[46]Ibid.

[47]Examples from Amy Saunders, "A Creative Approach to Work," *Columbus Dispatch* (May 2, 2008), pp. C1, C9; Shellenbarger, op. cit. (2007); and Michelle Conlin and Jay Greene, "How to Make a Microserf Smile," *Business Week* (September 10, 2007), pp. 57–59.

[48]"A Saner Workplace," *Business Week* (June 1, 2009), pp. 66–69.

[49]Erin Hatton, "The Rise of the Permanent Temp Economy," *New York Times* (January 26, 2013), nytimes.com (accessed April 16, 2013).

[50]Michael Orey, "They're Employees, No, They're Not," *Business Week* (November 16, 2009), pp. 73–74.

[51]Information and quotes from Peter Coy, Michelle Conlin, and Moira Herbst, "The Disposable Worker," *Business Week* (January 18, 2010), pp. 33–39.

[52]Quote from Sudeep Reddy, "Wary Companies Rely on Temporary Workers," *Wall Street Journal* (March 6–7, 2010), p. A. 4.

[53]See Kaja Whitehouse, "More Companies Offer Packages Linking Pay Plans to Performance," *Wall Street Journal* (December 13, 2005), p. B6.

[54]Ibid.

[55]Information and quotes from Lauren Weber and Rachel Emma Silverman, "Workers Share Their Salary Secrets," *Wall Street Journal* (April 17, 2013), p. B1

[56]Erin White, "How to Reduce Turnover," *Wall Street Journal* (November 21, 2005), p. B5.

[57]Information from Susan Pulliam, "New Dot-Com Mantra: 'Just Pay Me in Cash, Please,' " *Wall Street Journal* (November 28, 2000), p. C1.

[58]Nanette Byrnes, "Pain, but No Layoffs at Nucor," *Business Week* (March 26, 2009), www.businessweek.com.

[59]Information from www.intel.com; and "Stock Ownership for Everyone," *Hewitt Associates* (November 27, 2000): www.hewitt.com

[60]"Benefits: For Companies, the Runaway Train Is Slowing Down," *Business Week* (February 16, 2009), p. 15.

[61]For reviews, see Richard B. Freeman and James L. Medoff, *What Do Unions Do?* (New York: Basic Books, 1984); Charles C. Heckscher, *The New Unionism* (New York: Basic Books, 1988); and Barry T. Hirsch, *Labor Unions and the Economic Performance of Firms* (Kalamazoo, MI: W. E. Upjohn Institute for Employment Research, 1991).

[62]Melanie Trottmaa and Kris Maher, "Organized Labor Loses Members, *Wall Street Journal*" (January 24, 2013) p. A6.

[63]Example from Timothy Aeppel, "Pay Scales Divide Factory Floors," *Wall Street Journal* (April 9, 2008), p. B4.

[64]Matthew Dolan, "Ford to Begin Hiring at Much Lower Wages," *Wall Street Journal* (January 26, 2010), p. B1.

Feature Notes 11

Role Models—Information and quotes from Lorraine Monroe, "Leadership Is About Making Vision Happen—What I Call 'Vision Acts,'" *Fast Company* (March 2001), p. 98; Lorraine Monroe Leadership Institute Web site: www.lorrainemonroe.com. See also Lorraine Monroe, *Nothing's Impossible: Leadership Lessons from Inside and Outside the Classroom* (New York: Public Affairs Books, 1999), and *The Monroe Doctrine: An ABC Guide to What Great Bosses Do* (New York: PublicAffairs Books, 2003).

Facts to Consider—Information from "Many U.S. Employees Have Negative Attitudes to Their Jobs, Employers and Top Managers," Harris Poll #38 (May 6, 2005), retrieved from www.harrisinteractive.com.

Ethics Check—The zone of indifference is described by Chester Barnard in *Functions of the Executive* (Cambridge, MA: Harvard University Press, 1971), 30th Anniversary Edition.

Kraft Foods—Information and quotes from Irene Rosenfeld, "Irene Rosenfeld Drives Change with 'Rules of the Road'," *Wall Street Journal*, Special Advertising Section (October 6, 2009), p. A17; David Kesmodel and Ceceilie Rohwedder, "Sugar and Spice: A Clash of Two Change Agents," *Wall Street Journal* (September 8, 2009), p. A17; Ilan Brat, "A Jar of New Vegmite, a Window into Kraft," *Wall Street Journal* (September 30, 2009), pp. B1, B2; and Susan Verfield and Michael Arndt, "Kraft's Sugar Rush," *Business Week* (January 25, 2010), pp. 37–39.

Hot Topic—Information and incident from Julian Sancton, "Milgram at McDonald's," *Bloomberg BusinessWeek* (August 27–September 2, 2012), pp. 74–75.

Endnotes 11

[1]Abraham Zaleznick, "Leaders and Managers: Are They Different?" *Harvard Business Review* (May/June 1977), pp. 67–78.

[2]Tom Peters, "Rule #3: Leadership Is Confusing as Hell," *Fast Company* (March 2001), pp. 124–40.

[3]Quotations from Marshall Loeb, "Where Leaders Come From," *Fortune* (September 19, 1994), pp. 241–42; Genevieve Capowski, "Anatomy of a Leader: Where Are the Leaders of Tomorrow?" *Management Review* (March 1994), pp. 10–17. For additional thoughts, see Warren Bennis, *Why Leaders Can't Lead* (San Francisco: Jossey-Bass, 1996).

[4]See Jean Lipman-Blumen, *Connective Leadership: Managing in a Changing World* (New York: Oxford University Press, 1996), pp. 3–11.

[5]Rosabeth Moss Kanter, "Power Failure in Management Circuits," *Harvard Business Review* (July/August 1979), pp. 65–75.

[6]The classic treatment of these power bases is John R. P. French Jr. and Bertram Raven, "The Bases of Social Power," in Darwin Cartwright (ed.), *Group Dynamics: Research and Theory* (Evanson, IL: Row, Peterson, 1962), pp. 607–13.

[7]For managerial applications of this basic framework, see Gary Yukl and Tom Taber, "The Effective Use of Managerial Power," *Personnel,* vol. 60 (1983), pp. 37–49; and Robert C. Benfari, Harry E. Wilkinson, and Charles D. Orth, "The Effective Use of Power," *Business Horizons,* vol. 29 (1986), pp. 12–16. Gary A. Yukl, *Leadership in Organizations,* 4th ed. (Englewood Cliffs, NJ: Prentice-Hall, 1998), includes "information" as a separate, but related, power source.

[8]James M. Kouzes and Barry Z. Posner, "The Leadership Challenge," *Success* (April 1988), p. 68. See also their books *Credibility: How Leaders Gain and Lose It: Why People Demand It* (San Francisco: Jossey-Bass, 1996); *Encouraging the Heart: A Leader's Guide to Rewarding and Recognizing Others* (San Francisco: Jossey-Bass, 1999); and *The Leadership Challenge: How to Get Extraordinary Things Done in Organizations,* 3rd ed. (San Francisco: Jossey-Bass, 2002).

[9]Quote from Andy Serwer, "Game Changers: Legendary Basketball Coach John Wooden and Starbucks' Howard Schultz Talk About a Common Interest—Leadership," *Fortune* (August 11, 2008): www.cnnmoney.com.

[10]Burt Nanus, *Visionary Leadership: Creating a Compelling Sense of Vision for Your Organization* (San Francisco: Jossey-Bass, 1992).

[11]The early work on leader traits is well represented in Ralph M. Stogdill, "Personal Factors Associated with Leadership: A Survey of the Literature," *Journal of Psychology,* vol. 25 (1948), pp. 35–71. See also Edwin E. Ghiselli, *Explorations in Management Talent* (Santa Monica, CA: Goodyear, 1971); and Shirley A. Kirkpatrick and Edwin A. Locke, "Leadership: Do Traits Really Matter?" *Academy of Management Executive* (1991), pp. 48–60.

[12]See also John W. Gardner's article, "The Context and Attributes of Leadership," *New Management,* vol. 5 (1988), pp. 18–22; John P. Kotter, *The Leadership Factor* (New York: Free Press, 1988); and Bernard M. Bass, *Stogdill's Handbook of Leadership* (New York: Free Press, 1990).

[13]Kirkpatrick and Locke, op. cit. (1991).

[14]This terminology comes from Robert R. Blake and Jane Strygley Mouton, *The New Managerial Grid III* (Houston: Gulf Publishing, 1985) and the classic studies by Kurt Lewin and his associates at the University of Iowa. See, for example, K. Lewin and R. Lippitt, "An Experimental Approach to the Study of Autocracy and Democracy: A Preliminary Note," *Sociometry,* vol. 1 (1938), pp. 292–300; K. Lewin, "Field Theory and Experiment in Social Psychology: Concepts and Methods," *American Journal of Sociology,* vol. 44 (1939); and K. Lewin, R. Lippitt, and R. K. White, "Patterns of Aggressive Behavior in Experimentally Created Social Climates," *Journal of Social Psychology,* vol. 10 (1939), pp. 271–301.

[15]See Blake and Mouton, op. cit.

[16]For a good discussion of this theory, see Fred E. Fiedler, Martin M. Chemers, and Linda Mahar, *The Leadership Match Concept* (New York: Wiley, 1978); Fiedler's current contingency research with the cognitive resource theory is summarized in Fred E. Fiedler and Joseph E. Garcia, *New Approaches to Effective Leadership* (New York: Wiley, 1987).

[17]Paul Hersey and Kenneth H. Blanchard, *Management and Organizational Behavior* (Englewood Cliffs, NJ: Prentice-Hall, 1988). For an interview with Paul Hersey on the origins of the model, see John R. Schermerhorn Jr., "Situational Leadership: Conversations with Paul Hersey," *Mid-American Journal of Business* (Fall 1997), pp. 5–12.

[18]See Claude L. Graeff, "The Situational Leadership Theory: A Critical View," *Academy of Management Review,* vol. 8 (1983), pp. 285–91; and Carmen F. Fernandez and Robert P. Vecchio, "Situational Leadership Theory Revisited: A Test of an Across-Jobs Perspective," *Leadership Quarterly,* vol. 8 (summer 1997), pp. 67–84.

[19]See, for example, Robert J. House, "A Path-Goal Theory of Leader Effectiveness," *Administrative Sciences Quarterly,* vol. 16 (1971), pp. 321–38; and Robert J. House and Terrence R. Mitchell, "Path-Goal Theory of Leadership," *Journal of Contemporary Business* (Autumn 1974), pp. 81–97. The path-goal theory is reviewed by Bass, op. cit., and Yukl, op. cit. A supportive review of research is offered in Julie Indvik, "Path-Goal Theory of Leadership. A Meta-Analysis," in John A. Pearce II and Richard B. Robinson Jr. (eds.), *Academy of Management Best Paper Proceedings* (1986), pp. 189–92.

[20]See the discussions of path-goal theory in Yukl, op. cit.; and Bernard M. Bass, "Leadership: Good, Better, Best," *Organizational Dynamics* (Winter 1985), pp. 26–40.

[21]See Steven Kerr and John Jermier, "Substitutes for Leadership: Their Meaning and Measurement," *Organizational Behavior and Human Performance,* vol. 22 (1978), pp. 375–403; Jon P. Howell and Peter W. Dorfman, "Leadership and Substitutes for Leadership Among Professional and Nonprofessional Workers," *Journal of Applied Behavioral Science,* vol. 22 (1986), pp. 29–46.

[22]An early presentation of the theory is F. Dansereau Jr., G. Graen, and W. J. Haga, "A Vertical Dyad Linkage Approach to Leadership Within Formal Organizations: A Longitudinal Investigation of the Role Making Process," *Organizational Behavior and Human Performance,* vol. 13, pp. 46–78.

[23]This discussion is based on Yukl, op. cit., pp. 117–22.

[24]Ibid.

[25]Victor H. Vroom and Arthur G. Jago, *The New Leadership: Managing Participation in Organizations* (Englewood Cliffs, NJ: Prentice-Hall, 1988). This is based on earlier work by Victor H. Vroom, "A New Look in Managerial Decision-Making," *Organizational Dynamics* (Spring 1973), pp. 66–80; and Victor H. Vroom and Phillip Yetton, *Leadership and Decision-Making* (Pittsburgh: University of Pittsburgh Press, 1973).

[26]Vroom and Jago, op. cit.

[27]For a related discussion, see Edgar H. Schein, *Process Consultation Revisited: Building the Helping Relationship* (Reading, MA: Addison-Wesley, 1999).

[28]For a review, see Yukl, op. cit.

[29]See the discussion by Victor H. Vroom, "Leadership and the Decision Making Process," *Organizational Dynamics,* vol. 28 (2000), pp. 82–94.

[30]Survey data from Gallup Leadership Institute, *Briefings Report 2005-01* (Lincoln, NE: University of Nebraska–Lincoln); "The Stat," *Business Week* (September 12, 2005), p. 16; and "U.S. Job Satisfaction Keeps Falling, the Conference Board Reports Today," The Conference Board (February 28, 2005), retrieved from www.conference-board.org.

[31]Among the popular books addressing this point of view are Warren Bennis and Burt Nanus, *Leaders: The Strategies for Taking Charge* (New York: Harper Business 1997); Max DePree, *Leadership Is an Art* (New York: Doubleday, 1989); Kouzes and Posner, op. cit. (2002).

[32]The distinction was originally made by James McGregor Burns, *Leadership* (New York: Harper & Row, 1978) and was further developed by Bernard Bass, *Leadership and Performance Beyond Expectations* (New York: Free Press, 1985), and Bernard M. Bass. "Leadership: Good, Better, Best," *Organizational Dynamics* (Winter 1985), pp. 26–40. See also Bernard M. Bass, "Does the Transactional-Transformational Leadership Paradigm Transcend Organizational and National Boundaries?" *American Psychologist,* vol. 52 (February 1997), pp. 130–39.

[33]See the discussion in Bass, op. cit., 1997.

[34]This list is based on Kouzes and Posner, op. cit.; Gardner, op. cit.

[35]Daniel Goleman, "Leadership That Gets Results," *Harvard Business Review* (March/April 2000), pp. 78–90. See also his books *Emotional Intelligence* (New York: Bantam Books, 1995) and *Working with Emotional Intelligence* (New York: Bantam Books, 1998).

[36]Daniel Goleman, Annie McKee, and Richard E. Boyatzis, *Primal Leadership: Realizing the Power of Emotional Intelligence* (Boston, MA: Harvard Business School Press, 2002), p. 3.

[37]Daniel Goleman, "What Makes a Leader?" *Harvard Business Review* (November/December 1998), pp. 93–102.

[38]Goleman, Working with Emotional Intelligence, op. cit. (1998).

[39]Information from "Women and Men, Work and Power," *Fast Company,* issue 13 (1998), p. 71.

[40]Jane Shibley Hyde, "The Gender Similarities Hypothesis," *American Psychologist,* vol. 60, no. 6 (2005), pp. 581–92.

[41]A. H. Eagley, S. J. Daran, and M. G. Makhijani, "Gender and the Effectiveness of Leaders: A Meta-Analysis," *Psychological Bulletin,* vol. 117 (1995), pp. 125–45.

[42]Research on gender issues in leadership is reported in Sally Helgesen, *The Female Advantage: Women's Ways of Leadership* (New York: Doubleday, 1990); Judith B. Rosener, "Ways Women Lead," *Harvard Business Review* (November/December 1990), pp. 119–25; Alice H. Eagley, Steven J. Karau, and Blair T. Johnson, "Gender and Leadership Style Among School Principals: A Meta Analysis," *Administrative Science Quarterly,* vol. 27 (1992), pp. 76–102; Lipman-Blumen, op. cit.; Alice H. Eagley, Mary C. Johannesen-Smith, and Marloes L. van Engen, "Transformational, Transactional and Laissez-Faire Leadership: A Meta-Analysis of Women and Men," *Psychological Bulletin,* vol. 124, no. 4 (2003), pp. 569–591; and Carol Hymowitz, "Too Many Women Fall for Stereotypes of Selves, Study Says," *Wall Street Journal* (October 24, 2005), p. B. 1.

[43]Data reported by Rochelle Sharpe, "As Women Rule," *Business Week* (November 20, 2000), p. 75.

[44]Eagley et al., op. cit. (2003); Hymowitz, op. cit.; Rosener, op. cit.; Vroom, op. cit.,1973 and 2000; and, Ibarra and Obodaru, op. cit.

[45]Herminia Ibarra and Otilia Obodaru, "Women and the Vision Thing," *Harvard Business Review* (January, 2009): Reprint R0901E.

[46]Rosener, op. cit, (1990).

[47]See research summarized by Stephanie Armour, "Do Women Compete in Unhealthy Ways at Work?" *USA Today* (December 30, 2005), pp. B1–B2.

[48]Quote from "As Leaders, Women Rule," *Business Week* (November 20, 2000), pp. 75–84. Rosabeth Moss Kanter is the author of *Men and Women of the Corporation,* 2nd ed. (New York: Basic Books, 1993).

[49]See Del Jones, "Women CEOs Slowly Gain on Corporate America," *USA Today* (January 1, 2009): www.usatoday.com; Morice Mendoza, "Davos 2009: Where Are the Women?" *Business Week* (January 26, 2009): www.businessweek.com; and Susan Bulkeley Butler, *Women Count: A Guide to Changing the World* (South Bend, IN: Purdue University Press, 2010).

[50]Hyde, op. cit.; Hymowitz, op. cit.

[51]For debate on whether some transformational leadership qualities tend to be associated more with female than male leaders, see "Debate: Ways Women and Men Lead," *Harvard Business Review* (January/February 1991), pp. 150–60.

[52]See Terry Thomas, John R. Schermerhorn Jr., and John W. Dienhart, "Strategic Leadership of Ethical Behavior in Business," *Academy of Management Executive,* vol. 18 (May 2004), pp. 56–66.

[53]"Many U.S. Employees Have Negative Attitudes to Their Jobs, Employers and Top Managers," Harris Poll #38 (May 6, 2005), retrieved from www.harrisinteractive.com.

[54]Information from "The Stat," *Business Week* (September 12, 2005), p. 16.

[55]See Thomas et al., op. cit.

[56]Doug May, Adrian Chan, Timothy Hodges, and Bruce Avolio, "Developing the Moral Component of Authentic Leadership," *Organizational Dynamics,* vol. 32 (2003), pp. 247–60.

[57]Peter F. Drucker, "Leadership: More Doing than Dash," *Wall Street Journal* (January 6, 1988), p. 16.

[58]"Information from Southwest CEO Puts Emphasis on Character," *USA Today* (September 26, 2004), retrieved from www.usatoday/money/companies/management on December 12, 2005.

[59]Nitin Nohria, "The Big Question: What Should We Teach Our Business Leaders?" *Bloomberg BusinessWeek* (November 14–20, 2011), p. 68.

[60]Ibid.

[61]See Drucker, op cit., 1988.

[62]Robert K. Greenleaf and Larry C. Spears, *The Power of Servant Leadership: Essays* (San Francisco: Berrett-Koehler, 1996).

[63]Jay A. Conger, "Leadership: The Art of Empowering Others," *Academy of Management Executive,* vol. 3 (1989), pp. 17–24.

[64]Max DePree, "An Old Pro's Wisdom: It Begins with a Belief in People," *New York Times* (September 10, 1989), p. F2; DePree, op. cit.; David Woodruff, "Herman Miller: How Green Is My Factory," *Business Week* (September 16, 1991), pp. 54–56; and Max DePree, *Leadership Jazz* (New York: Doubleday, 1992).

[65]Lorraine Monroe, "Leadership Is About Making Vision Happen—What I Call 'Vision Acts,'" *Fast Company* (March 2001), p. 98; School Leadership Academy Web site: www.lorrainemonroe.com.

[66]Greenleaf and Spears, op. cit., p. 78.

Feature Notes 12

The Social Network—Eric Ditzian, "The Social Network: The Reviews are In!" mtv.com (October 1, 2010); and Ethan Smith, "'Social Network' Opens at No. 1," *Wall Street Journal* (October 4, 2010), p. B5.

Role Models—Information and quotes from corporate Web sites; The Entrepreneur's Hall of Fame: www.1tbn.com/halloffame.html; Knowledge@Wharton, "The Importance of Being Richard Branson," *Wharton School Publishing* (June 3, 2005), www.whartonsp.com; Diane Brady, "Richard Branson," *Bloomberg BusinessWeek* (November 22–28, 2010), p. 122; and http://www.virgin.com/.

Facts to Consider—Information from Rich Morin and Seth Model, "A Third of Americans Now Say They Are in the Lower Classes," *Pew Research Social & Demographic Trends* (September 10, 2012): pewsocialtrends.org (accessed April 29, 2013).

Spanx—Information from Andrew Ward, "Spanx Queen Firms Up the Bottom Line," *Financial Times* (November 30, 2006), p. 7; and Simona Covel, "A Dated Industry Gets a Modern Makeover," *Wall Street Journal* (August 7, 2008), p. B9.

Photo Essays—Bias—Information from Andrew M. Carton and Ashleigh Shelby Rosette, "Explaining Bias Against Black Leaders: Integrating Theory on Information Processing and Goal-Based Stereotyping," *Academy of Management Journal,* vol. 54, No. 6 (2011), pp. 1141–1158. Job Satisfaction—Information from PewResearch, "Take This Job and Love It," pewresearch.org (accessed October 2, 2012).

Hot Topic—Information from David Gelles, "The Mind Business," *Financial Times,* U.S. Kindle Edition (August 25, 2012).

Endnotes 12

[1]This example is reported in *Esquire* (December 1986), p. 243. Emphasis is added to the quotation. Note: Nussbaum became director of the Labor Department's Women's Bureau during the Clinton administration and subsequently moved to the AFL–CIO as head of the Women's Bureau.

[2]See H. R. Schiffman, *Sensation and Perception: An Integrated Approach,* 3rd ed. (New York: Wiley, 1990).

[3]Information from "Misconceptions About Women in the Global Arena Keep Their Numbers Low," Catalyst study: www.catalystwomen.org; Yochanan Altman and Susan Shortland, "Women and International Assignments: Taking Stock," *Human Resource Management,* vol. 47 (2008), pp. 196–216; and Sebastian Reiche, "Expatriatus," *IESE Business School Blog* (March 29, 2011): blog.iese.edu (accessed April 28, 2013).

[4]The classic work is Dewitt C. Dearborn and Herbert A. Simon, "Selective Perception: A Note on the Departmental Identification of Executives," *Sociometry,* vol. 21 (1958), pp. 140–44. See also J. P. Walsh, "Selectivity and Selective Perception: Belief Structures and Information Processing," *Academy of Management Journal,* vol. 24 (1988), pp. 453–70.

[5]Quote from Sheila O'Flanagan, "Underestimate Casual Dressers at Your Peril," *The Irish Times* (July 22, 2005).

[6]See William L. Gardner and Mark J. Martinko, "Impression Management in Organizations," *Journal of Management* (June 1988), pp. 332–43.

[7]Sandy Wayne and Robert Liden, "Effects of Impression Management on Performance Ratings," *Academy of Management Journal* (February 2005), pp. 232–52.

[8]Carl G. Jung, *Psychological Types,* H. G. Baynes trans. (Princeton, NJ: Princeton University Press, 1971).

[9]I. Briggs-Myers, *Introduction to Type* (Palo Alto, CA: Consulting Psychologists Press, 1980).

[10]See, for example, William L. Gardner and Mark J. Martinko, "Using the Myers-Briggs Type Indicator to Study Managers: A Literature Review and Research Agenda," *Journal of Management,* vol. 22 (1996), pp. 45–83; Naomi L. Quenk, *Essentials of Myers-Briggs Type Indicator Assessment* (New York: Wiley, 2000).

[11]See M. R. Barrick and M. K. Mount, "The Big Five Personality Dimensions and Job Performance: A Meta-Analysis," *Personnel Psychology,* vol. 44 (1991), pp. 1–26.

[12]For a sample of research, see G. M. Hurtz and J. J. Donovan, "Personality and Job Performance: The Big Five Revisited," *Journal of Applied Psychology,* vol. 85 (2000), pp. 869–79; and T. A. Judge and R. Ilies, "Relationship of Personality to Performance Motivation: A Meta-Analytic Review," *Journal of Applied Psychology,* vol. 87 (2002), pp. 797–807.

[13]This discussion based in part on John R. Schermerhorn Jr., James G. Hunt, and Richard N. Osborn, *Organizational Behavior,* 9th ed. (New York: Wiley, 2005), pp. 54–60.

[14]J. B. Rotter, "Generalized Expectancies for Internal versus External Control of Reinforcement," *Psychological Monographs,* vol. 80 (1966), pp. 1–28.

[15]T. W. Adorno, E. Frenkel-Brunswick, D. J. Levinson, and R. N. Sanford, *The Authoritarian Personality* (New York: Harper & Row, 1950).

[16]Niccolo Machiavelli, *The Prince,* trans. George Bull (Middlesex, UK: Penguin, 1961).

[17]See M. Snyder, *Public Appearances/Private Realities: The Psychology of Self-Monitoring* (New York: Freeman, 1987).

[18]See Arthur P. Brief, Randall S. Schuler, and Mary Van Sell, *Managing Job Stress* (Boston: Little, Brown, 1981), pp. 7, 8.

[19]The classic work is Meyer Friedman and Ray Roseman, *Type A Behavior and Your Heart* (New York: Knopf, 1974).

[20]Sue Shellenbarger, "Do We Work More or Not? Either Way, We Feel Frazzled," *Wall Street Journal* (July 30, 1997), p. B1; and "Argggyh! American Workers are at the Breaking Point," *The Pony Blog,* cnbc.com (April 9, 2013), accessed April 11, 2013.

[21]Ibid.

[22]See Hans Selye, *Stress in Health and Disease* (Boston: Butterworth, 1976).

[23]See Steve M. Jex, *Stress and Job Performance* (San Francisco: Jossey-Bass, 1998).

[24]Carol Hymowitz, "Can Workplace Stress Get *Worse?" Wall Street Journal* (January 16, 2001), pp. B1, B3.

[25]The extreme case of "workplace violence" is discussed by Richard V. Denenberg and Mark Braverman, *The Violence-Prone Workplace* (Ithaca, NY: Cornell University Press, 1999).

[26]David Gauthier-Villars and Leila Abboud, "In France, CEOs Can Become Hostages," *Wall Street Journal* (April 3, 2009), pp. B1, B4.

[27]See Daniel C. Ganster and Larry Murphy, "Workplace Interventions to Prevent Stress-Related Illness: Lessons from Research and Practice," Chapter 2 in Cary L. Cooper and Edwin A Locke (eds.), *Industrial and Organizational Psychology: Linking Theory with Practice* (Malden, MA: Blackwell Business, 2000); Jonathan D. Quick, Amy B. Henley, and James Campbell Quick, "The Balancing Act—At Work and at Home," *Organizational Dynamics,* vol. 33 (2004), pp. 426–37.

[28]Data from "Michael Mandel, "The Real Reasons You're Working So Hard," *Business Week* (October 3, 2005), pp. 60–70; "Many U.S. Employees Have Negative Attitudes to Their Jobs, Employers and Top Managers," *The Harris Poll #38* (May 6, 2005), retrieved from www.harrisinteractive.com; Sue Shellenbarger, "If You Need to Work Better, Maybe Try Working Less," *Wall Street Journal* (September 23, 2009), pp. D1, D2.

[29]See Melinda Beck, "Stress So Bad It Hurts—Really," *Wall Street Journal* (March 17, 2009), pp. D1, D6.

[30]Information and quote from Joann S. Lublin, "How One Black Woman Lands Her Top Jobs: Risks and Networking," *Wall Street Journal* (March 4, 2003), p. B1.

[31]Martin Fishbein and Icek Ajzen, *Belief, Attitude, Intention and Behavior: An Introduction to Theory and Research* (Reading, MA: Addison-Wesley, 1973).

[32]See Leon Festinger, *A Theory of Cognitive Dissonance* (Palo Alto, CA: Stanford University Press, 1957).

[33]For an overview, see Paul E. Spector, *Job Satisfaction* (Thousand Oaks, CA: Sage, 1997); Timothy A. Judge and Allan H. Church, "Job Satisfaction: Research and Practice," Chapter 7 in Cooper and Locke (eds.), op. cit. (2000); Timothy A. Judge, "Promote Job Satisfaction Through Mental Challenge," Chapter 6 in Edwin A. Locke (ed.), *The Blackwell Handbook of Principles of Organizational Behavior* (Malden, MA: Blackwell, 2004).

[34]Information in Stay Informed from Linda Grant, "Happy Workers, High Returns," *Fortune* (January 12, 1998), p. 81; Judge and Church op. cit. (2004); "U.S. Employees More Dissatisfied with Their Jobs," Associated Press (February 28, 2005), retrieved from www.msnbc.com; "U.S. Job Satisfaction Keeps Falling, the Conference Board Reports Today," *The Conference Board* (February 28, 2005), retrieved from www.conference-board.org; and Salary. com, "Survey Shows Impact of Downturn on Job Satisfaction," *OH&S: Occupational Health and Safety* (February 7, 2009): www.ohsonline.com.

[35]What Workers Want: A Worldwide Study of Attitudes to Work and Work-Life Balance (London: FDS International, 2007).

[36]Data reported in "When Loyalty Erodes, So Do Profits," *Business Week* (August 13, 2001), p. 8.

[37]Dennis W. Organ, *Organizational Citizenship Behavior: The Good Soldier Syndrome* (Lexington, MA: Lexington Books, 1988).

[38]See Mark C. Bolino and William H. Turnley, "Going the Extra Mile: Cultivating and Managing Employee Citizenship Behavior," *Academy of Management Executive,* vol. 17 (August 2003), pp. 60–67.

[39]Tony DiRomualdo, "The High Cost of Employee Disengagement" (July 7, 2004): www.wistechnology.com.

[40]These relationships are discussed in Charles N. Greene, "The Satisfaction-Performance Controversy," *Business Horizons,* vol. 15 (1982), pp. 31; Michelle T. Iaffaldano and Paul M. Muchinsky, "Job Satisfaction and Job Performance: A Meta Analysis," *Psychological Bulletin,* vol. 97 (1985), pp. 251–73.

[41]This discussion follows conclusions in Judge, op. cit. (2004). For a summary of the early research, see Iaffaldano and Muchinsky, op. cit.

[42]Daniel Goleman, "Leadership That Gets Results," *Harvard Business Review* (March–April 2000), pp. 78–90. See also his books *Emotional Intelligence* (New York: Bantam Books, 1995) and *Working with Emotional Intelligence* (New York: Bantam Books, 1998).

[43]"Charm Offensive: Why America's CEOs Are So Eager to Be Loved," *BusinessWeek* (June 26, 2006): businessweek.com (retrieved September 20, 2008).

[44]See Robert G. Lord, Richard J. Klimoski, and Ruth Knafer (eds.), *Emotions in the Workplace; Understanding the Structure and Role of Emotions in Organizational Behavior* (San Francisco: Jossey-Bass, 2002); Roy L. Payne and Cary L. Cooper (eds.), *Emotions at Work: Theory Research and Applications for Management* (Chichester, UK: Wiley, 2004); and Daniel Goleman and Richard Boyatzis, "Social Intelligence and the Biology of Leadership," *Harvard Business Review* (September 2008), Reprint R0809E.

[45]J. E. Bono and R. Ilies, "Charisma, Positive Emotions and Mood Contagion," *Leadership Quarterly,* vol. 17 (2006), pp. 317–34; and Goleman and Boyatzis, op. cit.

Feature Notes 13

Opening Quote—*J. K. Rowling, Harry Potter and the Half-Blood Prince*

Role Models—Information and quotes from Jennifer Fleming, "How to Distinguish Between the Different Types of Entrepreneurs," eHow website, April 24, 2011. ehow.com/how (Accessed November 18, 2012); Rosbeth Cantor, "Mark Zuckerberg and Misery as Motivation," *BusinessWeek,* November 1, 2010, http://www.bloomberg.com (Accessed November 18, 2012); and Colleen DeBaise, "How to Decide If Entrepreneurship Is Right for You," *Wall Street Journal* (December 2009), guides.wsj.com (Accessed November 18, 2012).

Facts to Consider—Information from "UK Headhunters Pledge New Focus on Gender," *Financial Times,* Kindle Edition (May 11, 2011); Joseph Schumpeter, "The Mommy Track," *The Economist,* Kindle Edition (August 25, 2012); Jill Parkin, "Women at Director Level Help to Make a Marque, *Financial Times,* Kindle Edition (May 22, 2012); "Gender Politics," The Economist, Kindle Edition (September 7, 2012); Joann S. Lublin, "Europe's Boards Recruit U.S. Women," *Wall Street Journal* (September 12, 2012), p. B8; James Fontanella-Khan, "EU Scraps Board Quotas for Women," *Financial Times,* Kindle Edition (October 24, 2012); and Jeff Green, "The Boardroom's Still the Boys' Room," *Bloomberg BusinessWeek* (October 29–November 4, 2012), pp. 25–26.

Ethics Check—Information on this situation from Jared Sandberg, "Why You May Regret Looking at Papers Left on the Office Copier," *Wall Street Journal* (June 20, 2006), p. B1.

HopeLab—Information from "HopeLab Video Games for Health," *Fast Company* (December, 2008/ January, 2009), p. 116; "Zamzee works! Research, Iteration and Positive New Results," (September 24, 2012): blog.hopelab.org; and hopelab.org.

Endnotes 13

[1]Melinda Beck, "If at First You Don't Succeed, You're in Excellent Company," *Wall Street Journal* (April 29, 2008), p. D1.

[2]See Abraham H. Maslow, *Eupsychian Management* (Homewood, IL: Richard D. Irwin, 1965); and Abraham H. Maslow, *Motivation and Person-*

ality, 2nd ed. (New York: Harper & Row, 1970). For a research perspective, see Mahmoud A. Wahba and Lawrence G. Bridwell, "Maslow Reconsidered: A Review of Research on the Need Hierarchy," *Organizational Behavior and Human Performance,* vol. 16 (1976), pp. 212–40.

[3]Clayton P. Alderfer, *Existence, Relatedness, and Growth* (New York: Free Press, 1972).

[4]Examples and quotes from Jane Hodges, "A Virtual Matchmaker for Volunteers," *Wall Street Journal* (February 12, 2009), p. D3; Dana Mattioli, "The Laid-Off Can Do Well Doing Good," *Wall Street Journal* (March 17, 2009), p. D1; Elizabeth Garone, "Paying It Forward Is a Full-Time Job," *Wall Street Journal* (March 17, 2009), p. D4.

[5]Developed originally from a discussion in Edward E. Lawler III, *Motivation in Work Organizations* (Monterey, CA: Brooks/Cole Publishing, 1973), pp. 30–36.

[6]For a collection of McClelland's work, see David C. McClelland, *The Achieving Society* (New York: Van Nostrand, 1961); "Business Drive and National Achievement," *Harvard Business Review,* vol. 40 (July/August 1962), pp. 99–112; David C. McClelland, *Human Motivation* (Glenview, IL: Scott, Foresman, 1985); David C. McClelland and Richard E. Boyatsis, "The Leadership Motive Pattern and Long-Term Success in Management," *Journal of Applied Psychology,* vol. 67 (1982), pp. 737–43.

[7]David C. McClelland and David H. Burnham, "Power Is the Great Motivator," *Harvard Business Review* (March/April 1976), pp. 100–10.

[8]The complete two-factor theory is in Frederick Herzberg, Bernard Mausner, and Barbara Block Synderman, *The Motivation to Work,* 2nd ed. (New York: Wiley, 1967); Frederick Herzberg, "One More Time: How Do You Motivate Employees?" *Harvard Business Review* (January/February 1968), pp. 53–62, and reprinted as an *HBR classic* (September/October 1987), pp. 109–20.

[9]Critical reviews are provided by Robert J. House and Lawrence A. Wigdor, "Herzberg's Dual-Factor Theory of Job Satisfaction and Motivation: A Review of the Evidence and a Criticism," *Personnel Psychology,* vol. 20 (Winter 1967), pp. 369–89; and Steven Kerr, Anne Harlan, and Ralph Stogdill, "Preference for Motivator and Hygiene Factors in a Hypothetical Interview Situation," *Personnel Psychology,* vol. 27 (Winter 1974), pp. 109–24. See also Frederick Herzberg, "Workers' Needs: The Same Around the World," *Industry Week* (September 21, 1987), pp. 29–32.

[10]See, for example, Greg R. Oldham and J. Richard Hackman, "Not What It Was and Not What It Will Be: The Future of Job Design Research," *Journal of Organizational Behavior,* vol. 31 (2010), pp. 463–479.

[11]See Herzberg et al., op. cit. (1967). The quotation is from Herzberg, op. cit. (1968).

[12]For a complete description of the core characteristics model, see J. Richard Hackman and Greg R. Oldham, *Work Redesign* (Reading, MA: Addison-Wesley, 1980).

[13]See, for example, J. Stacy Adams, "Toward an Understanding of Inequity," *Journal of Abnormal and Social Psychology,* vol. 67 (1963), pp. 422–36; and J. Stacy Adams, "Inequity in Social Exchange," in vol. 2, L. Berkowitz (ed.), *Advances in Experimental Social Psychology* (New York: Academic Press, 1965), pp. 267–300.

[14]See, for example, J. W. Harder, "Play for Pay: Effects of Inequity in a Pay-for-Performance Context," *Administrative Science Quarterly,* vol. 37 (1992), pp. 321–35.

[15]Information and quotes from Alistair Barr, "A Look at Some of the Most Luxurious Executive Perks," *Columbus Dispatch* (May 24, 2009), p. D1.

[16]Victor H. Vroom, *Work and Motivation* (New York: Wiley, 1964; republished by Jossey-Bass, 1994).

[17]"The Boss: Goal by Goal," *New York Times* (August 31, 2008), p. 10.

[18]The work on goal-setting theory is well summarized in Edwin A. Locke and Gary P. Latham, *Goal Setting: A Motivational Technique That Works!* (Englewood Cliffs, NJ: Prentice Hall, 1984). See also Edwin A. Locke, Kenneth N. Shaw, Lisa A. Saari, and Gary P. Latham, "Goal Setting and Task Performance 1969–1980," *Psychological Bulletin,* vol. 90 (1981), pp. 125–52; Mark E. Tubbs, "Goal Setting: A Meta-Analytic Examination of the Empirical Evidence," *Journal of Applied Psychology,* vol. 71 (1986), pp. 474–83; and Terence R. Mitchell, Kenneth R. Thompson, and Jane George-Falvy, "Goal Setting: Theory and Practice," Chapter 9 in Cary L. Cooper and Edwin A. Locke (eds.), *Industrial and Organizational Psychology: Linking Theory with Practice* (Malden, MA: Blackwell Business, 2000), pp. 211–49.

[19]For a recent critical discussion of goal-setting theory, see Lisa D. Ordonez, Maurice E. Schweitzer, Adam D. Galinsky, and Max H. Bazerman, "Goals Gone Wild: The Systematic Side Effects of Overprescribing Goal Setting," *Academy of Management Perspectives,* vol. 23 (February 2009), pp. 6–16; and Edwin A. Locke and Gary P. Latham, "Has Goal Setting Gone Wild, or Have Its Attackers Abandoned Good Scholarship?" *Academy of Management Perspectives,* vol. 23 (February, 2009), pp. 17–23.

[20]Gary P. Latham and Edwin A. Locke, "Self-Regulation Through Goal Setting," *Organizational Behavior and Human Decision Processes,* vol. 50 (1991), pp. 212–47.

[21]Edwin A. Locke, "Guest Editor's Introduction: Goal-Setting Theory and Its Applications to the World of Business," *Academy of Management Executive,* vol. 18, no. 4 (2004), pp. 124–25.

[22]E. L. Thorndike, *Animal Intelligence* (New York: Macmillan, 1911), p. 244.

[23]B. F. Skinner, *Walden Two* (New York: Macmillan, 1948); *Science and Human Behavior* (New York: Macmillan, 1953); *Contingencies of Reinforcement* (New York: Appleton-Century-Crofts, 1969).

[24]For a good review, see Lee W. Frederickson (ed.), *Handbook of Organizational Behavior Management* (New York: Wiley-Interscience, 1982); Fred Luthans and Robert Kreitner, *Organizational Behavior Modification* (Glenview, IL: Scott-Foresman, 1985); and Andrew D. Stajkovic and Fred Luthans, "A Meta-Analysis of the Effects of Organizational Behavior Modification on Task Performance 1975–95," *Academy of Management Journal,* vol. 40 (1997), pp. 1122–49.

[25]Knowledge@Wharton, "The Importance of Being Richard Branson," *Wharton School Publishing* (June 3, 2005): www.whartonsp.com.

[26]Richard Gibson, "Pitchman in the Corner Office," *Wall Street Journal* (October 24, 2007), p. D10. See also David Novak, *The Education of an Accidental CEO: Lessons Learned from the Trailer Park to the Corner Office* (New York: Crown Business, 2007).

[27]Michael Mankins, Alan Bird, and James Root, "Making Star Teams Out of Star Players," *Harvard Business Review,* vol. 91 (January–February 2013), pp. 74–78.

[28]Edwin A. Locke, "The Myths of Behavior Mod in Organizations," *Academy of Management Review,* vol. 2 (October 1977), pp. 543–53.

Feature Notes 14

Role Models—Information and quotes from Robert D. Hof, "Amazon's Risky Bet," *Business Week* (November 13, 2006), p. 52; Jon Neale, "Jeff Bezos," *Business Wings* (February 16, 2007): www.businesswings.com.uk; Alan Deutschman, "Inside the Mind of Jeff Bezos," *Fast Company* (December 19, 2007): www.fastcompany.com; and http://en.wikipedia.org.

Facts to Consider—Information from "Two Wasted Days at Work," *CNNMoney.com* (March 16, 2005): www.cnnmoney.com.

Ethics Check—Some information from Williams, and Stephen Harkins, "Many Hands Make Light the Work: The Causes and Consequences of Social Loafing," *Journal of Personality and Social Psychology*, vol. 37 (1978), pp. 822–32; and W. Jack Duncan, "Why Some People Loaf in Groups and Others Loaf Alone," *Academy of Management Executive*, vol. 8 (1994), pp. 79–80.

Hot Topic—Information from Ravi Mattu, "Be a Good Sport and You Might be a Better Manager," *Financial Times*, Kindle Edition (October 11, 2012); and Andrew Hill, "The Right Number of Stars for a Team," *Financial Times*, Kindle Edition (August 12, 2012). See also Mark de Rond, *There is an I in Team: What Elite Athletes and Coaches Really Know about High Performance* (Cambridge, MA: Harvard Business Review Press, 2012).

Endnotes 14

[1]See, for example, Edward E. Lawler III, Susan Albers Mohrman, and Gerald E. Ledford Jr., *Employee Involvement and Total Quality Management: Practices and Results in Fortune 1000 Companies* (San Francisco: Jossey-Bass, 1992); Susan A. Mohrman, Susan A. Cohen, and Monty A. Mohrman, *Designing Team-Based Organizations: New Forms for Knowledge Work* (San Francisco: Jossey-Bass, 1995).

[2]Jon R. Katzenbach and Douglas K. Smith, *The Wisdom of Teams: Creating the High Performance Organization* (Boston: Harvard Business School Press, 1993).

[3]See Edward E. Lawler III, *From the Ground Up: Six Principles for Building the New Logic Corporation* (San Francisco: Jossey-Bass, 1996), p. 131.

[4]Data from Lynda C. McDermott, Nolan Brawley, and William A. Waite, *World-Class Teams: Working Across Borders* (New York: Wiley, 1998), p. 5; survey reported in "Meetings Among Top Ten Time Wasters," *San Francisco Business Times* (April 7, 2003); www.bizjournals.com.

[5]Information from Scott Thurm, "Teamwork Raises Everyone's Game," *Wall Street Journal* (November 7, 2005), p. B7.

[6]Harold J. Leavitt, "Suppose We Took Groups More Seriously," in Eugene L. Cass and Frederick G. Zimmer (eds.), *Man and Work in Society* (New York: Van Nostrand Reinhold, 1975), pp. 67–77.

[7]See Marvin E. Shaw, *Group Dynamics: The Psychology of Small Group Behavior*, 2nd ed. (New York: McGraw-Hill, 1976); Leavitt, op. cit.

[8]A classic work is Bib Latané, Kipling Williams, and Stephen Harkins, "Many Hands Make Light the Work: The Causes and Consequences of Social Loafing," *Journal of Personality and Social Psychology*, vol. 37 (1978), pp. 822–32. See also John M. George, "Extrinsic and Intrinsic Origins of Perceived Social Loafing in Organizations," *Academy of Management Journal* (March 1992), pp. 191–202; and W. Jack Duncan, "Why Some People Loaf in Groups While Others Loaf Alone," *Academy of Management Executive*, vol. 8 (1994), pp. 79–80.

[9]The "linking pin" concept is introduced in Rensis Likert, *New Patterns of Management* (New York: McGraw-Hill, 1962).

[10]See discussion by Susan G. Cohen and Don Mankin, "The Changing Nature of Work," in Susan Albers Mohrman, Jay R. Galbraith, Edward E. Lawler III, and associates, *Tomorrow's Organization: Crafting Winning Capabilities in a Dynamic World* (San Francisco: Jossey-Bass, 1998), pp. 154–78.

[11]Information from "Diversity: America's Strength," special advertising section, *Fortune* (June 23, 1997); and American Express corporate communication (1998).

[12]See Susan D. Van Raalte, "Preparing the Task Force to Get Good Results," *S.A.M. Advanced Management Journal*, vol. 47 (Winter 1982), pp. 11–16; Walter Kiechel III, "The Art of the Corporate Task Force," *Fortune* (January 28, 1991), pp. 104–06.

[13]Developed from Eric Matson, "The Seven Sins of Deadly Meetings," *Fast Company* (April/May 1996), p. 122.

[14]Mohrman et al., op. cit. (1998).

[15]Matt Golosinski, "With Teamwork, Gregg Steinhafel Hits the Bull's-Eye at Target," *Kellogg* (Summer 2007), p. 32.

[16]For a good discussion of quality circles, see Edward E. Lawler III and Susan A. Mohrman, "Quality Circles After the Fad," *Harvard Business Review*, vol. 63 (January/February 1985), pp. 65–71; Edward E. Lawler III and Susan Albers Mohrman, "Employee Involvement, Reengineering, and TQM: Focusing on Capability Development," in Mohrman et al. (1998), pp. 179–208.

[17]William M. Bulkeley, "Computerizing Dull Meetings Is Touted as an Antidote to the Mouth That Bored," *Wall Street Journal* (January 28, 1992), pp. B1, B2.

[18]See Wayne F. Cascio, "Managing a Virtual Workplace," *Academy of Management Executive*, vol. 14 (2000), pp. 81–90.

[19]Robert D. Hof, "Teamwork, Supercharged," *Business Week* (November 21, 2005), pp. 90–92.

[20]See Sheila Simsarian Webber, "Virtual Teams: A Meta-Analysis," http://www.shrm.org.

[21]See Stacie A. Furst, Martha Reeves, Benson Rosen, and Richard S. Blackburn, "Managing the Life Cycle of Virtual Teams," *Academy of Management Executive*, vol. 18, no. 2 (2004), pp. 6–11.

[22]R. Brent Gallupe and William H. Cooper, "Brainstorming Electronically," *Sloan Management Review* (Winter 1997), pp. 11–21; Cascio, op. cit.

[23]Cascio, op. cit.; Furst et al., op. cit.

[24]See, for example, Paul S. Goodman, Rukmini Devadas, and Terri L. Griffith Hughson, "Groups and Productivity: Analyzing the Effectiveness of Self-Managing Teams," in John R. Campbell and Richard J. Campbell, *Productivity in Organizations* (San Francisco: Jossey-Bass, 1988); Jack Orsbrun, Linda Moran, Ed Musslewhite, and John H. Zenger, with Craig Perrin, *Self-Directed Work Teams: The New American Challenge* (Homewood, IL: Business One Irwin, 1990); Dale E. Yeatts and Cloyd Hyten, *High Performing Self-Managed Work Teams* (Thousand Oaks, CA: Sage, 1997).

[25]See, for example, J. Richard Hackman and Nancy Katz, "Group Behavior and Performance," in Susan T. Fiske, Daniel T. Gilbert, and Gardner Lindzey (eds.), *Handbook of Social Psychology*, 5th ed. (Hoboken, NJ: Wiley, 2010), pp. 1208–51.

[26]Goodman et al., op. cit.; Orsbrun et al., op. cit.; Yeatts and Hyten, op. cit.; and Lawler et al., op. cit., 1992.

[27]For a review of research on group effectiveness, see J. Richard Hackman, "The Design of Work Teams," in Jay W. Lorsch (ed.), *Handbook of Organizational Behavior* (Englewood Cliffs, NJ: Prentice-Hall, 1987), pp. 315–42; and J. Richard Hackman, Ruth Wageman, Thomas M. Ruddy, and Charles L. Ray, "Team Effectiveness in Theory and Practice," in Cary L. Cooper and Edwin A. Locke, *Industrial and Organizational Psychology: Linking Theory with Practice* (Malden, MA: Blackwell, 2000).

[28]For a discussion of effectiveness in the context of top management teams, see Edward E. Lawler III, David Finegold, and Jay A. Conger, "Corporate Boards: Developing Effectiveness at the Top," in Mohrman, op. cit. (1998), pp. 23–50.

[29]Quote from Alex Markels, "Money & Business," *U.S. News online* (October 22, 2006).

[30]See for example, Michael Mankins, Alan Bird, and James Root, "Making Star Teams Out of Star Players," *Harvard Business Review*, vol. 91 (January–February, 2013), pp. 74–78.

[31]"Dream Teams," *Northwestern* (Winter 2005), p. 10; Matt Golosinski, "Teamwork Takes Center Stage," *Northwestern* (Winter 2005), p. 39.

[32]Golosinski, op. cit., p. 39.

[33]See for example, Warren Watson. "Cultural Diversity's Impact on Interaction Process and Performance" *Academy of Management Journal*, vol. 16 (1993); Christopher Earley and Elaine Mosakowski, "Creating Hybrid Team Structures: An Empirical Test of Transnational Team Functioning," *Academy of Management Journal*, vol. 5 (February 2000), pp. 26–49; Eric Kearney, Diether Gebert, and Sven C. Voilpel, "When and How Diversity Benefits Teams: The Importance of Team Members' Need for Cognition," *Academy of Management Journal*, vol. 52 (2009), pp. 582–98; and Aparna Joshi and Hyuntak Roh, "The Role of Context in Work Team Diversity Research: A Meta-Analytic Approach," *Academy of Management Journal*, vol. 52 (2009), pp. 599–628.

[34]Information from Susan Carey, "Racing to Improve," *Wall Street Journal* (March 24, 2006), pp. B1, B6.

[35]Daniel Goleman, "Emotional Intelligence Teams," danielgoleman.info (January 27, 2007): accessed October 6, 2012.

[36]J. Steven Heinen and Eugene Jacobson, "A Model of Task Group Development in Complex Organizations and a Strategy of Implementation," *Academy of Management Review*, vol. 1 (1976), pp. 98–111; Bruce W. Tuckman, "Developmental Sequence in Small Groups," *Psychological Bulletin*, vol. 63 (1965), pp. 384–99; Bruce W. Tuckman and Mary Ann C. Jensen, "Stages of Small-Group Development Revisited," *Group & Organization Studies*, vol. 2 (1977), pp. 419–27.

[37]See Warren Watson, "Cultural Diversity's Impact on Interaction Process and Performance," *Academy of Management Journal*, vol. 16 (1993); Christopher Earley and Elaine Mosakowski, "Creating Hybrid Team Structures: An Empirical Test of Transnational Team Functioning," *Academy of Management Journal*, vol. 5 (February 2000), pp. 26–49; Eric Kearney, Diether Gebert, and Sven C. Voilpel, "When and How Diversity Benefits Teams: The Importance of Team Members' Need for Cognition," *Academy of Management Journal*, vol. 52 (2009), pp. 582–598; and Aparna Joshi and Hyuntak Roh, "The Role of Context in Work Team Diversity Research: A Meta-Analytic Approach," *Academy of Management Journal*, vol. 52 (2009), pp. 599–628.

[38]See, for example, Edgar Schein, *Process Consultation* (Reading, MA: Addison-Wesley, 1988); and Linda C. McDermott, Nolan Brawley, and William A. Waite, *World-Class Teams: Working Across Borders* (New York: Wiley, 1998).

[39]For a good discussion, see Robert F. Allen and Saul Pilnick, "Confronting the Shadow Organization: How to Detect and Defeat Negative Norms," *Organizational Dynamics* (Spring 1973), pp. 13–16.

[40]See Schein, op. cit., pp. 76–79.

[41]Marvin E. Shaw, *Group Dynamics: The Psychology of Small Group Behavior* (New York: McGraw-Hill, 1976).

[42]A classic work in this area is K. Benne and P. Sheets, "Functional Roles of Group Members," *Journal of Social Issues*, vol. 2 (1948), pp. 42–47; see also Likert, op. cit., pp. 166–69; Schein, op. cit., pp. 49–56.

[43]Based on John R. Schermerhorn Jr., James G. Hunt, and Richard N. Osborn, *Organizational Behavior*, 7th ed. (New York: Wiley, 2000), pp. 345–46.

44Schein, op. cit., pp. 69–75.

45A good overview is William D. Dyer, *Team-Building* (Reading, MA: Addison-Wesley, 1977).

46Quote from Terah Shelton Harris, "True Grit: How a Little Mud & Muscle Can Inspire Leaders and Build Teams," *ConventionSouth*, vol. 29 (February, 2013), p. 10–11.

47Schein, op. cit., pp. 69–75.

48Victor H. Vroom and Arthur G. Jago, *The New Leadership: Managing Participation in Organizations* (Englewood Cliffs, NJ: Prentice Hall, 1988); Victor H. Vroom, "A New Look in Managerial Decision-Making," *Organizational Dynamics* (Spring 1973), pp. 66–80; Victor H. Vroom and Phillip Yetton, *Leadership and Decision-Making* (Pittsburgh: University of Pittsburgh Press, 1973).

49See Kathleen M. Eisenhardt, Jean L. Kahwajy, and L. J. Bourgeois III, "How Management Teams Can Have a Good Fight," *Harvard Business Review* (July/August 1997), pp. 77–85.

50Michael A. Roberto, "Why Making the Decisions the Right Way Is More Important Than Making the Right Decisions," *Ivey Business Journal* (September/October 2005), pp. 1–7.

51See Irving L. Janis, "Groupthink," *Psychology Today* (November 1971), pp. 43–46; and *Victims of Groupthink*, 2nd ed. (Boston: Houghton Mifflin, 1982).

52See also Michael Harvey, M. Ronald Buckley, Milorad M. Novicevic, and Jonathon R. B. Halbesleben, "The Abilene Paradox After Thirty Years: A Global Perspective," *Organizational Dynamics*, vol. 33 (2004), pp. 215–26.

53Janis, op. cit.

54Ibid.

55Richard E. Walton, *Interpersonal Peacemaking: Confrontations and Third-Party Consultation* (Reading, MA: Addison-Wesley, 1969), p. 2.

56See Kenneth W. Thomas, "Conflict and Conflict Management," in M. D. Dunnett (ed.), *Handbook of Industrial and Organizational Behavior* (Chicago: Rand McNally, 1976), pp. 889–935.

57See Robert R. Blake and Jane Strygley Mouton, "The Fifth Achievement," *Journal of Applied Behavioral Science*, vol. 6 (1970), pp. 413–27; Alan C. Filley, *Interpersonal Conflict Resolution* (Glenview, IL: Scott, Foresman, 1975); and L. David Brown, *Managing Conflict at Organizational Interfaces* (Reading, MA: Addison-Wesley, 1983).

58Filley, op. cit.

Feature Notes 15

Opening Photo—Quote from Claire Suddath, "Inside the Elephant in the Room," *Bloomberg BusinessWeek* (December 10–December 16, 2012), pp. 83–85.

The Devil Wears Prada—W. C. Byham, "Start Networking Right Away (Even if You Hate It)." *Harvard Business Review*, vol. 22 (January 2009).

Role Models—Information and quotes from Adam Bryant, "Give Your Staff a Reason to Work for You," *International Herald Tribune* (July 5, 2010), p. 17.

Facts to Consider—Information from American Management Association, "Electronic Monitoring & Surveillance Survey" (February 8, 2008): www.press.amanet.org; and Liz Wolgemuth, "Why Web Surfing Is a No Problem," *U.S. News & World Report* (August 22, 2008): www.usnews.com.

Ethics Check—Information from Bridget Jones, "Blogger Fire Fury," CNN.com (July 19, 2006); and Bobbie Johnson, "Briton Sacked for Writing Paris Blog Wins Tribunal Case," *The Guardian* (March 29, 2007): guardian.co.uk.

Find Inspiration—Information and quotes from John Jurgensen, "The State of Jay-Z's Empire," *Wall Street Journal* (October 22, 2010), pp. D1, D2.

Photo Essay—Undercover Boss—Information and quotes from "Undercover Boss Gets the Communication Message," *Financial Times* (June 9, 2009).

Hot Topic—Information and quotes from Parminder Bahra, "The Science Behind Persuading People," *Wall Street Journal* (December 27, 2012), p. D5.

Endnotes 15

1See Henry Mintzberg, *The Nature of Managerial Work* (New York: Harper & Row, 1973 and Harper-Collins, 1997; John P. Kotter, "What Effective General Managers Really Do," *Harvard Business Review*, vol. 60 (November/December 1982), pp. 156–157; and *The General Managers* (New York: Macmillan, 1986).

2Mintzberg, op cit.

3Information from American Management Association (AMA), "The Passionate Organization Fast-Response Survey" (September 25–29, 2000), and organization Web site: http://www.amanet.org.

4Survey information from "What Do Recruiters Want?" *BizEd* (November/December 2002), p. 9; "Much to Learn, Professors Say," *USA Today* (July 5, 2001), p. 8D; and AMA, op. cit.

5Jay A. Conger, *Winning 'Em Over: A New Model for Managing in the Age of Persuasion* (New York: Simon & Schuster, 1998), pp. 24–79.

6Ibid.

7John Antonakis, Marika Fenley, and Sue Liechti, "Learning Charisma," *Harvard Business Review*, vol. 90 (June 2012), pp. 127–130; and Alicia Clegg, "The Subtle Secrets of Charisma," *Financial Times*, Kindle Edition (January 3, 2013).

8Information from Paul Davidson, "Managers to Millennials: Job Interview No Time to Text," *USA Today* (April 29, 2013), cnbc.com: accessed April 29, 2013.

9Ibid.

10See Robert H. Lengel and Richard L. Daft, "The Selection of Communication Media as an Executive Skill," *Academy of Management Executive*, vol. 2 (August 1988), pp. 225–32.

11Information from Sam Dillon, "What Corporate America Can't Build: A Sentence," *New York Times* (December 7, 2004).

12See Eric Matson, "Now That We Have Your Complete Attention," *Fast Company* (February/March 1997), pp. 124–32.

13David McNeill, *Hand and Mind: What Gestures Reveal About Thought* (Chicago: University of Chicago Press, 1992).

14Martin J. Gannon, *Paradoxes of Culture and Globalization* (Los Angeles: Sage, 2008), p. 76.

15McNeill, op. cit.

16Janelle Harris, "The Body Language of Business," *Black MBA* (Winter/Spring, 2012), pp. 34–37.

17Tom Peters and Nancy Austin, *A Passion for Excellence* (New York: Random House, 1985). "Epigrams and Insights from the Original Modern Guru," *Financial Times*, Kindle edition (March 4, 2010). See also Tom Peters, *The Little Big Things: 163 Ways to Pursue Excellence* (New York: HarperStudio, 2010).

18Suggested by an incident from Richard V. Farace, Peter R. Monge, and Hamish M. Russell, *Communicating and Organizing* (Reading, MA: Addison-Wesley, 1977), pp. 97–98.

19Examples and quotes from *Business Week* (July 8, 1991), pp. 60–61; www.ccl.org/leadership/programs/profiles/lisaDitullio.aspx (retrieved August 12, 2008); and Joe Walker, "Executives Learn New Skills to Improve Their Communication," *Wall Street Journal* (May 6, 2010), p. B3.

20Quote from Andy Serwer, "Game Changers: Legendary Basketball Coach John Wooden and Starbucks' Howard Schultz Talk about a Common Interest—Leadership," *Fortune* (August 11, 2008): www.cnnmoney.com.

21This discussion is based on Carl R. Rogers and Richard E. Farson, "Active Listening" (Chicago: Industrial Relations Center of the University of Chicago, n.d.); see also Carl R. Rogers and Fritz J. Roethlisberger, "Barriers and Gateways to Communication," *Harvard Business Review* (November/December, 2001), Reprint 91610.

22Ibid.

23A useful source of guidelines is John J. Gabarro and Linda A. Hill, "Managing Performance," Note 9-96-022 (Boston, MA: Harvard Business School Publishing, n.d.).

24Developed from John Anderson, "Giving and Receiving Feedback," in Paul R. Lawrence, Louis B. Barnes, and Jay W. Lorsch, eds., *Organizational Behavior and Administration*, 3rd ed. (Homewood, IL: Richard D. Irwin, 1976), p. 109.

25Sue DeWine, *The Consultant's Craft* (Boston: Bedford/St. Martin's Press, 2001), pp. 307–14.

26A classic work on proxemics is Edward T. Hall's book *The Hidden Dimension* (Garden City, NY: Doubleday, 1986).

27Information and quote from Rachel Emma Silverman, "When Water-Cooler Chats Aren't Enough," *Wall Street Journal* (May 1, 2013), p. B6.

28Information and quotes from Ben Kesling and James R. Hagerty, "Say Goodbye to the Office Cubicle," *Wall Street Journal* (April 3, 2013), pp. B1, 2.

29Information and quotes from Adam Bryant, "Creating Trust by Destroying Hierarchy," *Global Edition of the New York Times* (February 15, 2010), p. 19.

[30]Information and quote from Kelly K. Spors, "Top Small Workplaces 2009," *Wall Street Journal* (September 28, 2009), pp. R1–R4.

[31]Information and quotes from Sarah E. Needleman, "Thnx for the IView! I Wud Luv to Work 4 U!!;)," *Wall Street Journal Online* (July 31, 2008).

[32]Kevin Joy, "Online Introduction," *Columbus Dispatch* (April 19, 2013), pp. D1, D2.

[33]Information and quotes from, Rhymer Rigby, "Assume that Every Employer Is Looking at Your Profiles," *Financial Times*, Kindle Edition (April 22, 2013).

[34]Information and quotes from Michelle Conlin and Douglas MacMillan, "Managing the Tweets," *Business Week* (June 1, 2009), pp. 20–21. For P. Smith and Filiz Tabak, "Monitoring Employee E-Mails: Is There Any Room for Privacy?" *Academy of Management Perspectives*, vol. 23 (November, 2009), pp. 33–48.

[35]Information from Carol Hymowitz, "More American Chiefs Are Taking Top Posts at Overseas Concerns," *Wall Street Journal* (October 17, 2005), p. B1.

[36]Examples reported in Martin J. Gannon, *Paradoxes of Culture and Globalization* (Los Angeles: Sage Publications, 2008), p. 80.

[37]Information from Ben Brown, "Atlanta Out to Mind Its Manners," *USA Today* (March 14, 1996), p. 7.

Feature Notes 16

Finding Forrester—Project Implicit (https://implicit.harvard.edu).

Role Models—Information and quotes from Eric Shenninger, "Khan Academy: Friend or Foe?" *Huffington Post*, April 24, 2012. http://www.huffingtonpost.com (Accessed November 24, 2012); Aaron Saenz, "Yes, The Khan Academy IS the Future of Education. *SingularityHub.com*, "February 13, 2011, http://singularityhub.com (Accessed November 24, 2012); Michael Noer, "One Man One Computer 10 Million Students: How Khan Academy is Reinventing Education," *Forbes*, November 2, 2012, http://www.forbes.com (Accessed November 24, 2012); and Somini Sengupta, "Online Learning Personalized," *New York Times*, December 4, 2011. http://www.nytimes.com (Accessed November 24, 2012).

Facts to Consider—Information from *What Workers Want: A Worldwide Study of Attitudes to Work and Work-Life Balance* (London: FDS International Limited, 2007).

Ethics Check—Information and quotes from Susan Chandler, " 'Fair Trade' Label Enters Retail Market," *Columbus Dispatch* (October 16, 2006), p. G6; and www.fairindigo.com.

Massmart and Wal-Mart—Information and quotes from Robb M. Stewart, "Wal-Mart Checks Out a New Continent," *Wall Street Journal* (October 27, 2010), pp. B1, B2; and Robb M. Stewart, "Wal-Mart Sets Africa Deal," *Wall Street Journal* (November 30, 2010), p. B2.

Photo Essay—Silent Language Skills—Information from Eric Spitznagel, "How to Impress Your Chinese Boss," *Bloomberg BusinessWeek* (January 5, 2012): BusinessWeek.com.

Hot Topic—Survey data from Christine Porath and Christine Pearson, "The Price of Incivility: Lack of Respect Hurts Morale and the Bottom Line," *Harvard Business Review*, vol. 91 (January–February, 2013), pp. 114–121.

Endnotes 16

[1]Laura B. Shrestha and Elayne J. Heisler, *The Changing Demographic Profile of the United States* (Washington: Congressional Research Service, 2011); Conor Dougherty and Mriam Jordan, "Minority Births are New Majority," *Wall Street Journal* (May 17, 2012), p. A4; and Laura Meckler, "Hispanic Future in the Cards," *Wall Street Journal* (December 13, 2012), p. A3.

[2]Lee Gardenswartz and Anita Rowe, *Managing Diversity: A Complete Desk Reference and Planning Guide* (Chicago: Irwin, 1993).

[3]R. Roosevelt Thomas Jr., *Beyond Race and Gender* (New York: AMACOM, 1992), p. 10; see also R. Roosevelt Thomas Jr., " 'From Affirmative Action' to 'Affirming Diversity,' " *Harvard Business Review* (November/December 1990), pp. 107–17; R. Roosevelt Thomas Jr., with Marjorie I. Woodruff, *Building a House for Diversity* (New York: AMACOM, 1999).

[4]Oliver, op. cit.

[5]Gardenswartz and Rowe, op. cit., p. 220.

[6]Survey reported in "The Most Inclusive Workplaces Generate the Most Loyal Employees," *Gallup Management Journal* (December 2001), retrieved from http://gmj.gallup.com.

[7]Carol Stephenson, "Leveraging Diversity to Maximum Advantage: The Business Case for Appointing More Women to Boards," *Ivey Business Journal* (September/October 2004), Reprint #9B04TE03, pp. 1–8.

[8]Donald H. Oliver, "Achieving Results Through Diversity: A Strategy for Success," *Ivey Business Journal* (March/April, 2005), Reprint #9B05TB09, pp. 1–6.

[9]Thomas Kochan, Katerina Bezrukova, Robin Ely, Susan Jackson, Aparna Joshi, Karen Jehn, Jonathan Leonard, David Levine, and David Thomas, "The Effects of Diversity on Business Performance: Report of the Diversity Research Network," reported in *SHRM Foundation Research Findings* (retrieved from www.shrm.org/foundation/findings.asp). Full article published in *Human Resource Management*, vol. 42 (2003), pp. 3–21.

[10]Taylor Cox Jr., *Cultural Diversity in Organizations* (San Francisco: Berrett Koehler, 1994).

[11]Nanette Byrnes and Roger O. Crockett, "An Historic Succession at Xerox," *Business Week* (June 9, 2008), pp. 18–21.

[12]Rob Walker, "Sex vs. Ethics," *Fast Company* (June, 2008), pp. 72–78.

[13]Sue Shellenbarger, "The XX Factor: What's Holding Women Back?" *The Wall Street Journal* (May 7, 2012), pp. B7-B12.

[14]Sue Shellenbarger, "More Women Pursue Claims of Pregnancy Discrimination," *The Wall Street Journal* (March 27, 2008), p. D1.

[15]"Bias Cases by Workers Increase by 9%," *The Wall Street Journal* (March 6, 2008), p. D6.

[16]See Anthony Robbins and Joseph McClendon III, *Unlimited Power: A Black Choice* (New York: Free Press, 1997); and Augusto Failde and William Doyle, *Latino Success: Insights from America's Most Powerful Latino Executives* (New York: Free Press, 1996).

[17]About CQ (Cultural Intelligence)," *Cultural Intelligence Center*, culture.com (Accessed May 4, 2013).

[18]Barbara Benedict Bunker, "Appreciating Diversity and Modifying Organizational Cultures: Men and Women at Work," in Suresh Srivastava and David L. Cooperrider, *Appreciative Management and Leadership* (San Francisco: Jossey-Bass, 1990), Chapter 5.

[19]See Gary N. Powell, *Women-Men in Management* (Thousand Oaks, CA: Sage, 1993); and Cliff Cheng (ed.), *Masculinities in Organizations* (Thousand Oaks, CA: Sage, 1996). For added background, see also Sally Helgesen, *Everyday Revolutionaries: Working Women and the Transformation of American Life* (New York: Doubleday, 1998).

[20]"Demographics: The Young and the Restful," *Harvard Business Review* (November 2004), p. 25. "Many U.S. Employees Have Negative Attitudes to Their Jobs, Employers and Top Managers," *The Harris Poll #38* (May 6, 2005), available from www.harrisinteractive.com; and "U. S. Job Satisfaction Keeps Falling," *The Conference Board Reports Today* (February 25, 2005; retrieved from www.conference-board.org).

[21]Mayo Clinic, "Workplace Generation Gap: Understand Differences Among Colleagues" (July 6, 2005), retrieved from http://www.cnn.com.

[22]Thomas, op. cit. (1990, 1992).

[23]Quotes from Thomas, op. cit. (1992), p. 17.

[24]Information from "100 Best Corporate Citizens," *Business Ethics* online (retrieved from www.business-ethics.com, November 1, 2005).

[25]Thomas, op. cit. (1992), p. 17.

[26]Thomas and Woodruff, op. cit. (1999), pp. 211–26.

[27]"Diversity Today: Corporate Recruiting Practices in Inclusive Workplaces," *Fortune* (June 12, 2000), p. S4.

[28]Bunker, op. cit.,

[29]Ibid., pp. 127–49.

[30]Examples reported in Neil Chesanow, *The World-Class Executive* (New York: Rawson Associates, 1985).

[31]P. Christopher Earley and Elaine Mosakowski, "Toward Cultural Intelligence: Turning Cultural Differences into Workplace Advantage," *Academy of Management Executive*, vol. 18 (2004), pp. 151–57.

[32]Example from Julian E. Barnes, "U.S., Vietnam Exchange War Relics," *The Wall Street Journal* (June 5, 2012), p. A. 15.

[33]Edward T. Hall, *Beyond Culture* (New York: Doubleday, 1976).

[34]Edward T. Hall, *Hidden Differences* (New York: Doubleday, 1990).

[35]Michele J. Gelfand, Lisa H. Nishii, and Jana L. Raver, "On the Nature and Importance of Cultural Tightness-Looseness," *Journal of Applied Psychology*, vol. 91 (2006), pp. 1225–1244.

[36]Michele J. Gelfand and 42 co-authors, "Differences Between Tight and Loose Cultures: A 33 Nation Study," *Science,* vol. 332 (May 2011), pp. 100–1104.

[37]See, for example, Fons Trompenaars, *Riding the Waves of Culture: Understanding Cultural Diversity in Business* (London: Nicholas Brealey Publishing, 1993); Harry C. Triandis, *Culture and Social Behavior* (New York: McGraw-Hill, 1994); Steven H. Schwartz, "A Theory of Cultural Values and Some Implications for Work," *Applied Psychology: An International Review,* vol. 48 (1999), pp. 23–49; Martin J. Gannon, *Understanding Global Cultures,* 3rd ed. (Thousand Oaks, CA: Sage, 2004); and Robert J. House, Paul J. Hanges, Mansour Javidan, Peter W. Dorfman, and Vipin Gupta (eds.), *Culture, Leadership and Organizations: The GLOBE Study of 62 Societies* (Thousand Oaks, CA: Sage Publications, Inc., 2004).

[38]Geert Hofstede, *Culture's Consequences* (Beverly Hills, CA: Sage, 1984), and *Culture's Consequences: Comparing Values, Behaviors, Institutions and Organizations Across Nations,* 2nd ed. (Thousand Oaks, CA: Sage, 2001). See also Michael H. Hoppe, "An Interview with Geert Hofstede," *Academy of Management Executive,* vol. 18 (2004), pp. 75–79.

[39]Geert Hofstede and Michael H. Bond, "The Confucius Connection: From Cultural Roots to Economic Growth," *Organizational Dynamics,* vol. 16 (1988), pp. 4–21.

[40]This dimension is explained more thoroughly by Geert Hofstede et al., *Masculinity and Femininity: The Taboo Dimension of National Cultures* (Thousand Oaks, CA.: Sage, 1998).

[41]Information from "The Conundrum of the Glass Ceiling," op cit.; and "Japan's Diversity Problem," *Wall Street Journal* (October 24, 2005), pp. B1, B5.

[42]See Hofstede and Bond, op. cit.

[43]See Geert Hofstede, *Culture and Organizations: Software of the Mind* (London: McGraw-Hill, 1991).

[44]Discussion based on Allan Bird, Mark Mendenhall, Michael J. Stevens, and Gary Oddou, "Defining the Content Domain of Intercultural Competence for Global Leaders," *Journal of Managerial Psychology,* vol. 25 (2010), pp. 810–28.

Feature Notes 17

Opening Quote—International Labour Organization, *Facts on Child Labor 2010* (Geneva, Switzerland: April 1, 2010).

The Amazing Race—E. R. Goldstein, "What If 'English Only' Isn't Wrong?" *Wall Street Journal* (August 2010). Retrieved December 8, 2010 from http://online.wsj.com.

Role Models—Information and quotes from Muhammad Yunus, *Creating a World Without Poverty: Social Business and the Future of Capitalism* (New York: Public Affairs, 2009); "Fighting Poverty with $30 Loans," *USA Today* (April 25, 2013), p. 11A; and, David Bornstein, "Beyond Profit: A Talk with Muhammad Yunus," *New York Times,* opinionator.blogs.nytimes.com (April 17, 2013), accessed May 5, 2013.

Facts to Consider—Information from Transparency International, "Corruption Perceptions Index 2011," and "Bribe Payers Index (2011)" www.transparency.org (accessed may 5, 2013).

Ethics Check—Information from Raul Burgoa, "Bolivia Seizes Control of Oil and Gas Fields," *Bangkok Post* (May 3, 2006), p. B5.

Manager's Library—Information and quotes from Janet Maslin, "Formatting a world with No Secrets," *New York Times* (April 25, 2013), nytimes.com: accessed May 6, 2013; Liz Gannes, "What Assange, Slim, Kissinger and Other Told Eric Schmidt for his New book," *All Things D,* allthingsd.com (April 23, 2013), accessed May 7,2013; and Sam Gustin, "The Internet Doesn't Hurt People—People Do: 'The New Digital Age'," *Business & Money,* businesstimes.com (April 26, 2013), accessed May 7, 2013.

Hot Topic—Information and quotes from David Rocks and Nick Leiber, "Made in China? Not Worth the Trouble," *Bloomberg BusinessWeek* (June 25–July 1, 2012), pp. 49–50; and "The End of Cheap China," *The Economist* (March 10, 2012): www.economist.com (accessed January 9, 2013).

Endnotes 17

[1]Sample articles include "Globalization Bites Boeing," *Business Week* (March 24, 2008), p. 32; "One World, One Car, One Name," *Business Week* (March 24, 2008), p. 32; Eric Bellman and Jackie Range, "Indian-Style Mergers: Buy a Brand, Leave it Alone," *Wall Street Journal* (March 22–23, 2008), pp. A9,

A14; David Kiley, "One Ford for the Whole Wide World," *Business Week* (June 15, 2009), pp. 58–59; and, "Boeing: Faster, Faster, Faster," *The Economist,* Kindle Edition (January 29, 2012).

[2]Pietra Rivoli, *The Travels of a T-Shirt in the Global Economy,* 2nd ed. (Hoboken, NJ: Wiley, 2009).

[3]See for example Kenichi Ohmae's books *The Borderless World: Power and Strategy in the Interlinked Economy* (New York: Harper, 1989); *The End of the Nation State* (New York: Free Press, 1996); *The Invisible Continent: Four Strategic Imperatives of the New Economy* (New York: Harper, 1999); and *The Next Global Stage: Challenges and Opportunities in Our Borderless World* (Philadelphia: Wharton School Publishing, 2006).

[4]For a discussion of globalization, see Thomas L. Friedman, *The Lexus and the Olive Tree: Understanding Globalization* (New York: Bantam Doubleday Dell, 2000); John Micklethwait and Adrian Woodridge, *A Future Perfect: The Challenges and Hidden Promise of Globalization* (New York: Crown, 2000); and Thomas L. Friedman, *The World Is Flat: A Brief History of the Twenty-First Century* (New York: Farrar, Straus and Giroux, 2005).

[5]Rosabeth Moss Kanter, *World Class: Thinking Locally in the Global Economy* (New York: Simon & Schuster, 1995), preface.

[6]Paul Wilson, "Foreign Companies Big Employers in Ohio," *Columbus Dispatch* (December 26, 2005), p. F6.

[7] Jose W. Fernandez, "Foreign Direct Investment Supports U.S. Jobs," *DipNote: U.S. Department of State Official Blog* (October 07, 2011), accessed March 3, 2012.

[8]Quote from John A. Byrne, "Visionary vs. Visionary," *Business Week* (August 28, 2000), p. 210.

[9]See Mauro F. Guillén and Esteban García-Canal, "The American Model of the Multinational Firm and the 'New' Multinationals from Emerging Economies," *Academy of Management Perspectives,* vol. 23 (2009), pp. 23–35.

[10]Information from newbalance.com/corporate.

[11]Information and quote from Steve Hamm, "Into Africa: Capitalism from the Ground Up," *Business Week* (May, 4 2009), pp. 60–61.

[12]David Murphy, "A Foxconn Breakdown: It's Strengths, Strangeness, and Scrutiny," *PC Magazine* (January 22, 2012): pcmag.com.

[13]Information and quote from Syed Zain Al-Muhammad, Christina Passareiello, and Preetika Rana , "The Global Garment Trail: From Bangladesh to a Mall Near You," *Wall Street Journal* (May 4–5, 2013), pp. A1,A11.

[14]Information and quote from "More then a Third of Large Manufacturers Are Considering Reshoring from China to the U.S.," *Boston Consulting Group press release,* bcg.com (April 20, 2012): accessed May 5, 2013; and, "A Revolution in the Making," *The Wall Street Journal* (June 11, 2013), pp. R1, R2.

[15]"Survey: Intellectual Property Theft Now Accounts for 31% of Global Counterfeiting." *Gieschen Consultancy,* February 25, 2005.

[16]Information from "Not Exactly Counterfeit," *Fortune* (April 26, 2006): oney.cnn.com.

[17]Criteria for choosing joint venture partners developed from Anthony J. F. O'Reilly, "Establishing Successful Joint Ventures in Developing Nations: A CEO's Perspective," *Columbia Journal of World Business* (Spring 1988), pp. 65–71; and "Best Practices for Global Competitiveness," *Fortune* (March 30, 1998), pp. S1–S3, special advertising section.

[18]Karby Leggett, "U.S. Auto Makers Find Promise—and Peril—in China," *Wall Street Journal* (June 19, 2003), p. B1; "Did Spark Spark a Copycat?" *Business Week* (February 7, 2005), p. 64; and "Overview: Chery Automobile Co., Ltd.," *Cheryinterngtional.com* (accessed May 5, 2013).

[19]"Starbucks Wins Trademark Case," *The Economic Times,* Bangalore (January 3, 2006), p. 8.

[20]This index is reported in "Big Mac Index: Bun fight," *The Economist*: economist.com (February 2, 2013).

[21]Many newspapers and magazines publish annual lists of the world's largest multinational corporations. *Fortune's* annual listing is available from www.fortune.com.

[22]See Fortune.com and Ftimes.com.

[23]See Peter F. Drucker, "The Global Economy and the Nation-State," *Foreign Affairs,* vol. 76 (September/October 1997), pp. 159–71.

[24]Information from Steve Hamm, "IBM vs. TATA: Which Is More American?" *Business Week* (May 5, 2008), p. 28.

[25]Michael Mandel, "Multinationals: Are They Good for America?" *Business Week* (February 28, 2008): businessweek.com.

26"Count: Really Big Business," *Fast Company* (December, 2008/ January, 2009), p. 46.

27Mandel, op cit.

28Adapted from R. Hall Mason, "Conflicts Between Host Countries and Multinational Enterprise," *California Management Review,* vol. 17 (1974), pp. 6, 7.

29Headlines from Matthew Boyle and Joel Rosenblatt, "Avon Products Says It Fired Four Executives Over Bribes to China Officials" *Bloomberg* (May 5, 2011): bloomberg.com; Migual Guterary and Elisor Comlag, "Mexico Starts Investigation in Wal-Mart Bribery Case," news, yahoo.com (April 25, 2012).

30See Dionne Searcey, "U.S. Cracks Down on Corporate Bribes," *Wall Street Journal* (May 26, 2009), pp. A1–A4.

31Quote from Carol Matlack, "The Peril and Promise of Investing in Russia," *BusinessWeek* (October 5, 2009), pp. 48–51.

32"The Paradox of Bangladesh," *Bloomberg BusinessWeek* (May 13–May 19, 2013), pp. 14–15.

33Information and quote from Andrew Morse and Nick Wingfield, "Microsoft Will Investigate Conditions at Chinese Plant," *Wall Street Journal* (April 16, 2010), p. B7; and "About Us: Institute for Global Labour and Human Rights," globallabourrights.org (accessed May 5, 2013)

34"An Industry Monitors Child Labour," *New York Times* (October 16, 1997), pp. B1, B9; and Rugmark International Web site: www.rugmark.de.

35International Labour Organization, *Facts on Child Labor 2010* (Geneva, Switzerland: April 1, 2010).

36Information and quote from Andrew Morse and Nick Wingfield, "Apple Audits Labor Practices," *Wall Street Journal* (March 1, 2010), p. B3.

37See Robert B. Reich, "Who Is Them?" *Harvard Business Review* (March/April 1991), pp. 77–88.

38Carol Hymowitz, "The New Diversity," *Wall Street Journal* (November 14, 2005), p. R1.

39See for example, Melissa Korn, "Yale Redefines Global," *Wall Street Journal* (June 7, 2012), p. B9.

40This summary is based on Mansour Javidan, P. Dorfman, Mary Sully de Luque, and Robert J. House, "In the Eye of the Beholder: Cross Cultural Lessons in Leadership from Project GLOBE," *Academy of Management Perspectives* (February 2006), pp. 67–90; and Martin J. Gannon, *Paradoxes of Culture and Globalization* (Thousand Oaks, CA: Sage, 2008), p. 52.

41John Koten, "A Revolution in the Making," *The Wall Street Journal* (June 11, 2013), pp. R1, R2.

42Ibid.

Feature Notes 18

Opening Quote—"Charlie Rose Talks to Nick D' Aloisio," *Bloomberg BusinessWeek* (April 1–April 7, 2013), p. 40

Role Models—Information and quotes from "A Startup's New Prescription for Eyewear," *Bloomberg BusinessWeek* (July 4–10, 2011), pp. 49–551; (January 12, 2013); and warbyparker.com.

Facts to Consider—Data reported by Karen E. Klein, "Minority Start Ups: A Measure of Progress," *Business Week* (August 25, 2005), retrieved from www.businessweekonline; and press release, Minority Business Development Agency (March 5, 2009): www.mbda.gov; "Minority-Owned Business Growth & Global Reach," U. S. Department of Commerce MBDA: www.mdba.org (revised March, 2011); and Leah Yomtovian, "The Funding Landscape for Minority Entrepreneurs," *ideacrossing.org* (February 16, 2011).

Ethics Check—Information from Jessica Shambora, "The Story Behind the World's Hottest Shoemaker," *Financial Times,* Kindle edition (March 21, 2010); www.toms.com, and John Tozzi, "The Ben & Jerrys' Law: Principles Before Profit," *Bloomberg Businessweek* (April 26–May 2, 2010), pp. 69, 70.

Photo Essays—Etsy—Information from Etsy.com; and "Space Oddities," *Bloomberg BusinessWeek* (February 13–1, 2012), pp. 78–79. Shark Tank—Information from Carolyn T. Geer, "Innovation 101," *Wall Street Journal* (October 17, 2011), p. R5.

Hot Topic—Information and quotes from "Crowdfunding Students: Start Me Up," *The Economist* (June 15, 2013), economist.com (accessed June 20, 2013).

Endnotes 18

1Information from Gwen Moran, "How Military Veterans Are Finding Success in Small Business," *Entrepreneur* (February 20, 2012), entrepreneur.com (accessed January 11, 2013). See also, Ian Mount, "Open for Business," *USAA Magazine* (Summer 2012), pp. 20–24.

2Information from "Women Business Owners Receive First-Ever Micro Loans Via the Internet," *Business Wire* (August 9, 2000); Jim Hopkins, "Non-Profit Loan Group Takes Risks on Women in Business," *USA Today* (August 9, 2000), p. 2B; and "Women's Group Grants First Loans to Entrepreneurs," *Columbus Dispatch* (August 10, 2000), p. B2.

3Speech at the Lloyd Greif Center for Entrepreneurial Studies, Marshall School of Business, University of Southern California, 1996.

4Ibid.

5Information from Thomas Heath, "Value Added: The Nonprofit Entrepreneur," voices.washingtonpost.com.

6Information and quotes from the corporate websites; "Disruptor of the Day: Caterina Fake—Because She Had a Flickr of a Hunch about an Etsy," *Daily Disruption* (January 31, 2012), dailydisruption.com; Entrepreneur's Hall of Fame at www.1tbn.com; Anita Roddick, *Business as Unusual: My Entrepreneurial Journey, Profits with Principles* (West Sussex, England: Anita Roddick Books, 2005); Zack O'Malley Greenburg, "Jay-Z's Business Commandments" (March 16, 2011): forbes.com; and "Shawn 'Jay Z' Carter," BlackEntrepreneurProfile.com (accessed March 8, 2012): www.hunch.com.

7This list is developed from Jeffry A. Timmons, *New Venture Creation: Entrepreneurship for the 21st Century* (New York: Irwin/McGraw-Hill, 1999), pp. 47–48; and Robert D. Hisrich and Michael P. Peters, *Entrepreneurship,* 4th ed. (New York: Irwin/McGraw-Hill, 1998), pp. 67–70.

8For a review and discussion of the entrepreneurial mind, see Timmons, op. cit., pp. 219–225.

9Timothy Butler and James Waldroop, "Job Sculpting: The Art of Retaining Your Best People," *Harvard Business Review* (September/October 1999), pp. 144–52.

10Based on research summarized by Hisrich and Peters, op. cit., pp. 70–74.

11 Data in Arnaud Bertrand, "Age Verses the Cult of Youth Entrepreneurship," *Financial Times,* Kindle Edition (December 13 2012).

12Gwen Moran, "How Military Veterans are Finding Success in Small Business," *Entrepreneur* (February 20, 2012): entrepreneur.com (accessed January 11, 2013).

13See the review by Hisrich and Peters, op. cit.; and Paulette Thomas, "Entrepreneurs' Biggest Problems and How They Solve Them," *Wall Street Journal Reports* (March 17, 2003), pp. R1, R2.

14Ibid.

15Quote from www.anitaroddick.com/aboutanita.php (accessed April 24, 2010).

16*Paths to Entrepreneurship: New Directions for Women in Business* (New York: Catalyst, 1998) as summarized on the National Foundation for Women Business Owners Web site: www.nfwbo.org.; and *Women Business Owners of Color: Challenges and Accomplishments* (Washington, DC: National Foundation for Women Business Owners, 1998).

17"New Census Data Reinforces the Economic Power of Women-Owned Businesses in the U.S. says NAWBO," National Association of Women Business Owners press release (July 15, 2010); nawbo.org; Mark D. Wolf, "Women-Owned Business: America's New Job Creation Engine," *Forbes.com* (January 12, 2010); and *Paths to Entrepreneurship,* op. cit.

18"Wanted: More Black Entrepreneurs," *Bloomberg BusinessWeek* (January 23–29, 2012), pp. 4–16.

19Information from www.mbda.gov; and Leah Yomtovian, "The Funding Landscape for Minority Entrepreneurs," *ideacrossing.org* (February 16, 2011).

20David Bornstein, *How to Change the World: Social Entrepreneurs and the Power of New Ideas* (Oxford, UK: Oxford University Press, 2004).

21See Laura D'Andrea Tyson, "Good Works—With a Business Plan," *Business Week* (May 3, 2004), retrieved from *Business Week Online* (November 14, 2005) at www.businessweek.com.

22David Bornstein, *How to Change the World: Social Entrepreneurs and the Power of New Ideas* (Oxford, UK: Oxford University Press, 2004).

[23]See "The 10 Best Social Enterprises of 2009," *Fast Company* (December 1, 2009): fastcompany.com.

[24]Examples are from "Growing Green Business," *Northwestern* (Winter 2007), p. 19; and Regina McEnery, "Cancer Patients Getting the White-Glove Treatment," *Columbus Dispatch* (March 1, 2008).

[25]*The Facts About Small Business 1999* (Washington, DC: U.S. Small Business Administration, Office of Advocacy).

[26]Reported by Sue Shellenbarger, "Plumbing for Joy? Be Your Own Boss," *Wall Street Journal* (September 16, 2009), pp. D1, D2.

[27]Ibid.

[28]See U.S. Small Business Administration Web site: www.sba.gov; and *Statistical Abstract of the United States* (Washington, DC: U.S. Census Bureau, 1999).

[29]Charles Kenny, "Small Isn't Beautiful," *Bloomberg BusinessWeek* (October 3–9, 2011), pp. 10–11.

[30]Information and quotes from Steve Lohr, "The Rise of the Fleet-Footed Start-Up," *New York Times* (April 23, 2010): www.nytimes.com.

[31]Discussion based on "The Life Cycle of Entrepreneurial Firms," in Ricky Griffin (ed.), *Management,* 6th ed. (New York: Houghton Mifflin, 1999), pp. 309–10; and Neil C. Churchill and Virginia L. Lewis, "The Five Stages of Small Business Growth," *Harvard Business Review* (May/June 1993), pp. 30–50.

[32]Information reported in "The Rewards," *Inc. State of Small Business* (May 20–21, 2001), pp. 50–51.

[33]"The Business of Education," *Financial Times,* Kindle Edition (January 14, 2013); and The Family Firm Institute: www.ffi.org (accessed May 16, 2013).

[34]Conversation from the case "Am I My Uncle's Keeper?" by Paul I. Karofsky (Northeastern University Center for Family Business) and published at www.fambiz.com/contprov.cfm? ContProvCode=NECFB&ID=140.

[35]*Survey of Small and Mid-Sized Businesses: Trends for 2000,* conducted by Arthur Andersen and National Small Business United.

[36]Ibid.

[37]See U.S. Small Business Administration Web site: www.sba.gov.

[38]See Deborah Gage, "Venture Capital's Secret—3 out of 4 Start-Ups Fail," *Wall Street Journal* (September 20, 2012), pp. B1, B2.

[39]Based on Norman M. Scarborough and Thomas W. Zimmerer, *Effective Small Business Management* (Englewood Cliffs, NJ: Prentice-Hall, 2000), pp. 25–30; and Scott Clark, "Most Small-Business Failures Tied to Poor Management," *Business Journal* (April 10, 2000).

[40]Anne Field, "Business Incubators Are Growing Up," *Business Week* (November 16, 2009), p. 76.

[41]See www.sba.gov/aboutsba.

[42]Developed from William S. Sahlman, "How to Write a Great Business Plan," *Harvard Business Review* (July/August 1997), pp. 98–108.

[43]Marcia H. Pounds, "Business Plan Sets Course for Growth," *Columbus Dispatch* (March 16, 1998), p. 9; see also firm Web site: www.calcustoms.com.

[44]Standard components of business plans are described in many books, such as Linda Pinson, *Anatomy of a Business Plan: The Step-by-Step Guide to Building the Business and Securing Your Company's Future* (Tustin, CA: Out of Your Mind . . . and Into the Marketplace, 2008). Scarborough and Zimmerer, op. cit.; and on Web sites such as American Express Small Business Services, Business Town.com., and BizPlanIt.com.

[45]Angus Loten. "With New Law, Profits Take a Back Seat," *Wall Street Journal* (January 19, 2012): wsj.com (accessed November 24, 2012); Mark Underberg, "Benefit Corporations vs. 'Regular' Corporations: A Harmful Dichotomy" (June 18, 2012): *Businessethics.com* (accessed November 24, 2012); and Angus Loten, "Can Firms Aim to Do Good If It Hurts Profits?" *Wall Street Journal* (April 11, 2013), p. B6.

[46]As of this writing the B-Corp is legal in 12 states and is being considered in 20 others. For an update see Certified B Corporation: www.bcorporation.net.

[47]"You've Come a Long Way Baby," *Business Week Frontier* (July 10, 2000).

[48]See kickstarter.com and angel.co.

[49]See Jean Eaglesham, "Crowdfunding Efforts Draw Suspicion," *Wall Street Journal* (January 18, 2013), p. C1.

[50]Information from "Should Equity-Based Crowd Funding Be Legal?" *Wall Street Journal* (March 19, 2012), p. R3; and Angus Loten, "Avoiding the Equity Crowd Funding," *Wall Street Journal* (March 29, 2012); wsj.com.

Case 1 Trader Joe's

Elaine Misonzhink, "Retail Real Estate Pros Laud Trader Joe's Upsized Aspirations" (November 3, 2011), *Retail Traffic Magazine.* http://retailtrafficmag.com (Accessed 8/24/12).

Amy Groth, "Trader Joe's Is Run by This Ultra-Secretive German Family," *BusinessInsider.com* (August 1, 2011), http://articles.businessinsider.com (Accessed 8/21/12).

David Nusbaum, "Two Buck Chuck Price Goes Up, *Los Angeles Business Journal* (January 16, 2013), http://labusinessjournal.com (Accessed 2/7/13).

Christopher Palmeri, "Trader Joe's Recipe for Success," *Businessweek* (February 20, 2008), http://www.businessweek.com (Accessed 8/21/12).

Beth Kowitt, "Inside the Secret World of Trader Joe's," *Fortune* (February 23, 2010), http://money.cnn.com (Accessed 8/22/12).

Jena McGregor, "Leading Listener: Trader Joe's" (October 1, 2004), http://www.fastcompany.com (Accessed 2/7/13).

Blanca Torres, "Safeway Escalates Food Fight," *San Francisco Business Times* (March 30, 2012), http://www.bizjournals.com (Accessed 8/22/12).

"Trader Joe's Store Manager Salary," Glassdoor.com, http://www.glassdoor.com (Accessed 7/7/13).

Trader Joe's Website, "About," http://www.traderjoes.com (Accessed 8/22/12).

Trader Joe's Website, "Store Management," http://www.traderjoes.com (Accessed 8/23/12).

Matthew Enis, *Supermarket News* (July 19, 2010), v58 i29 pNA.

Kara Zuaro, "The 10 Best Trader Joe's Store-Brand Items," *L Magazine* (February 22, 2012), http://www.thelmagazine.com (Accessed 8/23/12).

http://wholefoodsmarket.com (Accessed 8/25/12).

"Trader Joe's Private Label World Revealed," *Store Brand Decisions* (August 24, 2010), http://www.storebrandsdecisions.com (Accessed 8/23/12).

Chobani

Diana Ramson, "Chobani Yogurt's Success Starts Where a Giant Left Off," *Entrepreneur Magazine* (May 25, 2012), http://www.entrepreneur.com (Accessed 8/25/12).

Megan Walsh, "Chobani Takes Gold in the Yogurt Aisle," *BusinessWeek* (July 31, 2012), http://www.businessweek.com (Accessed 8/25/12).

Philip Butta, "The World's 50 Most Innovative Companies," *Fast Company* (March 2012), http://www.fastcompany.com (Accessed 8/25/12).

Christopher Steiner, "The $700 Million Yogurt Startup," *Forbes* (September 8, 2011), http://www.forbes.com (Accessed 8/25/12).

Sarah Needleman, "Old Factory, Snap Decision Spawn Greek-Yogurt Craze," *Wall Street Journal* (June 20, 2012), http://online.wsj.com (Accessed 8/25/12).

Samantha Cortez, "INSTANT MBA: The Recipe for Success Requires a Lot of Experimentation," *Business Insider* (July 19, 2012), http://www.businessinsider.com (Accessed 8/25/12).

Sheridan Prasso, "Chobani: The Unlikely King of Yogurt, "*Fortune* (November 30, 2011), http://money.cnn.com (Accessed 8/27/12).

Case 2 Zara International

Zara International "Fashion Forward," *Economist* (March 24, 2012), http://www.economist.com (Accessed 8/26/12).

David Roman and William Kemble-Diaz, "Owner of Fast-Fashion Retailer Zara Keeps Up Emerging-Markets Push," *Wall Street Journal* (June 13, 2012), http://online.wsj.com (Accessed 8/26/12).

"Inditex's Agility, Scale Behind Growth, Analyst Says," *Bloomberg Business Video* (June 13, 2012), http://www.businessweek.com (Accessed 8/26/12).

Stephen Burgen, "Fashion chain Zara helps Inditex lift first quarter profits by 30%," *TheGuardian* (August 17, 2012), http://www.guardian.co.uk (Accessed 9/5/12).

Marissa Tom, *FabSugar Website* (June 26, 2012), http://www.fabsugar.com (Accessed 10/15/12).

Top 100: Zara, *Retail Customer Experience*, http://www.retailcustomerexperience.com (Accessed 10/15/12).

"Zara, A Spanish Success Story," *CNN* (June 15, 2001), http://edition.cnn.com (Accessed 10/15/12).

Inditex Press Dossier: www.inditex.com/en (Accessed 5/17/09).

"Zara Grows as Retail Rivals Struggle," *Wall Street Journal* (March 26, 2009).

Cecile Rohwedder and Keith Johnson, "Pace-setting Zara Seeks More Speed to Fight Its Rising Cheap-Chic Rivals," *Wall Street Journal* (February 20, 2008), p. B1.

"Zara: Taking the Lead in Fast Fashion," *BusinessWeek* (April 4, 2006).

"OurGroup," Inditex, http://inditex.com/en (Accessed 9/5/12).

Uniqlo

Dana Matioli, "Uniqlo Expansion Takes Retailer out to West Coast," *Wall Street Journal* (April 9, 2012), http://online.wsj.com (Accessed 8/28/12).

"A Message from Tadashi Yanai," *Uniqlo Website*, http://www.fastretailing.com (Accessed 8/28/12).

Tina Gaudoin, "Uniqlo: Cheap and Very Cheerful," *Wall Street Journal* (April 19, 2012), http://online.wsj.com (Accessed 8/28/12).

"Conquering the world with discipline, politeness and Japan-ness," *Economist* (June 26, 2010), http://www.economist.com (Accessed 8/28/12).

Jeff Chu, "Cheap Chic and Made for All: How Uniqlo intends to take over fashion," *Fast Company* (June 18, 2012), http://www.fastcompany.com (Accessed 8/28/12).

Case 3   Patagonia

Monte Burke, "Wal-Mart, Patagonia Team to Green Business," *Forbes*, Posted 5/6/10, http://www.forbes.com/forbes/2010/0524/rebuilding-sustainability-eco-friendly-mr-green-jeans.html. Accessed 2/2/11.

Kent Garber, "Yvon Chouinard: Patagonia Founder Fights for the Environment," *U.S. News*, Posted 10/22/09, http://www.usnews.com/news/best-leaders/articles/2009/10/22/yvon-chouinard-patagonia-founder-fights-for-the-environment. Accessed 2/2/11.

Diana Random, "Finding Success by Putting Company Culture First," *Entrepreneur*, Posted 4/19/11, http://www.entrepreneur.com/article/219509. Accessed 3/1/12.

Jennifer Wang, "Patagonia, From the Ground Up," *Entrepreneur*, Posted 6/10, http://www.entrepreneur.com/magazine/entrepreneur/2010/june/206536.html. Accessed 2/2/11.

"Environmental Internships," *Patagonia*, http://www.patagonia.com/eu/enSE/patagonia.go?assetid=9153. Accessed 2/3/11.

Philanthrocapitalism

Richard Riordan, "Giving Till it Works," *Wall Street Journal* (October 10, 2008), http://online.wsj.com/article/SB122359567803921177.html (Accessed August 30, 2012).

Bruce Watson, *Daily Finance*, "The New Age of Philanthropy: How Billionaires Are Giving Back" (March 26, 2011).

"The Birth of Philanthrocapitalism," *The Economist* (February 23, 2006), http://www.economist.com/node/5517656 (Accessed August 30, 2012).

http://www.gatesfoundation.org/Who-We-Are/General-Information/Foundation-Factsheet (Accessed March 23, 2013).

Leslie Lenkowsky. "A Buffet Rule Worth Following," *Wall Street Journal* (March 28, 2013), p. A13.

Case 4   Amazon

SC Digest Editorial Staff, Logistics News: In Astounding Move, Amazon.com Buys Robotic Material Handling Provider Kiva, *SC Digest.com* (March 21, 2012), http://www.scdigest.com (Accessed 9/6/12).

Mark Brohan, "Amazon plans a 40% expansion in distribution center space, report says," *InternetRetailer* (January 18, 2011), http://www.internetretailer.com (Accessed 9/6/12).

"2012 Earnings: Third Quarter Amazon.com," *New York Times* (August 28, 2012), http://topics.nytimes.com (Accessed 9/6/12).

Ian Sherr and Ben Fox Rubin, "Amazon Adds Epix Content in Blow to Netflix," *The Wall Street Journal* (September 4, 2012), http://online.wsj.com (Accessed 9/6/12).

"Retailers Talk Pros and Cons of Selling on Amazon," *Outdoor Industry Association* (March 8, 2012), http://www.outdoorindustry.org (Accessed 9/7/12).

Ron Miller, "Amazon Prime includes lots of free content," *Fierce Content Management* (August 28, 2012), Accessed 9/7/12.

David Meerman Scott, "The Flip Side of Free," *eContent*, vol. 28, no. 10 October 2005.

"Amazon CEO Takes Long View," *USA Today* (July 6, 2005). http://usatoday30.usatoday.com (Accessed 9/7/12).

Thomas Ricker, "Amazon Adds Audible to its Digital Empire," http://www.engadget.com (Accessed 9/7/12).

Tim O Reilly, "Why Kindle Should Be an Open Book," *Forbes*, http://www.forbes.com (Accessed 9/17/12).

Netflix

Andrew Goldman, "Reed Hastings Knows He Messed Up," *New York Times* (October 20, 2011), http://www.nytimes.com (Accessed 9/7/12).

William Cohan, "Seeing Red," *Vanity Fair Magazine* (February 22, 2012), http://www.vanityfair.com (Accessed 9/7/12).

Michael Liedtke, "Netflix CEO Reed Hastings on Mistakes, Biggest Competition," *Huffington Post* (December 7, 2011), http://www.huffingtonpost.com (Accessed 9/7/12).

Brian Stelter and Nick Wingfield, "How Netflix Lost 800,000 Members, and Good Will," *New York Times* (October 24, 2011), http://www.nytimes.com (Accessed 9/7/12).

Case 5   Nordstrom

Zacks Equity Search, "Nordstrom's Comps Rise Again," Zacks Investment Research (January 6, 2012), http://www.zacks.com (Accessed 9/10/12).

"Nordstrom Management Discusses Q4 2011 Results—Earnings Call Transcript," *Seeking Alpha*, Posted 2/16/12, http://seekingalpha.com (Accessed 9/10/12).

Stephanie Clifford, "Nordstrom Links Online Inventory to Real World," *New York Times* (August 23, 2010), http://www.nytimes.com (Accessed 9/10/12).

Cotton Timberlake, "Nordstrom Tries an Extreme Makeover with Topshop," *BusinessWeek* (July 12, 2012), http://www.businessweek.com (Accessed 9/10/12).

Cotton Timberlake, "How Nordstrom Bests Its Retail Rivals," *BusinessWeek* (August 11, 2011), http://www.businessweek.com (Accessed 9/10/12).

2011 Nordstrom Annual Report, https://materials.proxyvote.com (Accessed 9/10/12).

Cotton Timberlake, "Nordstrom Beats Macy's and Saks by Moving Inventories," *Bloomberg*, Posted 4/08/09, http://www.bloomberg.com (Accessed 2/14/12).

Stephanie Clifford, "Nordstrom Uses Web to Locate Items and Increase Sales," *The New York Times* (August 23, 2010), http://www.nytimes.com (Accessed 2/14/12).

Jake Bastell, "Nordstrom gets in step with tracking its inventory," *The Seattle Times*, Posted 2/10/02, http://community.seattletimes.nwsource.com (Accessed 2/14/12).

Global Supply Chains

"Japan and the Global Supply Chain—Broken Links," *Economist* (March 31, 2011), http://www.economist.com (Accessed 9/12/12).

Jonathan Welsh, "Japan Earthquake Hobbles Car Makers," *The Wall Street Journal* (March 13, 2011), http://blogs.wsj.com (Accessed 9/12/12).

"Just-in-Time—Philosophy of complete elimination of waste," *Toyota Website* (October 21, 2011), http://www.toyota-global.com (Accessed 9/12/12).

Yoshio Takahashi, "Lessons Learned: Japanese Car Makers a Year After Quake," *Wall Street Journal*, (March 7, 2012), http://blogs.wsj.com (Accessed 9/12/12).

Iason Dalavagas, "The Impact of Japan's Disaster on Toyota, Honda, and Nissan," *Value Line* (May 29, 2011), http://www.valueline.com (Accessed 9/11/11).

Case 6   Chipotle

Steven Russollilo, "Chipotle Shares Tank on Slowdown Fears," *Wall Street Journal* (July 20, 2012), http://blogs.wsj.com (Accessed 9/17/12).

Annie Gasparro, "Restaurant Chains Feel the Need for Speed," *Wall Street Journal* (September 4, 2012), http://online.wsj.com (Accessed 9/17/12).

Miriam Jordan, "A CEO's Demand: Fix Immigration," *Wall Street Journal* (December 19, 2011), http://online.wsj.com (Accessed 9/17/12).

"Heard on the Street: Overheard: Chipotle's Bean Counters," *Wall Street Journal* (February 27, 2011), http://online.wsj.com/article (Accessed 9/17/12).

Steve Van Tiem, "Superior Management a Key Ingredient to Chipotle's Success," *The Motley Fool* (June 20, 2012), http://beta.fool.com (Accessed 9/17/12).

Allison Aubrey, "Antibiotic-Free Meat Business Is Booming, Thanks to Chipotle," *NPR Website* (May 31, 2012), http://www.npr.org (Accessed 9/17/12).

"Full of Beans: How a Classically Trained Chef Reinvented Fast Food," *Knowledge at Wharton* (January 20, 2010), http://knowledge.wharton.upenn.edu (Accessed 9/17/12).

Mint.com

"40 Under 40," *Money CNN* (March 26, 2010), http://money.cnn.com (Accessed 9/14/12).

"Intuit to Acquire Mint.com," Intuit website press release (September 14, 2009), http://investors.intuit.com (Accessed 9/14/12).

T. Schweitzer, "The Number Cruncher," *Inc.* (September 17, 2008), http://www.inc.com (Accessed 9/14/12).

"Paying Off Debt Made Easier with Mint.com," *Intuit.com website*, http://investors.intuit.com (Accessed 9/14/12).

Case 7   Dunkin' Donuts

R. Jai Krishna and Rumman Ahmed, "Dunkin' Brands Looks at Emerging Markets," *Wall Street Journal* (May 30, 2012), http://blogs.wsj.com (Accessed 9/28/12).

Annalyn Censky, "Dunkin' Donuts to double U.S. locations," *CNN Money* (January 4, 2012), http://money.cnn.com (Accessed 9/28/12).

Vanessa Wong, "Q&A: Dunkin' Donuts' Creative Willy Wonka," *BusinessWeek* (September 24, 2012), http://www.businessweek.com (Accessed 9/28/12).

Carolyn Walkup, "Nigel Travel Talks Dunkin's Strategy," *QSR* (September 2010), http://www.qsrmagazine.com (Accessed 9/28/12).

"Menu," *DunkinDonuts website*, http://www.dunkindonuts.com (Accessed 9/28/12).

"Company Snapshot," *Dunkin' Donuts website*, http://www.dunkindonuts.com (Accessed 9/28/12).

Susan Spielberg, "For Snack Chains, Coffee Drinks the Best Way to Sweeten Profits," *Nation's Restaurant News* (June 27, 2005).

Dunkin' Donuts Press Kit, *Dunkin' Donuts website*, http://news.dunkindonuts.com (Accessed 9/28/12).

"Investor Overview, *Starbucks website*, http://investor.starbucks.com (Accessed 9/28/12).

Janet Adamy, "Starbucks Takes Plunge into Instant Coffee," *Wall Street Journal* (February 13, 2009), http://professional.wsj.com (Accessed 9/28/12).

Jamba Juice

Rick Aristotle Munarriz, "Jamba Juice's Sweet Future: Could It Be the Next Starbucks?" *DailyFinance* (May 1, 2012), http://www.dailyfinance.com (Accessed 9/28/12).

Galileo Russell, "Interview with James D. White, CEO/Turnaround Master of Jamba Juice." *Seeking Alpha* (September 19, 2012), http://seekingalpha.com (Accessed 9/28/12).

Case 8   Law Firms

John Gapper, "Law firms have struck the limits of partnership," *Financial Times* (May 9, 2012), http://www.ft.com (Accessed 10/2/12).

Mark Harris, "Why More Law Firms Will Go the Way of Dewey & LeBoeuf," *Fortune* (May 8, 2012), http://www.forbes.com (Accessed 10/2/12).

Daniel Fisher, "New Precedent for Law Firms," *Forbes* (June 8, 2011), http://www.forbes.com (Accessed 10/3/12).

"Technology Offers 50 Ways to Leave Your Lawyer," *Economist* (August 13, 2011), http://www.economist.com (Accessed 10/2/12).

Drew Combs, "The Disruptive Innovation at Axiom's Legal Outsourcing Division," *The American Lawyer* (July 2, 2012). http://www.law.com (Accessed 10/3/12).

Andrew Ross Sorkin, "Big Law Steps into Uncertain Times," *New York Times* (September 24, 2012), http://dealbook.nytimes.com (Accessed 10/3/12).

Goodbye Office

Haya El Nasser, "The Office is Shrinking as Tech Creates Workplace Everywhere," *USA Today* (June 5, 2012). http://usatoday30.usatoday.com (Accessed 10/8/12).

Newman Crane, "Business-Insurance: The Officeless Office Trend," *Newmancrane.com website* (Posted 5/22/12), http://www.newmancraneins.com (Accessed 10/8/12).

Rachel Emma Silverman and Robin Sidel, "Warming Up to the Officeless Office," *Wall Street Journal* (April 17, 2012), http://professional.wsj.com (Accessed 10/8/12).

Kelly Eggers, "Open Offices Aren't for Everyone," *Wall Street Journal* (April 17, 2012), http://online.wsj.com (Accessed 10/8/12).

Case 9   LinkedIn

Josh Bersin, "Facebook vs. LinkedIn—What's the Difference?" *Forbes* (May 21, 2012), http://www.forbes.com (Accessed 10/9/12).

Rick Vancouver, "Five Benefits of LinkedIn for Organizations (and IT Pros), *TechRepublic* (Posted 5/19/09), http://www.techrepublic.com (Accessed 10/9/12).

Paul Alofs, "8 Rules for Creating a Passionate Work Culture," *Fast Company* (May 21, 2012), http://www.fastcompany.com (Accessed 10/9/12).

David Lidsky, "The World's 50 Most Innovative Companies," *Fast Company* (October 2012), http://www.fastcompany.com (Accessed 10/9/12)

E. B. Boyd, "After LinkedIn's IPO: What It Will Have to Do to Earn Its $4.3 Billion Valuation." *Fast Company* (May 19, 2011), http://www.fastcompany.com (Accessed 10/9/12).

Ben Parr, "LinkedIn Launches Tool to Visualize Your Business Network," *Mashable* (Posted 1/24/11). http://mashable.com (Accessed 10/9/12).

Lena Rao, "Greylock Gives Super Angel Turned VC Reid Hoffman a 20 Million Seed Fund," *TechCrunch.com* website. (Posted 9/27/10), http://techcrunch.com (Accessed 10/9/12).

Jessi Hempel, "How LinkedIn Will Fire Up Your Career," *Fortune* (March 25, 2010), http://money.cnn.com (Accessed 10/9/12).

Sarah Lacy, "Attention Entrepreneurs: Mark Zuckerberg Isn't the Role Model. Reid Hoffman Is," *TechCrunch (*Posted 5/18/11), http://techcrunch.com (Accessed 10/9/12).

Liz Gannes, "Reid Hoffman and Jeff Weiner on LinkedIn, Perhaps the Only Even-Keeled Consumer Internet Company," *All Things Digital* (Posted 5/30/12), http://allthingsd.com (Accessed 10/9/12).

Gamers Welcome

Debra Weiss, "Management Trend Is Gamification of the Workplace," *ABA Journal* (Posted 11/17/11), http://www.abajournal.com (Accessed 10/11/12).

Rachel Emma Silverman, "Latest Game Theory: Mixing Work and Play," *Wall Street Journal* (October 10, 2011), http://professional.wsj.com (Accessed 10/11/12).

Rachel King, "The Games Companies Play," *BusinessWeek* (April 4, 2011), http://www.businessweek.com (Accessed 10/12/12).

Ryan Kim, "Real Rewards Help Gamification Take Flight," *Gigaom.com* (Posted 3/17/12), http://gigaom.com (Accessed 10/11/12).

Case 10   Chief Executive Mom

Lisa Miller, "Can Marissa Mayer Really Have it All?" *New York Magazine* (October 15, 2012), http://nymag.com (Accessed 10/21/12).

Amir Efrati, "Yahoo to Pay Mayer $100 Million over Five Years," *Wall Street Journal* (July 20, 2012), http://online.wsj.com (Accessed 10/21/12).

Amir Efrati, "A Makeover in Google's Image," *Wall Street Journal* (August 9, 2012), http://online.wsj.com (Accessed 10/21/12).

Jessica Gross, "How Relevant Is Marissa Mayer's Maternity Leave? Not Very," *BusinessWeek* (October 18, 2012), http://www.businessweek.com (Accessed 10/21/12).

Sue Shellenbarger, "More Women Pursue Claims of Pregnancy Discrimination," *Wall Street Journal* (March 27, 2008), http://professional.wsj.com (Accessed 10/23/12).

Vicki Elmer, "Workplace Pregnancy Discrimination Suits on the Rise," *The Washington Post* (April 8, 2012), http://www.washingtonpost.com (Accessed 10/27/12).

Hanny Lerner, "Negotiating Success: What to Learn from Marissa Mayer's Compensation Package," *Forbes* (August 15, 2012), http://www.forbes.com (Accessed 10/25/12).

Emanuella Grinberg, "If Marissa Mayer Can Have It All, Can You?" *CNN.com* (Posted 7/19/12). http://www.cnn.com (Accessed 10/26/12).

New Workplace Perks

Cotton Delo, "Why Companies Are Cozying Up to Napping at Work," *Fortune* (August 11, 2012), http://management.fortune.cnn.com (Accessed October 17, 2012).

"Napping Gets a Nod at the Workplace," *BusinessWeek (*August 26, 2010), http://www.businessweek.com (Accessed 10/29/12).

Danielle Gaines, "Workplace Napping Hits the Mainstream," *GreatReporter.com website* (Posted on 3/9/08), http://greatreporter.com (Accessed 10/19/12).

Case 11   Apple, Inc.

"About Cupidtino," Cupidtino Website. http://cupidtino.com (Accessed 10/31/12).

Larry Dignan, "Steve Jobs Resigns: Now Apple's Succession Plan to Be Put to Test," *ZDNet.com* Posted 8/24/11. http://www.zdnet.com (Accessed 10/31/12).

Yukari Iwatani Kane, "Jobs Maintains Grip at Apple," *Wall Street Journal* (April 11, 2009), http://professional.wsj.com (Accessed 10/28/12).

Spencer E. Ante and Jena McGregor, "Apple's Succession Plan: Nobody's Business," *Bloomberg Businessweek* (January 15, 2009), http://www.businessweek.com (Accessed 10/28/12).

Jessica Vascellaro, "Apple in his Own Image" (November 2, 2011), http://professional.wsj.com (Accessed 10/31/12).

John Martellaro, "Apple CEO Tim Cook: A Report Card," *The Mac Observer.* Posted 5/23/12. http://www.macobserver.com (Accessed 10/31/12).

Jessica Vascellaro, "Cook Is Making Apple His Own," *Wall Street Journal* (November 2, 2011), http://professional.wsj.com (Accessed 10/31/12).

Samantha Murphy, "Apple Experts: Stop Comparing Tim Cook to Steve Jobs," *Mashable*, Posted 10/5/12, http://news.yahoo.com (Accessed 10/31/12).

"Double Bind"

"How Can Young Women Develop a Leadership Style?" *Wall Street Journal* (March 19, 2009), http://guides.wsj.com (Accessed 11/3/12).

"Women and Leadership: Delicate Balancing Act," *Womens Media*, Posted 4/2/09, http://www.womensmedia.com (Accessed 10/31/12).

Case 12   Businesses in Trouble

Jonathan Berr, "McDonald's CEO: Relax, Ronald's not Bad," money.msn.com (May 23, 2013): Accessed June 24, 2013.

W. Keith Campbell and Constantine Sedikides. "Self-threat magnifies the self-serving bias: A meta-analytic integration," *Review of General Psychology*, vol. 3, no. 1 (1999), pp. 23–43. doi:10.1037/1089-2680.3.1.23.

Ben Austen, "The End of Borders and the Future of Books," *BusinessWeek* (November 10, 2011), http://www.businessweek.com (Accessed 11/4/12).

Marc Santora, "Teenagers' Suit Says McDonald's Made Them Obese," *New York Times* (November 21, 2002). http://www.nytimes.com (Accessed 11/5/12).

Leadership IQ

"What Makes a Good Leader?" Daniel Goleman Website, Posted 7/6/09, http://danielgoleman.info (Accessed 11/9/12).

Nick Tasler and Travis Bradberry, "Emotional Intelligence: Skills Worth Learning" (March 27, 2009), *BusinessWeek*, http://www.businessweek.com (Accessed 11/9/12).

Daniel Goleman, "What Makes a Leader?" *Harvard Business Review* (January 2004), http://hbr.org (Accessed 11/11/12).

Case 13   Salesforce.com

"Salesforce.com Signs Definitive Agreement to Acquire Rypple—First Step Toward Human Capital Management for the Social Enterprise," *Wall Street Journal* (December 15, 2011), http://professional.wsj.com (Accessed 11/12/12).

Don Tapscott, "Supervising Net Gen," *BusinessWeek* (December 8, 2008), http://www.businessweek.com (Accessed 11/12/12).

"Motivate," *Work.com,* http://work.com (Accessed 11/12/12).

Kate Abbot, "How I Got Here: Salesforce Rypple's Daniel Debow," *Bloomberg BusinessWeek* (June 27, 2012), http://www.businessweek.com (Accessed 11/12/12).

Rachel Emma Silverman, "Yearly Reviews? Try Weekly," *Wall Street Journal* (September 6, 2011), http://online.wsj.com (Accessed 11/12/12).

Samuel Culbert, "Get Rid of the Performance Review," *Wall Street Journal* (June 21, 2012), http://professional.wsj.com (Accessed 11/12/12).

Lena Rao, "Salesforce Debuts Rypple Powered Work to Help Companies Manage Talent," *TechCrunch,* Posted 9/19/12, http://techcrunch.com (Accessed 11/12/12).

Free Lunch

Shira Ovide, "Work Perk: Free Meal Rule Widens," *Wall Street Journal* (July 11, 2012), http://online.wsj.com (Accessed 11/11/12).

Kara Swisher, "In Week Two, Marissa Mayer Googifies Yahoo: Free Food! Friday Afternoon All-Hands! New Work Spaces! Fab Swag!" *All Things D*, Posted 7/29/12 (Accessed 11/11/12).

"100 Best Companies to Work for 2012: Best Benefits: Unusual Perks," *Fortune*, http://money.cnn.com (Accessed 11/11/12).

Case 14   Whole Foods

Lesley Patton and Bryan Gruley, "Whole Foods' Recession Lessons," *BusinessWeek* (August 9, 2012), http://www.businessweek.com (Accessed 9/12/12).

"Quality Standards," *Whole Foods Market* Website, http://www.wholefoodsmarket.com (Accessed 9/12/12).

"Our Mission and Culture," Whole Foods Market Website, http://www.wholefoodsmarket.com (Accessed 9/12/12).

Gary Hamel, "What Google, Whole Foods Do Best," *CNN Money* (September 27, 2007), http://money.cnn.com (Accessed 11/14/12).

"Mission Statement," *Whole Foods Market* Website, http://www.wholefoodsmarket.com (Accessed 11/14/12).

Jennifer Liberto, "CEO pay is 380 times average worker's—AFL-CIO," *MoneyCNN.com*, Posted 4/9/12, http://money.cnn.com (Accessed 11/24/12).

"Whole Foods Market, Inc. (WFM:NASDAQ GS)," http://investing.businessweek.com (Accessed 2/16/12).

Federal Reserve

Luca Di Leo and Jon Hilsenrath, "Bernanke on Fed Disagreements, Group Decision Making," *Wall Street Journal* (September 30, 2010), http://blogs.wsj.com (Accessed 9/5/12).

Jon Hilsenrath, "Bernanke's Imprint on Fed not Easily Erased," *Wall Street Journal* (January 30, 2012), http://online.wsj.com (Accessed 9/5/12).

Charles Fishman, "Whole Foods is all Teams," *Fast Company* (April 30, 1996), http://www.fastcompany.com (Accessed 11/13/12).

Case 15   Twitter

Lauren Duggan, "Twitter to Surpass 500 million Registered Users," Posted 2/21/12, *Media Bistro,* http://www.mediabistro.com (Accessed 1/15/13).

Sean Ludwig, "Ten Corporate Accounts Worth Following," *PC Magazine* (February 28, 2009), http://www.pcmag.com (Accessed 1/15/13). Pew Research, "The Demographics of Twitter Users," The results of this report are based on data from telephone interviews conducted by Princeton Survey Research Associates International from January 20 to February 19, 2012, among a sample of 2,253 adults, http://www.mindjumpers.com (Accessed 1/15/13). "Using Twitter for your Organization," (May 5, 2012), Kevin Bondelli, http://www.kevinbondelli.com (Accessed 1/15/13).

Charlie Minato, The Top 20 Brands on Twitter, Ranked by Influence with Customers," *BusinessInsider.com* (Posted 7/2/12), http://www.businessinsider.com (Accessed 1/16/13). "Twitter Turns Six," Twitter Blog, http://blog.twitter.com (Accessed 1/16/13).

Yammer

"Yammer: Changing the Way we Communicate at Work" (Posted 2/15/11), *Building43.com* website, http://www.businessinsider.com (Accessed 1/17/12). "Yammer Business Benefits," https://www.yammer.com (Accessed 1/17/13).

Case 16   Cultural Charades

Veenu Sandhu, " For young BPO workers, it's a close call with abuse," *Hindustan Times* (January 12, 2008), http://www.hindustantimes.com (Accessed 11/27/12).

R. Sanjeev Kumar, "BPO culture: Good or bad for Indian youth?" *MeriNews* (May 11, 2008), http://www.merinews.com (Accessed 11/27/12).

Andrew Marantz, "My Summer at an Indian Call Center," *Mother Jones* (July/August 2011), (December 7, 2011). http://www.motherjones.com (Accessed 11/27/12).

Kirti Kamboj, "Mother Jones falls short: My Summer in an Indian Call Center," *Hyphen* magazine (Posted 7/18/11), http://www.hyphenmagazine.com (Accessed 11/2/12).

Sarah Whitmire, "How Call Centers 'De-Indianize' Workers," *Newser* (Posted 7/10/11), (Accessed 11/12/12).

Suresh Yannamani, "The Changing Face of Indian BPO Industry," *SiliconIndia* (April 8, 2011), http://www.siliconindia.com (Accessed 11/12/12).

Christy Petty, "Gartner Says Worldwide BPO Growth Continues Despite Mixed Fortunes in Developed Countries," *Gartner Report* (August 22, 2011), http://www.gartner.com (Accessed 11/26/11).

Shehzad Nadeem, *Dead Ringers: How Outsourcing is Changing the Way Indians Understand Themselves* (Princeton, NJ: Princeton University Press, 2011).

Goutam Das and Sunny Sen, "Born Again: India's BPO Industry Losing Voice, Finds Life Elsewhere," *Business Today* (April 1, 2012), http://businesstoday.intoday.in (Accessed 11/26/12).

Beyond Race and Gender

Kevin Whitelaw, "Defining Diversity Beyond Race and Gender," National Public Radio (Posted 1/13/10), http://www.npr.org (Accessed 11/24/12).

"Corporate Responsibility Diversity and Inclusion," *Motorola Website*, http://responsibility.motorola.com (Accessed 11/24/12). "Abbott Careers: Diversity and Inclusion," *Abbott Website*, https://www.abbott.com (Accessed 11/24/12).

Transcript of Civil Rights Act (1964) http://www.ourdocuments.gov (Accessed 11/24/12).

Case 17   Harley-Davidson

Rick Barrett, "Harley-Davidson is changing to adapt here and globally," *Journal Sentinel* (April 30, 2011), http://www.jsonline.com (Accessed 11/25/12).

"Bikers go hog-wild as Harley-Davidson opens first store in China," *USA Today* (April 8, 2006), http://usatoday30.usatoday.com (Accessed 11/25/06).

Paula M. Miller, "An American Icon Revs Up Its Fan Base and Sales in China," *China Business Review online* (January–March 2012). www.chinabusinessreview.com (Accessed 11/25/12).

Sara Sidner, "Harley Davidson to Build Bikes in India," *CNN* (Posted 11/4/10). http://www.cnn.com (Accessed 11/25/12).

"Harley Davidson 100th Anniversary," *Harley Davidson Website*, http://110.harley-davidson.com (Accessed 11/25/12).

"Investor Relations," *Harley-Davidson Website*, http://investor.harley-davidson.com (Accessed 11/25/12).

NOT Made in China

David Rocks and Nick Leiber, "Small U.S. Manufacturers Give Up on 'Made in China,'" *BusinessWeek* (June 21, 2012), http://www.businessweek.com (Accessed 11/24/12).

John Bussey, "Will Costs Drive Firms Home?" *Wall Street Journal* (May 5, 2011), http://professional.wsj.com (Accessed 11/24/12).

Timothy Aeppel, "Candle Maker Feels Burned," *Wall Street Journal* (May 5, 2011), http://professional.wsj.com (Accessed 11/24/12).

Case 18   Angel Investors

Erik Sofge, "The Good, the Bad and the Crowd Funded," *Wall Street Journal* (August 18, 2012), http://professional.wsj.com (Accessed 11/24/12).

Scott Lowe and Ben Popper, "How Much Accountability Should Your Kickstarter Pledge Buy?" *The Verge.com* (September 14, 2012), http://www.theverge.com (Accessed 11/24/12).

Rachel Arndt, "The World's 50 Most Innovative Entrepreneurs," *Fast Company*, http://www.fastcompany.com. (Accessed 11/24/12).

Roger Yu, "Crowd funding fuels businesses, charities, creative ventures," *USA Today* (May 31, 2012), http://usatoday30.usatoday.com (Accessed 11/24/12).

Michael Farrell, "Kickstarter Propels Local Entrepreneurs," *The Boston Globe* (September 9, 2012), http://www.boston.com (Accessed 11/24/12).

Bethany Clough, "Kickstarter Proves Useful for Entrepreneurs," *Fresno Bee* (September 30, 2012), http://www.hispanicbusiness.com (Accessed 11/24/12).

Ben Hamilton, *PleaseFund.Us website* (September 9, 2011), http://www.pleasefund.us (Accessed 11/24/12).

"Project Guidelines," *Kickstarter.com website*, http://www.kickstarter.com (Accessed 11/25/12).

Rob Walker, "The Trivialities and Transcendence of Kickstarter," *The New York Times* (August 5, 2011), http://www.nytimes.com (Accessed 11/25/12).

Accidental Entrepreneurs

"About / The FlavorX Story," FlavorX website, http://flavorx.com (Accessed 11/24/12).

Leigh Buchanan, "The Heart of a Company," *Inc.* (June 1, 2003), http://www.inc.com (Accessed 11/24/12).

Justine Griffin, "More Retailers Offering Pet Meds," *Sun Sentinel* (July 1, 2012), http://www.postandcourier.com (Accessed 11/24/12).

SKILL BUILDING PORTFOLIO

Self-Assessment Notes

[1]Some items included in *Outcome Measurement Project, Phase I and Phase II Reports* (St. Louis: American Assembly of Collegiate Schools of Business, 1986).

[2]Item list from James Weber, "Management Value Orientations: A Typology and Assessment," *International Journal of Value Based Management*, vol. 3, no. 2 (1990), pp. 37–54.

[3]AIM Survey (El Paso, TX: ENFP Enterprises, 1989). Copyright © 1989 by Weston H. Agor. Used by permission.

[4]Suggested by a discussion in Robert Quinn, Sue R. Faerman, Michael P. Thompson, and Michael R. McGrath, *Becoming a Master Manager: A Contemporary Framework* (New York: Wiley, 1990), pp. 75–76.

[5]Julian P. Rotter, "External Control and Internal Control," *Psychology Today* (June, 1971), p. 42. Used by permission.

[6]Joseph A. Devito, *Messages: Building Interpersonal Communication Skills*, 3rd ed. (New York: HarperCollins, 1996), referencing William Haney, *Communicational Behavior: Text and Cases*, 3rd ed. (Homewood, IL: Irwin, 1973). Reprinted by permission.

[7]Questionnaire adapted from L. Steinmetz and R. Todd, *First Line Management*, 4th ed. (Homewood, IL: BPI/Irwin, 1986), pp. 64–67. Used by permission.

[8]Based on S. Budner, "Intolerance of Ambiguity as a Personality Variable," *Journal of Personality*, vol. 30, no. 1 (1962), pp. 29–50.

[9]Developed in part from Robert E. Quinn, Sue R. Faerman, Michael P. Thompson, and Michael R. McGrath, *Becoming a Master Manager! A Contemporary Framework* (New York: Wiley, 1990), p. 187. Used by permission.

[10]Fred E. Fiedler and Martin M. Chemers, *Improving Leadership Effectiveness: The Leader Match Concept*, 2nd ed. (New York: Wiley, 1984). Used by permission.

[11]Adapted from R. W. Bortner, "A Short Rating Scale as a Potential Measure of Type A Behavior," *Journal of Chronic Diseases*, vol. 22 (1966), pp. 87–91. Used by permission.

[12]Developed from Lynda McDermott, Nolan Brawley, and William Waite, *World-Class Teams: Working Across Borders* (New York: Wiley, 1998).

[13]Douglas T. Hall, Donald D. Bowen, Roy J. Lewicki, and Francine S. Hall, *Experiences in Management and Organizational Behavior*, 2nd ed. (New York: Wiley, 1985). Used by permission.

[14]Developed from "Is Your Company Really Global?" *Business Week* (December 1, 1997).

[15]Instrument adapted from Norman M. Scarborough and Thomas W. Zimmerer, *Effective Small Business Management*, 3rd ed. (Columbus: Merrill, 1991), pp. 26–27.

Class Exercise Notes

[1]Adapted from John R. Schermerhorn Jr., James G. Hunt, and Richard N. Osborn, *Managing Organizational Behavior*, 3rd ed. (New York: Wiley, 1988), pp. 32–33. Used by permission.

[2]Developed from Sara L. Rynes, Tamara L. Giluk, and Kenneth G. Brown, "The Very Separate Worlds of Academic and Practitioner Periodicals in Human Resource Management: Implications for Evidence-Based Management," *Academy of Management Journal*, vol. 50 (October 2008), p. 986.

[3]Adapted from "Lost at Sea: A Consensus-Seeking Task," in the 1975 Handbook for Group Facilitators. Used with permission of University Associates, Inc.

[4]Suggested by an exercise in John F. Veiga and John N. Yanouzas, *The Dynamics of Organization Theory: Gaining a Macro Perspective* (St. Paul, MN: West, 1979), pp. 69–71.

[5]Developed from Eugene Owens, "Upward Appraisal: An Exercise in Subordinate's Critique of Superior's Performance," *Exchange: The Organizational Behavior Teaching Journal*, vol. 3 (1978), pp. 41–42.

[6]Adapted from Roy J. Lewicki, Donald D. Bowen, Douglas T. Hall, and Francine S. Hall, "What Do You Value in Work?" *Experiences in Management and Organizational Behavior*, 3rd ed. (New York: Wiley, 1988), pp. 23–26. Used by permission.

[7]Developed from Brian Dumaine, "Why Do We Work?" *Fortune* (December 26, 1994), pp. 196–204.

[8]Adapted from William Dyer, *Team Building*, 2nd ed. (Reading, MA: Addison-Wesley, 1987), pp. 123–25.

[9]Suggested by feedback questionnaire in Judith R. Gordon, *A Diagnostic Approach to Organizational Behavior*, 3rd ed. (Boston: Allyn & Bacon, 1991), p. 298.

[10]From Sidney B. Simon, Howard Kirschenbaum, and Leland Howe, *Values Clarification, The Handbook*, rev. ed. © 1991, Values Press, P.O. Box 450, Sunderland, MA. 01375.

[11]Quote from woopidoo.com/businessquotes (retrieved September 16, 2006). See also Michael Gerber, *The E-Myth Revisited: Why Most Small Businesses Don't Work and What to Do About It* (New York: HarperCollins, 2001).

Team Project Notes

[1]Developed in part from Roy J. Lewicki, Donald D. Bowen, Douglas T. Hall, and Francine S. Hall, *Experiences in Management and Organizational Behavior*, 3rd ed. (New York: Wiley, 1988), pp. 261–67. Used by permission.

[2]Developed from Roy J. Lewicki, Donald D. Bowen, Douglas T. Hall, and Francine S. Hall, *Experiences in Management and Organizational Behavior*, 4th ed. (New York: Wiley, 1997), pp. 195–97.

Name Index

Organization Index

Subject Index

{ SPECIAL CHAPTER FEATURES

MANAGER'S LIBRARY

Delivering Happiness: A Path to Profits, Passion, and Purpose by Tony Hsieh

Outliers: The Story of Success by Malcolm Gladwell

Conscious Capitalism: Liberating the Heroic Spirit of Business by John Mackey and Raj Sisodia

The Shallows: What the Internet is Doing to Our Brains by Nicholas Carr

Analytics at Work: Smarter Decisions, Better Results by Thomas Davenport, Jeanne Harris, and Robert Morison

Lean In: Women, Work and the Will to Lead by Sheryl Sandberg

Rebooting Work: Transform How You Work in the Age of Entrepreneurship by Maynard Webb

The Truth About Middle Managers: Heroes, Villains, and the Reinvention of Middle Management by Paul Osterman

Change by Design: How Design Thinking Transforms Organizations and Inspires Innovation by Tim Brown

Fast Future: How the Millennial Generation is Shaping Our World by David Burstein

Power: Why Some People Have It and Others Don't by Jeffrey Pfeffer

Women Count: A Guide to Changing the World by Susan Bulkeley Butler

Drive: The Surprising Truth About What Motivates Us by Daniel H. Pink

Crowdsourcing: Why the Power of the Cloud is Driving the Future of Business by Jeff Howe

Collaboration: How Leaders Avoid the Traps, Build Common Ground, and Reap Big Results by Morten Hansen

Half the Sky: Turning Oppression into Opportunity for Women Worldwide by Nicholas D. Kristof and Sheryl WuDunn

The New Digital Age: Reshaping the Future of People, Nations and Business by Eric Schmidt and Jared Cohen

In-N-Out Burger: A Behind-the-Counter Look at the Fast-Food Chain that Breaks all the Rules by Stacy Perman

ETHICS CHECK

Watch out for bad apples at farmers' markets

Cyberslackers find company time great for internet surfing

Signing on to a green supply chain

Left to die on Mt. Everest

E-waste graveyards offer easy way out

Global privacy and censorship worries

Life and death at an outsourcing factory

Flattened into exhaustion

Facebook follies versus corporate culture

CEO gets $96.1 million pay package

When the boss asks too much

Is personality testing in your future?

Information goldmine is an equity dilemma

Danger! Social loafing may be closer than you think

Blogging is easy, but bloggers beware

Fair-trade fashion

Nationalism and protectionism

Entrepreneurship and social good

ROLE MODELS

Ursula Burns—Xerox

Oprah Winfrey—Oprah's Angel Network

Gary Hirshberg—Stonyfield Farms

Indra Nooyi—Pepsi

Don Thompson—McDonald's

Bill Gates—Microsoft

Wendy Kopp—Teach for America

Alan Mulally—Ford

Tom Szaky—TerraCycle

Dave Goldberg—Survey Monkey

Lorraine Monroe—Leadership Academy

Richard Branson—Virgin Group

Blake Mycoskie—TOMS

Jeff Bezos—Amazon

Linda Heasley—The Limited

Salman Khan—Khan Academy

Muhammad Yunus—Grameen Bank

David Gilboa, Niel Blumenthal, Andrew Hunt, Jeffrey Raider—Warby Parker

FACTS TO CONSIDER

Employment contradictions in workforce diversity

Generations differ when rating their bosses

Manager behavior key to an ethical workplace

American workers talk about their biggest fears

Policies on office romances vary widely

Distractions can be goal killers

Disposable workers are indispensible to business profits

Bosses may be overestimating their managing skills

Organization cultures face up to work-life trends

Human resource executives worry about performance measurement

Workers report shortcomings of leaders and top managers

Survey shows dissatisfaction and pessimism in lower economic classes

Europe turns to quotas to increase female board members

Unproductive meetings are major time wasters

Employees should worry about electronic monitoring

Employee morale varies around the world

Corruption and bribes haunt global business

Minority entrepreneurs are on the move

{ ACTIVE LEARNING RESOURCES

CASES FOR CRITICAL THINKING

1 Trader Joe's
2 Zara International
3 Patagonia
4 Amazon.com
5 Nordstrom
6 Chipotle
7 Dunkin' Donuts
8 Law Firms
9 LinkedIn
10 Chief Executive Mom
11 Apple, Inc.
12 Businesses in Trouble
13 Salesforce.com
14 Whole Foods
15 Twitter
16 Cultural Charades
17 Harley-Davidson
18 Angel Investors

SELF-ASSESSMENTS

Personal Career Readiness
Managerial Assumptions
Terminal Values Survey
Intuitive Ability
Time Management Profile
Internal/External Control
Handling Facts and Inferences
Empowering Others
Tolerance for Ambiguity
Performance Review Assumptions
Least-Preferred Co-Worker Scale
Stress Test
Two-Factor Profile
Team Leader Skills
Feedback and Assertiveness
Diversity Awareness
Global Intelligence
Entrepreneurship Orientation

CLASS EXERCISES

My Best Manager
Evidence-Based Management Quiz
Confronting Ethical Dilemmas
Lost at Sea
The Future Workplace
Stakeholder Maps
Strategic Scenarios
Organizational Metaphors
Force-Field Analysis
Upward Appraisal
Leading by Participation
Job Satisfaction Preferences
Why We Work
Understanding Team Dynamics
Communication and Teamwork Dilemmas
Alligator River Story
American Football
Entrepreneurs Among Us

TEAM PROJECTS

Managing Millennials
Management in Popular Culture
Organizational Commitment to Sustainability
Crisis Management Realities
Personal Career Planning
After Meeting/Project Review
Contrasting Strategies
"Network U"
Organizational Culture Walk
The Future of Labor Unions
Leadership Believe-It-or-Not
Difficult Personalities
CEO Pay
Superstars on the Team
How Words Count
Job Satisfaction Around the World
Globalization Pros and Cons
Community Entrepreneurs

HOT TOPICS

Time to turn the workplace into a fun place?
Raising expectations and getting better feedback.
Sustainability ranks low among chief executive challenges.
Stuck-in-rut executive finds creativity in the cloud.
Keep the career plan tight and focused, or loosen up?
Should parents pay for children's grades?
How about a "double Irish" with a "Dutch sandwich"?
Crowdsourcing evaluations as a way to flatten structures.
"Move over old timer, time to make room for GenY."
When the boss says "Do it." consider saying "No!"
Some employers provide time for Yoga and meditation.
Does disharmony help build a better team?
Gain influence by tapping the science of persuading.
Use punishment to sting incivility in the workplace.
Avoid China problems by reshoring our manufacturing.